SAS® Procedures Guide

Version 8

SAS Institute

The correct bibliographic citation for this manual is as follows: SAS Institute Inc., *SAS®* *Procedures Guide, Version 8,* Cary, NC: SAS Institute Inc., 1999. 1643 pp.

SAS® Procedures Guide, Version 8

Copyright © 1999 by SAS Institute Inc., Cary, NC, USA.

ISBN 1–58025–482–9

SAS Institute Inc., SAS Campus Drive, Cary, North Carolina 27513.

1st printing, October 1999

The Institute is a private company devoted to the support and further development of its software and related services.

Contents

x

Changes and Enhancements

Changes and Enhancements for All Operating Environments

This section describes the features of base SAS procedures that have been implemented or enhanced since Release 6.12. Version 8 changes and enhancements are preceded by **V8**. All other changes and enhancements described were included in Version 7. If you use SAS software in an OS/390, CMS, or OpenVMS VAX environment, then also see "Additional Version 7 Changes and Enhancements for OS/390, CMS, and OpenVMS VAX" on page xxiv.

For information about changes and enhancements to base SAS procedures that are relevant only to a particular operating environment, see the SAS documentation for that operating environment.

Changes That Affect Multiple Procedures

Output Delivery System

The Output Delivery System (ODS) is a new feature that enhances your ability to manage procedure output. Procedures that fully support ODS

- □ store links to each piece of output in the Results folder in the SAS Explorer
- □ can generate HTML output
- □ can generate output for a high-resolution printer
- □ can generate output data sets from procedure output
- □ provide a way for you to customize the procedure output by creating templates that you can use whenever you run the procedure.

For more information on ODS, see "Output Delivery System" on page 19.

Integrity Constraints

Integrity constraints are a set of rules that modifications to data sets (tables) must follow in order to guarantee the validity of the data. You can create integrity constraints with the DATASETS and SQL procedures. Integrity constraints have implications for other procedures, such as PROC SORT and PROC CPORT. (See the information on individual procedures.)

Generation Data Sets

Generation data sets enable you to keep historical versions of SAS data sets, SAS data views, SAS catalogs, and SAS/ACCESS files. In addition, a historical record of changes is provided so that you can audit the changes that have been made to these files.

PROC DATASETS manages the generation group — the set of generation data sets (see Chapter 14, "The DATASETS Procedure," on page 329). Other procedures can use the GENNUM= data set option to read a specific version of the data.

Changes to the Behavior of the WEIGHT Statement

Prior to Version 7 of the SAS System, all base procedures except PROC REPORT used a value of 0 for missing weights. PROC REPORT and most SAS/STAT procedures, such as PROC GLM, excluded observations with missing weight from the analysis. Now all procedures exclude observations with missing weights from the analysis.

PROC REPORT and most SAS/STAT procedures have always excluded not only observations with missing weights but also observations with negative and zero weights from the analysis. Now, base procedures that do not, by default, exclude observations with negative and 0 weights support the EXCLNPWGT option in the PROC statement. EXCLNPWGT excludes observations with negative and 0 weights.

For more information, see "WEIGHT" on page 73.

New Procedures

□ **V8** The DBCSTAB procedureChapter 15, "The DBCSTAB Procedure," on page 407 produces conversion tables for the double-byte character sets that SAS supports.

□ The FSLIST procedure on page 605 is now a part of base SAS software. You no longer need a SAS/FSP license to run the procedure.

□ The EXPORT procedure on page 423 reads data from a SAS data set and writes it to an external data source.

□ The IMPORT procedure on page 611 reads data from an external data source and writes it to a SAS data set.

□ The REGISTRY procedure on page 849 maintains the SAS Registry.

Changes to Existing Procedures

PROC CATALOG

□ The PROC CATALOG statement supports this new option:

FORCE
    forces statements to execute when the catalog has been opened by a process other than the current one.

□ The COPY statement on page 160 supports the NEW option, which overwrites the destination catalog (specified by OUT=) if it already exists.

PROC CIMPORT

- ☐ The CIMPORT procedure transports integrity constraints, passwords, and generation data sets.
- ☐ The PROC CIMPORT on page 212 statement supports these new options:

  MEMTYPE=
  > specifies to move only data sets or only catalogs during a library import.

  NEW
  > creates a new catalog for the imported transport file, and deletes any existing catalog with the same name.

- ☐ The SELECT statement on page 216 and the EXCLUDE statement on page 214 replace the SELECT= option and the EXCLUDE= option.

PROC CORR

- ☐ **V8** The WEIGHT statement now excludes observations with missing weight values from the analysis.
- ☐ **V8** The EXCLNPWGT option in the PROC CORR statement excludes observations with nonpositive weights from the analysis.

PROC CPORT

- ☐ The procedure transports integrity constraints, passwords, and generation data sets.
- ☐ The SELECT statement on page 319 and the EXCLUDE statement on page 318 replace the SELECT= option and the EXCLUDE= option.

PROC DATASETS

The SAS System now supports the creation and maintenance of generations of SAS data sets. A generation group consists of the base version of the file and a set of historical versions. You can use PROC DATASETS to manage generation data sets.

The SAS System now supports the creation of integrity constraints. Integrity constraints are a set of rules that modifications to a data set (table) must follow in order to guarantee the validity of the data. You can use PROC DATASETS to create and delete integrity constraints.

For more information on using PROC DATASETS with generation data sets and integrity constraints, see Chapter 14, "The DATASETS Procedure," on page 329.

- ☐ PROC DATASETS supports these new statements:

  V8 AUDIT"AUDIT Statement" on page 343
  > initiates and controls event logging to an audit file.

  IC CREATE"IC CREATE Statement" on page 360
  > creates an integrity constraint.

  IC DELETE"IC DELETE Statement" on page 361
  > deletes an integrity constraint.

  IC REACTIVATE"IC REACTIVATE Statement" on page 362
  > reactivates a foreign key integrity constraint that has been set to inactive.

  INDEX CENTILES"INDEX CENTILES" on page 362
  > updates centiles information for indexed variables.

- ☐ The APPEND statement on page 339 supports this new option:

APPENDVER=V6
> uses the Version 6 behavior for appending observations to the BASE= data set.

☐ The CHANGE statement on page 345 supports this new option:

GENNUM=
> restricts processing to a single generation file or to the entire generation group.

☐ The CONTENTS statement on page 346 supports these new options:

CENTILES
> prints centiles information for indexed variables.

V8 OUT2=
> names an output data set to contain information about indexes and integrity constraints.

☐ The COPY statement on page 349 supports this new option:

CONSTRAINT=
> specifies whether to copy all integrity constraints when copying a data set.

☐ The DELETE statement on page 354 supports this new option:

GENNUM=
> restricts processing to the specified generation files

☐ The INDEX CREATE on page 363 statement supports this new option:

UPDATECENTILES=
> specifies when the centiles are updated.

☐ The IC DELETE"IC DELETE Statement" on page 361 statement supports this new option:

V8 _ALL_
> deletes all constraints.

☐ The INDEX DELETE"INDEX DELETE Statement" on page 365 statement supports this new option:

V8 _ALL_
> deletes all indexes, except for indexes that are owned by an integrity constraint.

☐ The MODIFY statement on page 367 supports these new options:

GENMAX=
> sets the maximum number of generation files in a generation group.

GENNUM=
> restricts processing to the specified generation file.

☐ The REPAIR statement on page 371 supports this new option:

GENNUM=
> restricts processing to the specified generation files.

PROC FORMAT

☐ The PICTURE statement on page 441 supports these new options:

DATATYPE=
> specifies that the picture value is a template for formatting date, time, or datetime values.

DECSEP=
> specifies the separator character for the fractional part of a number. By default, this character is a period (.)

DIG3SEP=
> specifies the character that separates each group of three digits in a number. By default, this character is a comma (,).

MULTILABEL
> indicates that multiple labels for the same range are allowed. Secondary labels can be used by certain applications that are designed to handle multilabel formats. For all other applications, the secondary labels are ignored.
>
> When MULTILABEL is specified, overlapping ranges are also permitted.

□ The VALUE statement on page 450 supports this new option:

MULTILABEL
> indicates that multiple labels for the same range are allowed. Secondary labels can be used by certain applications that are designed to handle multilabel formats. For all other applications, the secondary labels are ignored.
>
> When MULTILABEL is specified, overlapping ranges are also permitted.

PROC FREQ

□ In PROC FREQ, the method for calculating the standard error for common relative risks has been revised.

□ PROC FREQ supports a new statement, the TEST statement on page 523. It provides asymptotic tests for some measures of association and measures of agreement. The TEST statement supports the following statistics.

MEASURES
> provides tests for all the measures of association. To select individual measures of association, use one or more of these options:
>
> GAMMA
>
> KENTB
>
> PCORR
>
> SCORR
>
> SMDCR
>
> SMDRC
>
> STUTC

AGREE
> provides tests for all the measures of agreement. To select individual measures of agreement, use one or more of these options:
>
> KAPPA
>
> WTKAP

□ The TABLES statement on page 514 supports these new options:

PRINTKWT
> prints the kappa coefficient weights.

SCOROUT
> displays the row and column scores when statistics are computed two-way tables.

BINOMIAL
>   computes binomial proportions, asymptotic standard error, and asymptotic confidence bounds for one-way tables.

The AGREE option in the TABLES statement on page 514 supports a parameter that specifies the type of weights that PROC FREQ uses to compute the weighted kappa coefficient. You can specify Cicchetti-Allison weights or Fleiss-Cohen weights.

□ The EXACT statement on page 507 now computes an exact chi-square goodness-of-fit test for one-way tables as well as an exact chi-square test for two-way tables. It also supports these new options:

V8 ALPHA=
>   specifies the confidence level for the confidence limits for the Monte Carlo p-value estimates.

MAXTIME=
>   specifies the amount of time that PROC FREQ uses to compute an exact *p*-value before timing out.

V8 MC
>   requests Monte Carlo estimation of exact *p*-values, instead of direct exact *p*-value computation.

V8 N=
>   specifies the number of samples for Monte Carlo estimation.

V8 SEED=
>   specifies the initial seed for random number generation for Monte Carlo estimation.

PROC MEANS

□ PROC MEANS supports these new statements:

TYPES
>   specifies which combinations of class variables PROC MEANS uses to subgroup the data (see "TYPES Statement" on page 646).

WAYS
>   specifies how many class variables PROC MEANS combines to subgroup the data (see "WAYS Statement" on page 647).

□ The PROC MEANS statement on page 627 supports these new options:

CHARTYPE
>   specifies that the _TYPE_ variable contains character values.

CLASSDATA=
>   specifies a data set that contains the combinations of class variable values to include in analysis.

COMPLETETYPES
>   creates all possible combinations of class variable values.

EXCLNPWGT
>   excludes observations with nonpositive weights from the analysis.

EXCLUSIVE
>   excludes from the analysis all class variable combinations that are not in the CLASSDATA= data set.

NOTRAP
: disables floating point exception (FPE) recovery during data processing.

PRINTALLTYPES
: displays all valid combinations of class variables in the output.

PRINTIDVARS
: prints the value of the ID variables.

QMARKERS=
: specifies the default number of markers to use for the P^2 quantile estimation method.

QMETHOD=
: specifies the method to process the input data to compute quantiles.

QNTLDEF=
: specifies the mathematical definition used to compute quantiles.

SUMSIZE=
: specifies the amount of memory available for data summarization with class variables.

☐ PROC MEANS now supports multiple CLASS statements. The CLASS statement (only in the MEANS, SUMMARY, and TABULATE procedures) supports the following new options:

ASCENDING
: specifies to sort the class variable levels in ascending order.

DESCENDING
: specifies to sort the class variable levels in descending order.

EXCLUSIVE
: excludes from the analysis all class variable values that are not found in the preloaded range of user-defined formats.

GROUPINTERNAL
: specifies not to apply formats to the class variables when PROC MEANS sorts the values to create combinations of class variables.

MISSING
: considers missing values as valid class variable levels.

V8 MLF
: enables PROC MEANS to use the primary and secondary format labels for a given range or overlapping ranges to create the subgroup combinations when a multilabel format is assigned to a class variable.

ORDER=
: specifies the sort order for the levels of the class variables in the output.

PRELOADFMT
: specifies to preload all the formats for the class variables.

☐ **V8** The OUTPUT statement on page 640: by default the statistics in the output data set automatically inherit the analysis variable's format, informat, and label. However, statistics computed for N, NMISS, SUMWGT, USS, CSS, VAR, CV, T, PROBT, SKEWNESS, and KURTOSIS will not inherit the analysis variable's format because this format may be invalid for these statistics (e.g. dollar or datetime formats).

The OUTPUT statement supports these new options:

V8 AUTOLABEL

specifies that PROC MEANS append the statistic name to the end of the variable label. If an analysis variable has no label, PROC MEANS creates a label by appending the statistic name to the analysis variable name.

AUTONAME

automatically resolves conflicts in the names of the variables in the OUT= data set.

IDGROUP

combines the features of the ID statement and the IDMIN option in the PROC MEANS statement.

INHERIT

specifies that statistics in the output data set inherit the attributes (label, length, and format) of the analysis variable that PROC MEANS uses to derive them.

V8 KEEPLEN

specifies that statistics in the output data set inherit the length of the analysis variable that PROC MEANS uses to derive them.

LEVELS

includes a variable named _LEVEL_ in the output data set. This variable contains a value from 1 to *n* that indicates a unique combination of the values of class variables (the values of the _TYPE_ variable).

V8 NOINHERIT

specifies that the variables in the output data set that contain statistics do not inherit the attributes (label and format) of the analysis variables which are used to derive them.

WAYS

includes a variable named _WAY_ in the output data set. This variable contains a value from 1 to the maximum number of CLASS variables that indicates how many CLASS variables PROC MEANS combines to create the TYPE value.

□ The VAR statement on page 646 supports this new option:

WEIGHT=

specifies a numeric variable whose values weight the variables that are specified in the VAR statement.

□ The WEIGHT statement on page 73 now excludes observations with missing weight values from the analysis.

□ PROC MEANS supports these new statistics:

MEDIAN

P1

P5

P10

P90

P95

P99

Q1

Q3

QRANGE

PROC OPTIONS

The OPTION= option in the PROC OPTIONS statement on page 687 supports two new suboptions, DEFINE and VALUE, that provide additional information about the specified option.

PROC PMENU

PROC PMENU supports submenus to enable multiple items to point to a common submenu.

PROC PRINT

☐ The PROC PRINT statement on page 786 supports this new option:

> OBS=
>> specifies a column header for the column that identifies each observation by number.

☐ The N= option in the PROC PRINT statement on page 786 has been enhanced so that you can specify explanatory text to print with the value of N.

PROC REPORT

☐ The PROC REPORT statement on page 879 supports this new option:

> FORMCHAR=
>> defines the characters to use as line-drawing characters in the report.

☐ The COMPUTE statement on page 905 supports this new option:

> _PAGE_
>> places information at the top or bottom of each page.

☐ If you use the Output Delivery System to create HTML files or printer output from PROC REPORT, you can set the style that the procedure uses for various parts of the report. Styles determine attributes like font face, font weight, color, and so forth. Information on the attributes that you can set for a style is in "Customizing the Style Definition That ODS Uses" on page 42.

> You specify styles for PROC REPORT with the STYLE= option. You can use this option in the following statements:

> ☐ PROC REPORT on page 879
> ☐ BREAK on page 893
> ☐ CALL DEFINE on page 899
> ☐ COMPUTE on page 905(with a location and LINE statements)
> ☐ DEFINE on page 908
> ☐ RBREAK on page 918

PROC SQL

☐ Some PROC SQL views are now updateable. The view must be based on a single DBMS table or SAS data file and must not contain a join, an ORDER BY clause, or a subquery.

☐ Whenever possible, PROC SQL passes joins to the DBMS rather than doing the joins itself. This enhances performance.

☐ You can now store DBMS connection information in a view with the USING LIBNAME clause.

□ A new option, DQUOTE=ANSI, enables you to use names that are not normally permissible in PROC SQL.

□ A PROC SQL query can now reference up to 32 views or tables. PROC SQL can perform joins on up to 32 tables.

□ PROC SQL can now create and update tables that contain integrity constraints.

For more information, see Chapter 34, "The SQL Procedure," on page 1021

PROC STANDARD

□ The PROC STANDARD statement supports this new option:

EXCLNPWGT

> excludes observations with nonpositive weights from the analysis.

□ The WEIGHT statement on page 73 now excludes observations with missing weight values from the analysis.

PROC SUMMARY

□ The PROC SUMMARY statement supports this new option:

EXCLNPWGT

> excludes observations with nonpositive weights from the analysis.

□ The WEIGHT statement on page 73 now excludes observations with missing weight values from the analysis.

PROC TABULATE

□ The PROC TABULATE statement on page 1158 supports these new options:

CLASSDATA=

> specifies a data set that contains the combinations of class variable values to include in analysis.

V8 CONTENTS=

> allows you to name the link in the HTML table of contents that points to the ODS output of the first table produced.

EXCLNPWGT

> excludes observations with nonpositive weights from the analysis.

EXCLUSIVE

> excludes from the analysis all class variable combinations that are not in the CLASSDATA= data set.

NOTRAP

> disables trapping mathematical errors due to overflow.

OUT=

> names the output data set.

QMARKERS=

> specifies the default number of markers to use for the P^2 (fixed space) quantile estimation method.

QMETHOD

> specifies the method to process the input data to compute quantiles.

QNTLDEF=

> specifies the mathematical definition used to compute quantiles.

V8 TRAP

enables trapping mathematical errors due to overflow.

□ PROC TABULATE now supports multiple CLASS statements. For a discussion of the options that the CLASS statement supports, see the discussion of PROC MEANS and the CLASS statement on page xvii. The CLASS statement has this new option:

V8 MLF

allows you to make use of multiple labels when a multilabel format is assigned to a class variable in PROC FORMAT.

□ In the TABLE statement "TABLE Statement" on page 1173, the following options have been enhanced:

V8 CONDENSE

prints multiple logical pages on a physical page.

V8 CONTENTS=

allows you to name the link in the HTML table of contents that points to the ODS output of the table produced using the TABLE statement.

V8 NOCONTINUED

suppresses the printing of the "(Continued)" continuation message for tables that span physical pages.

□ PROC TABULATE supports these new statistics:

V8 COLPCNT

V8 COLPCTSUM

MEDIAN

P1

P5

P10

P90

P95

P99

V8 PAGEPCTN

V8 PAGEPCTSUM

Q1

Q3

QRANGE

V8 REPPCTN

V8 REPPCTSUM

V8 ROWPCTN

V8 ROWPCTSUM

□ If you use the Output Delivery System to create HTML files or printer output from PROC TABULATE, you can set the style that the procedure uses for various parts of the report. Styles determine attributes like font face, font weight, color, and so forth. Information on the attributes that you can set for a style is in "Customizing the Style Definition That ODS Uses" on page 42.

You specify styles for PROC TABULATE with the STYLE= option. You can use this option in several locations in the procedure. For details see Chapter 37, "The TABULATE Procedure," on page 1151. In addition, there are two new styles:

V8 BeforeCaption
controls the look and feel of page dimension text.

V8 AfterCaption style
controls the look and feel of the "(Continued)" continuation message.

☐ PROC TABULATE supports multiple VAR statements. The VAR statement on page 646 supports this new option:

WEIGHT=
specifies a numeric variable whose values weight the variables that are specified in the VAR statement.

☐ The WEIGHT statement on page 73 now excludes observations with missing weight values from the analysis.

PROC UNIVARIATE

☐ **V8** PROC UNIVARIATE now supports high resolution graphical displays. You can generate histograms and comparative histograms and optionally superimpose fitted probabilty density curves for various distributions and kernel density estimates. You can generate quantile-quantile plots (Q-Q plots) and probability plots to compare a data distribution with various theoretical distributions. You also have the ability to inset summary statistics in the graphical displays.

☐ The WEIGHT statement on page 73 now excludes observations with missing weight values from the analysis.

☐ The output from PROC UNIVARIATE has been reorganized and includes some new tables:

The Moments table displays only those statistics that are related to sample moments.

A new table, Tests for Location, shows the Student's t test, the sign test, and the signed rank test.

A new table, Basic Statistical Measures, provides basic measures of location and variability.

☐ The UNIVARIATE procedure supports these new statements:

V8 CLASS statement
specifies one or two class variables for the analysis.
You can use the CLASS statement with a HISTOGRAM, PROBPLOT, or QQPLOT statement to create one-way and two-way high resolution comparative plots. When you use a single class variable, PROC UNIVARIATE displays an array of componentplots (stacked or side-by-side), for each level of the class variable. When you use two class variables, PROC UNIVARIATE displays a matrix of component plots, one for each combination of levels of the class variables

V8 HISTOGRAM statement
creates a high resolution graph of a histogram and optionally includes parametric and nonparametric density curve estimates. You can use the HISTOGRAM statement to specify the midpoints for histogram intervals, display density curves for fitted theoretical distributions (beta, exponential, gamma, lognormal, normal, and Weibull) on histograms, request goodness-of-fit tests for fitted distributions, display kernel density estimates on histograms, save histogram intervals and parameters of fitted distributions in output data sets, and request graphical enhancements.

V8 INSET statement
Places a box or table of summary statistics, called an *inset*, directly in the graphical display. The inset can display statistics that PROC UNIVARIATE

calculates or display values that you provide in a SAS data set. The INSET statement does not produce the graphical display. You must specify a HISTOGRAM, PROBPLOT, or QQPLOT statement. You can use options in the INSET statement to specify the position of the inset, to specify a header for the inset, and to specify graphical enhancements, such as background colors, text colors, text height, text font, and drop shadows

V8 PROBPLOT statement

creates a high-resolution graphics display of a probability plot, which compares ordered variable values with the percentiles of a specified theoretical distribution.

V8 QQPLOT statement

Creates a graphical display of a quantile-quantile plot (Q-Q plot), which compares ordered variable values with quantiles of a specified theoretical distribution.

☐ The PROC UNIVARIATE statement on page 1325 statement supports these new options:

V8 ANNOTATE=

specifies an input data set that contains annotate variables as described in SAS/GRAPH documentation. You can use this data set to add features to your high resolution graphics. PROC UNIVARIATE adds the features in this data set to every high resolution graph produced in the PROC step.

EXCLNPWGT

excludes observations with nonpositive weights from the analysis.

V8 GOUT=

specifies the SAS catalog in which to save the high resolution graphics output that the UNIVARIATE procedure produces.

PROC UNIVARIATE also supports the following enhancements:

☐ The ALL option requests tables of confidence limits, frequency, modes, and extreme values, and plots. For unweighted analysis variables, it also requests location counts, tests for normality, and robust estimators of scale and location.

☐ The CIBASIC option produces the Basic Statistical Measures table. This table provides basic measures of location and variability.

☐ The EXCLNPWGT option excludes observations with nonpositive weights from the analysis.

☐ The LOCCOUNT option produces the Location Counts table. This table shows the numbers of observations greater than, less than, and equal to the value of the new MU0= option. Formerly, this information was in the Moments table. The default value for MU0= is 0.

☐ Mode is no longer shown for continuous data. If there are multiple modes, the lowest mode is still shown. The MODES option in the PROC UNIVARIATE statement displays a table of all modes.

☐ The NORMAL option produces a table of Tests for Normality. These tests include empirical distribution function (EDF) goodness-of-fit tests. The Shapiro-Wilk test is included only if the sample size is less than or equal to 2000. The Kolmogorov test is always included.

☐ The ROBUSTSCALE option produces a table with robust estimates of scale.

☐ The TRIM= option produces a table of trimmed means.

☐ The WINSOR= option produces a table of winsorized means.

□ A new table, Basic Confidence Limits, provides basic confidence intervals for the mean, the standard deviation, and the variance.

□ You can request confidence intervals for quantiles with these options:

CIPCTLNORMAL

requests confidence intervals that are based on the assumption that the data are normal.

CIPCTLDF

requests confidence intervals that are distribution free.

□ The Extremes table is replaced by two tables:

Extreme Observations table

displays the n lowest observations and n highest observations, where n is specified with the new option NEXTROBS= in the PROC UNIVARIATE statement. FREQ and ID variables change the table.

Extreme Values table

displays the n lowest unique and n highest unique values, where n is specified with the new option NEXTRVAL= in the PROC UNIVARIATE statement.

Additional Version 7 Changes and Enhancements for OS/390, CMS, and OpenVMS VAX

For OS/390 (MVS), CMS, and OpenVMS VAX, the last release of base SAS software was the 6.09 Enhanced Release. Some changes and enhancements that were implemented for the other operating environments in the 6.10, 6.11, and 6.12 releases were not implemented for the OS/390, CMS, or OpenVMS VAX until Version 7. This section describes those additional features for the base procedures.

PROC FREQ

□ The EXACT statement on page 507 now provides statistical keywords that request exact p-values for the simple kappa coefficient, the weight kappa coefficient, and the odds ratio for 2x2 tables. The new statistic keywords are KAPPA, WTKAP, and OR, respectively.

□ The TABLES statement on page 514 supports these new options:

CL

requests confidence bounds for measures of association.

RELRISK

requests just the relative risk measures for 2x2 tables.

RISKDIFF

requests column 1 and column 2 risk (or bionomial proportions), risk differences, and confidence bounds for 2x2 tables.

TESTF=

requests a chi-square statistic to test for equal or specified frequencies for one-way tables.

TESTP=

requests a chi-square statistic to test for equal or specified proportions for one-way tables.

PROC REPORT

A new window, the EXPLORE window on page 934, lets you experiment with your data. For example, you can subset your data or suppress the display of a column. If you like the results, you can apply them to the report.

CHAPTER

28

The PRINT Procedure

Overview

The PRINT procedure prints the observations in a SAS data set, using all or some of the variables. You can create a variety of reports ranging from a simple listing to a highly customized report that groups the data and calculates totals and subtotals for numeric variables.

Output 28.1 on page 783 illustrates the simplest kind of report that you can produce. The statements that produce the output follow. A DATA step on page 798 creates the data set EXPREV.

```
options nodate pageno=1 linesize=64
        pagesize=60;
proc print data=exprev;
run;
```

Output 28.1   Simple Report Produced with PROC PRINT

```
                          The SAS System                              1

     Obs    Region     State    Month     Expenses    Revenues

      1     Southern    GA      JAN95       2000        8000
      2     Southern    GA      FEB95       1200        6000
      3     Southern    FL      FEB95       8500       11000
      4     Northern    NY      FEB95       3000        4000
      5     Northern    NY      MAR95       6000        5000
      6     Southern    FL      MAR95       9800       13500
      7     Northern    MA      MAR95       1500        1000
```

Output 28.2 on page 784 is a customized report that is produced by PROC PRINT. The statements that create this report

- ☐ customize the title and the column headings
- ☐ place dollar signs and commas in numeric output
- ☐ selectively include and control the order of variables in the report
- ☐ group the data by JobCode
- ☐ sum the values for Salary for each job code and for all job codes.

For an explanation of the program that produces this report, see Example 8 on page 813.

Output 28.2 Customized Report Produced with PROC PRINT

```
                        Expenses Incurred for                    1
              Salaries for Flight Attendants and Mechanics

                  Job Code    Gender    Annual Salary
                  ========    ======    =============

                    FA1         F         $23,177.00
                                F         $22,454.00
                                M         $22,268.00
                  --------                -------------
                    FA1                   $67,899.00

                    FA2         F         $28,888.00
                                F         $27,787.00
                                M         $28,572.00
                  --------                -------------
                    FA2                   $85,247.00

                    FA3         F         $32,886.00
                                F         $33,419.00
                                M         $32,217.00
                  --------                -------------
                    FA3                   $98,522.00

                    ME1         M         $29,769.00
                                M         $28,072.00
                                M         $28,619.00
                  --------                -------------
                    ME1                   $86,460.00

                    ME2         F         $35,108.00
                                F         $34,929.00
                                M         $35,345.00
                                M         $36,925.00
                                M         $35,090.00
                                M         $35,185.00
                  --------                -------------
                    ME2                   $212,582.00

                    ME3         M         $43,025.00
                                          =============
                                          $593,735.00
```

Procedure Syntax

Tip: Supports the Output Delivery System (see Chapter 2, "Fundamental Concepts for Using Base SAS Procedures")

Reminder: You can use the ATTRIB, FORMAT, LABEL, and WHERE statements. See Chapter 3, "Statements with the Same Function in Multiple Procedures," for details. You can also use any global statements as well. See Chapter 2, "Fundamental Concepts for Using Base SAS Procedures," for a list.

PROC PRINT <*option(s)*>;

    BY <DESCENDING> *variable-1* <...<DESCENDING> *variable-n*>
      <NOTSORTED>;

PAGEBY *BY-variable*;
SUMBY *BY-variable*;
ID *variable(s)*;
SUM *variable(s)*;
VAR *variable(s)*;

To do this	Use this statement
Produce a separate section of the report for each BY group	BY
Identify observations by the formatted values of the variables that you list instead of by observation numbers	ID
Control page ejects that occur before a page is full	PAGEBY
Limit the number of sums that appear in the report	SUMBY
Total values of numeric variables	SUM
Select variables that appear in the report and determine their order	VAR

PROC PRINT Statement

PROC PRINT *<option(s)>*;

To do this	Use this option
Specify the input data set	DATA=
Control general format	
Write a blank line between observations	DOUBLE
Print the number of observations in the data set, in BY groups, or both, and specify explanatory text to print with the number	N=
Suppress the column in the output that identifies each observation by number	NOOBS
Specify a column header for the column that identifies each observation by number	OBS=
Round unformatted numeric values to two decimal places	ROUND
Control page format	
Format the rows on a page	ROWS=
Use each variable's formatted width as its column width on all pages	WIDTH=UNIFORM

To do this	Use this option
Control column format	
Control the orientation of the column headings	HEADING=
Use variables' labels as column headings	LABEL or SPLIT=
Specify the split character, which controls line breaks in column headings	SPLIT=
Determine the column width for each variable	WIDTH=

Options

DATA=*SAS-data-set*
specifies the SAS data set to print.

Main discussion: "Input Data Sets" on page 18

DOUBLE
writes a blank line between observations.

Alias: D

Restriction: This option has no effect on the HTML output.

Featured in: Example 1 on page 798

HEADING=*direction*
controls the orientation of the column headings, where *direction* is one of the following:

HORIZONTAL
prints all column headings horizontally.

Alias: H

VERTICAL
prints all column headings vertically.

Alias: V

Default: Headings are either all horizontal or all vertical. If you omit HEADING=, PROC PRINT determines the direction of the column headings as follows:

- □ If you do not use LABEL, spacing dictates whether column headings are vertical or horizontal.

- □ If you use LABEL and at least one variable has a label, all headings are horizontal.

LABEL
uses variables' labels as column headings.

Alias: L

Default: If you omit LABEL, PROC PRINT uses the variable's name as the column heading even if the PROC PRINT step contains a LABEL statement. If a variable does not have a label, PROC PRINT uses the variable's name as the column heading.

Interaction: By default, if you specify LABEL and at least one variable has a label, PROC PRINT prints all column headings horizontally. Therefore, using LABEL may increase the number of pages of output. (Use HEADING=VERTICAL in the PROC PRINT statement to print vertical column headings.)

Interaction: PROC PRINT sometimes conserves space by splitting labels across multiple lines. Use SPLIT= in the PROC PRINT statement to control where these splits occur. You do not need to use LABEL if you use SPLIT=.

Tip: To create a blank column header for a variable, use this LABEL statement in your PROC PRINT step:

```
label variable-name='00'x;
```

See also: For information on using the LABEL statement to create temporary labels in procedures see Chapter 3, "Statements with the Same Function in Multiple Procedures," on page 67.

For information on using the LABEL statement in a DATA step to create permanent labels, see the section on statements in *SAS Language Reference: Dictionary*.

Featured in: Example 3 on page 801

Note: The SAS system option LABEL must be in effect in order for any procedure to use labels. For more information see the section on system options in *SAS Language Reference: Dictionary* △

N<="*string-1*" <"*string-2*">>

prints the number of observations in the data set, in BY groups, or both and specifies explanatory text to print with the number.

If you use the N option ...	PROC PRINT ...
with neither a BY nor a SUM statement	prints the number of observations in the data set at the end of the report and labels the number with the value of *string-1*.
with a BY statement	prints the number of observations in the BY group at the end of each BY group and labels the number with the value of *string-1*.
with a BY statement and a SUM statement	prints the number of observations in the BY group at the end of each BY group and prints the number of observations in the data set at the end of the report. The numbers for BY groups are labeled with *string-1*; the number for the entire data set is labeled with *string-2*.

Featured in: Example 2 on page 799 (alone)

Example 3 on page 801 (with a BY statement)
Example 4 on page 803 (with a BY statement and a SUM statement)

NOOBS

suppresses the observation number in the output.

Featured in: Example 3 on page 801

OBS="*column-header*"

specifies a column header for the column that identifies each observation by number.

Tip: OBS= honors the split character (see the discussion of SPLIT= on page 790).

Featured in: Example 2 on page 799

ROUND

rounds unformatted numeric values to two decimal places. (Formatted values are already rounded by the format to the specified number of decimal places.) For both formatted and unformatted variables, PROC PRINT uses these rounded values to calculate any sums in the report.

If you omit ROUND, PROC PRINT adds the actual values of the rows to obtain the sum *even though it displays the formatted (rounded) values.* Any sums are also rounded by the format, but they include only one rounding error, that of rounding the sum of the actual values. The ROUND option, on the other hand, rounds values before summing them, so there may be multiple rounding errors. The results without ROUND are more accurate, but ROUND is useful for published reports where it is important for the total to be the sum of the printed (rounded) values.

Be aware that the results from PROC PRINT with the ROUND option may differ from the results of summing the same data with other methods such as PROC MEANS or the DATA step. Consider a simple case in which

□ the data set contains three values for X: .003, .004, and .009.

□ X has a format of 5.2.

Depending on how you calculate the sum, you can get three different answers: 0.02, 0.01, and 0.016. Figure 28.1 on page 789 shows the results of calculating the sum with PROC PRINT (without and with the ROUND option) and PROC MEANS.

Figure 28.1 Three Methods of Summing Variables

Actual Values	PROC PRINT without the ROUND option		PROC PRINT with the ROUND option		PROC MEANS
	OBS	X	OBS	X	Analysis Variable : X
.003	1	0.00	1	0.00	Sum
.004	2	0.00	2	0.00	------------
.009	3	0.01	3	0.01	0.0160000
=====		=====		=====	------------
.016		0.02		0.01	

Notice that the sum produced without the ROUND option (.02) is closer to the actual result (0.16) than the sum produced with ROUND (0.01). However, the sum produced with ROUND reflects the numbers displayed in the report.

Alias: R

CAUTION:
Do not use ROUND with PICTURE formats. ROUND is for use with numeric values. SAS procedures treat variables that have picture formats as character variables. Using ROUND with such variables may lead to unexpected results. △

ROWS=*page-format*
formats rows on a page. Currently, PAGE is the only value that you can use for *page-format*:

PAGE
prints only one row of variables for each observation per page. When you use ROWS=PAGE, PROC PRINT does not divide the page into sections; it prints as many observations as possible on each page. If the observations do not fill the last page of the output, PROC PRINT divides the last page into sections and prints all the variables for the last few observations.

Restriction: Physical page size does not mean the same thing in HTML output as it does in traditional procedure output. Therefore, HTML output from PROC PRINT appears the same whether or not you use ROWS=.

Tip: The PAGE value can reduce the number of pages in the output if the data set contains large numbers of variables and observations. However, if the data set contains a large number of variables but few observations, the PAGE value can increase the number of pages in the output.

See also: "Page Layout" on page 795 for discussion of the default layout.

Featured in: Example 7 on page 810

SPLIT='*split-character*'
specifies the split character, which controls line breaks in column headers. It also uses labels as column headers. PROC PRINT breaks a column heading when it reaches the split character and continues the header on the next line. The split character is not part of the column heading although each occurrence of the split character counts toward the 256-character maximum for a label.

Alias: S=

Interaction: You do not need to use both LABEL and SPLIT= because SPLIT= implies the use of labels.

Interaction: The OBS= option honors the split character. (See the discussion of OBS= on page 788).

Featured in: Example 2 on page 799

Note: PROC PRINT does not split labels of BY variables in the heading preceding each BY group even if you specify SPLIT=. Instead, PROC PRINT treats the split character as part of the label. Therefore, you probably want to avoid using a split character when you are using the BY statement. △

UNIFORM
See WIDTH=UNIFORM on page 790.

WIDTH='*column-width*'
determines the column width for each variable. The value of *column-width* must be one of the following:

FULL
uses a variable's formatted width as the column width. If the variable does not have a format that explicitly specifies a field width, PROC PRINT uses the default width. For a character variable, the default width is the length of the variable. For a numeric variable, the default width is 12. When you use WIDTH=FULL, the column widths do not vary from page to page.

Tip: Using WIDTH=FULL can reduce execution time.

MINIMUM
uses for each variable the minimum column width that accommodates all values of the variable.

Alias: MIN

UNIFORM
uses each variable's formatted width as its column width on all pages. If the variable does not have a format that explicitly specifies a field width, PROC PRINT uses the widest data value as the column width. When you specify WIDTH=UNIFORM, PROC PRINT normally needs to read the data set twice. However, if all the variables in the data set have formats that explicitly specify a field width (for example, BEST12. but not BEST.), PROC PRINT reads the data set only once.

Alias: U

Tip: If the data set is large and you want a uniform report, you can save computer resources by using formats that explicitly specify a field width so that PROC PRINT reads the data only once.

Tip: WIDTH=UNIFORM is the same as UNIFORM.

Restriction: When not all variables have formats that explicitly specify a width, you cannot use WIDTH=UNIFORM with an engine that supports concurrent access if another user is updating the data set at the same time.

UNIFORMBY

formats all columns uniformly within a BY group, using each variable's formatted width as its column width. If the variable does not have a format that explicitly specifies a field width, PROC PRINT uses the widest data value as the column width.

Alias: UBY

Restriction: You cannot use UNIFORMBY with a sequential data set.

Default: If you omit WIDTH= and do not specify the UNIFORM option, PROC PRINT individually constructs each page of output. The procedure analyzes the data for a page and decides how best to display them. Therefore, column widths may differ from one page to another.

Tip: Column width is affected not only by variable width but also by the length of column headings. Long column headings may lessen the usefulness of WIDTH=.

See also: For a discussion of default column widths, see "Column Width" on page 797.

BY Statement

Produces a separate section of the report for each BY group.

Main discussion: "BY" on page 68

Featured in: Example 3 on page 801, Example 4 on page 803, Example 5 on page 805, Example 6 on page 808, and Example 8 on page 813

    BY <DESCENDING> *variable-1*
       <...<DESCENDING> *variable-n*>
       <NOTSORTED>;

Required Arguments

variable

specifies the variable that the procedure uses to form BY groups. You can specify more than one variable. If you do not use the NOTSORTED option in the BY statement, the observations in the data set must either be sorted by all the variables that you specify, or they must be indexed appropriately. Variables in a BY statement are called *BY variables*.

Options

DESCENDING
> specifies that the data set is sorted in descending order by the variable that immediately follows the word DESCENDING in the BY statement.

NOTSORTED
> specifies that observations are not necessarily sorted in alphabetic or numeric order. The data are grouped in another way, for example, chronological order.
>
> The requirement for ordering or indexing observations according to the values of BY variables is suspended for BY-group processing when you use the NOTSORTED option. In fact, the procedure does not use an index if you specify NOTSORTED. The procedure defines a BY group as a set of contiguous observations that have the same values for all BY variables. If observations with the same values for the BY variables are not contiguous, the procedure treats each contiguous set as a separate BY group.

Using the BY Statement with an ID Statement

PROC PRINT uses a special layout if all BY variables appear in the same order at the beginning of the ID statement. (See Example 8 on page 813.)

Using the BY Statement with the NOBYLINE Option

If you use the BY statement with the SAS system option NOBYLINE, which suppresses the BY line that normally appears in output produced with BY-group processing, PROC PRINT always starts a new page for each BY group. This behavior ensures that if you create customized BY lines by putting BY-group information in the title and suppressing the default BY lines with NOBYLINE, the information in the titles matches the report on the pages. (See "Creating Titles That Contain BY-Group Information" on page 54.)

ID Statement

Identifies observations by using the formatted values of the variables that you list instead of by using observation numbers.

Featured in: Example 7 on page 810 and Example 8 on page 813

ID *variable(s)*;

Required Arguments

variable(s)
> specifies one or more variables to print instead of the observation number at the beginning of each row of the report.
>
> **Restriction:**   If the ID variables occupy so much space that no room remains on the line for at least one other variable, PROC PRINT writes a warning to the SAS log and does not treat all ID variables as ID variables.

Interaction: If a variable in the ID statement also appears in the VAR statement, the output contains two columns for that variable.

Using the BY Statement with an ID Statement

PROC PRINT uses a special layout if all BY variables appear in the same order at the beginning of the ID statement. (See Example 8 on page 813.)

PAGEBY Statement

Controls page ejects that occur before a page is full.

Requirements: BY statement

Featured in: Example 3 on page 801

PAGEBY *BY-variable*;

Required Arguments

BY-variable
> identifies a variable appearing in the BY statement in the PROC PRINT step. If the value of the BY variable changes, or if the value of any BY variable that precedes it in the BY statement changes, PROC PRINT begins printing a new page.

> **Interaction:** If you use the BY statement with the SAS system option NOBYLINE, which suppresses the BY line that normally appears in output produced with BY-group processing, PROC PRINT always starts a new page for each BY group. This behavior ensures that if you create customized BY lines by putting BY-group information in the title and suppressing the default BY lines with NOBYLINE, the information in the titles matches the report on the pages. (See "Creating Titles That Contain BY-Group Information" on page 54.)

SUM Statement

Totals values of numeric variables.

Featured in: Example 4 on page 803, Example 5 on page 805, Example 6 on page 808, and Example 8 on page 813

SUM *variable(s)*;

Required Arguments

variable(s)
  identifies the numeric variables to total in the report.

Using the SUM and BY Statements Together

When you use a SUM statement and a BY statement with one BY variable, PROC PRINT sums the SUM variables for each BY group that contains more than one observation and totals them over all BY groups (see Example 4 on page 803).

When you use a SUM statement and a BY statement with multiple BY variables, PROC PRINT sums the SUM variables for each BY group that contains more than one observation, just as it does if you use only one BY variable. However, it provides sums only for those BY variables whose values change when the BY group changes. (See Example 5 on page 805.)

Note: When the value of a BY variable changes, the SAS System considers that the values of all variables listed after it in the BY statement also change. △

SUMBY Statement

Limits the number of sums that appear in the report.

Requirements: BY statement

Featured in: Example 6 on page 808

SUMBY *BY-variable*;

Required Arguments

BY-variable
  identifies a variable that appears in the BY statement in the PROC PRINT step. If the value of the BY variable changes, or if the value of any BY variable that precedes it in the BY statement changes, PROC PRINT prints the sums of all variables listed in the SUM statement.

What Variables Are Summed?

If you use a SUM statement, PROC PRINT subtotals only the SUM variables. Otherwise, PROC PRINT subtotals all the numeric variables in the data set except those listed in the ID and BY statements.

VAR Statement

Selects variables that appear in the report and determines their order.

Tip: If you omit the VAR statement, PROC PRINT prints all variables in the data set.

Featured in: Example 1 on page 798 and Example 8 on page 813

VAR *variable(s)*;

Required Arguments

variable(s)
> identifies the variables to print. PROC PRINT prints the variables in the order that you list them.
>
> **Interaction:** In the PROC PRINT output, variables that are listed in the ID statement precede variables that are listed in the VAR statement. If a variable in the ID statement also appears in the VAR statement, the output contains two columns for that variable.

Results

Procedure Output

PROC PRINT always produces a printed report. You control the appearance of the report with statements and options. See "Examples" on page 798 for a sampling of the types of reports that the procedure produces.

Page Layout

By default, PROC PRINT uses an identical layout for all observations on a page of output. First, it attempts to print observations on a single line (see Figure 28.2 on page 795).

Figure 28.2 Printing Observations on a Single Line

				1
Obs	Var_1	Var_2	Var_3	
1	~~~~	~~~~	~~~~	
2	~~~~	~~~~	~~~~	
3	~~~~	~~~~	~~~~	
4	~~~~	~~~~	~~~~	
5	~~~~	~~~~	~~~~	
6	~~~~	~~~~	~~~~	

If PROC PRINT cannot fit all the variables on a single line, it splits the observations into two or more sections and prints the observation number or the ID variables at the beginning of each line. For example, in Figure 28.3 on page 796, PROC PRINT prints the values for the first three variables in the first section of each page and the values for the second three variables in the second section of each page.

Figure 28.3   Splitting Observations into Multiple Sections on One Page

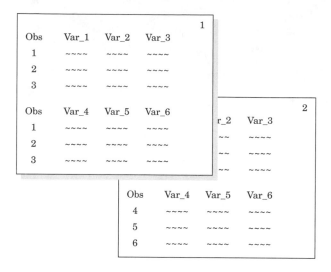

If PROC PRINT cannot fit all the variables on one page, the procedure prints subsequent pages with the same observations until it has printed all the variables. For example, in Figure 28.4 on page 796, PROC PRINT uses the first two pages to print values for the first three observations and the second two pages to print values for the rest of the observations.

Figure 28.4   Splitting Observations across Multiple Pages

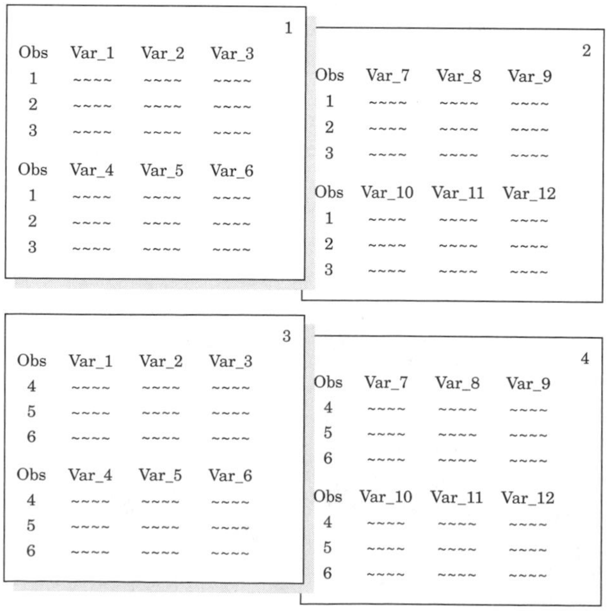

Note: You can alter the page layout with the ROWS= option in the PROC PRINT statement (see the discussion of ROWS= on page 789). △

Note: PROC PRINT may produce slightly different output if the data set is not RADIX addressable. Version 6 compressed files are not RADIX addressable, while, beginning with Version 7, compressed files are RADIX addressable. (The integrity of the data is not compromised; the procedure simply numbers the observations differently.) △

Column Headings

By default, spacing dictates whether PROC PRINT prints column headings horizontally or vertically. Figure 28.2 on page 795, Figure 28.3 on page 796, and Figure 28.4 on page 796 all illustrate horizontal headings. Figure 28.5 on page 797 illustrates vertical headings.

Figure 28.5 Using Vertical Headings

```
                              1
           V     V     V
           a     a     a
    O      r     r     r
    b      –     –     –
    s      1     2     3

    1    ~~~~  ~~~~  ~~~~
    2    ~~~~  ~~~~  ~~~~
    3    ~~~~  ~~~~  ~~~~
    4    ~~~~  ~~~~  ~~~~
    5    ~~~~  ~~~~  ~~~~
    6    ~~~~  ~~~~  ~~~~
```

Note: If you use LABEL and at least one variable has a label, PROC PRINT prints all column headings horizontally unless you specify HEADING=VERTICAL. △

Column Width

By default, PROC PRINT uses a variable's formatted width as the column width. (The WIDTH= option overrides this default behavior.) If the variable does not have a format that explicitly specifies a field width, PROC PRINT uses the widest data value for that variable on that page as the column width.

If the formatted value of a character variable or the data width of an unformatted character variable exceeds the linesize minus the length of all the ID variables, PROC PRINT may truncate the value. Consider the following situation:

- The linesize is 80.
- IdNumber is a character variable with a length of 10. It is used as an ID variable.
- State is a character variable with a length of 2. It is used as an ID variable.
- Comment is a character variable with a length of 200.

When PROC PRINT prints these three variables on a line, it uses 14 print positions for the two ID variables and the space after each one. This leaves 80–14, or 66, print positions for COMMENT. Longer values of COMMENT are truncated.

WIDTH= controls the column width.

Note: Column width is affected not only by variable width but also by the length of column headings. Long column headings may lessen the usefulness of WIDTH=. △

Examples

Example 1: Selecting Variables to Print

Procedure features:
  PROC PRINT statement options:
    DOUBLE
  VAR statement

This example
- [ ] selects three variables for the report
- [ ] uses variable labels as column headings
- [ ] double spaces between rows of the report.

Program

```
options nodate pageno=1 linesize=70 pagesize=60;
```

The data set EXPREV contains information on a company's monthly expenses and revenues for two regions of the United States.

```
data exprev;
   input Region $ State $ Month monyy5.
       Expenses Revenues;
   format month monyy5.;
   datalines;
Southern GA JAN95 2000   8000
Southern GA FEB95 1200   6000
Southern FL FEB95 8500  11000
Northern NY FEB95 3000   4000
Northern NY MAR95 6000   5000
Southern FL MAR95 9800  13500
Northern MA MAR95 1500   1000
;
```

DOUBLE writes a blank line between observations. (This option has no effect on the HTML output.)

```
proc print data=exprev double;
```

The VAR statement creates columns for Month, State, and Expenses, in that order.

```
     var month state expenses;
```

The TITLE statement specifies a title for the report.

```
     title 'Monthly Expenses for Offices in Each State';
run;
```

Output

By default, PROC PRINT identifies each observation by number under the column heading **Obs**.

```
            Monthly Expenses for Offices in Each State              1

                 Obs     Month     State     Expenses

                  1      JAN95      GA          2000

                  2      FEB95      GA          1200

                  3      FEB95      FL          8500

                  4      FEB95      NY          3000

                  5      MAR95      NY          6000

                  6      MAR95      FL          9800

                  7      MAR95      MA          1500
```

Example 2: Customizing Text in Column Headers

Procedure features:
   PROC PRINT statement options:
      N
      OBS=
      SPLIT=
Other features:
   LABEL statement
Data set: EXPREV on page 798

This example

□ customizes and underlines the text in column headings for variables

□ customizes the column header for the column that identifies observations by number

□ shows the number of observations in the report

□ writes the values of Expenses with commas.

Program

```
options nodate pageno=1 linesize=70 pagesize=60;
```

SPLIT= identifies the asterisk as the character that starts a new line in column headers. The N option prints the number of observations at the end of the report. OBS= specifies the column header for the column that identifies each observation by number. The split character (*) starts a new line in the column heading. Therefore, the equal signs (=) in the value of OBS= underline the column header.

```
proc print data=exprev split='*' n obs='Observation*Number*===========';
```

The VAR statement creates columns for Month, State, and Expenses, in that order.

```
var month state expenses;
```

The LABEL statement associates a label with each variable for the duration of the PROC PRINT step. When you use SPLIT= in the PROC PRINT statement, the procedure uses labels for column headers. The split character (*) starts a new line in the column heading. Therefore, the equal signs (=) in the labels underline the column headers.

```
label month='Month**====='
      state='State**====='
      expenses='Expenses**=======';
```

The FORMAT statement assigns a format to use for Expenses in the report. The TITLE statement specifies a title.

```
format expenses comma10.;
title 'Monthly Expenses for Offices in Each State';
run;
```

Output

```
      Monthly Expenses for Offices in Each State              1

   Observation    Month    State     Expenses
     Number

   ===========    =====    =====     ========

        1         JAN95     GA         2,000
        2         FEB95     GA         1,200
        3         FEB95     FL         8,500
        4         FEB95     NY         3,000
        5         MAR95     NY         6,000
        6         MAR95     FL         9,800
        7         MAR95     MA         1,500

            N = 7
```

Example 3: Creating Separate Sections of a Report for Groups of Observations

Procedure features:
    PROC PRINT statement options:
        LABEL
        N=
        NOOBS
    BY statement
    PAGEBY statement
Other features:
    SORT procedure
    LABEL statement
Data set: EXPREV on page 798

This example
  □ suppresses the printing of observation numbers at the beginning of each row
  □ presents the data for each state in a separate section of the report
  □ begins a new page for each region.

Program

```
options pagesize=60 pageno=1 nodate linesize=70;
```

PROC SORT sorts the observations by Region, State, and Month.

```
proc sort data=exprev;
    by region state month;
```

```
run;
```

N= prints the number of observations in a BY group at the end of that BY group. The explanatory text that the N= option provides precedes the number. NOOBS suppresses the printing of observation numbers at the beginning of the rows. LABEL uses variables' labels as column headings.

```
proc print data=exprev n='Number of observations for the state: '
          noobs label;
```

The VAR statement creates columns for Month, Expenses, and Revenues, in that order.

```
var month expenses revenues;
```

The BY statement produces a separate section of the report for each BY group and prints a heading above each one. The PAGEBY statement starts a new page each time the value of Region changes.

```
by region state;
pageby region;
```

The LABEL statement associates a label with the variable Region for the duration of the PROC PRINT step. When you use the LABEL option in the PROC PRINT statement, the procedure uses labels for column headings.

```
label region='Sales Region';
```

The FORMAT statement assigns a format to Expenses and Revenues for this report. The TITLE statement specifies a title.

```
format revenues expenses comma10.;
title 'Sales Figures Grouped by Region and State';
run;
```

Output

```
                    Sales Figures Grouped by Region and State                1

------------------- Sales Region=Northern State=MA -------------------

            Month        Expenses        Revenues

            MAR95          1,500           1,000

        Number of observations for the state: 1


------------------- Sales Region=Northern State=NY -------------------

            Month        Expenses        Revenues

            FEB95          3,000           4,000
            MAR95          6,000           5,000

        Number of observations for the state: 2
```

```
                    Sales Figures Grouped by Region and State                2

------------------- Sales Region=Southern State=FL -------------------

            Month        Expenses        Revenues

            FEB95          8,500          11,000
            MAR95          9,800          13,500

        Number of observations for the state: 2


------------------- Sales Region=Southern State=GA -------------------

            Month        Expenses        Revenues

            JAN95          2,000           8,000
            FEB95          1,200           6,000

        Number of observations for the state: 2
```

Example 4: Summing Numeric Variables with One BY Group

Procedure features:
    PROC PRINT statement options:
      N=
    BY statement
    SUM statement
Other features:
    SORT procedure
    TITLE statement
      #BYVAL specification
    SAS system options :

BYLINE
NOBYLINE

Data set: EXPREV on page 798

This example

☐ sums expenses and revenues for each region and for all regions

☐ shows the number of observations in each BY group and in the whole report

☐ creates a customized title, containing the name of the region. This title replaces the default BY line for each BY group.

Program

The SAS system option NOBYLINE suppresses the printing of the default BY line. When you use PROC PRINT with NOBYLINE, each BY group starts on a new page.

```
options nodate pageno=1 linesize=70 pagesize=60 nobyline;
```

PROC SORT sorts the observations by Region.

```
proc sort data=exprev;
   by region;
run;
```

NOOBS suppresses the printing of observation numbers at the beginning of the rows. N= prints the number of observations in a BY group at the end of that BY group and (because of the SUM statement) prints the number of observations in the data set at the end of the report. The first piece of explanatory text that N= provides precedes the number for each BY group. The second piece of explanatory text that N= provides precedes the number for the entire data set.

```
proc print data=exprev noobs
           n='Number of observations for the state: '
             'Number of observations for the data set: ';
```

The SUM statement alone sums the values of Expenses and Revenues for the entire data set. Because the PROC PRINT step contains a BY statement, the SUM statement also sums the values of Expenses and Revenues for each region that contains more than one observation.

```
   sum expenses revenues;
   by region;
```

The FORMAT statement assigns the COMMA10. format to Expenses and Revenues for this report.

```
   format revenues expenses comma10.;
```

The TITLE statement specifies a title. The #BYVAL specification places the current value of the BY variable Region in the title. Because NOBYLINE is in effect, each BY group starts on a new page, and the title serves as a BY line.

```
    title 'Revenue and Expense Totals for the
#byval(region) Region';
run;
```

The SAS system option BYLINE resets the printing of the default BY line.

```
options byline;
```

Output

```
        Revenue and Expense Totals for the Northern Region        1

        State     Month     Expenses        Revenues

        NY        FEB95        3,000           4,000
        NY        MAR95        6,000           5,000
        MA        MAR95        1,500           1,000
        ------              ----------      ----------
        Region              10,500          10,000

          Number of observations for the state: 3
```

```
        Revenue and Expense Totals for the Southern Region        2

        State     Month     Expenses        Revenues

        GA        JAN95        2,000           8,000
        GA        FEB95        1,200           6,000
        FL        FEB95        8,500          11,000
        FL        MAR95        9,800          13,500
        ------              ----------      ----------
        Region              21,500          38,500
                            ==========      ==========
                            32,000          48,500

      Number of observations for the state: 4
  Number of observations for the data set: 7
```

Example 5: Summing Numeric Variables with Multiple BY Variables

Procedure features:
  BY statement
  SUM statement
Other features: SORT procedure

Data set: EXPREV on page 798

This example

☐ sums expenses and revenues for

  ☐ each region

  ☐ each state with more than one row in the report

  ☐ all rows in the report.

☐ shows the number of observations in each BY group and in the whole report.

Program

```
options nodate pageno=1 linesize=70 pagesize=60;
```

PROC SORT sorts the observations by Region and State.

```
proc sort data=exprev;
   by region state;
run;
```

The N option prints the number of observations in a BY group at the end of that BY group and prints the total number of observations used in the report at the bottom of the report. NOOBS suppresses the printing of observation numbers at the beginning of the rows.

```
proc print data=exprev n noobs;
```

The BY statement produces a separate section of the report for each BY group. The SUM statement alone sums the values of Expenses and Revenues for the entire data set. Because the program contains a BY statement, the SUM statement also sums the values of Expenses and Revenues for each BY group that contains more than one observation.

```
by region state;
sum expenses revenues;
```

The LABEL statement associates a label with the variable Region for the duration of the PROC PRINT step. The BY line at the beginning of each BY group uses the label. The FORMAT statement assigns a format to Expenses and Revenues for this report. The TITLE statement specifies a title.

```
label  region='Sales Region';
format revenues expenses comma10.;
title 'Revenue and Expense Totals for Each State and Region';
run;
```

Output

The report uses default column headers (variable names) because neither the SPLIT= nor the LABEL option is used. Nevertheless, the BY line at the top of each section of the report shows the BY variables' labels and their values. The name of a BY variable identifies the subtotals in the report.

PROC PRINT sums Expenses and Revenues for each BY group that contains more than one observation. However, sums are shown only for the BY variables whose values change from one BY group to the next. For example, in the third BY group, where the sales region is **Southern** and the state is **FL**, expenses and revenues are summed only for the state because the next BY group is for the same region.

```
                 Revenue and Expense Totals for Each State and Region        1

------------------- Sales Region=Northern State=MA --------------------

               Month       Expenses       Revenues

               MAR95          1,500          1,000

                             N = 1


------------------- Sales Region=Northern State=NY --------------------

               Month       Expenses       Revenues

               FEB95          3,000          4,000
               MAR95          6,000          5,000
               ------      ----------     ----------
               State          9,000          9,000
               Region        10,500         10,000

                             N = 2


------------------- Sales Region=Southern State=FL --------------------

               Month       Expenses       Revenues

               FEB95          8,500         11,000
               MAR95          9,800         13,500
               ------      ----------     ----------
               State         18,300         24,500

                             N = 2


------------------- Sales Region=Southern State=GA --------------------

               Month       Expenses       Revenues

               JAN95          2,000          8,000
               FEB95          1,200          6,000
               ------      ----------     ----------
               State          3,200         14,000
               Region        21,500         38,500
                           ==========     ==========
                             32,000         48,500

                             N = 2
                     Total N = 7
```

Example 6: Limiting the Number of Sums in a Report

Features:
    BY statement
    SUM statement
    SUMBY statement

Other features:
    SORT procedure
    LABEL statement

Data set: EXPREV on page 798

This example

☐ creates a separate section of the report for each combination of state and region

☐ sums expenses and revenues only for each region and for all regions, not for individual states.

Program

```
options nodate pageno=1 linesize=70 pagesize=60;
```

PROC SORT sorts the observations by Region and State.

```
proc sort data=exprev;
   by region state;
run;
```

NOOBS suppresses the printing of observation numbers at the beginning of the rows.

```
proc print data=exprev noobs;
```

The SUM and BY statements work together to sum the values of Revenues and Expenses for each BY group as well as for the whole report. The SUMBY statement limits the subtotals to one for each region.

```
   by region state;
   sum revenues expenses;
   sumby region;
```

The LABEL statement associates a label with the variable Region for the duration of the PROC PRINT step. This label is used in the BY lines.

```
   label region='Sales Region';
```

The FORMAT statement assigns the COMMA10. format to Expenses and Revenues for this
report. The TITLE statement specifies the title.

```
    format revenues expenses comma10.;
    title 'Revenue and Expense Figures for Each Region';
run;
```

Output

The report uses default column headers (variable names) because neither the SPLIT= nor the
LABEL option is used. Nevertheless, the BY line at the top of each section of the report shows
the BY variables' labels and their values. The name of a BY variable identifies the subtotals in
the report.

```
                 Revenue and Expense Figures for Each Region                1

------------------- Sales Region=Northern State=MA -------------------

               Month       Expenses        Revenues

               MAR95          1,500           1,000


------------------- Sales Region=Northern State=NY -------------------

               Month       Expenses        Revenues

               FEB95          3,000           4,000
               MAR95          6,000           5,000
               ------      ----------      ----------
               Region        10,500          10,000


------------------- Sales Region=Southern State=FL -------------------

               Month       Expenses        Revenues

               FEB95          8,500          11,000
               MAR95          9,800          13,500


------------------- Sales Region=Southern State=GA -------------------

               Month       Expenses        Revenues

               JAN95          2,000           8,000
               FEB95          1,200           6,000
               ------      ----------      ----------
               Region        21,500          38,500
                           ==========      ==========
                              32,000          48,500
```

Example 7: Controlling the Layout of a Report with Many Variables

Procedure features:
 PROC PRINT statement options:
  ROWS=
 ID statement
Other features:
 SAS data set options:
  OBS=

This example shows two ways of printing a data set with a large number of variables: one is the default, and the other uses ROWS=. For detailed explanations of the layouts of these two reports, see the ROWS= option on page 789 and see "Page Layout" on page 795.

These reports use a pagesize of 24 and a linesize of 64 to help illustrate the different layouts.

Note: When the two reports are written as HTML output, they do not differ. △

Program

```
options nodate pageno=1 linesize=64 pagesize=24 ;
```

The data set EMPDATA contains personal and job-related information about a company's employees. A DATA step on page 1501 creates this data set.

```
data empdata;
   input IdNumber $ 1-4 LastName $ 9-19 FirstName $ 20-29
         City $ 30-42 State $ 43-44 /
         Gender $ 1 JobCode $ 9-11 Salary 20-29 @30 Birth date7.
         @43 Hired date7. HomePhone $ 54-65;
   format birth hired date7.;
   datalines;
1919    Adams      Gerald   Stamford    CT
M       TA2        34376    15SEP48     07JUN75    203/781-1255
1653    Alexander  Susan    Bridgeport  CT
F       ME2        35108    18OCT52     12AUG78    203/675-7715

. . . more lines of data . . .

1407    Grant      Daniel   Mt. Vernon  NY
M       PT1        68096    26MAR57     21MAR78    914/468-1616
1114    Green      Janice   New York    NY
F       TA2        32928    21SEP57     30JUN75    212/588-1092
;
```

The OBS= data set option uses only the first 12 observations to create the report. (This is just to conserve space here.) The ID statement identifies observations with the formatted value of IdNumber rather than with the observation number. This report is in Output 28.3 on page 811.

```
proc print data=empdata(obs=12);
   id idnumber;
   title 'Personnel Data';
run;
```

ROWS=PAGE prints only one row of variables for each observation on a page. This report is in Output 28.4 on page 812.

```
proc print data=empdata(obs=12) rows=page;
   id idnumber;
   title 'Personnel Data';
run;
```

Output

Output 28.3 Default Layout for a Report with Many Variables

In the traditional procedure output, each page of this report contains values for all variables in each observation. In the HTML output, this report is identical to the report that uses ROWS=PAGE.

Note that PROC PRINT automatically splits the variable names that are used as column headers at a change in capitalization if the entire name does not fit in the column. Compare, for example, the column headers for LastName (which fits in the column) and FirstName (which does not fit in the column).

```
                         Personnel Data                              1

 Id                   First
Number    LastName    Name          City         State    Gender

 1919     Adams       Gerald     Stamford         CT         M
 1653     Alexander   Susan      Bridgeport       CT         F
 1400     Apple       Troy       New York         NY         M
 1350     Arthur      Barbara    New York         NY         F
 1401     Avery       Jerry      Paterson         NJ         M
 1499     Barefoot    Joseph     Princeton        NJ         M
 1101     Baucom      Walter     New York         NY         M

 Id       Job
Number    Code    Salary       Birth      Hired      HomePhone

 1919     TA2      34376     15SEP48    07JUN75    203/781-1255
 1653     ME2      35108     18OCT52    12AUG78    203/675-7715
 1400     ME1      29769     08NOV55    19OCT78    212/586-0808
 1350     FA3      32886     03SEP53    01AUG78    718/383-1549
 1401     TA3      38822     16DEC38    20NOV73    201/732-8787
 1499     ME3      43025     29APR42    10JUN68    201/812-5665
 1101     SCP      18723     09JUN50    04OCT78    212/586-8060
```

```
                        Personnel Data                            2
     Id                    First
   Number    LastName      Name          City        State    Gender

   1333      Blair         Justin        Stamford      CT        M
   1402      Blalock       Ralph         New York      NY        M
   1479      Bostic        Marie         New York      NY        F
   1403      Bowden        Earl          Bridgeport    CT        M
   1739      Boyce         Jonathan      New York      NY        M

     Id      Job
   Number    Code    Salary      Birth      Hired      HomePhone

   1333      PT2     88606     02APR49    13FEB69    203/781-1777
   1402      TA2     32615     20JAN51    05DEC78    718/384-2849
   1479      TA3     38785     25DEC56    08OCT77    718/384-8816
   1403      ME1     28072     31JAN57    24DEC79    203/675-3434
   1739      PT1     66517     28DEC52    30JAN79    212/587-1247
```

Output 28.4   Layout Produced by the ROWS=PAGE Option

Each page of this report contains values for only some of the variables
in each observation. However, each page contains values for more
observations than the default report does.

```
                        Personnel Data                            1
     Id                    First
   Number    LastName      Name          City        State    Gender

   1919      Adams         Gerald        Stamford      CT        M
   1653      Alexander     Susan         Bridgeport    CT        F
   1400      Apple         Troy          New York      NY        M
   1350      Arthur        Barbara       New York      NY        F
   1401      Avery         Jerry         Paterson      NJ        M
   1499      Barefoot      Joseph        Princeton     NJ        M
   1101      Baucom        Walter        New York      NY        M
   1333      Blair         Justin        Stamford      CT        M
   1402      Blalock       Ralph         New York      NY        M
   1479      Bostic        Marie         New York      NY        F
   1403      Bowden        Earl          Bridgeport    CT        M
   1739      Boyce         Jonathan      New York      NY        M
```

```
                        Personnel Data                    2

  Id       Job
Number     Code    Salary     Birth     Hired     HomePhone

  1919     TA2     34376     15SEP48   07JUN75   203/781-1255
  1653     ME2     35108     18OCT52   12AUG78   203/675-7715
  1400     ME1     29769     08NOV55   19OCT78   212/586-0808
  1350     FA3     32886     03SEP53   01AUG78   718/383-1549
  1401     TA3     38822     16DEC38   20NOV73   201/732-8787
  1499     ME3     43025     29APR42   10JUN68   201/812-5665
  1101     SCP     18723     09JUN50   04OCT78   212/586-8060
  1333     PT2     88606     02APR49   13FEB69   203/781-1777
  1402     TA2     32615     20JAN51   05DEC78   718/384-2849
  1479     TA3     38785     25DEC56   08OCT77   718/384-8816
  1403     ME1     28072     31JAN57   24DEC79   203/675-3434
  1739     PT1     66517     28DEC52   30JAN79   212/587-1247
```

Example 8: Creating a Customized Layout with BY Groups and ID Variables

Procedure features:
   BY statement
   ID statement
   SUM statement
   VAR statement

Other features:
   SORT procedure

Data set: EMPDATA on page 810

This customized report
   □ selects variables to include in the report and controls their order
   □ selects observations to include in the report
   □ groups the selected observations by JobCode
   □ sums the salaries for each job code and for all job codes
   □ displays numeric data with commas and dollar signs.

Program

PROC SORT creates a temporary data set in which the observations are sorted by JobCode and Gender.

```
options nodate pageno=1 linesize=64 pagesize=60;
proc sort data=empdata out=tempemp;
   by jobcode gender;
run;
```

SPLIT= identifies the asterisk as the character that starts a new line in column headers.

```
proc print data=tempemp split='*';
```

The VAR statement and the ID statement together select the variables to include in the report. The ID statement and the BY statement produce the special format.

```
id jobcode;
by jobcode;
var gender salary;
```

The SUM statement totals the values of Salary for each BY group and for the whole report.

```
sum salary;
```

The LABEL statement associates a label with each variable for the duration of the PROC PRINT step. When you use SPLIT= in the PROC PRINT statement, the procedure uses labels for column headings.

```
label jobcode='Job Code*========'
      gender='Gender*======'
      salary='Annual Salary*=============';
```

The FORMAT statement assigns a format to Salary for this report. The WHERE statement selects for the report only the observations for job codes that contain the letters 'FA' or 'ME'. The TITLE statements specify two titles.

```
format salary dollar11.2;
where jobcode contains 'FA' or jobcode contains 'ME';
title 'Expenses Incurred for';
title2 'Salaries for Flight Attendants and Mechanics';
run;
```

Output

The ID and BY statements work together to produce this layout. The ID variable is listed only once for each BY group. The BY lines are suppressed. Instead, the value of the ID variable, JobCode, identifies each BY group.

```
                      Expenses Incurred for                      1
            Salaries for Flight Attendants and Mechanics

              Job Code      Gender      Annual Salary
              ========      ======      =============

                FA1           F           $23,177.00
                              F           $22,454.00
                              M           $22,268.00
              --------                  -------------
                FA1                       $67,899.00

                FA2           F           $28,888.00
                              F           $27,787.00
                              M           $28,572.00
              --------                  -------------
                FA2                       $85,247.00

                FA3           F           $32,886.00
                              F           $33,419.00
                              M           $32,217.00
              --------                  -------------
                FA3                       $98,522.00

                ME1           M           $29,769.00
                              M           $28,072.00
                              M           $28,619.00
              --------                  -------------
                ME1                       $86,460.00

                ME2           F           $35,108.00
                              F           $34,929.00
                              M           $35,345.00
                              M           $36,925.00
                              M           $35,090.00
                              M           $35,185.00
              --------                  -------------
                ME2                      $212,582.00

                ME3           M           $43,025.00
                                         =============
                                         $593,735.00
```

Example 9: Printing All the Data Sets in a SAS Library

Features:
   Macro facility
   DATASETS procedure
   PRINT procedure

Data set: EXPREV on page 798 and LIST on page 492

This example prints all the data sets in a SAS library. You can use the same programming logic with any procedure. Just replace the PROC PRINT step near the end of the example with whatever procedure step you want to execute. The example uses the macro language. For details about the macro language, see *SAS Guide to Macro Processing, Version 6, Second Edition.*

Program

```
libname printlib 'SAS-data-library'
options nodate pageno=1 linesize=80 pagesize=60;
```

PROC DATASETS copies two data sets out of the WORK library into the PRINTLIB library to limit the number of data sets available to the example.

```
proc datasets library=work memtype=data nolist;
   copy out=printlib;
      select list exprev;
run;
```

The %MACRO statement creates the macro PRINTALL. When you call the macro, you can pass it one or two parameters. The first parameter is the name of the library whose data set you want to print. The second parameter is a library used by the macro. If you do not specify this parameter, the WORK library is the default.

```
%macro printall(libname,worklib=work);
```

The %LOCAL statement creates two local macro variables, NUM and I, to use in a loop.

```
   %local num i;
```

This PROC DATASETS step reads the library LIBNAME that you specify as a parameter when you invoke the macro. The CONTENTS statement produces an output data set called TEMP1 in WORKLIB. This data set contains an observation for each variable in each data set in the library LIBNAME. By default, each observation includes the name of the data set that the variable is in as well as other information about the variable. However, the KEEP= data set option writes only the name of the data set to TEMP1.

```
   proc datasets library=&libname memtype=data nodetails;
      contents out=&worklib..temp1(keep=memname) data=_all_ noprint;
   run;
```

This DATA step increments the value of N each time that it reads the last occurrence of a data set name (when IF LAST.MEMNAME is true). The CALL SYMPUT statement uses the current value of N to create a macro variable for each unique value of MEMNAME in the data set TEMP1. The TRIM function removes extra blanks in the TITLE statement in the PROC PRINT step that follows.

```
   data _null_;
      set &worklib..temp1 end=final;
```

```
      by memname notsorted;
      if last.memname;
      n+1;
      call symput('ds'||left(put(n,8.)),trim(memname));
```

When it reads the last observation in the data set (when FINAL is true), the DATA step assigns the value of N to the macro variable NUM. At this point in the program, the value of N is the number of observations in the data set.

```
      if final then call symput('num',put(n,8.));
```

The RUN statement is crucial. It forces the DATA step to run, thus creating the macro variables used in the CALL SYMPUT statements before the %DO loop, which uses them, executes.

```
   run;
```

The %DO loop issues a PROC PRINT step for each data set. The %MEND statement ends the macro.

```
   %do i=1 %to &num;
      proc print data=&libname..&&ds&i noobs;
         title "Data Set &libname..&&ds&i";
      run;
   %end;
%mend printall;
```

This invocation of the PRINTALL macro prints all the data sets in the library PRINTLIB.

```
options nodate pageno=1 linesize=70 pagesize=60;
%printall(printlib)
```

Output

```
                  Data Set printlib.EXPREV                      1

      Region    State    Month    Expenses    Revenues

      Northern    MA     MAR95      1500        1000
      Northern    NY     FEB95      3000        4000
      Northern    NY     MAR95      6000        5000
      Southern    FL     FEB95      8500       11000
      Southern    FL     MAR95      9800       13500
      Southern    GA     JAN95      2000        8000
      Southern    GA     FEB95      1200        6000
```

```
                        Data Set printlib.LIST                        2

Name                  Street              City         State   Zip

Gabrielli, Theresa    24 Ridgetop Rd.     Westboro     MA      01581
Clayton, Aria         314 Bridge St.      Hanover      NH      03755
Dix, Martin L.        4 Shepherd St.      Norwich      VT      05055
Slater, Emily C.      2009 Cherry St.     York         PA      17407
Ericson, Jane         211 Clancey Court   Chapel Hill  NC      27514
An, Ing               95 Willow Dr.       Charlotte    NC      28211
Jacobson, Becky       7 Lincoln St.       Tallahassee  FL      32312
Misiewicz, Jeremy     43-C Lakeview Apts. Madison      WI      53704
Ahmadi, Hafez         5203 Marston Way    Boulder      CO      80302
Archuleta, Ruby       Box 108             Milagro      NM      87429
```

CHAPTER

29

The PRINTTO Procedure

Overview

The PRINTTO procedure defines destinations for SAS procedure output and for the SAS log. By default, SAS procedure output and the SAS log are routed to the default procedure output file and the default SAS log file for your method of operation. See Table 29.1 on page 819. You can store the SAS log or procedure output in an external file or in a SAS catalog entry. With additional programming, you can use SAS output as input data within the same job.

Table 29.1 Default Destinations for SAS Log and Procedure Output

Method of running the SAS System	SAS log destination	Procedure output destination
windowing environment	the LOG window	the OUTPUT window
interactive line mode	the display monitor (as statements are entered)	the display monitor (as each step executes)
noninteractive mode or batch mode	depends on the host operating system	depends on the operating environment

Operating Environment Information: For information and examples specific to your operating system or environment, see the appropriate SAS Companion or technical report. △

Procedure Syntax

PROC PRINTTO *<option(s)>*;

PROC PRINTTO Statement

Tip: To reset the destination for the SAS log and procedure output to the default, use the PROC PRINTTO statement without options.

Tip: To route the SAS log and procedure output to the same file, specify the same file with both the LOG= and PRINT= options.

PROC PRINTTO *<option(s)>*;

To do this	Use this option
provide a description for a SAS log or procedure output stored in a SAS catalog entry	LABEL=
route the SAS log to a permanent external file or SAS catalog entry	LOG=
combine the SAS log and procedure output into a single file	LOG= and PRINT= with same destination
replace the file instead of appending to it	NEW=
route procedure output to a permanent external file or SAS catalog entry	PRINT=

Without Options

Using a PROC PRINTTO statement with no options
□ closes any files opened by a PROC PRINTTO statement
□ points both the SAS log and SAS procedure output to their default destinations.

Interaction: To close the appropriate file and to return only the SAS log or procedure output to its default destination, use LOG=LOG or PRINT=PRINT.

Featured in: Example 1 on page 823 and Example 2 on page 825

Options

LABEL=*'description'*
provides a description for a catalog entry that contains a SAS log or procedure output.

Range: 1 to 40 characters

Interaction: Use the LABEL= option only when you specify a catalog entry as the value for the LOG= or the PRINT= option.

Featured in: Example 2 on page 825

LOG=LOG | *file-specification* | *SAS-catalog-entry*
routes the SAS log to one of three locations:

LOG
routes the SAS log to its default destination.

file-specification
routes the SAS log to an external file. It is one of the following:

'external-file'
the name of an external file specified in quotation marks.

fileref
a fileref previously assigned to an external file.

SAS-catalog-entry
routes the SAS log to a SAS catalog entry. By default, *libref* is SASUSER, *catalog* is PROFILE, and *type* is LOG. Express *SAS-catalog-entry* in one of the following ways:

libref.catalog.entry<.LOG>
a SAS catalog entry stored in the SAS data library and SAS catalog specified.

catalog.entry<.LOG>
a SAS catalog entry stored in the specified SAS catalog in the default SAS data library SASUSER.

entry.LOG
a SAS catalog entry stored in the default SAS library and catalog: SASUSER.PROFILE.

Default: LOG.

Tip: After routing the log to an external file or a catalog entry, you can specify LOG to route the SAS log back to its default destination.

Tip: When routing the SAS log, include a RUN statement in the PROC PRINTTO statement. If you omit the RUN statement, the first line of the following DATA or PROC step is not routed to the new file. (This occurs because a statement does not execute until a step boundary is crossed.)

Interaction: The NEW option replaces the existing contents of a file with the new log. Otherwise, the new log is appended to the file.

Interaction: To route the SAS log and procedure output to the same file, specify the same file with both the LOG= and PRINT= options.

Interaction: When routing the log to a SAS catalog entry, you can use the LABEL option to provide a description for the entry in the catalog directory.

Featured in: Example 1 on page 823, Example 2 on page 825, and Example 3 on page 829

NEW
clears any information that exists in a file and prepares the file to receive the SAS log or procedure output.

Default: If you omit NEW, the new information is appended to the existing file.

Interaction: If you specify both LOG= and PRINT=, NEW applies to both.

Featured in: Example 1 on page 823, Example 2 on page 825, and Example 3 on page 829

PRINT= PRINT | *file-specification* | *SAS-catalog-entry*
routes procedure output to one of three locations:

PRINT

routes procedure output to its default destination. After routing it to an external file or a catalog entry, you can specify PRINT to route subsequent procedure output to its default destination.

file-specification

routes procedure output to an external file. It is one of the following:

'external-file'

the name of an external file specified in quotation marks.

fileref

a fileref previously assigned to an external file.

SAS-catalog-entry

routes procedure output to a SAS catalog entry. By default, *libref* is SASUSER, *catalog* is PROFILE, and *type* is LOG. Express *SAS-catalog-entry* in one of the following ways:

libref.catalog.entry<.LOG>

a SAS catalog entry stored in the SAS data library and SAS catalog specified.

catalog.entry<.LOG>

a SAS catalog entry stored in the specified SAS catalog in the default SAS data library SASUSER.

entry.LOG

a SAS catalog entry stored in the default SAS library and catalog: SASUSER.PROFILE.

Aliases: FILE=, NAME=

Default: PRINT

Interaction: The NEW option replaces the existing contents of a file with the new procedure output. If you omit NEW, the new output is appended to the file.

Interaction: To route the SAS log and procedure output to the same file, specify the same file with both the LOG= and PRINT= options.

Interaction: When routing procedure output to a SAS catalog entry, you can use the LABEL option to provide a description for the entry in the catalog directory.

Featured in: Example 3 on page 829

UNIT=*nn*

routes the output to the file identified by the fileref FT*nn*F001, where *nn* is an integer between 1 and 99.

Range: 1 to 99, integer only.

Tip: You can define this fileref yourself; however, some operating systems predefine certain filerefs in this form.

Concepts

Page Numbering

□ When the SAS system option NUMBER is in effect, there is a single page-numbering sequence for all output in the current job or session. When NONUMBER is in effect, output pages are not numbered.

☐ You can specify the beginning page number for the output you are currently producing by using the PAGENO= in an OPTIONS statement.

Examples

Example 1: Routing to External Files

Procedure features:
    PRINTTO statement:
      Without options
      Options:
        LOG=
        NEW
        PRINT=

This example uses PROC PRINTTO to route the log and procedure output to an external file and then reset both destinations to the default.

Program

SOURCE writes the lines of source code to the default destination for the SAS log. See Output 29.1 on page 824.

```
options nodate pageno=1 linesize=80 pagesize=60 source;
```

PROC PRINTTO uses LOG= to route the SAS log to an external file. By default, this log is appended to the current contents of **log-file**. See Output 29.2 on page 824.

```
proc printto log='log-file';
   run;
```

The DATA step creates the NUMBERS data set.

```
data numbers;
   input x y z;
   datalines;
14.2    25.2     96.8
10.8    51.6     96.8
 9.5    34.2    138.2
 8.8    27.6     83.2
```

```
     11.5    49.4   287.0
      6.3    42.0   170.7
   ;
```

PROC PRINTTO routes output to an external file. Because NEW is specified, any output written to **output-file** will overwrite the file's current contents. The PROC PRINT output is written to the specified external file. See Output 29.3 on page 825.

```
proc printto print='output-file' new;
run;
```

```
proc print data=numbers;
   title 'Listing of NUMBERS Data Set';
run;
```

PROC PRINTTO routes subsequent logs and procedure output to their default destinations and closes both of the current files. See Output 29.1 on page 824.

```
proc printto;
run;
```

Log

Output 29.1   Portion of Log Routed to the Default Destination

```
1         options nodate pageno=1 linesize=80 pagesize=60 source;
2         proc printto log='log-file';
3         run;
```

Output 29.2 Portion of Log Routed to an External File

```
5
6             data numbers;
7                input x y z;
8                datalines;

NOTE: The data set WORK.NUMBERS has 6 observations and 3 variables.
NOTE: DATA statement used:
      real time              0.00 seconds
      cpu time               0.00 seconds


15           ;
16           proc printto print='output-file' new;
16
17           run;

NOTE: PROCEDURE PRINTTO used:
      real time              0.00 seconds
      cpu time               0.00 seconds


18
19           proc print data=numbers;
20               title 'Listing of NUMBERS Data Set';
21           run;

NOTE: The PROCEDURE PRINT printed page 1.
NOTE: PROCEDURE PRINT used:
      real time              0.00 seconds
      cpu time               0.00 seconds


22
23           proc printto;
24           run;
```

Output

Output 29.3 Procedure Output Routed to an External File

```
                    Listing of NUMBERS Data Set                    1

                   OBS      x       y       z

                    1     14.2    25.2    96.8
                    2     10.8    51.6    96.8
                    3      9.5    34.2   138.2
                    4      8.8    27.6    83.2
                    5     11.5    49.4   287.0
                    6      6.3    42.0   170.7
```

Example 2: Routing to SAS Catalog Entries

Procedure features:

PRINTTO statement:

Without options

Options:

LABEL=

LOG=

NEW

PRINT=

This example uses PROC PRINTTO to route the SAS log and procedure output to a SAS catalog entry and then to reset both destinations to the default.

Program

```
libname lib1 'SAS-data-library';

options nodate pageno=1 linesize=80 pagesize=60 source;
```

PROC PRINTTO routes the SAS log to a SAS catalog entry named
SASUSER.PROFILE.TEST.LOG. The PRINTTO procedure uses the default libref and catalog
SASUSER.PROFILE because only the entry name and type are specified. LABEL= assigns a
description for the catalog entry. See Output 29.4 on page 828.

```
proc printto log=test.log label='Inventory program' new;
run;
```

The DATA step creates a permanent SAS data set.

```
data lib1.inventry;
   length Dept $ 4 Item $ 6 Season $ 6 Year 4;
   input dept item season year @@;
   datalines;
3070 20410   spring 1996 3070 20411   spring 1997
3070 20412   spring 1997 3070 20413   spring 1997
3070 20414   spring 1996 3070 20416   spring 1995
3071 20500   spring 1994 3071 20501   spring 1995
3071 20502   spring 1996 3071 20503   spring 1996
3071 20505   spring 1994 3071 20506   spring 1994
3071 20507   spring 1994 3071 20424   spring 1994
;
```

PROC PRINTTO routes procedure output from the subsequent PROC REPORT to the SAS
catalog entry LIB1.CAT1.INVENTRY.OUTPUT. LABEL= assigns a description for the catalog
entry. See Output 29.5 on page 828.

```
proc printto print=lib1.cat1.inventry.output
             label='Inventory program' new;
run;

proc report data=lib1.inventry nowindows headskip;
   column dept item season year;
   title 'Current Inventory Listing';
run;
```

PROC PRINTTO closes the current files opened by PROC PRINTTO and reroutes subsequent
SAS logs and procedure output to their default destinations.

```
proc printto;
run;
```

Log

Output 29.4   SAS Log Routed to SAS Catalog Entry SASUSER.PROFILE.TEST.LOG.

You can view this catalog entry in the BUILD window of the SAS Explorer.

```
8
9    data lib1.inventry;
10      length Dept $ 4 Item $ 6 Season $ 6 Year 4;
11      input dept item season year @@;
12      datalines;

NOTE: SAS went to a new line when INPUT statement reached past the end of a
      line.
NOTE: The data set LIB1.INVENTRY has 14 observations and 4 variables.
NOTE: DATA statement used:
      real time              0.00 seconds
      cpu time               0.00 seconds


20   ;
21
22   proc printto print=lib1.cat1.inventry.output
23      label='Inventory program' new;
24   run;

NOTE: PROCEDURE PRINTTO used:
      real time              0.00 seconds
      cpu time               0.00 seconds


25
26   proc report data=lib1.inventry nowindows headskip;
27      column dept item season year;
28      title 'Current Inventory Listing';
29   run;

NOTE: PROCEDURE REPORT used:
      real time              0.00 seconds
      cpu time               0.00 seconds


30
31   proc printto;
32   run;
```

Output

Output 29.5   Procedure Output Routed to SAS Catalog Entry LIB1.CAT1.INVENTRY.OUTPUT.

You can view this catalog entry in the BUILD window of the SAS Explorer.

```
                    Current Inventory Listing                    1

              Dept   Item    Season      Year

              3070   20410   spring      1996
              3070   20411   spring      1997
              3070   20412   spring      1997
              3070   20413   spring      1997
              3070   20414   spring      1996
              3070   20416   spring      1995
              3071   20500   spring      1994
              3071   20501   spring      1995
              3071   20502   spring      1996
              3071   20503   spring      1996
              3071   20505   spring      1994
              3071   20506   spring      1994
              3071   20507   spring      1994
              3071   20424   spring      1994
```

Example 3: Using Procedure Output as an Input File

Procedure features:
  PRINTTO statement:
    Without options
    Options:
      LOG=
      NEW
      PRINT=

This example uses PROC PRINTTO to route procedure output to an external file and then uses that file as input to a DATA step.

The DATA step uses the RANUNI function to randomly generate values for variables X and Y in data set A.

```
data test;
   do n=1 to 1000;
      x=int(ranuni(77777)*7);
      y=int(ranuni(77777)*5);
      output;
   end;
run;
```

The FILENAME statement assigns a fileref to an external file. PROC PRINTTO routes subsequent procedure output to the file referenced by the fileref ROUTED. See Output 29.6 on page 830.

```
filename routed 'output-filename';
```

```
proc printto print=routed new;
run;
```

PROC FREQ computes frequency counts and a chi-square analysis on variables X and Y in data set TEST. This output is routed to the file referenced as ROUTED.

```
proc freq data=test;
   tables x*y / chisq;
run;
```

You must use another PROC PRINTTO to close the file referenced by fileref ROUTED so that the following DATA step can read it. The step also routes subsequent procedure output to the default destination. PRINT= causes the step to affect only procedure output, not the SAS log.

```
proc printto print=print;
run;
```

The DATA step uses ROUTED, the file containing PROC FREQ output, as an input file and creates data set PROBTEST. This DATA step reads all records in ROUTED but creates an observation only from a record that begins with `Chi-Squa`.

```
data probtest;
   infile routed;
   input word1 $ @;
   if word1='Chi-Squa' then
      do;
         input df chisq prob;
         keep chisq prob;
         output;
      end;
run;
```

PROC PRINT produces a simple listing of data set PROBTEST. This output is routed to the default destination. See Output 29.7 on page 831.

```
proc print data=probtest;
   title 'Chi-Square Analysis for Table of X by Y';
run;
```

Output 29.6 PROC FREQ Output Routed to the External File Referenced as ROUTED

```
                              The FREQ Procedure

                              Table of x by y


         x           y

         Frequency|
         Percent  |
         Row Pct  |
         Col Pct  |      0|      1|      2|      3|      4| Total
         ---------+--------+--------+--------+--------+--------+
              0 |     29 |     33 |     12 |     25 |     27 |    126
                |   2.90 |   3.30 |   1.20 |   2.50 |   2.70 |  12.60
                |  23.02 |  26.19 |   9.52 |  19.84 |  21.43 |
                |  15.18 |  16.18 |   6.25 |  11.74 |  13.50 |
         ---------+--------+--------+--------+--------+--------+
              1 |     23 |     26 |     29 |     20 |     19 |    117
                |   2.30 |   2.60 |   2.90 |   2.00 |   1.90 |  11.70
                |  19.66 |  22.22 |  24.79 |  17.09 |  16.24 |
                |  12.04 |  12.75 |  15.10 |   9.39 |   9.50 |
         ---------+--------+--------+--------+--------+--------+
              2 |     28 |     26 |     32 |     30 |     25 |    141
                |   2.80 |   2.60 |   3.20 |   3.00 |   2.50 |  14.10
                |  19.86 |  18.44 |  22.70 |  21.28 |  17.73 |
                |  14.66 |  12.75 |  16.67 |  14.08 |  12.50 |
         ---------+--------+--------+--------+--------+--------+
              3 |     26 |     24 |     36 |     32 |     45 |    163
                |   2.60 |   2.40 |   3.60 |   3.20 |   4.50 |  16.30
                |  15.95 |  14.72 |  22.09 |  19.63 |  27.61 |
                |  13.61 |  11.76 |  18.75 |  15.02 |  22.50 |
         ---------+--------+--------+--------+--------+--------+
              4 |     25 |     31 |     28 |     36 |     29 |    149
                |   2.50 |   3.10 |   2.80 |   3.60 |   2.90 |  14.90
                |  16.78 |  20.81 |  18.79 |  24.16 |  19.46 |
                |  13.09 |  15.20 |  14.58 |  16.90 |  14.50 |
         ---------+--------+--------+--------+--------+--------+
              5 |     32 |     29 |     26 |     33 |     27 |    147
                |   3.20 |   2.90 |   2.60 |   3.30 |   2.70 |  14.70
                |  21.77 |  19.73 |  17.69 |  22.45 |  18.37 |
                |  16.75 |  14.22 |  13.54 |  15.49 |  13.50 |
         ---------+--------+--------+--------+--------+--------+
              6 |     28 |     35 |     29 |     37 |     28 |    157
                |   2.80 |   3.50 |   2.90 |   3.70 |   2.80 |  15.70
                |  17.83 |  22.29 |  18.47 |  23.57 |  17.83 |
                |  14.66 |  17.16 |  15.10 |  17.37 |  14.00 |
         ---------+--------+--------+--------+--------+--------+
         Total        191      204      192      213      200     1000
                    19.10    20.40    19.20    21.30    20.00   100.00
```

2

```
                              The FREQ Procedure

                          Statistics for Table of x by y


         Statistic                      DF       Value        Prob
         ------------------------------------------------------------
         Chi-Square                     24      27.2971      0.2908
         Likelihood Ratio Chi-Square    24      28.1830      0.2524
         Mantel-Haenszel Chi-Square      1       0.6149      0.4330
         Phi Coefficient                        0.1652
         Contingency Coefficient                0.1630
         Cramer's V                             0.0826


                            Sample Size = 1000
```

Output 29.7   PROC PRINT Output of Data Set PROBTEST, Routed to Default Destination

```
                    Chi-Square Analysis for Table of X by Y                    3

                      Obs      chisq      prob

                       1      27.297     0.291
```

CHAPTER

30

The RANK Procedure

Overview

The RANK procedure computes ranks for one or more numeric variables across the observations of a SAS data set and outputs the ranks to a new SAS data set. PROC RANK by itself produces no printed output.

Output 30.1 on page 833 shows the results of ranking the values of one variable with a simple PROC RANK step. In this example, the new ranking variable shows the order of finish of five golfers over a four-day competition. The player with the lowest number of strokes finishes in first place. The following statements produce the output:

```
proc rank data=golf out=rankings;
   var strokes;
   ranks Finish;
run;

proc print data=rankings;
run;
```

Output 30.1   Assignment of the Lowest Rank Value to the Lowest Variable Value

```
                        The SAS System                          1

            OBS    Player    Strokes    Finish

             1     Jack       279         2
             2     Jerry      283         3
             3     Mike       274         1
             4     Randy      296         4
             5     Tito       302         5
```

In Output 30.2 on page 834, the candidates for city council are ranked by district according to the number of votes that they received in the election and according to the number of years that they have served in office.

This example shows how PROC RANK can

□ reverse the order of the rankings so that the highest value receives the rank of 1, the next highest value receives the rank of 2, and so on

□ rank the observations separately by values of multiple variables

□ rank the observations within BY groups

□ handle tied values.

For an explanation of the program that produces this report, see Example 2 on page 842.

Output 30.2   Assignment of the Lowest Rank Value to the Highest Variable Value within Each BY Group

```
                  Results of City Council Election                1
-------------------------------- District=1 --------------------------------

                                              Vote      Years
            OBS    Candidate    Vote   Years  Rank      Rank

             1     Cardella     1689     8      1         1
             2     Latham       1005     2      3         2
             3     Smith        1406     0      2         3
             4     Walker        846     0      4         3

                            N = 4


-------------------------------- District=2 --------------------------------

                                              Vote      Years
            OBS    Candidate    Vote   Years  Rank      Rank

             5     Hinkley       912     0      3         3
             6     Kreitemeyer  1198     0      2         3
             7     Lundell      2447     6      1         1
             8     Thrash        912     2      3         2

                            N = 4
```

Procedure Syntax

Reminder: You can use the ATTRIB, FORMAT, LABEL, and WHERE statements. See Chapter 3, "Statements with the Same Function in Multiple Procedures," for details. You can also use any global statements as well. See Chapter 2, "Fundamental Concepts for Using Base SAS Procedures," for a list.

PROC RANK <*option(s)*>;
  BY <DESCENDING> *variable-1*
     <...<DESCENDING> *variable-n*>
     <NOTSORTED>;
  VAR *data-set-variables(s)*;
  RANKS *new-variables(s)*;

PROC RANK Statement

PROC RANK <*option(s)*>;

To do this	Use this option
Specify the input data set	DATA=
Create an output data set	OUT=
Specify the ranking method	
Compute fractional ranks	FRACTION or NPLUS1
Partition observations into groups	GROUPS=
Compute normal scores	NORMAL=
Compute percentages	PERCENT
Compute Savage scores	SAVAGE
Reverse the order of the rankings	DESCENDING
Specify how to rank tied values	TIES=

Note: You can specify only one ranking method in a single PROC RANK step. △

Options

DATA=*SAS-data-set*
  specifies the input SAS data set.
  Main discussion: "Input Data Sets" on page 18
  Restriction: You cannot use PROC RANK with an engine that supports concurrent access if another user is updating the data set at the same time.

DESCENDING

reverses the direction of the ranks. With DESCENDING, the largest value receives a rank of 1, the next largest value receives a rank of 2, and so on. Otherwise, values are ranked from smallest to largest.

Featured in: Example 1 on page 840 and Example 2 on page 842

FRACTION

computes fractional ranks by dividing each rank by the number of observations having nonmissing values of the ranking variable.

Alias: F

Interaction: TIES=HIGH is the default with the FRACTION option. With TIES=HIGH, fractional ranks can be considered values of a right-continuous empirical cumulative distribution function.

See also: NPLUS1 option

GROUPS=*number-of-groups*

assigns group values ranging from 0 to *number-of-groups* minus 1. Common specifications are GROUPS=100 for percentiles, GROUPS=10 for deciles, and GROUPS=4 for quartiles. For example, GROUPS=4 partitions the original values into four groups, with the smallest values receiving, by default, a quartile value of 0 and the largest values receiving a quartile value of 3.

The formula for calculating group values is

$$\mathrm{FLOOR}\left(rank * k / (n + 1)\right)$$

where FLOOR is the FLOOR function, *rank* is the value's order rank, k is the value of GROUPS=, and n is the number of observations having nonmissing values of the ranking variable.

If the number of observations is evenly divisible by the number of groups, each group has the same number of observations, provided there are no tied values at the boundaries of the groups. Grouping observations by a variable that has many tied values can result in unbalanced groups because PROC RANK always assigns observations with the same value to the same group.

Tip: Use DESCENDING to reverse the order of the group values.

Featured in: Example 3 on page 844

NORMAL=BLOM | TUKEY | VW

computes normal scores from the ranks. The resulting variables appear normally distributed. The formulas are

BLOM	$y_i = \Phi^{-1}(r_i - 3/8)/(n + 1/4)$
TUKEY	$y_i = \Phi^{-1}(r_i - 1/3)/(n + 1/3)$
VW	$y_i = \Phi^{-1}(r_i)/(n + 1)$

where Φ^{-1} is the inverse cumulative normal (PROBIT) function, r_i is the rank of the ith observation, and n is the number of nonmissing observations for the ranking variable.

VW stands for van der Waerden. With NORMAL=VW, you can use the scores for a nonparametric location test. All three normal scores are approximations to the exact expected order statistics for the normal distribution, also called *normal scores*. The BLOM version appears to fit slightly better than the others (Blom 1958; Tukey 1962).

NPLUS1

computes fractional ranks by dividing each rank by the denominator $n+1$, where n is the number of observations having nonmissing values of the ranking variable.

Aliases: FN1, N1

Interaction: TIES=HIGH is the default with the NPLUS1 option.

See also: FRACTION option

OUT=*SAS-data-set*

names the output data set. If *SAS-data-set* does not exist, PROC RANK creates it. If you omit OUT=, the data set is named using the DATA*n* naming convention.

PERCENT

divides each rank by the number of observations having nonmissing values of the variable and multiplies the result by 100 to get a percentage.

Alias: P

Interaction: TIES=HIGH is the default with the PERCENT option.

Tip: You can use PERCENT to calculate cumulative percentages, but use GROUPS=100 to compute percentiles.

SAVAGE

computes Savage (or exponential) scores from the ranks by the following formula (Lehman 1975):

$$y_i = \left[\sum_{j=n-r_i+1} \left(\frac{1}{j} \right) \right] - 1$$

TIES=HIGH | LOW | MEAN

specifies the rank for tied values.

HIGH

assigns the largest of the corresponding ranks.

LOW

assigns the smallest of the corresponding ranks.

MEAN

assigns the mean of the corresponding ranks.

Default: MEAN (unless the FRACTION or PERCENT option is in effect)

Featured in: Example 1 on page 840 and Example 2 on page 842

BY Statement

Produces a separate set of ranks for each BY group.

Main discussion: "BY" on page 68

Featured in: Example 2 on page 842 and Example 3 on page 844

BY <DESCENDING> *variable-1*
  <...<DESCENDING> *variable-n*>
  <NOTSORTED>;

Required Arguments

variable
> specifies the variable that the procedure uses to form BY groups. You can specify more than one variable. If you do not use the NOTSORTED option in the BY statement, the observations in the data set must either be sorted by all the variables that you specify, or they must be indexed appropriately. Variables in a BY statement are called *BY variables*.

Options

DESCENDING
> specifies that the observations are sorted in descending order by the variable that immediately follows the word DESCENDING in the BY statement.

NOTSORTED
> specifies that observations are not necessarily sorted in alphabetic or numeric order. The observations are grouped in another way, for example, chronological order.
>
> The requirement for ordering or indexing observations according to the values of BY variables is suspended for BY-group processing when you use the NOTSORTED option. In fact, the procedure does not use an index if you specify NOTSORTED. The procedure defines a BY group as a set of contiguous observations that have the same values for all BY variables. If observations with the same values for the BY variables are not contiguous, the procedure treats each contiguous set as a separate BY group.

RANKS Statement

Creates new variables for the rank values.

Requirement: If you use the RANKS statement, you must also use the VAR statement.

Default: If you omit the RANKS statement, the rank values replace the original variable values in the output data set.

Featured in: Example 1 on page 840 and Example 2 on page 842

RANKS *new-variables(s)*;

Required Arguments

new-variable(s)
> specifies one or more new variables that contain the ranks for the variable(s) listed in the VAR statement. The first variable listed in the RANKS statement contains the ranks for the first variable listed in the VAR statement, the second variable listed in the RANKS statement contains the ranks for the second variable listed in the VAR statement, and so forth.

VAR Statement

Specifies the input variables.

Default: If you omit the VAR statement, PROC RANK computes ranks for all numeric variables in the input data set.

Featured in: Example 1 on page 840, Example 2 on page 842, and Example 3 on page 844

VAR *data-set-variables(s)*;

Required Arguments

data-set-variable(s)
    specifies one or more variables for which ranks are computed.

Using the VAR Statement with the RANKS Statement

The VAR statement is required when you use the RANKS statement. Using these statements together creates the ranking variables named in the RANKS statement that correspond to the input variables specified in the VAR statement. If you omit the RANKS statement, the rank values replace the original values in the output data set.

Concepts

Computer Resources

PROC RANK stores all values in memory of the variables for which it computes ranks.

Statistical Applications

Ranks are useful for investigating the distribution of values for a variable. The ranks divided by n or $n+1$ form values in the range 0 to 1, and these values estimate the cumulative distribution function. You can apply inverse cumulative distribution functions to these fractional ranks to obtain probability quantile scores, which you can compare to the original values to judge the fit to the distribution. For example, if a set of data has a normal distribution, the normal scores should be a linear function of the original values, and a plot of scores versus original values should be a straight line.

Many nonparametric methods are based on analyzing ranks of a variable:

□ A two-sample t–test applied to the ranks is equivalent to a Wilcoxon rank sum test using the t approximation for the significance level. If you apply the t–test to the normal scores rather than to the ranks, the test is equivalent to the van der Waerden test. If you apply the t–test to median scores (GROUPS=2), the test is equivalent to the median test.

□ A one-way analysis of variance applied to ranks is equivalent to the Kruskal-Wallis *k*-sample test; the F–test generated by the parametric procedure applied to the ranks is often better than the X^2 approximation used by Kruskal-Wallis. This test can be extended to other rank scores (Quade 1966).

□ You can obtain a Friedman's two-way analysis for block designs by ranking within BY groups and then performing a main-effects analysis of variance on these ranks (Conover 1980).

□ You can investigate regression relationships by using rank transformations with a method described by Iman and Conover (1979).

Results

Missing Values

Missing values are not ranked and are left missing when ranks or rank scores replace the original values in the output data set.

Output Data Set

The RANK procedure creates a SAS data set containing the ranks or rank scores but does not create any printed output. You can use PROC PRINT, PROC REPORT, or another SAS reporting tool to print the output data set.

The output data set contains all the variables from the input data set plus the variables named in the RANKS statement. If you omit the RANKS statement, the rank values replace the original variable values in the output data set.

Examples

Example 1: Ranking Values of Multiple Variables

Procedure features:
  PROC RANK statement options:

   DESCENDING
   TIES=

  RANKS statement

  VAR statement

Other features:
  PRINT procedure

This example

☐ reverses the order of the ranks so that the highest value receives the rank of 1

☐ assigns tied values the best possible rank

☐ creates ranking variables and prints them with the original variables.

Program

```
options nodate pageno=1 linesize=80 pagesize=60;
```

The data set CAKE contains each participant's last name, score for presentation, and score for taste in a cake-baking contest.

```
data cake;
   input Name $ 1-10 Present 12-13 Taste 15-16;
   datalines;
Davis      77 84
Orlando    93 80
Ramey      68 72
Roe        68 75
Sanders    56 79
Simms      68 77
Strickland 82 79
;
```

DESCENDING reverses the order of the ranks so that the high score receives the rank of 1. TIES=LOW gives tied values the best possible rank. OUT= creates the output data set ORDER.

```
proc rank data=cake out=order descending ties=low;
```

The new variables PresentRank and TasteRank contain the respective ranks for the variables Present and Taste.

```
   var present taste;
   ranks PresentRank TasteRank;
run;
```

PROC PRINT prints the ORDER data set.

```
proc print data=order;
   title "Rankings of Participants' Scores";
run;
```

Output

```
                      Rankings of Participants' Scores                        1

                                                Present       Taste
           OBS    Name         Present   Taste    Rank         Rank

            1     Davis          77       84        3           1
            2     Orlando        93       80        1           2
            3     Ramey          68       72        4           7
            4     Roe            68       75        4           6
            5     Sanders        56       79        7           3
            6     Simms          68       77        4           5
            7     Strickland     82       79        2           3
```

Example 2: Ranking Values within BY Groups

Procedure features:
PROC RANK statement options:
 DESCENDING
 TIES=
BY statement
RANKS statement
VAR statement

Other features:
PRINT procedure

This example
- □ ranks observations separately within BY groups
- □ reverses the order of the ranks so that the highest value receives the rank of 1
- □ assigns tied values the best possible rank
- □ creates ranking variables and prints them with the original variables.

Program

```
options nodate pageno=1 linesize=80 pagesize=60;
```

The data set ELECT contains each candidate's last name, district number, vote total, and number of years experience on the city council.

```
data elect;
   input Candidate $ 1-11 District 13 Vote 15-18 Years 20;
   datalines;
Cardella    1 1689 8
Latham      1 1005 2
Smith       1 1406 0
```

```
Walker       1  846 0
Hinkley      2  912 0
Kreitemeyer  2 1198 0
Lundell      2 2447 6
Thrash       2  912 2
;
```

DESCENDING reverses the order of the ranks so that the highest vote total receives the rank of 1. TIES=LOW gives tied values the best possible rank. OUT= creates the output data set RESULTS.

```
proc rank data=elect out=results ties=low descending;
```

The BY statement separates the rankings by values of District.

```
   by district;
```

The new variables VoteRank and YearsRank contain the respective ranks for the variables Vote and Years.

```
   var vote years;
   ranks VoteRank YearsRank;
run;
```

PROC PRINT prints the RESULTS data set. The N option prints the number of observations in each BY group.

```
proc print data=results n;
   by district;
   title 'Results of City Council Election';
run;
```

Output

In the second district, Hinkley and Thrash tied with 912 votes. They both receive a rank of 3 because TIES=LOW.

```
                    Results of City Council Election                      1

------------------------------ District=1 -----------------------------------

                                            Vote      Years
            OBS    Candidate    Vote  Years  Rank      Rank

             1     Cardella     1689    8      1         1
             2     Latham       1005    2      3         2
             3     Smith        1406    0      2         3
             4     Walker        846    0      4         3

                              N = 4


------------------------------ District=2 -----------------------------------

                                            Vote      Years
            OBS    Candidate    Vote  Years  Rank      Rank

             5     Hinkley       912    0      3         3
             6     Kreitemeyer  1198    0      2         3
             7     Lundell      2447    6      1         1
             8     Thrash        912    2      3         2

                              N = 4
```

Example 3: Partitioning Observations into Groups Based on Ranks

Procedure features:
   PROC RANK statement option:
      GROUPS=
   BY statement
   VAR statement
Other features:
   PRINT procedure
   SORT procedure

This example
   □ partitions observations into groups on the basis of values of two input variables
   □ groups observations separately within BY groups
   □ replaces the original variable values with the group values.

Program

```
options nodate pageno=1 linesize=80 pagesize=60;
```

The data set SWIM contains swimmers' first names and their times, in seconds, for the backstroke and the freestyle. This example groups the swimmers into pairs, within male and female classes, based on times in both strokes so that every swimmer is paired with someone who has a similar time for each stroke.

```
data swim;
   input Name $ 1-7 Gender $ 9 Back 11-14 Free 16-19;
   datalines;
Andrea  F 28.6 30.3
Carole  F 32.9 24.0
Clayton M 27.0 21.9
Curtis  M 29.0 22.6
Doug    M 27.3 22.4
Ellen   F 27.8 27.0
Jan     F 31.3 31.2
Jimmy   M 26.3 22.5
Karin   F 34.6 26.2
Mick    M 29.0 25.4
Richard M 29.7 30.2
Sam     M 27.2 24.1
Susan   F 35.1 36.1
;
```

PROC SORT sorts the data set by Gender. This is required to obtain a separate set of ranks for each group.

```
proc sort data=swim out=pairs;
   by gender;
run;
```

GROUPS=3 assigns one of three possible group values (0,1,2) to each swimmer for each stroke.

```
proc rank data=pairs out=rankpair groups=3;
```

The BY statement ranks the times separately by Gender.

```
   by gender;
```

The VAR statement specifies the input variables. With no RANKS statement, PROC RANK replaces the original variable values with the group values in the output data set.

```
   var back free;
run;
```

PROC PRINT prints the RANKPAIR data set. The N option prints the number of observations in each BY group.

```
proc print data=rankpair n;
   by gender;
```

```
        title 'Pairings of Swimmers for Backstroke and Freestyle';
run;
```

Output

The group values pair up swimmers with similar times to work on each stroke. For example, Andrea and Ellen work together on the backstroke because they have the fastest times in the female class. The groups of male swimmers are unbalanced because there are seven male swimmers; for each stroke, one group has three swimmers.

```
                Pairings of Swimmers for Backstroke and Freestyle              1

------------------------------- Gender=F -------------------------------

            OBS      Name      Back     Free

             1       Andrea     0        1
             2       Carole     1        0
             3       Ellen      0        1
             4       Jan        1        2
             5       Karin      2        0
             6       Susan      2        2

                        N = 6


------------------------------- Gender=M -------------------------------

            OBS      Name      Back     Free

             7       Clayton    0        0
             8       Curtis     2        1
             9       Doug       1        0
            10       Jimmy      0        1
            11       Mick       2        2
            12       Richard    2        2
            13       Sam        1        1

                        N = 7
```

References

Blom, G. (1958), *Statistical Estimates and Transformed Beta Variables*, New York: John Wiley & Sons, Inc.

Conover, W.J. (1980), *Practical Nonparametric Statistics*, Second Edition, New York: John Wiley & Sons, Inc.

Conover, W.J. and Iman, R.L. (1976), "On Some Alternative Procedures Using Ranks for the Analysis of Experimental Designs," *Communications in Statistics*, A5, 14, 1348–1368.

Conover, W.J. and Iman, R.L. (1981), "Rank Transformations as a Bridge between Parametric and Nonparametric Statistics," *The American Statistician*, 35, 124–129.

Iman, R.L. and Conover, W.J. (1979), "The Use of the Rank Transform in Regression," *Technometrics*, 21, 499–509.

Lehman, E.L. (1975), *Nonparametrics: Statistical Methods Based on Ranks*, San Francisco: Holden-Day.

Quade, D. (1966), "On Analysis of Variance for the k-Sample Problem," *Annals of Mathematical Statistics*, 37, 1747–1758.

Tukey, John W. (1962), "The Future of Data Analysis," *Annals of Mathematical Statistics*, 33, 22.

CHAPTER

31

The REGISTRY Procedure

Overview

The REGISTRY procedure maintains the SAS Registry. The registry consists of two parts. One part is stored in the SASHELP library, and the other part is stored in the SASUSER library.

Procedure Syntax

PROC REGISTRY <*option(s)*>;

PROC REGISTRY Statement

PROC REGISTRY <*option(s)*>;

To do this	Use this statement
Erase the contents of the SASUSER registry	CLEARSASUSER
Compare the contents of a registry to a file	COMPARETO
Enable registry debugging	DEBUGON
Disable registry debugging	DEBUGOFF

To do this	Use this statement
Write the contents of a registry to the specified file	EXPORT=
Provide additional information in the SAS log about the results of the IMPORT= and the UNINSTALL options	FULLSTATUS
Import the specified file to a registry	IMPORT=
Write the contents of the entire registry to the SAS log	LIST
Write the contents of the SASHELP portion of the registry to the SAS log	LISTHELP
Write the contents of the SASUSER portion of the registry to the SAS log	LISTUSER
Start exporting or writing the contents of a registry at the specified key	STARTAT=
Delete from the specified registry all the keys and values that are in the specified file	UNINSTALL
Perform the specified operation on the SASHELP portion of the SAS Registry	USESASHELP

Options

CLEARSASUSER
erases the content of the SASUSER portion of the SAS Registry.

COMPARETO=*file-specification*
compares the contents of a file to a registry. It returns information about keys and values that it finds in the file that are not in the registry. It reports as differences

  □ keys that are defined in the external file but not in the registry

  □ value names for a given key that are in the external file but not in the registry

  □ differences in the content of like-named values in like-named keys.
COMPARETO= does not report as differences any keys and values that are in the registry but not in the file because the registry could easily be composed of pieces from many different files.
file-specification is one of the following:

'external-file'
is the name of an external file that contains the registry information.

fileref
is a fileref that has been assigned to an external file. Use the FILENAME statement to assign a fileref. (For information on the FILENAME statement, see the section on statements in *SAS Language Reference: Dictionary*.)

Interaction: By default, PROC REGISTRY compares *file-specification* to the SASUSER portion of the registry. Use USESASHELP to compare *file-specification* to the SASHELP portion of the registry.

See also: For information on how to structure a file that contains registry information, see "Creating Registry Files" on page 852.

DEBUGON
enables registry debugging.

DEBUGOFF
disables registry debugging.

EXPORT=*file-specification*
writes the contents of a registry to the specified file, where
file-specification is one of the following:

'external-file'
is the name of an external file that contains the registry information.

fileref
is a fileref that has been assigned to an external file. Use the FILENAME
statement to assign a fileref. (For information on the FILENAME statement, see
the section on statements in *SAS Language Reference: Dictionary*.)

If *file-specification* already exists, PROC REGISTRY overwrites it. Otherwise,
PROC REGISTRY creates the file.

Interaction: By default, EXPORT= writes the SASUSER portion of the registry to
the specified file. Use USESASHELP to write the SASHELP portion of the registry.

Interaction: Use the STARTAT= option to export a single key and all of its subkeys.

FULLSTATUS
provides additional information in the SAS log about the results of the IMPORT=
and the UNINSTALL options.

IMPORT=*file-specification*
specifies the file to import into the SAS Registry. PROC REGISTRY does not
overwrite the existing registry. Instead, it updates the existing registry with the
contents of the specified file.

file-specification is one of the following:

'external-file'
is the name of an external file that contains the registry information.

fileref
is a fileref that has been assigned to an external file. Use the FILENAME
statement to assign a fileref. (For information on the FILENAME statement, see
the section on statements in *SAS Language Reference: Dictionary*.)

Interaction: By default, IMPORT= imports the file to the SASUSER portion of the
SAS registry. Use USESASHELP to import the file to the SASHELP portion of the
registry. You must have write permission to SASHELP to use USESASHELP.

Interaction: Use FULLSTATUS to obtain additional information in the SAS log as
you import a file.

See also: For information on how to structure a file that contains registry
information, see "Creating Registry Files" on page 852.

LIST
writes the contents of the entire SAS Registry to the SAS log.

Interaction: Use the STARTAT= option to write a single key and all of its subkeys.

LISTHELP
writes the contents of the SASHELP portion of the registry to the SAS log.

Interaction: Use the STARTAT= option to write a single key and all of its subkeys.

LISTUSER
writes the contents of the SASUSER portion of the registry to the SAS log.

Interaction: Use the STARTAT= option to write a single key and all of its subkeys.

STARTAT='*key-name*'
exports or writes the contents of a single key and all of its subkeys.

Interaction: USE STARTAT= with the EXPORT=, LIST, LISTHELP, or LISTUSER option.

UNINSTALL=*file-specification*
deletes from the specified registry all the keys and values that are in the specified file. *file-specification* is one of the following:

'*external-file*'
is the name of an external file that contains the keys and values to delete.

fileref
is a fileref that has been assigned to an external file. Use the FILENAME statement to assign a fileref. (For information on the FILENAME statement, see the section on statements in *SAS Language Reference: Dictionary*.)

Interaction: By default, UNINSTALL deletes the keys and values from the SASUSER portion of the SAS registry. Use USESASHELP to delete the keys and values from the SASHELP portion of the registry. You must have write permission to SASHELP to use this option.

Interaction: Use FULLSTATUS to obtain additional information in the SAS log as you uninstall a registry.

See also: For information on how to structure a file that contains registry information, see "Creating Registry Files" on page 852.

USESASHELP
performs the specified operation on the SASHELP portion of the SAS Registry.

Interaction: Use USESASHELP with the IMPORT=, EXPORT=, COMPARETO, or UNINSTALL option. To use USESASHELP with IMPORT= or UNINSTALL, you must have write permission to SASHELP.

Creating Registry Files

You can create registry files with the SAS Registry Editor or with any text editor.
A registry file must have a particular structure. Each entry in the registry file consists of a key name, followed on the next line by one or more values. The key name identifies the key or subkey that you are defining. Any values that follow specify the names or data to associate with the key.

For more information on the SAS Registry and the Registry Editor, see the SAS online Help.

Specifying Key names

Key names are entered on a single line between square brackets ([and]). To specify a subkey, enter multiple key names between the brackets, starting with the root key. Separate the names in a sequence of key names with a backslash (\). The length of a single key name or a sequence of key names cannot exceed 255 characters (including the square brackets and the backslashes). Key names can contain any character except the backslash.

Examples of valid key name sequences follow. These sequences are typical of the SAS Registry:

[CORE\EXPLORER\MENUS\ENTRIES\CLASS]

[CORE\EXPLORER\NEWMEMBER\CATALOG]

[CORE\EXPLORER\NEWENTRY\CLASS]

[CORE\EXPLORER\ICONS\ENTRIES\LOG]

Specifying Values for Keys

Enter each value on the line following the key name that it is associated with. You can specify multiple values for each key, but each value must be on a separate line.

The general form of a value is

value-name=value-content

A *value-name* can be an at sign (@), which indicates the default value name, or it can be any text string in double quotation marks. If the text contains an ampersand (&), the character (either uppercase or lowercase) that follows the ampersand is a shortcut for the value name. See Example 1 on page 854.

A value cannot contain more than 255 characters (including quotation marks and ampersands). It can contain any character except a backslash (\).

Value-content can be any of the following:

□ a string (inside double quotation marks). You can put anything inside the quotes, including nothing ("").

   Note: To include a backslash character in the quoted string, use two adjacent backslashes. To include a double quotation mark, use two adjacent double quotation marks. △

□ the string **int:** followed by a signed long integer value.

□ the string **uint:** followed by an unsigned long integer value.

□ the string **dword:** followed by an unsigned long hexadecimal value.

□ the string **hex:** followed by any number of hexadecimal characters separated by commas. If you extend the hexadecimal characters beyond a single line, end the line with a backslash to indicate that the data continues on the next line.

□ the string **double:** followed by a double value.

The following examples illustrate and explain some of the different types of values that are currently stored in the SAS Registry:

"&Open"="BUILD %8b.%32b.%32b.%8b MSG=NO"
   This value is a quoted string that issues the BUILD command on the selected object.
   The character **o** is a shortcut for this action.

"P&rint"="GSUBMIT 'PROC PRINT DATA=%8b.%32b;RUN;';LISTING;DLGPRT;"
   This value is a quoted string that executes the GSUBMIT command, which in turn executes the PRINT procedure and the LISTING and DLGPRT statements.
   The character **r** is a shortcut for this action.

"&Edit"="IMAGEEDIT;IMPORT'%s' 'FORMAT=GIF'"
   This value is a quoted string that imports the selected GIF file into the SAS Image Editor.
   The character **E** is a shortcut for this action.

"Brick"=hex:02,03,00,f4,00,01
   The value of 'Brick' is hex values.

Examples

Example 1: Example of a Registry Entry

This example stores three values in the subkey named TOOLBOX:

The key name sequence identifies a subkey.

```
[CORE\EXPLORER\MENUS\ENTRIES\TOOLBOX]
```

The default value executes the TOOLEDIT command on the selected TOOLBOX entry.

```
@="TOOLEDIT %8b.%32b.%32b"
```

This value defines Open, which is the same as the default. The character **o** is a shortcut for the action.

```
"&Open"="TOOLEDIT %8b.%32b.%32b"
```

This value defines Load, which executes the TOOLLOAD command on the selected TOOLBOX entry.

```
"Load"="TOOLLOAD %8b.%32b.%32b"
```

Example 2: Importing a File to the Registry

Procedure features: IMPORT=
Other features: FILENAME statement

This example imports a file into the SASUSER portion of the SAS Registry.

Program

The FILENAME statement assigns the fileref **source** to the external file that contains the text to read into the registry.

```
filename source 'external-file';
```

IMPORT= imports the file that is associated with the fileref **source**. By default, IMPORT= writes to the SASUSER portion of the SAS Registry.

```
proc registry
   import=source;
run;
```

SAS Log

```
1   filename source 'external-file';
2   proc registry
3      import=source;
4   run;
Parsing REG file and loading the registry please wait....
Registry IMPORT is now complete.
```

Example 3: Listing and Exporting the Registry

Procedure features:
> EXPORT=
> LISTUSER

This example lists the SASUSER portion of the SAS Registry and exports it to an external file.

Program

LISTUSER writes the contents of the SASUSER portion of the registry to the SAS log.

```
proc registry
   listuser
```

EXPORT= exports the registry to the specified file. By default, EXPORT= writes the SASUSER portion of the SAS Registry.

```
   export='external-file';
run;
```

SAS Log

```
1  proc registry listuser export='external-file';
2  run;
Starting to write out the registry file, please wait...
The export to file external-file is now complete.
Contents of SASUSER REGISTRY.
[  HKEY_USER_ROOT]
[    CORE]
[      EXPLORER]
[        CONFIGURATION]
         Initialized= "True"
[        FOLDERS]
[          UNXHOST1]
           Closed= "658"
           Icon= "658"
           Name= "Home Directory"
           Open= "658"
           Path= "~"
```

Example 4: Comparing the Registry to an External File

Procedure features: COMPARETO=

Other features: FILENAME statement

This example compares the SASUSER portion of the SAS Registry to an external file.

Program

The FILENAME statement assigns the fileref **testreg** to the external file that contains the text to compare to the registry.

```
filename testreg 'external-file';
```

COMPARETO compares the file that is associated with the fileref **testreg** to the SASUSER portion of the SAS Registry.

```
proc registry
   compareto=testreg;
run;
```

SAS Log

This SAS log shows two differences between the SASUSER portion of the registry and the specified external file. In the registry, the value of "Initialized" is "True"; in the external file, it is "False". In the registry, the value of "Icon" is "658"; in the external file it is "343".

```
1    filename testreg 'external-file';
2    proc registry
3      compareto=testreg;
4  run;
Parsing REG file and comparing the registry please wait....
COMPARE DIFF: Value "Initialized" in
[HKEY_USER_ROOT\CORE\EXPLORER\CONFIGURATION]: REGISTRY TYPE=STRING, CURRENT
VALUE="True"
COMPARE DIFF: Value "Initialized" in
[HKEY_USER_ROOT\CORE\EXPLORER\CONFIGURATION]: FILE TYPE=STRING, FILE
VALUE="False"
COMPARE DIFF: Value "Icon" in
[HKEY_USER_ROOT\CORE\EXPLORER\FOLDERS\UNXHOST1]: REGISTRY TYPE=STRING,
CURRENT VALUE="658"
COMPARE DIFF: Value "Icon" in
[HKEY_USER_ROOT\CORE\EXPLORER\FOLDERS\UNXHOST1]: FILE TYPE=STRING, FILE
VALUE="343"
Registry COMPARE is now complete.
COMPARE: There were differences between the registry and the file.
```

CHAPTER

32

The REPORT Procedure

Overview

The REPORT procedure combines features of the PRINT, MEANS, and TABULATE procedures with features of the DATA step in a single report-writing tool that can produce a variety of reports. You can use PROC REPORT in three ways:

□ in a windowing environment with a prompting facility that guides you as you build a report.

□ in a windowing environment without the prompting facility.

□ in a nonwindowing environment. In this case, you submit a series of statements with the PROC REPORT statement, just as you do in other SAS procedures.

   You can submit these statements from the PROGRAM EDITOR window with the NOWINDOWS option in the PROC REPORT statement, or you can run SAS in batch, noninteractive, or interactive line mode (see the information on running the SAS System in *SAS Language Reference: Concepts*).

This section provides reference information about using PROC REPORT in a windowing or nonwindowing environment. Similar information is also available online through the Help facility. For task-oriented documentation for the nonwindowing environment, see SAS Technical Report P-258, *Using the REPORT Procedure in a Nonwindowing Environment, Release 6.07*.

Types of Reports

A *detail report* contains one row for every observation selected for the report. Each of these rows is a *detail row*. A *summary report* consolidates data so that each row represents multiple observations. Each of these rows is also called a detail row.

Both detail and summary reports can contain *summary lines* as well as detail rows. A summary line summarizes numerical data for a set of detail rows or for all detail rows. PROC REPORT provides both default and customized summaries (see "Using Break Lines" on page 874).

This overview illustrates the kinds of reports that PROC REPORT can produce. The statements that create the data sets and formats used in these reports are in Example 1 on page 958. The formats are stored in a permanent SAS data library. See "Examples" on page 958 for more reports and for the statements that create them.

A Sampling of Reports

The data set that these reports use contains one day's sales figures for eight stores in a chain of grocery stores.

A simple PROC REPORT step produces a report similar to one produced by a simple PROC PRINT step. Figure 32.1 on page 862 illustrates the simplest kind of report that you can produce with PROC REPORT. The statements that produce the report follow. The data set and formats that the program uses are created in Example 1 on page 958. Although the WHERE and FORMAT statements are not essential, here they limit the amount of output and make the values easier to understand.

```
libname proclib 'SAS-data-library';
```

```
options nodate pageno=1 linesize=64 pagesize=60
     fmtsearch=(proclib);
```

```
proc report data=grocery nowd;
   where sector='se';
   format sector $sctrfmt.;
   format manager $mgrfmt.;
   format dept $deptfmt.;
   format sales dollar10.2;
run;
```

Figure 32.1   Simple Detail Report with a Detail Row for Each Observation

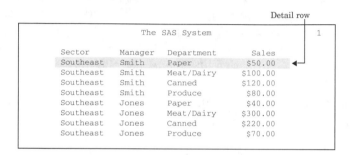

The report in Figure 32.2 on page 862 uses the same observations as those in Figure 32.1 on page 862. However, the statements that produce this report

- ☐ order the rows by the values of Manager and Department
- ☐ create a default summary line for each value of Manager
- ☐ create a customized summary line for the whole report. A customized summary lets you control the content and appearance of the summary information, but you must write additional PROC REPORT statements to create one.

For an explanation of the program that produces this report, see Example 2 on page 961.

Figure 32.2   Ordered Detail Report with Default and Customized Summaries

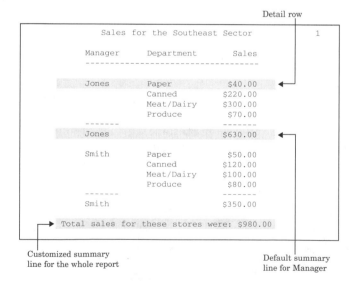

The summary report in Figure 32.3 on page 863 contains one row for each store in the northern sector. Each detail row represents four observations in the input data set—one for each department. Information about individual departments does not appear in this report. Instead, the value of Sales in each detail row is the sum of the values of Sales in all four departments. In addition to consolidating multiple observations into one row of the report, the statements that create this report

- □ customize the text of the column headers
- □ create default summaries that total the sales for each sector of the city
- □ create a customized summary that totals the sales for both sectors.

For an explanation of the program that produces this report, see Example 4 on page 967.

Figure 32.3 Summary Report with Default and Customized Summaries

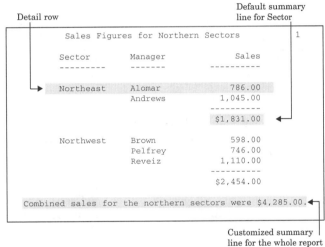

The summary report in Figure 32.4 on page 864 is similar to Figure 32.3 on page 863. The major difference is that it also includes information for individual departments. Each selected value of Department forms a column in the report. In addition, the statements that create this report

- □ compute and display a variable that is not in the input data set
- □ double-space the report
- □ put blank lines in some of the column headers.

For an explanation of the program that produces this report, see Example 5 on page 970.

Figure 32.4 Summary Report with a Column for Each Value of a Variable

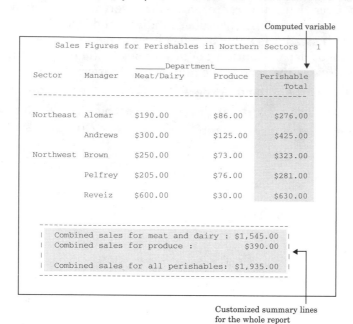

Computed variable

```
     Sales Figures for Perishables in Northern Sectors    1

                         _____Department_____
     Sector   Manager   Meat/Dairy      Produce   Perishable
                                                      Total
     ------------------------------------------------------------

     Northeast Alomar    $190.00         $86.00      $276.00

               Andrews   $300.00        $125.00      $425.00

     Northwest Brown     $250.00         $73.00      $323.00

               Pelfrey   $205.00         $76.00      $281.00

               Reveiz    $600.00         $30.00      $630.00


         --------------------------------------------------
         |  Combined sales for meat and dairy : $1,545.00  |
         |  Combined sales for produce :           $390.00  |
         |                                                  |
         |  Combined sales for all perishables: $1,935.00  |
         --------------------------------------------------
```

Customized summary lines
for the whole report

The customized report in Figure 32.5 on page 865 shows each manager's store on a separate page. Only the first two pages appear here. The statements that create this report create

- □ a customized header for each page of the report

- □ a computed variable (Profit) that is not in the input data set

- □ a customized summary with text that is dependent on the total sales for that manager's store.

For an explanation of the program that produces this report, see Example 9 on page 979.

Figure 32.5 Customized Summary Report

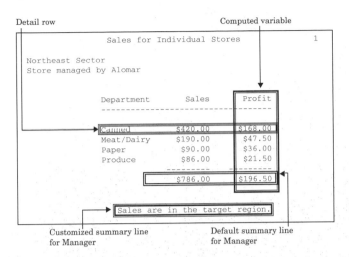

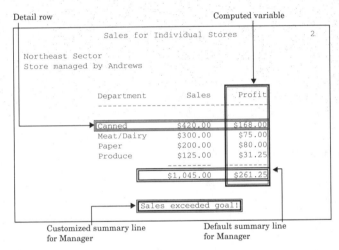

The report in Figure 32.6 on page 866 uses customized style elements to control things like font faces, font sizes, and justification, as well as the width of the border of the table and the width of the spacing between cells. This report was created by using the HTML destination of the Output Delivery System (ODS) and the STYLE= option in several statements in the procedure.

For an explanation of the program that produces this report, see Example 16 on page 999. For information on ODS, see "Output Delivery System" on page 19.

Figure 32.6 HTML Output

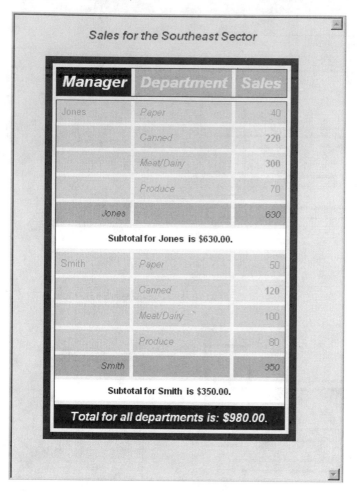

Concepts

Laying Out a Report

Report writing is simplified if you approach it with a clear understanding of what you want the report to look like. The most important thing to figure out is the layout of the report. To determine the layout, ask yourself the following kinds of questions:

- ☐ What do I want to display in each column of the report?
- ☐ In what order do I want the columns to appear?
- ☐ Do I want to display a column for each value of a particular variable?
- ☐ Do I want a row for every observation in the report, or do I want to consolidate information for multiple observations into one row?
- ☐ In what order do I want the rows to appear?

Once you understand the layout of the report, use the COLUMN and DEFINE statements in PROC REPORT to construct the layout.

The COLUMN statement lists the items that appear in the columns of the report, describes the arrangement of the columns, and defines headers that span multiple columns. A report item can be

□ a data set variable

□ a statistic calculated by the procedure

□ a variable that you compute based on other items in the report.

Omit the COLUMN statement if you want to include all variables in the input data set in the same order as they occur in the data set.

Note: If you start PROC REPORT in the windowing environment without the COLUMN statement, the initial report includes only as many variables as will fit on one page. △

The DEFINE statement (or, in the windowing environment, the DEFINITION window) defines the characteristics of an item in the report. These characteristics include how PROC REPORT uses the item in the report, the text of the column header, and the format to use to display values.

Usage of Variables in a Report

Much of a report's layout is determined by the usages that you specify for variables in the DEFINE statements or DEFINITION windows. For data set variables, these usages are

DISPLAY

ORDER

ACROSS

GROUP

ANALYSIS

A report can contain variables that are not in the input data set. These variables must have a usage of COMPUTED.

Display Variables

A report that contains one or more display variables has a row for every observation in the input data set. Display variables do not affect the order of the rows in the report. If no order variables appear to the left of a display variable, the order of the rows in the report reflects the order of the observations in the data set. By default, PROC REPORT treats all character variables as display variables.

Featured in: Example 1 on page 958

Order Variables

A report that contains one or more order variables has a row for every observation in the input data set. If no display variable appears to the left of an order variable, PROC REPORT orders the detail rows according to the ascending, formatted values of the order variable. You can change the default order with ORDER= and DESCENDING in the DEFINE statement or with the DEFINITION window.

If the report contains multiple order variables, PROC REPORT establishes the order of the detail rows by sorting these variables from left to right in the report. PROC REPORT does not repeat the value of an order variable from one row to the next if the value does not change.

Featured in: Example 2 on page 961

Across Variables

PROC REPORT creates a column for each value of an across variable. PROC REPORT orders the columns by the ascending, formatted values of the across variable. You can change the default order with ORDER= and DESCENDING in the DEFINE statement or with the DEFINITION window. If no other variable helps define the column (see "COLUMN Statement" on page 903), PROC REPORT displays the N statistic (the number of observations in the input data set that belong to that cell of the report).

If you are familiar with procedures that use class variables, you will see that across variables are class variables that are used in the column dimension.

Featured in: Example 5 on page 970

Group Variables

If a report contains one or more group variables, PROC REPORT tries to consolidate into one row all observations from the data set that have a unique combination of formatted values for all group variables.

When PROC REPORT creates groups, it orders the detail rows by the ascending, formatted values of the group variable. You can change the default order with ORDER= and DESCENDING in the DEFINE statement or with the DEFINITION window.

If the report contains multiple group variables, the REPORT procedure establishes the order of the detail rows by sorting these variables from left to right in the report. PROC REPORT does not repeat the values of a group variable from one row to the next if the value does not change.

If you are familiar with procedures that use class variables, you will see that group variables are class variables that are used in the row dimension.

Note: You cannot always create groups. PROC REPORT cannot consolidate observations into groups if the report contains any order variables or any display variables that do not have one or more statistics associated with them (see "COLUMN Statement" on page 903). In the windowing environment, if PROC REPORT cannot immediately create groups, it changes all display and order variables to group variables so that it can create the group variable that you requested. In the nonwindowing environment, it returns to the SAS log a message that explains why it could not create groups. Instead, it creates a detail report that displays group variables the same way as it displays order variables. Even if PROC REPORT creates a detail report, the variables that you defined as group variables retain that usage in their definitions. △

Featured in: Example 4 on page 967

Analysis Variables

An analysis variable is a numeric variable that is used to calculate a statistic for all the observations represented by a cell of the report. (Across variables, in combination with group variables or order variables, determine which observations a cell represents.) You associate a statistic with an analysis variable in the variable's definition or in the COLUMN statement. By default, PROC REPORT uses numeric variables as analysis variables that are used to calculate the Sum statistic.

The value of an analysis variable depends on where it appears in the report:

☐ In a detail report, the value of an analysis variable in a detail row is the value of the statistic associated with that variable calculated for a single observation. Calculating a statistic for a single observation is not practical; however, using the variable as an analysis variable enables you to create summary lines for sets of observations or for all observations.

□ In a summary report, the value displayed for an analysis variable is the value of the statistic that you specify calculated for the set of observations represented by that cell of the report.

□ In a summary line for any report, the value of an analysis variable is the value of the statistic that you specify calculated for all observations represented by that cell of the summary line.

See also: "BREAK Statement" on page 893 and "RBREAK Statement" on page 918

Featured in: Example 2 on page 961, Example 3 on page 964, Example 4 on page 967, and Example 5 on page 970

CAUTION:
Using dates in a report. Be careful when you use SAS dates in reports that contain summary lines. SAS dates are numeric variables. Unless you explicitly define dates as some other kind of variable, PROC REPORT summarizes them. △

Computed Variables

Computed variables are variables that you define for the report. They are not in the input data set, and PROC REPORT does not add them to the input data set. However, computed variables are included in an output data set if you create one.

In the windowing environment, you add a computed variable to a report from the COMPUTED VAR window.

In the nonwindowing environment, you add a computed variable by

□ including the computed variable in the COLUMN statement

□ defining the variable's usage as COMPUTED in the DEFINE statement

□ computing the value of the variable in a compute block associated with the variable.

Featured in: Example 5 on page 970, Example 10 on page 983, and Example 13 on page 991

Interactions of Position and Usage

The position and usage of each variable in the report determine the report's structure and content. PROC REPORT orders the detail rows of the report according to the values of order and group variables, considered from left to right in the report. Similarly, PROC REPORT orders columns for an across variable from top to bottom, according to the values of the variable.

Several items can collectively define the contents of a column in a report. For instance, in Figure 32.7 on page 870, the values that appear in the third and fourth columns are collectively determined by Sales, an analysis variable, and by Department, an across variable. You create this kind of report with the COLUMN statement or, in the windowing environment, by placing report items above or below each other. This is called stacking items in the report because each item generates a header, and the headers are stacked one above the other.

Figure 32.7   Stacking Department and Sales

```
┌─────────────────────────────────────────────────────┐
│     Sales Figures for Perishables in Northern Sectors │
│                                                       │
│                        _____Department_____       │
│        Sector   Manager   Meat/Dairy   Produce  Perishable │
│                                                   Total │
│        ------------------------------------------------- │
│                                                       │
│        Northeast Alomar    $190.00     $86.00    $276.00 │
│                                                       │
│                  Andrews   $300.00     $125.00   $425.00 │
│                                                       │
│        Northwest Brown     $250.00     $73.00    $323.00 │
│                                                       │
│                  Pelfrey   $205.00     $76.00    $281.00 │
│                                                       │
│                  Reveiz    $600.00     $30.00    $630.00 │
└─────────────────────────────────────────────────────┘
```

When you use multiple items to define the contents of a column, at most one of the following can be in a column:

- □ a display variable with or without a statistic above or below it
- □ an analysis variable with or without a statistic above or below it
- □ an order variable
- □ a group variable
- □ a computed variable.

More than one of these items in a column creates a conflict for PROC REPORT about which values to display.

Table 32.1 on page 870 shows which report items can share a column.

Note: You cannot stack group or order variables with other report items. △

Table 32.1   Report Items That Can Share Columns

	Display	**Analysis**	**Order**	**Group**	**Computed**	**Across**	**Statistic**
Display						X[*]	X
Analysis						X	X
Order							
Group							
Computed variable						X	
Across	X[*]	X			X	X	X
Statistic	X	X				X	

[*]When a display variable and an across variable share a column, the report must also contain another variable that is not in the same column.

The following items can stand alone in a column:

- □ display variable
- □ analysis variable
- □ order variable
- □ group variable

- ☐ computed variable
- ☐ across variable
- ☐ N statistic.

Note: The values in a column occupied only by an across variable are frequency counts. △

Statistics Available in PROC REPORT

N	CSS
NMISS	STDERR
MEAN	CV
STD	T
MIN	PRT
MAX	VAR
RANGE	SUMWGT
SUM	PCTN
USS	PCTSUM

Every statistic except N must be associated with a variable. You associate a statistic with a variable either by placing the statistic above or below a numeric display variable or by specifying the statistic as a usage option in the DEFINE statement or in the DEFINITION window for an analysis variable.

You can place N anywhere because it is the number of observations in the input data set that contributes to the value in a cell of the report. The value of N does not depend on a particular variable.

For definitions of these statistics, see "Keywords and Formulas" on page 1458.

Note: If you use the MISSING option in the PROC REPORT statement, N includes observations with missing group, order, or across variables. △

Using Compute Blocks

A *compute block* is one or more programming statements that appear either between a COMPUTE and an ENDCOMP statement or in a COMPUTE window. PROC REPORT executes these statements as it builds the report. A compute block can be associated with a report item (a data set variable, a statistic, or a computed variable) or with a location (at the top or bottom of the report; before or after a set of observations). You create a compute block with the COMPUTE window or with the COMPUTE statement. One form of the COMPUTE statement associates the compute block with a report item. Another form associates the compute block with a location in the report (see "Using Break Lines" on page 874).

Note: When you use the COMPUTE statement, you do not have to use a corresponding BREAK or RBREAK statement. (See Example 2 on page 961, which uses COMPUTE AFTER but does not use the RBREAK statement). Use these statements only when you want to implement one or more BREAK statement or RBREAK statement options (see Example 9 on page 979, which uses both COMPUTE AFTER MANAGER and BREAK AFTER MANAGER. △

The Purpose of Compute Blocks

A compute block that is associated with a report item can

☐ define a variable that appears in a column of the report but is not in the input data set

☐ define display attributes for a report item (see "CALL DEFINE Statement" on page 899).

A compute block that is associated with a location can write a customized summary. In addition, all compute blocks can use SAS language elements to perform calculations (see "The Contents of Compute Blocks" on page 872). A PROC REPORT step can contain multiple compute blocks.

The Contents of Compute Blocks

In the windowing environment, a compute block is in a COMPUTE window. In the nonwindowing environment, a compute block begins with a COMPUTE statement and ends with an ENDCOMP statement. Within a compute block, you can use these SAS language elements:

☐ DM statement

☐ %INCLUDE statement

☐ these DATA step statements:

assignment	LENGTH
CALL	LINK
DO (all forms)	RETURN
END	SELECT
GO TO	sum
IF-THEN/ELSE	

☐ comments

☐ null statements

☐ macro variables and macro invocations

☐ all DATA step functions.

For information about SAS language elements see the appropriate section in *SAS Language Reference: Dictionary*.

Within a compute block, you can also use these PROC REPORT features:

☐ Compute blocks for a customized summary can contain one or more LINE statements, which place customized text and formatted values in the summary. (See "LINE Statement" on page 917.)

☐ Compute blocks for a report item can contain one or more CALL DEFINE statements, which set attributes like color and format each time a value for the item is placed in the report. (See "CALL DEFINE Statement" on page 899.)

☐ Any compute block can contain the automatic variable _BREAK_ (see "The Automatic Variable _BREAK_" on page 875.

Four Ways to Reference Report Items in a Compute Block

A compute block can reference any report item that forms a column in the report (whether or not the column is visible). You reference report items in a compute block in one of four ways:

- □ by name.
- □ by a compound name that identifies both the variable and the name of the statistic that you calculate with it. A compound name has this form

    variable-name.statistic

- □ by an alias that you create in the COLUMN statement or in the DEFINITION window.
- □ by column number, in the form

    _Cn_

    where *n* is the number of the column (from left to right) in the report.

    Note: Even though the columns that you define with NOPRINT and NOZERO do not appear in the report, you must count them when you are referencing columns by number. See the discussion of NOPRINT on page 913 and NOZERO on page 913. △

CAUTION:
Referencing variables that have missing values leads to missing values. If a compute block references a variable that has a missing value, PROC REPORT displays that variable as a blank (for character variables) or as a period (for numeric variables). △

The following table shows how to use each type of reference in a compute block.

If the variable that you reference is this type...	Then refer to it by...	For example...
group	name[*]	Department
order	name[*]	Department
computed	name[*]	Department
display	name[*]	Department
display sharing a column with a statistic	a compound name[*]	Sales.sum
analysis	a compound name[*]	Sales.mean
any type sharing a column with an across variable	column number[**]	_c3_

[*]If the variable has an alias, you must reference it with the alias.

[**]Even if the variable has an alias, you must reference it by column number.

Featured in: Example 3 on page 964, which references analysis variables by their aliases; Example 5 on page 970, which references variables by column number; and Example 10 on page 983, which references group variables and computed variables by name.

Compute Block Processing

PROC REPORT processes compute blocks in two different ways.

- □ If a compute block is associated with a location, PROC REPORT executes the compute block only at that location. Because PROC REPORT calculates statistics for groups before it actually constructs the rows of the report, statistics for sets of detail rows are available before or after the rows are displayed, as are values for any variables based on these statistics.

□ If a compute block is associated with a report item, PROC REPORT executes the compute block on every row of the report when it comes to the column for that item. The value of a computed variable in any row of a report is the last value assigned to that variable during that execution of the DATA step statements in the compute block. PROC REPORT assigns values to the columns in a row of a report from left to right. Consequently, you cannot base the calculation of a computed variable on any variable that appears to its right in the report.

Note: PROC REPORT recalculates computed variables at breaks. For details on compute block processing see "How PROC REPORT Builds a Report" on page 946. △

Using Break Lines

Break lines are lines of text (including blanks) that appear at particular locations, called *breaks*, in a report. A report can contain multiple breaks. Generally, break lines are used to visually separate parts of a report, to summarize information, or both. They can occur

□ at the beginning or end of a report

□ at the top or bottom of each page

□ between sets of observations (whenever the value of a group or order variable changes).

Break lines can contain

□ text

□ values calculated for either a set of rows or for the whole report.

Creating Break Lines

There are two ways to create break lines. The first way is simpler. It produces a default summary. The second way is more flexible. It produces a customized summary and provides a way to slightly modify a default summary. Default summaries and customized summaries can appear at the same location in a report.

Default summaries are produced with the BREAK statement, the RBREAK statement, or the BREAK window. You can use default summaries to visually separate parts of the report, to summarize information for numeric variables, or both. Options provide some control over the appearance of the break lines, but if you choose to summarize numeric variables, you have no control over the content and the placement of the summary information. (A break line that summarizes information is a summary line.)

Customized summaries are produced in a compute block. You can control both the appearance and content of a customized summary, but you must write the code to do so.

Order of Break Lines

You control the order of the lines in a customized summary. However, PROC REPORT controls the order of lines in a default summary and the placement of a customized summary relative to a default summary. When a default summary contains multiple break lines, the order in which the break lines appear is

1 overlining or double overlining

2 summary line

3 underlining or double underlining

4 blank line

5 page break.

If you define a customized summary for the same location, customized break lines appear after underlining or double underlining.

The Automatic Variable _BREAK_

PROC REPORT automatically creates a variable called _BREAK_. This variable contains

- □ a blank if the current line is not part of a break
- □ the value of the break variable if the current line is part of a break between sets of observations
- □ the value **RBREAK** if the current line is part of a break at the beginning or end of the report.

Using Style Elements in PROC REPORT

If you use the Output Delivery System to create HTML output or Printer output from PROC REPORT, you can specify style elements for the procedure to use for various parts of the report. Style elements determine presentation attributes like font face, font weight, color, and so forth. Information about the attributes that you can set for a style is in "Customizing the Style Definition That ODS Uses" on page 42.

You specify style elements for PROC REPORT with the STYLE= option. Table 32.2 on page 875 shows where you can use this option. Specifications on a statement other than the PROC REPORT statement override the same specification in the PROC REPORT statement. However, any style attributes that you specify in the PROC REPORT statement and do not override in another statement are inherited. For instance, if you specify a blue background and a white foreground for all column headers in the PROC REPORT statement, and you specify a gray background for the column headers of a variable in the DEFINE statement, the background for that particular column header is gray, and the foreground is white (as specified in the PROC REPORT statement).

Detailed information about STYLE= is provided in the documentation for individual statements.

Table 32.2 Using the STYLE= Option in PROC REPORT

To set the style element for	Use STYLE= in this statement
The report as a whole, including attributes of the table itself (like the spacing between cells) as well as style elements for column headers, cells, default summaries, customized summaries, and individual cells defined by CALL DEFINE statements	PROC REPORT
Column headers and cells for a particular variable	DEFINE
Default summary lines	BREAK
	RBREAK
Customized summary lines	COMPUTE (with a location and LINE statements)
Individual cells of the report	CALL DEFINE

Printing a Report

Printing from the REPORT Window

By default, if you print from the REPORT window, the report is routed directly to your printer. If you want, you can specify a form to use for printing (see "Printing with a Form" on page 876). Forms specify things like the type of printer that you are using, text format, and page orientation.

Note: Forms are available only when you run SAS from a windowing environment. △

Operating Environment Information: Printing is implemented differently in different operating environments. For information related to printing, consult *SAS Language Reference: Concepts*. Additional information may be available in the SAS documentation for your operating environment. △

Printing with a Form

To print with a form from the REPORT window:

1 Specify a form. You can specify a form with the FORMNAME command or, in some cases, through the File menu.

2 Specify a print file if you want the output to go to a file instead of directly to the printer. You can specify a print file with the PRTFILE command or, in some cases, through the **File** pull-down menu.

3 Issue the PRINT or PRINT PAGE command from the command line or from the **File** pull-down menu.

4 If you specified a print file,

    a Free the print file. You can free a file with the FREE command or, in some cases, through **Print utilities** in the **File** pull-down menu. You cannot view or print the file until you free it.

    b Use operating environment commands to send the file to the printer.

Printing from the OUTPUT Window

If you are running PROC REPORT with the NOWINDOWS option, the default destination for the output is the OUTPUT window. Use the commands in the **File** pull-down menu to print the report.

Printing from Noninteractive or Batch Mode

If you use noninteractive or batch mode, SAS writes the output either to the display or to external files, depending on the operating environment and on the SAS options that you use. Refer to the SAS documentation for your operating environment for information about how these files are named and where they are stored.

You can print the output file directly or use PROC PRINTTO to redirect the output to another file. In either case, no form is used, but carriage control characters are written if the destination is a print file.

Use operating environment commands to send the file to the printer.

Printing from Interactive Line Mode

If you use interactive line mode, by default the output and log are displayed on the screen immediately following the programming statements. Use PROC PRINTTO to redirect the output to an external file. Then use operating environment commands to send the file to the printer.

Using PROC PRINTTO

PROC PRINTTO defines destinations for the SAS output and the SAS log (see Chapter 29, "The PRINTTO Procedure," on page 819).

PROC PRINTTO does not use a form, but it does write carriage control characters if you are writing to a print file.

CAUTION:

You need two PROC PRINTTO steps. The first PROC PRINTTO step precedes the PROC REPORT step. It redirects the output to a file. The second PROC PRINTTO step follows the PROC REPORT step. It reestablishes the default destination and frees the output file. You cannot print the file until PROC PRINTTO frees it. △

Storing and Reusing a Report Definition

The OUTREPT= option in the PROC REPORT statement stores a report definition in the specified catalog entry. If you are working in the nonwindowing environment, the definition is based on the PROC REPORT step that you submit. If you are in the windowing environment, the definition is based on the report that is in the REPORT window when you end the procedure. The SAS System assigns an entry type of REPT to the entry.

In the windowing environment, you can save the definition of the current report by selecting

File ▶ Save Report

A report definition may differ from the SAS program that creates the report (see the discussion of OUTREPT= on page 887).

You can use a report definition to create an identically structured report for any SAS data set that contains variables with the same names as the ones used in the report definition. Use the REPORT= option in the PROC REPORT statement to load a report definition when you start PROC REPORT. In the windowing environment, load a report definition from the LOAD REPORT window by selecting

File ▶ Open Report

Procedure Syntax

Tip: Supports the Output Delivery System. (See Chapter 2, "Fundamental Concepts for Using Base SAS Procedures" for information on the Output Delivery System.)

Reminder: You can use the ATTRIB, FORMAT, LABEL, and WHERE statements. See Chapter 3, "Statements with the Same Function in Multiple Procedures," for details. You can also use any global statements as well. See Chapter 2, "Fundamental Concepts for Using Base SAS Procedures," for a list.

PROC REPORT *<option(s)>*;

    BREAK *location break-variable</ option(s)>*;

BY <DESCENDING> *variable-1*
 <...<DESCENDING> *variable-n*> <NOTSORTED>;
COLUMN *column-specification(s)*;
 COMPUTE *location* <*target*>
  </ STYLE=<*style-element-name*>
  <[*style–attribute -specification(s)*]>>;
 LINE *specification(s)*;
 . . . *select SAS language elements* . . .
 ENDCOMP;
 COMPUTE *report-item* </ *type-specification*>;
 CALL DEFINE (*column-id*, '*attribute-name*', *value*);
 . . . *select SAS language elements* . . .
 ENDCOMP;
DEFINE *report-item* / <*usage*>
 <*attribute(s)*>
 <*option(s)*>
 <*justification*>
 <COLOR=*color*>
 <'*column-header-1*' <...'*column-header-n*'>>
 <*style*>;
FREQ *variable*;
RBREAK *location* </ *option(s)*>;
WEIGHT *variable*;

To do this	Use this statement
Produce a default summary at a change in the value of a group or order variable	BREAK
Create a separate report for each BY group	BY
Set the value of an attribute for a particular column in the current row	CALL DEFINE
Describe the arrangement of all columns and of headers that span more than one column	COLUMN
Specify one or more programming statements that PROC REPORT executes as it builds the report	COMPUTE and ENDCOMP
Describe how to use and display a report item	DEFINE
Treat observations as if they appear multiple times in the input data set	FREQ
Provide a subset of features of the PUT statement for writing customized summaries	LINE

To do this	Use this statement
Produce a default summary at the beginning or end of a report or at the beginning and end of each BY group	RBREAK
Specify weights for analysis variables in the statistical calculations	WEIGHT

PROC REPORT Statement

PROC REPORT *<option(s)>*;

To do this	Use this option
Specify the input data set	DATA=
Specify the output data set	OUT=
Select the windowing or the nonwindowing environment	WINDOWS| NOWINDOWS
Specify the divisor to use in the calculation of variances	VARDEF=
Exclude observations with nonpositive weight values from the analysis.	EXCLNPWGT
Use a report that was created before compute blocks required aliases (before Release 6.11)	NOALIAS
Specify one or more style elements (for the Output Delivery System) to use for different parts of the report	STYLE=
Control the layout of the report	
Use formatting characters to add line-drawing characters to the report	BOX
Specify whether to center or left-justify the report and summary text	CENTER|NOCENTER
Specify the default number of characters for columns containing computed variables or numeric data set variables	COLWIDTH=
Define the characters to use as line-drawing characters in the report	FORMCHAR=
Specify the length of a line of the report	LS=
Consider missing values as valid values for group, order, or across variables	MISSING
Specify the number of panels on each page of the report	PANELS=

To do this	Use this option
Specify the number of lines in a page of the report	PS=
Specify the number of blank characters between panels	PSPACE=
Override options in the DEFINE statement that suppress the display of a column	SHOWALL
Specify the number of blank characters between columns	SPACING=
Display one value from each column of the report, on consecutive lines if necessary, before displaying another value from the first column	WRAP
Customize column headers	
Underline all column headers and the spaces between them	HEADLINE
Write a blank line beneath all column headers	HEADSKIP
Suppress column headers	NOHEADER
Write *name=* in front of each value in the report, where *name=* is the column header for the value	NAMED
Specify the split character	SPLIT=
Store and retrieve report definitions, PROC REPORT statements, and your report profile	
Write to the SAS log the PROC REPORT code that creates the current report	LIST
Suppress the building of the report	NOEXEC
Store in the specified catalog the report definition defined by the PROC REPORT step that you submit	OUTREPT=
Identify the report profile to use	PROFILE=
Specify the report definition to use	REPORT=
Control the windowing environment	
Display command lines rather than menu bars in all REPORT windows	COMMAND

To do this	Use this option
Identify the library and catalog containing user-defined help for the report	HELP=
Open the REPORT window and start the PROMPT facility	PROMPT

Options

BOX

uses formatting characters to add line-drawing characters to the report. These characters

- □ surround each page of the report
- □ separate column headers from the body of the report
- □ separate rows and columns from each other
- □ separate values in a summary line from other values in the same columns
- □ separate a customized summary from the rest of the report.

Restriction: This option has no effect on the HTML or Printer output.

Interaction: You cannot use BOX if you use WRAP in the PROC REPORT statement or in the ROPTIONS window or if you use FLOW in any item definition.

See also: the discussion of FORMCHAR= on page 882

Featured in: Example 12 on page 989

CENTER | NOCENTER

specifies whether to center or left-justify the report and summary text (customized break lines).

PROC REPORT honors the first of these centering specifications that it finds:

- □ the CENTER or NOCENTER option in the PROC REPORT statement or the CENTER toggle in the ROPTIONS window
- □ the CENTER or NOCENTER option stored in the report definition that is loaded with REPORT= in the PROC REPORT statement
- □ the SAS system option CENTER or NOCENTER.

Restriction: This option has no effect on the HTML or Printer output.

Interaction: When CENTER is in effect, PROC REPORT ignores spacing that precedes the leftmost variable in the report.

COLWIDTH=*column-width*

specifies the default number of characters for columns containing computed variables or numeric data set variables.

Default: 9

Range: 1 to the linesize

Restriction: This option has no effect on the HTML or Printer output.

Interaction: When setting the width for a column, PROC REPORT first looks at WIDTH= in the definition for that column. If WIDTH= is not present, PROC REPORT uses a column width large enough to accommodate the format for the item. (For information about formats see the discussion of FORMAT= on page 912.)

If no format is associated with the item, the column width depends on variable type:

If the variable is a ...	Then the column width is the ...
character variable in the input data set	length of the variable
numeric variable in the input data set	value of the COLWIDTH= option
computed variable (numeric or character)	value of the COLWIDTH= option

Featured in: Example 2 on page 961

COMMAND
displays command lines rather than menu bars in all REPORT windows.

After you have started PROC REPORT in the windowing environment, you can display the menu bars in the current window by issuing the COMMAND command. You can display the menu bars in all PROC REPORT windows by issuing the PMENU command. The PMENU command affects all the windows in your SAS session. Both of these commands are toggles.

You can store a setting of COMMAND in your report profile. PROC REPORT honors the first of these settings that it finds:

☐ the COMMAND option in the PROC REPORT statement

☐ the setting in your report profile.

Restriction: This option has no effect in the nonwindowing environment.

DATA=*SAS-data-set*
specifies the input data set.

Main discussion: "Input Data Sets" on page 18

EXCLNPWGT
excludes observations with nonpositive weight values (zero or negative) from the analysis. By default, PROC REPORT treats observations with negative weights like those with zero weights and counts them in the total number of observations.

Alias: EXCLNPWGTS

Requirement: You must use a WEIGHT statement.

See also: "WEIGHT Statement" on page 922

FORMCHAR <(*position(s)*)>='*formatting-character(s)*'
defines the characters to use as line-drawing characters in the report.

position(s)
identifies the position of one or more characters in the SAS formatting-character string. A space or a comma separates the positions.

Default: Omitting (*position(s)*) is the same as specifying all 20 possible SAS formatting characters, in order.

Range: PROC REPORT uses 12 of the 20 formatting characters that SAS provides. Table 32.3 on page 883 shows the formatting characters that PROC REPORT uses. Figure 32.8 on page 884 illustrates the use of some commonly used formatting character in the output from PROC REPORT.

formatting-character(s)
lists the characters to use for the specified positions. PROC REPORT assigns characters in *formatting-character(s)* to *position(s)*, in the order that they are listed. For instance, the following option assigns the asterisk (*) to the third formatting character, the pound sign (#) to the seventh character, and does not alter the remaining characters:

```
formchar(3,7)='*#'
```

Restriction: This option has no effect on the HTML or Printer output.

Interaction: The SAS system option FORMCHAR= specifies the default formatting characters. The system option defines the entire string of formatting characters. The FORMCHAR= option in a procedure can redefine selected characters.

Tip: You can use any character in *formatting-characters*, including hexadecimal characters. If you use hexadecimal characters, you must put an **x** after the closing quote. For instance, the following option assigns the hexadecimal character 2D to the third formatting character, the hexadecimal character 7C to the seventh character, and does not alter the remaining characters:

```
formchar(3,7)='2D7C'x
```

Table 32.3 Formatting Characters Used by PROC REPORT

Position	Default	Used to draw
1	|	the right and left borders and the vertical separators between columns
2	-	the top and bottom borders and the horizontal separators between rows; also underlining and overlining in break lines as well as the underlining that the HEADLINE option draws
3	-	the top character in the left border
4	-	the top character in a line of characters that separates columns
5	-	the top character in the right border
6	|	the leftmost character in a row of horizontal separators
7	+	the intersection of a column of vertical characters and a row of horizontal characters
8	|	the rightmost character in a row of horizontal separators
9	-	the bottom character in the left border
10	-	the bottom character in a line of characters that separate columns
11	-	the bottom character in the right border
13	=	double overlining and double underlining in break lines

Figure 32.8 Formatting Characters in PROC REPORT Output

```
          Sales for Northern Sectors              1


     Sector      Manager        Sales      ⊝2
     ------------------------------⊝

     Northeast   Alomar          786.00
                 Andrews       1,045.00
                              ---------⊝
                              1,831.00  ⊝2
                              ---------⊝

     Northwest   Brown           598.00
                 Pelfrey         746.00
                 Reveiz        1,110.00
                              ---------
                              2,454.00
                              ---------


                              ========⊜
                              4,285.00  ⊜13
                              ========⊜
```

HEADLINE

underlines all column headers and the spaces between them at the top of each page of the report.

The HEADLINE option underlines with the second formatting character. (See the discussion of FORMCHAR= on page 882 .)

Default: hyphen (–)

Restriction: This option has no effect on the HTML or Printer output.

Tip: In traditional (monospace) SAS output, you can underline column headers without underlining the spaces between them, by using two hyphens (`'--'`) as the last line of each column header instead of using HEADLINE.

Featured in: Example 2 on page 961 and Example 8 on page 977

HEADSKIP

writes a blank line beneath all column headers (or beneath the underlining that the HEADLINE option writes) at the top of each page of the report.

Restriction: This option has no effect on the HTML or Printer output.

Featured in: Example 2 on page 961

HELP=*libref.catalog*

identifies the library and catalog containing user-defined help for the report. This help can be in CBT or HELP catalog entries. You can write a CBT or HELP entry for each item in the report with the BUILD procedure in SAS/AF software. Store all such entries for a report in the same catalog.

Specify the entry name for help for a particular report item in the DEFINITION window for that report item or in a DEFINE statement.

Restriction: This option has no effect in the nonwindowing environment or on the HTML or Printer output.

LIST

writes to the SAS log the PROC REPORT code that creates the current report. This listing may differ in these ways from the statements that you submit:

- □ It shows some defaults that you may not have specified.
- □ It omits some statements that are not specific to the REPORT procedure, whether you submit them with the PROC REPORT step or had previously submitted them. These statements include

  BY

  FOOTNOTE

  FREQ

  TITLE

  WEIGHT

  WHERE

- □ It omits these PROC REPORT statement options:

  LIST

  OUT=

  OUTREPT=

  PROFILE=

  REPORT=

  WINDOWS | NOWINDOWS

- □ It omits SAS system options.
- □ It resolves automatic macro variables.

Restriction: This option has no effect in the windowing environment. Selecting

| Tools | ▶ | Report Statements |

serves a similar purpose. It writes the report definition for the report that is currently in the REPORT window to the SOURCE window.

LS=*line-size*

specifies the length of a line of the report.

PROC REPORT honors the first of these line size specifications that it finds:

- □ the LS= option in the PROC REPORT statement or Linesize= in the ROPTIONS window
- □ the LS= setting stored in the report definition loaded with REPORT= in the PROC REPORT statement
- □ the SAS system option LINESIZE=.

Range: 64-256 (integer)

Restriction: This option has no effect on the HTML or Printer output.

Featured in: Example 6 on page 973 and Example 8 on page 977

MISSING

considers missing values as valid values for group, order, or across variables. Special missing values used to represent numeric values (the letters A through Z and the underscore (_) character) are each considered as a different value. A group for each missing value appears in the report. If you omit the MISSING option, PROC REPORT does not include observations with a missing value for any group, order, or across variables in the report.

See also: For information about special missing values, see the section on missing values in *SAS Language Reference: Concepts*.

Featured in: Example 11 on page 986

NAMED

writes *name=* in front of each value in the report, where *name* is the column header for the value.

Interaction: When you use the NAMED option, PROC REPORT automatically uses the NOHEADER option.

Tip: Use NAMED in conjunction with the WRAP option to produce a report that wraps all columns for a single row of the report onto consecutive lines rather than placing columns of a wide report on separate pages.

Featured in: Example 7 on page 975

lets you use a report that was created before compute blocks required aliases (before Release 6.11). If you use NOALIAS, you cannot use aliases in compute blocks.

NOCENTER

See CENTER|NOCENTER on page 881.

NOEXEC

suppresses the building of the report. Use NOEXEC with OUTREPT= to store a report definition in a catalog entry. Use NOEXEC with LIST and REPORT= to display a listing of the specified report definition.

NOHEADER

suppresses column headers, including those that span multiple columns.

Once you suppress the display of column headers in the windowing environment, you cannot select any report items.

NOWINDOWS

Alias: NOWD

See WINDOWS|NOWINDOWS on page 893.

OUT=*SAS-data-set*

names the output data set. If this data set does not exist, PROC REPORT creates it. The data set contains one observation for each detail row of the report and one observation for each unique summary line. If you use both customized and default summaries at the same place in the report, the output data set contains only one observation because the two summaries differ only in how they present the data. Information about customization (underlining, color, text, and so forth) is not data and is not saved in the output data set.

The output data set contains one variable for each column of the report. PROC REPORT tries to use the name of the report item as the name of the corresponding variable in the output data set. However, this is not possible if a data set variable is under or over an across variable or if a data set variable appears multiple times in the COLUMN statement without aliases. In these cases, the name of the variable is based on the column number (_C1_, _C2_, and so forth).

Output data set variables that are derived from input data set variables retain the formats of their counterparts in the input data set. PROC REPORT derives labels for these variables from the corresponding column headers in the report unless the only item defining the column is an across variable. In that case, the variables have no label. If multiple items are stacked in a column, the labels of the corresponding output data set variables come from the analysis variable in the column.

The output data set also contains a variable named _BREAK_. If an observation in the output data set derives from a detail row in the report, the value of _BREAK_ is missing. If it derives from a summary line, the value of _BREAK_ is the name of the break variable associated with the summary line, or _RBREAK_.

Interaction: You cannot use OUT= in a PROC REPORT step that uses a BY statement.

Featured in: Example 12 on page 989 and Example 13 on page 991

OUTREPT=*libref.catalog.entry*
stores in the specified catalog entry the REPORT definition defined by the PROC REPORT step that you submit. PROC REPORT assigns the entry a type of REPT.

The stored report definition may differ in these ways from the statements that you submit:

□ It omits some statements that are not specific to the REPORT procedure, whether you submit them with the PROC REPORT step or whether they are already in effect when you submit the step. These statements include

BY

FOOTNOTE

FREQ

TITLE

WEIGHT

WHERE

□ It omits these PROC REPORT statement options:

LIST

NOALIAS

OUT=

OUTREPT=

PROFILE=

REPORT=

WINDOWS | NOWINDOWS

□ It omits SAS system options.

□ It resolves automatic macro variables.

Featured in: Example 7 on page 975

PANELS=*number-of-panels*
specifies the number of panels on each page of the report. If the width of a report is less than half of the line size, you can display the data in multiple sets of columns so that rows that would otherwise appear on multiple pages appear on the same page. Each set of columns is a *panel*. A familiar example of this kind of report is a telephone book, which contains multiple panels of names and telephone numbers on a single page.

When PROC REPORT writes a multipanel report, it fills one panel before beginning the next.

The number of panels that fits on a page depends on the

□ width of the panel

□ space between panels

□ line size.

Restriction: This option has no effect on the HTML or Printer destination.

Default: 1

Tip: If *number-of-panels* is larger than the number of panels that can fit on the page, PROC REPORT creates as many panels as it can. Let PROC REPORT put your data in the maximum number of panels that can fit on the page by specifying a large number of panels (for example, 99).

See also: For information about the space between panels and the line size, see the discussions of PSPACE= on page 889 and the discussion of LS= on page 885.

Featured in: Example 8 on page 977

PROFILE=*libref.catalog*

identifies the report profile to use. A profile

- □ specifies the location of menus that define alternative menu bars and pull-down menus for the REPORT and COMPUTE windows.

- □ sets defaults for WINDOWS, PROMPT, and COMMAND.

PROC REPORT uses the entry REPORT.PROFILE in the catalog that you specify as your profile. If no such entry exists, or if you do not specify a profile, PROC REPORT uses the entry REPORT.PROFILE in SASUSER.PROFILE. If you have no profile, PROC REPORT uses default menus and the default settings of the options.

You create a profile from the PROFILE window while using PROC REPORT in a windowing environment. To create a profile

1 Invoke PROC REPORT with the WINDOWS option.

2 Select `Tools` → `Report Profile`.

3 Fill in the fields to suit your needs.

4 Select `OK` to exit the PROFILE window. When you exit the window, PROC REPORT stores the profile in SASUSER.PROFILE.REPORT.PROFILE. Use the CATALOG procedure or the Explorer window to copy the profile to another location.

Note: If you open the PROFILE window and decide not to create a profile, select `CANCEL` to close the window. △

PROMPT

opens the REPORT window and starts the PROMPT facility. This facility guides you through creating a new report or adding more data set variables or statistics to an existing report.

If you start PROC REPORT with prompting, the first window gives you a chance to limit the number of observations that are used during prompting. When you exit the prompter, PROC REPORT removes the limit.

Restriction: When you use the PROMPT option, you open the REPORT window. When the REPORT window is open, you cannot send procedure output to the HTML or Printer destination.

Tip: You can store a setting of PROMPT in your report profile. PROC REPORT honors the first of these settings that it finds:

- □ the PROMPT option in the PROC REPORT statement

- □ the setting in your report profile.

If you omit PROMPT from the PROC REPORT statement, the procedure uses the setting in your report profile, if you have one. If you do not have a report profile, PROC REPORT does not use the prompt facility. For information on report profiles, see "PROFILE" on page 936.

PS=*page-size*

   specifies the number of lines in a page of the report.

   PROC REPORT honors the first of these page size specifications that it finds:

   □ the PS= option in the PROC REPORT statement

   □ the PS= setting in the report definition specified with REPORT= in the PROC REPORT statement

   □ the SAS system option PAGESIZE=.

   Range: 15-32,767 (integer)

   Restriction: This option has no effect on the HTML or Printer output.

   Featured in: Example 6 on page 973 and Example 8 on page 977

PSPACE=*space-between-panels*

   specifies the number of blank characters between panels. PROC REPORT separates all panels in the report by the same number of blank characters. For each panel, the sum of its width and the number of blank characters separating it from the panel to its left cannot exceed the line size.

   Default: 4

   Restriction: This option has no effect on the HTML or Printer output.

   Featured in: Example 8 on page 977

REPORT=*libref.catalog.entry*

   specifies the report definition to use. PROC REPORT stores all report definitions as entries of type REPT in a SAS catalog.

   Interaction: If you use REPORT=, you cannot use the COLUMN statement.

   See also: OUTREPT= on page 887

   Featured in: Example 7 on page 975

SHOWALL

   overrides options in the DEFINE statement that suppress the display of a column.

   See also: NOPRINT and NOZERO in "DEFINE Statement" on page 908

SPACING=*space-between-columns*

   specifies the number of blank characters between columns. For each column, the sum of its width and the blank characters between it and the column to its left cannot exceed the line size.

   Default: 2

   Restriction: This option has no effect on the HTML or Printer output.

   Interaction: PROC REPORT separates all columns in the report by the number of blank characters specified by SPACING= in the PROC REPORT statement unless you use SPACING= in the DEFINE statement to change the spacing to the left of a specific item.

   Interaction: When CENTER is in effect, PROC REPORT ignores spacing that precedes the leftmost variable in the report.

   Featured in: Example 2 on page 961

SPLIT='*character*'

   specifies the split character. PROC REPORT breaks a column header when it reaches that character and continues the header on the next line. The split character itself is not part of the column header although each occurrence of the split character counts toward the 256-character maximum for a label.

   Default: slash (/)

> **Interaction:** The FLOW option in the DEFINE statement honors the split character.
>
> **Featured in:** Example 5 on page 970

STYLE<(*location(s)*)>=<*style-element-name*><[*style-attribute-specification(s)*]>
specifies the style element to use for the specified locations in the report.

> *Note:* You can use braces ({ and }) instead of square brackets ([and]). △

location
identifies the part of the report that the STYLE= option affects. Table 32.4 on page 890 shows the available locations and the other statements that you can specify them in. Specifications in a statement other than the PROC REPORT statement override the same specification in the PROC REPORT statement. However, any style attributes that you specify in the PROC REPORT statement and do not override in another statement are inherited. For instance, if you specify a blue background and a white foreground for all column headers in the PROC REPORT statement, and you specify a gray background for the column headers of a variable in the DEFINE statement, the background for that particular column header is gray, and the foreground is white (as specified in the PROC REPORT statement).

Table 32.4 Specifying Locations in the STYLE= Option

This *location*	Affects this part of the report	And can also be specified for individual items in this statement
CALLDEF	all cells that are identified by a CALL DEFINE statement	CALL DEFINE
COLUMN	the cells of all columns	DEFINE
HEADER	all column headers and all spanning headers	DEFINE (for column headers)
LINES	all LINE statements in all compute blocks	COMPUTE (with one or more LINE statements)
REPORT	the structural part of the report, that is, the underlying table. Use REPORT to set things such as the width of the border and the space between cells	none
SUMMARY	all default summary lines produced by a BREAK or an RBREAK statement	BREAK RBREAK

style-element-name
is the name of a style element that is part of a style definition that is registered with the Output Delivery System. SAS Institute provides some style definitions. Users can create their own style definitions with PROC TEMPLATE. For information about Institute-supplied style definitions, see "What Style Definitions Are Shipped with the Software?" on page 43. For information about PROC

TEMPLATE and the Output Delivery System, see *The Complete Guide to the SAS Output Delivery System.*

Default: Table 32.5 on page 891 shows the default style element for each location:

Table 32.5   The Default Style Element for Each Location in PROC REPORT

Location	Default style element
CALLDEF	Data
COLUMN	Data
HEADER	Header
LINES	NoteContent
REPORT	Table
SUMMARY	DataEmphasis

style-attribute-specification

describes the style attribute to change. Each *style-attribute-specification* has this general form:

style-attribute-name=style-attribute-value

You can set these style attributes in the REPORT location:

BACKGROUND=	FONT_WIDTH=*
BACKGROUNDIMAGE=	FOREGROUND=*
BORDERCOLOR=	FRAME=
BORDERCOLORDARK=	HTMLCLASS=
BORDERCOLORLIGHT=	JUST=
BORDERWIDTH=	OUTPUTWIDTH=
CELLPADDING=	POSTHTML=
CELLSPACING=	POSTIMAGE=
FONT=*	POSTTEXT=
FONT_FACE=*	PREHTML=
FONT_SIZE=*	PREIMAGE=
FONT_STYLE=*	PRETEXT=
FONT_WEIGHT=*	RULES=

* When you use these attributes in this location, they affect only the text that is specified with the PRETEXT=, POSTTEXT=, PREHTML=, and POSTHTML= attributes. To alter the foreground color or the font for the text that appears in the table, you must set the corresponding attribute in a location that affects the cells rather than the table.

You can set these style attributes in the CALLDEF, COLUMN, HEADER, LINES, and SUMMARY locations:

ASIS=	FONT_WIDTH=
BACKGROUND=	HREFTARGET=
BACKGROUNDIMAGE=	HTMLCLASS=
BORDERCOLOR=	JUST=
BORDERCOLORDARK=	NOBREAKSPACE=
BORDERCOLORLIGHT=	POSTHTML=
BORDERWIDTH=	POSTIMAGE=
CELLHEIGHT=	POSTTEXT=
CELLWIDTH=	PREHTML=
FLYOVER=	PREIMAGE=
FONT=	PRETEXT=
FONT_FACE=	PROTECTSPECIALCHARS=
FONT_SIZE=	TAGATTR=
FONT_STYLE=	URL=
FONT_WEIGHT=	VJUST=

For information about style attributes, see "What Style Attributes Can Base Procedures Specify?" on page 43.

Restriction: This option affects only the HTML and Printer output.

Featured in: Example 15 on page 996 and Example 16 on page 999

VARDEF=*divisor*
specifies the divisor to use in the calculation of the variance and standard deviation. Table 32.6 on page 892 shows the possible values for *divisor* and associated divisors.

Table 32.6   Possible Values for VARDEF=

Value	Divisor	Formula for Divisor
DF	degrees of freedom	$n - 1$
N	number of observations	n
WDF	sum of weights minus one	$(\Sigma_i \, w_i) - 1$
WEIGHT |WGT	sum of weights	$\Sigma_i \, w_i$

The procedure computes the variance as $CSS/divisor$, where CSS is the corrected sums of squares and equals $\sum (x_i - \overline{x})^2$. When you weight the analysis variables, CSS equals $\sum w_i (x_i - \overline{x}_w)^2$, where $\overline{x}_w$ is the weighted mean.

Default: DF

Requirement: To compute the standard error of the mean and Student's *t*-test, use the default value of VARDEF=.

Tip: When you use the WEIGHT statement and VARDEF=DF, the variance is an estimate of σ^2, where the variance of the *i*th observation is $var(x_i) = \sigma^2/w_i$ and

w_i is the weight for the ith observation. This yields an estimate of the variance of an observation with unit weight.

Tip: When you use the WEIGHT statement and VARDEF=WGT, the computed variance is asymptotically (for large n) an estimate of $\sigma^2/\overline{w}$, where $\overline{w}$ is the average weight. This yields an asymptotic estimate of the variance of an observation with average weight.

See also: "WEIGHT" on page 73

WINDOWS | NOWINDOWS

selects a windowing or nonwindowing environment.

When you use WINDOWS, SAS opens the REPORT window, which enables you to modify a report repeatedly and to see the modifications immediately. When you use NOWINDOWS, PROC REPORT runs without the REPORT window and sends its output to the SAS procedure output.

Alias: WD | NOWD

Restriction: When you use the WINDOWS option, you cannot send procedure output to the HTML or Printer destination.

Tip: You can store a setting of WINDOWS in your report profile, if you have one. If you do not specify WINDOWS or NOWINDOWS in the PROC REPORT statement, the procedure uses the setting in your report profile. If you do not have a report profile, PROC REPORT looks at the setting of the SAS system option DMS. If DMS is ON, PROC REPORT uses the windowing environment; if DMS is OFF, it uses the nonwindowing environment.

See also: For a discussion of the report profile see the discussion of PROFILE= on page 888.

Featured in: Example 1 on page 958

WRAP

displays one value from each column of the report, on consecutive lines if necessary, before displaying another value from the first column. By default, PROC REPORT displays values for only as many columns as it can fit on one page. It fills a page with values for these columns before starting to display values for the remaining columns on the next page.

Restriction: This option has no effect on the HTML or Printer output.

Interaction: When WRAP is in effect, PROC REPORT ignores PAGE in any item definitions.

Tip: Typically, you use WRAP in conjunction with the NAMED option in order to avoid wrapping column headers.

Featured in: Example 7 on page 975

BREAK Statement

Produces a default summary at a break (a change in the value of a group or order variable). The information in a summary applies to a set of observations. The observations share a unique combination of values for the break variable and all other group or order variables to the left of the break variable in the report.

Featured in: Example 4 on page 967 and Example 5 on page 970.

BREAK *location break-variable</ option(s)>*;

To do this	Use this option
Specify the color of the break lines in the REPORT window	COLOR=
Double overline each value	DOL
Double underline each value	DUL
Overline each value	OL
Start a new page after the last break line	PAGE
Write a blank line for the last break line	SKIP
Specify a style element for default summary lines, customized summary lines or both	STYLE=
Write a summary line in each group of break lines	SUMMARIZE
Suppress the printing of the value of the break variable in the summary line and of any underlining or overlining in the break lines in the column containing the break variable	SUPPRESS
Underline each value	UL

Required Arguments

location
> controls the placement of the break lines and is either

> AFTER
>> places the break lines immediately after the last row of each set of rows that have the same value for the break variable.

> BEFORE
>> places the break lines immediately before the first row of each set of rows that have the same value for the break variable.

break-variable
> is a group or order variable. The REPORT procedure writes break lines each time the value of this variable changes.

Options

COLOR=*color*
> specifies the color of the break lines in the REPORT window. You can use the following colors:

BLACK	MAGENTA
BLUE	ORANGE
BROWN	PINK
CYAN	RED

GRAY   WHITE

GREEN   YELLOW

Default: The color of **Foreground** in the SASCOLOR window. (For more information, see the online help for the SASCOLOR window.)

Restriction: This option has no effect on the HTML or Printer output.

Note: Not all operating environments and devices support all colors, and on some operating systems and devices, one color may map to another color. For example, if the DEFINITION window displays the word BROWN in yellow characters, selecting BROWN results in a yellow item. △

DOL

(for double overlining) uses the thirteenth formatting character to overline each value

□ that appears in the summary line

□ that would appear in the summary line if you specified the SUMMARIZE option.

Default: equals sign (=)

Restriction: This option has no effect on the HTML or Printer output.

Interaction: If you specify both the OL and DOL options, PROC REPORT honors only OL.

See also: the discussion of FORMCHAR= on page 882.

DUL

(for double underlining) uses the thirteenth formatting character to underline each value

□ that appears in the summary line

□ that would appear in the summary line if you specified the SUMMARIZE option.

Default: equals sign (=)

Restriction: This option has no effect on the HTML or Printer output.

Interaction: If you specify both the UL and DUL options, PROC REPORT honors only UL.

See also: the discussion of FORMCHAR= on page 882.

OL

(for overlining) uses the second formatting character to overline each value

□ that appears in the summary line

□ that would appear in the summary line if you specified the SUMMARIZE option.

Default: hyphen (–)

Restriction: This option has no effect on the HTML or Printer output.

Interaction: If you specify both the OL and DOL options, PROC REPORT honors only OL.

See also: the discussion of FORMCHAR= on page 882.

Featured in: Example 2 on page 961 and Example 9 on page 979

PAGE

starts a new page after the last break line.

Interaction: If you use PAGE in the BREAK statement and you create a break at the end of the report, the summary for the whole report appears on a separate page.

Featured in: Example 9 on page 979

SKIP
>   writes a blank line for the last break line.
>
>   **Restriction:**   This option has no effect on the HTML or Printer output.
>
>   **Featured in:**   Example 2 on page 961, Example 4 on page 967, Example 5 on page
>   970, and Example 8 on page 977

STYLE=<*style-element-name*><[*style-attribute-specification(s)*]>
>   specifies the style element to use for default summary lines that are created with the
>   BREAK statement. You can alter the default style element of the summary lines or
>   specify another style element entirely.
>
>   *Note:*   You can use braces ({ and }) instead of square brackets ([and]). △

>   *style-element-name*
>   >   is the name of a style element that is part of a style definition that is registered
>   >   with the Output Delivery System. SAS Institute provides some styles definitions.
>   >   Users can create their own style definitions with PROC TEMPLATE.
>   >
>   >   Default: If you do not specify a style element, PROC REPORT uses DataEmphasis.
>   >
>   >   See also: For information about Institute-supplied style definitions, see "What
>   >   Style Definitions Are Shipped with the Software?" on page 43.
>   >   For information about PROC TEMPLATE and the Output Delivery System,
>   >   see *The Complete Guide to the SAS Output Delivery System*.

>   *style-attribute-specification*
>   >   describes the style attribute to change. Each *style-attribute-specification* has this
>   >   general form:
>   >
>   >   >   *style-attribute-name=style-attribute-value*
>   >
>   >   You can set these attributes:

ASIS=	FONT_WIDTH=
BACKGROUND=	HREFTARGET=
BACKGROUNDIMAGE=	HTMLCLASS=
BORDERCOLOR=	JUST=
BORDERCOLORDARK=	NOBREAKSPACE=
BORDERCOLORLIGHT=	POSTHTML=
BORDERWIDTH=	POSTIMAGE=
CELLHEIGHT=	POSTTEXT=
CELLWIDTH=	PREHTML=
FLYOVER=	PREIMAGE=
FONT=	PRETEXT=
FONT_FACE=	PROTECTSPECIALCHARS=
FONT_SIZE=	TAGATTR=
FONT_STYLE=	URL=
FONT_WEIGHT=	VJUST=

>   >   For information about style attributes, see "What Style Attributes Can Base
>   >   Procedures Specify?" on page 43.
>   >
>   >   **Restriction:**   This option affects only the HTML and Printer output.

SUMMARIZE
> writes a summary line in each group of break lines. A summary line for a set of observations contains values for
>> □ the break variable (which you can suppress with the SUPPRESS option)
>> □ other group or order variables to the left of the break variable
>> □ statistics
>> □ analysis variables
>> □ computed variables.
>
> The following table shows how PROC REPORT calculates the value for each kind of report item in a summary line created by the BREAK statement:

If the report item is ...	Then its value is ...
the break variable	the current value of the variable (or a missing value if you use SUPPRESS)
a group or order variable to the left of the break variable	the current value of the variable
a group or order variable to the right of the break variable, or a display variable anywhere in the report	missing*
a statistic	the value of the statistic over all observations in the set
an analysis variable	the value of the statistic specified as the usage option in the item's definition. PROC REPORT calculates the value of the statistic over all observations in the set. The default usage is SUM.
a computed variable	the results of the calculations based on the code in the corresponding compute block (see "COMPUTE Statement" on page 905).

* If you reference a variable with a missing value in a customized summary line, PROC REPORT displays that variable as a blank (for character variables) or a period (for numeric variables).

> *Note:* PROC REPORT cannot create groups in a report that contains order or display variables. △
>
> **Featured in:** Example 2 on page 961, Example 4 on page 967, and Example 9 on page 979

SUPPRESS
> suppresses printing of
>> □ the value of the break variable in the summary line
>> □ any underlining and overlining in the break lines in the column containing the break variable.
>
> **Interaction:** If you use SUPPRESS, the value of the break variable is unavailable for use in customized break lines unless you assign a value to it in the compute block associated with the break (see "COMPUTE Statement" on page 905).
>
> **Featured in:** Example 4 on page 967

UL
> (for underlining) uses the second formatting character to underline each value
>> □ that appears in the summary line
>> □ that would appear in the summary line if you specified the SUMMARIZE option.

Default: hyphen (–)

Restriction: This option has no effect on the HTML or Printer output.

Interaction: If you specify both the UL and DUL options, PROC REPORT honors only UL.

See also: the discussion of FORMCHAR= on page 882.

Order of Break Lines

When a default summary contains more than one break line, the order in which the break lines appear is

1 overlining or double overlining (OL or DOL)

2 summary line (SUMMARIZE)

3 underlining or double underlining (UL or DUL)

4 skipped line (SKIP)

5 page break (PAGE).

Note: If you define a customized summary for the break, customized break lines appear after underlining or double underlining. For more information about customized break lines, see "COMPUTE Statement" on page 905 and "LINE Statement" on page 917. △

BY Statement

Creates a separate report on a separate page for each BY group.

Restriction: If you use the BY statement, you must use the NOWINDOWS option in the PROC REPORT statement.

Restriction: You cannot use the OUT= option when you use a BY statement.

Interaction: If you use the RBREAK statement in a report that uses BY processing, PROC REPORT creates a default summary for each BY group. In this case, you cannot summarize information for the whole report.

Tip: Using the BY statement does not make the FIRST. and LAST. variables available in compute blocks.

Main discussion: "BY" on page 68

BY <DESCENDING> *variable-1*
    <...<DESCENDING> *variable-n*> <NOTSORTED>;

Required Arguments

variable
    specifies the variable that the procedure uses to form BY groups. You can specify more than one variable. If you do not use the NOTSORTED option in the BY statement, the observations in the data set must either be sorted by all the variables that you specify, or they must be indexed appropriately. Variables in a BY statement are called *BY variables*.

Options

DESCENDING
specifies that the data set is sorted in descending order by the variable that immediately follows the word DESCENDING in the BY statement.

NOTSORTED
specifies that observations are not necessarily sorted in alphabetic or numeric order. The data are grouped in another way, for example, chronological order.

The requirement for ordering or indexing observations according to the values of BY variables is suspended for BY-group processing when you use the NOTSORTED option. In fact, the procedure does not use an index if you specify NOTSORTED. The procedure defines a BY group as a set of contiguous observations that have the same values for all BY variables. If observations with the same values for the BY variables are not contiguous, the procedure treats each contiguous set as a separate BY group.

CALL DEFINE Statement

Sets the value of an attribute for a particular column in the current row.

Restriction: Valid only in a compute block that is attached to a report item.

Featured in: Example 4 on page 967

CALL DEFINE (*column-id*, *'attribute-name'*, *value*);

The CALL DEFINE statement is often used to write report definitions that other people will use in a windowing environment. Only the FORMAT, URL, URLBP, and URLP attributes have an effect in the nonwindowing environment. In fact, URL, URLBP, and URLP are effective only in the nonwindowing environment. The STYLE= attribute is effective only when you are using the Output Delivery System to create HTML or Printer output. (See Table 32.7 on page 900 for descriptions of the available attributes.)

Required Arguments

column-id
specifies a column name or a column number. A column ID can be one of the following:
  □ a character literal (in quotation marks)
  □ a character expression
  □ a numeric literal
  □ a numeric expression
  □ a name of the form _Cn_, where n is the column number
  □ the automatic variable _COL_. This variable identifies the column containing the report item that the compute block is attached to.

attribute-name
is the attribute to define. For attribute names, refer to Table 32.7 on page 900.

value

sets the value for the attribute. For values for each attribute, refer to Table 32.7 on page 900.

Table 32.7 Attribute Descriptions

Attribute	Description	Values	Affects
BLINK	Controls blinking of current value	1 turns blinking on; 0 turns it off	windowing environment
COLOR	Controls the color of the current value in the REPORT window	'blue', 'red', 'pink', 'green', 'cyan', 'yellow', 'white', 'orange', 'black', 'magenta', 'gray', 'brown'	windowing environment
COMMAND	Specifies that a series of commands follows	a quoted string of SAS commands to submit to the command line	windowing environment
FORMAT	Specifies a format for the column	a SAS format or a user-defined format	windowing and nonwindowing environments
HIGHLIGHT	Controls highlighting of the current value	1 turns highlighting on; 0 turns it off	windowing environment
RVSVIDEO	Controls display of the current value	1 turns reverse video on; 0 turns it off	windowing environment
STYLE=	Specifies the style element for the Output Delivery System	See "Using the STYLE= Attribute" on page 901	HTML and Printer output
URL	Makes the contents of each cell of the column a link to the specified Uniform Resource Locator (URL)*	a quoted URL (either single or double quotation marks can be used)	HTML output

Attribute	Description	Values	Affects
URLBP	Makes the contents of each cell of the column a link. The link points to a Uniform Resource Locator that is a concatenation of 1 the string that is specified by the BASE= option in the ODS HTML statement 2 the string that is specified by the PATH= option in the ODS HTML statement 3 the value of the URLBP attribute[*,#]	a quoted URL (either single or double quotation marks can be used)	HTML output
URLP	Makes the contents of each cell of the column a link. The link points to a Uniform Resource Locator that is a concatenation of 1 the string that is specified by the PATH= option in the ODS HTML statement 2 the value of the URLP attribute[*,#]	a quoted URL (either single or double quotation marks can be used)	HTML output

* The total length of the URL that you specify (including any characters that come from the BASE= and PATH= options) cannot exceed the line size. Use the LS= option in the PROC REPORT statement to alter the line size for the PROC REPORT step. (See the discussion of LS= on page 885.)

\# For information on the BASE= and PATH= options, see the documentation for the ODS HTML statement in *The Complete Guide to the SAS Output Delivery System.*

Note: The attributes BLINK, HIGHLIGHT, and RVSVIDEO do not work on all devices. △

Using the STYLE= Attribute

The STYLE= attribute specifies the style element to use in the cells that are affected by the CALL DEFINE statement.

The STYLE= attribute functions like the STYLE= option in other statements in PROC REPORT. However, instead of acting as an option in a statement, it becomes the value for the STYLE= attribute. For instance, the following CALL DEFINE statement sets the background color to yellow and the font size to 7:

```
call define(_col_, "style",
            "style=[background=yellow font_size=7]");
```

The general form for the value of the style attribute is

STYLE=<*style-element-name*><[*style-attribute-specification(s)*]>

Note: You can use braces ({ and }) instead of square brackets ([and]). △

style-element-name

is the name of a style element that is part of a style definition that is registered with the Output Delivery System. SAS Institute provides some style definitions. Users can create their own style definitions and style elements with PROC TEMPLATE.

Default: If you do not specify a style element, PROC REPORT uses Data.

See also: For information about Institute-supplied style definitions, see "What Style Definitions Are Shipped with the Software?" on page 43.

For information about PROC TEMPLATE and the Output Delivery System, see *The Complete Guide to the SAS Output Delivery System*.

style-attribute-specification

describes one or more style attributes to change. Each *style-attribute-specification* has this general form:

style-attribute-name=style-attribute-value

You can set the following style attributes in the CALL DEFINE statement:

ASIS=	FONT_WIDTH=
BACKGROUND=	HREFTARGET=
BACKGROUNDIMAGE=	HTMLCLASS=
BORDERCOLOR=	JUST=
BORDERCOLORDARK=	NOBREAKSPACE=
BORDERCOLORLIGHT=	POSTHTML=
BORDERWIDTH=	POSTIMAGE=
CELLHEIGHT=	POSTTEXT=
CELLWIDTH=	PREHTML=
FLYOVER=	PREIMAGE=
FONT=	PRETEXT=
FONT_FACE=	PROTECTSPECIALCHARS=
FONT_SIZE=	TAGATTR=
FONT_STYLE=	URL=
FONT_WEIGHT=	VJUST=

For information about style attributes, see "What Style Attributes Can Base Procedures Specify?" on page 43.

Retriction: This option affects only the HTML and Printer output.

Interaction: If you set a style element for the CALLDEF location in the PROC REPORT statement and you want to use that exact style element in a CALL DEFINE statement, use an empty string as the value for the STYLE attribute, as shown here:

```
call define (_col_, "STYLE", "" );
```

Featured in: Example 16 on page 999

COLUMN Statement

Describes the arrangement of all columns and of headers that span more than one column.

Restriction: You cannot use the COLUMN statement if you use REPORT= in the PROC REPORT statement.

Featured in: Example 1 on page 958, Example 3 on page 964, Example 5 on page 970, Example 6 on page 973, Example 10 on page 983, and Example 11 on page 986

COLUMN *column-specification(s)*;

Required Arguments

column-specification(s)
  is one or more of the following:

  □ *report-item(s)*

  □ *report-item-1*, *report-item-2* <. . . , *report-item-n*>

  □ *('header-1 '< . . . 'header-n '> report-item(s))*

  □ *report-item=name*

  where *report-item* is the name of a data set variable, a computed variable, or a statistic. Available statistics are

N	CSS
NMISS	STDERR
MEAN	CV
STD	T
MIN	PRT
MAX	VAR
RANGE	SUMWGT
SUM	PCTN
USS	PCTSUM

  For definitions of these statistics, see "Keywords and Formulas" on page 1458. To compute standard error and the Student's *t* test you must use the default value of VARDEF= which is DF.

report-item(s)
  identifies items that each form a column in the report.

  Featured in: Example 1 on page 958 and Example 11 on page 986

report-item-1, *report-item-2* <. . . , *report-item-n*>
  identifies report items that collectively determine the contents of the column or columns. These items are said to be stacked in the report because each item generates a header, and the headers are stacked one above the other. The header for the leftmost item is on top. If one of the items is an analysis variable, a

computed variable, or a statistic, its values fill the cells in that part of the report. Otherwise, PROC REPORT fills the cells with frequency counts.

If you stack a statistic with an analysis variable, the statistic that you name in the column statement overrides the statistic in the definition of the analysis variable. For example, the following PROC REPORT step produces a report that contains the minimum value of Sales for each sector:

```
proc report data=grocery;
   column sector sales,min;
   define sector/group;
   define sales/analysis sum;
run;
```

Interaction: A series of stacked report items can include only one analysis variable or statistic. If you include more than one, PROC REPORT returns an error because it cannot determine which values to put in the cells of the report.

Tip: You can use parentheses to group report items whose headers should appear at the same level rather than stacked one above the other.

Featured in: Example 5 on page 970, Example 6 on page 973, and Example 10 on page 983

('header-1 '< . . . 'header-n '> report-item(s))
creates one or more headers that span multiple columns.

header
is a string of characters that spans one or more columns in the report. PROC REPORT prints each header on a separate line. You can use split characters in a header to split one header over multiple lines. See the discussion of SPLIT= on page 889.

In traditional (monospace) SAS output, if the first and last characters of a header are one of the following characters, PROC REPORT uses that character to expand the header to fill the space over the column or columns:

:– = _ .* +

Similarly, if the first character of a header is < and the last character is >, or vice-versa, PROC REPORT expands the header to fill the space over the column by repeating the first character before the text of the header and the last character after it.

report-item(s)
specifies the columns to span.

Featured in: Example 10 on page 983

report-item=name
specifies an alias for a report item. You can use the same report item more than once in a COLUMN statement. However, you can use only one DEFINE statement for any given name. (The DEFINE statement designates characteristics such as formats and customized column headers. If you omit a DEFINE statement for an item, the REPORT procedure uses defaults.) Assigning an alias in the COLUMN statement does not by itself alter the report. However, it does enable you to use separate DEFINE statements for each occurrence of a variable or statistic.

Featured in: Example 3 on page 964

CAUTION:
You cannot always use an alias. When you refer in a compute block to a report item that has an alias, you must usually use the alias. However, if the report item shares

a column with an across variable, you must reference it by column number (see "Four Ways to Reference Report Items in a Compute Block" on page 872). △

COMPUTE Statement

Starts a *compute block*. **A compute block contains one or more programming statements that PROC REPORT executes as it builds the report.**

Interaction: An ENDCOMP statement must mark the end of the group of statements in the compute block.

Featured in: Example 2 on page 961, Example 3 on page 964, Example 4 on page 967, Example 5 on page 970, Example 9 on page 979, and Example 10 on page 983

COMPUTE *location* <*target*>
    </ STYLE=<*style-element-name*>
    <[*style-attribute-specification(s)*]>>;

  LINE *specification(s)*;
  . . . *select SAS language elements* . . .
  ENDCOMP;

COMPUTE *report-item* </ *type-specification*>;
  CALL DEFINE (*column-id, 'attribute-name', value*);
  . . . *select SAS language elements* . . .
  ENDCOMP;

A compute block can be associated with a report item or with a location (at the top or bottom of a report; at the top or bottom of a page; before or after a set of observations). You create a compute block with the COMPUTE window or with the COMPUTE statement. One form of the COMPUTE statement associates the compute block with a report item. Another form associates the compute block with a location.

For a list of the SAS language elements that you can use in compute blocks, see "The Contents of Compute Blocks" on page 872.

Required Arguments

You must specify either a location or a report item in the COMPUTE statement.

location
  determines where the compute block executes in relation to *target*.

AFTER
  executes the compute block at a break in one of the following places:

    □ immediately after the last row of a set of rows that have the same value for the variable that you specify as *target* or, if there is a default summary on that variable, immediately after the creation of the preliminary summary line (see "How PROC REPORT Builds a Report" on page 946).

    □ near the bottom of each page, immediately before any footnotes, if you specify _PAGE_ as *target*

    □ at the end of the report if you omit a target.

BEFORE

executes the compute block at a break in one of the following places:

□ immediately before the first row of a set of rows that have the same value for the variable that you specify as *target* or, if there is a default summary on that variable, immediately after the creation of the preliminary summary line (see "How PROC REPORT Builds a Report" on page 946).

□ near the top of each page, between any titles and the column headers, if you specify _PAGE_ as *target*

□ immediately before the first detail row if you omit a target.

Featured in: Example 3 on page 964 and Example 9 on page 979

report-item

specifies a data set variable, a computed variable, or a statistic to associate the compute block with. If you are working in the nonwindowing environment, you must include the report item in the COLUMN statement. If the item is a computed variable, you must include a DEFINE statement for it.

Featured in: Example 4 on page 967 and Example 5 on page 970

CAUTION:

The position of a computed variable is important. PROC REPORT assigns values to the columns in a row of a report from left to right. Consequently, you cannot base the calculation of a computed variable on any variable that appears to its right in the report. △

Options

STYLE=<*style-element-name*><[*style-attribute-specification(s)*]>

specifies the style to use for the text that is created by any LINE statements in this compute block.

Note: You can use braces ({ and }) instead of square brackets ([and]). △

style-element-name

is the name of a style element that is part of a style definition that is registered with the Output Delivery System. SAS Institute provides some style definitions. Users can create their own style definitions and style elements with PROC TEMPLATE.

Default: If you do not specify a style element, PROC REPORT uses NoteContent.

See also: For information about Institute-supplied style definitions, see "What Style Definitions Are Shipped with the Software?" on page 43.

For information about PROC TEMPLATE and the Output Delivery System, see *The Complete Guide to the SAS Output Delivery System*.

style-attribute-specification

describes one or more style attributes to change. Each *style-attribute-specification* has this general form:

style-attribute-name=style-attribute-value

You can set the following style attributes in the STYLE= option in the COMPUTE statement:

ASIS=	FONT_WIDTH=
BACKGROUND=	HREFTARGET=
BACKGROUNDIMAGE=	HTMLCLASS=
BORDERCOLOR=	JUST=
BORDERCOLORDARK=	NOBREAKSPACE=
BORDERCOLORLIGHT=	POSTHTML=
BORDERWIDTH=	POSTIMAGE=
CELLHEIGHT=	POSTTEXT=
CELLWIDTH=	PREHTML=
FLYOVER=	PREIMAGE=
FONT=	PRETEXT=
FONT_FACE=	PROTECTSPECIALCHARS=
FONT_SIZE=	TAGATTR=
FONT_STYLE=	URL=
FONT_WEIGHT=	VJUST=

Retriction: This option affects only the HTML and Printer output.

Featured in: Example 16 on page 999

target

controls when the compute block executes. If you specify a location (BEFORE or AFTER) for the COMPUTE statement, you can also specify *target*, which can be one of the following:

break-variable

is a group or order variable.

When you specify a break variable, PROC REPORT executes the statements in the compute block each time the value of the break variable changes.

PAGE </ justification>

causes the compute block to execute once for each page, either immediately after printing any titles or immediately before printing any footnotes. *justification* controls the placement of text and values. It can be one of the following:

CENTER	centers each line that the compute block writes.
LEFT	left-justifies each line that the compute block writes.
RIGHT	right-justifies each line that the compute block writes.

Default: CENTER

Featured in: Example 9 on page 979

type-specification

specifies the type and, optionally, the length of *report-item*. If the report item associated with a compute block is a computed variable, PROC REPORT assumes that it is a numeric variable unless you use a type specification to specify that it is a character variable. A type specification has the form

CHARACTER <LENGTH=*length*>

where

CHARACTER
specifies that the computed variable is a character variable. If you do not specify a length, the variable's length is 8.

Alias: CHAR

Featured in: Example 10 on page 983

LENGTH=*length*
specifies the length of a computed character variable.

Default: 8

Range: 1 to 200

Interaction: If you specify a length, you must use CHARACTER to indicate that the computed variable is a character variable.

Featured in: Example 10 on page 983

DEFINE Statement

Describes how to use and display a report item.

Tip: If you do not use a DEFINE statement, PROC REPORT uses default characteristics.

Featured in: Example 2 on page 961, Example 3 on page 964, Example 4 on page 967, Example 5 on page 970, Example 6 on page 973, Example 9 on page 979, and Example 10 on page 983

DEFINE *report-item* / *<usage>*
    <attribute(s)>
    <option(s)>
    <justification>
    <COLOR=color>
    <'column-header-1' <...'column-header-n'>>
    <style>;

To do this	Use this option
Specify how to use a report item (see "Usage of Variables in a Report" on page 867)	
Define the item, which must be a data set variable, as an across variable	ACROSS
Define the item, which must be a data set variable, as an analysis variable	ANALYSIS
Define the item as a computed variable	COMPUTED
Define the item, which must be a data set variable, as a display variable	DISPLAY
Define the item, which must be a data set variable, as a group variable	GROUP

To do this	Use this option
Define the item, which must be a data set variable, as an order variable	ORDER
Specify style attribute s for a report item	
Assign a SAS or user-defined format to the item	FORMAT=
Reference a HELP or CBT entry that contains Help information for the report item	ITEMHELP=
Order the values of a group, order, or across variable according to the specified order	ORDER=
Define the number of blank characters to leave between the column being defined and the column immediately to its left	SPACING=
Associate a statistic with an analysis variable	
Define the width of the column in which PROC REPORT displays the report item	WIDTH=
Specify options for a report item	
Reverse the order in which PROC REPORT displays rows or values of a group, order, or across variable	DESCENDING
Wrap the value of a character variable in its column	FLOW
Specify that the item that you are defining is an ID variable	ID
Suppress the display of the report item	NOPRINT
Suppress the display of the report item if its values are all zero or missing	NOZERO
Insert a page break just before printing the first column containing values of the report item	PAGE
Control the placement of values and column headers	
Center the formatted values of the report item within the column width and center the column header over the values	CENTER
Left-justify the formatted values of the report item within the column width and left-justify the column headers over the values	LEFT
Right-justify the formatted values of the report item within the column width and right-justify the column headers over the values	RIGHT
Specify the color in the REPORT window of the column header and of the values of the item that you define	COLOR=
Define the column header for the report item	*column-header*
Specify a style element (for the Output Delivery System) for the report item	STYLE=

Required Arguments

report-item
>   specifies the name or alias (established in the COLUMN statement) of the data set
>   variable, computed variable, or statistic to define.

>   *Note:*   Do not specify a usage option in the definition of a statistic. The name of the
>   statistic tells PROC REPORT how to use it. △

Options

ACROSS
>   defines *item*, which must be a data set variable, as an across variable. (See "Across
>   Variables" on page 868.)
>   **Featured in:**   Example 5 on page 970

ANALYSIS
>   defines *item*, which must be a data set variable, as an analysis variable. (See
>   "Analysis Variables" on page 868.)
>   By default, PROC REPORT calculates the Sum statistic for an analysis variable.
>   Specify an alternate statistic with the *statistic* option in the DEFINE statement.

>   *Note:*   Naming a statistic in the DEFINE statement implies the ANALYSIS
>   option, so you never need to specify ANALYSIS. However, specifying ANALYSIS may
>   make your code easier for novice users to understand. △
>   **Featured in:**   Example 2 on page 961, Example 3 on page 964, and Example 4 on
>   page 967

CENTER
>   centers the formatted values of the report item within the column width and centers
>   the column header over the values. This option has no effect on the CENTER option
>   in the PROC REPORT statement, which centers the report on the page.

COLOR=*color*
>   specifies the color in the REPORT window of the column header and of the values of
>   the item that you are defining. You can use the following colors:

BLACK	MAGENTA
BLUE	ORANGE
BROWN	PINK
CYAN	RED
GRAY	WHITE
GREEN	YELLOW

>   **Default:**   The color of **Foreground** in the SASCOLOR window. (For more
>   information, see the online Help for the SASCOLOR window.)
>   **Restriction:**   This option has no effect on the HTML or Printer output.
>   *Note:*   Not all operating environments and devices support all colors, and in some
>   operating environments and devices, one color may map to another color. For
>   example, if the DEFINITION window displays the word BROWN in yellow
>   characters, selecting BROWN results in a yellow item. △

column-header
>   defines the column header for the report item. Enclose each header in single or
>   double quotation marks. When you specify multiple column headers, PROC REPORT

uses a separate line for each one. The split character also splits a column header over multiple lines.

In traditional (monospace) SAS output, if the first and last characters of a header are one of the following characters, PROC REPORT uses that character to expand the header to fill the space over the column:

`:- = \_ .* +`

Similarly, if the first character of a header is < and the last character is >, or vice-versa, PROC REPORT expands the header to fill the space over the column by repeating the first character before the text of the header and the last character after it.

Default:

Item	Header
variable without a label	variable name
variable with a label	variable label
statistic	statistic name

Tip: If you want to use names when labels exist, submit the following SAS statement before invoking PROC REPORT:

```
options nolabel;
```

Tip: HEADLINE underlines all column headers and the spaces between them. In traditional (monospace) SAS outut, you can underline column headers without underlining the spaces between them, by using the special characters `'--'` as the last line of each column header instead of using HEADLINE (see Example 4 on page 967).

See also: SPLIT= on page 889

Featured in: Example 3 on page 964, Example 4 on page 967, and Example 5 on page 970

COMPUTED

defines the specified item as a computed variable. Computed variables are variables that you define for the report. They are not in the input data set, and PROC REPORT does not add them to the input data set.

In the windowing environment, you add a computed variable to a report from the COMPUTED VAR window.

In the nonwindowing environment, you add a computed variable by

□ including the computed variable in the COLUMN statement

□ defining the variable's usage as COMPUTED in the DEFINE statement

□ computing the value of the variable in a compute block associated with the variable.

Featured in: Example 5 on page 970 and Example 10 on page 983

DESCENDING

reverses the order in which PROC REPORT displays rows or values of a group, order, or across variable.

Tip: By default, PROC REPORT orders group, order, and across variables by their formatted values. Use the ORDER= option in the DEFINE statement to specify an alternate sort order.

DISPLAY

defines *item*, which must be a data set variable, as a display variable.

FLOW

wraps the value of a character variable in its column. The FLOW option honors the split character. If the text contains no split character, PROC REPORT tries to split text at a blank.

Restriction: This option has no effect on the HTML or Printer output.

Featured in: Example 10 on page 983

FORMAT=*format*

assigns a SAS or user-defined format to the item. This format applies to *item* as PROC REPORT displays it; the format does not alter the format associated with a variable in the data set. For data set variables, PROC REPORT honors the first of these formats that it finds:

   □ the format assigned with FORMAT= in the DEFINE statement

   □ the format assigned in a FORMAT statement when you invoke PROC REPORT

   □ the format associated with the variable in the data set.

If none of these is present, PROC REPORT uses BEST*w.* for numeric variables and $*w.* for character variables. The value of *w* is the default column width. For character variables in the input data set, the default column width is the variable's length. For numeric variables in the input data set and for computed variables (both numeric and character), the default column width is the value specified by COLWIDTH= in the PROC REPORT statement or in the ROPTIONS window.

In the windowing environment, if you are unsure what format to use, type a question mark (?) in the format field in the DEFINITION window to access the FORMATS window.

Featured in: Example 2 on page 961 and Example 6 on page 973

GROUP

defines *item*, which must be a data set variable, as a group variable. (See "Group Variables" on page 868.)

Featured in: Example 4 on page 967, Example 6 on page 973, and Example 14 on page 994

ID

specifies that the item that you are defining is an ID variable. An ID variable and all columns to its left appear at the left of every page of a report. ID ensures that you can identify each row of the report when the report contains more columns than will fit on one page.

Featured in: Example 6 on page 973

ITEMHELP=*entry-name*

references a HELP or CBT entry that contains help information for the report item. Use PROC BUILD in SAS/AF software to create a HELP or CBT entry for a report item. All HELP and CBT entries for a report must be in the same catalog, and you must specify that catalog with the HELP= option in the PROC REPORT statement or from the **User Help** fields in the ROPTIONS window.

Of course, you can access these entries only from a windowing environment. To access a Help entry from the report, select the item and issue the HELP command. PROC REPORT first searches for and displays an entry named *entry-name*.CBT. If no such entry exists, it searches for *entry-name*.HELP. If neither a CBT nor a HELP entry for the selected item exists, the opening frame of the Help for PROC REPORT is displayed.

LEFT

left-justifies the formatted values of the report item within the column width and left-justifies the column headers over the values. If the format width is the same as the width of the column, the LEFT option has no effect on the placement of values.

NOPRINT
suppresses the display of the report item. Use this option
- □ if you do not want to show the item in the report but you need to use its values to calculate other values that you use in the report
- □ to establish the order of rows in the report
- □ if you do not want to use the item as a column but want to have access to its values in summaries (see Example 9 on page 979).

Interaction: Even though the columns that you define with NOPRINT do not appear in the report, you must count them when you are referencing columns by number (see "Four Ways to Reference Report Items in a Compute Block" on page 872).

Interaction: SHOWALL in the PROC REPORT statement or the ROPTIONS window overrides all occurrences of NOPRINT.

Featured in: Example 3 on page 964, Example 9 on page 979, and Example 12 on page 989

NOZERO
suppresses the display of the report item if its values are all zero or missing.

Interaction: Even though the columns that you define with NOZERO do not appear in the report, you must count them when you are referencing columns by number (see "Four Ways to Reference Report Items in a Compute Block" on page 872).

Interaction: SHOWALL in the PROC REPORT statement or in the ROPTIONS window overrides all occurrences of NOZERO.

ORDER
defines *item*, which must be a data set variable, as an order variable. (See "Order Variables" on page 867.)

Featured in: Example 2 on page 961

ORDER=DATA | FORMATTED | FREQ | INTERNAL
orders the values of a group, order, or across variable according to the specified order, where

DATA
orders values according to their order in the input data set.

FORMATTED
orders values by their formatted (external) values. By default, the order is ascending.

FREQ
orders values by ascending frequency count.

INTERNAL
orders values by their unformatted values, which yields the same order that PROC SORT would yield. This order is operating environment-dependent. This sort sequence is particularly useful for displaying dates chronologically.

Default: FORMATTED

Interaction: DESCENDING in the item's definition reverses the sort sequence for an item.

Featured in: Example 2 on page 961

CAUTION:
Default for the ORDER= Option. In other SAS procedures, the default is ORDER=INTERNAL. The default for the option in PROC REPORT may change in

a future release to be consistent with other procedures. Therefore, in production jobs where it is important to order report items by their formatted values, specify ORDER=FORMATTED even though it is currently the default. Doing so ensures that PROC REPORT will continue to produce the reports you expect even if the default changes. △

PAGE

inserts a page break just before printing the first column containing values of the report item.

Interaction: PAGE is ignored if you use WRAP in the PROC REPORT statement or in the ROPTIONS window.

RIGHT

right-justifies the formatted values of the specified item within the column width and right-justifies the column headers over the values. If the format width is the same as the width of the column, RIGHT has no effect on the placement of values.

SPACING=*horizontal-positions*

defines the number of blank characters to leave between the column being defined and the column immediately to its left. For each column, the sum of its width and the blank characters between it and the column to its left cannot exceed the line size.

Default: 2

Restriction: This option has no effect on the HTML or Printer output.

Interaction: When PROC REPORT's CENTER option is in effect, PROC REPORT ignores spacing that precedes the leftmost variable in the report.

Interaction: SPACING= in an item's definition overrides the value of SPACING= in the PROC REPORT statement or in the ROPTIONS window.

statistic

associates a statistic with an analysis variable. You must associate a statistic with every analysis variable in its definition. PROC REPORT uses the statistic you specify to calculate values for the analysis variable for the observations represented by each cell of the report. You cannot use *statistic* in the definition of any other kind of variable.

Default: SUM

Note: PROC REPORT uses the name of the analysis variable as the default header for the column. You can customize the column header with the *column-header* option in the DEFINE statement. △

Use one of the following values for *statistic*:

N	CSS
NMISS	STDERR
MEAN	CV
STD	T
MIN	PRT
MAX	VAR
RANGE	SUMWGT
SUM	PCTN
USS	PCTSUM

Requirement: To compute standard error and the Student's *t*-test you must use the default value of VARDEF= which is DF.

See also: For definitions of these statistics, see "Keywords and Formulas" on page 1458.

Featured in: Example 2 on page 961, Example 3 on page 964, and Example 4 on page 967

STYLE<(*location(s)*)>=<*style-element-name*><[*style-attribute-specification(s)*]>
specifies the style element to use for column headers and for text inside cells for this report item.

> *Note:* You can use braces ({ and }) instead of square brackets ([and]). △

location
identifies the areas of the column that the STYLE= option affects. *location* can be

COLUMN
affects all text that is inside the cells of the table for this report item.

HEADER
affects the column header for this report item.

Default: If you do not specify a location, STYLE= affects both the column header and the text in the cells.

style-element-name
is the name of a style element that is part of a style definition that is registered with the Output Delivery System. SAS Institute provides some style definitions. Users can create their own style definitions and style elements with PROC TEMPLATE.

Default: If you do not specify a style element, PROC REPORT uses Data for the COLUMN location and Header for the HEADER location.

See also: For information about Institute-supplied style definitions, see "What Style Definitions Are Shipped with the Software?" on page 43.

For information about PROC TEMPLATE and the Output Delivery System, see *The Complete Guide to the SAS Output Delivery System*.

style-attribute-specification
describes the style attribute to change. Each *style-attribute-specification* has this general form:

> *style-attribute-name=style-attribute-value*

You can set these style attributes:

ASIS=	FONT_WIDTH=
BACKGROUND=	HREFTARGET=
BACKGROUNDIMAGE=	HTMLCLASS=
BORDERCOLOR=	JUST=
BORDERCOLORDARK=	NOBREAKSPACE=
BORDERCOLORLIGHT=	POSTHTML=
BORDERWIDTH=	POSTIMAGE=
CELLHEIGHT=	POSTTEXT=
CELLWIDTH=	PREHTML=
FLYOVER=	PREIMAGE=

FONT=	PRETEXT=
FONT_FACE=	PROTECTSPECIALCHARS=
FONT_SIZE=	TAGATTR=
FONT_STYLE=	URL=
FONT_WEIGHT=	VJUST=

For information about style attributes, see "What Style Attributes Can Base Procedures Specify?" on page 43.

Restriction: This option affects only the HTML and Printer output.

Featured in: Example 16 on page 999

WIDTH=*column-width*
defines the width of the column in which PROC REPORT displays *item*.

Default: A column width that is just large enough to handle the format. If there is no format, PROC REPORT uses the value of COLWIDTH=.

Range: 1 to the value of the SAS system option LINESIZE=

Restriction: This option has no effect on the HTML or Printer output.

Interaction: WIDTH= in an item definition overrides the value of COLWIDTH= in the PROC REPORT statement or the ROPTIONS window.

Tip: When you stack items in the same column in a report, the width of the item that is at the bottom of the stack determines the width of the column.

Featured in: Example 10 on page 983

ENDCOMP Statement

Marks the end of one or more programming statements that PROC REPORT executes as it builds the report.

Restriction: A COMPUTE statement must precede the ENDCOMP statement.

ENDCOMP;

See also: COMPUTE statement

Featured in: Example 2 on page 961

FREQ Statement

Treats observations as if they appear multiple times in the input data set.

Tip: The effects of the FREQ and WEIGHT statements are similar except when calculating degrees of freedom.

See also: For an example that uses the FREQ statement, see "Example" on page 71

FREQ *variable*;

Required Arguments

variable
> specifies a numeric variable whose value represents the frequency of the observation. If you use the FREQ statement, the procedure assumes that each observation represents *n* observations, where *n* is the value of *variable*. If *n* is not an integer, the SAS System truncates it. If *n* is less than 1 or is missing, the procedure does not use that observation to calculate statistics.

Frequency Information Is Not Saved

When you store a report definition, PROC REPORT does not store the FREQ statement.

LINE Statement

Provides a subset of the features of the PUT statement for writing customized summaries.

Restriction: This statement is valid only in a compute block that is associated with a location in the report.

Restriction: You cannot use the LINE statement in conditional statements (IF-THEN, IF-THEN/ELSE, and SELECT) because it does not take effect until PROC REPORT has executed all other statements in the compute block.

Featured in: Example 2 on page 961, Example 3 on page 964, and Example 9 on page 979

LINE *specification(s)*;

Required Arguments

specification(s)
> can have one of the following forms. You can mix different forms of specifications in one LINE statement.

> *item item-format*
>> specifies the item to display and the format to use to display it, where

item

is the name of a data set variable, a computed variable, or a statistic in the report. For information about referencing report items see "Four Ways to Reference Report Items in a Compute Block" on page 872.

item-format

is a SAS or user-defined format. You must specify a format for each item.

Featured in: Example 2 on page 961

'character-string'

specifies a string of text to display. When the string is a blank and nothing else is in *specification(s)*, PROC REPORT prints a blank line.

Featured in: Example 2 on page 961

number-of-repetitions*'character-string'

specifies a character string and the number of times to repeat it.

Featured in: Example 3 on page 964

pointer-control

specifies the column in which PROC REPORT displays the next specification. You can use either of the following forms for pointer controls:

@column-number

specifies the number of the column in which to begin displaying the next item in the specification list.

+column-increment

specifies the number of columns to skip before beginning to display the next item in the specification list.

Both *column-number* and *column-increment* can be either a variable or a literal value.

Restriction: The pointer controls are designed for monospace output. They have no effect on the HTML or Printer output. Do not use pointer controls if you are writing to the HTML or Printer destination.

Featured in: Example 3 on page 964 and Example 5 on page 970

Differences between the LINE and PUT Statements

The LINE statement does not support the following features of the PUT statement:

□ automatic labeling signaled by an equals sign (=), also known as named output

□ the _ALL_, _INFILE_, and _PAGE_ arguments and the OVERPRINT option

□ grouping items and formats to apply one format to a list of items

□ pointer control using expressions

□ line pointer controls (# and /)

□ trailing at signs (@ and @@)

□ format modifiers

□ array elements.

RBREAK Statement

Produces a default summary at the beginning or end of a report or at the beginning and end of each BY group.

Featured in: Example 1 on page 958 and Example 10 on page 983

RBREAK *location </ option(s)>*;

To do this	Use this option
Specify the color of the break lines in the REPORT window	COLOR=
Double overline each value	DOL
Double underline each value	DUL
Overline each value	OL
Start a new page after the last break line of a break located at the beginning of the report	PAGE
Write a blank line for the last break line of a break located at the beginning of the report	SKIP
Specify a style element (for the Output Delivery System) for default summary lines, customized summary lines, or both	STYLE=
Include a summary line as one of the break lines	SUMMARIZE
Underline each value	UL

Required Arguments

location
> controls the placement of the break lines and is either of the following:

> AFTER
>> places the break lines at the end of the report.

> BEFORE
>> places the break lines at the beginning of the report.

Options

COLOR=*color*
> specifies the color of the break lines in the REPORT window. You can use the following colors:

BLACK	MAGENTA
BLUE	ORANGE
BROWN	PINK
CYAN	RED
GRAY	WHITE
GREEN	YELLOW

> **Default:** The color of **Foreground** in the SASCOLOR window. (For more information, see the online Help for the SASCOLOR window.)

Restriction: This option has no effect on the HTML or Printer output.

Note: Not all operating environments and devices support all colors, and in some operating environments and devices, one color may map to another color. For example, if the DEFINITION window displays the word BROWN in yellow characters, selecting BROWN results in a yellow item. △

DOL

(for double overlining) uses the thirteenth formatting character to overline each value

□ that appears in the summary line

□ that would appear in the summary line if you specified the SUMMARIZE option.

Default: equals sign (=)

Restriction: This option has no effect on the HTML or Printer output.

Interaction: If you specify both the OL and DOL options, PROC REPORT honors only OL.

See also: the discussion of FORMCHAR= on page 882.

Featured in: Example 1 on page 958

DUL

(for double underlining) uses the thirteenth formatting character to underline each value

□ that appears in the summary line

□ that would appear in the summary line if you specified the SUMMARIZE option.

Default: equals sign (=)

Restriction: This option has no effect on the HTML or Printer output.

Interaction: If you specify both the UL and DUL options, PROC REPORT honors only UL.

See also: the discussion of FORMCHAR= on page 882.

OL

(for overlining) uses the second formatting character to overline each value

□ that appears in the summary line

□ that would appear in the summary line if you specified the SUMMARIZE option.

Default: hyphen (–)

Restriction: This option has no effect on the HTML or Printer output.

Interaction: If you specify both the OL and DOL options, PROC REPORT honors only OL.

See also: the discussion of FORMCHAR= on page 882.

Featured in: Example 10 on page 983

PAGE

starts a new page after the last break line of a break located at the beginning of the report.

SKIP

writes a blank line after the last break line of a break located at the beginning of the report.

Restriction: This option has no effect on the HTML or Printer output.

STYLE=<*style-element-name*><[*style-attribute-specification(s)*]>

specifies the style element to use for default summary lines that are created with the RBREAK statement. You can alter the default style element of the summary lines or specify another style element entirely.

Note: You can use braces ({ and }) instead of square brackets ([and]). △

style-element-name
is the name of a style element that is part of a style definition that is registered with the Output Delivery System. SAS Institute provides some style definitions. Users can create their own style definitions and style elements with PROC TEMPLATE.

Default: If you do not specify a style element, PROC REPORT uses DataEmphasis.

See also: For information about Institute-supplied style definitions, see "What Style Definitions Are Shipped with the Software?" on page 43.

For information about PROC TEMPLATE and the Output Delivery System, see *The Complete Guide to the SAS Output Delivery System.*

style-attribute-specification
describes one or more style attributes to change. Each *style-attribute-specification* has this general form:

style-attribute-name=style-attribute-value

You can set these style attributes:

ASIS=	FONT_WIDTH=
BACKGROUND=	HREFTARGET=
BACKGROUNDIMAGE=	HTMLCLASS=
BORDERCOLOR=	JUST=
BORDERCOLORDARK=	NOBREAKSPACE=
BORDERCOLORLIGHT=	POSTHTML=
BORDERWIDTH=	POSTIMAGE=
CELLHEIGHT=	POSTTEXT=
CELLWIDTH=	PREHTML=
FLYOVER=	PREIMAGE=
FONT=	PRETEXT=
FONT_FACE=	PROTECTSPECIALCHARS=
FONT_SIZE=	TAGATTR=
FONT_STYLE=	URL=
FONT_WEIGHT=	VJUST=

For information about style attributes, see "What Style Attributes Can Base Procedures Specify?" on page 43.

Restriction: This option affects only the HTML and Printer output.

SUMMARIZE
includes a summary line as one of the break lines. A summary line at the beginning or end of a report contains values for

☐ statistics

☐ analysis variables

☐ computed variables.

The following table shows how PROC REPORT calculates the value for each kind of report item in a summary line created by the RBREAK statement:

If the report item is ...	Then its value is ...
a statistic	the value of the statistic over all observations in the set
an analysis variable	the value of the statistic specified as the usage option in the DEFINE statement. PROC REPORT calculates the value of the statistic over all observations in the set. The default usage is SUM.
a computed variable	the results of the calculations based on the code in the corresponding compute block (see "COMPUTE Statement" on page 905).

Featured in: Example 1 on page 958 and Example 10 on page 983

UL

(for underlining) uses the second formatting character to underline each value

□ that appears in the summary line

□ that would appear in the summary line if you specified the SUMMARIZE option.

Default: hyphen (–)

Restriction: This option has no effect on the HTML or Printer output.

Interaction: If you specify both the UL and DUL options, PROC REPORT honors only UL.

See also: the discussion of FORMCHAR= on page 882.

Order of Break Lines

When a default summary contains more than one break line, the order in which the break lines appear is

1 overlining or double overlining (OL or DOL)

2 summary line (SUMMARIZE)

3 underlining or double underlining (UL or DUL)

4 skipped line (SKIP)

5 page break (PAGE).

Note: If you define a customized summary for the break, customized break lines appear after underlining or double underlining. For more information about customized break lines, see "COMPUTE Statement" on page 905 and "LINE Statement" on page 917. △

WEIGHT Statement

Specifies weights for analysis variables in the statistical calculations.

See also: For information about calculating weighted statistics see "Calculating Weighted Statistics" on page 74. For an example that uses the WEIGHT statement, see "Example" on page 74.

WEIGHT *variable*;

Required Arguments

variable
    specifies a numeric variable whose values weight the values of the analysis variables. The value of the variable does not have to be an integer. If the value of *variable* is

Weight value...	PROC REPORT...
0	counts the observation in the total number of observations
less than 0	converts the value to zero and counts the observation in the total number of observations
missing	excludes the observation

To exclude observations that contain negative and zero weights from the analysis, use EXCLNPWGT. Note that most SAS/STAT procedures, such as PROC GLM, exclude negative and zero weights by default.

Tip: When you use the WEIGHT statement, consider which value of the VARDEF= option is appropriate. See VARDEF= on page 892 and the calculation of weighted statistics in "Keywords and Formulas" on page 1458 for more information.

Note: Prior to Version 7 of the SAS System, the procedure did not exclude the observations with missing weights from the count of observations. △

Weight Information Is Not Saved

When you store a report definition, PROC REPORT does not store the WEIGHT statement.

PROC REPORT Windows

The windowing environment in PROC REPORT provides essentially the same functionality as the statements, with one major exception. You cannot use the Output Delivery System from the windowing environment.

BREAK

Controls PROC REPORT's actions at a change in the value of a group or order variable or at the top or bottom of a report.

Path

Edit ▶ Summarize information

After you select **Summarize Information**, PROC REPORT offers you four choices for the location of the break:

□ **Before Item**

□ **After Item**

□ **At the top**

□ **At the bottom.**

After you select a location, the BREAK window opens.

Note: To create a break before or after detail lines (when the value of a group or order variable changes), you must select a variable before you open the BREAK window. △

Description

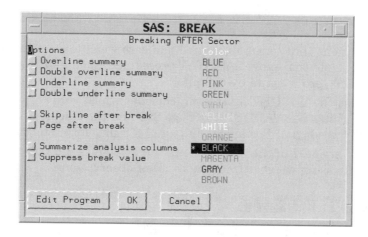

Note: For information about changing the formatting characters that are used by the line drawing options in this window, see the discussion of FORMCHAR= on page 882. △

Options

Overline summary
uses the second formatting character to overline each value

□ that appears in the summary line

□ that would appear in the summary line if you specified the SUMMARIZE option.

Default: hyphen (-)

Interaction: If you specify options to overline and to double overline, PROC REPORT overlines.

Double overline summary
uses the thirteenth formatting character to overline each value

□ that appears in the summary line

□ that would appear in the summary line if you specified the SUMMARIZE option.

Default: equals sign (=)

Interaction: If you specify options to overline and to double overline, PROC REPORT overlines.

Underline summary

uses the second formatting character to underline each value

☐ that appears in the summary line

☐ that would appear in the summary line if you specified the SUMMARIZE option.

Default: hyphen (-)

Interaction: If you specify options to underline and to double underline, PROC REPORT underlines.

Double underline summary

uses the thirteenth formatting character to underline each value

☐ that appears in the summary line

☐ that would appear in the summary line if you specified the SUMMARIZE option.

Default: equals sign (=)

Interaction: If you specify options to overline and to double overline, PROC REPORT overlines.

Skip line after break

writes a blank line for the last break line.

This option has no effect if you use it in a break at the end of a report.

Page after break

starts a new page after the last break line. This option has no effect in a break at the end of a report.

Interaction: If you use this option in a break on a variable and you create a break at the end of the report, the summary for the whole report is on a separate page.

Summarize analysis columns

writes a summary line in each group of break lines. A summary line contains values for

☐ statistics

☐ analysis variables

☐ computed variables.

A summary line between sets of observations also contains

☐ the break variable (which you can suppress with **Suppress break value**)

☐ other group or order variables to the left of the break variable.

The following table shows how PROC REPORT calculates the value for each kind of report item in a summary line created by the BREAK window:

If the report item is ...	Then its value is ...
the break variable	the current value of the variable (or a missing value if you select **suppress break value**)
a group or order variable to the left of the break variable	the current value of the variable
a group or order variable to the right of the break variable, or a display variable anywhere in the report	missing[*]
a statistic	the value of the statistic over all observations in the set
an analysis variable	the value of the statistic specified as the usage option in the item's definition. PROC REPORT calculates the value of the statistic over all observations in the set. The default usage is SUM.

If the report item is ...	Then its value is ...
a computed variable	the results of the calculations based on the code in the corresponding compute block (see "COMPUTE Statement" on page 905).

*If you reference a variable with a missing value in a customized summary line, PROC REPORT displays that variable as a blank (for character variables) or a period (for numeric variables).

Suppress break value

suppresses printing of

☐ the value of the break variable in the summary line

☐ any underlining and overlining in the break lines in the column containing the break variable.

If you select **Suppress break value**, the value of the break variable is unavailable for use in customized break lines unless you assign it a value in the compute block associated with the break.

Color

From the list of colors, select the one to use in the REPORT window for the column header and the values of the item that you are defining.

Default: The color of **Foreground** in the SASCOLOR window. (For more information, see the online Help for the SASCOLOR window.)

Note: Not all operating environments and devices support all colors, and in some operating environments and devices, one color may map to another color. For example, if the DEFINITION window displays the word BROWN in yellow characters, selecting BROWN results in a yellow item.

Pushbuttons

|Edit Program|
opens the COMPUTE window and enables you to associate a compute block with a location in the report.

|OK|
applies the information in the BREAK window to the report and closes the window.

|Cancel|
closes the BREAK window without applying information to the report.

COMPUTE

Attaches a compute block to a report item or to a location in the report. Use the SAS Text Editor commands to manipulate text in this window.

Path

From Edit Program in the COMPUTED VAR, DEFINITION, or BREAK window.

Description

For information about the SAS language features that you can use in the COMPUTE window, see "The Contents of Compute Blocks" on page 872.

COMPUTED VAR

Adds a variable that is not in the input data set to the report.

Path

Select a column. Then select

After you select **Computed Column**, PROC REPORT prompts you for the location of the computed column relative to the column that you have selected. After you select a location, the COMPUTED VAR window opens.

Description

Enter the name of the variable at the prompt. If it is a character variable, select the **Character data** check box and, if you want, enter a value in the **Length** field. The length can be any integer between 1 and 200. If you leave the field blank, PROC REPORT assigns a length of 8 to the variable.

After you enter the name of the variable, select Edit Program to open the COMPUTE window. Use programming statements in the COMPUTE window to define the computed variable. After closing the COMPUTE and COMPUTED VAR windows, open the DEFINITION window to describe how to display the computed variable.

CAUTION:

The Position of a Computed Variable Is Important. PROC REPORT assigns values to the columns in a row of a report from left to right. Consequently, you cannot base the calculation of a computed variable on any variable that appears to its right in the report. △

DATA COLUMNS

Lists all variables in the input data set so that you can add one or more data set variables to the report.

Path

Select a report item. Then select

After you select **Data column**, PROC REPORT prompts you for the location of the computed column relative to the column that you have selected. After you select a location, the DATA COLUMNS window opens.

Description

Select one or more variables to add to the report. When you select the first variable, it moves to the top of the list in the window. If you select multiple variables, subsequent selections move to the bottom of the list of selected variables. An asterisk (*) identifies each selected variable. The order of selected variables from top to bottom determines their order in the report from left to right.

DATA SELECTION

Loads a data set into the current report definition.

Path

Description

The first list box in the DATA SELECTION window lists all the librefs defined for your SAS session. The second one lists all the SAS data sets in the selected library.

CAUTION:
Use Data Compatible with the Current Report Definition. The data set that you load must contain variables whose names are the same as the variable names in the current report definition. △

Pushbuttons

OK
:   loads the selected data set into the current report definition.

Cancel
:   closes the DATA SELECTION window without loading new data.

DEFINITION

Displays the characteristics associated with an item in the report and lets you change them.

Path

Select a report item. Then select

 Edit ▶ Define

Note: Alternatively, double-click on the selected item. (Not all operating environments support this method of opening the DEFINITION window.) △

Description

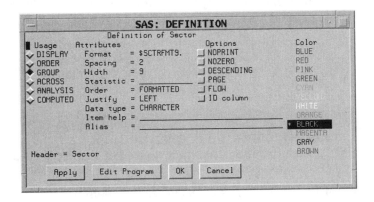

Usage

For an explanation of each type of usage see "Laying Out a Report" on page 866.

DISPLAY
defines the selected item as a display variable. DISPLAY is the default for character variables.

ORDER
defines the selected item as an order variable.

GROUP
defines the selected item as a group variable.

ACROSS
defines the selected item as an across variable.

ANALYSIS
defines the selected item as an analysis variable. You must specify a statistic (see the discussion of statistic= on page 930) for an analysis variable. ANALYSIS is the default for numeric variables.

COMPUTED
defines the selected item as a computed variable. Computed variables are variables that you define for the report. They are not in the input data set, and PROC REPORT does not add them to the input data set. However, computed variables are included in an output data set if you create one.

In the windowing environment, you add a computed variable to a report from the COMPUTED VAR window.

Attributes

Format=
> assigns a SAS or user-defined format to the item. This format applies to the selected item as PROC REPORT displays it; the format does not alter the format associated with a variable in the data set. For data set variables, PROC REPORT honors the first of these formats that it finds:
> - □ the format assigned with FORMAT= in the DEFINITION window
> - □ the format assigned in a FORMAT statement when you start PROC REPORT
> - □ the format associated with the variable in the data set.
>
> If none of these is present, PROC REPORT uses BESTw. for numeric variables and w. for character variables. The value of w is the default column width. For character variables in the input data set, the default column width is the variable's length. For numeric variables in the input data set and for computed variables (both numeric and character), the default column width is the value of the COLWIDTH= attribute in the ROPTIONS window.
>
> If you are unsure what format to use, type a question mark (?) in the format field in the DEFINITION window to access the FORMATS window.

Spacing=
> defines the number of blank characters to leave between the column being defined and the column immediately to its left. For each column, the sum of its width and the blank characters between it and the column to its left cannot exceed the line size.
>
> **Default:** 2
>
> **Interaction:** When PROC REPORT's CENTER option is in effect, PROC REPORT ignores spacing that precedes the leftmost variable in the report.
>
> **Interaction:** SPACING= in an item definition overrides the value of SPACING= in the PROC REPORT statement or the ROPTIONS window.

Width=
> defines the width of the column in which PROC REPORT displays the selected item.
>
> **Range:** 1 to the value of the SAS system option LINESIZE=
>
> **Default:** A column width that is just large enough to handle the format. If there is no format, PROC REPORT uses the value of COLWIDTH=.
>
> *Note:* When you stack items in the same column in a report, the width of the item that is at the bottom of the stack determines the width of the column. △

Statistic=
> associates a statistic with an analysis variable. You must associate a statistic with every analysis variable in its definition. PROC REPORT uses the statistic that you specify to calculate values for the analysis variable for the observations represented by each cell of the report. You cannot use *statistic* in the definition of any other kind of variable.
>
> **Default:** SUM
>
> *Note:* PROC REPORT uses the name of the analysis variable as the default header for the column. You can customize the column header with the **Header** field of the DEFINITION window. △
>
> You can use the following values for *statistic*:

N	CSS
NMISS	STDERR
MEAN	CV
STD	T
MIN	PRT

MAX	VAR
RANGE	SUMWGT
SUM	PCTN
USS	PCTSUM

Requirement: To compute standard error and the Student's *t*-test you must use the default value of VARDEF= which is DF.

See also: For definitions of these statistics, see "Keywords and Formulas" on page 1458.

Order=
orders the values of a GROUP, ORDER, or ACROSS variable according to the specified order, where

DATA
orders values according to their order in the input data set.

FORMATTED
orders values by their formatted (external) values. By default, the order is ascending.

FREQ
orders values by ascending frequency count.

INTERNAL
orders values by their unformatted values, which yields the same order that PROC SORT would yield. This order is operating environment-dependent. This sort sequence is particularly useful for displaying dates chronologically.

Default: FORMATTED

Interaction: DESCENDING in the item's definition reverses the sort sequence for an item.

CAUTION:
Default for the ORDER= Option. In other SAS procedures, the default is ORDER=INTERNAL. The default for the option in PROC REPORT may change in a future release to be consistent with other procedures. Therefore, in production jobs where it is important to order report items by their formatted values, specify ORDER=FORMATTED even though it is currently the default. Doing so ensures that PROC REPORT will continue to produce the reports you expect even if the default changes. △

Justify=
You can justify the placement of the column header and of the values of the item that you are defining within a column in one of three ways:

LEFT
left-justifies the formatted values of the item that you are defining within the column width and left-justifies the column header over the values. If the format width is the same as the width of the column, LEFT has no effect on the placement of values.

RIGHT
right-justifies the formatted values of the item that you are defining within the column width and right-justifies the column header over the values. If the format width is the same as the width of the column, RIGHT has no effect on the placement of values.

CENTER

centers the formatted values of the item that you are defining within the column width and centers the column header over the values. This option has no effect on the setting of the SAS system option CENTER.

When justifying values, PROC REPORT justifies the field width defined by the format of the item within the column. Thus, numbers are always aligned.

Data type=

shows you if the report item is numeric or character. You cannot change this field.

Item Help=

references a HELP or CBT entry that contains help information for the selected item. Use PROC BUILD in SAS/AF software to create a HELP or CBT entry for a report item. All HELP and CBT entries for a report must be in the same catalog, and you must specify that catalog with the HELP= option in the PROC REPORT statement or from the **User Help** fields in the ROPTIONS window.

To access a help entry from the report, select the item and issue the HELP command. PROC REPORT first searches for and displays an entry named *entry-name*.CBT. If no such entry exists, PROC REPORT searches for *entry-name*.HELP. If neither a CBT nor a HELP entry for the selected item exists, the opening frame of the help for PROC REPORT is displayed.

Alias=

By entering a name in the **Alias** field, you create an alias for the report item that you are defining. Aliases let you distinguish between different uses of the same report item. When you refer in a compute block to a report item that has an alias, you must use the alias (see Example 3 on page 964).

Options

NOPRINT

suppresses the display of the item that you are defining. Use this option

☐ if you do not want to show the item in the report but you need to use the values in it to calculate other values you use in the report

☐ to establish the order of rows in the report

☐ if you do not want to use the item as a column but want to have access to its values in summaries (see Example 9 on page 979).

Interaction: Even though the columns that you define with NOPRINT do not appear in the report, you must count them when you are referencing columns by number (see "Four Ways to Reference Report Items in a Compute Block" on page 872).

Interaction: SHOWALL in the PROC REPORT statement or the ROPTIONS window overrides all occurrences of NOPRINT.

NOZERO

suppresses the display of the item that you are defining if its values are all zero or missing.

Interaction: Even though the columns that you define with NOZERO do not appear in the report, you must count them when you are referencing columns by number (see "Four Ways to Reference Report Items in a Compute Block" on page 872).

Interaction: SHOWALL in the PROC REPORT statement or the ROPTIONS window overrides all occurrences of NOZERO.

DESCENDING

reverses the order in which PROC REPORT displays rows or values of a group, order, or across variable.

PAGE

inserts a page break just before printing the first column containing values of the selected item.

Interaction: PAGE is ignored if you use WRAP in the PROC REPORT statement or in the ROPTIONS window.

FLOW

wraps the value of a character variable in its column. The FLOW option honors the split character. If the text contains no split character, PROC REPORT tries to split text at a blank.

ID column

specifies that the item that you are defining is an ID variable. An ID variable and all columns to its left appear at the left of every page of a report. ID ensures that you can identify each row of the report when the report contains more columns than will fit on one page.

Color

From the list of colors, select the one to use in the REPORT window for the column header and the values of the item that you are defining.

Default: The color of **Foreground** in the SASCOLOR window. (For more information, see the online Help for the SASCOLOR window.)

Note: Not all operating environments and devices support all colors, and in some operating environments and devices, one color may map to another color. For example, if the DEFINITION window displays the word BROWN in yellow characters, selecting BROWN results in a yellow item.

Pushbuttons

|Apply|

applies the information in the open window to the report and keeps the window open.

|Edit Program|

opens the COMPUTE window and enables you to associate a compute block with the variable that you are defining.

|OK|

applies the information in the DEFINITION window to the report and closes the window.

|Cancel|

closes the DEFINITION window without applying changes made with |APPLY|.

DISPLAY PAGE

Displays a particular page of the report.

Path

Description

You can get to the last page of the report by entering a large number for the page number. When you are on the last page of the report, PROC REPORT sends a note to the message line of the REPORT window.

EXPLORE

Lets you experiment with your data.

Restriction: You cannot open the EXPLORE window unless your report contains at least one group or order variable.

Path

Description

In the EXPLORE window you can
- subset the data with list boxes
- suppress the display of a column with the **Remove Column** checkbox
- change the order of the columns with Rotate columns .

Note: The results of your manipulations in the EXPLORE window appear in the REPORT window but are not saved in report definitions.   △

Window Features

list boxes
The EXPLORE window contains three list boxes. These boxes contain the value "All levels" as well as actual values for the first three group or order variables in your report. The values reflect any WHERE clause processing that is in effect. For example, if you use a WHERE clause to subset the data so that it includes only the northeast and northwest sectors, the only values that appear in the list box for Sector are **All levels**, **Northeast**, and **Northwest**. Selecting **All levels** in this case displays rows of the report for only the northeast and northwest sectors. To see data for all the sectors, you must clear the WHERE clause before you open the EXPLORE window.

Selecting values in the list boxes restricts the display in the REPORT window to the values that you select. If you select incompatible values, PROC REPORT returns an error.

Remove Column

Above each list box in the EXPLORE window is a check box labeled `Remove Column`. Selecting this check box and applying the change removes the column from the REPORT window. You can easily restore the column by clearing the check box and applying that change.

Pushbuttons

OK
applies the information in the EXPLORE window to the report and closes the window.

Apply
applies the information in the EXPLORE window to the report and keeps the window open.

Rotate columns
changes the order of the variables displayed in the list boxes. Each variable that can move one column to the left does; the leftmost variable moves to the third column.

Cancel
closes the EXPLORE window without applying changes made with APPLY.

FORMATS

Displays a list of formats and provides a sample of each one.

Path

From the DEFINE window, type a question mark (?) in the `Format` field and select any of the pushbuttons except `Cancel`, or press RETURN.

Description

When you select a format in the FORMATS window, a sample of that format appears in the `Sample:` field. Select the format that you want to use for the variable that you are defining.

Pushbuttons

OK
writes the format that you have selected into the `Format` field in the DEFINITION window and closes the FORMATS window. To see the format in the report, select Apply in the DEFINITION window.

Cancel
closes the FORMATS window without writing a format into the `Format` field.

LOAD REPORT

Loads a stored report definition.

Path

Description

The first list box in the LOAD REPORT window lists all the librefs defined for your SAS session. The second one lists all the catalogs in the selected library. The third one lists descriptions of all the stored report definitions (entry types of REPT) in the selected catalog. If there is no description for an entry, the list box contains the entry's name.

Pushbuttons

OK
   loads the current data into the selected report definition.

Cancel
   closes the LOAD REPORT window without loading a new report definition.

Note: Issuing the END command in the REPORT window returns you to the previous report definition (with the current data). △

MESSAGES

Automatically opens to display notes, warnings, and errors returned by PROC REPORT.

You must close the MESSAGES window by selecting OK before you can continue to use PROC REPORT.

PROFILE

Customizes some features of the PROC REPORT environment by creating a report profile.

Path

Description

The PROFILE window creates a report profile that

☐ specifies the SAS library, catalog, and entry that define alternative menus to use in the REPORT and COMPUTE windows. Use PROC PMENU to create catalog entries of type PMENU that define these menus. PMENU entries for both windows must be in the same catalog.

□ sets defaults for WINDOWS, PROMPT, and COMMAND. PROC REPORT uses the default option whenever you start the procedure unless you specifically override the option in the PROC REPORT statement.

Specify the catalog that contains the profile to use with the PROFILE= option in the PROC REPORT statement (see the discussion of PROFILE= on page 888).

Pushbuttons

[OK]

stores your profile in a file that is called SASUSER.PROFILE.REPORT.PROFILE.

Note: Use PROC CATALOG or the EXPLORER window to copy the profile to another location. △

[Cancel]

closes the window without storing the profile.

PROMPTER

Prompts you for information as you add items to a report.

Path

Specify the PROMPT option when you start PROC REPORT or select PROMPT from the ROPTIONS window. The PROMPTER window opens the next time that you add an item to the report.

Description

The prompter guides you through parts of the windows most commonly used to build a report. As the content of the PROMPTER window changes, the title of the window changes to the name of the window that you would use to perform a task if you were not using the prompter. The title change is to help you begin to associate the windows with their functions and to learn what window to use if you later decide to change something.

If you start PROC REPORT with prompting, the first window gives you a chance to limit the number of observations used during prompting. When you exit the prompter, PROC REPORT removes the limit.

Pushbuttons

[OK]

applies the information in the open window to the report and continues the prompting process.

Note: When you select [OK] from the last prompt window, PROC REPORT removes any limit on the number of observations that it is working with. △

Apply
> applies the information in the open window to the report and keeps the window open.

Backup
> returns you to the previous PROMPTER window.

Exit Prompter
> closes the PROMPTER window without applying any more changes to the report. If you have limited the number of observations to use during prompting, PROC REPORT removes the limit.

REPORT

Is the surface on which the report appears.

Path

Use WINDOWS or PROMPT in the PROC REPORT statement.

Description

You cannot write directly in any part of the REPORT window except column headers. To change other aspects of the report, you select a report item as the target of the next command and issue the command. To select an item, use a mouse or cursor keys to position the cursor over it. Then click the mouse button or press RETURN. To execute a command, make a selection from the menu bar at the top of the REPORT window. PROC REPORT displays the effect of a command immediately unless the DEFER option is on.

Note: Issuing the END command in the REPORT window returns you to the previous report definition with the current data. If there is no previous report definition, END closes the REPORT window. △

ROPTIONS

Displays choices that control the layout and display of the entire report and identifies the SAS data library and catalog containing CBT or HELP entries for items in the report.

Path

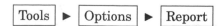

Tools ▶ Options ▶ Report

Description

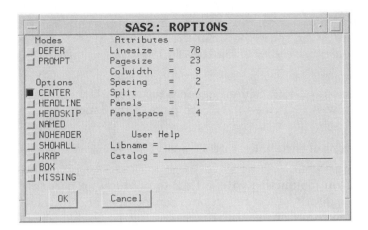

Modes

DEFER

stores the information for changes and makes the changes all at once when you turn DEFER mode off or select

    DEFER is particularly useful when you know that you need to make several changes to the report but do not want to see the intermediate reports.

    By default, PROC REPORT redisplays the report in the REPORT window each time you redefine the report by adding or deleting an item, by changing information in the DEFINITION window, or by changing information in the BREAK window.

PROMPT

opens the PROMPTER window the next time that you add an item to the report.

Options

CENTER

centers the report and summary text (customized break lines). If CENTER is not selected, the report is left-justified.

    PROC REPORT honors the first of these centering specifications that it finds:

- □ the CENTER or NOCENTER option in the PROC REPORT statement or the CENTER toggle in the ROPTIONS window

- □ the CENTER or NOCENTER option stored in the report definition loaded with REPORT= in the PROC REPORT statement

- □ the SAS system option CENTER or NOCENTER.

    When PROC REPORT's CENTER option is in effect, PROC REPORT ignores spacing that precedes the leftmost variable in the report.

HEADLINE

underlines all column headers and the spaces between them at the top of each page of the report.

    HEADLINE underlines with the second formatting character. (See the discussion of FORMCHAR= on page 882.)

Default: hyphen (-)

Tip: In traditional (monospace) SAS output, you can underline column headers without underlining the spaces between them, by using '--' as the last line of each column header instead of using HEADLINE.

HEADSKIP

writes a blank line beneath all column headers (or beneath the underlining that the HEADLINE option writes) at the top of each page of the report.

NAMED

writes *name=* in front of each value in the report, where *name* is the column header for the value.

Tip: Use NAMED in conjunction with WRAP to produce a report that wraps all columns for a single row of the report onto consecutive lines rather than placing columns of a wide report on separate pages.

Interaction: When you use NAMED, PROC REPORT automatically uses NOHEADER.

NOHEADER

suppresses column headers, including those that span multiple columns.

Once you suppress the display of column headers in the windowing environment, you cannot select any report items.

SHOWALL

overrides the parts of a definition that suppress the display of a column (NOPRINT and NOZERO). You define a report item with a DEFINE statement or in the DEFINITION window.

WRAP

displays one value from each column of the report, on consecutive lines if necessary, before displaying another value from the first column. By default, PROC REPORT displays values for only as many columns as it can fit on one page. It fills a page with values for these columns before starting to display values for the remaining columns on the next page.

Interaction: When WRAP is in effect, PROC REPORT ignores PAGE in any item definitions.

Tip: Typically, you use WRAP in conjunction with NAMED to avoid wrapping column headers.

BOX

uses formatting characters to add line-drawing characters to the report. These characters

□ surround each page of the report

□ separate column headers from the body of the report

□ separate rows and columns from each other.

Interaction: You cannot use BOX if you use WRAP in the PROC REPORT statement or ROPTIONS window or if you use FLOW in any item's definition.

See also: For information about formatting characters, see the discussion of FORMCHAR= on page 882.

MISSING

considers missing values as valid values for group, order, or across variables. Special missing values that are used to represent numeric values (the letters A through Z and the underscore (_) character) are each considered as a different value. A group for each missing value appears in the report. If you omit the MISSING option, PROC REPORT does not include observations with a missing value for one or more group, order, or across variables in the report.

Attributes

Linesize
> specifies the line size for a report. PROC REPORT honors the first of these line-size specifications that it finds:
> - □ LS= in the PROC REPORT statement or Linesize= in the ROPTIONS window
> - □ the LS= setting stored in the report definition loaded with REPORT= in the PROC REPORT statement
> - □ the SAS system option LINESIZE=.
>
> **Range:** 64-256 (integer)
>
> **Tip:** If the line size is greater than the width of the REPORT window, use SAS windowing environment commands RIGHT and LEFT to display portions of the report that are not currently in the display.

Pagesize
> specifies the page size for a report. PROC REPORT honors the first of these pagesize specifications that it finds
> - □ PS= in the PROC REPORT statement or **Pagesize=** in the ROPTIONS window
> - □ the PS= setting stored in the report definition loaded with REPORT= in the PROC REPORT statement
> - □ the SAS system option PAGESIZE=.
>
> **Range:** 15-32,767 (integer)

Colwidth
> specifies the default number of characters for columns containing computed variables or numeric data set variables.
>
> **Range:** 1 to the linesize
>
> **Default:** 9
>
> **Interaction:** When setting the width for a column, PROC REPORT first looks at WIDTH= in the definition for that column. If WIDTH= is not present, PROC REPORT uses a column width large enough to accommodate the format for the item. (For information about formats, see the discussion of Format= on page 930.) If no format is associated with the item, the column width depends on variable type:

If the variable is a ...	Then the column width is the ...
character variable in the input data set	length of the variable
numeric variable in the input data set	value of the COLWIDTH= option
computed variable (numeric or character)	value of the COLWIDTH= option

SPACING=*space-between-columns*
> specifies the number of blank characters between columns. For each column, the sum of its width and the blank characters between it and the column to its left cannot exceed the line size.
>
> **Default:** 2
>
> **Interaction:** PROC REPORT separates all columns in the report by the number of blank characters specified by SPACING= in the PROC REPORT statement or the

ROPTIONS window unless you use SPACING= in the definition of a particular item to change the spacing to the left of that item.

Interaction: When CENTER is in effect, PROC REPORT ignores spacing that precedes the leftmost variable in the report.

SPLIT='*character*'

specifies the split character. PROC REPORT breaks a column header when it reaches that character and continues the header on the next line. The split character itself is not part of the column header although each occurrence of the split character counts toward the 40-character maximum for a label.

Default: slash (/)

Interaction: The FLOW option in the DEFINE statement honors the split character.

Note: If you are typing over a header (rather than entering one from the PROMPTER or DEFINITION window), you do not see the effect of the split character until you refresh the screen by adding or deleting an item, by changing the contents of a DEFINITION or a BREAK window, or by selecting

PANELS=*number-of-panels*

specifies the number of panels on each page of the report. If the width of a report is less than half of the line size, you can display the data in multiple sets of columns so that rows that would otherwise appear on multiple pages appear on the same page. Each set of columns is a *panel*. A familiar example of this kind of report is a telephone book, which contains multiple panels of names and telephone numbers on a single page.

When PROC REPORT writes a multipanel report, it fills one panel before beginning the next.

The number of panels that fits on a page depends on the

□ width of the panel

□ space between panels

□ line size.

Default: 1

Tip: If *number-of-panels* is larger than the number of panels that can fit on the page, PROC REPORT creates as many panels as it can. Let PROC REPORT put your data in the maximum number of panels that can fit on the page by specifying a large number of panels (for example, 99).

See also: For information about specifying the space between panels see the discussion of PSPACE= on page 942. For information about setting the linesize, see the discussion of Linesize on page 941).

PSPACE=*space-between-panels*

specifies the number of blank characters between panels. PROC REPORT separates all panels in the report by the same number of blank characters. For each panel, the sum of its width and the number of blank characters separating it from the panel to its left cannot exceed the line size.

Default: 4

User Help

identifies the library and catalog containing user-defined help for the report. This help can be in CBT or HELP catalog entries. You can write a CBT or HELP entry for each item in the report with the BUILD procedure in SAS/AF software. You must store all such entries for a report in the same catalog.

Specify the entry name for help for a particular report item in the DEFINITION window for that report item or in a DEFINE statement.

SAVE DATA SET

Lets you specify an output data set in which to store the data from the current report.

Path

Description

To specify an output data set, enter the name of the SAS data library and the name of the data set (called **member** in the window) that you want to create in the Save Data Set window.

Pushbuttons

OK
Creates the output data set and closes the Save Data Set window.

Cancel
Closes the Save Data Set window without creating an output data set.

SAVE DEFINITION

Saves a report definition for subsequent use with the same data set or with a similar data set.

Path

Description

The SAVE DEFINITION window prompts you for the complete name of the catalog entry in which to store the definition of the current report and for an optional description of the report. This description shows up in the LOAD REPORT window and helps you to select the appropriate report.

SAS stores the report definition as a catalog entry of type REPT. You can use a report definition to create an identically structured report for any SAS data set that contains variables with the same names as those used in the report definition.

Pushbuttons

OK
Creates the report definition and closes the SAVE DEFINITION window.

Cancel
Closes the SAVE DEFINITION window without creating a report definition.

SOURCE

Lists the PROC REPORT statements that build the current report.

Path

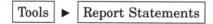

Tools ▶ Report Statements

STATISTICS

Displays statistics that are available in PROC REPORT.

Path

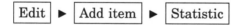

Edit ▶ Add item ▶ Statistic

After you select **Statistic**, PROC REPORT prompts you for the location of the statistic relative to the column that you have selected. After you select a location, the STATISTICS window opens.

Description

Select the statistics that you want to include in your report and close the window. When you select the first statistic, it moves to the top of the list in the window. If you select multiple statistics, subsequent selections move to the bottom of the list of selected statistics. The order of selected statistics from top to bottom determines their order in the report from left to right.

Note: If you double-click on a statistic, PROC REPORT immediately adds it to the report. The STATISTICS window remains open. △

To compute standard error and the Student's *t* test you must use the default value of VARDEF= which is DF.

WHERE

Selects observations from the data set that meet the conditions that you specify.

Path

Subset ► Where

Description

Enter a *where-expression* in the **Enter where clause** field. A *where-expression* is an arithmetic or logical expression that generally consists of a sequence of operands and operators. For information about constructing a *where-expression*, see the documentation of the WHERE statement in the section on statements in *SAS Language Reference: Dictionary*.

Note: You can clear all *where-expressions* by leaving the **Enter where clause** field empty and by selecting OK. △

Pushbuttons

OK
Applies the *where-expression* to the report and closes the WHERE window.

Cancel
Closes the WHERE window without altering the report.

WHERE ALSO

Selects observations from the data set that meet the conditions that you specify and any other conditions that are already in effect.

Path

Subset ► Where Also

Description

Enter a *where-expression* in the **Enter where clause** field. A *where-expression* is an arithmetic or logical expression that generally consists of a sequence of operands and operators. For information about constructing a *where-expression*, see the documentation of the WHERE statement in the chapter on statements in *SAS Language Reference: Dictionary*.

Pushbuttons

OK
Adds the *where-expression* to any other *where-expressions* that are already in effect and applies them all to the report. It also closes the WHERE ALSO window.

Cancel
Closes the WHERE ALSO window without altering the report.

How PROC REPORT Builds a Report

This section first explains the process of building a report. Following this explanation are illustrations of how PROC REPORT creates two sample reports. The examples use programming statements; you can construct the same reports in the windowing environment.

To understand the process of building a report, you must understand the difference between report variables and DATA step variables. Variables that appear only in one or more compute blocks are *DATA step variables*. Variables that appear in one or more columns of the report are *report variables*. A report variable may or may not appear in a compute block.

Sequence of Events

PROC REPORT constructs a report as follows:

1 It consolidates the data by group, order, and across variables. It calculates all statistics for the report, those for detail rows as well as those for summary lines in breaks. Statistics include those computed for analysis variables. PROC REPORT calculates statistics for summary lines whether or not they appear in the report. It stores all this information in a temporary file.

2 It initializes all DATA step variables to missing.

3 It begins constructing the rows of the report.

   a At the beginning of each row, it initializes all report variables to missing.
   b It fills in values for report variables from left to right.
      □ Values for computed variables come from executing the statements in the corresponding compute blocks.
      □ Values for all other variables come from the temporary file created at the beginning of the report-building process.

   c Whenever it comes to a break, PROC REPORT first constructs the break lines created with the BREAK or RBREAK statement or with options in the BREAK window. It then executes the statements in the compute block attached to the break (if there is one).

   Note: Because of the way PROC REPORT builds a report, you can
      □ use group statistics in compute blocks for a break before the group variable.
      □ use statistics for the whole report in a compute block at the beginning of the report.

This document references these statistics with the appropriate compound name. For information about referencing report items in a compute block, see "Four Ways to Reference Report Items in a Compute Block" on page 872. △

Construction of Summary Lines

PROC REPORT constructs a summary line for a break if either of the following conditions is true:

- ☐ You summarize numeric variables in the break.
- ☐ You use a compute block at the break. (You can attach a compute block to a break without using a BREAK or RBREAK statement or without selecting any options in the BREAK window.)

> For more information about using compute blocks, see "Using Compute Blocks" on page 871 and the discussion of the COMPUTE statement on page 905.

The summary line that PROC REPORT constructs at this point is preliminary. If no compute block is attached to the break, the preliminary summary line becomes the final summary line. However, if a compute block is attached to the break, the statements in the compute block can alter the values in the preliminary summary line.

PROC REPORT prints the summary line only if you summarize numeric variables in the break.

Using Compound Names

When you use a statistic in a report, you generally refer to it in compute blocks by a compound name like Sales.sum. However, in different parts of the report, that same name has different meanings. Consider the report in Output 32.1 on page 947. The statements that create the output follow. The user-defined formats that are used are created by a PROC FORMAT step on page 960.

```
libname proclib 'SAS-data-library';


options nodate pageno=1 linesize=64
        pagesize=60 fmtsearch=(proclib);
proc report data=grocery nowindows;
   column sector manager sales;
   define sector / group format=$sctrfmt.;
   define sales  / analysis sum
                   format=dollar9.2;
   define manager / group format=$mgrfmt.;
   break after sector / summarize skip ol;
   rbreak after / summarize dol dul;
   compute after;
      sector='Total:';
   endcomp;
run;
```

Output 32.1   Three Different Meanings of Sales.sum

```
                        The SAS System                        1

         Sector      Manager      Sales
         Northeast   Alomar      $786.00        ❶
                     Andrews   $1,045.00
         ---------             ---------
         Northeast             $1,831.00        ❷

         Northwest   Brown       $598.00
                     Pelfrey     $746.00
                     Reveiz    $1,110.00
         ---------             ---------
         Northwest             $2,454.00

         Southeast   Jones       $630.00
                     Smith       $350.00
         ---------             ---------
         Southeast               $980.00

         Southwest   Adams       $695.00
                     Taylor      $353.00
         ---------             ---------
         Southwest             $1,048.00

         =========             =========
         Total:                $6,313.00        ❸
         =========             =========
```

Here Sales.sum has three different meanings:

1 In detail rows, the value is the sales for one manager's store in a sector of the city. For example, the first detail row of the report shows that the sales for the store that Alomar manages were $786.00.

2 In the group summary lines, the value is the sales for all the stores in one sector. For example, the first group summary line shows that sales for the Northeast sector were $1,831.00.

3 In the report summary line, the value ($6,313.00) is the sales for all stores in the city.

CAUTION:

When to Use an Alias   Unless you use the NOALIAS option in the PROC REPORT statement, when you refer in a compute block to a statistic that has an alias, you do not use a compound name. Generally, you must use the alias. However, if the statistic shares a column with an across variable, you must reference it by column number (see "Four Ways to Reference Report Items in a Compute Block" on page 872). △

Building a Report That Uses Groups and a Report Summary

The report in Output 32.2 on page 949 contains five columns:

□ Sector and Department are group variables.

□ Sales is an analysis variable that is used to calculate the Sum statistic.

□ Profit is a computed variable whose value is based on the value of Department.

□ The N statistic indicates how many observations each row represents.

At the end of the report a break summarizes the statistics and computed variables in the report and assigns to Sector the value of **TOTALS:**.

The following statements produce Output 32.2 on page 949. The user-defined formats that are used are created by a PROC FORMAT step on page 960.

```
libname proclib 'SAS-data-library';



options nodate pageno=1 linesize=64
        pagesize=60 fmtsearch=(proclib);
proc report data=grocery headline headskip;
   column sector department sales Profit N;
   define sector / group format=$sctrfmt.;
   define department   / group format=$deptfmt.;
   define sales  / analysis sum
                   format=dollar9.2;
   define profit / computed format=dollar9.2;

   compute profit;
      if department='np1' or department='np2'
         then profit=0.4*sales.sum;
      else profit=0.25*sales.sum;
   endcomp;

   rbreak after / dol dul summarize;
   compute after;
      sector='TOTALS:';
   endcomp;

   where sector contains 'n';
   title 'Report for Northeast and Northwest Sectors';
run;
```

Output 32.2   Report with Groups and a Report Summary

```
        Report for Northeast and Northwest Sectors        1

   Sector     Department     Sales      Profit         N
   -----------------------------------------------------------

   Northeast  Canned        $840.00     $336.00        2
              Meat/Dairy    $490.00     $122.50        2
              Paper         $290.00     $116.00        2
              Produce       $211.00      $52.75        2
   Northwest  Canned      $1,070.00     $428.00        3
              Meat/Dairy  $1,055.00     $263.75        3
              Paper         $150.00      $60.00        3
              Produce       $179.00      $44.75        3
   =========              =========   =========  =========
   TOTALS:               $4,285.00   $1,071.25         20
   =========              =========   =========  =========
```

A description of how PROC REPORT builds this report follows:

1 PROC REPORT starts building the report by consolidating the data (Sector and Department are group variables) and by calculating the statistics (Sales.sum and N) for each detail row and for the break at the end of the report. It stores these values in a temporary file.

2 Now, PROC REPORT is ready to start building the first row of the report. This report does not contain a break at the beginning of the report or a break before any groups, so the first row of the report is a detail row. The procedure initializes all report variables to missing, as Figure 32.9 on page 950 illustrates. Missing values for a character variable are represented by a blank, and missing values for a numeric variable are represented by a period.

Figure 32.9   First Detail Row with Values Initialized

Sector	Department	Sales	Profit	N
		.	.	.

3 Figure 32.10 on page 950 illustrates the construction of the first three columns of the row. PROC REPORT fills in values for the row from left to right. Values come from the temporary file created at the beginning of the report-building process.

Figure 32.10   First Detail Row with Values Filled in from Left to Right

Sector	Department	Sales	Profit	N
Northeast		.	.	.

Sector	Department	Sales	Profit	N
Northeast	Canned	.	.	.

Sector	Department	Sales	Profit	N
Northeast	Canned	$840.00	.	.

4 The next column in the report contains the computed variable Profit. When it gets to this column, PROC REPORT executes the statements in the compute block that is attached to Profit. Nonperishable items (which have a value of **np1** or **np2**) return a profit of 40%; perishable items (which have a value of **p1** or **p2**) return a profit of 25%.

```
if department='np1' or department='np2'
   then profit=0.4*sales.sum;
else profit=0.25*sales.sum;
```

The row now looks like Figure 32.11 on page 951.

CAUTION:

The position of a computed variable is important. PROC REPORT assigns values to the columns in a row of a report from left to right. Consequently, you cannot base the calculation of a computed variable on any variable that appears to its right in the report. △

Figure 32.11 A Computed Variable Added to the First Detail Row

Sector	Department	Sales	Profit	N
Northeast	Canned	$840.00	$336.00	.

5 Next, PROC REPORT fills in the value for the N statistic. The value comes from the temporary file created at the beginning of the report-building process. Figure 32.12 on page 951 illustrates the completed row.

Figure 32.12 First Complete Detail Row

Sector	Department	Sales	Profit	N
Northeast	Canned	$840.00	$336.00	2

6 The procedure writes the completed row to the report.

7 PROC REPORT repeats steps 2, 3, 4, 5, and 6 for each detail row in the report.

8 At the break at the end of the report, PROC REPORT constructs the break lines described by the RBREAK statement. These lines include double underlining, double overlining, and a preliminary version of the summary line. The statistics for the summary line were calculated earlier (see step 1). The value for the computed variables is calculated when PROC REPORT reaches the appropriate column, just as it is in detail rows. PROC REPORT uses these values to create the preliminary version of the summary line (see Figure 32.13 on page 951).

Figure 32.13 Preliminary Summary Line

Sector	Department	Sales	Profit	N
		$4,285.00	$1,071.25	20

9 If no compute block is attached to the break, the preliminary version of the summary line is the same as the final version. However, in this example, a compute block is attached to the break. Therefore, PROC REPORT now executes the statements in that compute block. In this case, the compute block contains one statement:

```
sector='TOTALS:';
```

This statement replaces the value of Sector, which in the summary line is missing by default, with the word **TOTALS:**. After PROC REPORT executes the statement, it modifies the summary line to reflect this change to the value of Sector. The final version of the summary line appears in Figure 32.14 on page 952.

Figure 32.14   Final Summary Line

Sector	Department	Sales	Profit	N
TOTALS:		$4,285.00	$1,071.25	20

10 Finally, PROC REPORT writes all the break lines–underlining, overlining, and the final summary line–to the report.

Building a Report That Uses DATA Step Variables

PROC REPORT initializes report variables to missing at the beginning of each row of the report. The value for a DATA step variable is initialized to missing before PROC REPORT begins to construct the rows of the report, and it remains missing until you specifically assign a value to it. PROC REPORT retains the value of a DATA step variable from the execution of one compute block to another.

Because all compute blocks share the current values of all variables, you can initialize DATA step variables at a break at the beginning of the report or at a break before a break variable. This report initializes the DATA step variable Sctrtot at a break before Sector.

CAUTION:
   Timing at Breaks. PROC REPORT creates a preliminary summary line for a break before it executes the corresponding compute block. If the summary line contains computed variables, the computations are based on the values of the contributing variables in the preliminary summary line. If you want to recalculate computed variables based on values you set in the compute block, you must do so explicitly in the compute block. This report illustrates this technique.
   If no compute block is attached to a break, the preliminary summary line becomes the final summary line. △

The report in Output 32.3 on page 953 contains five columns:

□ Sector and Department are group variables.

□ Sales is an analysis variable that is used twice in this report: once to calculate the Sum statistic, and once to calculate the Pctsum statistic.

□ Sctrpct is a computed variable whose values are based on the values of Sales and a DATA step variable, Sctrtot, which is the total sales for a sector.

At the beginning of the report, a customized report summary tells what the sales for all stores are. At a break before each group of observations for a department, a default summary summarizes the data for that sector. At the end of each group a break inserts a blank line.

The following statements produce Output 32.3 on page 953. The user-defined formats that are used are created by a PROC FORMAT step on page 960.

Note: Calculations of the percentages do not multiply their results by 100 because PROC REPORT prints them with the PERCENT. format. △

```
libname proclib 'SAS-data-library';


options nodate pageno=1 linesize=64
        pagesize=60 fmtsearch=(proclib);
proc report data=grocery noheader nowindows;
  column sector department sales
         Sctrpct sales=Salespct;

  define sector     / 'Sector' group
                        format=$sctrfmt.;
  define department / group format=$deptfmt.;
  define sales      / analysis sum
                        format=dollar9.2 ;
  define sctrpct    / computed
                        format=percent9.2 ;
  define salespct   / pctsum format=percent9.2;

  compute before;
     line ' ';
     line @16 'Total for all stores is '
          sales.sum dollar9.2;
     line ' ';
     line @29 'Sum of' @40 'Percent'
          @51 'Percent of';
     line @6 'Sector' @17 'Department'
          @29 'Sales'
          @40 'of Sector' @51 'All Stores';
     line @6 55*'=';
     line ' ';
  endcomp;

  break before sector / summarize ul;
  compute before sector;
     sctrtot=sales.sum;
     sctrpct=sales.sum/sctrtot;
  endcomp;

  compute sctrpct;
     sctrpct=sales.sum/sctrtot;
  endcomp;

  break after sector/skip;
  where sector contains 'n';
  title 'Report for Northeast and Northwest Sectors';
run;
```

Output 32.3   Report with DATA Step Variables

```
              Report for Northeast and Northwest Sectors              1


              Total for all stores is $4,285.00

                          Sum of      Percent    Percent of
     Sector    Department Sales       of Sector  All Stores
     ===========================================================

     Northeast             $1,831.00  100.00%     42.73%
     ---------             ---------  ---------   ---------
     Northeast  Canned       $840.00   45.88%     19.60%
                Meat/Dairy   $490.00   26.76%     11.44%
                Paper        $290.00   15.84%      6.77%
                Produce      $211.00   11.52%      4.92%

     Northwest             $2,454.00  100.00%     57.27%
     ---------             ---------  ---------   ---------
     Northwest  Canned     $1,070.00   43.60%     24.97%
                Meat/Dairy $1,055.00   42.99%     24.62%
                Paper        $150.00    6.11%      3.50%
                Produce      $179.00    7.29%      4.18%
```

A description of how PROC REPORT builds this report follows:

1 PROC REPORT starts building the report by consolidating the data (Sector and Department are group variables) and by calculating the statistics (Sales.sum and Sales.pctsum) for each detail row, for the break at the beginning of the report, for the breaks before each group, and for the breaks after each group. It stores these values in a temporary file.

2 PROC REPORT initializes the DATA step variable, Sctrtot, to missing (see Figure 32.15 on page 954).

Figure 32.15   Initialized DATA Step Variables

Report Variables					DATA Step Variable
Sector	**Department**	**Sales.sum**	**Sctrpct**	**Sales.pctsum**	**Sctrtot**
		.	.	.	.

3 Because this PROC REPORT step contains a COMPUTE BEFORE statement, the procedure constructs a preliminary summary line for the break at the beginning of the report. This preliminary summary line contains values for the statistics (Sales.sum and Sales.pctsum) and the computed variable (Sctrpct).

   At this break, Sales.sum is the sales for all stores, and Sales.pctsum is the percentage those sales represent for all stores (100%). PROC REPORT takes the values for these statistics from the temporary file that it created at the beginning of the report-building process.

   The value for Sctrpct comes from executing the statements in the corresponding compute block. Because the value of Sctrtot is missing, PROC REPORT cannot calculate a value for Sctrpct. Therefore, in the preliminary summary line (which is not printed in this case), this variable also has a missing value (see Figure 32.16 on page 955).

The statements in the COMPUTE BEFORE block do not alter any variables. Therefore, the final summary line is the same as the preliminary summary line.

Note: The COMPUTE BEFORE statement creates a break at the beginning of the report. You do not need to use an RBREAK statement. △

Figure 32.16 Preliminary and Final Summary Line for the Break at the Beginning of the Report

		Report Variables			DATA Step Variable
Sector	Department	Sales.sum	Sctrpct	Sales.pctsum	Sctrtot
		$4,285.00	.	100.00%	.

4 Because the program does not include an RBREAK statement with the SUMMARIZE option, PROC REPORT does not write the final summary line to the report. Instead, it uses LINE statements to write a customized summary that embeds the value of Sales.sum into a sentence and to write customized column headers. (The NOHEADER option in the PROC REPORT statement suppresses the default column headers, which would have appeared before the customized summary.)

5 Next, PROC REPORT constructs a preliminary summary line for the break before the first group of observations. (This break both uses the SUMMARIZE option in the BREAK statement and has a compute block attached to it. Either of these conditions generates a summary line.) The preliminary summary line contains values for the break variable (Sector), the statistics (Sales.sum and Sales.pctsum), and the computed variable (Sctrpct). At this break, Sales.sum is the sales for one sector (the northeast sector). PROC REPORT takes the values for Sector, Sales.sum, and Sales.pctsum from the temporary file that it created at the beginning of the report-building process.

The value for Sctrpct comes from executing the statements in the corresponding compute blocks. Because the value of Sctrtot is still missing, PROC REPORT cannot calculate a value for Sctrpct. Therefore, in the preliminary summary line, Sctrpct has a missing value (see Figure 32.17 on page 955).

Figure 32.17 Preliminary Summary Line for the Break before the First Group of Observations

		Report Variables			DATA Step Variable
Sector	Department	Sales.sum	Sctrpct	Sales.pctsum	Sctrtot
Northeast		$1,831.00	.	42.73%	.

6 PROC REPORT creates the final version of the summary line by executing the statements in the COMPUTE BEFORE SECTOR compute block. These statements execute once each time the value of Sector changes.

□ The first statement assigns the value of Sales.sum, which in that part of the report represents total sales for one Sector, to the variable Sctrtot.

□ The second statement completes the summary line by recalculating Sctrpct from the new value of Sctrtot. Figure 32.18 on page 956 shows the final summary line.

CAUTION:

> **Recalculating Values in the Final Summary Line.** If you do not recalculate the value for Sctrpct, it will be missing because the value of Sctrtot is missing at the time that the COMPUTE Sctrpct block executes. △

Figure 32.18   Final Summary Line for the Break before the First Group of Observations

		Report Variables			DATA Step Variable
Sector	Department	Sales.sum	Sctrpct	Sales.pctsum	Sctrtot
Northeast		$1,831.00	100.00%	42.73%	$1,831.00

7 Because the program contains a BREAK BEFORE statement with the SUMMARIZE option, PROC REPORT writes the final summary line to the report. The UL option in the BREAK statement underlines the summary line.

8 Now, PROC REPORT is ready to start building the first detail row of the report. It initializes all report variables to missing. Values for DATA step variables do not change. Figure 32.19 on page 956 illustrates the first detail row at this point.

Figure 32.19   First Detail Row with Initialized Values

		Report Variables			DATA Step Variable
Sector	Department	Sales.sum	Sctrpct	Sales.pctsum	Sctrtot
		.	.	.	$1,831.00

9 Figure 32.20 on page 956 illustrates the construction of the first three columns of the row. PROC REPORT fills in values for the row from left to right. The values come from the temporary file it created at the beginning of the report-building process.

Figure 32.20   Filling in Values from Left to Right

		Report Variables			DATA Step Variable
Sector	Department	Sales.sum	Sctrpct	Sales.pctsum	Sctrtot
Northeast		.	.	.	$1,831.00

		Report Variables			DATA Step Variable
Sector	Department	Sales.sum	Sctrpct	Sales.pctsum	Sctrtot
Northeast	Canned	.	.	.	$1,831.00

		Report Variables			DATA Step Variable
Sector	Department	Sales.sum	Sctrpct	Sales.pctsum	Sctrtot
Northeast	Canned	$840.00	.	.	$1,831.00

10 The next column in the report contains the computed variable Sctrpct. When it gets to this column, PROC REPORT executes the statement in the compute block attached to Sctrpct. This statement calculates the percentage of the sector's total sales that this department accounts for:

```
sctrpct=sales.sum/sctrtot;
```

The row now looks like Figure 32.21 on page 957.

Figure 32.21   First Detail Row with the First Computed Variable Added

		Report Variables			DATA Step Variable
Sector	Department	Sales.sum	Sctrpct	Sales.pctsum	Sctrtot
Northeast	Canned	$840.00	45.88%	.	$1,831.00

11 The next column in the report contains the statistic Sales.pctsum. PROC REPORT gets this value from the temporary file. The first detail row is now complete (see Figure 32.22 on page 957).

Figure 32.22   First Complete Detail Row

		Report Variables			DATA Step Variable
Sector	Department	Sales.sum	Sctrpct	Sales.pctsum	Sctrtot
Northeast	Canned	$840.00	45.88%	19.60%	$1,831.00

12 PROC REPORT writes the detail row to the report. It repeats steps 8, 9, 10, 11, and 12 for each detail row in the group.

13 After writing the last detail row in the group to the report, PROC REPORT constructs the default group summary. Because no compute block is attached to this break and because the BREAK AFTER statement does not include the SUMMARIZE option, PROC REPORT does not construct a summary line. The only action at this break is that the SKIP option in the BREAK AFTER statement writes a blank line after the last detail row of the group.

14 Now the value of the break variable changes from **Northeast** to **Northwest**. PROC REPORT constructs a preliminary summary line for the break before this group of observations. As at the beginning of any row, PROC REPORT initializes all report variables to missing but retains the value of the DATA step variable. Next, it completes the preliminary summary line with the appropriate values for the break variable (Sector), the statistics (Sales.sum and Sales.pctsum), and the computed variable (Sctrpct). At this break, Sales.sum is the sales for the Northwest sector. Because the COMPUTE BEFORE Sector block has not yet executed, the value of Sctrtot is still $1,831.00, the value for the Northeast sector. Thus, the value that PROC REPORT calculates for Sctrpct in this preliminary summary line is incorrect (see Figure 32.23 on page 958). The statements in the compute block for this break calculate the correct value (see the following step).

Figure 32.23   Preliminary Summary Line for the Break before the Second Group of Observations

		Report Variables			DATA Step Variable
Sector	Department	Sales.sum	Sctrpct	Sales.pctsum	Sctrtot
Northwest		$2,454.00	134.00%	57.27%	$1,831.00

CAUTION:

Synchronizing Values for Computed Variables in Break Lines. If the PROC REPORT step does not recalculate Sctrpct in the compute block attached to the break, the value in the final summary line will not be synchronized with the other values in the summary line, and the report will be incorrect. △

15 PROC REPORT creates the final version of the summary line by executing the statements in the COMPUTE BEFORE Sector compute block. These statements execute once each time the value of Sector changes.

  □ The first statement assigns the value of Sales.sum, which in that part of the report represents sales for the Northwest sector, to the variable Sctrtot.

  □ The second statement completes the summary line by recalculating Sctrpct from the new, appropriate value of Sctrtot. Figure 32.24 on page 958 shows the final summary line.

Figure 32.24   Final Summary Line for the Break before the Second Group of Observations

		Report Variables			DATA Step Variable
Sector	Department	Sales.sum	Sctrpct	Sales.pctsum	Sctrtot
Northwest		$2,454.00	100.00%	57.27%	$2,454.00

Because the program contains a BREAK BEFORE statement with the SUMMARIZE option, PROC REPORT writes the final summary line to the report. The UL option in the BREAK statement underlines the summary line.

16 Now, PROC REPORT is ready to start building the first row for this group of observations. It repeats steps 8 through 16 until it has processed all observations in the input data set (stopping with step 14 for the last group of observations).

Examples

Example 1: Selecting Variables for a Report

Procedure features:
  PROC REPORT statement options:
    NOWD

COLUMN statement
    default variable usage
RBREAK statement options:
  DOL
  SUMMARIZE
Other features:
  FORMAT statement
  FORMAT procedure:
    LIBRARY=
  SAS system options:
    FMTSEARCH=
  Automatic macro variables:
    SYSDATE

This example uses a permanent data set and permanent formats to create a report that contains

- □ one row for every observation
- □ a default summary for the whole report.

Program

```
libname proclib 'SAS-data-library';
```

```
options nodate pageno=1 linesize=64 pagesize=60;
```

The data set GROCERY contains one day's sales figures for eight stores in the Grocery Mart chain. Each observation contains one day's sales data for one department in one store.

```
data grocery;
   input Sector $ Manager $ Department $ Sales @@;
   datalines;
se 1 np1 50    se 1 p1 100    se 1 np2 120    se 1 p2 80
se 2 np1 40    se 2 p1 300    se 2 np2 220    se 2 p2 70
nw 3 np1 60    nw 3 p1 600    nw 3 np2 420    nw 3 p2 30
nw 4 np1 45    nw 4 p1 250    nw 4 np2 230    nw 4 p2 73
nw 9 np1 45    nw 9 p1 205    nw 9 np2 420    nw 9 p2 76
sw 5 np1 53    sw 5 p1 130    sw 5 np2 120    sw 5 p2 50
sw 6 np1 40    sw 6 p1 350    sw 6 np2 225    sw 6 p2 80
ne 7 np1 90    ne 7 p1 190    ne 7 np2 420    ne 7 p2 86
ne 8 np1 200   ne 8 p1 300    ne 8 np2 420    ne 8 p2 125
;
```

PROC FORMAT creates permanent formats for Sector, Manager, and Department. The LIBRARY= option specifies a permanent storage location so that the formats are available in subsequent SAS sessions. These formats are used for examples throughout this section.

```
proc format library=proclib;
   value $sctrfmt 'se' = 'Southeast'
                  'ne' = 'Northeast'
                  'nw' = 'Northwest'
                  'sw' = 'Southwest';

   value $mgrfmt '1' = 'Smith'   '2' = 'Jones'
                 '3' = 'Reveiz'  '4' = 'Brown'
                 '5' = 'Taylor'  '6' = 'Adams'
                 '7' = 'Alomar'  '8' = 'Andrews'
                 '9' = 'Pelfrey';

   value $deptfmt 'np1' = 'Paper'
                  'np2' = 'Canned'
                  'p1'  = 'Meat/Dairy'
                  'p2'  = 'Produce';
run;
```

The SAS system option FMTSEARCH= adds the SAS data library PROCLIB to the search path that is used to locate formats.

```
options fmtsearch=(proclib);
```

The NOWD option runs the REPORT procedure without the REPORT window and sends its output to the SAS procedure output.

```
proc report data=grocery nowd;
```

The report contains a column for Manager, Department, and Sales. Because there is no DEFINE statement for any of these variables, PROC REPORT uses the character variables (Manager and Department) as display variables and the numeric variable (Sales) as an analysis variable that is used to calculate the sum statistic.

```
column manager department sales;
```

The RBREAK statement produces a default summary at the end of the report. DOL writes a line of equal signs (=) above the summary information. SUMMARIZE sums the value of Sales for all observations in the report.

```
rbreak after / dol summarize;
```

The WHERE statement selects for the report only the observations for stores in the southeast sector.

```
where sector='se';
```

The FORMAT statement assigns formats to use in the report. You can use the FORMAT statement only with data set variables.

```
      format manager $mgrfmt.;
      format department $deptfmt.;
      format sales dollar11.2;
```

SYSDATE is an automatic macro variable that returns the date when the SAS job or SAS session began. The TITLE2 statement uses double rather than single quotes so that the macro variable resolves.

```
      title 'Sales for the Southeast Sector';
      title2 "for &sysdate";
   run;
```

Output

```
                    Sales for the Southeast Sector           1
                            for 14MAY98

            Manager   Department        Sales
            Smith     Paper            $50.00
            Smith     Meat/Dairy      $100.00
            Smith     Canned          $120.00
            Smith     Produce          $80.00
            Jones     Paper            $40.00
            Jones     Meat/Dairy      $300.00
            Jones     Canned          $220.00
            Jones     Produce          $70.00
                                  ===========
                                     $980.00
```

Example 2: Ordering the Rows in a Report

Procedure features:
   PROC REPORT statement options:

   COLWIDTH=
   HEADLINE
   HEADSKIP
   SPACING=

   BREAK statement options:

   OL
   SKIP
   SUMMARIZE

   COMPUTE statement arguments:

   AFTER

   DEFINE statement options:

   ANALYSIS
   FORMAT=
   ORDER
   ORDER=
   SUM

ENDCOMP statement

LINE statement:

with quoted text
with variable values

Data set: GROCERY on page 959

Formats: $MGRFMT. and $DEPTFMT. on page 960

This example

☐ arranges the rows alphabetically by the formatted values of Manager and the internal values of Department (so that sales for the two departments that sell nonperishable goods precede sales for the two departments that sell perishable goods)

☐ controls the default column width and the spacing between columns

☐ underlines the column headers and writes a blank line beneath the underlining

☐ creates a default summary of Sales for each manager

☐ creates a customized summary of Sales for the whole report.

Program

```
libname proclib 'SAS-data-library';
```

```
options nodate pageno=1 linesize=64 pagesize=60
        fmtsearch=(proclib);
```

The NOWD option runs PROC REPORT without the REPORT window and sends its output to the SAS procedure output. COLWIDTH=10 sets the default column width to 10 characters. SPACING= puts five blank characters between columns. HEADLINE underlines all column headers and the spaces between them at the top of each page of the report. HEADSKIP writes a blank line beneath the underlining that HEADLINE writes.

```
proc report data=grocery nowd
            colwidth=10
            spacing=5
            headline headskip;
```

The report contains a column for Manager, Department, and Sales.

```
column manager department sales;
```

The values of all variables with the ORDER option in the DEFINE statement determine the order of the rows in the report. In this report, PROC REPORT arranges the rows first by the value of Manager (because it is the first variable in the COLUMN statement) and then by the values of Department.

ORDER= specifies the sort order for a variable. This report arranges the rows according to the formatted values of Manager and the internal values of Department (np1, np2, p1, and p2). FORMAT= specifies the formats to use in the report.

```
define manager / order order=formatted format=$mgrfmt.;
define department / order order=internal format=$deptfmt.;
```

Sum calculates the sum statistic for all observations represented by the current row of the row. In this report each row represents only one observation. Therefore, the Sum statistic is the same as the value of Sales for that observation in the input data set. Using Sales as an analysis variable in this report enables you to summarize the values for each group and at the end of the report.

```
define sales / analysis sum format=dollar7.2;
```

This BREAK statement produces a default summary after the last row for each manager. OL writes a row of hyphens above the summary line. SUMMARIZE writes the value of Sales (the only analysis or computed variable) in the summary line. PROC REPORT sums the values of Sales for each manager because Sales is an analysis variable used to calculate the Sum statistic. SKIP writes a blank line after the summary line.

```
break after manager / ol
                      summarize
                      skip;
```

This COMPUTE statement begins a compute block that produces a customized summary at the end of the report. The LINE statement places the quoted text and the value of Sales.sum (with the DOLLAR9.2 format) in the summary. An ENDCOMP statement must end the compute block.

```
compute after;
   line 'Total sales for these stores were: '
        sales.sum dollar9.2;
endcomp;
```

The WHERE statement selects for the report only the observations for stores in the southeast sector.

```
where sector='se';
```

The TITLE statement specifies the title.

```
   title 'Sales for the Southeast Sector';
run;
```

Output

```
                     Sales for the Southeast Sector                    1

              Manager        Department        Sales
              ---------------------------------------

              Jones          Paper              $40.00
                             Canned            $220.00
                             Meat/Dairy        $300.00
                             Produce            $70.00
              -------                          -------
              Jones                            $630.00

              Smith          Paper              $50.00
                             Canned            $120.00
                             Meat/Dairy        $100.00
                             Produce            $80.00
              -------                          -------
              Smith                            $350.00

         Total sales for these stores were:    $980.00
```

Example 3: Using Aliases to Obtain Multiple Statistics for the Same Variable

Procedure features:
>   COLUMN statement:
>>   with aliases
>   COMPUTE statement arguments:
>>   AFTER
>   DEFINE statement options:
>>   ANALYSIS
>>   MAX
>>   MIN
>>   NOPRINT
>>   customizing column headers
>   LINE statement:
>>   pointer controls
>>   quoted text
>>   repeating a character string
>>   variable values and formats
>>   writing a blank line

Other features:
>   automatic macro variables:
>>   SYSDATE

Data set: GROCERY on page 959

Formats: $MGRFMT. and $DEPTFMT. on page 960

The customized summary at the end of this report displays the minimum and maximum values of Sales over all departments for stores in the southeast sector. To determine these values, PROC REPORT needs the MIN and MAX statistic for Sales in every row of the report. However, to keep the report simple, the display of these statistics is suppressed.

Program

```
libname proclib 'SAS-data-library';


options nodate pageno=1 linesize=64 pagesize=60
        fmtsearch=(proclib);
```

The NOWD option runs PROC REPORT without the REPORT window and sends its output to the SAS procedure output. HEADLINE underlines all column headers and the spaces between them at the top of each page of the report. HEADSKIP writes a blank line beneath the underlining that HEADLINE writes.

```
proc report data=grocery nowd headline headskip;
```

The report contains columns for Manager and Department. It also contains three columns for Sales. The column specifications SALES=SALESMIN and SALES=SALESMAX create aliases for Sales. These aliases enable you to use a separate definition of Sales for each of the three columns.

```
column manager department sales
        sales=salesmin
        sales=salesmax;
```

The values of all variables with the ORDER option in the DEFINE statement determine the order of the rows in the report. In this report, PROC REPORT arranges the rows first by the value of Manager (because it is the first variable in the COLUMN statement) and then by the values of Department. The ORDER= option specifies the sort order for a variable. This report arranges the values of Manager by their formatted values and arranges the values of Department by their internal values (np1, np2, p1, and p2). FORMAT= specifies the formats to use in the report. Text in quotation marks specifies column headers.

```
define manager / order
                order=formatted
                format=$mgrfmt.
                'Manager';
define department   / order
                order=internal
                format=$deptfmt.
                'Department';
```

The value of an analysis variable in any row of a report is the value of the statistic associated with it (in this case Sum) calculated for all observations represented by that row. In a detail report each row represents only one observation. Therefore, the Sum statistic is the same as the value of Sales for that observation in the input data set.

```
define sales / analysis sum format=dollar7.2 'Sales';
```

These DEFINE statements use aliases from the COLUMN statement to create separate columns for the MIN and MAX statistics for the analysis variable Sales. NOPRINT suppresses the printing of these statistics. Although PROC REPORT does not print these values in columns, it has access to them so that it can print them in the summary.

```
define salesmin / analysis min noprint;
define salesmax / analysis max noprint;
```

This COMPUTE statement begins a compute block that executes at the end of the report. The first LINE statement writes a blank line. The second LINE statement writes 53 hyphens (-), beginning in column 7.

```
compute after;
   line ' ';
   line @7 53*'-';
```

The first line of this LINE statement writes the text in quotation marks, beginning in column 7. The second line writes the value of Salesmin with the DOLLAR7.2 format, beginning in the next column. The cursor then moves one column to the right (+1), where PROC REPORT writes the text in quotation marks. Again, the cursor moves one column to the right, and PROC REPORT writes the value of Salesmax with the DOLLAR7.2 format. (Note that the program must reference the variables by their aliases.) The third line writes the text in quotation marks, beginning in the next column.

```
   line @7 '| Departmental sales ranged from'
        salesmin dollar7.2  +1 'to' +1 salesmax dollar7.2
        '. |';
   line @7 53*'-';
```

An ENDCOMP statement must end the compute block.

```
   endcomp;
```

The WHERE statement selects for the report only the observations for stores in the southeast sector. The TITLE statements specify two titles. SYSDATE is an automatic macro variable that returns the date when the SAS job or SAS session began. The TITLE2 statement uses double rather than single quotes so that the macro variable resolves.

```
   where sector='se';
   title 'Sales for the Southeast Sector';
   title2 ''for &sysdate'';
run;
```

Output

```
                    Sales for the Southeast Sector            1
                            for 27MAY98

                Manager   Department     Sales
                --------------------------------

                Jones     Paper         $40.00
                          Canned       $220.00
                          Meat/Dairy   $300.00
                          Produce       $70.00
                Smith     Paper         $50.00
                          Canned       $120.00
                          Meat/Dairy   $100.00
                          Produce       $80.00


        -------------------------------------------------
        | Departmental sales ranged from $40.00 to $300.00. |
        -------------------------------------------------
```

Example 4: Consolidating Multiple Observations into One Row of a Report

Procedure features:
    BREAK statement options:

        OL
        SKIP
        SUMMARIZE
        SUPPRESS

    CALL DEFINE statement

    Compute block

        associated with a data set variable

    COMPUTE statement arguments:

        AFTER
        a data set variable as *report-item*

    DEFINE statement options:

        ANALYSIS
        GROUP
        SUM
        customizing column headers

    LINE statement:

        quoted text
        variable values

Data set: GROCERY on page 959

Formats: $MGRFMT. and $DEPTFMT. on page 960

This example creates a summary report that

☐ consolidates information for each combination of Sector and Manager into one row of the report

☐ contains default summaries of sales for each sector

□ contains a customized summary of sales for all sectors

□ uses one format for sales in detail rows and a different format in summary rows

□ uses customized column headers.

Program

```
libname proclib 'SAS-data-library';
```

The NOWD option runs PROC REPORT without the REPORT window and sends its output to the SAS procedure output. HEADLINE underlines all column headers and the spaces between them at the top of each page of the report. HEADSKIP writes a blank line beneath the underlining that HEADLINE writes..

```
options nodate pageno=1 linesize=64 pagesize=60
        fmtsearch=(proclib);

proc report data=grocery nowd headline headskip;
```

The report contains columns for Sector, Manager, and Sales.

```
column sector manager sales;
```

In this report, Sector and Manager are group variables. Sales is an analysis variable used to calculate the Sum statistic. Each detail row represents a set of observations that have a unique combination of formatted values for all group variables. The value of Sales in each detail row is the sum of Sales for all observations in the group. FORMAT= specifies the format to use in the report. Text in quotation marks in a DEFINE statement specifies the column header.

```
define sector / group
                format=$sctrfmt.
                'Sector';
define manager / group
                 format=$mgrfmt.
                 'Manager';
define sales / analysis sum
               format=comma10.2
               'Sales';
```

This BREAK statement produces a default summary after the last row for each sector. OL writes a row of hyphens above the summary line. SUMMARIZE writes the value of Sales in the summary line. PROC REPORT sums the values of Sales for each manager because Sales is an analysis variable used to calculate the Sum statistic. SUPPRESS prevents PROC REPORT from displaying the value of Sector in the summary line. SKIP writes a blank line after the summary line.

```
break after sector / ol
                     summarize
                     suppress
```

```
        skip;
```

This compute block creates a customized summary at the end of the report. The LINE statement writes the quoted text and the value of Sales.sum (with a format of DOLLAR9.2) in the summary. An ENDCOMP statement must end the compute block.

```
compute after;
   line 'Combined sales for the northern sectors were '
        sales.sum dollar9.2 '.';
endcomp;
```

In detail rows, PROC REPORT displays the value of Sales with the format specified in its definition (COMMA10.2). The compute block specifies an alternate format to use in the current column on summary rows. Summary rows are identified as a value other than a blank for _BREAK_.

```
compute sales;
   if _break_ ne ' ' then
   call define(_col_,"format","dollar11.2");
endcomp;
```

The WHERE statement selects for the report only the observations for stores in the northeast and northwest sectors. The TITLE statement specifies the title.

```
where sector contains 'n';
title 'Sales Figures for Northern Sectors';
run;
```

Output

```
                Sales Figures for Northern Sectors            1

             Sector     Manager      Sales
             ------------------------------

             Northeast  Alomar       786.00
                        Andrews    1,045.00
                                  ----------
                                  $1,831.00

             Northwest  Brown        598.00
                        Pelfrey      746.00
                        Reveiz     1,110.00
                                  ----------
                                  $2,454.00

       Combined sales for the northern sectors were $4,285.00.
```

Example 5: Creating a Column for Each Value of a Variable

Procedure features:
    PROC REPORT statement options:
      SPLIT=
    BREAK statement options:
      SKIP
    COLUMN statement:
      stacking variables
    COMPUTE statement arguments:
      with a computed variable as *report-item*
      AFTER
    DEFINE statement options:
      ACROSS
      ANALYSIS
      COMPUTED
      SUM
    LINE statement:
      pointer controls

Data set: GROCERY on page 959

Formats: $SCTRFMT., $MGRFMT., and $DEPTFMT. on page 960

The report in this example

□ consolidates multiple observations into one row

□ contains a column for each value of Department that is selected for the report (the departments that sell perishable items)

□ contains a variable that is not in the input data set

□ uses customized column headers, some of which contain blank lines

□ double-spaces between detail rows

□ uses pointer controls to control the placement of text and variable values in a customized summary.

Program

```
libname proclib 'SAS-data-library';
```

```
options nodate pageno=1 linesize=64 pagesize=60
        fmtsearch=(proclib);
```

The NOWD option runs PROC REPORT without the REPORT window and sends its output to the SAS procedure output. HEADLINE underlines the column headers. HEADSKIP writes a blank line beneath the underlining that HEADLINE writes. SPLIT= defines the split character as an asterisk (*) because the default split character (/) is part of the name of a department.

```
proc report data=grocery nowd
             headline
             headskip
             split='*';
```

Department and Sales are separated by a comma in the COLUMN statement, so they collectively determine the contents of the column that they define. Each item generates a header, but the header for Sales is set to blank in its definition. Because Sales is an analysis variable, its values fill the cells created by these two variables.

```
column sector manager department,sales perish;
```

In this report, Sector and Manager are group variables. Each detail row of the report consolidates the information for all observations with the same values of the group variables. FORMAT= specifies the formats to use in the report. Text in quotation marks in the DEFINE statements specifies column headers. These statements illustrate two ways to write a blank line in a column header. `'Sector' ''` writes a blank line because each quoted string is a line of the column header. The two adjacent quotation marks write a blank line for the second line of the header. `'Manager* '` writes a blank line because the split character (*) starts a new line of the header. That line contains only a blank.

```
define sector / group format=$sctrfmt. 'Sector' '';
define manager / group format=$mgrfmt. 'Manager* ';
```

PROC REPORT creates a column and a column header for each formatted value of the across variable Department. PROC REPORT orders the columns by these values. PROC REPORT also generates a column header that spans all these columns. Quoted text in the DEFINE statement for Department customizes this header. In traditional (monospace) SAS output, PROC REPORT expands the header with underscores to fill all columns created by the across variable. Sales is an analysis variable that is used to calculate the sum statistic. In each case, the value of Sales is the sum of Sales for all observations in one department in one group. (In this case, the value represents a single observation.)

```
define department / across format=$deptfmt. '_Department_';
define sales / analysis sum format=dollar11.2 ' ';
```

The COMPUTED option indicates that PROC REPORT must compute values for Perish. You compute the variable's values in a compute block associated with Perish.

```
define perish / computed format=dollar11.2
                'Perishable*Total';
```

This BREAK statement creates a default summary after the last row for each value of Manager. The only option in use is SKIP, which writes a blank line. You can use this technique to double-space in many reports that contains a group or order variable.

```
break after manager / skip;
```

This compute block computes the value of Perish from the values for the Meat/Dairy department and the Produce department. Because the variables Sales and Department collectively define these columns, there is no way to identify the values to PROC REPORT by name. Therefore, the assignment statement uses column numbers to unambiguously specify the values to use. Each time PROC REPORT needs a value for Perish, it sums the values in the third and fourth columns of that row of the report.

```
compute perish;
   perish=_c3_+_c4_;
endcomp;
```

This compute block creates a customized summary at the end of the report. The first LINE statement writes 57 hyphens (-) starting in column 4. Subsequent LINE statements write the quoted text in the specified columns and the values of the variables _C3_, _C4_, and _C5_ with the DOLLAR11.2 format.

```
compute after;
   line @4 57*'-';
   line @4 '|   Combined sales for meat and dairy : '
        @46 _c3_ dollar11.2 '    |';
   line @4 '|   Combined sales for produce : '
        @46 _c4_ dollar11.2 '    |';
   line @4 '|' @60 '|';
   line @4 '|   Combined sales for all perishables: '
        @46 _c5_ dollar11.2 '    |';
   line @4 57*'-';
endcomp;
```

The WHERE statement selects for the report only the observations for departments **p1** and **p2** in stores in the northeast or northwest sector. The TITLE statement specifies the title.

```
where sector contains 'n'
      and (department='p1' or department='p2');
   title "Sales Figures for Perishables in Northern Sectors";
run;
```

Output

```
     Sales Figures for Perishables in Northern Sectors          1
                          _____Department_____
                                                  Perishable
     Sector     Manager    Meat/Dairy    Produce      Total

     -----------------------------------------------------------

     Northeast  Alomar      $190.00      $86.00    $276.00

                Andrews     $300.00     $125.00    $425.00

     Northwest  Brown       $250.00      $73.00    $323.00

                Pelfrey     $205.00      $76.00    $281.00

                Reveiz      $600.00      $30.00    $630.00

     -----------------------------------------------------------
    |  Combined sales for meat and dairy :    $1,545.00         |
    |  Combined sales for produce :             $390.00         |
    |                                                           |
    |  Combined sales for all perishables:    $1,935.00         |
     -----------------------------------------------------------
```

Example 6: Displaying Multiple Statistics for One Variable

Procedure features:
  PROC REPORT statement options:

  LS=
  PS=
  COLUMN statement:

  specifying statistics for stacked variables
  DEFINE statement options:

  FORMAT=
  GROUP
  ID
Data set: GROCERY on page 959
Formats: $MGRFMT. on page 960

The report in this example displays six statistics for the sales for each manager's store. The output is too wide to fit all the columns on one page, so three of the statistics appear on the second page of the report. In order to make it easy to associate the statistics on the second page with their group, the report repeats the values of Manager and Sector on every page of the report.

Program

```
libname proclib 'SAS-data-library';
```

```
options nodate pageno=1 linesize=80 pagesize=60
        fmtsearch=(proclib);
```

The NOWD option runs PROC REPORT without the REPORT window and sends its output to the SAS procedure output. HEADLINE underlines all column headers and the spaces between them at the top of each page of the report. HEADSKIP writes a blank line beneath the underlining that HEADLINE writes. LS= sets the line size for the report to 66, and PS= sets the page size to 18.

```
proc report data=grocery nowd headline headskip
            ls=66 ps=18;
```

This COLUMN statement creates a column for Sector, Manager, and each of the six statistics associated with Sales.

```
column sector manager (Sum Min Max Range Mean Std),sales;
```

ID specifies that Manager is an ID variable. An ID variable and all columns to its left appear at the left of every page of a report. In this report, Sector and Manager are group variables. Each detail row of the report consolidates the information for all observations with the same values of the group variables. FORMAT= specifies the formats to use in the report.

```
define manager / group format=$mgrfmt. id;
define sector / group format=$sctrfmt.;
define sales / format=dollar11.2 ;
```

The TITLE statement specifies a title for the report.

```
    title 'Sales Statistics for All Sectors';
run;
```

Output

```
                    Sales Statistics for All Sectors                1

                              Sum          Min          Max
         Sector    Manager    Sales        Sales        Sales
         -------------------------------------------------------------

         Northeast Alomar      $786.00      $86.00      $420.00
                   Andrews   $1,045.00     $125.00      $420.00
         Northwest Brown       $598.00      $45.00      $250.00
                   Pelfrey     $746.00      $45.00      $420.00
                   Reveiz    $1,110.00      $30.00      $600.00
         Southeast Jones       $630.00      $40.00      $300.00
                   Smith       $350.00      $50.00      $120.00
         Southwest Adams       $695.00      $40.00      $350.00
                   Taylor      $353.00      $50.00      $130.00
```

```
                Sales Statistics for All Sectors                 2

                              Range        Mean         Std
        Sector    Manager     Sales        Sales        Sales
        -------------------------------------------------------

        Northeast Alomar     $334.00      $196.50      $156.57
                  Andrews    $295.00      $261.25      $127.83
        Northwest Brown      $205.00      $149.50      $105.44
                  Pelfrey    $375.00      $186.50      $170.39
                  Reveiz     $570.00      $277.50      $278.61
        Southeast Jones      $260.00      $157.50      $123.39
                  Smith       $70.00       $87.50       $29.86
        Southwest Adams      $310.00      $173.75      $141.86
                  Taylor      $80.00       $88.25       $42.65
```

Example 7: Storing and Reusing a Report Definition

Procedure features:
   PROC REPORT statement options:

   NAMED
   OUTREPT=
   REPORT=
   WRAP

Other features:
   TITLE statement

   WHERE statement

Data set: GROCERY on page 959

Formats: $SCTRFMT., $MGRFMT. and $DEPTFMT. on page 960

The first PROC REPORT step in this example creates a report that displays one value from each column of the report, using two rows to do so, before displaying another value from the first column. (By default, PROC REPORT displays values for only as many columns as it can fit on one page. It fills a page with values for these columns before starting to display values for the remaining columns on the next page.)

Each item in the report is identified in the body of the report rather than in a column header.

The report definition created by the first PROC REPORT step is stored in a catalog entry. The second PROC REPORT step uses it to create a similar report for a different sector of the city.

Program to Store a Report Definition

```
libname proclib 'SAS-data-library';


options nodate pageno=1 linesize=80 pagesize=60
       fmtsearch=(proclib);
```

The NOWD option runs PROC REPORT without the REPORT window and sends its output to the SAS procedure output. NAMED writes *name=* in front of each value in the report, where *name=* is the column header for the value. When you use NAMED, PROC REPORT suppresses the display of column headers at the top of each page.

```
proc report data=grocery nowd
            named
            wrap
            ls=64 ps=36
            outrept=proclib.reports.namewrap;
```

The report contains a column for Sector, Manager, Department, and Sales.

```
column sector manager department sales;
```

Because no usage is specified in the DEFINE statements, PROC REPORT uses the defaults. The character variables (Sector, Manager, and Department) are display variables. Sales is an analysis variable that is used to calculate the sum statistic. FORMAT= specifies the formats to use in the report.

```
define sector / format=$sctrfmt.;
define manager / format=$mgrfmt.;
define department / format=$deptfmt.;
define sales / format=dollar11.2;
```

A report definition may differ from the SAS program that creates the report. In particular, PROC REPORT stores neither WHERE statements nor TITLE statements.

```
    where manager='1';
    title "Sales Figures for Smith on &sysdate";
run;
```

Output

This is the output from the first PROC REPORT step, which creates the report definition.

```
            Sales Figures for Smith on 01OCT98              1

Sector=Southeast  Manager=Smith    Department=Paper
Sales=      $50.00
Sector=Southeast  Manager=Smith    Department=Meat/Dairy
Sales=     $100.00
Sector=Southeast  Manager=Smith    Department=Canned
Sales=     $120.00
Sector=Southeast  Manager=Smith    Department=Produce
Sales=      $80.00
```

Program to Use a Report Definition

REPORT= uses the report definition stored in PROCLIB.REPORTS.NAMEWRAP to produce the report. The second report differs from the first one because it uses different WHERE and TITLE statements.

```
options nodate pageno=1 fmtsearch=(proclib);
proc report data=grocery report=proclib.reports.namewrap
            nowd;
   where sector='sw';
   title "Sales Figures for the Southwest Sector on &sysdate";
run;
```

Output

```
        Sales Figures for the Southwest Sector on 01OCT98        1

     Sector=Southwest   Manager=Taylor    Department=Paper
     Sales=      $53.00
     Sector=Southwest   Manager=Taylor    Department=Meat/Dairy
     Sales=     $130.00
     Sector=Southwest   Manager=Taylor    Department=Canned
     Sales=     $120.00
     Sector=Southwest   Manager=Taylor    Department=Produce
     Sales=      $50.00
     Sector=Southwest   Manager=Adams     Department=Paper
     Sales=      $40.00
     Sector=Southwest   Manager=Adams     Department=Meat/Dairy
     Sales=     $350.00
     Sector=Southwest   Manager=Adams     Department=Canned
     Sales=     $225.00
     Sector=Southwest   Manager=Adams     Department=Produce
     Sales=      $80.00
```

Example 8: Condensing a Report into Multiple Panels

Procedure features:
    PROC REPORT statement options:

        FORMCHAR=
        HEADLINE
        LS=
        PANELS=
        PS=
        PSPACE=

    BREAK statement options:

        SKIP

Other features:
    SAS system option FORMCHAR=

Data set: GROCERY on page 959

Formats: $MGRFMT. and $DEPTFMT. on page 960

The report in this example

□ uses panels to condense a two-page report to one page. Panels compactly present information for long, narrow reports by placing multiple rows of information side by side.

□ uses a default summary to place a blank line after the last row for each manager.

□ changes the default underlining character for the duration of this PROC REPORT step.

Program

```
libname proclib 'SAS-data-library';
```

```
options nodate pageno=1 linesize=80 pagesize=60
        fmtsearch=(proclib);
```

The NOWD option runs PROC REPORT without the REPORT window and sends its output to the SAS procedure output. HEADLINE underlines all column headers and the spaces between them at the top of each panel of the report. FORMCHAR= sets the value of the second formatting character (the one that HEADLINE uses) to the tilde (~). Therefore, the tilde underlines the column headers in the output. HEADSKIP writes a blank line beneath the underlining that HEADLINE writes. LS= sets the line size for the report to 64, and PS= sets the page size to 18. PANELS= creates a multipanel report. Specifying PANELS=99 ensures that PROC REPORT fits as many panels as possible on one page. PSPACE=8 places 8 spaces between panels.

```
proc report data=grocery nowd headline
            formchar(2)='~'
            panels=99 pspace=6
            ls=64 ps=18;
```

The report contains a column for Manager, Department, and Sales.

```
column manager department sales;
```

The values of all variables with the ORDER option in the DEFINE statement determine the order of the rows in the report. In this report, PROC REPORT arranges the rows first by the value of Manager (because it is the first variable in the COLUMN statement) and then, within each value of Manager, by the values of Department. The ORDER= option specifies the sort order for a variable. This report arranges the values of Manager by their formatted values and arranges the values of Department by their internal values (np1, np2, p1, and p2). FORMAT= specifies the formats to use in the report.

```
define manager / order
                 order=formatted
```

```
                    format=$mgrfmt.;
define department / order
                order=internal
                format=$deptfmt.;
define sales / format=dollar7.2;
```

This BREAK statement produces a default summary after the last row for each manager. Because SKIP is the only option in the BREAK statement, each break consists of only a blank line.

```
break after manager / skip;
```

The WHERE statement selects for the report only the observations for stores in the northwest or southwest sector. The TITLE statement specifies a title for the report.

```
where sector='nw' or sector='sw';
title "Sales for the Western Sectors";
run;
```

Output

```
                Sales for the Western Sectors              1

Manager  Department   Sales      Manager  Department   Sales
~~~~~~~~~~~~~~~~~~~~~~~~~~~~      ~~~~~~~~~~~~~~~~~~~~~~~~~~~~
Adams    Paper        $40.00
         Canned      $225.00     Reveiz   Paper        $60.00
         Meat/Dairy  $350.00              Canned      $420.00
         Produce      $80.00              Meat/Dairy  $600.00
                                          Produce      $30.00
Brown    Paper        $45.00
         Canned      $230.00     Taylor   Paper        $53.00
         Meat/Dairy  $250.00              Canned      $120.00
         Produce      $73.00              Meat/Dairy  $130.00
                                          Produce      $50.00
Pelfrey  Paper        $45.00
         Canned      $420.00
         Meat/Dairy  $205.00
         Produce      $76.00
```

Example 9: Writing a Customized Summary on Each Page

Procedure features:
    BREAK statement options:
        OL
        PAGE
        SUMMARIZE
    COMPUTE statement arguments:

with a computed variable as *report-item*
BEFORE *break-variable*
AFTER *break-variable* with conditional logic
BEFORE _PAGE_
DEFINE statement options:
NOPRINT
LINE statement:

pointer controls
quoted text
repeating a character string
variable values and formats

Data set: GROCERY on page 959

Formats: $SCTRFMT., $MGRFMT., and $DEPTFMT. on page 960

The report in this example displays a record of one day's sales for each store. The rows are arranged so that all the information about one store is together, and the information for each store begins on a new page. Some variables appear in columns. Others appear only in the page header that identifies the sector and the store's manager.

The header that appears at the top of each page is created with the _PAGE_ argument in the COMPUTE statement.

Profit is a computed variable based on the value of Sales and Department.

The text that appears at the bottom of the page depends on the total of Sales for the store. Only the first two pages of the report appear here.

Program

```
libname proclib 'SAS-data-library';
```

```
options nodate pageno=1 linesize=64 pagesize=30
        fmtsearch=(proclib);
```

The NOWD option runs PROC REPORT without the REPORT window and sends its output to the SAS procedure output. NOHEADER in the PROC REPORT statement suppresses the default column headers.

```
proc report data=grocery nowd
            headline headskip;
```

The TITLE statement specifies a title for the report.

```
    title 'Sales for Individual Stores';
```

The report contains a column for Sector, Manager, Department, Sales, and Profit, but the NOPRINT option suppresses the printing of the columns for Sector and Manager. The page header (created later in the program) includes their values. To get these variable values into the page header, Sector and Manager must be in the COLUMN statement.

```
column sector manager department sales Profit;
```

In this report, Sector, Manager, and Department are group variables. Each detail row of the report consolidates the information for all observations with the same values of the group variables. Profit is a computed variable whose values are calculated in the next section of the program. FORMAT= specifies the formats to use in the report.

```
define sector / group noprint;
define manager / group noprint;
define profit / computed format=dollar11.2;
define sales / analysis sum format=dollar11.2;
define department / group format=$deptfmt.;
```

Profit is computed as a percentage of Sales. For nonperishable items, the profit is 40% of the sale price. For perishable items the profit is 25%. Notice that in the compute block you must reference the variable Sales with a compound name (Sales.sum) that identifies both the variable and the statistic that you calculate with it.

```
compute profit;
    if department='np1' or department='np2'
        then profit=0.4*sales.sum;
    else profit=0.25*sales.sum;
endcomp;
```

This compute block executes at the top of each page, after PROC REPORT writes the title. It writes the page header for the current manager's store. The LEFT option left-justifies the text in the LINE statements. Each LINE statement writes the text in quotation marks just as it appears in the statement. The LINE statement writes a variable value with the format specified immediately after the variable's name. The at sign (@) specifies the column to write in.

```
compute before _page_ / left;
    line sector $sctrfmt. ' Sector';
    line 'Store managed by ' manager $mgrfmt.;
    line ' ';
    line ' ';
    line ' ';
endcomp;
```

This BREAK statement creates a default summary after the last row for each manager. OL writes a row of hyphens above the summary line. SUMMARIZE writes the value of Sales (the only analysis or computed variable) in the summary line. The PAGE option starts a new page after each default summary so that the page header created in the preceding compute block always pertains to the correct manager.

```
break after manager / ol summarize page;
```

This compute block places conditional text in a customized summary that appears after the last detail row for each manager.

```
compute after manager;
```

The LENGTH statement assigns a length of 35 to the DATA step variable TEXT. In this particular case, the LENGTH statement is unnecessary because the longest version appears in the first IF/THEN statement. However, using the LENGTH statement ensures that even if the order of the conditional statements changes, TEXT will be long enough to hold the longest version.

```
length text $ 35;
```

You cannot use the LINE statement in conditional statements (IF-THEN, IF-THEN/ELSE, and SELECT) because it does not take effect until PROC REPORT has executed all other statements in the compute block. These IF-THEN/ELSE statements assign a value to TEXT based on the value of Sales.sum in the summary row. A LINE statement writes that variable, whatever its value happens to be.

```
        if sales.sum lt 500 then
            text='Sales are below the target region.';
        else if sales.sum ge 500 and sales.sum lt 1000 then
            text='Sales are in the target region.';
        else if sales.sum ge 1000 then
            text='Sales exceeded goal!';
        line ' ';
        line text $35.;
    endcomp;
    run;
```

Output

```
                   Sales for Individual Stores                    1

Northeast Sector
Store managed by Alomar



          Department          Sales         Profit
          ------------------------------------------

          Canned             $420.00        $168.00
          Meat/Dairy         $190.00         $47.50
          Paper               $90.00         $36.00
          Produce             $86.00         $21.50
                             ----------     ----------
                             $786.00        $196.50

          Sales are in the target region.
```

```
                    Sales for Individual Stores                      2

Northeast Sector
Store managed by Andrews



              Department          Sales        Profit
              ---------------------------------------

              Canned            $420.00       $168.00
              Meat/Dairy        $300.00        $75.00
              Paper             $200.00        $80.00
              Produce           $125.00        $31.25
                              -----------   -----------
                              $1,045.00       $261.25

                    Sales exceeded goal!
```

Example 10: Calculating Percentages

Procedure features:

    COLUMN statement arguments:

        PCTSUM

        SUM

        spanning heads

    COMPUTE statement options:

        CHAR

        LENGTH=

    DEFINE statement options:

        COMPUTED

        FLOW

        WIDTH=

    RBREAK statement options:

        OL

        SUMMARIZE

Other features:

    TITLE statement

Data set: GROCERY on page 959

Formats: $MGRFMT. and $DEPTFMT. on page 960

The summary report in this example shows the total sales for each store and the percentage that these sales represent of sales for all stores. Each of these columns has its own header. A single header also spans all the columns. This header looks like a title, but it differs from a title because it would be stored in a report definition. You must submit a null TITLE statement whenever you use the report definition, or the report will contain both a title and the spanning header.

The report includes a computed character variable, COMMENT, that flags stores with an unusually high percentage of sales. The text of COMMENT wraps across multiple rows. It makes sense to compute COMMENT only for individual stores.

Therefore, the compute block that does the calculation includes conditional code that prevents PROC REPORT from calculating COMMENT on the summary line.

Program

```
libname proclib 'SAS-data-library';
```

```
options nodate pageno=1 linesize=64 pagesize=60
        fmtsearch=(proclib);
```

The NOWD option runs PROC REPORT without the REPORT window and sends its output to the SAS procedure output. HEADLINE underlines all column headers and the spaces between them at the top of each page of the report. The null TITLE statement suppresses the title for the report.

```
proc report data=grocery nowd headline;
   title;
```

The COLUMN statement uses the text in quotation marks as a spanning header. The header spans all the columns in the report because they are all included in the pair of parentheses that contains the header. The COLUMN statement associates two statistics with Sales: Sum and Pctsum. The Sum statistic sums the values of Sales for all observations that are included in a row of the report. The Pctsum statistic shows what percentage that sum is of Sales for all observations in the report.

```
column ('Individual Store Sales as a Percent of All Sales'
        sector manager sales,(sum pctsum) comment);
```

In this report, Sector and Manager are group variables. Each detail row represents a set of observations that have a unique combination of formatted values for all group variables. Sales is, by default, an analysis variable used to calculate the Sum statistic. However, because statistics are associated with Sales in the column statement, those statistics override the default. FORMAT= specifies the formats to use in the report. Text between quotation marks specifies the column header.

```
define manager / group
                   format=$mgrfmt.;
define sector / group
                   format=$sctrfmt.;
define sales / format=dollar11.2
                 '';
define sum / format=dollar9.2
             'Total Sales';
```

The DEFINE statement for Pctsum specifies a column header, a format, and a column width of 8. The PERCENT. format presents the value of Pctsum as a percentage rather than a decimal. The DEFINE statement for COMMENT defines it as a computed variable and assigns it a column width of 20 and a blank column header. The FLOW option wraps the text for COMMENT onto multiple lines if it exceeds the column width.

```
define pctsum / 'Percent of Sales' format=percent6. width=8;
define comment / computed width=20 '' flow;
```

Options in the COMPUTE statement define COMMENT as a character variable with a length of 40.

```
compute comment / char length=40;
```

This compute block creates a comment that says "Sales substantially above expectations." for every store where sales exceeded 15% of the sales for all stores. Of course, on the summary row for the report, the value of Pctsum is 100. However, it is inappropriate to flag this row as having exceptional sales. The automatic variable _BREAK_ distinguishes detail rows from summary rows. In a detail row, the value of _BREAK_ is blank. The THEN statement executes only on detail rows where the value of Pctsum exceeds 0.15.

```
    if sales.pctsum gt .15 and _break_ = ' '
    then comment='Sales substantially above expectations.';
    else comment=' ';
endcomp;
```

This RBREAK statement creates a default summary at the end of the report. OL writes a row of hyphens above the summary line. SUMMARIZE writes the values of Sales.sum and Sales.pctsum in the summary line.

```
    rbreak after / ol summarize;
run;
```

Output

```
                                                                    1

           Individual Store Sales as a Percent of All Sales

                              Total    Percent
      Sector      Manager     Sales    of Sales
      -----------------------------------------------------------------
      Northeast   Alomar     $786.00      12%
                  Andrews  $1,045.00      17%    Sales substantially
                                                 above expectations.

      Northwest   Brown      $598.00       9%
                  Pelfrey    $746.00      12%
                  Reveiz   $1,110.00      18%    Sales substantially
                                                 above expectations.

      Southeast   Jones      $630.00      10%
                  Smith      $350.00       6%
      Southwest   Adams      $695.00      11%
                  Taylor     $353.00       6%
                           ---------    --------
                         $6,313.00      100%
```

Example 11: How PROC REPORT Handles Missing Values

Procedure features:
　　PROC REPORT statement options:
　　　　MISSING
　　COLUMN statement
　　　　with the N statistic
Other features:
　　TITLE statement
Formats:　$MGRFMT. on page 960

This example illustrates the difference between the way PROC REPORT handles missing values for group (or order or across) variables with and without the MISSING option. The differences in the reports are apparent if you compare the values of N for each row and compare the totals in the default summary at the end of the report.

Program with Data Set with No Missing Values

```
libname proclib 'SAS-data-library';


options nodate pageno=1 linesize=64 pagesize=60
        fmtsearch=(proclib);
```

GROCMISS is identical to GROCERY except that it contains some observations with missing values for Sector, Manager, or both.

```
data grocmiss;
   input Sector $ Manager $ Department $ Sales @@;
datalines;
se 1 np1 50      .  1 p1 100    se . np2 120    se 1 p2 80
se 2 np1 40     se 2 p1 300     se 2 np2 220    se 2 p2 70
nw 3 np1 60     nw 3 p1 600      . 3 np2 420    nw 3 p2 30
nw 4 np1 45     nw 4 p1 250     nw 4 np2 230    nw 4 p2 73
nw 9 np1 45     nw 9 p1 205     nw 9 np2 420    nw 9 p2 76
sw 5 np1 53     sw 5 p1 130     sw 5 np2 120    sw 5 p2 50
 .  . np1 40    sw 6 p1 350     sw 6 np2 225    sw 6 p2 80
ne 7 np1 90     ne . p1 190     ne 7 np2 420    ne 7 p2 86
ne 8 np1 200    ne 8 p1 300     ne 8 np2 420    ne 8 p2 125
;
```

The NOWD option runs PROC REPORT without the REPORT window and sends its output to the SAS procedure output. HEADLINE underlines all column headers and the spaces between them.

```
proc report data=grocmiss nowd headline;
```

The report contains a column for Sector, Manager, the N statistic, and Sales.

```
   column sector manager N sales;
```

In this report, Sector and Manager are group variables. Sales is, by default, an analysis variable used to calculate the Sum statistic. Each detail row represents a set of observations that have a unique combination of formatted values for all group variables. The value of Sales in each detail row is the sum of Sales for all observations in the group. In this PROC REPORT step, the procedure does not include observations with a missing value for the group variable. FORMAT= specifies formats to use in the report.

```
   define sector / group format=$sctrfmt.;
   define manager / group format=$mgrfmt.;
   define sales / format=dollar9.2;
```

This RBREAK statement creates a default summary at the end of the report. DOL writes a row of equals signs above the summary line. SUMMARIZE writes the values of N and Sales.sum in the summary line.

```
   rbreak after / dol summarize;
```

The TITLE statement specifies a title for the report.

```
   title 'Summary Report for All Sectors and Managers';
run;
```

Output with No Missing Values

```
           Summary Report for All Sectors and Managers             1

            Sector      Manager          N       Sales
            ----------------------------------------------
            Northeast   Alomar           3      $596.00
                        Andrews          4    $1,045.00
            Northwest   Brown            4      $598.00
                        Pelfrey          4      $746.00
                        Reveiz           3      $690.00
            Southeast   Jones            4      $630.00
                        Smith            2      $130.00
            Southwest   Adams            3      $655.00
                        Taylor           4      $353.00
                                     =========  =========
                                        31    $5,443.00
```

Program with Data Set with Missing Values

The MISSING option in the second PROC REPORT step includes the observations with missing values for the group variable.

```
proc report data=grocmiss nowd headline missing;
   column sector manager N sales;
   define sector / group format=$sctrfmt.;
   define manager / group format=$mgrfmt.;
   define sales / format=dollar9.2;
   rbreak after / dol summarize;
run;
```

Output with Missing Values

```
                                                                   3

            Sector      Manager          N       Sales
            ----------------------------------------------
                                         1       $40.00
                        Reveiz           1      $420.00
                        Smith            1      $100.00
            Northeast                    1      $190.00
                        Alomar           3      $596.00
                        Andrews          4    $1,045.00
            Northwest   Brown            4      $598.00
                        Pelfrey          4      $746.00
                        Reveiz           3      $690.00
            Southeast                    1      $120.00
                        Jones            4      $630.00
                        Smith            2      $130.00
            Southwest   Adams            3      $655.00
                        Taylor           4      $353.00
                                     =========  =========
                                        36    $6,313.00
```

Example 12: Creating and Processing an Output Data Set

Procedure features:

PROC REPORT statement options:

BOX

OUT=

DEFINE statement options:

ANALYSIS

GROUP

NOPRINT

SUM

Other features:

Data set options:

WHERE=

Data set: GROCERY on page 959

Formats: $MGRFMT. on page 960

This example uses WHERE processing as it builds an output data set. This technique enables you to do WHERE processing after you have consolidated multiple observations into a single row.

The first PROC REPORT step creates a report (which it does not display) in which each row represents all the observations from the input data set for a single manager. The second PROC REPORT step builds a report from the output data set. This report uses line-drawing characters to separate the rows and columns.

Program to Create Output Data Set

```
libname proclib 'SAS-data-library';
```

```
options nodate pageno=1 linesize=64 pagesize=60
        fmtsearch=(proclib);
```

The NOWD option runs PROC REPORT without the REPORT window and sends its output to the SAS procedure output. OUT= creates the output data set TEMP. The output data set contains a variable for each column in the report (Manager and Sales) as well as for the variable _BREAK_, which is not used in this example. Each observation in the data set represents a row of the report. Because Manager is a group variable and Sales is an analysis variable used to calculate the Sum statistic, each row in the report (and therefore each observation in the output data set) represents multiple observations from the input data set. In particular, each value of Sales in the output data set is the total of all values of Sales for that manager. The WHERE= data set option in the OUT= option filters those rows as PROC REPORT creates the output data set. Only those observations with sales that exceed $1,000 become observations in the output data set.

```
proc report data=grocery nowd
            out=temp( where=(sales gt 1000) );
```

```
     column manager sales;
```

Because the definitions of all report items in this report include the NOPRINT option, PROC REPORT does not print a report. However, the PROC REPORT step does execute and create an output data set.

```
     define manager / group noprint;
     define sales / analysis sum noprint;
  run;
```

Output Showing the Output Data Set

This is the output data set that PROC REPORT creates. It is used as the input DATA step in the next PROC REPORT step.

```
                           The Data Set TEMP                              1

     Manager       Sales  _____BREAK_____
     3             1110
     8             1045
```

Program That Uses the Output Data Set

DATA= specifies the output data set from the previous PROC REPORT step as the input data set for this report. The BOX option draws an outline around the output, separates the column headers from the body of the report, and separates rows and columns of data. The TITLE statements specify a title for the report.

```
  proc report data=temp box nowd;
     column manager sales;
     define manager / group format=$mgrfmt.;
     define sales / analysis sum format=dollar11.2;
     title 'Managers with Daily Sales';
     title2 'of over';
     title3 'One Thousand Dollars';
  run;
```

Report Based on the Output Data Set

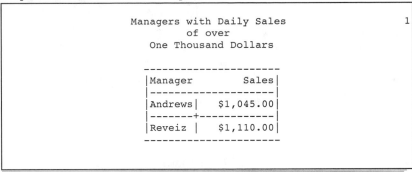

```
                    Managers with Daily Sales                    1
                            of over
                    One Thousand Dollars

              ---------------------
              |Manager       Sales|
              |-------------------|
              |Andrews|   $1,045.00|
              |-------+-----------|
              |Reveiz |   $1,110.00|
              ---------------------
```

Example 13: Storing Computed Variables as Part of a Data Set

Procedure features:
    PROC REPORT statement options:
      OUT=
    COMPUTE statement:
      with a computed variable as *report-item*
    DEFINE statement options:
      COMPUTED
Other features: CHART procedure
Data set: GROCERY on page 959
Formats: $SCTRFMT. on page 960

The report in this example
- creates a computed variable
- stores it in an output data set
- uses that data set to create a chart based on the computed variable.

Program that Creates the Output Data Set

```
libname proclib 'SAS-data-library';
```

```
options nodate pageno=1 linesize=64 pagesize=60
        fmtsearch=(proclib);
```

The NOWD option runs PROC REPORT without the REPORT window and sends its output to the SAS procedure output. OUT= creates the output data set PROFIT.

```
title;
proc report data=grocery nowd out=profit;
```

The report contains a column for Manager, Department, Sales, and Profit, which is not in the input data set. Because the purpose of this report is to generate an output data set to use in another procedure, the report layout simply uses the default usage for all the data set variables to list all the observations. DEFINE statements for the data set variables are unnecessary.

```
column sector manager department sales Profit;
```

The COMPUTED option tells PROC REPORT that Profit is defined in a compute block somewhere in the PROC REPORT step.

```
define profit / computed;
```

Profit is computed as a percentage of Sales. For nonperishable items, the profit is 40% of the sale price. For perishable items the profit is 25%. Notice that in the compute block, you must reference the variable Sales with a compound name (Sales.sum) that identifies both the variable and the statistic that you calculate with it.

```
    /* Compute values for Profit. */
compute profit;
    if department='np1' or department='np2' then profit=0.4*sales.sum;
    else profit=0.25*sales.sum;
endcomp;
run;
```

The Output Data Set

This is the output data set created by PROC REPORT. It is used as input for PROC CHART.

```
                        The Data Set PROFIT                       1

Sector     Manager    Department       Sales       Profit   _BREAK__
  se          1        np1               50           20
  se          1        p1               100           25
  se          1        np2              120           48
  se          1        p2                80           20
  se          2        np1               40           16
  se          2        p1               300           75
  se          2        np2              220           88
  se          2        p2                70         17.5
  nw          3        np1               60           24
  nw          3        p1               600          150
  nw          3        np2              420          168
  nw          3        p2                30          7.5
  nw          4        np1               45           18
  nw          4        p1               250         62.5
  nw          4        np2              230           92
  nw          4        p2                73        18.25
  nw          9        np1               45           18
  nw          9        p1               205        51.25
  nw          9        np2              420          168
  nw          9        p2                76           19
  sw          5        np1               53         21.2
  sw          5        p1               130         32.5
  sw          5        np2              120           48
  sw          5        p2                50         12.5
  sw          6        np1               40           16
  sw          6        p1               350         87.5
  sw          6        np2              225           90
  sw          6        p2                80           20
  ne          7        np1               90           36
  ne          7        p1               190         47.5
  ne          7        np2              420          168
  ne          7        p2                86         21.5
  ne          8        np1              200           80
  ne          8        p1               300           75
  ne          8        np2              420          168
  ne          8        p2               125        31.25
```

Program That Uses the Output Data Set

PROC CHART uses the output data set from the previous PROC REPORT step to chart the sum of Profit for each sector.

```
title;
options nodate pageno=1 linesize=80 pagesize=60
        fmtsearch=(proclib);
proc chart data=profit;
   block sector / sumvar=profit;
   format sector $sctrfmt.;
   format profit dollar7.2;
run;
```

Output from Processing the Output Data Set

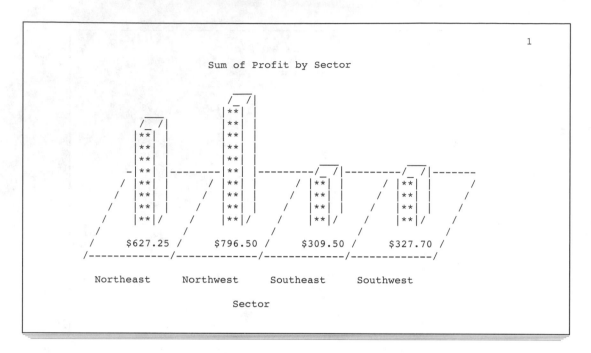

Example 14: Using a Format to Create Groups

Procedure features:
    DEFINE statement options:
        GROUP

Other features: FORMAT procedure

Data set: GROCERY on page 959

Formats: $MGRFMT. on page 960

This example shows how to use formats to control the number of groups that PROC REPORT creates. The program creates a format for Department that classifies the four departments as one of two types: perishable or nonperishable. Consequently, when Department is an across variable, PROC REPORT creates only two columns instead of four. The column header is the formatted value of the variable.

Program

```
libname proclib 'SAS-data-library';
```

```
options nodate pageno=1 linesize=64 pagesize=60
        fmtsearch=(proclib);
```

PROC FORMAT creates a format for Department. This variable has four different values in the data set, but the format has only two values.

```
proc format;
   value $perish 'p1','p2'='Perishable'
                 'np1','np2'='Nonperishable';
run;
```

The NOWD option runs the REPORT procedure without the REPORT window and sends its output to the SAS procedure output. HEADLINE underlines all column headers and the spaces between them at the top of each page of the report. HEADSKIP writes a blank line beneath the underlining that HEADLINE writes.

```
proc report data=grocery nowd
     headline
     headskip;
```

Department and Sales are separated by a comma in the COLUMN statement, so they collectively determine the contents of the column that they define. Because Sales is an analysis variable, its values fill the cells created by these two variables. The report also contains a column for Manager and a column for Sales by itself (which is the sales for all departments).

```
     column manager department,sales sales;
```

Manager is a group variable. Each detail row of the report consolidates the information for all observations with the same value of Manager. Department is an across variable. PROC REPORT creates a column and a column header for each formatted value of Department. ORDER=FORMATTED arranges the values of Manager and Department alphabetically according to their formatted values. FORMAT= specifies the formats to use. The empty quotation marks in the definition of Department specify a blank column header, so no header spans all the departments. However, PROC REPORT uses the formatted values of Department to create a column header for each individual department.

```
     define manager / group order=formatted
                   format=$mgrfmt.;
     define department / across order=formatted
               format=$perish. '';
```

Sales is an analysis variable used to calculate the Sum statistic. Sales appears twice in the COLUMN statement, and the same definition applies to both occurrences. FORMAT= specifies the format to use in the report. WIDTH= specifies the width of the column. Notice that the column headers for the columns that both Department and Sales create are a combination of the header for Department and the (default) header for Sales.

```
     define sales / analysis sum
               format=dollar9.2 width=13;
```

This COMPUTE statement begins a compute block that produces a customized summary at the end of the report. The LINE statement places the quoted text and the value of Sales.sum (with the DOLLAR9.2 format) in the summary. An ENDCOMP statement must end the compute block.

```
compute after;
   line ' ';
   line 'Total sales for these stores were: '
        sales.sum dollar9.2;
endcomp;
```

The TITLE statement specifies a title for the report.

```
title 'Sales Summary for All Stores';
run;
```

Output

```
                 Sales Summary for All Stores                    1


              Nonperishable      Perishable
   Manager          Sales            Sales            Sales
   ---------------------------------------------------------------


   Adams          $265.00          $430.00          $695.00
   Alomar         $510.00          $276.00          $786.00
   Andrews        $620.00          $425.00        $1,045.00
   Brown          $275.00          $323.00          $598.00
   Jones          $260.00          $370.00          $630.00
   Pelfrey        $465.00          $281.00          $746.00
   Reveiz         $480.00          $630.00        $1,110.00
   Smith          $170.00          $180.00          $350.00
   Taylor         $173.00          $180.00          $353.00

      Total sales for these stores were: $6,313.00
```

Example 15: Specifying Style Elements for HTML Output in the PROC REPORT Statement

Procedure features: STYLE= option in the PROC REPORT statement

Other features: ODS HTML statement

Data set: GROCERY on page 959

Formats: $MGRFMT. and $DEPTFMT. on page 960

This example creates HTML files and sets the style elements for each location in the report in the PROC REPORT statement.

Program

```
libname proclib 'SAS-data-library';
```

```
options nodate fmtsearch=(proclib);
```

The ODS HTML statement produces output that is written in HTML. The output from PROC REPORT goes to the body file.

```
ods html body='external-file';
```

The NOWD option runs PROC REPORT without the REPORT window. In this case, SAS writes the output to both the traditional procedure output and to the HTML body file.

```
proc report data=grocery nowd headline headskip
```

This STYLE= option sets the style element for the structural part of the report. Because no style element is specified, PROC REPORT uses all the style attributes of the default style element for this location except for CELLSPACING=, BORDERWIDTH=, and BORDERCOLOR=.

```
style(report)=[cellspacing=5 borderwidth=10 bordercolor=blue]
```

This STYLE= option sets the style element for all column headers. Because no style element is specified, PROC REPORT uses all the style attributes of the default style element for this location except for those that are specified here.

```
style(header)=[foreground=yellow font_face=lucida
               font_style=italic font_size=6]
```

This STYLE= option sets the style element for all the cells in all the columns. Because no style element is specified, PROC REPORT uses all the style attributes of the default style element for this location except for those that are specified here.

```
style(column)=[foreground=moderate brown
               font_face=helvetica font_size=4]
```

This STYLE= option sets the style element for all the LINE statement in all compute blocks. Because no style element is specified, PROC REPORT uses all the style attributes of the default style element for this location except for those that are specified here.

```
style(lines)=[foreground=white background=black font_face=lucida
              font_style=italic font_weight=bold font_size=5]
```

This STYLE= option sets the style element for all the default summary lines. Because no style element is specified, PROC REPORT uses all the style attributes of the default style element for this location except for those that are specified here.

```
style(summary)=[foreground=cx3e3d73 background=cxaeadd9
                font_face=helvetica font_size=3 just=r];
```

The report contains a column for Manager, Department, and Sales.

```
    column manager department sales;
```

In this report Manager is an order variable. PROC REPORT arranges the rows first by the value of Manager (because it is the first variable in the COLUMN statement). ORDER= specifies that values of Manager are arranged according to their formatted values. FORMAT= specifies the format to use for this variable. Text in quotation marks specifies the column headers.

```
    define manager / order
                     order=formatted
```

```
                                    format=$mgrfmt.
                                    'Manager';
```

In this report Department is an order variable. PROC REPORT arranges the rows first by the value of Manager (because it is the first variable in the COLUMN statement), then by the value of Department. ORDER= specifies that values of Department are arranged according to their internal values. FORMAT= specifies the format to use for this variable. Text in quotation marks specifies the column header.

```
    define department / order
                        order=internal
                        format=$deptfmt.
                        'Department';
```

The BREAK statement produces a default summary after the last row for each manager. SUMMARIZE writes the values of Sales (the only analysis or computed variable in the report) in the summary line. PROC REPORT sums the values of Sales for each manager because Sales is an analysis variable that is used to calculate the Sum statistic.

```
    break after manager / summarize;
```

The COMPUTE statement begins a compute block that produces a customized summary after each value of Manager. The LINE statement places the quoted text and the values of Manager and Sales.sum (with the formats $MGRFMT. and DOLLAR7.2) in the summary. An ENDCOMP statement must end the compute block.

```
    compute after manager;
        line 'Subtotal for ' manager $mgrfmt. 'is '
                sales.sum dollar7.2 '.';
    endcomp;
```

This COMPUTE statement begins a compute block that executes at the end of the report. The LINE statement writes the quoted text and the value of Sales.sum (with the DOLLAR7.2 format). An ENDCOMP statement must end the compute block.

```
    compute after;
        line 'Total for all departments is: '
                sales.sum dollar7.2 '.';
    endcomp;
```

The WHERE statement selects for the report only the observations for stores in the southeast sector.

```
    where sector='se';
```

The TITLE statement specifies the title.

```
    title 'Sales for the Southeast Sector';
run;
```

The ODS HTML statement closes the HTML destination.

```
ods html close;
```

HTML Body File

This report uses customized style elements to control things like font faces, font sizes, and justification, as well as the width of the border of the table and the width of the spacing between the cells. All these customizations are done in the PROC REPORT statement.

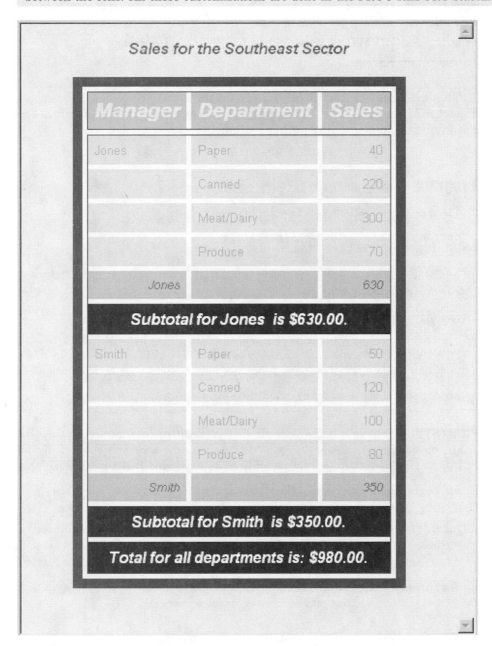

Example 16: Specifying Style Elements for HTML Output in Multiple Statements

Procedure features:

   STYLE= option in

        PROC REPORT statement
        CALL DEFINE statement

> COMPUTE statement
> DEFINE statement

Other features: ODS HTML statement

Data set: GROCERY on page 959

Formats: $MGRFMT. on page 960 and $DEPTFMT. on page 960

This example creates HTML files and sets the style elements for each location in the report in the PROC REPORT statement. It then overrides some of these settings by specifying style elements in other statements.

Program

```
libname proclib 'SAS-data-library';

options nodate fmtsearch=(proclib);
```

The ODS HTML statement produces output that is written in HTML. The output from PROC REPORT goes to the body file.

```
ods html body='external-file';
```

The NOWD option runs PROC REPORT without the REPORT window. In this case, SAS writes the output to both the traditional procedure output and to the HTML body file.

```
proc report data=grocery nowd headline headskip
```

This STYLE= option sets the style element for the structural part of the report. Because no style element is specified, PROC REPORT uses all the style attributes of the default style element for this location except for CELLSPACING= and BORDERWIDTH=.

```
style(report)=[cellspacing=5 borderwidth=10 bordercolor=blue]
```

This STYLE= option sets the style element for all column headers. Because no style element is specified, PROC REPORT uses all the style attributes of the default style element for this location except for those that are specified here.

```
style(header)=[foreground=yellow font_face=lucida
               font_style=italic font_size=6]
```

This STYLE= option sets the style element for all the cells in all the columns. Because no style element is specified, PROC REPORT uses all the style attributes of the default style element for this location except for those that are specified here.

```
style(column)=[foreground=moderate brown
               font_face=helvetica font_size=4]
```

This STYLE= option sets the style element for all the LINE statement in all compute blocks. Because no style element is specified, PROC REPORT uses all the style attributes of the default style element for this location except for those that are specified here.

```
style(lines)=[foreground=white background=black font_face=lucida
              font_style=italic font_weight=bold font_size=5]
```

This STYLE= option sets the style element for all the default summary lines. Because no style element is specified, PROC REPORT uses all the style attributes of the default style element for this location except for those that are specified here.

```
style(summary)=[foreground=cx3e3d73 background=cxaeadd9
               font_face=helvetica font_size=3 just=r];
```

The report contains a column for Manager, Department, and Sales.

```
column manager department sales;
```

In this report Manager is an order variable. PROC REPORT arranges the rows first by the value of Manager (because it is the first variable in the COLUMN statement). ORDER= specifies that values of Manager are arranged according to their formatted values. FORMAT= specifies the format to use for this variable. Text in quotation marks specifies the column headers.

```
define manager / order
               order=formatted
               format=$mgrfmt.
               'Manager'
```

The STYLE= option sets the foreground and background colors of the column header for Manager. The other style attributes for the column header will match those that were established for the HEADER location in the PROC REPORT statement.

```
style(header)=[foreground=white
               background=black];
```

In this report Department is an order variable. PROC REPORT arranges the rows first by the value of Manager (because it is the first variable in the COLUMN statement), then by the value of Department. ORDER= specifies that values of Department are arranged according to their internal values. FORMAT= specifies the format to use for this variable. Text in quotation marks specifies the column header.

```
define department / order
                  order=internal
                  format=$deptfmt.
                  'Department'
```

The STYLE= option sets the font of the cells in the column Department to **italic**. The other style attributes for the cells will match those that were established for the COLUMN location in the PROC REPORT statement.

```
style(column)=[font_style=italic];
```

The BREAK statement produces a default summary after the last row for each manager. SUMMARIZE writes the values of Sales (the only analysis or computed variable in the report) in the summary line. PROC REPORT sums the values of Sales for each manager because Sales is an analysis variable that is used to calculate the Sum statistic.

```
break after manager / summarize;
```

The COMPUTE statement begins a compute block that produces a customized summary at the end of the report. This STYLE= option specifies the style element to use for the text that is created by the LINE statement in this compute block. This style element switches the foreground and background colors that were specified for the LINES location in the PROC REPORT statement. It also changes the font style, the font weight, and the font size.

```
compute after manager
        / style=[font_style=roman font_size=3 font_weight=bold
          background=white foreground=black];
```

The LINE statement places the quoted text and the values of Manager and Sales.sum (with the formats $MGRFMT. and DOLLAR7.2) in the summary. An ENDCOMP statement must end the compute block.

```
line 'Subtotal for ' manager $mgrfmt. 'is '
      sales.sum dollar7.2 '.';
endcomp;
```

This compute block specifies a background color and a bold font for all cells in the Sales column that contain values of 100 or greater and that are not summary lines.

```
compute sales;
   if sales.sum>100 and _break_=' ' then
   call define(_col_, "style",
               "style=[background=yellow
                      font_face=helvetica
                      font_weight=bold]");
endcomp;
```

This COMPUTE statement begins a compute block that executes at the end of the report. The LINE statement writes the quoted text and the value of Sales.sum (with the DOLLAR7.2 format). An ENDCOMP statement must end the compute block.

```
compute after;
   line 'Total for all departments is: '
        sales.sum dollar7.2 '.';
endcomp;
```

The WHERE statement selects for the report only the observations for stores in the southeast sector.

```
where sector='se';
```

The TITLE statement specifies the title.

```
title 'Sales for the Southeast Sector';
run;
```

The ODS HTML statement closes the HTML destination.

```
ods html close;
```

HTML Body File

Display 32.1 HTML Body File

This report uses customized style elements to control things like font faces, font sizes, and justification, as well as the width of the border of the table and the width of the spacing between cells. Some of these customizations are done in the PROC REPORT statement. Others are set in subordinate statements.

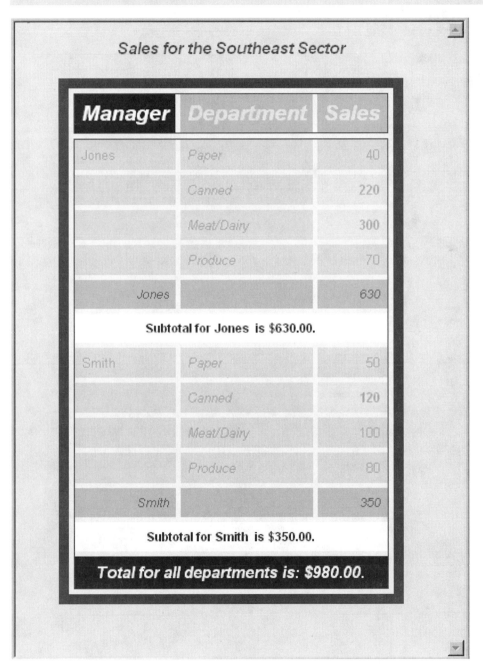

CHAPTER

33

The SORT Procedure

Overview

The SORT procedure sorts observations in a SAS data set by one or more character or numeric variables, either replacing the original data set or creating a new, sorted data set. PROC SORT by itself produces no printed output.

Output 33.1 on page 1005 shows the results of sorting a data set with the most basic form of a PROC SORT step. In this example, PROC SORT replaces the original data set, sorted alphabetically by last name, with a data set that is sorted by employee identification number. The statements that produce the output follow:

```
proc sort data=employee;
   by idnumber;
run;

proc print data=employee;
run;
```

Output 33.1   Observations Sorted by the Values of One Variable

```
                   The SAS System                        1

          Obs     Name          IDnumber

           1      Belloit         1988
           2      Wesley          2092
           3      Lemeux          4210
           4      Arnsbarger      5466
           5      Pierce          5779
           6      Capshaw         7338
```

Output 33.2 on page 1006 shows the results of a more complicated sort by three variables. The businesses in this example are sorted by town, then by debt from highest amount to lowest amount, then by account number. For an explanation of the program that produces this output, see Example 2 on page 1016.

Output 33.2   Observations Sorted by the Values of Multiple Variables

```
               Customers with Past-Due Accounts             1
              Listed by Town, Amount, Account Number

                                                    Account
     Obs     Company              Town        Debt   Number

      1      Paul's Pizza         Apex        83.00   1019
      2      Peter's Auto Parts   Apex        65.79   7288
      3      Watson Tabor Travel  Apex        37.95   3131
      4      Tina's Pet Shop      Apex        37.95   5108
      5      Apex Catering        Apex        37.95   9923
      6      Deluxe Hardware      Garner     467.12   8941
      7      Boyd & Sons Accounting Garner   312.49   4762
      8      World Wide Electronics Garner   119.95   1122
      9      Elway Piano and Organ  Garner    65.79   5217
     10      Ice Cream Delight    Holly Springs 299.98 2310
     11      Tim's Burger Stand   Holly Springs 119.95 6335
     12      Strickland Industries Morrisville  657.22 1675
     13      Pauline's Antiques   Morrisville   302.05 9112
     14      Bob's Beds           Morrisville   119.95 4998
```

Note: The sorting capabilities that are described in this chapter are available on all operating environments. In addition, if you use the HOST value of the SAS system option SORTPGM=, you may be able to use other sorting options available only in your operating environment. Refer to the SAS documentation for your operating environment for information on other sorting capabilities. For more information about the SAS system option SORTPGM=, see the chapter on SAS system options in *SAS Language Reference: Dictionary.* △

Procedure Syntax

Requirements: BY statement

Reminder: You can use the ATTRIB, FORMAT, LABEL, and WHERE statements. See Chapter 3, "Statements with the Same Function in Multiple Procedures," for details. You can also use any global statements as well. See Chapter 2, "Fundamental Concepts for Using Base SAS Procedures," for a list.

PROC SORT *<option(s)> <collating-sequence-option>*;

   BY <DESCENDING> *variable-1* <...<DESCENDING> *variable-n*>;

PROC SORT Statement

PROC SORT *<option(s)> <collating-sequence-option>*;

To do this	Use this option
Specify the input data set	DATA=
Create an output data set	OUT=
Specify the collating sequence	
Specify ASCII	ASCII
Specify EBCDIC	EBCDIC
Specify Danish	DANISH
Specify Finnish	FINNISH
Specify Norwegian	NORWEGIAN
Specify Swedish	SWEDISH
Specify a customized sequence	NATIONAL
Specify any of these collating sequences: ASCII, EBCDIC, DANISH, FINNISH, ITALIAN, NORWEGIAN, SPANISH, SWEDISH	SORTSEQ=
Specify the output order	
Reverse the order for character variables	REVERSE
Maintain the order within BY groups	EQUALS
Allow for variation within BY groups	NOEQUALS
Eliminate duplicate observations	
Delete observations with common BY values	NODUPKEY
Delete observations that have duplicate values	NODUPRECS
Specify the available memory	SORTSIZE=

To do this	Use this option
Force redundant sorting	FORCE
Reduce temporary disk usage	TAGSORT

Options

ASCII

sorts character variables using the ASCII collating sequence. You need this option only when you sort by ASCII on a system where EBCDIC is the native collating sequence.

Restriction: You can specify only one collating sequence option in a PROC SORT step.

See also: "Sorting Orders for Character Variables" on page 1012

Default: NO

DANISH
NORWEGIAN

sort characters according to the Danish and Norwegian national standard.

The Danish and Norwegian collating sequence is shown in Figure 33.1 on page 1011.

Operating Environment Information: For information about operating environment-specific behavior, see the SAS documentation for your operating environment. △

Restriction: You can specify only one collating sequence option in a PROC SORT step.

DATA= *SAS-data-set*

identifies the input SAS data set.

Main discussion: "Input Data Sets" on page 18

EBCDIC

sorts character variables using the EBCDIC collating sequence. You need this option only when you sort by EBCDIC on a system where ASCII is the native collating sequence.

Restriction: You can specify only one collating sequence option in a PROC SORT step.

See also: "Sorting Orders for Character Variables" on page 1012

EQUALS | NOEQUALS

specifies the order of the observations in the output data set. For observations with identical BY-variable values, EQUALS maintains the order from the input data set in the output data set. NOEQUALS does not necessarily preserve this order in the output data set.

Default: EQUALS

Interaction: When you use NODUPRECS to remove consecutive duplicate observations in the output data set, the choice of EQUALS or NOEQUALS can have an effect on which observations are removed.

Tip: Using NOEQUALS can save CPU time and memory.

FINNISH
SWEDISH

sort characters according to the Finnish and Swedish national standard. The Finnish and Swedish collating sequence is shown in Figure 33.1 on page 1011.

Operating Environment Information: For information about operating environment-specific behavior, see the SAS documentation for your operating environment. △

Restriction: You can specify only one collating sequence option in a PROC SORT step.

FORCE

sorts and replaces an indexed or subsetted data set when the OUT= option is not specified. Without the FORCE option, PROC SORT does not sort and replace an indexed data set because sorting destroys user-created indexes for the data set. When you specify FORCE, PROC SORT sorts and replaces the data set and destroys all user-created indexes for the data set. Indexes that were created or required by integrity constraints are preserved.

Tip: Since, by default, PROC SORT does not sort a data set according to how it is already sorted, you can use FORCE to override this behavior. This might be necessary if the SAS System cannot verify the sort specification in the data set option SORTEDBY=. For information about SORTEDBY=, see the section on SAS system options in *SAS Language Reference: Dictionary*.

Restriction: You cannot use PROC SORT with the FORCE option and without the OUT= option on data sets that were created with the Version 5 compatibility engine or with a sequential engine such as a tape format engine.

NATIONAL

sorts character variables using an alternate collating sequence, as defined by your installation, to reflect a country's National Use Differences. To use this option, your site must have a customized national sort sequence defined. Check with the SAS Installation Representative at your site to determine if a customized national sort sequence is available.

Restriction: You can specify only one collating sequence option in a PROC SORT step.

NODUPKEY

checks for and eliminates observations with duplicate BY values. If you specify this option, PROC SORT compares all BY values for each observation to those for the previous observation written to the output data set. If an exact match is found, the observation is not written to the output data set.

Operating Environment Information: If you use the VMS operating environment sort, the observation that is written to the output data set is not always the first observation of the BY group. △

See also: NODUPRECS

Featured in: Example 3 on page 1018

NODUPRECS

checks for and eliminates duplicate observations. If you specify this option, PROC SORT compares all variable values for each observation to those for the previous observation that was written to the output data set. If an exact match is found, the observation is not written to the output data set.

Alias: NODUP

Interaction: When you are removing consecutive duplicate observations in the output data set with NODUPRECS, the choice of EQUALS or NOEQUALS can have an effect on which observations are removed.

Interaction: The action of NODUPRECS is directly related to the setting of the SORTDUP data set option. When SORTDUP= is set to LOGICAL, NODUPRECS removes only the duplicate variables that are present in the input data set after a

DROP or KEEP operation. Setting SORTDUP=LOGICAL increases the number of duplicate records that are removed because it eliminates variables before record comparisons takes place. Also, setting SORTDUP=LOGICAL can improve performance because dropping variables before sorting reduces the amount of memory required to perform the sort. When SORTDUP= is set to PHYSICAL, NODUPRECS removes all duplicate variables in the data set, regardless if they have been kept or dropped. For more information about the data set option SORTDUP=, see *SAS Language Reference: Dictionary*.

Tip: Because NODUPRECS checks only consecutive observations, some nonconsecutive duplicate observations may remain in the output data set. You can remove all duplicates with this option by sorting on all variables.

See also: NODUPKEY

NOEQUALS
See EQUALS | NOEQUALS.

NORWEGIAN
See DANISH.

OUT=*SAS-data-set*
names the output data set. If *SAS-data-set* does not exist, PROC SORT creates it.

Default: Without OUT=, PROC SORT overwrites the original data set.

Tip :   You can use data set options with OUT=.

Featured in: Example 1 on page 1014

REVERSE
sorts character variables using a collating sequence that is reversed from the normal collating sequence.

Interaction: Using REVERSE with the DESCENDING option in the BY statement restores the sequence to the normal order.

See also: The DESCENDING option in the BY statement. The difference is that the DESCENDING option can be used with both character and numeric variables.

SORTSEQ= *collating-sequence*
specifies the collating sequence. The value of *collating-sequence* can be any one of the individual options in the PROC SORT statement that specify a collating sequence, or the value can be the name of a translation table, either a default translation table or one that you have created in the TRANTAB procedure. For an example of using PROC TRANTAB and PROC SORT with SORTSEQ=, see Example 6 on page 1311 . The available translation tables are

Danish

Finnish

Italian

Norwegian

Spanish

Swedish

To see how the alphanumeric characters in each language will sort, refer to Figure 33.1 on page 1011.

Restriction: You can specify only one collating sequence, either by SORTSEQ= or by one of the individual options that are available in the PROC SORT statement.

Figure 33.1   National Collating Sequences of Alphanumeric Characters

```
Danish:      0123456789ABCDEFGHIJKLMNOPQRSTUVWXYZÆØÅabcdefghijklmnopqrstuvwxyzæøå

Finnish:     0123456789ABCDEFGHIJKLMNOPQRSTUVWXYZÅÄÖabcdefghijklmnopqrstuvwxyzåäö

Italian:     0123456789AÀBCÇDEÉÈFGHIÌJKLMNOÒPQRSTUÙVWXYZaàbcçdeéèfghiìjklmnoòpqrstuùvwxyz

Norwegian:   0123456789ABCDEFGHIJKLMNOPQRSTUVWXYZÆØÅabcdefghijklmnopqrstuvwxyzæøå

Spanish:     0123456789AÁaáBbCcDdEÉeéFfGgHhIÍiíJjKkLlMmNnÑñOÓoóPpQqRrSsTtUÚuúÜüVvWwXxYyZz

Swedish:     0123456789ABCDEFGHIJKLMNOPQRSTUVWXYZÅÄÖabcdefghijklmnopqrstuvwxyzåäö
```

SORTSIZE=*memory-specification*
> specifies the maximum amount of memory that is available to PROC SORT.
> *memory-specification* is one of the following:

MAX
> specifies that all available memory can be used.

n
> specifies the amount of memory in bytes, where n is a real number.

nK
> specifies the amount of memory in kilobytes, where n is a real number.

nM
> specifies the amount of memory in megabytes, where n is a real number.

nG
> specifies the amount of memory in gigabytes, where n is a real number.
> Specifying the SORTSIZE= option in the PROC SORT statement temporarily overrides the SAS system option SORTSIZE=. For information about the system option, see the section on SAS system options in *SAS Language Reference: Dictionary*

> *Operating Environment Information:*   Some system sort utilities may treat this option differently. Refer to the SAS documentation for your operating environment. △

> **Default:**   the value of the SAS system option SORTSIZE=

> **Tip:**   This option can help improve sort performance by restricting the virtual memory paging that the operating environment controls. If PROC SORT needs more memory, it uses a temporary utility file. As a general rule, the value of SORTSIZE should not exceed the amount of physical memory that will be available to the sorting process.

SWEDISH
> See FINNISH.

TAGSORT
> stores only the BY variables and the observation numbers in temporary files. The BY variables and the observation numbers are called *tags*. At the completion of the sorting process, PROC SORT uses the tags to retrieve records from the input data set in sorted order.

> **Tip:**   When the total length of BY variables is small compared with the record length, TAGSORT reduces temporary disk usage considerably. However, processing time may be much higher.

BY Statement

Specifies the sorting variables.

Featured in: Example 1 on page 1014, Example 2 on page 1016, and Example 3 on page 1018

BY <DESCENDING> *variable-1* <...<DESCENDING> *variable-n*>;

Required Arguments

variable
specifies the variable by which PROC SORT sorts the observations. PROC SORT first arranges the data set by the values in ascending order, by default, of the first BY variable. PROC SORT then arranges any observations that have the same value of the first BY variable by the values in ascending order of the second BY variable. This sorting continues for every specified BY variable.

Option

DESCENDING
reverses the sort order for the variable that immediately follows in the statement so that observations are sorted from the largest value to the smallest value.

Featured in: Example 2 on page 1016

Concepts

Sorting Orders for Numeric Variables

For numeric variables, the smallest-to-largest comparison sequence is
1 SAS System missing values (shown as a period or special missing value)
2 negative numeric values
3 zero
4 positive numeric values.

Sorting Orders for Character Variables

PROC SORT uses either the EBCDIC or the ASCII collating sequence when it compares character values, depending on the environment under which the procedure is running.

EBCDIC Order

The operating environments that use the EBCDIC collating sequence include CMS and OS/390.

The sorting order of the English-language EBCDIC sequence is

blank . < (+ | & ! $ *); ¬ - / , % _ > ?: # @ '= "

a b c d e f g h i j k l m n o p q r ~ s t u v w x y z

{ A B C D E F G H I } J K L M N O P Q R \ S T

U V W X Y Z

0 1 2 3 4 5 6 7 8 9

The main features of the EBCDIC sequence are that lowercase letters are sorted before uppercase letters, and uppercase letters are sorted before digits. Note also that some special characters interrupt the alphabetic sequences. The blank is the smallest displayable character.

ASCII Order

The operating environments that use the ASCII collating sequence include

Macintosh

MS-DOS

OpenVMS

OS/2

PC DOS

UNIX and its derivatives

Windows

From the smallest to largest displayable character, the English-language ASCII sequence is

blank ! " # $ % & ' ( )* + , - . /0 1 2 3 4 5 6 7 8 9 : ; < = > ? @

A B C D E F G H I J K L M N O P Q R S T U V W X Y Z[\] ^_

a b c d e f g h i j k l m n o p q r s t u v w x y z { } ~

The main features of the ASCII sequence are that digits are sorted before uppercase letters, and uppercase letters are sorted before lowercase letters. The blank is the smallest displayable character.

Stored Sort Information

PROC SORT records the BY variables, collating sequence, and character set that it uses to sort the data set. This information is stored with the data set to help avoid unnecessary sorts.

Before PROC SORT sorts a data set, it checks the stored sort information. If you try to sort a data set the way that it is currently sorted, PROC SORT does not perform the sort and writes a message to the log to that effect. To override this behavior, use the FORCE option. If you try to sort a data set the way that it is currently sorted and you specify an OUT= data set, PROC SORT simply makes a copy of the DATA= data set.

To override the sort information that PROC SORT stores, use the _NULL_ value with the SORTEDBY= data set option. For information about SORTEDBY=, see the section on data set options in *SAS Language Reference: Dictionary*.

If you want to change the sort information for an existing data set, use the SORTEDBY= data set option in the MODIFY statement in the DATASETS procedure.

To access the sort information that is stored with a data set, use the CONTENTS statement in PROC DATASETS. For details, see Chapter 14, "The DATASETS Procedure," on page 329.

Integrity Constraints

Sorting the data set in place without OUT= preserves both referential and general integrity constraints, as well as any indexes that they may require. A sort using the OUT= option will not preserve any integrity constraints or indexes. For more information on integrity constraints, see the section on SAS files in *SAS Language Reference: Concepts*.

Results

Procedure Output

PROC SORT produces only an output data set. To see the output data set, you can use PROC PRINT, PROC REPORT, or another of the many available methods of printing in the SAS System.

Output Data Set

When you specify the OUT= option, PROC SORT creates a new data set that contains the sorted observations. Without OUT=, PROC SORT replaces the original data set with the sorted observations as soon as the procedure executes without errors. Even when a data set is replaced, there must be at least enough space in the data library for a second copy of the original data set.

You can also sort compressed data sets. If you specify a compressed data set as the input data set and omit the OUT= option, the input data set is sorted and remains compressed. If you specify an OUT= data set, the resulting data set is compressed only if you choose a compression method with the COMPRESS= data set option. For more information about the data set option COMPRESS=, see the section on SAS data set options in *SAS Language Reference: Dictionary*.

Note: If the SAS system option NOREPLACE is in effect, you cannot replace the original data set with the sorted version. You must either use the OUT= option or specify the SAS system option REPLACE in an OPTIONS statement. △

Examples

Example 1: Sorting by the Values of Multiple Variables

Procedure features:
    PROC SORT statement option:

OUT=
BY statement
Other features:
PROC PRINT

This example
- sorts the observations by the values of two variables
- creates an output data set for the sorted observations
- prints the results.

Program

```
options nodate pageno=1 linesize=80 pagesize=60;
```

The data set ACCOUNT contains the name of each business that owes money, the amount of money that it owes on its account, the account number, and the town where the business is located.

```
data account;
    input Company $ 1-22 Debt 25-30 AccountNumber 33-36
          Town $ 39-51;
    datalines;
Paul's Pizza            83.00 1019  Apex
World Wide Electronics  119.95 1122  Garner
Strickland Industries   657.22 1675  Morrisville
Ice Cream Delight       299.98 2310  Holly Springs
Watson Tabor Travel     37.95 3131  Apex
Boyd & Sons Accounting  312.49 4762  Garner
Bob's Beds              119.95 4998  Morrisville
Tina's Pet Shop         37.95 5108  Apex
Elway Piano and Organ   65.79 5217  Garner
Tim's Burger Stand      119.95 6335  Holly Springs
Peter's Auto Parts      65.79 7288  Apex
Deluxe Hardware         467.12 8941  Garner
Pauline's Antiques      302.05 9112  Morrisville
Apex Catering           37.95 9923  Apex
;
```

OUT= creates a new data set for the sorted observations.

```
proc sort data=account out=bytown;
```

The BY statement first sorts the observations alphabetically by town, then by company.

```
    by town company;
run;
```

PROC PRINT prints the data set BYTOWN.

```
proc print data=bytown;
```

The VAR statement specifies the variables and their order in the output.

```
    var company town debt accountnumber;
    title 'Customers with Past-Due Accounts';
    title2 'Listed Alphabetically within Town';
run;
```

Output

```
                        Customers with Past-Due Accounts                    1
                        Listed Alphabetically within Town


                                                            Account
        Obs   Company                  Town          Debt   Number

         1    Apex Catering            Apex          37.95    9923
         2    Paul's Pizza             Apex          83.00    1019
         3    Peter's Auto Parts       Apex          65.79    7288
         4    Tina's Pet Shop          Apex          37.95    5108
         5    Watson Tabor Travel      Apex          37.95    3131
         6    Boyd & Sons Accounting   Garner       312.49    4762
         7    Deluxe Hardware          Garner       467.12    8941
         8    Elway Piano and Organ    Garner        65.79    5217
         9    World Wide Electronics   Garner       119.95    1122
        10    Ice Cream Delight        Holly Springs 299.98   2310
        11    Tim's Burger Stand       Holly Springs 119.95   6335
        12    Bob's Beds               Morrisville   119.95   4998
        13    Pauline's Antiques       Morrisville   302.05   9112
        14    Strickland Industries    Morrisville   657.22   1675
```

Example 2: Reversing the Order of the Sorted Values

Procedure features:
   BY statement option:
      DESCENDING

Other features
   PROC PRINT

Data set: ACCOUNT on page 1015

This example

□ sorts the observations by the values of three variables

□ reverses the sorting order for one of the variables

□ prints the results.

Program

```
options nodate pageno=1 linesize=80 pagesize=60;
```

OUT= creates a new data set for the sorted observations.

```
proc sort data=account out=sorted;
```

The BY statement first sorts the observations alphabetically by town, then by descending values of amount owed, then by ascending values of the account number.

```
    by town descending debt accountnumber;
run;
```

PROC PRINT prints the data set SORTED.

```
proc print data=sorted;
```

The VAR statement specifies the variables and their order in the output.

```
    var company town debt accountnumber;
    title  'Customers with Past-Due Accounts';
    title2 'Listed by Town, Amount, Account Number';
run;
```

Output

Note that sorting last by AccountNumber puts the businesses in Apex with a debt of $37.95 in order of account number.

```
                        Customers with Past-Due Accounts                     1
                       Listed by Town, Amount, Account Number

                                                              Account
           Obs    Company               Town           Debt    Number

            1     Paul's Pizza          Apex           83.00    1019
            2     Peter's Auto Parts    Apex           65.79    7288
            3     Watson Tabor Travel   Apex           37.95    3131
            4     Tina's Pet Shop       Apex           37.95    5108
            5     Apex Catering         Apex           37.95    9923
            6     Deluxe Hardware       Garner        467.12    8941
            7     Boyd & Sons Accounting Garner       312.49    4762
            8     World Wide Electronics Garner       119.95    1122
            9     Elway Piano and Organ  Garner        65.79    5217
           10     Ice Cream Delight     Holly Springs 299.98    2310
           11     Tim's Burger Stand    Holly Springs 119.95    6335
           12     Strickland Industries Morrisville   657.22    1675
           13     Pauline's Antiques    Morrisville   302.05    9112
           14     Bob's Beds            Morrisville   119.95    4998
```

Example 3: Displaying the First Observation of Each BY Group

Procedure features:

PROC SORT statement option:

NODUPKEY

BY statement

Other features:

PROC PRINT

Data set: ACCOUNT   on page 1015

In this example, PROC SORT creates an output data set that contains only the first observation of each BY group. The NODUPKEY option removes an observation from the output data set when its BY value is identical to the previous observation's BY value. The resulting report contains one observation for each town where the businesses are located.

Program

```
options nodate pageno=1 linesize=80 pagesize=60;
```

NODUPKEY writes only the first observation of each BY group to the new data set TOWNS.

```
proc sort data=account out=towns nodupkey;
```

The BY statement sorts the observations by town.

```
    by town;
 run;
```

PROC PRINT prints the data set TOWNS.

```
 proc print data=towns;
```

The VAR statement specifies the variables and their order in the output.

```
    var town company debt accountnumber;
    title 'Towns of Customers with Past-Due Accounts';
 run;
```

Output

The output data set contains only four observations, one for each town in the input data set.

```
              Towns of Customers with Past-Due Accounts                 1

                                                         Account
    Obs    Town            Company               Debt    Number

     1     Apex            Paul's Pizza          83.00    1019
     2     Garner          World Wide Electronics 119.95  1122
     3     Holly Springs   Ice Cream Delight     299.98   2310
     4     Morrisville     Strickland Industries 657.22   1675
```

CHAPTER

34

The SQL Procedure

Overview

The SQL procedure implements Structured Query Language (SQL) for the SAS System. SQL is a standardized, widely used language that retrieves and updates data in tables and views based on those tables.

The SAS System's SQL procedure enables you to

- □ retrieve and manipulate data that are stored in tables or views.

- □ create tables, views, and indexes on columns in tables.

- □ create SAS macro variables that contain values from rows in a query's result.

□ add or modify the data values in a table's columns or insert and delete rows. You can also modify the table itself by adding, modifying, or dropping columns.

□ send DBMS-specific SQL statements to a database management system (DBMS) and to retrieve DBMS data.

Figure 34.1 on page 1023 summarizes the variety of source material that you can use with PROC SQL and what the procedure can produce.

Figure 34.1 PROC SQL Input and Output

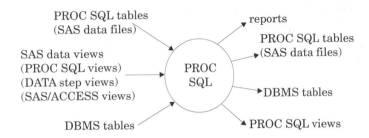

What Are PROC SQL Tables?

A PROC SQL *table* is synonymous with a SAS data file and has a member type of DATA. You can use PROC SQL tables as input into DATA steps and procedures.

You create PROC SQL tables from SAS data files, from SAS data views, or from DBMS tables using PROC SQL's Pass-Through Facility. The Pass-Through Facility is described in "Connecting to a DBMS Using the SQL Procedure Pass-Through Facility" on page 1095.

In PROC SQL terminology, a *row* in a table is the same as an *observation* in a SAS data file. A *column* is the same as a *variable*.

What Are Views?

A *SAS data view* defines a virtual data set that is named and stored for later use. A view contains no data but describes or defines data that are stored elsewhere. There are three types of SAS data views:

□ PROC SQL views

□ SAS/ACCESS views

□ DATA step views.

You can refer to views in queries as if they were tables. The view derives its data from the tables or views that are listed in its FROM clause. The data accessed by a view are a subset or superset of the data in its underlying table(s) or view(s).

A PROC SQL view is a SAS data set of type VIEW created by PROC SQL. A PROC SQL view contains no data. It is a stored query expression that reads data values from its underlying files, which can include SAS data files, SAS/ACCESS views, DATA step views, other PROC SQL views, or DBMS data. When executed, a PROC SQL view's output can be a subset or superset of one or more underlying files.

SAS/ACCESS views and DATA step views are similar to PROC SQL views in that they are both stored programs of member type VIEW. SAS/ACCESS views describe data in DBMS tables from other software vendors. DATA step views are stored DATA step programs.

You can update data through a PROC SQL or SAS/ACCESS view with certain restrictions. See "Updating PROC SQL and SAS/ACCESS Views" on page 1097. You can use all types of views as input to DATA steps and procedures.

Note: In this chapter, the term *view* collectively refers to PROC SQL views, DATA step views, and SAS/ACCESS views, unless otherwise noted. △

SQL Procedure Coding Conventions

Because PROC SQL implements Structured Query Language, it works somewhat differently from other base SAS procedures, as described here:

☐ You do not need to repeat the PROC SQL statement with each SQL statement. You need only to repeat the PROC SQL statement if you execute a DATA step or another SAS procedure between statements.

☐ SQL procedure statements are divided into clauses. For example, the most basic SELECT statement contains the SELECT and FROM clauses. Items within clauses are separated with commas in SQL, not with blanks as in the SAS System. For example, if you list three columns in the SELECT clause, the columns are separated with commas.

☐ The SELECT statement, which is used to retrieve data, also outputs the data automatically unless you specify the NOPRINT option in the PROC SQL statement. This means you can display your output or send it to a list file without specifying the PRINT procedure.

☐ The ORDER BY clause sorts data by columns. In addition, tables do not need to be presorted by a variable for use with PROC SQL. Therefore, you do not need to use the SORT procedure with your PROC SQL programs.

☐ A PROC SQL statement runs when you submit it; you do not have to specify a RUN statement. If you follow a PROC SQL statement with a RUN statement, the SAS System ignores the RUN statement and submits the statements as usual.

Procedure Syntax

Tip: Supports the Output Delivery System. (See Chapter 2, "Fundamental Concepts for Using Base SAS Procedures" for information on the Output Delivery System.)

Reminder: See Chapter 3, "Statements with the Same Function in Multiple Procedures," for details. You can also use any global statements as well. See Chapter 2, "Fundamental Concepts for Using Base SAS Procedures," for a list.

Note:

Regular type indicates the name of a component that is described in "Component Dictionary" on page 1056.

view-name indicates a SAS data view of any type.

PROC SQL *<option(s)>*;
   ALTER TABLE *table-name*
      <constraint-clause> <,constraint-clause>...>;
    <**ADD** column-definition *<,column-definition>...>*
    <**MODIFY** column-definition
      <,column-definition>...>

<**DROP** *column* <,*column*>...>;

CREATE <**UNIQUE**> **INDEX** *index-name*
   ON *table-name (column* <,*column*>...);

CREATE TABLE *table-name* (column-definition <,column-definition>...);
   (column-specification , ...<*constraint-specification* > ,...) ;

CREATE TABLE *table-name* **LIKE** *table-name*;

CREATE TABLE *table-name* **AS** query-expression
   <**ORDER BY** *order-by-item* <,*order-by-item*>...>;

CREATE VIEW *proc-sql-view* **AS** query-expression
   <**ORDER BY** *order-by-item* <,*order-by-item*>...>;
   <**USING** *libname-clause*<, *libname-clause*>...>;

DELETE
   FROM *table-name | proc-sql-view | sas / access-view* <**AS** *alias*>
      <**WHERE** sql-expression>;

DESCRIBE TABLE*table-name*<,*table-name*>... ;

DESCRIBE TABLE CONSTRAINTS *table-name* <, *table-name*>... ;

DESCRIBE VIEW *proc-sql-view* <,*proc-sql-view*>... ;

DROP INDEX *index-name* <,*index-name*>...
      FROM *table-name*;

DROP TABLE *table-name* <,*table-name*>...;

DROP VIEW *view-name* <,*view-name*>...;

INSERT INTO *table-name | sas / access-view | proc-sql-view* <(*column*<,*column*>...) >
   SET *column*=sql-expression
      <,*column*=sql-expression>...
      <**SET** *column*=sql-expression
      <,*column*=sql-expression>...>;

INSERT INTO *table-name | sas / access-view | proc-sql-view*<(*column*<,*column*>...)>
   VALUES (*value*<,*value*>...)
      <**VALUES** (*value* <,*value*>...)>...;

INSERT INTO *table-name | sas / access-view | proc-sql-view*
   <(*column*<,*column*>...)> query-expression;

RESET <*option(s)*>;

SELECT <DISTINCT> *object-item* <,*object-item*>...
      <**INTO** :*macro-variable-specification*
         <, :*macro-variable-specification*>...>
      FROM *from-list*
      <**WHERE** sql-expression>
      <**GROUP BY** *group-by-item*
         <,*group-by-item*>...>
      <**HAVING** sql-expression>
      <**ORDER BY** *order-by-item*
         <,*order-by-item*>...>;

UPDATE *table-name | sas / access-view | proc-sql-view* <**AS** *alias*>
   SET *column*=sql-expression
      <,*column*=sql-expression>...
      <**SET***column*=sql-expression
         <,*column*=sql-expression>...>
   <**WHERE** sql-expression>;

VALIDATE*query-expression*;

To connect to a DBMS and send it a DBMS-specific nonquery SQL statement, use this form:

PROC SQL;
    <**CONNECT TO** *dbms-name* <AS *alias*><
        <(*connect-statement-argument-1=value*
        ...<*connect-statement-argument-n=value*>)>>
        <(*dbms-argument-1=value*
        ...<*dbms-argument-n=value*>)>>;
    EXECUTE (*dbms-SQL-statement*)
        BY *dbms-name* | *alias*;
    <**DISCONNECT FROM** *dbms-name* | *alias*;>
  <**QUIT**;>

To connect to a DBMS and query the DBMS data, use this form:

PROC SQL;
    <**CONNECT TO** *dbms-name* <AS *alias*><
        <(*connect-statement-argument-1=value*
        ...<*connect-statement-argument-n=value*>)>>
        <(*dbms-argument-1=value*
        ...<*dbms-argument-n=value*>)>>;
    SELECT *column-list*
      FROM CONNECTION TO *dbms-name* | *alias*
        (*dbms-query*)
        optional PROC SQL clauses;
    <**DISCONNECT FROM** *dbms-name* | *alias*;>
  <**QUIT**;>

To do this	Use this statement
Modify, add, or drop columns	ALTER TABLE
Establish a connection with a DBMS	CONNECT
Create an index on a column	CREATE INDEX
Create a PROC SQL table	CREATE TABLE
Create a PROC SQL view	CREATE VIEW
Delete rows	DELETE
Display a definition of a table or view	DESCRIBE
Terminate the connection with a DBMS	DISCONNECT
Delete tables, views, or indexes	DROP
Send a DBMS-specific nonquery SQL statement to a DBMS	EXECUTE
Add rows	INSERT
Reset options that affect the procedure environment without restarting the procedure	RESET

To do this	Use this statement
Select and execute rows	SELECT
Query a DBMS	CONNECTION TO
Modify values	UPDATE
Verify the accuracy of your query	VALIDATE

PROC SQL Statement

PROC SQL *<option(s)>*;

To do this	Use this option
Control output	
Double-space the report	DOUBLE|NODOUBLE
Write a statement to the SAS log that expands the query	FEEDBACK|NOFEEDBACK
Flow characters within a column	FLOW|NOFLOW
Include a column of row numbers	NUMBER|NONUMBER
Specify whether PROC SQL prints the query's result	PRINT|NOPRINT
Specify whether PROC SQL should display sorting information	SORTMSG|NOSORTMSG
Specify a collating sequence	SORTSEQ=
Control execution	
Allow PROC SQL to use names other than SAS names	DQUOTE=
Specify whether PROC SQL should stop executing after an error	ERRORSTOP|NOERRORSTOP
Specify whether PROC SQL should execute statements	EXEC|NOEXEC
Restrict the number of input rows	INOBS=
Restrict the number of output rows	OUTOBS=
Restrict the number of loops	LOOPS=
Specify whether PROC SQL prompts you when a limit is reached with the INOBS=, OUTOBS=, or LOOPS= options	PROMPT|NOPROMPT

To do this	Use this option
Specify whether PROC SQL writes timing information to the SAS log	STIMER | NOSTIMER
Specify how PROC SQL handles updates when there is an interruption	UNDO_POLICY=

Options

DOUBLE | NODOUBLE
double-spaces the report.

Default: NODOUBLE

Featured in: Example 5 on page 1108

DQUOTE=ANSI | SAS
specifies whether PROC SQL treats values within double-quotes as variables or strings. With DQUOTE=ANSI, PROC SQL treats a quoted value as a variable. This enables you to use the following as table names, column names, or aliases:

□ reserved words such as AS, JOIN, GROUP, and so on.

□ DBMS names and other names not normally permissible in SAS.

The quoted value can contain any character.
With DQUOTE=SAS, values within quotes are treated as strings.

Default: SAS

ERRORSTOP | NOERRORSTOP
specifies whether PROC SQL stops executing if it encounters an error. In a batch or noninteractive session, ERRORSTOP instructs PROC SQL to stop executing the statements but to continue checking the syntax after it has encountered an error.

NOERRORSTOP instructs PROC SQL to execute the statements and to continue checking the syntax after an error occurs.

Default: NOERRORSTOP in an interactive SAS session; ERRORSTOP in a batch or noninteractive session

Interaction: This option is useful only when the EXEC option is in effect.

Tip: ERRORSTOP has an effect only when SAS is running in the batch or noninteractive execution mode.

Tip: NOERRORSTOP is useful if you want a batch job to continue executing SQL procedure statements after an error is encountered.

EXEC | NOEXEC
specifies whether a statement should be executed after its syntax is checked for accuracy.

Default: EXEC

Tip: NOEXEC is useful if you want to check the syntax of your SQL statements without executing the statements.

See also: ERRORSTOP on page 1028 option

FEEDBACK | NOFEEDBACK
specifies whether PROC SQL displays a statement after it expands view references or makes certain transformations on the statement.

This option expands any use of an asterisk (for example, **SELECT** *) into the list of qualified columns that it represents. Any PROC SQL view is expanded into the underlying query, and parentheses are shown around all expressions to further indicate their order of evaluation.

Default: NOFEEDBACK

FLOW<=*n* <*m*>>|NOFLOW

specifies that character columns longer than *n* are flowed to multiple lines. PROC SQL sets the column width at *n* and specifies that character columns longer than *n* are flowed to multiple lines. When you specify FLOW=*n m*, PROC SQL floats the width of the columns between these limits to achieve a balanced layout. FLOW is equivalent to FLOW=12 200.

Default: NOFLOW

INOBS=*n*

restricts the number of rows (observations) that PROC SQL retrieves from any single source.

Tip: This option is useful for debugging queries on large tables.

LOOPS=*n*

restricts PROC SQL to *n* iterations through its inner loop. You use the number of iterations reported in the SQLOOPS macro variable (after each SQL statement is executed) to discover the number of loops. Set a limit to prevent queries from consuming excessive computer resources. For example, joining three large tables without meeting the join-matching conditions could create a huge internal table that would be inefficient to execute.

See also: "Using Macro Variables Set by PROC SQL" on page 1096

NODOUBLE

See DOUBLE|NODOUBLE on page 1028.

NOERRORSTOP

See ERRORSTOP|NOERRORSTOP on page 1028.

NOEXEC

See EXEC|NOEXEC on page 1028.

NOFEEDBACK

See FEEDBACK|NOFEEDBACK on page 1028.

NOFLOW

See FLOW|NOFLOW on page 1029.

NONUMBER

See NUMBER|NONUMBER on page 1029.

NOPRINT

See PRINT|NOPRINT on page 1030.

NOPROMPT

See PROMPT|NOPROMPT on page 1030.

NOSORTMSG

See SORTMSG|NOSORTMSG on page 1030.

NOSTIMER

See STIMER|NOSTIMER on page 1030.

NUMBER|NONUMBER

specifies whether the SELECT statement includes a column called ROW, which is the row (or observation) number of the data as they are retrieved.

Default: NONUMBER

Featured in: Example 4 on page 1106

OUTOBS=*n*

restricts the number of rows (observations) in the output. For example, if you specify OUTOBS=10 and insert values into a table using a query-expression, the SQL procedure inserts a maximum of 10 rows. Likewise, OUTOBS=10 limits the output to 10 rows.

PRINT|NOPRINT

specifies whether the output from a SELECT statement is printed.

Default: PRINT

Tip: NOPRINT is useful when you are selecting values from a table into macro variables and do not want anything to be displayed.

PROMPT|NOPROMPT

modifies the effect of the INOBS=, OUTOBS=, and LOOPS= options. If you specify the PROMPT option and reach the limit specified by INOBS=, OUTOBS=, or LOOPS=, PROC SQL prompts you to stop or continue. The prompting repeats if the same limit is reached again.

Default: NOPROMPT

SORTMSG|NOSORTMSG

Certain operations, such as ORDER BY, may sort tables internally using PROC SORT. Specifying SORTMSG requests information from PROC SORT about the sort and displays the information in the log.

Default: NOSORTMSG

SORTSEQ=*sort-table*

specifies the collating sequence to use when a query contains an ORDER BY clause. Use this option only if you want a collating sequence other than your system's or installation's default collating sequence.

See also: SORTSEQ= option in *SAS Language Reference: Dictionary*.

STIMER|NOSTIMER

specifies whether PROC SQL writes timing information to the SAS log for each statement, rather than as a cumulative value for the entire procedure. For this option to work, you must also specify the SAS system option STIMER. Some operating environments require that you specify this system option when you invoke SAS. If you use the system option alone, you receive timing information for the entire SQL procedure, not on a statement-by-statement basis.

Default: NOSTIMER

UNDO_POLICY=NONE|OPTIONAL|REQUIRED

specifies how PROC SQL handles updated data if errors occur while you are updating data. You can use UNDO_POLICY= to control whether your changes will be permanent:

NONE

keeps any updates or inserts.

OPTIONAL

reverses any updates or inserts that it can reverse reliably.

REQUIRED

undoes all inserts or updates that have been done to the point of the error. In some cases, the UNDO operation cannot be done reliably. For example, when a program uses a SAS/ACCESS view, it may not be able to reverse the effects of the

INSERT and UPDATE statements without reversing the effects of other changes at the same time. In that case, PROC SQL issues an error message and does not execute the statement. Also, when a SAS data set is accessed through a SAS/ SHARE server and is opened with the data set option CNTLLEV=RECORD, you cannot reliably reverse your changes.

This option may enable other users to update newly inserted rows. If an error occurs during the insert, PROC SQL can delete a record that another user updated. In that case, the statement is not executed, and an error message is issued.

Default: REQUIRED

Note: Options can be added, removed, or changed between PROC SQL statements with the RESET statement. △

ALTER TABLE Statement

Adds columns to, drops columns from, and changes column attributes in an existing table. Adds, modifies, and drops integrity constraints from an existing table.

Restriction: You cannot use any type of view in an ALTER TABLE statement.

Restriction: You cannot use ALTER TABLE on a table that is accessed via an engine that does not support UPDATE processing.

Featured in: Example 3 on page 1104

ALTER TABLE *table-name*
    <*constraint-clause*> <, *constraint-clause*>...>;
  <**ADD** column-definition <,column-definition>...>
  <**MODIFY** column-definition
      <,column-definition>...>
  <**DROP** *column* <,*column*>...>;

where each *constraint-clause* is one of the following:

ADD <CONSTRAINT *constraint-name*> *constraint*

DROP CONSTRAINT *constraint-name*

DROP FOREIGN KEY *constraint-name* [Note: This is a DB2 extension.]

DROP PRIMARY KEY [Note: This is a DB2 extension.]

where *constraint* can be one of the following:

NOT NULL (*column*)

CHECK (*WHERE-clause*)

PRIMARY KEY (*columns*)

DISTINCT (*columns*)

UNIQUE (*columns*)

FOREIGN KEY (*columns*)
    REFERENCES *table-name*
    <ON DELETE *referential-action* > <ON UPDATE *referential-action*>

Arguments

column
names a column in *table-name*.

column-definition
See "column-definition" on page 1059.

constraint-name
specifies the name for the constraint being specified.

referential-action
specifies the type of action to be performed on all matching foreign key values.

RESTRICT
occurs only if there are matching foreign key values. This is the default referential action.

SET NULL
sets all matching foreign key values to NULL.

table-name
refers to the name of table containing the primary key referenced by the foreign key.

WHERE-clause
specifies a SAS WHERE-clause.

Specifying Initial Values of New Columns

When the ALTER TABLE statement adds a column to the table, it initializes the column's values to missing in all rows of the table. Use the UPDATE statement to add values to the new column(s).

Changing Column Attributes

If a column is already in the table, you can change the following column attributes using the MODIFY clause: length, informat, format, and label. The values in a table are either truncated or padded with blanks (if character data) as necessary to meet the specified length attribute.

You cannot change a character column to numeric and vice versa. To change a column's data type, drop the column and then add it (and its data) again, or use the DATA step.

Note: You cannot change the length of a numeric column with the ALTER TABLE statement. Use the DATA step instead. △

Renaming Columns

To change a column's name, you must use the SAS data set option RENAME=. You cannot change this attribute with the ALTER TABLE statement. RENAME= is described in the section on SAS data set options in *SAS Language Reference: Dictionary*.

Indexes on Altered Columns

When you alter the attributes of a column and an index has been defined for that column, the values in the altered column continue to have the index defined for them. If you drop a column with the ALTER TABLE statement, all the indexes (simple and composite) in which the column participates are also dropped. See "CREATE INDEX Statement" on page 1033 for more information on creating and using indexes.

Integrity Constraints

Use ALTER TABLE to modify integrity constraints for existing tables. Use the CREATE TABLE statement to attach integrity constraints to new tables. For more information on integrity constraints, see the section on SAS files in *SAS Language Reference: Concepts*.

CONNECT Statement

Establishes a connection with a DBMS that is supported by SAS/ACCESS software.

Requirement: SAS/ACCESS software is required. For more information on this statement, refer to your SAS/ACCESS documentation.

See also: "Connecting to a DBMS Using the SQL Procedure Pass-Through Facility" on page 1095

CONNECT TO *dbms-name* <AS *alias*> <(<*connect-statement-arguments*> <*database-connection-arguments*>)>;

Arguments

alias
    specifies an alias that has 1 to 32 characters. The keyword AS must precede *alias*. Some DBMSs allow more than one connection. The optional AS clause enables you to name the connections so that you can refer to them later.

connect-statement-arguments
    specifies arguments that indicate whether you can make multiple connections, shared or unique connections, and so on to the database. These arguments are optional, but if they are included, they must be enclosed in parentheses.

database-connection-arguments
    specifies the DBMS-specific arguments that are needed by PROC SQL to connect to the DBMS. These arguments are optional for most databases, but if they are included, they must be enclosed in parentheses.

dbms-name
    identifies the DBMS that you want to connect to (for example, ORACLE or DB2).

CREATE INDEX Statement

Creates indexes on columns in tables.

Restriction: You cannot use CREATE INDEX on a table accessed via an engine that does not support UPDATE processing.

CREATE <UNIQUE> INDEX *index-name*
  ON *table-name (column <, column>...)*;

Arguments

column
  specifies a column in *table-name*.

index-name
  names the index that you are creating. If you are creating an index on one column only, *index-name* must be the same as *column*. If you are creating an index on more than one column, *index-name* cannot be the same as any column in the table.

table-name
  specifies a PROC SQL table.

Indexes in PROC SQL

An *index* stores both the values of a table's columns and a system of directions that enable access to rows in that table by index value. Defining an index on a column or set of columns enables SAS, under certain circumstances, to locate rows in a table more quickly and efficiently. Indexes enable PROC SQL to execute the following classes of queries more efficiently:

☐ comparisons against a column that is indexed

☐ an IN subquery where the column in the inner subquery is indexed

☐ correlated subqueries, where the column being compared with the correlated reference is indexed

☐ join-queries, where the join-expression is an equals comparison and all the columns in the join-expression are indexed in one of the tables being joined.

SAS maintains indexes for all changes to the table, whether the changes originate from PROC SQL or from some other source. Therefore, if you alter a column's definition or update its values, the same index continues to be defined for it. However, if an indexed column in a table is dropped, the index on it is also dropped.

You can create simple or composite indexes. A *simple index* is created on one column in a table. A simple index must have the same name as that column. A *composite index* is one index name that is defined for two or more columns. The columns can be specified in any order, and they can have different data types. A composite index name cannot match the name of any column in the table. If you drop a composite index, the index is dropped for all the columns named in that composite index.

UNIQUE Keyword

The UNIQUE keyword causes the SAS System to reject any change to a table that would cause more than one row to have the same index value. Unique indexes guarantee that data in one column, or in a composite group of columns, remain unique for every row in a table. For this reason, a unique index cannot be defined for a column that includes NULL or missing values.

Managing Indexes

You can use the CONTENTS statement in the DATASETS procedure to display a table's index names and the columns for which they are defined. You can also use the

DICTIONARY tables INDEXES, TABLES, and COLUMNS to list information about indexes. See "DICTIONARY tables" on page 1062.

See the section on SAS files in *SAS Language Reference: Dictionary* for a further description of when to use indexes and how they affect SAS statements that handle BY-group processing.

CREATE TABLE Statement

Creates PROC SQL tables.

Featured in: Example 1 on page 1101 and Example 2 on page 1103

❶**CREATE TABLE** *table-name* (column-definition <,column-definition>...);

(column-specification ,...<*constraint-specification*> ,...) ;

> where *column-specification* is

> column-definition <*column-attribute*>

> where *constraint-specification* is

> **CONSTRAINT** *constraint-name constraint*

> *column-attribute* is one of the following:

> **UNIQUE**

> **DISTINCT** [Note: This is a DB2 extension. DISTINCT is the same as UNIQUE.]

> **NOT NULL**

> **CHECK** (*WHERE-clause*)

> **PRIMARY KEY**

> **REFERENCES** *table-name*
> > <**ON DELETE** *referential-action* > <**ON UPDATE** *referential-action* >

constraint is one of the following:

> **NOT NULL** (*column*)

> **CHECK** (*WHERE-clause*)

> **PRIMARY KEY** (*columns*)

> **DISTINCT** (*columns*)

> **UNIQUE** (*columns*)

> **FOREIGN KEY** (*columns*)
> > **REFERENCES** *table-name*
> > <ON DELETE *referential-action*> <ON UPDATE *referential-action*>

❷**CREATE TABLE***table-name* **LIKE** *table-name*;

❸**CREATE TABLE** *table-name* **AS** query-expression
> <**ORDER BY** *order-by-item* <,*order-by-item*>...>;

Arguments

column-definition
See "column-definition" on page 1059.

constraint-name
is the name for the constraint being specified.

order-by-item
See ORDER BY Clause on page 1053.

query-expression
See "query-expression" on page 1075.

referential-action
specifies the type of action to be performed on all matching foreign key values.

RESTRICT
occurs only if there are matching foreign key values. This is the default referential action.

SET NULL
sets all matching foreign key values to NULL.

table-name
is the name of the table containing the primary key referenced by the foreign key.

WHERE *clause*
specifies a SAS WHERE-clause.

Creating a Table without Rows

1 The first form of the CREATE TABLE statement creates tables that automatically map SQL data types to those supported by the SAS System. Use this form when you want to create a new table with columns that are not present in existing tables. It is also useful if you are running SQL statements from an SQL application in another SQL-based database.

2 The second form uses a LIKE clause to create a table that has the same column names and column attributes as another table. To drop any columns in the new table, you can specify the DROP= data set option in the CREATE TABLE statement. The specified columns are dropped when the table is created. Indexes are not copied to the new table.

Both of these forms create a table without rows. You can use an INSERT statement to add rows. Use an ALTER statement to modify column attributes or to add or drop columns.

Creating a Table from a Query Expression

3 The third form of the CREATE TABLE statement stores the results of any query-expression in a table and does not display the output. It is a convenient way to create temporary tables that are subsets or supersets of other tables.

When you use this form, a table is physically created as the statement is executed. The newly created table does not reflect subsequent changes in the underlying tables (in the query-expression). If you want to continually access the most current data, create a view from the query expression instead of a table. See "CREATE VIEW Statement" on page 1037.

Integrity Constraints

You can attach integrity constraints when you create a new table. To modify integrity constraints, use the ALTER TABLE statement. For more information on integrity constraints, see the section on SAS files in *SAS Language Reference: Concepts*.

CREATE VIEW Statement

Creates a PROC SQL view from a query-expression.

See also: "What Are Views?" on page 1023
Featured in: Example 8 on page 1116

CREATE VIEW *proc-sql-view* **AS** query-expression
  <ORDER BY *order-by-item* <,*order-by-item*>...>
    <USING *statement*<, *libname-clause*> ... > ;

where each *libname-clause* is one of the following:

LIBNAME *libref* <*engine*> '*SAS-data-library*' <*option(s)*> <*engine-host-option(s)*>

LIBNAME *libref* *SAS/ACCESS-engine-name* <*SAS/ACCESS-engine-connection-option(s)*> <*SAS/ACCESS-engine-LIBNAME-option(s)*>

Arguments

order-by-item
    See ORDER BY Clause on page 1053.

query-expression
    See "query-expression" on page 1075.

proc-sql-view
    specifies the name for the PROC SQL view that you are creating. See "What Are Views?" on page 1023 for a definition of a PROC SQL view.

Sorting Data Retrieved by Views

PROC SQL allows you to specify the ORDER BY clause in the CREATE VIEW statement. Every time a view is accessed, its data are sorted and displayed as specified by the ORDER BY clause. This sorting on every access has certain performance costs, especially if the view's underlying tables are large. It is more efficient to omit the ORDER BY clause when you are creating the view and specify it as needed when you reference the view in queries.

Note: If you specify the NUMBER option in the PROC SQL statement when you create your view, the ROW column appears in the output. However, you cannot order by the ROW column in subsequent queries. See the description of the NUMBER option on page 1030. △

Librefs and Stored Views

You can refer to a table name alone (without the libref) in the FROM clause of a CREATE VIEW statement if the table and view reside in the same SAS data library, as in this example:

```
create view proclib.view1 as
    select *
        from invoice
        where invqty>10;
```

In this view, VIEW1 and INVOICE are stored permanently in the SAS data library referenced by PROCLIB. Specifying a libref for INVOICE is optional.

Updating Views

You can update a view's underlying data with some restrictions. See "Updating PROC SQL and SAS/ACCESS Views" on page 1097.

Embedded LIBNAME Statements

The USING clause allows you to store DBMS connection information in a view by *embedding* the SAS/ACCESS LIBNAME statement inside the view. When PROC SQL executes the view, the stored query assigns the libref and establishes the DBMS connection using the information in the LIBNAME statement. The scope of the libref is local to the view, and will not conflict with any identically named librefs in the SAS session. When the query finishes, the connection to the DBMS is terminated and the libref is deassigned.

The USING clause must be the last clause in the SELECT statement. Multiple LIBNAME statements can be specified, separated by commas. In the following example, a connection is made and the libref ACCREC is assigned to an ORACLE database.

```
create view proclib.view1 as
    select *
        from accrec.invoices as invoices
        using libname accrec oracle
            user=username pass=password
            path='dbms-path';
```

For more information on the SAS/ACCESS LIBNAME statement, see the SAS/ACCESS documentation for your DBMS.

You can also embed a SAS LIBNAME statement in a view with the USING clause. This enables you to store SAS libref information in the view. Just as in the embedded SAS/ACCESS LIBNAME statement, the scope of the libref is local to the view, and it will not conflict with an identically named libref in the SAS session.

```
create view work.tableview as
    select * from proclib.invoices
        using libname proclib 'sas-data-library';
```

DELETE Statement

Removes one or more rows from a table or view that is specified in the FROM clause.

Restriction: You cannot use DELETE FROM on a table accessed via an engine that does not support UPDATE processing.

Featured in: Example 5 on page 1108

DELETE
   FROM *table-name* | *sas/access-view* | *proc-sql-view* <**AS** *alias*>
      <**WHERE**sql-expression>;

Arguments

alias
   assigns an alias to *table-name*, *sas/access-view*, or *proc-sql-view*.

sas/access-view
   specifies a SAS/ACCESS view that you are deleting rows from.

proc-sql-view
   specifies a PROC SQL view that you are deleting rows from.

sql-expression
   See "sql-expression" on page 1081.

table-name
   specifies the table that you are deleting rows from.

Deleting Rows Through Views

You can delete one or more rows from a view's underlying table, with some restrictions. See "Updating PROC SQL and SAS/ACCESS Views" on page 1097.

CAUTION:
   If you omit a WHERE clause, the DELETE statement deletes all the rows from the specified table or the table described by a view. △

DESCRIBE Statement

Displays a PROC SQL definition in the SAS log.

Restriction: PROC SQL views are the only type of view allowed in a DESCRIBE VIEW statement.

Featured in: Example 6 on page 1111

DESCRIBE TABLE *table-name* <,*table-name*>... ;

DESCRIBE VIEW *proc-sql-view* <,*proc-sql-view*>... ;

DESCRIBE TABLE CONSTRAINTS *table-name* <, *table-name*>... ;

Arguments

table-name
  specifies a PROC SQL table.

proc-sql-view
  specifies a PROC SQL view.

Details

  □ The DESCRIBE TABLE statement writes a CREATE TABLE statement to the
    SAS log for the table specified in the DESCRIBE TABLE statement, regardless of
    how the table was originally created (for example, with a DATA step). If
    applicable, SAS data set options are included with the table definition. If indexes
    are defined on columns in the table, CREATE INDEX statements for those indexes
    are also written to the SAS log.

    When you are transferring a table to a DBMS that is supported by SAS/
    ACCESS software, it is helpful to know how it is defined. To find out more
    information on a table, use the FEEDBACK option or the CONTENTS statement
    in the DATASETS procedure.

  □ The DESCRIBE VIEW statement writes a view definition to the SAS log. If you
    use a PROC SQL view in the DESCRIBE VIEW statement that is based on or
    derived from another view, you may want to use the FEEDBACK option in the
    PROC SQL statement. This option displays in the SAS log how the underlying
    view is defined and expands any expressions that are used in this view definition.
    The CONTENTS statement in DATASETS procedure can also be used with a view
    to find out more information.

  □ The DESCRIBE TABLE CONSTRAINTS statement lists the integrity constraints
    that are defined for the specified table(s).

DISCONNECT Statement

Ends the connection with a DBMS that is supported by a SAS/ACCESS interface.

Requirement: SAS/ACCESS software is required. For more information on this
statement, refer to your SAS/ACCESS documentation.

See also: "Connecting to a DBMS Using the SQL Procedure Pass-Through Facility" on
page 1095

DISCONNECT FROM *dbms-name* | *alias*;

Arguments

alias
specifies the alias that is defined in the CONNECT statement.

dbms-name
specifies the DBMS from which you want to end the connection (for example, DB2 or ORACLE). The name you specify should match the name that is specified in the CONNECT statement.

Details

□ An implicit COMMIT is performed before the DISCONNECT statement ends the DBMS connection. If a DISCONNECT statement is not submitted, implicit DISCONNECT and COMMIT actions are performed and the connection to the DBMS is broken when PROC SQL terminates.

□ PROC SQL continues executing until you submit a QUIT statement, another SAS procedure, or a DATA step.

DROP Statement

Deletes tables, views, or indexes.

Restriction: You cannot use DROP TABLE or DROP INDEX on a table accessed via an engine that does not support UPDATE processing.

DROP TABLE *table-name* <,*table-name*>...;

DROP VIEW *view-name* <,*view-name*>...;

DROP INDEX *index-name* <,*index-name*>...
    FROM *table-name*;

Arguments

index-name
specifies an index that exists on *table-name*.

table-name
specifies a PROC SQL table.

view-name
specifies a SAS data view of any type: PROC SQL view, SAS/ACCESS view, or DATA step view.

Details

□ If you drop a table that is referenced in a view definition and try to execute the view, an error message is written to the SAS log stating that the table does not exist. Therefore, remove references in queries and views to any table(s) and view(s) that you drop.

□ If you drop a table with indexed columns, all the indexes are automatically dropped. If you drop a composite index, the index is dropped for all the columns that are named in that index.

□ You cannot use the DROP statement to drop a table or view in an external database that is described by a SAS/ACCESS view.

EXECUTE Statement

Sends a DBMS-specific SQL statement to a DBMS that is supported by a SAS/ACCESS interface.

Requirement: SAS/ACCESS software is required. For more information on this statement, refer to your SAS/ACCESS documentation.

See also: "Connecting to a DBMS Using the SQL Procedure Pass-Through Facility" on page 1095 and the SQL documentation for your DBMS.

EXECUTE (*dbms-SQL-statement*)
   BY *dbms-name* | *alias*;

Arguments

alias
   specifies an optional alias that is defined in the CONNECT statement. Note that *alias* must be preceded by the keyword BY.

dbms-name
   identifies the DBMS to which you want to direct the DBMS statement (for example, ORACLE or DB2).

dbms-SQL-statement
   is any DBMS-specific SQL statement, except the SELECT statement, that can be executed by the DBMS-specific dynamic SQL.

Details

□ If your DBMS supports multiple connections, you can use the alias that is defined in the CONNECT statement. This alias directs the EXECUTE statements to a specific DBMS connection.

□ Any return code or message that is generated by the DBMS is available in the macro variables SQLXRC and SQLXMSG after the statement completes.

INSERT Statement

Adds rows to a new or existing table or view.

Restriction: You cannot use INSERT INTO on a table accessed via an engine that does not support UPDATE processing.

Featured in: Example 1 on page 1101

❶**INSERT INTO***table-name* | *sas* / *access-view* | *proc-sql-view*
    <(column<,column>...)><,user-name>...;

  SET *column*=sql-expression
      <,column=sql-expression>...
      <**SET** *column*=sql-expression
      <,column=sql-expression>...>;

❷**INSERT INTO** *table-name* | *sas* / *access-view* | *proc-sql-view* *<(column<,column>...)>*
  VALUES *(value <, value>...)*
      <**VALUES** *(value <, value>...)>*...;

❸**INSERT INTO** *table-name* | *sas* / *access-view* | *proc-sql-view*
    <(column<,column>...)> query-expression;

Arguments

column
  specifies the column into which you are inserting rows.

sas/access-view
  specifies a SAS/ACCESS view into which you are inserting rows.

proc-sql-view
  specifies a PROC SQL view into which you are inserting rows.

sql-expression
  See "sql-expression" on page 1081.

table-name
  specifies a PROC SQL table into which you are inserting rows.

value
  is a data value.

Methods for Inserting Values

1 The first form of the INSERT statement uses the SET clause, which specifies or alters the values of a column. You can use more than one SET clause per INSERT statement, and each SET clause can set the values in more than one column. Multiple SET clauses are not separated by commas. If you specify an optional list of columns, you can set a value only for a column that is specified in the list of columns to be inserted.

2 The second form of the INSERT statement uses the VALUES clause. This clause can be used to insert lists of values into a table. You can either give a value for

each column in the table or give values just for the columns specified in the list of column names. One row is inserted for each VALUES clause. Multiple VALUES clauses are not separated by commas. The order of the values in the VALUES clause matches the order of the column names in the INSERT column list or, if no list was specified, the order of the columns in the table.

3   The third form of the INSERT statement inserts the results of a query-expression into a table. The order of the values in the query-expression matches the order of the column names in the INSERT column list or, if no list was specified, the order of the columns in the table.

Note: If the INSERT statement includes an optional list of column names, only those columns are given values by the statement. Columns that are in the table but not listed are given missing values. △

Inserting Rows through Views

You can insert one or more rows into a table through a view, with some restrictions. See "Updating PROC SQL and SAS/ACCESS Views" on page 1097.

Adding Values to an Indexed Column

If an index is defined on a column and you insert a new row into the table, that value is added to the index. You can display information about indexes with

□   the CONTENTS statement in the DATASETS procedure. See "CONTENTS Statement" on page 346.

□   the DICTIONARY.INDEXES table. See "DICTIONARY tables" on page 1062 for more information.

For more information on creating and using indexes, see "CREATE INDEX Statement" on page 1033.

RESET Statement

Resets PROC SQL options without restarting the procedure.

Featured in: Example 5 on page 1108

RESET <*option(s)*>;

The RESET statement enables you to add, drop, or change the options in PROC SQL without restarting the procedure. See "PROC SQL Statement" on page 1027 for a description of the options.

SELECT Statement

Selects columns and rows of data from tables and views.

See also: "table-expression" on page 1094, "query-expression" on page 1075

SELECT <DISTINCT> *object-item* <,*object-item*>...
　　<**INTO** :*macro-variable-specification*
　　　　<, :*macro-variable-specification*>...>
　　FROM *from-list*
　　<**WHERE** sql-expression>
　　<**GROUP BY** *group-by-item*
　　　　<, *group-by-item*>...>
　　<**HAVING** sql-expression>
　　<**ORDER BY** *order-by-item*
　　　　<,*order-by-item*>...>;

SELECT Clause

Lists the columns that will appear in the output.

See Also: "column-definition" on page 1059

Featured in: Example 1 on page 1101 and Example 2 on page 1103

SELECT <DISTINCT> *object-item* <,*object-item*>...

□ *object-item* is one of the following:

　　*

　　case-expression <**AS** *alias*>

　　column-name <**AS** *alias*>
　　　　<column-modifier <column-modifier>...>

　　sql-expression <**AS** *alias*>
　　　　<column-modifier <column-modifier>...>

　　*table-name.**

　　*table-alias.**

　　*view-name.**

　　*view-alias.**

Arguments

case-expression
　　See "CASE expression" on page 1058.

column-modifier
　　See "column-modifier" on page 1060.

column-name
　　See "column-name" on page 1061.

DISTINCT
　　eliminates duplicate rows.

Featured in: Example 13 on page 1126

sql-expression
See "sql-expression" on page 1081.

table-alias
is an alias for a PROC SQL table.

table-name
specifies a PROC SQL table.

view-name
specifies any type of SAS data view.

view-alias
specifies the alias for any type of SAS data view.

Asterisk(*) Notation

The asterisk (*) represents all columns of the table(s) listed in the FROM clause. When an asterisk is not prefixed with a table name, all the columns from all tables in the FROM clause are included; when it is prefixed (for example, *table-name.** or *table-alias.**), all the columns from that table only are included.

Column Aliases

A column alias is a temporary, alternate name for a column. Aliases are specified in the SELECT clause to name or rename columns so that the result table is clearer or easier to read. Aliases are often used to name a column that is the result of an arithmetic expression or summary function. An alias is one word only. If you need a longer column name, use the LABEL= column-modifier, as described in "column-modifier" on page 1060. The keyword AS is required with a column alias to distinguish the alias from other column names in the SELECT clause.

Column aliases are optional, and each column name in the SELECT clause can have an alias. After you assign an alias to a column, you can use the alias to refer to that column in other clauses.

If you use a column alias when creating a PROC SQL view, the alias becomes the permanent name of the column for each execution of the view.

INTO Clause

Stores the value of one or more columns for use later in another PROC SQL query or SAS statement.

Restriction: An INTO clause cannot be used in a CREATE TABLE statement.

See also: "Using Macro Variables Set by PROC SQL" on page 1096

INTO :*macro-variable-specification*
    <, :*macro-variable-specification*>...

□   :*macro-variable-specification* is one of the following:

:*macro-variable* <SEPARATED BY '*character*' <NOTRIM>>;

:*macro-variable-1* – :*macro-variable-n* <NOTRIM>;

Arguments

macro-variable
  specifies a SAS macro variable that stores the values of the rows that are returned.

NOTRIM
  protects the leading and trailing blanks from being deleted from the macro variable value when the macro variables are created.

SEPARATED BY *'character'*
  specifies a character that separates the values of the rows.

Details

  □ Use the INTO clause only in the outer query of a SELECT statement and not in a subquery.
  □ You can put multiple rows of the output into macro variables. You can check the PROC SQL macro variable SQLOBS to see the number of rows produced by a query-expression. See "Using Macro Variables Set by PROC SQL" on page 1096 for more information on SQLOBS.

Examples

These examples use the PROCLIB.HOUSES table:

```
                        The SAS System                              1

                     Style       SqFeet
                     ------------------
                     CONDO          900
                     CONDO         1000
                     RANCH         1200
                     RANCH         1400
                     SPLIT         1600
                     SPLIT         1800
                     TWOSTORY      2100
                     TWOSTORY      3000
```

With the *macro-variable-specification*, you can do the following:
  □ You can create macro variables based on the first row of the result.

```
proc sql noprint;
   select style, sqfeet
       into :style, :sqfeet
       from proclib.houses;

%put &style &sqfeet;
```

The results are written to the SAS log:

```
1    proc sql noprint;
2      select style, sqfeet
3          into :style, :sqfeet
4          from proclib.houses;
5
6    %put &style &sqfeet;
CONDO         900
```

☐ You can create one new macro variable per row in the result of the SELECT statement. This example shows how you can request more values for one column than for another. The hyphen (-) is used in the INTO clause to imply a range of macro variables. You can use either the keywords THROUGH or THRU instead of a hyphen.

The following PROC SQL step puts the values from the first four rows of the PROCLIB.HOUSES table into macro variables:

```
proc sql noprint;
select distinct Style, SqFeet
    into :style1 - :style3, :sqfeet1 - :sqfeet4
    from proclib.houses;

%put &style1 &sqfeet1;
%put &style2 &sqfeet2;
%put &style3 &sqfeet3;
%put &sqfeet4;
```

The %PUT statements write the results to the SAS log:

```
1    proc sql noprint;
2    select distinct style, sqfeet
3        into :style1 - :style3, :sqfeet1 - :sqfeet4
4        from proclib.houses;
5
6    %put &style1 &sqfeet1;
CONDO 900
7    %put &style2 &sqfeet2;
CONDO 1000
8    %put &style3 &sqfeet3;
CONDO 1200
9    %put &sqfeet4;
1400
```

☐ You can concatenate the values of one column into one macro variable. This form is useful for building up a list of variables or constants.

```
proc sql;
    select distinct style
        into :s1 separated by ','
        from proclib.houses;

%put &s1;
```

The results are written to the SAS log:

```
3    proc sql;
4       select distinct style
5          into :s1 separated by ','
6          from proclib.houses;
7
8    %put &s1

CONDO,RANCH,SPLIT,TWOSTORY
```

□ The leading and trailing blanks are trimmed from the values before the macro variables are created. If you do not want the blanks to be trimmed, add NOTRIM, as shown in the following example:

```
proc sql noprint;
   select style, sqfeet
      into :style1 - :style4 notrim,
          :sqfeet separated by ',' notrim
      from proclib.houses;

%put *&style1* *&sqfeet*;
%put *&style2* *&sqfeet*;
%put *&style3* *&sqfeet*;
%put *&style4* *&sqfeet*;
```

The results are written to the SAS log, as shown in Output 34.1 on page 1049.

Output 34.1 Macro Variable Values

```
3    proc sql noprint;
4       select style, sqfeet
5          into :style1 - :style4 notrim,
6              :sqfeet separated by ',' notrim
7          from proclib.houses;
8
9    %put *&style1* *&sqfeet*;
*CONDO   * *     900,    1000,    1200,    1400,    1600,    1800,    2100,
 3000*
10   %put *&style2* *&sqfeet*;
*CONDO   * *     900,    1000,    1200,    1400,    1600,    1800,    2100,
 3000*
11   %put *&style3* *&sqfeet*;
*RANCH   * *     900,    1000,    1200,    1400,    1600,    1800,    2100,
 3000*
12   %put *&style4* *&sqfeet*;
*RANCH   * *     900,    1000,    1200,    1400,    1600,    1800,    2100,
 3000*
```

FROM Clause

Specifies source tables or views.

Featured in: Example 1 on page 1101, Example 4 on page 1106, Example 9 on page 1118, and Example 10 on page 1121

FROM *from-list*

□ *from-list* is one of the following:

table-name <<**AS**> *alias*>

view-name <<**AS**> *alias*>

joined-table

(query-expression) <<AS> alias
<(*column* <,*column*>...)>>

CONNECTION TO

Arguments

column
names the column that appears in the output. The column names that you specify are matched by position to the columns in the output.

CONNECTION TO
See "CONNECTION TO" on page 1062.

joined-table
See "joined-table" on page 1068.

query-expression
See "query-expression" on page 1075.

table-name
specifies a PROC SQL table.

view-name
specifies any type of SAS data view.

Table Aliases

A table alias is a temporary, alternate name for a table that is specified in the FROM clause. Table aliases are prefixed to column names to distinguish between columns that are common to multiple tables. Table aliases are always required when joining a table with itself. Column names in other kinds of joins must be prefixed with table aliases or table names unless the column names are unique to those tables.

The optional keyword AS is often used to distinguish a table alias from other table names.

In-Line Views

The FROM clause can itself contain a query-expression that takes an optional table alias. This kind of nested query-expression is called an *in-line view*. An in-line view is any query-expression that would be valid in a CREATE VIEW statement. PROC SQL can support many levels of nesting, but it is limited to 32 tables in any one query. The 32–table limit includes underlying tables that may contribute to views that are specified in the FROM clause.

An in-line view saves you a programming step. Rather than creating a view and referring to it in another query, you can specify the view *in-line* in the FROM clause.

Characteristics of in-line views include the following:

□ An in-line view is not assigned a permanent name, although it can take an alias.

□ An in-line view can be referred to only in the query in which it is defined. It cannot be referenced in another query.

□ You cannot use an ORDER BY clause in an in-line view.

□ The names of columns in an in-line view can be assigned in the object-item list of that view or with a parenthesized list of names following the alias. This syntax can be useful for renaming columns. See Example 10 on page 1121 for an example.

WHERE Clause

Subsets the output based on specified conditions.

Featured in: Example 4 on page 1106 and Example 9 on page 1118

WHERE sql-expression

Argument

sql-expression
See "sql-expression" on page 1081.

Details

□ When a condition is met (that is, the condition resolves to true), those rows are displayed in the result table; otherwise, no rows are displayed.

□ You cannot use summary functions that specify only one column. For example:

```
where max(measure1) > 50;
```

However, this WHERE clause will work:

```
where max(measure1,measure2) > 50;
```

Writing Efficient WHERE Clauses

Here are some guidelines for writing efficient WHERE clauses that enable PROC SQL to use indexes effectively:

□ Avoid using LIKE predicates that begin with % or _:

```
/* inefficient:*/ where country like '%INA'
/* efficient: */  where country like 'A%INA'
```

□ Avoid using arithmetic expressions in a predicate:

```
/* inefficient:*/ where salary>12*4000
/* efficient: */  where salary>48000
```

□ First put the expression that returns the fewest number of rows. In the following query, there are fewer rows where miles>3800 than there are where boarded>100.

```
where miles>3800 and boarded>100
```

GROUP BY Clause

Specifies how to group the data for summarizing.

Featured in: Example 8 on page 1116 and Example 12 on page 1124

GROUP BY *group-by-item* <,*group-by-item*>...

□ *group-by-item* is one of the following:

integer

column-name

sql-expression

Arguments

integer
equates to a column's position.

column-name
See "column-name" on page 1061.

sql-expression
See "sql-expression" on page 1081.

Details

□ You can specify more than one *group-by-item* to get more detailed reports. Both the grouping of multiple items and the BY statement of a PROC step are evaluated in similiar ways. If more than one *group-by-item* is specified, the first one determines the major grouping.

□ Integers can be substituted for column names (that is, SELECT object-items) in the GROUP BY clause. For example, if the *group-by-item* is 2, the results are grouped by the values in the second column of the SELECT clause list. Using integers can shorten your coding and enable you to group by the value of an unnamed expression in the SELECT list.

□ The data do not have to be sorted in the order of the group-by values because PROC SQL handles sorting automatically. You can use the ORDER BY clause to specify the order in which rows are displayed in the result table.

□ If you specify a GROUP BY clause in a query that does not contain a summary function, your clause is transformed into an ORDER BY clause and a message to that effect is written to the SAS log.

□ A *group-by-item* cannot be a summary function. For example, the following GROUP BY clause is not valid:

```
group by sum(x)
```

HAVING Clause

Subsets grouped data based on specified conditions.

Featured in: Example 8 on page 1116 and Example 12 on page 1124

HAVING sql-expression

Argument

sql-expression
See "sql-expression" on page 1081.

Subsetting Grouped Data

The HAVING clause is used with at least one summary function and an optional GROUP BY clause to summarize groups of data in a table. A HAVING clause is any valid SQL expression that is evaluated as either true or false for each group in a query. Or, if the query involves remerged data, the HAVING expression is evaluated for each row that participates in each group. The query must include one or more summary functions.

Typically, the GROUP BY clause is used with the HAVING expression and defines the group(s) to be evaluated. If you omit the GROUP BY clause, the summary function and the HAVING clause treat the table as one group.

The following PROC SQL step uses the PROCLIB.PAYROLL table (shown in Example 2 on page 1103) and groups the rows by SEX to determine the oldest employee of each sex. In SAS, dates are stored as integers. The lower the birthdate as an integer, the greater the age. The expression **birth=min(birth)** is evaluated for each row in the table. When the minimum birthdate is found, the expression becomes true and the row is included in the output.

```
proc sql;
   title 'Oldest Employee of Each Gender';
   select *
      from proclib.payroll
      group by sex
      having birth=min(birth);
```

Note: This query involves remerged data because the values returned by a summary function are compared to values of a column that is not in the GROUP BY clause. See "Remerging Data" on page 1090 for more information about summary functions and remerging data. △

ORDER BY Clause

Specifies the order in which rows are displayed in a result table.

See also: "query-expression" on page 1075
Featured in: Example 11 on page 1122

ORDER BY *order-by-item* <,*order-by-item*>...;

□ *order-by-item* is one of the following:

    integer <ASC|DESC>

    column-name <ASC|DESC>

    sql-expression <ASC|DESC>

Arguments

ASC
orders the data in ascending order. This is the default order.

column-name
See "column-name" on page 1061.

DESC
orders the data in descending order.

integer
equates to a column's position.

sql-expression
See "sql-expression" on page 1081.

Details

□ The ORDER BY clause sorts the result of a query expression according to the order specified in that query. When this clause is used, the default ordering sequence is ascending, from the lowest value to the highest. You can use the SORTSEQ= option to change the collating sequence for your output. See "PROC SQL Statement" on page 1027.

□ If an ORDER BY clause is omitted, the SAS System's default collating sequence and your operating environment determine the order of a result table's rows. Therefore, if you want your result table to appear in a particular order, use the ORDER BY clause.

□ Using an ORDER BY clause has certain performance costs, as does any sorting procedure. If you are querying large tables, and the order of their results is not important, your queries will run faster without an ORDER BY clause.

□ If more than one *order-by-item* is specified (separated by commas), the first one determines the major sort order. For example, if the *order-by-item* is 2 (an integer), the results are ordered by the values of the second column. If a query-expression includes a set operator (for example, UNION), use integers to specify the order. Doing so avoids ambiguous references to columns in the table expressions.

□ In the ORDER BY clause, you can specify any column of a table or view that is specified in the FROM clause of a query-expression, regardless of whether that column has been included in the query's SELECT clause. For example, this query produces a report ordered by the descending values of the population change for each country from 1990 to 1995:

```
proc sql;
   select country
```

```
               from census
               order by pop95-pop90 desc;


      NOTE: The query as specified involves
            ordering by an item that
            doesn't appear in its SELECT clause.
```

☐ You can order the output by the values that are returned by a function, for example:

```
proc sql;
   select *
      from measure
         order by put(pol_a,fmt_a.);
```

UPDATE Statement

Modifies a column's values in existing rows of a table or view.

Restriction: You cannot use UPDATE on a table accessed via an engine that does not support UPDATE processing.

Featured in: Example 3 on page 1104

UPDATE *table-name* | *sas/access-view* | *proc-sql-view* **<AS** *alias***>**

   SET *column*=sql-expression
       <,*column*=sql-expression>...

   <**SET***column*=sql-expression
       <,*column*=sql-expression>...>

   <**WHERE**sql-expression>;

Arguments

alias
   assigns an alias to *table-name*, *sas/access-view*, or *proc-sql-view*.

column
   specifies a column in *table-name*, *sas/access-view*, or *proc-sql-view*.

sas/access-view
   specifies a SAS/ACCESS view.

sql-expression
   See "sql-expression" on page 1081.

table-name
   specifies a PROC SQL table.

proc-sql-view
   specifies a PROC SQL view.

Updating Tables through Views

You can update one or more rows of a table through a view, with some restrictions. See "Updating PROC SQL and SAS/ACCESS Views" on page 1097.

Details

□ Any column that is not modified retains its original values, except in certain queries using the CASE expression. See "CASE expression" on page 1058 for a description of CASE expressions.

□ To add, drop, or modify a column's definition or attributes, use the ALTER TABLE statement, described in "ALTER TABLE Statement" on page 1031.

□ In the SET clause, a column reference on the left side of the equal sign can also appear as part of the expression on the right side of the equal sign. For example, you could use this expression to give employees a $1,000 holiday bonus:

```
set salary=salary + 1000
```

□ If you omit the WHERE clause, all the rows are updated. When you use a WHERE clause, only the rows that meet the WHERE condition are updated.

□ When you update a column and an index has been defined for that column, the values in the updated column continue to have the index defined for them.

VALIDATE Statement

Checks the accuracy of a query-expression's syntax without executing the expression.

VALIDATE query-expression;

Argument

query-expression
See "query-expression" on page 1075.

Details

□ The VALIDATE statement writes a message in the SAS log that states that the query is valid. If there are errors, VALIDATE writes error messages to the SAS log.

□ The VALIDATE statement can also be included in applications that use the macro facility. When used in such an application, VALIDATE returns a value that indicates the query-expression's validity. The value is returned through the macro variable SQLRC (a short form for SQL return code). For example, if a SELECT statement is valid, the macro variable SQLRC returns a value of 0. See "Using Macro Variables Set by PROC SQL" on page 1096 for more information.

Component Dictionary

This section describes the components that are used in SQL procedure statements. *Components* are the items in PROC SQL syntax that appear in roman type.

Most components are contained in clauses within the statements. For example, the basic SELECT statement is composed of the SELECT and FROM clauses, where each clause contains one or more components. Components can also contain other components.

For easy reference, components appear in alphabetical order, and some terms are referred to before they are defined. Use the index or the "See Also" references to refer to other statement or component descriptions that may be helpful.

BETWEEN condition

Selects rows where column values are within a range of values.

sql-expression <NOT> **BETWEEN** sql-expression
    AND sql-expression

□ sql-expression is described in "sql-expression" on page 1081.

Details

□ The sql-expressions must be of compatible data types. They must be either all numeric or all character types.

□ Because a BETWEEN condition evaluates the boundary values as a range, it is not necessary to specify the smaller quantity first.

□ You can use the NOT logical operator to exclude a range of numbers, for example, to eliminate customer numbers between 1 and 15 (inclusive) so that you can retrieve data on more recently acquired customers.

□ PROC SQL supports the same comparison operators that the DATA step supports. For example:

```
x between 1 and 3
x between 3 and 1
1<=x<=3
x>=1 and x<=3
```

CALCULATED

Refers to columns already calculated in the SELECT clause.

CALCULATED *column-alias*

□ *column-alias* is the name assigned to the column in the SELECT clause.

Referencing a CALCULATED Column

CALCULATED enables you to use the results of an expression in the same SELECT clause or in the WHERE clause. It is valid only when used to refer to columns that are calculated in the immediate query expression.

CASE expression

Selects result values that satisfy specified conditions.

Featured in: Example 3 on page 1104 and Example 13 on page 1126

CASE <*case-operand*>
    WHEN *when-condition* **THEN** *result-expression*
    <**WHEN** *when-condition* **THEN** *result-expression*>...
    <**ELSE** *result-expression*>
    END

    □   *case-operand*, *when-condition*, and *result-expression* must be valid sql-expressions. See "sql-expression" on page 1081.

Details

The CASE expression selects values if certain conditions are met. A CASE expression returns a single value that is conditionally evaluated for each row of a table (or view). Use the WHEN-THEN clauses when you want to execute a CASE expression for some but not all of the rows in the table that is being queried or created. An optional ELSE expression gives an alternative action if no THEN expression is executed.

When you omit *case-operand*, *when-condition* is evaluated as a Boolean (true or false) value. If *when-condition* returns a nonzero, nonmissing result, the WHEN clause is true. If *case-operand* is specified, it is compared with *when-condition* for equality. If *case-operand* equals *when-condition*, the WHEN clause is true.

If the *when-condition* is true for the row being executed, the *result-expression* following THEN is executed. If *when-condition* is false, PROC SQL evaluates the next *when-condition* until they are all evaluated. If every *when-condition* is false, PROC SQL executes the ELSE expression, and its result becomes the CASE expression's result. If no ELSE expression is present and every *when-condition* is false, the result of the CASE expression is a missing value.

You can use CASE expressions in the SELECT, UPDATE, and INSERT statements.

Example

The following two PROC SQL steps show two equivalent CASE expressions that create a character column with the strings in the THEN clause. The CASE expression in the second PROC SQL step is a shorthand method that is useful when all the comparisons are with the same column.

Example Code 34.1

```
proc sql;
   select *, case
                when degrees > 80 then 'Hot'
                when degrees < 40 then 'Cold'
                else 'Mild'
                end
      from temperatures;

proc sql;
   select *, case Degrees
                when > 80 then 'Hot'
                when < 40 then 'Cold'
                else 'Mild'
                end
      from temperatures;
```

column-definition

Defines PROC SQL's data types and dates.

See also: "column-modifier" on page 1060

Featured in: Example 1 on page 1101

column CHARACTER|VARCHAR *<(width)>*
     <column-modifier <column-modifier>...>

column INTEGER|SMALLINT
     <column-modifier <column-modifier>...>

column DECIMAL|NUMERIC|FLOAT *<(width<,ndec>)>*
     <column-modifier <column-modifier>...>

column REAL|DOUBLE PRECISION
     <column-modifier <column-modifier>...>

column DATE <column-modifier>

□ column-modifier is described in "column-modifier" on page 1060.

□ *ndec* is the number of decimals. PROC SQL ignores *ndec*. It is included for compatibility with SQL from other software.

□ *width* is the width of the column. The *width* field on a character column specifies the width of that column; it defaults to eight characters. PROC SQL ignores a *width* field on a numeric column. All numeric columns are created with the maximum precision allowed by the SAS System. If you want to create numeric columns that use less storage space, use the LENGTH statement in the DATA step.

Details

□ SAS supports many but not all of the data types that SQL-based databases support. The SQL procedure defaults to the SAS data types NUM and CHAR.

□ The CHARACTER, INTEGER, and DECIMAL data types can be abbreviated to CHAR, INT, and DEC, respectively.

□ A column declared with DATE is a SAS numeric variable with a date informat or format. You can use any of the column-modifiers to set the appropriate attributes for the column being defined. See *SAS Language Reference: Dictionary* for more information on dates.

---

column-modifier

Sets column attributes.

See also: "column-definition" on page 1059 and SELECT Clause on page 1045

Featured in: Example 1 on page 1101 and Example 2 on page 1103

< **INFORMAT**=*informatw.d*>

<**FORMAT**–*formatw.d*>

< **LABEL**=*'label'*>

< **LENGTH**=*length*>

Specifying Informats for Columns (INFORMAT=)

INFORMAT= specifies the informat to be used when SAS accesses data from a table or view. You can change one permanent informat to another by using the ALTER statement. PROC SQL stores informats in its table definitions so that other SAS procedures and the DATA step can use this information when they reference tables created by PROC SQL.

Specifying Formats for Columns (FORMAT=)

FORMAT= determines how character and numeric values in a column are displayed by the query-expression. If the FORMAT= modifier is used in the ALTER, CREATE TABLE, or CREATE VIEW statements, it specifies the permanent format to be used when SAS displays data from that table or view. You can change one permanent format to another by using the ALTER statement.

See *SAS Language Reference: Dictionary* for more information on informats and formats.

Specifying Labels for Columns (LABEL=)

LABEL= associates a label with a column heading. If the LABEL= modifier is used in the ALTER, CREATE TABLE, or CREATE VIEW statements, it specifies the permanent label to be used when displaying that column. You can change one permanent label to another by using the ALTER statement.

If you refer to a labeled column in the ORDER BY or GROUP BY clause, you must use either the column name (not its label), the column's alias, or its ordering integer (for example, **ORDER BY 2**). See the section on SAS statements in *SAS Language Reference: Dictionary* for more information on labels.

A label can begin with the following characters: a through z, A through Z, 0 through 9, an underscore (_), or a blank space. If you begin a label with any other character, such as pound sign (#), that character is used as a split character and it splits the label onto the next line wherever it appears. For example:

```
select dropout label=
'#Percentage of#Students Who#Dropped Out'
   from educ(obs=5);
```

If you need a special character to appear as the first character in the output, precede it with a space or a forward slash (/).

You can omit the LABEL= part of the column-modifier and still specify a label. Be sure to enclose the label in quotes. For example:

```
select empname "Names of Employees"
   from sql.employees;
```

If you need an apostrophe in the label, type it twice so that the SAS System reads the apostrophe as a literal. Or, you can use single and double quotes alternately (for example, "Date Rec'd").

---

column-name

Specifies the column to select.

See also: "column-modifier" on page 1060 and SELECT Clause on page 1045

---

column-name is one of the following:

column

table-name.column

table-alias.column

view-name.column

view-alias.column

Qualifying Column Names

A column can be referred to by its name alone if it is the only column by that name in all the tables or views listed in the current query-expression. If the same column name exists in more than one table or view in the query expression, you must *qualify* each use of the column name by prefixing a reference to the table that contains it. Consider the following examples:

```
SALARY        /* name of the column */
EMP.SALARY    /* EMP is the table or view name */
E.SALARY      /* E is an alias for the table
                 or view that contains the
                 SALARY column */
```

CONNECTION TO

Retrieves and uses DBMS data in a PROC SQL query or view.

Tip: You can use CONNECTION TO in the SELECT statement's FROM clause as part of the from-list.

See also: "Connecting to a DBMS Using the SQL Procedure Pass-Through Facility" on page 1095 and your SAS/ACCESS documentation.

CONNECTION TO *dbms-name (dbms-query)*

CONNECTION TO *alias (dbms-query)*

- □   *alias* specifies an alias, if one was defined in the CONNECT statement.
- □   *dbms-name* identifies the DBMS you are using.
- □   *dbms-query* specifies the query to send to a DBMS. The query uses the DBMS's dynamic SQL. You can use any SQL syntax that the DBMS understands, even if that is not valid for PROC SQL. However, your DBMS query cannot contain a semicolon because that represents the end of a statement to the SAS System.

  The number of tables that you can join with *dbms-query* is determined by the DBMS. Each CONNECTION TO component counts as one table toward the 32-table PROC SQL limit for joins.

CONTAINS condition

Tests whether a string is part of a column's value.

Restriction: The CONTAINS condition is used only with character operands.

Featured in: Example 7 on page 1112

---

sql-expression<NOT> **CONTAINS** sql-expression

For more information, see "sql-expression" on page 1081.

DICTIONARY tables

Retrieve information about elements associated with the current SAS session.

Restriction: You cannot use SAS data set options with DICTIONARY tables.

Restriction: DICTIONARY tables are read-only objects.

Featured in: Example 6 on page 1111

DICTIONARY. *table-name*

☐ *table-name* is one of the following:

CATALOGS	**MEMBERS**
COLUMNS	OPTIONS
EXTFILES	TABLES
INDEXES	TITLES
MACROS	VIEWS

Querying DICTIONARY Tables

The DICTIONARY tables component is specified in the FROM clause of a SELECT statement. DICTIONARY is a reserved libref for use only in PROC SQL. Data from DICTIONARY tables are generated at run time.

You can use a PROC SQL query to retrieve or subset data from a DICTIONARY table. You can save that query as a PROC SQL view for use later. Or, you can use the existing SASHELP views that are created from the DICTIONARY tables.

To see how each DICTIONARY table is defined, submit a DESCRIBE TABLE statement. After you know how a table is defined, you can use its column names in a subsetting WHERE clause to get more specific information. For example:

```
proc sql;
    describe table dictionary.indexes;
```

The results are written to the SAS log:

```
1    proc sql;
2        describe table dictionary.indexes;
NOTE: SQL table DICTIONARY.INDEXES was created like:

create table DICTIONARY.INDEXES
  (
   libname char(8) label='Library Name',
   memname char(32) label='Member Name',
   memtype char(8) label='Member Type',
   name char(32) label='Column Name',
   idxusage char(9) label='Column Index Type',
   indxname char(32) label='Index Name',
   indxpos num label='Position of Column in Concatenated Key',
   nomiss char(3) label='Nomiss Option',
   unique char(3) label='Unique Option'
  );
```

You specify a DICTIONARY table in a PROC SQL query or view to retrieve information about its objects. For example, the following query returns a row for each index in the INDEXES DICTIONARY table:

```
proc sql;
    title 'DICTIONARY.INDEXES Table';
    select * from dictionary.indexes;
```

Subsetting Data from DICTIONARY Tables

DICTIONARY tables are often large. Therefore, if you are looking for specific information, use a WHERE clause to retrieve a subset of the rows in a DICTIONARY table. In the following example, only the rows with the member name **ADBDBI** are displayed from the DICTIONARY.CATALOGS table:

```
proc sql ;
title 'Subset of the DICTIONARY.CATALOGS Table';
title2 'Rows with Member Name ADBDBI ';
   select * from dictionary.catalogs
       where memname ='ADBDBI';
```

Creating PROC SQL Views from DICTIONARY Tables

To use DICTIONARY tables in other SAS procedures or in the DATA step, use PROC SQL views that are based on the DICTIONARY tables.

You can either create a PROC SQL view on a DICTIONARY table or you can use the SASHELP views, as described in "Accessing DICTIONARY Tables with SASHELP Views" on page 1065. You can then use the view in a DATA or PROC step. The following example creates a PROC SQL view on the DICTIONARY.OPTIONS table. Output 34.2 on page 1064 displays the view with PROC PRINT:

```
options linesize=120 nodate pageno=1;

proc sql;
   create view work.options as
       select * from dictionary.options;


proc print data=work.options(obs=10) noobs;
   title 'Listing of the View WORK.OPTIONS';
   title2 'First 10 Rows Only';
run;
```

Output 34.2   DICTIONARY.OPTIONS Table (partial output)

```
                              Listing of the View WORK.OPTIONS                                    1
                                     First 10 Rows Only


    optname          setting        optdesc
                                                                                        level

    BATCH            NOBATCH        Use the batch set of default values for SAS system options
                                                                                        Portable
    BINDING          DEFAULT        Controls the binding edge for duplexed output
                                                                                        Portable
    BOTTOMMARGIN                    Bottom margin for printed output
                                                                                        Portable
    BUFNO            1              Number of buffers for each SAS data set
                                                                                        Portable
    BUFSIZE          0              Size of buffer for page of SAS data set
                                                                                        Portable
    BYERR            BYERR          Set the error flag if a null data set is input to the SORT procedure
                                                                                        Portable
    BYLINE           BYLINE         Print the by-line at the beginning of each by-group
                                                                                        Portable
    CAPS             NOCAPS         Translate SAS source and data lines to uppercase
                                                                                        Portable
    CARDIMAGE        NOCARDIMAGE    Process SAS source and data lines as 80-byte records
                                                                                        Portable
    CATCACHE         0              Number of SAS catalogs to keep in cache memory
                                                                                        Portable
```

Accessing DICTIONARY Tables with SASHELP Views

You can use the permanent PROC SQL views that are available in the SASHELP data library to access DICTIONARY tables. Table 34.1 on page 1065 lists all of the permanent PROC SQL views in the SASHELP library as well as the CREATE VIEW statement that defines each view. You can reference these views and display their results using a PROC SQL query, other SAS procedure, or the DATA step.

Table 34.1 Views in DICTIONARY Tables

PROC SQL Views in the SASHELP LIBRARY	PROC SQL Statements to Create the Views
SASHELP.VCATALG	```create view sashelp.vcatalg as select * from dictionary.catalogs;```
SASHELP.VCOLUMN	```create view sashelp.vcolumn as select * from dictionary.columns;```
SASHELP.VEXTFL	```create view sashelp.vextfl as select * from dictionary.extfiles;```
SASHELP.VINDEX	```create view sashelp.vindex as select * from dictionary.indexes;```
SASHELP.VMACRO	```create view sashelp.vmacro as select * from dictionary.macros;```
SASHELP.VMEMBER	```create view sashelp.vmember as select * from dictionary.members;```
SASHELP.VOPTION	```create view sashelp.voption as select * from dictionary.options;```
SASHELP.VTABLE	```create view sashelp.vtable as select * from dictionary.tables;```
SASHELP.VTITLE	```create view sashelp.vtitle as select * from dictionary.titles;```
SASHELP.VVIEW	```create view sashelp.vview as select * from dictionary.views;```
SASHELP.VSACCES	```create view sashelp.vsacces as select libname, memname from dictionary.members where memtype='ACCESS' order by libname, memname;```
SASHELP.VSCATLG	```create view sashelp.vscatlg as select libname, memname from dictionary.members where memtype='CATALOG' order by libname, memname;```

PROC SQL Views in the SASHELP LIBRARY	PROC SQL Statements to Create the Views

SASHELP.VSLIB	`create`
	`view sashelp.vslib as`
	`    select distinct libname, path`
	`    from dictionary.members`
	`    order by libname;`

SASHELP.VSTABLE	`create`
	`view sashelp.vstable as`
	`    select libname, memname`
	`    from dictionary.members`
	`    where memtype='DATA'`
	`    order by libname, memname;`

SASHELP.VSTABVW	`create`
	`view sashelp.vstabvw as`
	`    select libname, memname, memtype`
	`    from dictionary.members`
	`    where memtype='VIEW' or memtype='DATA'`
	`    order by libname, memname;`

SASHELP.VSVIEW	`create`
	`view sashelp.vsview as`
	`    select libname, memname`
	`    from dictionary.members`
	`    where memtype='VIEW'`
	`    order by libname, memname;`

EXISTS condition

Tests if a subquery returns one or more rows.

See also: "Query Expressions (Subqueries)" on page 1083

<NOT> **EXISTS** (query-expression)

□ query-expression is described in "query-expression" on page 1075.

Details

The EXISTS condition is an operator whose right operand is a subquery. The result of an EXISTS condition is true if the subquery resolves to at least one row. The result of a NOT EXISTS condition is true if the subquery evaluates to zero rows. For example, the following query subsets PROCLIB.PAYROLL (which is shown in Example 2 on page 1103) based on the criteria in the subquery. If the value for STAFF.IDNUM is on the same row as the value **CT** in PROCLIB.STAFF (which is shown in Example 4 on page 1106), the matching IDNUM in PROCLIB.PAYROLL is included in the output. Thus, the query returns all the employees from PROCLIB.PAYROLL who live in **CT**.

```
proc sql;
   select *
```

```
from proclib.payroll p
where exists (select *
                  from proclib.staff s
                  where p.idnumber=s.idnum
                      and state='CT');
```

IN condition

Tests set membership.

Featured in: Example 4 on page 1106

---

sql-expression <NOT> **IN** (*constant* <,*constant*>...)

sql-expression <NOT> **IN** (query-expresssion)

- □ *constant* is a number or a quoted character string (or other special notation) that indicates a fixed value. Constants are also called *literals*.
- □ query-expression is described in "query-expression" on page 1075.
- □ sql-expression is described in "sql-expression" on page 1081.

Details

An IN condition tests if the column value that is returned by the sql-expression on the left is a member of the set (of constants or values returned by the query-expression) on the right. If so, it selects rows based upon the column value. That is, the IN condition is true if the value of the left-hand operand is in the set of values that are defined by the right-hand operand.

IS condition

Tests for a missing value.

Featured in: Example 5 on page 1108

---

sql-expression **IS** <NOT> **NULL**

sql-expression **IS** <NOT> **MISSING**

- □ sql-expression is described in "sql-expression" on page 1081.

Details

IS NULL and IS MISSING are predicates that test for a missing value. IS NULL and IS MISSING are used in the WHERE, ON, and HAVING expressions. Each predicate resolves to true if the sql-expression's result is missing and false if it is not missing.

SAS stores a numeric missing value as a period (.) and a character missing value as a blank space. Unlike missing values in some versions of SQL, missing values in SAS always appear first in the collating sequence. Therefore, in Boolean and comparison operations, the following expressions resolve to true in a predicate:

```
   3>null
  -3>null
   0>null
```

The SAS System way of evaluating missing values differs from that of the ANSI Standard for SQL. According to the Standard, these expressions are NULL. See "sql-expression" on page 1081 for more information on predicates and operators. See "PROC SQL and the ANSI Standard" on page 1098 for more information on the ANSI Standard.

joined-table

Joins a table with itself or with other tables.

Restrictions: Joins are limited to 32 tables.

See also: FROM Clause on page 1049 and "query-expression" on page 1075

Featured in: Example 4 on page 1106, Example 7 on page 1112, Example 9 on page 1118, Example 13 on page 1126, and Example 14 on page 1129

---

table-name <<**AS**> *alias*>, *table-name* <<**AS**> *alias*>
  <, *table-name* <<**AS**> *alias*>...>

table-name <**INNER**> **JOIN** *table-name*
  ON sql-expression

table-name **LEFT JOIN** *table-name* **ON** sql-expression

table-name **RIGHT JOIN** *table-name* **ON** sql-expression

table-name **FULL JOIN** *table-name* **ON** sql-expression

□ *alias* specifies an alias for *table-name*.

□ sql-expression is described in "sql-expression" on page 1081.

□ *table-name* can be one of the following:

  □ the name of a PROC SQL table.

  □ the name of a SAS data view.

  □ a query-expression. A query-expression in the FROM clause is usually referred to as an *in-line view*. See FROM Clause on page 1049 for more information on in-line views.

  □ a connection to a DBMS in the form of the CONNECTION TO component. See "CONNECTION TO" on page 1062 for more information.

Joining Tables

When multiple tables, views, or query-expressions are listed in the FROM clause, they are processed to form one table. The resulting table contains data from each contributing table. These queries are referred to as *joins*.

Conceptually, when two tables are specified, each row of table A is matched with all the rows of table B to produce an internal or intermediate table. The number of rows in the intermediate table (*Cartesian product*) is equal to the product of the number of rows in each of the source tables. The intermediate table becomes the input to the rest of the query in which some of its rows may be eliminated by the WHERE clause or summarized by a summary function.

A common type of join is an *equijoin*, in which the values from a column in the first table must equal the values of a column in the second table.

Table Limit

PROC SQL can process a maximum of 32 tables for a join. If you are using views in a join, the number of tables on which the views are based count toward the 32-table limit. Each CONNECTION TO component in the Pass-Through Facility counts as one table.

Specifying the Rows to Be Returned

The WHERE clause or ON clause contains the conditions (sql-expression) under which the rows in the Cartesian product are kept or eliminated in the result table. WHERE is used to select rows from inner joins. ON is used to select rows from inner or outer joins.

The expression is evaluated for each row from each table in the intermediate table described earlier in "Joining Tables" on page 1069. The row is considered to be matching if the result of the expression is true (a nonzero, nonmissing value) for that row.

Note: You can follow the ON clause with a WHERE clause to further subset the query result. See Example 7 on page 1112 for an example. △

Table Aliases

Table aliases are used in joins to distinguish the columns of one table from those in the other table(s). A table name or alias must be prefixed to a column name when you are joining tables that have matching column names. See FROM Clause on page 1049 for more information on table aliases.

Joining a Table with Itself

A single table can be joined with itself to produce more information. These joins are sometimes called *reflexive joins*. In these joins, the same table is listed twice in the FROM clause. Each instance of the table must have a table alias or you will not be able to distinguish between references to columns in either instance of the table. See Example 13 on page 1126 and Example 14 on page 1129 for examples.

Inner Joins

An *inner join* returns a result table for all the rows in a table that have one or more matching rows in the other table(s), as specified by the sql-expression. Inner joins can be performed on up to 32 tables in the same query-expression.

You can perform an inner join by using a list of table-names separated by commas or by using the INNER, JOIN, and ON keywords.

The LEFTTAB and RIGHTTAB tables are used to illustrate this type of join:

```
              Left Table - LEFTTAB

        Continent   Export    Country
        -------------------------------
        NA          wheat     Canada
        EUR         corn      France
        EUR         rice      Italy
        AFR         oil       Egypt
              Right Table- RIGHTTAB

        Continent   Export    Country
        -------------------------------
        NA          sugar     USA
        EUR         corn      Spain
        EUR         beets     Belgium
        ASIA        rice      Vietnam
```

The following example joins the LEFTTAB and RIGHTTAB tables to get the *Cartesian product* of the two tables. The Cartesian product is the result of combining every row from one table with every row from another table. You get the Cartesian product when you join two tables and do not subset them with a WHERE clause or ON clause.

```
proc sql;
   title 'The Cartesian Product of';
   title2 'LEFTTAB and RIGHTTAB';
   select *
      from lefttab, righttab;
```

```
                     The Cartesian Product of
                       LEFTTAB and RIGHTTAB

Continent   Export   Country   Continent   Export   Country
------------------------------------------------------------------
NA          wheat    Canada    NA          sugar    USA
NA          wheat    Canada    EUR         corn     Spain
NA          wheat    Canada    EUR         beets    Belgium
NA          wheat    Canada    ASIA        rice     Vietnam
EUR         corn     France    NA          sugar    USA
EUR         corn     France    EUR         corn     Spain
EUR         corn     France    EUR         beets    Belgium
EUR         corn     France    ASIA        rice     Vietnam
EUR         rice     Italy     NA          sugar    USA
EUR         rice     Italy     EUR         corn     Spain
EUR         rice     Italy     EUR         beets    Belgium
EUR         rice     Italy     ASIA        rice     Vietnam
AFR         oil      Egypt     NA          sugar    USA
AFR         oil      Egypt     EUR         corn     Spain
AFR         oil      Egypt     EUR         beets    Belgium
AFR         oil      Egypt     ASIA        rice     Vietnam
```

The LEFTTAB and RIGHTTAB tables can be joined by listing the table names in the FROM clause. The following query represents an equijoin because the values of Continent from each table are matched. The column names are prefixed with the table aliases so that the correct columns can be selected.

```
proc sql;
   title 'Inner Join';
```

```
select *
    from lefttab as l, righttab as r
    where l.continent=r.continent;
```

```
                              Inner Join

    Continent  Export   Country   Continent  Export   Country
    ---------------------------------------------------------------
    NA         wheat    Canada    NA         sugar    USA
    EUR        corn     France    EUR        corn     Spain
    EUR        corn     France    EUR        beets    Belgium
    EUR        rice     Italy     EUR        corn     Spain
    EUR        rice     Italy     EUR        beets    Belgium
```

The following PROC SQL step is equivalent to the previous one and shows how to write an equijoin using the INNER JOIN and ON keywords.

```
proc sql;
    title 'Inner Join';
    select *
        from lefttab as l inner join
                righttab as r
        on l.continent=r.continent;
```

See Example 4 on page 1106, Example 13 on page 1126, and Example 14 on page 1129 for more examples.

Outer Joins

Outer joins are inner joins that have been augmented with rows that did not match with any row from the other table in the join. The three types of outer joins are left, right, and full.

A left outer join, specified with the keywords LEFT JOIN and ON, has all the rows from the Cartesian product of the two tables for which the sql-expression is true, plus rows from the first (LEFTTAB) table that do not match any row in the second (RIGHTTAB) table.

```
proc sql;
    title 'Left Outer Join';
    select *
        from lefttab as l left join
                righttab as r
        on l.continent=r.continent;
```

```
                          Left Outer Join

    Continent  Export   Country   Continent  Export   Country
    ---------------------------------------------------------------
    AFR        oil      Egypt
    EUR        rice     Italy     EUR        beets    Belgium
    EUR        corn     France    EUR        beets    Belgium
    EUR        rice     Italy     EUR        corn     Spain
    EUR        corn     France    EUR        corn     Spain
    NA         wheat    Canada    NA         sugar    USA
```

A right outer join, specified with the keywords RIGHT JOIN and ON, has all the rows from the Cartesian product of the two tables for which the sql-expression is true, plus rows from the second (RIGHTTAB) table that do not match any row in the first (LEFTTAB) table.

```
proc sql;
   title 'Right Outer Join';
   select *
      from lefttab as l right join
           righttab as r
      on l.continent=r.continent;
```

```
                            Right Outer Join

Continent  Export      Country   Continent  Export    Country
------------------------------------------------------------------
                                 ASIA       rice      Vietnam
EUR        rice        Italy     EUR        beets     Belgium
EUR        rice        Italy     EUR        corn      Spain
EUR        corn        France    EUR        beets     Belgium
EUR        corn        France    EUR        corn      Spain
NA         wheat       Canada    NA         sugar     USA
```

A full outer join, specified with the keywords FULL JOIN and ON, has all the rows from the Cartesian product of the two tables for which the sql-expression is true, plus rows from each table that do not match any row in the other table.

```
proc sql;
   title 'Full Outer Join';
   select *
      from lefttab as l full join
           righttab as r
      on l.continent=r.continent;
```

```
                            Full Outer Join

Continent  Export      Country   Continent  Export    Country
------------------------------------------------------------------
AFR        oil         Egypt
                                 ASIA       rice      Vietnam
EUR        rice        Italy     EUR        beets     Belgium
EUR        rice        Italy     EUR        corn      Spain
EUR        corn        France    EUR        beets     Belgium
EUR        corn        France    EUR        corn      Spain
NA         wheat       Canada    NA         sugar     USA
```

See Example 7 on page 1112 for another example.

Joining More Than Two Tables

Inner joins are usually performed on two or three tables, but they can be performed on up to 32 tables in PROC SQL. A join on three tables is described here to explain how and why the relationships work among the tables.

In a three-way join, the sql-expression consists of two conditions: one relates the first table to the second table and the other relates the second table to the third table. It is possible to break this example into stages, performing a two-way join into a temporary table and then joining that table with the third one for the same result. However, PROC SQL can do it all in one step as shown in the next example.

The example shows the joining of three tables: COMM, PRICE, and AMOUNT. To calculate the total revenue from exports for each country, you need to multiply the amount exported (AMOUNT table) by the price of each unit (PRICE table), and you must know the commodity that each country exports (COMM table).

```
                          COMM Table

          Continent  Export    Country
          ------------------------------
          NA         wheat     Canada
          EUR        corn      France
          EUR        rice      Italy
          AFR        oil       Egypt
                     PRICE Table

                    Export        Price
                    ------------------
                    rice          3.56
                    corn          3.45
                    oil             18
                    wheat         2.98
```

```
                      AMOUNT Table

             Country    Quantity
             ------------------
             Canada       16000
             France        2400
             Italy          500
             Egypt        10000
```

```
proc sql;
   title  'Total Export Revenue';
   select c.Country, p.Export, p.Price,
          a.Quantity,a.quantity*p.price
          as Total
     from comm c, price p, amount a
     where c.export=p.export
          and c.country=a.country;
```

```
                   Total Export Revenue

       Country  Export     Price  Quantity    Total
       --------------------------------------------
       Italy    rice        3.56       500     1780
       France   corn        3.45      2400     8280
       Egypt    oil           18     10000   180000
       Canada   wheat       2.98     16000    47680
```

See Example 9 on page 1118 for another example.

Comparison of Joins and Subqueries

You can often use a subquery and a join to get the same result. However, it is often more efficient to use a join if the outer query and the subquery do not return duplicate rows. For example, the following queries produce the same result. The second query is more efficient:

```
proc sql;
   select IDNumber, Birth
      from proclib.payroll
      where IDNumber in (select idnum
                            from proclib.staff
                            where lname like 'B%');
```

```
proc sql;
   select  p.IDNumber, p.Birth
      from proclib.payroll p, proclib.staff s
      where p.idnumber=s.idnum
            and s.lname like 'B%';
```

Note: PROCLIB.PAYROLL is shown in Example 2 on page 1103. △

LIKE condition

Tests for a matching pattern.

sql-expression <NOT> **LIKE** sql-expression

□ sql-expression is described in "sql-expression" on page 1081.

Details

The LIKE condition selects rows by comparing character strings with a pattern-matching specification. It resolves to true and displays the matched string(s) if the left operand matches the pattern specified by the right operand.

Patterns for Searching

Patterns are composed of three classes of characters:

underscore (_)
   matches any single character.

percent sign (%)
   matches any sequence of zero or more characters.

any other character
   matches that character.

These patterns can appear before, after, or on both sides of characters that you want to match. The LIKE condition is case-sensitive.

The following list uses these values: `Smith`, `Smooth`, `Smothers`, `Smart`, and `Smuggle`.

`'Sm%'`
> matches `Smith`, `Smooth`, `Smothers`, `Smart`, `Smuggle`.

`'%th'`
> matches `Smith`, `Smooth`.

`'S__gg%'`
> matches `Smuggle`.

`'S_o'`
> matches a three-letter word, so it has no matches here.

`'S_o%'`
> matches `Smooth`, `Smothers`.

`'S%th'`
> matches `Smith`, `Smooth`.

`'Z'`
> matches the single, uppercase character `z` only, so it has no matches here.

Searching for Mixed-Case Strings

To search for mixed-case strings, use the UPCASE function to make all the names uppercase before entering the LIKE condition:

```
upcase(name) like 'SM%';
```

Note: When you are using the % character, be aware of the effect of trailing blanks. You may have to use the TRIM function to remove trailing blanks in order to match values. △

---

query-expression

Retrieves data from tables.

See also: "table-expression" on page 1094, "Query Expressions (Subqueries)" on page 1083, and "In-Line Views" on page 1050

---

table-expression <*set-operator* table-expression>...

- □ table-expression is described in "table-expression" on page 1094.
- □ *set-operator* is one of the following:

> **INTERSECT** <CORRESPONDING> <ALL>
>
> **OUTER UNION** <CORRESPONDING>
>
> **UNION** <CORRESPONDING> <ALL>
>
> **EXCEPT** <CORRESPONDING> <ALL>

Query Expressions and Table Expressions

A query-expression is one or more table-expressions. Multiple table expressions are linked by set operators. The following figure illustrates the relationship between table-expressions and query-expressions.

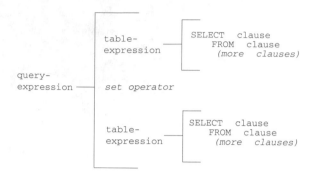

Set Operators

PROC SQL provides traditional set operators from relational algebra:

OUTER UNION
concatenates the query results.

UNION
produces all unique rows from both queries.

EXCEPT
produces rows that are part of the first query only.

INTERSECT
produces rows that are common to both query results.

A query-expression with set operators is evaluated as follows.

☐ Each table-expression is evaluated to produce an (internal) intermediate result table.

☐ Each intermediate result table then becomes an operand linked with a set operator to form an expression, for example, A UNION B.

☐ If the query-expression involves more than two table-expressions, the result from the first two becomes an operand for the next set operator and operand, for example, (A UNION B) EXCEPT C, ((A UNION B) EXCEPT C) INTERSECT D, and so on.

☐ Evaluating a query-expression produces a single output table.

Set operators follow this order of precedence unless they are overridden by parentheses in the expression(s): INTERSECT is evaluated first. OUTER UNION, UNION, and EXCEPT have the same level of precedence.

PROC SQL performs set operations even if the tables or views that are referred to in the table-expressions do not have the same number of columns. The reason for this is that the ANSI Standard for SQL requires that tables or views involved in a set operation have the same number of columns and that the columns have matching data types. If a set operation is performed on a table or view that has fewer columns than the one(s) with which it is being linked, PROC SQL extends the table or view with fewer columns by creating columns with missing values of the appropriate data type. This temporary alteration enables the set operation to be performed correctly.

CORRESPONDING (CORR) Keyword

The CORRESPONDING keyword is used only when a set operator is specified. CORR causes PROC SQL to match the columns in table-expressions *by name* and not by ordinal position. Columns that do not match by name are excluded from the result table, except for the OUTER UNION operator. See "OUTER UNION" on page 1077.

For example, when performing a set operation on two table-expressions, PROC SQL matches the first specified column-name (listed in the SELECT clause) from one table-expression with the first specified column-name from the other. If CORR is omitted, PROC SQL matches the columns by ordinal position.

ALL Keyword

The set operators automatically eliminate duplicate rows from their output tables. The optional ALL keyword preserves the duplicate rows, reduces the execution by one step, and thereby improves the query-expression's performance. You use it when you want to display all the rows resulting from the table-expressions, rather than just the rows that are output because duplicates have been deleted. The ALL keyword is used only when a set operator is also specified.

OUTER UNION

Performing an OUTER UNION is very similar to performing the SAS DATA step with a SET statement. The OUTER UNION concatenates the intermediate results from the table-expressions. Thus, the result table for the query-expression contains all the rows produced by the first table-expression followed by all the rows produced by the second table-expression. Columns with the same name are in separate columns in the result table.

For example, the following query expression concatenates the ME1 and ME2 tables but does not overlay like-named columns. Output 34.3 on page 1078 shows the result.

```
proc sql;
    title 'ME1 and ME2: OUTER UNION';
    select *
        from me1
    outer union
    select *
        from me2;
```

```
ME1

        IDnum     Jobcode     Salary      Bonus
        ---------------------------------------------
        1400      ME1         29769       587
        1403      ME1         28072       342
        1120      ME1         28619       986
        1120      ME1         28619       986
```

```
                        ME2

        IDnum     Jobcode     Salary
        -----------------------------------
        1653      ME2         35108
        1782      ME2         35345
        1244      ME2         36925
```

Output 34.3 OUTER UNION of ME1 and ME2 Tables

```
ME1 and ME2: OUTER UNION

    IDnum    Jobcode    Salary    Bonus  IDnum    Jobcode    Salary
    -----------------------------------------------------------------------
    1400     ME1        29769      587                                   .
    1403     ME1        28072      342                                   .
    1120     ME1        28619      986                                   .
    1120     ME1        28619      986                                   .
                                    .      .   1653     ME2        35108
                                    .      .   1782     ME2        35345
                                    .      .   1244     ME2        36925
```

To overlay columns with the same name, use the CORRESPONDING keyword.

```
proc sql;
    title 'ME1 and ME2: OUTER UNION CORRESPONDING';
    select *
        from me1
    outer union corr
    select *
        from me2;
```

```
ME1 and ME2: OUTER UNION CORRESPONDING

    IDnum    Jobcode    Salary    Bonus
    -------------------------------------------
    1400     ME1        29769      587
    1403     ME1        28072      342
    1120     ME1        28619      986
    1120     ME1        28619      986
    1653     ME2        35108        .
    1782     ME2        35345        .
    1244     ME2        36925        .
```

In the resulting concatenated table, notice the following:

- □ OUTER UNION CORRESPONDING retains all nonmatching columns.

- □ For columns with the same name, if a value is missing from the result of the first table-expression, the value in that column from the second table-expression is inserted.

- □ The ALL keyword is not used with OUTER UNION because this operator's default action is to include all rows in a result table. Thus, both rows from the table ME1 where IDnum is **1120** appear in the output.

UNION

The UNION operator produces a table that contains all the unique rows that result from both table-expressions. That is, the output table contains rows produced by the first table-expression, the second table-expression, or both.

Columns are appended by position in the tables, regardless of the column names. However, the data type of the corresponding columns must match or the union will not occur. PROC SQL issues a warning message and stops executing.

The names of the columns in the output table are the names of the columns from the first table-expression unless a column (such as an expression) has no name in the first table-expression. In such a case, the name of that column in the output table is the name of the respective column in the second table-expression.

In the following example, PROC SQL combines the two tables:

```
proc sql;
   title 'ME1 and ME2: UNION';
   select *
      from me1
   union
   select *
      from me2;
```

```
ME1 and ME2: UNION

        IDnum    Jobcode    Salary    Bonus
        ----------------------------------------
        1120     ME1        28619      986
        1244     ME2        36925        .
        1400     ME1        29769      587
        1403     ME1        28072      342
        1653     ME2        35108        .
        1782     ME2        35345        .
```

In the following example, ALL includes the duplicate row from ME1. In addition, ALL changes the sorting by specifying that PROC SQL make one pass only. Thus, the values from ME2 are simply appended to the values from ME1.

```
proc sql;
   title 'ME1 and ME2: UNION ALL';
   select *
      from me1
   union all
   select *
      from me2;
```

```
ME1 and ME2: UNION ALL

        IDnum    Jobcode    Salary    Bonus
        ----------------------------------------
        1400     ME1        29769      587
        1403     ME1        28072      342
        1120     ME1        28619      986
        1120     ME1        28619      986
        1653     ME2        35108        .
        1782     ME2        35345        .
        1244     ME2        36925        .
```

See Example 5 on page 1108 for another example.

EXCEPT

The EXCEPT operator produces (from the first table-expression) an output table that has unique rows that are not in the second table-expression. If the intermediate result from the first table-expression has at least one occurrence of a row that is not in the intermediate result of the second table-expression, that row (from the first table-expression) is included in the result table.

In the following example, the IN_USA table contains flights to cities within and outside the USA. The OUT_USA table contains flights only to cities outside the USA. This example returns only the rows from IN_USA that are not also in OUT_USA:

```
proc sql;
    title 'Flights from IN_USA';
    select * from in_usa
    except
    select * from out_usa;
```

```
IN_USA


           Flight    Dest
           ------------------
           145       ORD
           156       WAS
           188       LAX
           193       FRA
           207       LON
```

```
           OUT_USA

           Flight    Dest
           ------------------
           193       FRA
           207       LON
           311       SJA
```

```
           Flights from IN_USA

           Flight    Dest
           ------------------
           145       ORD
           156       WAS
           188       LAX
```

INTERSECT

The INTERSECT operator produces an output table that has rows that are common to both tables. For example, using the IN_USA and OUT_USA tables shown above, the following example returns rows that are in both tables:

```
proc sql;
    title 'Flights from IN_USA and OUT_USA';
    select * from in_usa
    intersect
    select * from out_usa;
```

```
Flights from IN_USA and OUT_USA

                 Flight    Dest
                 ------------------
                 193       FRA
                 207       LON
```

---

sql-expression

Produces a value from a sequence of operands and operators.

operand operator operand

 □ *operand* is one of the following:
  □ *constant* is a number or a quoted character string (or other special notation) that indicates a fixed value. Constants are also called *literals*. Constants are described in *SAS Language Reference: Dictionary*.
  □ column-name is described in "column-name" on page 1061.
  □ *SAS-function* is almost any SAS function. Functions are described in *SAS Language Reference: Dictionary*.
  □ The ANSI SQL function COALESCE is supported.
  □ summary-function is described in "summary-function" on page 1088.
  □ query-expression is described in "query-expression" on page 1075.
  □ USER is a literal that references the userid of the person who submitted the program. The userid that is returned is operating environment-dependent, but PROC SQL uses the same value that the &SYSJOBID macro variable has on the operating environment.
 □ *operator* is described in "Operators and the Order of Evaluation" on page 1082.

Note: SAS functions, including summary functions, can stand alone as SQL expressions. For example

```
select min(x) from table;
```

```
select scan(y,4) from table;
```

△

SAS Functions

PROC SQL supports the same SAS functions as the DATA step, except for the functions LAG, DIF, and SOUND. For example, the SCAN function is used in the following query:

```
select style, scan(street,1) format=$15.
  from houses;
```

See *SAS Language Reference: Dictionary* for complete documentation on SAS functions. Summary functions are also SAS functions. See "summary-function" on page 1088 for more information.

COALESCE Function

PROC SQL also supports the ANSI SQL function COALESCE. COALESCE accepts multiple column names of the same data type. The COALESCE function returns the first argument whose value is not a SAS missing value. In some SQL DBMSs, the COALESCE function is called the IFNULL function. See "PROC SQL and the ANSI Standard" on page 1098 for more information.

For an example that uses COALESCE, see Example 7 on page 1112.

USER Literal

USER can be specified in a view definition, for example, to create a view that restricts access to those in the user's department:

```
create view myemp as
   select * from dept12.employees
      where manager=user;
```

This view produces a different set of employee information for each manager who references it.

Operators and the Order of Evaluation

The order in which operations are evaluated is the same as in the DATA step with this one exception: NOT is grouped with the logical operators AND and OR in PROC SQL; in the DATA step, NOT is grouped with the unary plus and minus signs.

Unlike missing values in some versions of SQL, missing values in the SAS System always appear first in the collating sequence. Therefore, in Boolean and comparison operations, the following expressions resolve to true in a predicate:

```
 3>null
-3>null
 0>null
```

You can use parentheses to group values or to nest mathematical expressions. Parentheses make expressions easier to read and can also be used to change the order of evaluation of the operators. Evaluating expressions with parentheses begins at the deepest level of parentheses and moves outward. For example, SAS evaluates A+B*C as A+(B*C), although you can add parentheses to make it evaluate as (A+B)*C for a different result.

Higher priority operations are performed first: that is, group 0 operators are evaluated before group 5 operators. Table 34.2 on page 1082 shows the operators and their order of evaluation, including their priority groups.

Table 34.2 Operators and Order of Evaluation

Group	Operator	Description
0	( )	forces the expression enclosed to be evaluated first
1	case-expression	selects result values that satisfy specified conditions

Group	Operator	Description
2	**	raises to a power
	unary +, unary -	indicates a positive or negative number
3	*	multiplies
	/	divides
4	+	adds
	−	subtracts
5	||	concatenates
6	<NOT> BETWEEN condition	See "BETWEEN condition" on page 1057.
	<NOT> CONTAINS condition	see "CONTAINS condition" on page 1062.
	<NOT> EXISTS condition	See "EXISTS condition" on page 1066.
	<NOT> IN condition	See "IN condition" on page 1067.
	IS <NOT> condition	See "IS condition" on page 1067.
	<NOT> LIKE condition	See "LIKE condition" on page 1074.
7	=, eq	equals
	¬=, ^=, < >, ne	does not equal
	>, gt	is greater than
	<, lt	is less than
	>=, ge	is greater than or equal to
	<=, le	is less than or equal to
	=*	sounds like (use with character operands only). See Example 11 on page 1122.
8	&, AND	indicates logical AND
9	|, OR	indicates logical OR
10	¬, ^, NOT	indicates logical NOT

Symbols for operators may vary, depending on the operating environment. See *SAS Language Reference: Dictionary* for more information on operators and expressions.

Query Expressions (Subqueries)

Query-expressions are called *subqueries* when used in WHERE or HAVING clauses. A subquery is a query-expression that is nested as part of another query-expression. A subquery selects one or more rows from a table based on values in another table.

Depending on the clause that contains it, a subquery can return a single value or multiple values. If more than one subquery is used in a query-expression, the innermost query is evaluated first, then the next innermost query, and so on, moving outward.

PROC SQL allows a subquery (contained in parentheses) at any point in an expression where a simple column value or constant can be used. In this case, a subquery must return a *single value*, that is, one row with only one column. When a subquery returns one value, you can name the value with a column alias and refer to it by that name elsewhere in the query. This is useful for replacing values with other values returned using a subquery.

The following is an example of a subquery that returns one value. This PROC SQL step subsets the PROCLIB.PAYROLL table based on information in the PROCLIB.STAFF table. (PROCLIB.PAYROLL is shown in Example 2 on page 1103, and PROCLIB.STAFF is shown in Example 4 on page 1106.) PROCLIB.PAYROLL contains employee identification numbers (IdNumber) and their salaries (Salary) but does not contain their names. If you want to return only the row from PROCLIB.PAYROLL for one employee, you can use a subquery that queries the PROCLIB.STAFF table, which contains the employees' identification numbers and their names (Lname and Fname).

```
options ls=64 nodate nonumber;
proc sql;
    title 'Information for Earl Bowden';
    select *
        from proclib.payroll
        where idnumber=
            (select idnum
            from proclib.staff
            where upcase(lname)='BOWDEN');
```

```
Information for Earl Bowden

    Id
    Number  Sex  Jobcode   Salary   Birth    Hired
    ------------------------------------------------
    1403    M    ME1        28072   28JAN69  21DEC91
```

Subqueries can return *multiple values*. The following example uses the tables PROCLIB.DELAY and PROCLIB.MARCH. These tables contain information about the same flights and have the Flight column in common. The following subquery returns all the values for Flight in PROCLIB.DELAY for international flights. The values from the subquery complete the WHERE clause in the outer query. Thus, when the outer query is executed, only the international flights from PROCLIB.MARCH are in the output.

```
options ls=64 nodate nonumber;
proc sql outobs=5;
    title 'International Flights from';
    title2 'PROCLIB.MARCH';
    select Flight, Date, Dest, Boarded
        from proclib.march
        where flight in
            (select flight
             from proclib.delay
             where destype='International');
```

```
International Flights from
              PROCLIB.MARCH

     Flight    Date  Dest  Boarded
     -------------------------------
     219     01MAR94  LON      198
     622     01MAR94  FRA      207
     132     01MAR94  YYZ      115
     271     01MAR94  PAR      138
     219     02MAR94  LON      147
```

Sometimes it is helpful to compare a value with a set of values returned by a subquery. The keywords ANY or ALL can be specified before a subquery when the subquery is the right-hand operand of a comparison. If ALL is specified, the comparison is true only if it is true for all values returned by the subquery. If a subquery returns no rows, the result of an ALL comparison is true for each row of the outer query.

If ANY is specified, the comparison is true if it is true for any one of the values returned by the subquery. If a subquery returns no rows, the result of an ANY comparison is false for each row of the outer query.

The following example selects all those in PROCLIB.PAYROLL who earn more than the highest paid **ME3**:

```
options ls=64 nodate nonumber ;
proc sql;
title ''Employees who Earn More than'';
title2 ''All ME's'';
   select *
      from proclib.payroll
      where salary > all (select salary
                      from proclib.payroll
                      where jobcode='ME3');
```

```
               Employees who Earn More than
                       All ME's

     Id
     Number  Sex  Jobcode   Salary   Birth    Hired
     ----------------------------------------------------
     1333    M    PT2       88606   30MAR61  10FEB81
     1739    M    PT1       66517   25DEC64  27JAN91
     1428    F    PT1       68767   04APR60  16NOV91
     1404    M    PT2       91376   24FEB53  01JAN80
     1935    F    NA2       51081   28MAR54  16OCT81
     1905    M    PT1       65111   16APR72  29MAY92
     1407    M    PT1       68096   23MAR69  18MAR90
     1410    M    PT2       84685   03MAY67  07NOV86
     1439    F    PT1       70736   06MAR64  10SEP90
     1545    M    PT1       66130   12AUG59  29MAY90
     1106    M    PT2       89632   06NOV57  16AUG84
     1442    F    PT2       84536   05SEP66  12APR88
     1417    M    NA2       52270   27JUN64  07MAR89
     1478    M    PT2       84203   09AUG59  24OCT90
     1556    M    PT1       71349   22JUN64  11DEC91
```

```
                    Employees who Earn More than
                             All ME's

       Id
       Number   Sex   Jobcode   Salary    Birth     Hired
       --------------------------------------------------------
       1352     M     NA2       53798     02DEC60   16OCT86
       1890     M     PT2       91908     20JUL51   25NOV79
       1107     M     PT2       89977     09JUN54   10FEB79
       1830     F     PT2       84471     27MAY57   29JAN83
       1928     M     PT2       89858     16SEP54   13JUL90
       1076     M     PT1       66558     14OCT55   03OCT91
```

Note: See the first item in "Subqueries and Efficiency" on page 1087 for a note about efficiency when using ALL. △

Correlated Subqueries

In a correlated subquery, the WHERE expression in a subquery refers to values in a table in the outer query. The correlated subquery is evaluated for each row in the outer query. With correlated subqueries, PROC SQL executes the subquery and the outer query together.

The following example uses the PROCLIB.DELAY and PROCLIB.MARCH tables. A DATA step"PROCLIB.DELAY" on page 1506 creates PROCLIB.DELAY. PROCLIB.MARCH is shown in Example 13 on page 1126. PROCLIB.DELAY has the Flight, Date, Orig, and Dest columns in common with PROCLIB.MARCH:

```
proc sql outobs=5;
   title 'International Flights';
   select *
      from proclib.march
      where 'International' in
            (select destype
             from proclib.delay
             where march.Flight=delay.Flight);
```

The subquery resolves by substituting every value for MARCH.Flight into the subquery's WHERE clause, one row at a time. For example, when MARCH.Flight= **219**, the subquery resolves as follows:

1 PROC SQL retrieves all the rows from DELAY where Flight= **219** and passes their DESTYPE values to the WHERE clause.

2 PROC SQL uses the DESTYPE values to complete the WHERE clause:

```
      where 'International' in
         ('International','International', ...)
```

3 The WHERE clause checks to see if **International** is in the list. Because it is, all rows from MARCH that have a value of **219** for Flight become part of the output.

Output 34.4 on page 1086 contains the rows from MARCH for international flights only.

Output 34.4   International Flights for March

```
                           International Flights

       Flight    Date   Depart  Orig  Dest     Miles   Boarded  Capacity
       -----------------------------------------------------------------
       219     01MAR94    9:31   LGA   LON      3442      198      250
       622     01MAR94   12:19   LGA   FRA      3857      207      250
       132     01MAR94   15:35   LGA   YYZ       366      115      178
       271     01MAR94   13:17   LGA   PAR      3635      138      250
       219     02MAR94    9:31   LGA   LON      3442      147      250
```

Subqueries and Efficiency

☐ Use the MAX function in a subquery instead of the ALL keyword before the subquery. For example, the following queries produce the same result, but the second query is more efficient:

```
proc sql;
   select * from proclib.payroll
   where salary> all(select salary
                     from proclib.payroll
                     where jobcode='ME3');


proc sql;
   select * from proclib.payroll
   where salary> (select max(salary)
                  from proclib.payroll
                  where jobcode='ME3');
```

☐ With subqueries, use IN instead of EXISTS when possible. For example, the following queries produce the same result, but the second query is more efficient:

```
proc sql;
   select *
      from proclib.payroll p
      where exists (select *
                    from staff s
                    where p.idnum=s.idnum
                       and state='CT');


proc sql;
   select *
      from proclib.payroll
      where idnum in (select idnum
                      from staff
                      where state='CT');
```

summary-function

Performs statistical summary calculations.

Restriction: A summary function cannot appear in an ON clause or a WHERE clause.

See also: GROUP BY on page 1052, HAVING Clause on page 1053, SELECT Clause on page 1045, and "table-expression" on page 1094

Featured in: Example 8 on page 1116, Example 12 on page 1124, and Example 15 on page 1131

---

summary-function (<DISTINCT | ALL> sql-expression)

□   sql-expression is described in "sql-expression" on page 1081.

Summarizing Data

Summary functions produce a statistical summary of the entire table or view listed in the FROM clause or for each group specified in a GROUP BY clause. If GROUP BY is omitted, all the rows in the table or view are considered to be a single group. These functions reduce all the values in each row or column in a table to one *summarizing* or *aggregate* value. For this reason, these functions are often called *aggregate functions*. For example, the sum (one value) of a column results from the addition of all the values in the column.

Function Names and the Corresponding Statistics

Some functions have more than one name to accommodate both SAS and SQL conventions:

AVG, MEAN
   means or average of values

COUNT, FREQ, N
   number of nonmissing values

CSS
   corrected sum of squares

CV
   coefficient of variation (percent)

MAX
   largest value

MIN
   smallest value

NMISS
   number of missing values

PRT
   probability of a greater absolute value of Student's *t*

RANGE
   range of values

STD
standard deviation

STDERR
standard error of the mean

SUM
sum of values

SUMWGT
sum of the WEIGHT variable values*

T
Student's *t* value for testing the hypothesis that the population mean is zero

USS
uncorrected sum of squares

VAR
variance

For a description and the formulas used for these statistics, see Appendix 1, "SAS Elementary Statistics Procedures," on page 1457

Counting Rows

The COUNT function counts rows. COUNT(*) returns the total number of rows in a group or in a table. If you use a column name as an argument to COUNT, the result is the total number of rows in a group or in a table that have a nonmissing value for that column. If you want to count the unique values in a column, specify COUNT(DISTINCT *column*).

If the SELECT clause of a table-expression contains one or more summary functions and that table-expression resolves to no rows, then the summary function results are missing values. The following are exceptions that return zeros:

COUNT(*)

COUNT(<DISTINCT> sql-expression)

NMISS(<DISTINCT> sql-expression)

See Example 8 on page 1116 and Example 15 on page 1131 for examples.

Calculating Statistics Based on the Number of Arguments

The number of arguments specified in a summary function affects how the calculation is performed. If you specify a single argument, the values in the column are calculated. If you specify multiple arguments, the arguments or columns listed are calculated for each row. For example, consider calculations on the following table.

```
proc sql;
    title 'Summary Table';
    select * from summary;
```

---

* Currently, there is no way to designate a WEIGHT variable for a table in PROC SQL. Thus, each row (or observation) has a weight of 1.

```
                          Summary Table

                  X            Y            Z
        -----------------------------------
                  1            3            4
                  2            4            5
                  8            9            4
                  4            5            4
```

If you use one argument in the function, the calculation is performed on that column only. If you use more than one argument, the calculation is performed on each row of the specified columns. In the following PROC SQL step, the MIN and MAX functions return the minimum and maximum of the columns they are used with. The SUM function returns the sum of each row of the columns specified as arguments:

```
proc sql;
    select min(x) as Colmin_x,
           min(y) as Colmin_y,
           max(z) as Colmax_z,
           sum(x,y,z) as Rowsum
       from summary;
```

```
                          Summary Table

        Colmin_x  Colmin_y  Colmax_z    Rowsum
        ---------------------------------------
               1         3         5         8
               1         3         5        11
               1         3         5        21
               1         3         5        13
```

Remerging Data

When you use a summary function in a SELECT clause or a HAVING clause, you may see the following message in the SAS log:

```
NOTE: The query requires remerging summary
      statistics back with the original
      data.
```

The process of *remerging* involves two passes through the data. On the first pass, PROC SQL

- □ calculates and returns the value of summary functions. It then uses the result to calculate the arithmetic expressions in which the summary function participates.

- □ groups data according to the GROUP BY clause.

On the second pass, PROC SQL retrieves any additional columns and rows that it needs to show in the output.

The following examples use the PROCLIB.PAYROLL table (shown in Example 2 on page 1103) to show when remerging of data is and is not necessary.

The first query requires remerging. The first pass through the data groups the data by Jobcode and resolves the AVG function for each group. However, PROC SQL must make a second pass in order to retrieve the values of IdNumber and Salary.

```
proc sql outobs=10;
   title 'Salary Information';
   title2 '(First 10 Rows Only)';
   select  IdNumber, Jobcode, Salary,
           avg(salary) as AvgSalary
      from proclib.payroll
      group by jobcode;
```

```
                      Salary Information
                      (First 10 Rows Only)

        Id
        Number  Jobcode   Salary  AvgSalary
        -----------------------------------
        1845    BCK        25996  25794.22
        1673    BCK        25477  25794.22
        1834    BCK        26896  25794.22
        1389    BCK        25028  25794.22
        1100    BCK        25004  25794.22
        1677    BCK        26007  25794.22
        1663    BCK        26452  25794.22
        1383    BCK        25823  25794.22
        1704    BCK        25465  25794.22
        1132    FA1        22413  23039.36
```

You can change the previous query to return only the average salary for each jobcode. The following query does not require remerging because the first pass of the data does the summarizing and the grouping. A second pass is not necessary.

```
proc sql outobs=10;
   title 'Average Salary for Each Jobcode';
   select Jobcode, avg(salary) as AvgSalary
   from proclib.payroll
   group by jobcode;
```

```
                 Average Salary for Each Jobcode

                      Jobcode  AvgSalary
                      ------------------
                      BCK       25794.22
                      FA1       23039.36
                      FA2       27986.88
                      FA3       32933.86
                      ME1       28500.25
                      ME2       35576.86
                      ME3       42410.71
                      NA1        42032.2
                      NA2          52383
                      PT1          67908
```

When you use the HAVING clause, PROC SQL may have to remerge data to resolve the HAVING expression.

First, consider a query that uses HAVING but that does not require remerging. The query groups the data by values of Jobcode, and the result contains one row for each value of Jobcode and summary information for people in each Jobcode. On the first pass, the summary functions provide values for the **Number**, **Average Age**, and **Average Salary** columns. The first pass provides everything that PROC SQL needs to resolve the HAVING clause, so no remerging is necessary.

```
proc sql outobs=10;
title 'Summary Information for Each Jobcode';
title2 '(First 10 Rows Only)';
   select Jobcode,
           count(jobcode) as number
              label='Number',
           avg(int((today()-birth)/365.25))
              as avgage format=2.
              label='Average Age',
           avg(salary) as avgsal format=dollar8.
              label='Average Salary'
       from proclib.payroll
       group by jobcode
       having avgage ge 30;
```

```
            Summary Information for Each Jobcode                  1
                     (First 10 Rows Only)


                                  Average    Average
            Jobcode    Number         Age     Salary
            ------------------------------------------
            BCK             9          33    $25,794
            FA1            11          30    $23,039
            FA2            16          34    $27,987
            FA3             7          36    $32,934
            ME1             8          31    $28,500
            ME2            14          37    $35,577
            ME3             7          39    $42,411
            NA2             3          39    $52,383
            PT1             8          35    $67,908
            PT2            10          40    $87,925
```

In the following query, PROC SQL remerges the data because the HAVING clause uses the SALARY column in the comparison and SALARY is not in the GROUP BY clause.

```
proc sql outobs=10;
title 'Employees who Earn More than the';
title2 'Average for Their Jobcode';
title3 '(First 10 Rows Only)';
   select Jobcode, Salary,
           avg(salary) as AvgSalary
       from proclib.payroll
       group by jobcode
       having salary > AvgSalary;
```

```
         Employees who Earn More than the
             Average for Their Jobcode
                (First 10 Rows Only)

         Jobcode    Salary  AvgSalary
         ---------------------------
         BCK         25996   25794.22
         BCK         26896   25794.22
         BCK         26007   25794.22
         BCK         26452   25794.22
         BCK         25823   25794.22
         FA1         23738   23039.36
         FA1         23916   23039.36
         FA1         23644   23039.36
         FA1         23979   23039.36
         FA1         23177   23039.36
```

Keep in mind that PROC SQL remerges data when

- the values returned by a summary function are used in a calculation. For example, the following query returns the values of X and the percent of the total for each row. On the first pass, PROC SQL computes the sum of X, and on the second pass PROC SQL computes the percentage of the total for each value of X:

```
proc sql;
   title 'Percentage of the Total';
   select X, (100*x/sum(X)) as Pct_Total
      from summary;
```

```
                 Percentage of the Total

                     x   Pct_Total
                 -------------------
                    32    14.81481
                    86    39.81481
                    49    22.68519
                    49    22.68519
```

- the values returned by a summary function are compared to values of a column that is not specified in the GROUP BY clause. For example, the following query uses the PROCLIB.PAYROLL table. PROC SQL remerges data because the column Salary is not specified in the GROUP BY clause:

```
proc sql;
   select  jobcode,  salary,
           avg(salary) as avsal
      from proclib.payroll
      group by jobcode
      having salary > avsal;
```

- a column from the input table is specified in the SELECT clause and is not specified in the GROUP BY clause. This rule does not refer to columns used as arguments to summary functions in the SELECT clause.

For example, in the following query, the presence of IdNumber in the SELECT clause causes PROC SQL to remerge the data because IdNumber is not involved in grouping or summarizing during the first pass. In order for PROC SQL to retrieve the values for IdNumber, it must make a second pass through the data.

```
proc sql;
   select IdNumber, jobcode,
           avg(salary) as avsal
        from proclib.payroll
        group by jobcode;
```

table-expression

Defines part or all of a query-expression.

See also: "query-expression" on page 1075

SELECT <**DISTINCT**> *object-item*<,*object-item*>...
   <**INTO** :*macro-variable-specification*
        <, :*macro-variable-specification*>...>
   FROM *from-list*
   <**WHERE** sql-expression>
   <**GROUP BY** *group-by-item* <,*group-by-item*>...>
   <**HAVING** sql-expression>

See "SELECT Statement" on page 1044 for complete information on the SELECT statement.

Details

A table-expression is a SELECT statement. It is the fundamental building block of most SQL procedure statements. You can combine the results of multiple table-expressions with set operators, which creates a query-expression. Use one ORDER BY clause for an entire query-expression. Place a semicolon only at the end of the entire query-expression. A query-expression is often only one SELECT statement or table-expression.

Concepts

Using SAS Data Set Options with PROC SQL

PROC SQL can apply most of the SAS data set options, such as KEEP= and DROP=, to tables or SAS/ACCESS views. In the SQL procedure, SAS data set options that are separated by spaces are enclosed in parentheses, and they follow immediately after the table or SAS/ACCESS view name. You can also use SAS data set options on tables or SAS/ACCESS views listed in the FROM clause of a query. In the following PROC SQL

step, RENAME= renames LNAME to LASTNAME for the STAFF1 table. OBS=
restricts the number of rows written to STAFF1 to 15:

```
proc sql;
   create table
          staff1(rename=(lname=lastname)) as
      select *
          from staff(obs=15);
```

You cannot use SAS data set options with DICTIONARY tables because
DICTIONARY tables are read-only objects.

The only SAS data set options that you can use with PROC SQL views are those that
assign and provide SAS passwords: READ=, WRITE=, ALTER=, and PW=.

See *SAS Language Reference: Dictionary* for a description of SAS data set options.

Connecting to a DBMS Using the SQL Procedure Pass-Through Facility

The SQL Procedure Pass-Through Facility enables you to send DBMS-specific SQL
statements directly to a DBMS for execution. The Pass-Through Facility uses a SAS/
ACCESS interface engine to connect to the DBMS. Therefore, you must have SAS/
ACCESS software installed for your DBMS.

You submit SQL statements that are DBMS-specific. For example, you pass
Transact-SQL statements to a SYBASE database. The Pass-Through Facility's basic
syntax is the same for all the DBMSs. Only the statements that are used to connect to
the DBMS and the SQL statements are DBMS-specific.

With the Pass-Through Facility, you can perform the following tasks:

☐ establish a connection with the DBMS using a CONNECT statement and
terminate the connection with the DISCONNECT statement.

☐ send nonquery DBMS-specific SQL statements to the DBMS using the EXECUTE
statement.

☐ retrieve data from the DBMS to be used in a PROC SQL query with the
CONNECTION TO component in a SELECT statement's FROM clause.

You can use the Pass-Through Facility statements in a query, or you can store them
in a PROC SQL view. When a view is stored, any options that are specified in the
corresponding CONNECT statement are also stored. Thus, when the PROC SQL view
is used in a SAS program, the SAS System can automatically establish the appropriate
connection to the DBMS.

See "CONNECT Statement" on page 1033, "DISCONNECT Statement" on page 1040,
"EXECUTE Statement" on page 1042, "CONNECTION TO" on page 1062, and your
SAS/ACCESS documentation.

Return Codes

As you use PROC SQL statements that are available in the Pass-Through Facility,
any errors are written to the SAS log. The return codes and messages that are
generated by the Pass-Through Facility are available to you through the SQLXRC and
SQLXMSG macro variables. Both macro variables are described in "Using Macro
Variables Set by PROC SQL" on page 1096.

Connecting to a DBMS using the LIBNAME Statement

For many DBMSs, you can directly access DBMS data by assigning a libref to the
DBMS using the SAS/ACCESS LIBNAME statement. Once you have associated a libref

with the DBMS, you can specify a DBMS table in a two-level SAS name and work with the table like any SAS data set. You can also embed the LIBNAME statement in a PROC SQL view (see "CREATE VIEW Statement" on page 1037).

PROC SQL will take advantage of the capabilities of a DBMS by passing it certain operations whenever possible. For example, before implementing a join, PROC SQL checks to see if the DBMS can do the join. If it can, PROC SQL passes the join to the DBMS. This increases performance by reducing data movement and translation. If the DBMS cannot do the join, PROC SQL processes the join. Using the SAS/ACCESS LIBNAME statement can often provide you with the performance benefits of the SQL Procedure Pass-Through Facility without having to write DBMS-specific code.

To use the SAS/ACCESS LIBNAME statement, you must have SAS/ACCESS installed for your DBMS. For more information on the SAS/ACCESS LIBNAME statement, refer to your SAS/ACCESS documentation.

Using Macro Variables Set by PROC SQL

PROC SQL sets up macro variables with certain values after it executes each statement. These macro variables can be tested inside a macro to determine whether to continue executing the PROC SQL step. SAS/AF software users can also test them in a program after an SQL SUBMIT block of code, using the SYMGET function.

After each PROC SQL statement has executed, the following macro variables are updated with these values:

SQLOBS

contains the number of rows executed by an SQL procedure statement. For example, it contains the number of rows formatted and displayed in SAS output by a SELECT statement or the number of rows deleted by a DELETE statement.

SQLRC

contains the following status values that indicate the success of the SQL procedure statement:

0

PROC SQL statement completed successfully with no errors.

4

PROC SQL statement encountered a situation for which it issued a warning. The statement continued to execute.

8

PROC SQL statement encountered an error. The statement stopped execution at this point.

12

PROC SQL statement encountered an internal error, indicating a bug in PROC SQL that should be reported to SAS Institute. These errors can occur only during compile time.

16

PROC SQL statement encountered a user error. This error code is used, for example, when a subquery (that can only return a single value) evaluates to more than one row. These errors can only be detected during run time.

24

PROC SQL statement encountered a system error. This error is used, for example, if the system cannot write to a PROC SQL table because the disk is full. These errors can occur only during run time.

28
PROC SQL statement encountered an internal error, indicating a bug in PROC SQL that should be reported to SAS Institute. These errors can occur only during run time.

SQLOOPS
contains the number of iterations that the inner loop of PROC SQL executes. The number of iterations increases proportionally with the complexity of the query. See also the description of the LOOPS option on page 1029.

SQLXRC
contains the DBMS-specific return code that is returned by the Pass-Through Facility.

SQLXMSG
contains descriptive information and the DBMS-specific return code for the error that is returned by the Pass-Through Facility.

This example retrieves the data but does not display them in SAS output because of the NOPRINT option in the PROC SQL statement. The %PUT macro statement displays the macro variables values.

```
proc sql noprint;
   select *
       from proclib.payroll;


%put sqlobs=**&sqlobs**
     sqloops=**&sqloops**
     sqlrc=**&sqlrc**;
```

The message in Output 34.5 on page 1097 appears in the SAS log and gives you the macros' values.

Output 34.5 PROC SQL Macro Variable Values

```
1    options ls=80;
2    proc sql noprint;
3       select *
4           from proclib.payroll;
5
6    %put sqlobs=**&sqlobs**
7         sqloops=**&sqloops**
8         sqlrc=**&sqlrc**;
sqlobs=**1**        sqloops=**11**        sqlrc=**0**
```

Updating PROC SQL and SAS/ACCESS Views

You can update PROC SQL and SAS/ACCESS views using the INSERT, DELETE, and UPDATE statements, under the following conditions.

□ If the view accesses a DBMS table, you must have been granted the appropriate authorization by the external database management system (for example, DB2). You must have installed the SAS/ACCESS software for your DBMS. See the SAS/ACCESS interface guide for your DBMS for more information on SAS/ACCESS views.

□ You can update only a single table through a view. The table cannot be joined to another table or linked to another table with a set-operator. The view cannot contain a subquery.

□ You can update a column in a view using the column's alias, but you cannot update a derived column, that is, a column produced by an expression. In the following example, you can update the column SS, but not WeeklySalary.

```
create view EmployeeSalaries as
    select Employee, SSNumber as SS,
           Salary/52 as WeeklySalary
           from employees;
```

□ You cannot update a view containing an ORDER BY.

PROC SQL and the ANSI Standard

PROC SQL follows most of the guidelines set by the American National Standards Institute (ANSI) in its implementation of SQL. However, it is not fully compliant with the current ANSI Standard for SQL.*

The SQL research project at SAS Institute has focused primarily on the expressive power of SQL as a query language. Consequently, some of the database features of SQL have not yet been implemented in the SAS System.

This section describes

□ enhancements to SQL that SAS Institute has made through PROC SQL

□ the ways in which PROC SQL differs from the current ANSI Standard for SQL.

SQL Procedure Enhancements

Most of the enhancements described here are required by the current ANSI Standard.

Reserved Words

PROC SQL reserves very few keywords and then only in certain contexts. The ANSI Standard reserves all SQL keywords in all contexts. For example, according to the Standard you cannot name a column GROUP because of the keywords GROUP BY.

The following words are reserved in PROC SQL:

□ The keyword CASE is always reserved; its use in the CASE expression (an SQL2 feature) precludes its use as a column name.

  If you have a column named CASE in a table and you want to specify it in a PROC SQL step, you can use the SAS data set option RENAME= to rename that column for the duration of the query. You can also surround CASE in double quotes ("CASE") and set the PROC SQL option DQUOTE=ANSI.

□ The keywords AS, ON, FULL, JOIN, LEFT, FROM, WHEN, WHERE, ORDER, GROUP, RIGHT, INNER, OUTER, UNION, EXCEPT, HAVING, and INTERSECT cannot normally be used for table aliases. These keywords all introduce clauses that appear after a table name. Since the alias is optional, PROC SQL deals with this ambiguity by assuming that any one of these words introduces the corresponding clause and is not the alias. If you want to use one of these keywords as an alias, use the PROC SQL option DQUOTE=ANSI.

---

* International Organization for Standardization (ISO): *Database SQL*. Document ISO/IEC 9075:1992. Also available as American National Standards Institute (ANSI) Document ANSI X3.135-1992.

□ The keyword USER is reserved for the current userid. If you have a column named USER in a table and you want to specify it in a PROC SQL step, you can use the SAS data set option RENAME= to rename that column for the duration of the query. You can also surround USER in double quotes ("USER") and set the PROC SQL option DQUOTE=ANSI.

Column Modifiers

PROC SQL supports the SAS System's INFORMAT=, FORMAT=, and LABEL= modifiers for expressions within the SELECT clause. These modifiers control the format in which output data are displayed and labeled.

Alternate Collating Sequences

PROC SQL allows you to specify an alternate collating (sorting) sequence to be used when you specify the ORDER BY clause. See the description of the SORTSEQ= option in "PROC SQL Statement" on page 1027 for more information.

ORDER BY Clause in a View Definition

PROC SQL permits you to specify an ORDER BY clause in a CREATE VIEW statement. When the view is queried, its data are always sorted according to the specified order unless a query against that view includes a different ORDER BY clause. See "CREATE VIEW Statement" on page 1037 for more information.

In-Line Views

The ability to code nested query-expressions in the FROM clause is a requirement of the ANSI Standard. PROC SQL supports such nested coding.

Outer Joins

The ability to include columns that both match and do not match in a join-expression is a requirement of the ANSI Standard. PROC SQL supports this ability.

Arithmetic Operators

PROC SQL supports the SAS System exponentiation (**) operator. PROC SQL uses the notation < > to mean not equal.

Orthogonal Expressions

PROC SQL permits the combination of comparison, Boolean, and algebraic expressions. For example, (X=3)*7 yields a value of 7 if X=3 is true because true is defined to be 1. If X=3 is false, it resolves to 0 and the entire expression yields a value of 0.

PROC SQL permits a subquery in any expression. This feature is required by the ANSI Standard. Therefore, you can have a subquery on the left side of a comparison operator in the WHERE expression.

PROC SQL permits you to order and group data by any kind of mathematical expression (except those including summary functions) using ORDER BY and GROUP BY clauses. You can also group by an expression that appears on the SELECT clause by using the integer that represents the expression's ordinal position in the SELECT clause. You are not required to select the expression by which you are grouping or ordering. See ORDER BY Clause on page 1053 and GROUP BY Clause on page 1052 for more information.

Set Operators

The set operators UNION, INTERSECT, and EXCEPT are required by the ANSI Standard. PROC SQL provides these operators plus the OUTER UNION operator.

The ANSI Standard also requires that the tables being operated upon all have the same number of columns with matching data types. The SQL procedure works on tables that have the same number of columns, as well as on those that do not, by creating virtual columns so that a query can evaluate correctly. See "query-expression" on page 1075 for more information.

Statistical Functions

PROC SQL supports many more summary functions than required by the ANSI Standard for SQL.

PROC SQL supports the remerging of summary function results into the table's original data. For example, computing the percentage of total is achieved with $100*x/\text{SUM}(x)$ in PROC SQL. See "summary-function" on page 1088 for more information on the available summary functions and remerging data.

SAS System Functions

PROC SQL supports all the functions available to the SAS DATA step, except for LAG, DIF, and SOUND. Other SQL databases support their own set of functions.

SQL Procedure Omissions

PROC SQL differs from the ANSI Standard for SQL in the following ways.

COMMIT Statement

The COMMIT statement is not supported.

ROLLBACK Statement

The ROLLBACK statement is not supported. The UNDO_POLICY= option in the PROC SQL statement addresses rollback. See the description of the UNDO_POLICY= option in "PROC SQL Statement" on page 1027 for more information.

Identifiers and Naming Conventions

In the SAS System, table names, column names, and aliases are limited to 32 characters and can contain mixed case. For more information on SAS naming conventions, see *SAS Language Reference: Dictionary*. The ANSI Standard for SQL allows longer names.

Granting User Privileges

The GRANT statement, PRIVILEGES keyword, and authorization-identifier features of SQL are not supported. You may want to use operating environment-specific means of security instead.

Three-Valued Logic

ANSI-compatible SQL has three-valued logic, that is, special cases for handling comparisons involving NULL values. Any value compared with a NULL value evaluates to NULL.

PROC SQL follows the SAS System convention for handling missing values: when numeric NULL values are compared to non-NULL numbers, the NULL values are less than or smaller than all the non-NULL values; when character NULL values are compared to non-NULL characters, the character NULL values are treated as a string of blanks.

Embedded SQL

Currently there is no provision for embedding PROC SQL statements in other SAS programming environments, such as the DATA step or SAS/IML software.

Examples

Example 1: Creating a Table and Inserting Data into It

Procedure features:
    CREATE TABLE statement
        column-modifier
    INSERT statement
        VALUES clause
    SELECT clause
    FROM clause
Table: PROCLIB.PAYLIST

This example creates the table PROCLIB.PAYLIST and inserts data into it.

Program

```
libname proclib 'SAS-data-library';


options nodate pageno=1 linesize=80 pagesize=40;
```

The CREATE TABLE statement creates PROCLIB.PAYLIST with six empty columns. Each column definition indicates whether the column is character or numeric. The number in parentheses specifies the width of the column. INFORMAT= and FORMAT= assign date informats and formats to the Birth and Hired columns.

```
proc sql;
   create table proclib.paylist
       (IdNum char(4),
        Gender char(1),
        Jobcode char(3),
        Salary num,
        Birth num informat=date7.
               format=date7.,
        Hired num informat=date7.
               format=date7.);
```

The INSERT statement inserts data values into PROCLIB.PAYLIST according to the position in the VALUES clause. Therefore, in the first VALUES clause, **1639** is inserted into the first column, **F** into the second column, and so forth. Dates in SAS are stored as integers with 0 equal to January 1, 1960. Suffixing the date with a **d** is one way to use the internal value for dates.

```
insert into proclib.paylist
    values('1639','F','TA1',42260,'26JUN70'd,'28JAN91'd)
    values('1065','M','ME3',38090,'26JAN54'd,'07JAN92'd)
    values('1400','M','ME1',29769.'05NOV67'd,'16OCT90'd)
```

The value **null** represents a missing value for the character column Jobcode. The period represents a missing value for the numeric column Salary.

```
    values('1561','M',null,36514,'30NOV63'd,'07OCT87'd)
    values('1221','F','FA3',.,'22SEP63'd,'04OCT94'd);
```

The SELECT clause selects columns from PROCLIB.PAYLIST. The asterisk (*) selects all columns. The FROM clause specifies PROCLIB.PAYLIST as the table to select from.

```
title 'PROCLIB.PAYLIST Table';
select *
    from proclib.paylist;
```

Output Table

PROCLIB.PAYLIST

```
                        PROCLIB.PAYLIST Table                          1

       Id
       Num   Gender  Jobcode   Salary    Birth     Hired
       ------------------------------------------------------
       1639  F         TA1      42260   26JUN70   28JAN91
       1065  M         ME3      38090   26JAN54   07JAN92
       1400  M         ME1      29769   05NOV67   16OCT90
       1561  M                  36514   30NOV63   07OCT87
       1221  F         FA3          .   22SEP63   04OCT94
```

Example 2: Creating a Table from a Query's Result

Procedure features:
    CREATE TABLE statement
      AS query-expression
    SELECT clause
      column alias
      FORMAT= column-modifier
      object-item

Other features:
    data set option
      OBS=

Tables:
    PROCLIB.PAYROLL, PROCLIB.BONUS

This example builds a column with an arithmetic expression and creates the PROCLIB.BONUS table from the query's result.

Input Table

PROCLIB.PAYROLL (Partial Listing)

```
                        PROCLIB.PAYROLL
                        First 10 Rows Only

     Id
     Number  Sex  Jobcode   Salary    Birth      Hired
     ------------------------------------------------------
       1919   M    TA2       34376   12SEP60    04JUN87
       1653   F    ME2       35108   15OCT64    09AUG90
       1400   M    ME1       29769   05NOV67    16OCT90
       1350   F    FA3       32886   31AUG65    29JUL90
       1401   M    TA3       38822   13DEC50    17NOV85
       1499   M    ME3       43025   26APR54    07JUN80
       1101   M    SCP       18723   06JUN62    01OCT90
       1333   M    PT2       88606   30MAR61    10FEB81
       1402   M    TA2       32615   17JAN63    02DEC90
       1479   F    TA3       38785   22DEC68    05OCT89
```

Program

```
libname proclib 'SAS-data-library';


options nodate pageno=1 linesize=80 pagesize=40;
```

The CREATE TABLE statement creates the table PROCLIB.BONUS from the result of the subsequent query.

```
proc sql;
   create table proclib.bonus as
```

The SELECT clause specifies that three columns will be in the new table: IdNumber, Salary, and Bonus. FORMAT= assigns the DOLLAR8. format to Salary. The Bonus column is built with the SQL expression **salary*.025**.

```
select IdNumber, Salary format=dollar8.,
       salary*.025 as Bonus format=dollar8.
   from proclib.payroll;
```

The SELECT clause selects columns from PROCLIB.BONUS. The asterisk (*) selects all columns. The FROM clause specifies PROCLIB.BONUS as the table to select from. The OBS= data set option limits the printing of the output to 10 rows.

```
title 'BONUS Information';
select *
   from proclib.bonus(obs=10);
```

Output

PROCLIB.BONUS

```
                    BONUS Information                        1

         Id
         Number    Salary     Bonus
         --------------------------
         1919      $34,376      $859
         1653      $35,108      $878
         1400      $29,769      $744
         1350      $32,886      $822
         1401      $38,822      $971
         1499      $43,025    $1,076
         1101      $18,723      $468
         1333      $88,606    $2,215
         1402      $32,615      $815
         1479      $38,785      $970
```

Example 3: Updating Data in a PROC SQL Table

Procedure features:
    ALTER TABLE statement
        DROP clause

> MODIFY clause
>
> UPDATE statement
>
> SET clause
>
> CASE expression

Table: EMPLOYEES

This example updates data values in the EMPLOYEES table and drops a column.

Input

```
data Employees;
    input IdNum $4. +2 LName $11. FName $11. JobCode $3.
          +1 Salary 5. +1 Phone $12.;
    datalines;
1876  CHIN        JACK        TA1 42400 212/588-5634
1114  GREENWALD   JANICE      ME3 38000 212/588-1092
1556  PENNINGTON  MICHAEL     ME1 29860 718/383-5681
1354  PARKER      MARY        FA3 65800 914/455-2337
1130  WOOD        DEBORAH     PT2 36514 212/587-0013
;
```

Program

```
options nodate pageno=1 linesize=80 pagesize=40;
```

The SELECT clause displays the table before the updates. The asterisk (*) selects all columns for display. The FROM clause specifies EMPLOYEES as the table to select from.

```
proc sql;
    title 'Employees Table';
    select * from Employees;
```

The UPDATE statement updates the values in EMPLOYEES. The SET clause specifies that the data in the Salary column be multiplied by 1.04 when the job code ends with a **1** and 1.025 for all other job codes. (The two underscores represent any character.) The CASE expression returns a value for each row that completes the SET clause.

```
update employees
     set salary=salary*
     case when jobcode like '__1' then 1.04
          else 1.025
     end;
```

The ALTER TABLE statement specifies EMPLOYEES as the table to alter. The MODIFY clause permanently modifies the format of the Salary column. The DROP clause permanently drops the Phone column.

```
alter table employees
   modify salary num format=dollar8.
   drop phone;
```

The SELECT clause displays the EMPLOYEES table after the updates. The asterisk (*) selects all columns.

```
title 'Updated Employees Table';
select * from employees;
```

Output

```
                              Employees Table                               1

       Id                            Job
       Num   LName        FName       Code    Salary  Phone
       --------------------------------------------------------------
       1876  CHIN         JACK        TA1      42400  212/588-5634
       1114  GREENWALD    JANICE      ME3      38000  212/588-1092
       1556  PENNINGTON   MICHAEL     ME1      29860  718/383-5681
       1354  PARKER       MARY        FA3      65800  914/455-2337
       1130  WOOD         DEBORAH     PT2      36514  212/587-0013
```

```
                          Updated Employees Table                           2

        Id                            Job
        Num   LName        FName       Code    Salary
        ------------------------------------------------
        1876  CHIN         JACK        TA1     $44,096
        1114  GREENWALD    JANICE      ME3     $38,950
        1556  PENNINGTON   MICHAEL     ME1     $31,054
        1354  PARKER       MARY        FA3     $67,445
        1130  WOOD         DEBORAH     PT2     $37,427
```

Example 4: Joining Two Tables

Procedure features:
    FROM clause
        table alias
    inner join
    joined-table component
    PROC SQL statement option
        NUMBER
    WHERE clause
        IN condition
Tables: PROCLIB.STAFF, PROCLIB.PAYROLL

This example joins two tables in order to to get more information about data that are common to both tables.

Input Tables

PROCLIB.STAFF (Partial Listing)

```
                            PROCLIB.STAFF
                           First 10 Rows Only

Id
Num    Lname               Fname            City             State   Hphone
-----------------------------------------------------------------------------
1919   ADAMS               GERALD           STAMFORD         CT      203/781-1255
1653   ALIBRANDI           MARIA            BRIDGEPORT       CT      203/675-7715
1400   ALHERTANI           ABDULLAH         NEW YORK         NY      212/586-0808
1350   ALVAREZ             MERCEDES         NEW YORK         NY      718/383-1549
1401   ALVAREZ             CARLOS           PATERSON         NJ      201/732-8787
1499   BAREFOOT            JOSEPH           PRINCETON        NJ      201/812-5665
1101   BAUCOM              WALTER           NEW YORK         NY      212/586-8060
1333   BANADYGA            JUSTIN           STAMFORD         CT      203/781-1777
1402   BLALOCK             RALPH            NEW YORK         NY      718/384-2849
1479   BALLETTI            MARIE            NEW YORK         NY      718/384-8816
```

PROCLIB.PAYROLL (Partial Listing)

```
                          PROCLIB.PAYROLL
                         First 10 Rows Only

Id
Number  Sex  Jobcode   Salary    Birth     Hired
------------------------------------------------------
1919    M    TA2       34376    12SEP60   04JUN87
1653    F    ME2       35108    15OCT64   09AUG90
1400    M    ME1       29769    05NOV67   16OCT90
1350    F    FA3       32886    31AUG65   29JUL90
1401    M    TA3       38822    13DEC50   17NOV85
1499    M    ME3       43025    26APR54   07JUN80
1101    M    SCP       18723    06JUN62   01OCT90
1333    M    PT2       88606    30MAR61   10FEB81
1402    M    TA2       32615    17JAN63   02DEC90
1479    F    TA3       38785    22DEC68   05OCT89
```

Program

```
libname proclib 'SAS-data-library';
```

NUMBER adds a column that contains the row number.

```
proc sql number;
```

The SELECT clause selects the columns to output.

```
title 'Information for Certain Employees Only';
select Lname, Fname, City, State,
       IdNumber, Salary, Jobcode
```

The FROM clause lists the tables to select from.

```
from proclib.staff, proclib.payroll
```

The WHERE clause specifies that the tables are joined on the ID number from each table. WHERE also further subsets the query with the IN condition, which returns rows for only four employees.

```
where idnumber=idnum and idnum in
      ('1919','1400', '1350', '1333');
```

Output

```
                 Information for Certain Employees Only                  1


                                                            Id
      Row  Lname           Fname          City       State Number
           Salary  Jobcode
      --------------------------------------------------------------
       1   ADAMS           GERALD         STAMFORD    CT    1919
           34376   TA2

       2   ALHERTANI       ABDULLAH       NEW YORK    NY    1400
           29769   ME1

       3   ALVAREZ         MERCEDES       NEW YORK    NY    1350
           32886   FA3

       4   BANADYGA        JUSTIN         STAMFORD    CT    1333
           88606   PT2
```

Example 5: Combining Two Tables
Procedure features:

DELETE statement
IS condition
RESET statement option
     DOUBLE
UNION set operator

Tables: PROCLIB.NEWPAY, PROCLIB.PAYLIST, PROCLIB.PAYLIST2

This example creates a new table, PROCLIB.NEWPAY, by concatenating two other tables: PROCLIB.PAYLIST and PROCLIB.PAYLIST2.

Input Tables

PROCLIB.PAYLIST

```
                    PROCLIB.PAYLIST Table

     Id
     Num   Gender  Jobcode   Salary    Birth    Hired
     ------------------------------------------------------
     1639  F       TA1        42260   26JUN70  28JAN91
     1065  M       ME3        38090   26JAN54  07JAN92
     1400  M       ME1        29769   05NOV67  16OCT90
     1561  M                  36514   30NOV63  07OCT87
     1221  F       FA3            .   22SEP63  04OCT94
```

PROCLIB.PAYLIST2

```
                    PROCLIB.PAYLIST2 Table

     Id
     Num   Gender  Jobcode   Salary    Birth    Hired
     ------------------------------------------------------
     1919  M       TA2        34376   12SEP66  04JUN87
     1653  F       ME2        31896   15OCT64  09AUG92
     1350  F       FA3        36886   31AUG55  29JUL91
     1401  M       TA3        38822   13DEC55  17NOV93
     1499  M       ME1        23025   26APR74  07JUN92
```

Program

```
libname proclib 'SAS-data-library';


options nodate pageno=1 linesize=80 pagesize=60;
```

The SELECT clauses select all the columns from the tables listed in the FROM clauses. The UNION set operator concatenates the query results that are produced by the two SELECT clauses. UNION orders the result by IdNum.

```
proc sql;
   create table proclib.newpay as
      select * from proclib.paylist
      union
      select * from proclib.paylist2;
```

The DELETE statement deletes rows from PROCLIB.NEWPAY that satisfy the WHERE expression. The IS condition specifies rows that contain missing values in the Jobcode or Salary column.

```
delete
   from proclib.newpay
   where jobcode is missing or salary is missing;
```

RESET changes the procedure environment without stopping and restarting PROC SQL. The DOUBLE option double-spaces the output. (The DOUBLE option has no effect on ODS output.) The SELECT clause selects all columns from the newly created table, PROCLIB.NEWPAY.

```
reset double;
title 'Personnel Data';
select *
   from proclib.newpay;
```

Output

```
                              Personnel Data                              1

     Id
     Num   Gender   Jobcode   Salary    Birth     Hired
     ----------------------------------------------------------------
     1065  M        ME3        38090   26JAN54   07JAN92

     1350  F        FA3        36886   31AUG55   29JUL91

     1400  M        ME1        29769   05NOV67   16OCT90

     1401  M        TA3        38822   13DEC55   17NOV93

     1499  M        ME1        23025   26APR74   07JUN92

     1639  F        TA1        42260   26JUN70   28JAN91

     1653  F        ME2        31896   15OCT64   09AUG92

     1919  M        TA2        34376   12SEP66   04JUN87
```

Example 6: Reporting from DICTIONARY Tables

Procedure features:
> DESCRIBE TABLE statement
> DICTIONARY.*table-name* component

Table: DICTIONARY.MEMBERS

This example uses DICTIONARY tables to show a list of the SAS files in a SAS data library. If you do not know the names of the columns in the DICTIONARY table that you are querying, use a DESCRIBE TABLE statement with the table.

Program

```
libname proclib 'SAS-data-library';
```

SOURCE writes the programming statements to the SAS log.

```
options nodate pageno=1 source linesize=80 pagesize=60;
```

DESCRIBE TABLE writes the column names from DICTIONARY.MEMBERS to the SAS log.

```
proc sql;
   describe table dictionary.members;
```

The SELECT clause selects the MEMNAME and MEMTYPE columns. The FROM clause specifies DICTIONARY.MEMBERS as the table to select from. The WHERE clause subsets the output to include only those rows that have a libref of *PROCLIB* in the LIBNAME column.

```
title 'SAS Files in the PROCLIB Library';
select memname, memtype
   from dictionary.members
   where libname='PROCLIB';
```

Log

```
2   options nodate pageno=1 source linesize=80 pagesize=60;
3   proc sql;
4     describe table dictionary.members;
NOTE: SQL table DICTIONARY.MEMBERS was created like:

create table DICTIONARY.MEMBERS
  (
   libname char(8) label='Library Name',
   memname char(32) label='Member Name',
   memtype char(8) label='Member Type',
   engine char(8) label='Engine Name',
   index char(32) label='Indexes',
   path char(1024) label='Path Name'
  );

5     title 'SAS Files in the PROCLIB Library';
6     select memname, memtype
7        from dictionary.members
8        where libname='PROCLIB';
```

Output

```
              SAS Files in the PROCLIB Library                      1

                                       Member
                   Member Name         Type
                   ------------------------------------------
                   BONUS               DATA
                   BONUS95             DATA
                   DELAY               DATA
                   HOUSES              DATA
                   INTERNAT            DATA
                   JOBS                VIEW
                   MARCH               DATA
                   NEWPAY              DATA
                   PAYDATA             VIEW
                   PAYINFO             VIEW
                   PAYLIST             DATA
                   PAYLIST2            DATA
                   PAYROLL             DATA
                   PAYROLL2            DATA
                   SCHEDULE            DATA
                   SCHEDULE2           DATA
                   STAFF               DATA
                   STAFF2              DATA
                   SUPERV              DATA
                   SUPERV2             DATA
```

Example 7: Performing an Outer Join

Procedure features:
   joined-table component
   left outer join
   SELECT clause

COALESCE function
WHERE clause
    CONTAINS condition
Tables: PROCLIB.PAYROLL, PROCLIB.PAYROLL2

This example illustrates a left outer join of the PROCLIB.PAYROLL and PROCLIB.PAYROLL2 tables.

Input Tables

PROCLIB.PAYROLL (Partial Listing)

```
                         PROCLIB.PAYROLL
                         First 10 Rows Only

      Id
      Number  Sex  Jobcode   Salary    Birth     Hired
      ------------------------------------------------------
      1009    M    TA1        28880   02MAR59   26MAR92
      1017    M    TA3        40858   28DEC57   16OCT81
      1036    F    TA3        39392   19MAY65   23OCT84
      1037    F    TA1        28558   10APR64   13SEP92
      1038    F    TA1        26533   09NOV69   23NOV91
      1050    M    ME2        35167   14JUL63   24AUG86
      1065    M    ME2        35090   26JAN44   07JAN87
      1076    M    PT1        66558   14OCT55   03OCT91
      1094    M    FA1        22268   02APR70   17APR91
      1100    M    BCK        25004   01DEC60   07MAY88
```

PROCLIB.PAYROLL2

```
                         PROCLIB.PAYROLL2

      Id
      Num   Sex  Jobcode   Salary    Birth     Hired
      ------------------------------------------------------
      1036   F    TA3       42465   19MAY65   23OCT84
      1065   M    ME3       38090   26JAN44   07JAN87
      1076   M    PT1       69742   14OCT55   03OCT91
      1106   M    PT3       94039   06NOV57   16AUG84
      1129   F    ME3       36758   08DEC61   17AUG91
      1221   F    FA3       29896   22SEP67   04OCT91
      1350   F    FA3       36098   31AUG65   29JUL90
      1369   M    TA3       36598   28DEC61   13MAR87
      1447   F    FA1       22123   07AUG72   29OCT92
      1561   M    TA3       36514   30NOV63   07OCT87
      1639   F    TA3       42260   26JUN57   28JAN84
      1998   M    SCP       23100   10SEP70   02NOV92
```

Program

```
libname proclib 'SAS-data-library';


options nodate pageno=1 linesize=80 pagesize=60;
```

OUTOBS= limits the output to 10 rows. The SELECT clause lists the columns to select. Some column names are prefixed with a table alias because they are in both tables. LABEL= and FORMAT= are column modifiers.

```
proc sql outobs=10;
   title 'Most Current Jobcode and Salary Information';
   select p.IdNumber, p.Jobcode, p.Salary,
          p2.jobcode label='New Jobcode',
          p2.salary label='New Salary' format=dollar8.
```

The FROM clause lists the tables to join and assigns table aliases. The keywords LEFT JOIN specify the type of join. The order of the tables in the FROM clause is important. PROCLIB.PAYROLL is listed first and is considered the "left" table, PROCLIB.PAYROLL2 is the "right" table.

```
      from proclib.payroll as p left join proclib.payroll2 as p2
```

The ON clause specifies that the join be performed based on the values of the ID numbers from each table.

```
      on p.IdNumber=p2.idnum;
```

Output

As the output shows, all rows from the left table, PROCLIB.PAYROLL, are returned. PROC SQL assigns missing values for rows in the left table, PAYROLL, that have no matching values for IdNum in PAYROLL2.

```
              Most Current Jobcode and Salary Information              1

              Id                        New           New
              Number   Jobcode   Salary Jobcode       Salary
              -----------------------------------------------
              1009     TA1       28880                    .
              1017     TA3       40858                    .
              1036     TA3       39392  TA3       $42,465
              1037     TA1       28558                    .
              1038     TA1       26533                    .
              1050     ME2       35167                    .
              1065     ME2       35090  ME3       $38,090
              1076     PT1       66558  PT1       $69,742
              1094     FA1       22268                    .
              1100     BCK       25004                    .
```

The SELECT clause lists the columns to select. COALESCE overlays the like-named columns. For each row, COALESCE returns the first nonmissing value of either P2.JOBCODE or P.JOBCODE. Because P2.JOBCODE is the first argument, if there is a nonmissing value for P2.JOBCODE, COALESCE returns that value. Thus, the output contains the most recent jobcode information for every employee. LABEL= assigns a column label.

```
title 'Most Current Jobcode and Salary Information';
select p.idnumber, coalesce(p2.jobcode,p.jobcode)
       label='Current Jobcode',
```

For each row, COALESCE returns the first nonmissing value of either P2.SALARY or P.SALARY. Because P2.SALARY is the first argument, if there is a nonmissing value for P2.SALARY, COALESCE returns that value. Thus, the output contains the most recent salary information for every employee.

```
coalesce(p2.salary,p.salary) label='Current Salary'
            format=dollar8.
```

The FROM clause lists the tables to join and assigns table aliases. The keywords LEFT JOIN specify the type of join. The ON clause specifies that the join is based on the ID numbers from each table.

```
from proclib.payroll p left join proclib.payroll2 p2
on p.IdNumber=p2.idnum;
```

Output

```
            Most Current Jobcode and Salary Information              1

                   Id       Current   Current
                   Number   Jobcode   Salary
                   -------------------------
                   1009     TA1       $28,880
                   1017     TA3       $40,858
                   1036     TA3       $42,465
                   1037     TA1       $28,558
                   1038     TA1       $26,533
                   1050     ME2       $35,167
                   1065     ME3       $38,090
                   1076     PT1       $69,742
                   1094     FA1       $22,268
                   1100     BCK       $25,004
```

The WHERE clause subsets the left join to include only those rows containing the value **TA**.

```
title 'Most Current Information for Ticket Agents';
select p.IdNumber,
```

```
          coalesce(p2.jobcode,p.jobcode) label='Current Jobcode',
          coalesce(p2.salary,p.salary) label='Current Salary'
   from proclib.payroll p left join proclib.payroll2 p2
   on p.IdNumber=p2.idnum
   where p2.jobcode contains 'TA';
```

Output

```
              Most Current Information for Ticket Agents                1

                      Id      Current   Current
                      Number  Jobcode   Salary
                      -----------------------------
                      1036    TA3        42465
                      1369    TA3        36598
                      1561    TA3        36514
                      1639    TA3        42260
```

Example 8: Creating a View from a Query's Result

Procedure features:
    CREATE VIEW statement
    GROUP BY clause
    SELECT clause
        COUNT function
    HAVING clause

Other features:
    AVG summary function
    data set option
        PW=

Tables: PROCLIB.PAYROLL, PROCLIB.JOBS

This example creates the PROC SQL view PROCLIB.JOBS from the result of a query-expression.

Input Table

PROCLIB.PAYROLL (Partial Listing)

```
                      PROCLIB.PAYROLL
                     First 10 Rows Only

     Id
     Number  Sex  Jobcode  Salary   Birth    Hired
     -------------------------------------------------
     1009    M    TA1       28880   02MAR59  26MAR92
     1017    M    TA3       40858   28DEC57  16OCT81
     1036    F    TA3       39392   19MAY65  23OCT84
     1037    F    TA1       28558   10APR64  13SEP92
     1038    F    TA1       26533   09NOV69  23NOV91
     1050    M    ME2       35167   14JUL63  24AUG86
     1065    M    ME2       35090   26JAN44  07JAN87
     1076    M    PT1       66558   14OCT55  03OCT91
     1094    M    FA1       22268   02APR70  17APR91
     1100    M    BCK       25004   01DEC60  07MAY88
```

Program

```
libname proclib 'SAS-data-library';
```

```
options nodate pageno=1 linesize=80 pagesize=60;
```

CREATE VIEW creates the PROC SQL view PROCLIB.JOBS. The PW= data set option assigns password protection to the data generated by this view.

```
proc sql;
   create view proclib.jobs(pw=red) as
```

The SELECT clause specifies four columns for the view: Jobcode and three columns, Number, AVGAGE, and AVGSAL, whose values are the products of functions. COUNT returns the number of nonmissing values for each jobcode because the data are grouped by Jobcode. LABEL= assigns a label to the column.

```
      select Jobcode,
             count(jobcode) as number label='Number',
```

The AVG summary function calculates the average age and average salary for each jobcode.

```
             avg(int((today()-birth)/365.25)) as avgage
                format=2. label='Average Age',
             avg(salary) as avgsal
                format=dollar8. label='Average Salary'
```

The FROM clause specifies PAYROLL as the table to select from. PROC SQL assumes the libref of PAYROLL to be PROCLIB because PROCLIB is used in the CREATE VIEW statement.

```
from payroll
```

The GROUP BY clause groups the data by the values of Jobcode. Thus, any summary statistics are calculated for each grouping of rows by value of Jobcode. The HAVING clause subsets the grouped data and returns rows for job codes that contain an average age of greater than or equal to 30.

```
group by jobcode
having avgage ge 30;
```

The SELECT statement selects all columns from PROCLIB.JOBS. PW=RED is necessary because the view is password-protected.

```
title 'Current Summary Information for Each Job Category';
title2 'Average Age Greater Than Or Equal to 30';
select * from proclib.jobs(pw=red);
```

Output

```
                Current Summary Information for Each Job Category           1
                       Average Age Greater Than Or Equal to 30

                                       Average    Average
                 Jobcode    Number       Age       Salary
                 ------------------------------------------
                 BCK           9          33       $25,794
                 FA2          16          34       $27,987
                 FA3           7          35       $32,934
                 ME1           8          30       $28,500
                 ME2          14          36       $35,577
                 ME3           7          39       $42,411
                 NA2           3          38       $52,383
                 PT1           8          34       $67,908
                 PT2          10          39       $87,925
                 PT3           2          50       $10,505
                 SCP           7          34       $18,309
                 TA1           9          32       $27,721
                 TA2          20          33       $33,575
                 TA3          12          37       $39,680
```

Example 9: Joining Three Tables

Procedure features:
   FROM clause
   joined-table component
   WHERE clause

Tables: PROCLIB.STAFF2, PROCLIB.SCHEDULE2, PROCLIB.SUPERV2

This example joins three tables and produces a report that contains columns from each table.

Input Tables

PROCLIB.STAFF2

```
                              PROCLIB.STAFF2

Id
Num    Lname           Fname           City             State  Hphone
-------------------------------------------------------------------------
1106   MARSHBURN       JASPER          STAMFORD         CT     203/781-1457
1430   DABROWSKI       SANDRA          BRIDGEPORT       CT     203/675-1647
1118   DENNIS          ROGER           NEW YORK         NY     718/383-1122
1126   KIMANI          ANNE            NEW YORK         NY     212/586-1229
1402   BLALOCK         RALPH           NEW YORK         NY     718/384-2849
1882   TUCKER          ALAN            NEW YORK         NY     718/384-0216
1479   BALLETTI        MARIE           NEW YORK         NY     718/384-8816
1420   ROUSE           JEREMY          PATERSON         NJ     201/732-9834
1403   BOWDEN          EARL            BRIDGEPORT       CT     203/675-3434
1616   FUENTAS         CARLA           NEW YORK         NY     718/384-3329
```

PROCLIB.SCHEDULE2

```
                     PROCLIB.SCHEDULE2

                                        Id
            Flight    Date    Dest     Num
            -------------------------------
            132      01MAR94   BOS     1118
            132      01MAR94   BOS     1402
            219      02MAR94   PAR     1616
            219      02MAR94   PAR     1478
            622      03MAR94   LON     1430
            622      03MAR94   LON     1882
            271      04MAR94   NYC     1430
            271      04MAR94   NYC     1118
            579      05MAR94   RDU     1126
            579      05MAR94   RDU     1106
```

PROCLIB.SUPERV2

```
                        PROCLIB.SUPERV2

                  Supervisor            Job
                  Id          State     Category
                  --------------------------------
                  1417         NJ        NA
                  1352         NY        NA
                  1106         CT        PT
                  1442         NJ        PT
                  1118         NY        PT
                  1405         NJ        SC
                  1564         NY        SC
                  1639         CT        TA
                  1126         NY        TA
                  1882         NY        ME
```

Program

```
libname proclib 'SAS-data-library';
```

```
options nodate pageno=1 linesize=80 pagesize=60;
```

The SELECT clause specifies the columns to select. IdNum is prefixed with a table alias because it appears in two tables.

```
    proc sql;
 title 'All Flights for Each Supervisor';
    select s.IdNum, Lname, City 'Hometown', Jobcat,
          Flight, Date
```

The FROM clause lists the three tables for the join and assigns an alias to each table.

```
        from proclib.schedule2 s, proclib.staff2 t, proclib.superv2 v
```

The WHERE clause specifies the columns that join the tables. The STAFF2 and SCHEDULE2 tables have an IdNum column, which has related values in both tables. The STAFF2 and SUPERV2 tables have the IdNum and SUPID columns, which have related values in both tables.

```
        where s.idnum=t.idnum and t.idnum=v.supid;
```

Output

```
                     All Flights for Each Supervisor                    1

   Id                                   Job
   Num    Lname         Hometown        Category  Flight   Date
   -------------------------------------------------------------
   1106   MARSHBURN     STAMFORD        PT        579      05MAR94
   1118   DENNIS        NEW YORK        PT        132      01MAR94
   1118   DENNIS        NEW YORK        PT        271      04MAR94
   1126   KIMANI        NEW YORK        TA        579      05MAR94
   1882   TUCKER        NEW YORK        ME        622      03MAR94
```

Example 10: Querying an In-Line View

Procedure features:
FROM clause

in-line view

Tables: PROCLIB.STAFF, PROCLIB.SCHEDULE, PROCLIB.SUPERV

This example uses the query explained in Example 9 on page 1118 as an in-line view. The example also shows how to rename columns with an in-line view.

Program

```
libname proclib 'SAS-data-library';
```

```
options nodate pageno=1 linesize=80 pagesize=60;
```

The SELECT clause selects all columns returned by the query in the FROM clause.

```
proc sql outobs=10;
   title 'All Flights for Each Supervisor';
   select *
```

The query that joins the three tables is used in the FROM clause instead of the name of a table or view. In the in-line query, the SELECT clause lists the columns to select. IdNum is prefixed with a table alias because it appears in two tables. The FROM clause lists the three tables for the join and assigns an alias to each table. The WHERE clause specifies the columns that join the tables. The STAFF2 and SCHEDULE2 tables have an IdNum column, which has related values in both tables. The STAFF2 and SUPERV2 tables have the IdNum and SUPID columns, which have related values in both tables.

```
   from (select lname, s.idnum, city, jobcat,
                flight, date
```

```
            from proclib.schedule2 s, proclib.staff2 t,
                  proclib.superv2 v
            where s.idnum=t.idnum and t.idnum=v.supid)
```

> The alias THREE refers to the entire query. The names in parentheses become the names for the columns in the output. The label **Job Category** appears in the output instead of the name Jobtype because PROC SQL prints a column's label if the column has a label.

```
            as three (Surname, Emp_ID, Hometown,
                         Jobtype, FlightNumber, FlightDate);
```

Output

```
                            All Flights for Each Supervisor                          1

                                           Job
         Surname          Emp_ID  Hometown  Category  FlightNumber  FlightDate
         -----------------------------------------------------------------------
         MARSHBURN        1106    STAMFORD  PT        579           05MAR94
         DENNIS           1118    NEW YORK  PT        132           01MAR94
         DENNIS           1118    NEW YORK  PT        271           04MAR94
         KIMANI           1126    NEW YORK  TA        579           05MAR94
         TUCKER           1882    NEW YORK  ME        622           03MAR94
```

Example 11: Retrieving Values with the SOUNDS-LIKE Operator

Procedure features:
    ORDER BY clause
    SOUNDS-LIKE operator
Table: PROCLIB.STAFF

This example returns rows based on the functionality of the SOUNDS-LIKE operator in a WHERE clause.

Input Table

PROCLIB.STAFF

```
                             PROCLIB.STAFF
                            First 10 Rows Only

Id
Num    Lname           Fname           City            State  Hphone
-----------------------------------------------------------------------
1919   ADAMS           GERALD          STAMFORD        CT     203/781-1255
1653   ALIBRANDI       MARIA           BRIDGEPORT      CT     203/675-7715
1400   ALHERTANI       ABDULLAH        NEW YORK        NY     212/586-0808
1350   ALVAREZ         MERCEDES        NEW YORK        NY     718/383-1549
1401   ALVAREZ         CARLOS          PATERSON        NJ     201/732-8787
1499   BAREFOOT        JOSEPH          PRINCETON       NJ     201/812-5665
1101   BAUCOM          WALTER          NEW YORK        NY     212/586-8060
1333   BANADYGA        JUSTIN          STAMFORD        CT     203/781-1777
1402   BLALOCK         RALPH           NEW YORK        NY     718/384-2849
1479   BALLETTI        MARIE           NEW YORK        NY     718/384-8816
```

Program

```
libname proclib 'SAS-data-library';


options nodate pageno=1 linesize=80 pagesize=60;
```

The SELECT clause selects all columns from the table in the FROM clause, PROCLIB.STAFF.

```
proc sql;
    title "Employees Whose Last Name Sounds Like 'Johnson'";
    select *
       from proclib.staff
```

The WHERE clause uses the SOUNDS-LIKE operator to subset the table by those employees whose last name sounds like **Johnson**. The ORDER BY clause orders the output by the second column.

```
    where lname=*"Johnson"
    order by 2;
```

Output

```
        Employees Whose Last Name Sounds Like 'Johnson'              1

Id
Num    Lname           Fname           City            State  Hphone
-----------------------------------------------------------------------
1411   JOHNSEN         JACK            PATERSON        NJ     201/732-3678
1113   JOHNSON         LESLIE          NEW YORK        NY     718/383-3003
1369   JONSON          ANTHONY         NEW YORK        NY     212/587-5385
```

SOUNDS-LIKE is useful, but there may be instances where it does not return every row that seems to satisfy the condition. PROCLIB.STAFF has an employee with the last name **SANDERS** and an employee with the last name **SANYERS**. The algorithm does not find **SANYERS**, but it does find **SANDERS** and **SANDERSON**.

```
title "Employees Whose Last Name Sounds Like 'Sanders'";
select *
    from proclib.staff
    where lname=*"Sanders"
    order by 2;
```

```
                   Employees Whose Last Name Sounds Like 'Sanders'                    2
Id
Num   Lname              Fname            City            State  Hphone
----------------------------------------------------------------------------
1561  SANDERS            RAYMOND          NEW YORK        NY     212/588-6615
1414  SANDERSON          NATHAN           BRIDGEPORT      CT     203/675-1715
1434  SANDERSON          EDITH            STAMFORD        CT     203/781-1333
```

Example 12: Joining Two Tables and Calculating a New Value

Procedure features:
    GROUP BY clause
    HAVING clause
    SELECT clause

      ABS function
      FORMAT= column-modifier
      LABEL= column-modifier
      MIN summary function
      ** operator, exponentiation
      SQRT function

Tables: STORES, HOUSES

This example joins two tables in order to compare and analyze values that are unique to each table yet have a relationship with a column that is common to both tables.

```
options ls=80 ps=60 nodate pageno=1 ;
data stores;
  input Store $ x y;
  datalines;
store1 6 1
store2 5 2
store3 3 5
store4 7 5
```

```
    ;
data houses;
   input House $ x y;
   datalines;
house1 1 1
house2 3 3
house3 2 3
house4 7 7
   ;
```

Input Tables

STORES and HOUSES

The tables contain X and Y coordinates that represent the location of the stores and houses.

```
                         STORES Table                            1
                      Coordinates of Stores

                  Store            x          y
                  ----------------------------
                  store1           6          1
                  store2           5          2
                  store3           3          5
                  store4           7          5
```

```
                         HOUSES Table                            2
                      Coordinates of Houses

                  House            x          y
                  ----------------------------
                  house1           1          1
                  house2           3          3
                  house3           2          3
                  house4           7          7
```

Program

```
options nodate pageno=1 linesize=80 pagesize=60;
```

The SELECT clause specifies three columns: HOUSE, STORE, and DIST. The arithmetic expression uses the square root function (SQRT) to create the values of DIST, which contain the distance from HOUSE to STORE for each row. The double asterisk (**) represents exponentiation. LABEL= assigns a label to STORE and to DIST.

```
proc sql;
   title 'Each House and the Closest Store';
   select house, store label='Closest Store',
          sqrt((abs(s.x-h.x)**2)+(abs(h.y-s.y)**2)) as dist
```

```
                label='Distance' format=4.2
        from stores s, houses h
```

The minimum distance from each house to all the stores is calculated because the data are grouped by house. The HAVING clause specifies that each row be evaluated to determine if its value of DIST is the same as the minimum distance for that house to any store.

```
group by house
having dist=min(dist);
```

Output

```
                          Each House and the Closest Store                          1

                                  Closest
                      House       Store     Distance
                      ----------------------------------
                      house1      store2        4.12
                      house2      store3        2.00
                      house3      store3        2.24
                      house4      store4        2.00
```

Example 13: Producing All the Possible Combinations of the Values in a Column

Procedure features:
    CASE expression
    joined-table component
    SELECT clause
        DISTINCT keyword
Tables: PROCLIB.MARCH, FLIGHTS

This example joins a table with itself to get all the possible combinations of the values in a column.

Input Table

PROCLIB.MARCH (Partial Listing)

```
                           PROCLIB.MARCH
                         First 10 Rows Only

    Flight      Date  Depart  Orig  Dest      Miles  Boarded  Capacity
    ------------------------------------------------------------------
       114    01MAR94    7:10  LGA   LAX        2475      172       210
       202    01MAR94   10:43  LGA   ORD         740      151       210
       219    01MAR94    9:31  LGA   LON        3442      198       250
       622    01MAR94   12:19  LGA   FRA        3857      207       250
       132    01MAR94   15:35  LGA   YYZ         366      115       178
       271    01MAR94   13:17  LGA   PAR        3635      138       250
       302    01MAR94   20:22  LGA   WAS         229      105       180
       114    02MAR94    7:10  LGA   LAX        2475      119       210
       202    02MAR94   10:43  LGA   ORD         740      120       210
       219    02MAR94    9:31  LGA   LON        3442      147       250
```

Program

```
libname proclib 'SAS-data-library';
```

```
options nodate pageno=1 linesize=80 pagesize=60;
```

The CREATE TABLE statement creates the table FLIGHTS from the output of the query. The SELECT clause selects the unique values of Dest. DISTINCT specifies that only one row for each value of city be returned by the query and stored in the table FLIGHTS. The FROM clause specifies PROCLIB.MARCH as the table to select from.

```
proc sql;
   create table flights as
      select distinct dest
         from proclib.march;
```

```
   title 'Cities Serviced by the Airline';
```

```
select * from flights;
```

Output

FLIGHTS Table

```
                        Cities Serviced by the Airline                    1
                                     Dest
                                     ----
                                     FRA
                                     LAX
                                     LON
                                     ORD
                                     PAR
                                     WAS
                                     YYZ
```

The SELECT clause specifies three columns for the output. The prefixes on DEST are table aliases to specify which table to take the values of Dest from. The CASE expression creates a column that contains the character string **to and from**.

```
title 'All Possible Connections';
select f1.Dest, case
                  when f1.dest ne ' ' then 'to and from'
                end,
       f2.Dest
```

The FROM clause joins FLIGHTS with itself and creates a table that contains every possible combination of rows. The table contains two rows for each possible route, for example, **PAR <-> WAS** and **WAS <-> PAR**.

```
from flights as f1, flights as f2
```

The WHERE clause subsets the internal table by choosing only those rows where the name in F1.Dest sorts before the name in F2.Dest. Thus, there is only one row for each possible route.

```
where f1.dest < f2.dest
```

ORDER BY sorts the result by the values of F1.Dest.

```
order by f1.dest;
```

Output

```
                        All Possible Connections                          2

                        Dest                 Dest
                        ----------------------
                        FRA   to and from  WAS
                        FRA   to and from  YYZ
                        FRA   to and from  LAX
                        FRA   to and from  ORD
                        FRA   to and from  LON
                        FRA   to and from  PAR
                        LAX   to and from  PAR
                        LAX   to and from  LON
                        LAX   to and from  WAS
                        LAX   to and from  ORD
                        LAX   to and from  YYZ
                        LON   to and from  WAS
                        LON   to and from  PAR
                        LON   to and from  YYZ
                        LON   to and from  ORD
                        ORD   to and from  WAS
                        ORD   to and from  PAR
                        ORD   to and from  YYZ
                        PAR   to and from  YYZ
                        PAR   to and from  WAS
                        WAS   to and from  YYZ
```

Example 14: Matching Case Rows and Control Rows

Procedure features:
   joined-table component

Tables: MATCH_11 on page 1504, MATCH

This example uses a table that contains data for a case-control study. Each row contains information for a case or a control. To perform statistical analysis, you need a table with one row for each case-control pair. PROC SQL joins the table with itself in order to match the cases with their appropriate controls. After the rows are matched, differencing can be performed on the appropriate columns.

The input table MATCH_11 contains one row for each case and one row for each control. Pair contains a number that associates the case with its control. Low is 0 for the controls and 1 for the cases. The remaining columns contain information about the cases and controls.

Input Table

```
                              MATCH_11 Table
                             First 10 Rows Only

Pair      Low      Age      Lwt      Race     Smoke     Ptd      Ht       UI      race1     race2
--------------------------------------------------------------------------------------------------
  1        0       14       135       1        0         0        0        0        0         0
  1        1       14       101       3        1         1        0        0        0         1
  2        0       15        98       2        0         0        0        0        1         0
  2        1       15       115       3        0         0        0        1        0         1
  3        0       16        95       3        0         0        0        0        0         1
  3        1       16       130       3        0         0        0        0        0         1
  4        0       17       103       3        0         0        0        0        0         1
  4        1       17       130       3        1         1        0        1        0         1
  5        0       17       122       1        1         0        0        0        0         0
  5        1       17       110       1        1         0        0        0        0         0
```

Program

```
options nodate pageno=1 linesize=80 pagesize=60;
```

The SELECT clause specifies the columns for the table MATCH. SQL expressions in the SELECT clause calculate the differences for the appropriate columns and create new columns.

```
proc sql;
   create table match as
      select
         one.Low,
         one.Pair,
         (one.lwt - two.lwt) as Lwt_d,
         (one.smoke - two.smoke) as Smoke_d,
         (one.ptd - two.ptd) as Ptd_d,
         (one.ht - two.ht) as Ht_d,
         (one.ui - two.ui) as UI_d
```

The FROM clause lists the table MATCH_11 twice. Thus, the table is joined with itself. The WHERE clause returns only the rows for each pair that show the difference when the values for control are subtracted from the values for case.

```
      from match_11 one, match_11 two
      where (one.pair=two.pair and one.low>two.low);
```

The SELECT clause selects all the columns from MATCH. The OBS= data set option limits the printing of the output to five rows.

```
      title 'Differences for Cases and Controls';
      select *
         from match(obs=5);
```

Output

MATCH Table

```
              Differences for Cases and Controls                    1

      Low      Pair     Lwt_d   Smoke_d     Ptd_d      Ht_d      UI_d
      --------------------------------------------------------------
       1        1        -34       1          1         0         0
       1        2         17       0          0         0         1
       1        3         35       0          0         0         0
       1        4         27       1          1         0         1
       1        5        -12       0          0         0         0
```

Example 15: Counting Missing Values with a SAS Macro

Procedure feature:
    COUNT function
Table: SURVEY

This example uses a SAS macro to create columns. The SAS macro is not explained
here. See the SAS Guide to Macro Processing for complete documentation on the SAS
COUNTM macro.

Input Table

SURVEY contains data from a questionnaire about diet and exercise habits. SAS enables you to
use a special notation for missing values. In the EDUC column, the `.x` notation indicates that
the respondent gave an answer that is not valid, and `.n` indicates that the respondent did not
answer the question. A period as a missing value indicates a data entry error.

```
data survey;
   input id $ diet $ exer $ hours xwk educ;
   datalines;
1001 yes yes 1 3 1
1002 no   yes 1 4 2
1003 no   no   . . .n
1004 yes yes 2 3 .x
1005 no   yes 2 3 .x
1006 yes yes 2 4 .x
1007 no   yes .5 3 .
1008 no   no   . . .
;
```

Program

```
options nodate pageno=1 linesize=80 pagesize=60;
```

The COUNTM macro uses the COUNT function to perform various counts for a column. Each COUNT function uses a CASE expression to select the rows to be counted. The first COUNT function uses only the column as an argument to return the number of nonmissing rows.

```
%macro countm(col);
   count(&col) "Valid Responses for &col",
```

The IS MISSING keywords return the rows that have any type of missing value: **.n**, **.x**, or a period. The PUT function returns a character string to be counted.

```
count(case
         when &col is missing  then put(&col, 2.)
         end) "Missing or NOT VALID Responses for &col",
```

The last three COUNT functions use CASE expressions to count the occurrences of the three notations for missing values.

```
count(case
         when &col=.n  then put(&col, 2.)
         end) "Coded as NO ANSWER for &col",
count(case
         when &col=.x  then put(&col, 2.)
         end) "Coded as NOT VALID answers for &col",
count(case
         when &col=.  then put(&col, 1.)
         end) "Data Entry Errors for &col"
%mend;
```

The SELECT clause specifies the columns that are in the output. COUNT(*) returns the total number of rows in the table. The COUNTM macro uses the values of the EDUC column to create the columns defined in the macro.

```
proc sql;
   title 'Counts for Each Type of Missing Response';
   select count(*)  "Total No. of Rows",
          %countm(educ)
      from survey;
```

Output

			Counts for Each Type of Missing Response			1

Total No. of Rows	Valid Responses for educ	Missing or NOT VALID Responses for educ	Coded as NO ANSWER for educ	Coded as NOT VALID answers for educ	Data Entry Errors for educ
8	2	6	1	3	2

CHAPTER

35

The STANDARD Procedure

Overview

The STANDARD procedure standardizes variables in a SAS data set to a given mean and standard deviation, and it creates a new SAS data set containing the standardized values.

Output 35.1 on page 1135 shows a simple standardization where the output data set contains standardized student exam scores. The statements that produce the output follow:

```
proc standard data=score mean=75 std=5
            out=stndtest;
run;

proc print data=stndtest;
run;
```

Output 35.1   Standardized Test Scores Using PROC STANDARD

```
                    The SAS System                        1

          Obs      Student       Test1

           1       Capalleti     80.5388
           2       Dubose        64.3918
           3       Engles        80.9143
           4       Grant         68.8980
           5       Krupski       75.2816
           6       Lundsford     79.7877
           7       Mcbane        73.4041
           8       Mullen        78.6612
           9       Nguyen        74.9061
          10       Patel         71.9020
          11       Si            73.4041
          12       Tanaka        77.9102
```

Output 35.2 on page 1136 shows a more complex example that uses BY-group processing. PROC STANDARD computes Z scores separately for two BY groups by standardizing life-expectancy data to a mean of 0 and a standard deviation of 1. The data are 1950 and 1993 life expectancies at birth for 16 countries. The birth rates for each country, classified as stable or rapid, form the two BY groups. The statements that produce the analysis also

- □ print statistics for each variable to standardize
- □ replace missing values with the given mean
- □ calculate standardized values using a given mean and standard deviation
- □ print the data set with the standardized values.

For an explanation of the program that produces this output, see Example 2 on page 1145.

Output 35.2   Z Scores for Each BY Group Using PROC STANDARD

```
                         Life Expectancies by Birth Rate                      1

--------------------------- PopulationRate=Stable ----------------------------

                            Standard
Name            Mean        Deviation            N     Label

Life50      67.400000       1.854724             5     1950 life expectancy
Life93      74.500000       4.888763             6     1993 life expectancy


--------------------------- PopulationRate=Rapid -----------------------------

                            Standard
Name            Mean        Deviation            N     Label

Life50      42.000000       5.033223             8     1950 life expectancy
Life93      59.100000       8.225300            10     1993 life expectancy
                   Standardized Life Expectancies at Birth                     2
                        by a Country's Birth Rate

            Population
              Rate      Country         Life50       Life93

              Stable    France          -0.21567      0.51138
              Stable    Germany          0.32350      0.10228
              Stable    Japan           -1.83316      0.92048
              Stable    Russia           0.00000     -1.94323
              Stable    United Kingdom   0.86266      0.30683
              Stable    United States    0.86266      0.10228
              Rapid     Bangladesh       0.00000     -0.74161
              Rapid     Brazil           1.78812      0.96045
              Rapid     China           -0.19868      1.32518
              Rapid     Egypt            0.00000      0.10942
              Rapid     Ethiopia        -1.78812     -1.59265
              Rapid     India           -0.59604     -0.01216
              Rapid     Indonesia       -0.79472     -0.01216
              Rapid     Mozambique       0.00000     -1.47107
              Rapid     Philippines      1.19208      0.59572
              Rapid     Turkey           0.39736      0.83888
```

Procedure Syntax

Tip: Supports the Output Delivery System (see Chapter 2, "Fundamental Concepts for Using Base SAS Procedures")

Reminder: You can use the ATTRIB, FORMAT, LABEL, and WHERE statements. See Chapter 3, "Statements with the Same Function in Multiple Procedures," for details. You can also use any global statements as well. See Chapter 2, "Fundamental Concepts for Using Base SAS Procedures," for a list.

PROC STANDARD <*option(s)*>;

   BY <DESCENDING> *variable-1* <...<DESCENDING> *variable-n*>
     <NOTSORTED>;

   FREQ *variable*;

   VAR *variable(s)*;

   WEIGHT *variable*;

To do this	Use this statement
Calculate separate standardized values for each BY group	BY
Identify a variable whose values represent the frequency of each observation	FREQ
Select the variables to standardize and determine the order they appear in the printed output	VAR
Identify a variable whose values weight each observation in the statistical calculations	WEIGHT

PROC STANDARD Statement

PROC STANDARD <*option(s)*>;

To do this	Use this option
Specify the input data set	DATA=
Specify the output data set	OUT=
Computational options	
Exclude observations with nonpositive weights	EXCLNPWGT
Specify the mean value	MEAN=
Replace missing values with a variable mean or MEAN= value	REPLACE
Specify the standard deviation value	STD=
Specify the divisor for variance calculations	VARDEF=
Control printed output	
Print statistics for each variable to standardize	PRINT

Without Options

If you do not specify MEAN=, REPLACE, or STD=, the output data set is an identical copy of the input data set.

Options

DATA=*SAS-data-set*
  identifies the input SAS data set.

  Main discussion: "Input Data Sets" on page 18

  Restriction: You cannot use PROC STANDARD with an engine that supports concurrent access if another user is updating the data set at the same time.

EXCLNPWGT
> excludes observations with nonpositive weight values (zero or negative). The procedure does not use the observation to calculate the mean and standard deviation, but the observation is still standardized. By default, the procedure treats observations with negative weights like those with zero weights and counts them in the total number of observations.

MEAN=*mean-value*
> standardizes variables to a mean of *mean-value*.
>
> **Alias:** M=
>
> **Default:** mean of the input values
>
> **Featured in:** Example 1 on page 1143

OUT=*SAS-data-set*
> identifies the output data set. If *SAS-data-set* does not exist, PROC STANDARD creates it. If you omit OUT=, the data set is named DATA*n*, where *n* is the smallest integer that makes the name unique.
>
> **Default:** DATA*n*
>
> **Featured in:** Example 1 on page 1143

PRINT
> prints the original frequency, mean, and standard deviation for each variable to standardize.
>
> **Featured in:** Example 2 on page 1145

REPLACE
> replaces missing values with the variable mean.
>
> **Interaction:** If you use MEAN=, PROC STANDARD replaces missing values with the given mean.
>
> **Featured in:** Example 2 on page 1145

STD=*std-value*
> standardizes variables to a standard deviation of *std-value*.
>
> **Alias:** S=
>
> **Default:** standard deviation of the input values
>
> **Featured in:** Example 1 on page 1143

VARDEF=*divisor*
> specifies the divisor to use in the calculation of variances and standard deviation. Table 35.1 on page 1139 shows the possible values for *divisor* and the associated divisors.

Table 35.1 Possible Values for VARDEF=

Value	Divisor	Formula for Divisor
DF	degrees of freedom	$n - 1$
N	number of observations	n
WDF	sum of weights minus one	$(\Sigma_i w_i) - 1$
WEIGHT | WGT	sum of weights	$\Sigma_i w_i$

The procedure computes the variance as $CSS/divisor$, where CSS is the corrected sums of squares and equals $\sum(x_i - \overline{x})^2$. When you weight the analysis variables, CSS equals $\sum w_i(x_i - \overline{x}_w)^2$ where $\overline{x}_w$ is the weighted mean.

Default: DF

Tip: When you use the WEIGHT statement and VARDEF=DF, the variance is an estimate of σ^2, where the variance of the *i*th observation is $var(x_i) = \sigma^2/w_i$ and w_i is the weight for the *i*th observation. This yields an estimate of the variance of an observation with unit weight.

Tip: When you use the WEIGHT statement and VARDEF=WGT, the computed variance is asymptotically (for large *n*) an estimate of $\sigma^2/\overline{w}$, where $\overline{w}$ is the average weight. This yields an asymptotic estimate of the variance of an observation with average weight.

See also: "WEIGHT" on page 73

Main discussion: "Keywords and Formulas" on page 1458

BY Statement

Calculates standardized values separately for each BY group.

Main discussion: "BY" on page 68

Featured in: Example 2 on page 1145

BY <DESCENDING> *variable-1* <...<DESCENDING> *variable-n*><NOTSORTED>;

Required Arguments

variable
   specifies the variable that the procedure uses to form BY groups. You can specify more than one variable. If you do not use the NOTSORTED option in the BY statement, the observations in the data set must either be sorted by all the variables that you specify, or they must be indexed appropriately. These variables are called *BY variables*.

Options

DESCENDING
   specifies that the data set is sorted in descending order by the variable that immediately follows the word DESCENDING in the BY statement.

NOTSORTED
   specifies that observations are not necessarily sorted in alphabetic or numeric order. The data are grouped in another way, for example, chronological order.
   The requirement for ordering or indexing observations according to the values of BY variables is suspended for BY-group processing when you use the NOTSORTED option. In fact, the procedure does not use an index if you specify NOTSORTED. The procedure defines a BY group as a set of contiguous observations

that have the same values for all BY variables. If observations with the same values for the BY variables are not contiguous, the procedure treats each contiguous set as a separate BY group.

FREQ Statement

Specifies a numeric variable whose values represent the frequency of the observation.

Tip: The effects of the FREQ and WEIGHT statements are similar except when calculating degrees of freedom.

See also: For an example that uses the FREQ statement, see "FREQ" on page 70

FREQ *variable*;

Required Arguments

variable
   specifies a numeric variable whose value represents the frequency of the observation. If you use the FREQ statement, the procedure assumes that each observation represents n observations, where n is the value of *variable*. If n is not an integer, the SAS System truncates it. If n is less than 1 or is missing, the procedure does not use that observation to calculate statistics but the observation is still standardized.
   The sum of the frequency variable represents the total number of observations.

VAR Statement

Specifies the variables to standardize and their order in the printed output.

Default: If you omit the VAR statement, PROC STANDARD standardizes all numeric variables not listed in the other statements.

Featured in: Example 1 on page 1143

VAR *variable(s)*;

Required Arguments

variable(s)
   identifies one or more variables to standardize.

WEIGHT Statement

Specifies weights for analysis variables in the statistical calculations.

See also: For information on calculating weighted statistics and for an example that uses the WEIGHT statement, see "WEIGHT" on page 73

WEIGHT *variable*;

Required Arguments

variable
> specifies a numeric variable whose values weight the values of the analysis variables. The values of the variable do not have to be integers. If the value of the weight variable is

Weight value...	PROC STANDARD...
0	counts the observation in the total number of observations
less than 0	converts the weight value to zero and counts the observation in the total number of observations
missing	excludes the observation from the calculation of mean and standard deviation

> To exclude observations that contain negative and zero weights from the calculation of mean and standard deviation, use EXCLNPWGT. Note that most SAS/STAT procedures, such as PROC GLM, exclude negative and zero weights by default.

> **Tip:** When you use the WEIGHT statement, consider which value of the VARDEF= option is appropriate. See VARDEF= on page 1139 and the calculation of weighted statistics in "Keywords and Formulas" on page 1458 for more information.

> *Note:* Prior to Version 7 of the SAS System, the procedure did not exclude the observations with missing weights from the count of observations. △

Results

Missing Values

By default, PROC STANDARD excludes missing values for the analysis variables from the standardization process, and the values remain missing in the output data set. When you specify the REPLACE option, the procedure replaces missing values with the variable's mean or the MEAN= value.

If the value of the WEIGHT variable or the FREQ variable is missing then the procedure does not use the observation to calculate the mean and the standard deviation. However, the observation is standardized.

Output Data Set

PROC STANDARD always creates an output data set that stores the standardized values in the VAR statement variables, regardless of whether you specify the OUT= option. The output data set contains all the input data set variables, including those not standardized. PROC STANDARD does not print the output data set. Use PROC PRINT, PROC REPORT, or another SAS reporting tool to print the output data set.

Statistical Computations

Standardizing values removes the location and scale attributes from a set of data. The formula to compute standardized values is

$$x'_i = \frac{S * (x_i - \overline{x})}{s_x} + M$$

where

x'_i	is a new standardized value
S	is the value of STD=
M	is the value of MEAN=
x_i	is an observation's value
$\overline{x}$	is a variable's mean
s_x	is a variable's standard deviation.

PROC STANDARD calculates the mean ($\overline{x}$) and standard deviation (s_x) from the input data set. The resulting standardized variable has a mean of M and a standard deviation of S.

If the data are normally distributed, standardizing is also studentizing since the resulting data have a Student's t distribution.

Examples

Example 1: Standardizing to a Given Mean and Standard Deviation

Procedure features:
   PROC STANDARD statement options:
      MEAN=
      OUT=
      STD=
   VAR statement

Other features:
   PRINT procedure

This example
- □ standardizes two variables to a mean of 75 and a standard deviation of 5
- □ specifies the output data set
- □ combines standardized variables with original variables
- □ prints the output data set.

Program

The data set SCORE contains test scores for students who took two tests and a final exam. The FORMAT statement assigns the Z*w.d* format to StudentNumber. This format pads right-justified output with 0s instead of blanks. The LENGTH statement specifies the number of bytes to use to store values of Student.

```
options nodate pageno=1 linesize=80 pagesize=60;
data score;
   length Student $ 9;
   input Student $ StudentNumber Section $
         Test1 Test2 Final @@;
   format studentnumber z4.;
   datalines;
Capalleti 0545 1 94 91 87   Dubose      1252 2 51 65 91
Engles    1167 1 95 97 97   Grant       1230 2 63 75 80
Krupski   2527 2 80 69 71   Lundsford 4860 1 92 40 86
Mcbane    0674 1 75 78 72   Mullen      6445 2 89 82 93
Nguyen    0886 1 79 76 80   Patel       9164 2 71 77 83
Si        4915 1 75 71 73   Tanaka      8534 2 87 73 76
;
```

PROC STANDARD uses a mean of 75 and a standard deviation of 5 to standardize the values. OUT= identifies STNDTEST as the data set to contain the standardized values.

```
proc standard data=score mean=75 std=5
              out=stndtest;
```

The VAR statement specifies the variables to standardize.

```
   var test1 test2;
run;
```

PROC SQL joins SCORE and STNDTEST to create a table (COMBINED) that contains standardized and original test scores for each student. Using AS to rename the standardized variables NEW.TEST1 to StdTest1 and NEW.TEST2 to StdTest2 makes the variable names unique.

```
proc sql;
   create table combined as
   select old.student, old.studentnumber,
          old.section,
          old.test1, new.test1 as StdTest1,
          old.test2, new.test2 as StdTest2,
          old.final
   from score as old, stndtest as new
   where old.student=new.student;
```

PROC PRINT prints the COMBINED table. ROUND rounds the standardized values to two decimal places. The TITLE statement specifies a title.

```
proc print data=combined noobs round;
   title 'Standardized Test Scores for a College Course';
run;
```

Output

The data set contains variables with both standardized and original values. StdTest1 and StdTest2 store the standardized test scores that PROC STANDARD computes.

```
                  Standardized Test Scores for a College Course                 1

              Student                       Std           Std
Student       Number    Section    Test1    Test1   Test2   Test2   Final

Capalleti     0545         1         94      80.54    91     80.86    87
Dubose        1252         2         51      64.39    65     71.63    91
Engles        1167         1         95      80.91    97     82.99    97
Grant         1230         2         63      68.90    75     75.18    80
Krupski       2527         2         80      75.28    69     73.05    71
Lundsford     4860         1         92      79.79    40     62.75    86
Mcbane        0674         1         75      73.40    78     76.24    72
Mullen        6445         2         89      78.66    82     77.66    93
Nguyen        0886         1         79      74.91    76     75.53    80
Patel         9164         2         71      71.90    77     75.89    83
Si            4915         1         75      73.40    71     73.76    73
Tanaka        8534         2         87      77.91    73     74.47    76
```

Example 2: Standardizing BY Groups and Replacing Missing Values

Procedure features:
   PROC STANDARD statement options:
   PRINT
   REPLACE

BY statement
Other features:
FORMAT procedure
PRINT procedure
SORT procedure

This example

☐ calculates Z scores separately for each BY group using a mean of 1 and standard deviation of 0

☐ replaces missing values with the given mean

☐ prints the mean and standard deviation for the variables to standardize

☐ prints the output data set.

Program

PROC FORMAT creates a format to identify birth rates with a character value.

```
options nodate pageno=1 linesize=80 pagesize=60;
proc format;
   value popfmt 1='Stable'
                2='Rapid';
run;
```

Each observation in the LIFEXP data set contains information on 1950 and 1993 life expectancies at birth for 16 nations*. The birth rate for each nation is classified as stable (1) or rapid (2). The nations with missing data obtained independent status after 1950.

```
data lifexp;
   input PopulationRate Country $char14. Life50 Life93 @@;
   label life50='1950 life expectancy'
         life93='1993 life expectancy';
   datalines;
2 Bangladesh      .  53 2 Brazil         51 67
2 China          41 70 2 Egypt          42 60
2 Ethiopia       33 46 1 France         67 77
1 Germany        68 75 2 India          39 59
2 Indonesia      38 59 1 Japan          64 79
2 Mozambique      . 47 2 Philippines    48 64
1 Russia          . 65 2 Turkey         44 66
1 United Kingdom 69 76 1 United States  69 75
;
```

PROC SORT sorts the observations by the birth rate.

---

* Data are from VITAL SIGNS 1994: The Trends That Are Shaping Our Future by Lester R. Brown, Hal Kane, and David Malin Roodman, eds. Copyright (c) 1994 by Worldwatch Institute. Reprinted by permission of W.W. Norton & Company, Inc.

```
proc sort data=lifexp;
   by populationrate;
run;
```

PROC STANDARD standardizes all numeric variables to a mean of 1 and a standard deviation of 0. REPLACE replaces missing values. PRINT prints statistics.

```
proc standard data=lifexp mean=0 std=1 replace
              print out=zscore;
```

The BY statement standardizes the values separately by birth rate.

```
   by populationrate;
```

The FORMAT statement assigns a format to PopulationRate. The output data set contains formatted values. The TITLE statement specifies a title.

```
   format populationrate popfmt.;
   title1 'Life Expectancies by Birth Rate';
run;
```

PROC PRINT prints the standardized values.

```
proc print data=zscore noobs;
   title 'Standardized Life Expectancies at Birth';
   title2 'by a Country''s Birth Rate';
run;
```

Output

PROC STANDARD prints the variable name, mean, standard deviation, input frequency, and label of each variable to standardize for each BY group.

Life expectancies for Bangladesh, Mozambique, and Russia are no longer missing. The missing values are replaced with the given mean (0).

```
                        Life Expectancies by Birth Rate                           1

-------------------------- PopulationRate=Stable ----------------------------

                             Standard
Name            Mean        Deviation          N     Label

Life50       67.400000      1.854724           5     1950 life expectancy
Life93       74.500000      4.888763           6     1993 life expectancy


-------------------------- PopulationRate=Rapid -----------------------------

                             Standard
Name            Mean        Deviation          N     Label

Life50       42.000000      5.033223           8     1950 life expectancy
Life93       59.100000      8.225300          10     1993 life expectancy
                   Standardized Life Expectancies at Birth                        2
                        by a Country's Birth Rate

            Population
               Rate     Country          Life50      Life93

               Stable   France          -0.21567     0.51138
               Stable   Germany          0.32350     0.10228
               Stable   Japan           -1.83316     0.92048
               Stable   Russia           0.00000    -1.94323
               Stable   United Kingdom   0.86266     0.30683
               Stable   United States    0.86266     0.10228
               Rapid    Bangladesh       0.00000    -0.74161
               Rapid    Brazil           1.78812     0.96045
               Rapid    China           -0.19868     1.32518
               Rapid    Egypt            0.00000     0.10942
               Rapid    Ethiopia        -1.78812    -1.59265
               Rapid    India           -0.59604    -0.01216
               Rapid    Indonesia       -0.79472    -0.01216
               Rapid    Mozambique       0.00000    -1.47107
               Rapid    Philippines      1.19208     0.59572
               Rapid    Turkey           0.39736     0.83888
```

CHAPTER

36

The SUMMARY Procedure

Overview

The SUMMARY procedure provides data summarization tools that compute descriptive statistics for variables across all observations or within groups of observations. By default, PROC SUMMARY does not display output. The SUMMARY procedure is very similar to the MEANS procedure. Except for the differences discussed in the following section, all the information in Chapter 24, "The MEANS Procedure," on page 623 also applies to PROC SUMMARY.

Procedure Syntax

Tip: Supports the Output Delivery System (see Chapter 2, "Fundamental Concepts for Using Base SAS Procedures," on page 15)

Reminder: You can use the ATTRIB, FORMAT, LABEL, and WHERE statements. See Chapter 3, "Statements with the Same Function in Multiple Procedures," for details. You can also use any global statements as well. See Chapter 2, "Fundamental Concepts for Using Base SAS Procedures," for a list.

PROC SUMMARY *<option(s)> <statistic-keyword(s)>*;
  BY <DESCENDING> *variable-1*<...<DESCENDING> *variable-n*>
    <NOTSORTED>;
  CLASS *variable(s)* </ *option(s)*>;
  FREQ *variable*;
  ID *variable(s)*;
  OUTPUT <OUT=*SAS-data-set*><*output-statistic-specification(s)*>
    <*id-group-specification(s)*> <*maximum-id-specification(s)*>
    <*minimum-id-specification(s)*></ *option(s)*> ;
  TYPES *request(s)*;
  VAR *variable(s)*</ WEIGHT=*weight-variable*>;
  WAYS *list*;

WEIGHT *variable*;

PROC SUMMARY Statement

PRINT | NOPRINT
specifies whether PROC SUMMARY displays the descriptive statistics. By default, PROC SUMMARY produces no display output, but PROC MEANS does produce display output.

Default: NOPRINT

VAR Statement

Identifies the analysis variables and their order in the results.

Default: If you omit the VAR statement, PROC SUMMARY produces a simple count of observations, whereas PROC MEANS tries to analyze all the numeric variables that are not listed in the other statements.

CHAPTER

37

The TABULATE Procedure

Overview

The TABULATE procedure displays descriptive statistics in tabular format, using some or all of the variables in a data set. You can create a variety of tables ranging from simple to highly customized.

PROC TABULATE computes many of the same statistics that are computed by other descriptive statistical procedures such as MEANS, FREQ, and REPORT. PROC TABULATE provides

- □ simple but powerful methods to create tabular reports

- □ flexibility in classifying the values of variables and establishing hierarchical relationships between the variables

- □ mechanisms for labeling and formatting variables and procedure-generated statistics.

Output 37.1 on page 1152 shows a simple table that was produced by PROC TABULATE. The data set on page 1199 contains data on expenditures of energy by two types of customers, residential and business, in individual states in the Northeast (1) and West (4) regions of the United States. The table sums expenditures for states within a geographic division. (The RTS option provides enough space to display the column headers without hyphenating them.)

```
options nodate pageno=1 linesize=64
        pagesize=40;

proc tabulate data=energy;
   class region division type;
   var expenditures;
   table region*division, type*expenditures /
        rts=20;
run;
```

Output 37.1 Simple Table Produced by PROC TABULATE

```
                           The SAS System                        1
 --------------------------------------------------------
|              |              |           Type            |
|              |              |---------------------------|
|              |              |      1       |      2      |
|              |              |--------------+-------------|
|              |              | Expenditures | Expenditures|
|              |              |--------------+-------------|
|              |              |     Sum      |     Sum     |
|--------------+--------------+--------------+-------------|
| Region       | Division     |              |             |
|--------+-----+--------------|              |             |
| 1      |     | 1            |      7477.00 |     5129.00 |
|        |     |--------------+--------------+-------------|
|        |     | 2            |     19379.00 |    15078.00 |
|--------+-----+--------------+--------------+-------------|
| 4      |     | 3            |      5476.00 |     4729.00 |
|        |     |--------------+--------------+-------------|
|        |     | 4            |     13959.00 |    12619.00 |
 --------------------------------------------------------
```

Output 37.2 on page 1153 is a more complicated table using the same data set that was used to create Output 37.1 on page 1152. The statements that create this report

□ customize column and row headers

□ apply a format to all table cells

□ sum expenditures for residential and business customers

□ compute subtotals for each division

□ compute totals for all regions.

For an explanation of the program that produces this report, see Example 6 on page 1212.

Output 37.2 Complex Table Produced by PROC TABULATE

```
            Energy Expenditures for Each Region                1
                     (millions of dollars)

       -------------------------------------------------------------
       |                     |           Customer Base           |
       |                     |-----------------------------------|
       |                     |Residential | Business  |  All     |
       |                     | Customers  | Customers | Customers|
       |---------------------+------------+-----------+----------|
       |Region    |Division  |            |           |          |
       |----------+----------|            |           |          |
       |Northeast |New England|    7,477  |    5,129  |   12,606 |
       |          |----------+------------+-----------+----------|
       |          |Middle    |            |           |          |
       |          |Atlantic  |   19,379   |   15,078  |   34,457 |
       |          |----------+------------+-----------+----------|
       |          |Subtotal  |   26,856   |   20,207  |   47,063 |
       |----------+----------+------------+-----------+----------|
       |West      |Division  |            |           |          |
       |          |----------|            |           |          |
       |          |Mountain  |    5,476   |    4,729  |   10,205 |
       |          |----------+------------+-----------+----------|
       |          |Pacific   |   13,959   |   12,619  |   26,578 |
       |          |----------+------------+-----------+----------|
       |          |Subtotal  |   19,435   |   17,348  |   36,783 |
       |---------------------+------------+-----------+----------|
       |Total for All Regions |   $46,291 |   $37,555 |  $83,846 |
       -------------------------------------------------------------
```

Display 37.1 on page 1154 shows a table created with HTML. Beginning with Version 7 of the SAS System, you can use the Output Delivery System to create customized HTML files from PROC TABULATE. For an explanation of the program that produces this table, see Example 14 on page 1243.

Display 37.1 HTML Table Produced by PROC TABULATE

Terminology

Figure 37.1 on page 1155 illustrates some of the terms that are commonly used in discussions of PROC TABULATE.

Figure 37.1   Illustration of Terms Used to Discuss PROC TABULATE

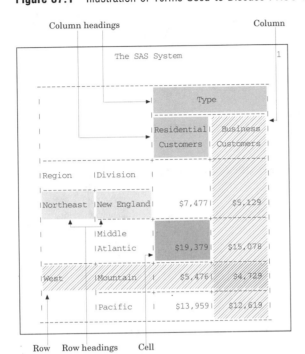

In addition, the following terms frequently appear in discussions of PROC TABULATE:

category
> the combination of unique values of class variables. The TABULATE procedure creates a separate category for each unique combination of values that exists in the observations of the data set. Each category that is created by PROC TABULATE is represented by one or more cells in the table where the pages, rows, and columns that describe the category intersect.
>
> The table in Figure 37.1 on page 1155 contains three class variables: Region, Division, and Type. These class variables form the eight categories listed in Table 37.1 on page 1156. (For convenience, the categories are described in terms of their formatted values.)

Table 37.1 Categories Created from Three Class Variables

Region	Division	Type
Northeast	New England	Residential Customers
Northeast	New England	Business Customers
Northeast	Middle Atlantic	Residential Customers
Northeast	Middle Atlantic	Business Customers
West	Mountain	Residential Customers
West	Mountain	Business Customers
West	Pacific	Residential Customers
West	Pacific	Business Customers

continuation message
   is the text that appears below the table if it spans multiple physical pages.
      A continuation message has a style. The default style is *Aftercaption*. For more information about using styles, see STYLE= on page 1164 in the PROC TABULATE statement and "Using Style Elements in PROC TABULATE" on page 1188.

nested variable
   a variable whose values appear in the table with each value of another variable.
      In Figure 37.1 on page 1155, Division is nested under Region.

page dimension text
   is the text that appears above the table if the table has a page dimension. However, if you specify BOX=_PAGE_ in the TABLE statement, the text that would appear above the table appears in the box.
      Page dimension text has a style. The default style is *Beforecaption*. For more information about using styles, see STYLE= on page 1164 in the PROC TABULATE statement and "Using Style Elements in PROC TABULATE" on page 1188.

subtable
   the group of cells that is produced by crossing a single element from each dimension of the TABLE statement when one or more dimensions contain concatenated elements.
      Figure 37.1 on page 1155 contains no subtables. For an illustration of a table that is composed of multiple subtables, see Figure 37.17 on page 1238.

Procedure Syntax

Requirements: At least one TABLE statement is required.

Requirements: Depending on the variables that appear in the TABLE statement, a CLASS statement, a VAR statement, or both are required.

Tip: Supports the Output Delivery System (see Chapter 2, "Fundamental Concepts for Using Base SAS Procedures")

Reminder: You can use the ATTRIB, FORMAT, LABEL, and WHERE statements. See Chapter 3, "Statements with the Same Function in Multiple Procedures," for details. You can also use any global statements as well. See Chapter 2, "Fundamental Concepts for Using Base SAS Procedures," for a list.

PROC TABULATE <*option(s)*>;

   BY <DESCENDING> *variable-1*
        <...<DESCENDING> *variable-n*>
        <NOTSORTED>;

   CLASS *variable(s)* </ *options*>;

   CLASSLEV *variable(s) / style* =<*style-element-name* | <PARENT>>
        <[*style-attribute-specification(s)*]>;

   FREQ *variable*;

   KEYLABEL *keyword-1='description-1'*
        <...*keyword-n='description-n'*>;

   KEYWORD *keyword(s) / style* =<*style-element-name* | <PARENT>>
        <[*style-attribute-specification(s)*]>;

   TABLE <<*page-expression,*> *row-expression,*> *column-expression* </ *table-option(s)*>;

   VAR *analysis-variable(s)*</ *options*>;

   WEIGHT *variable*;

To do this	Use this statement
Create a separate table for each BY group	BY
Identify variables in the input data set as class variables	CLASS
Specify a style for class variable level value headings	CLASSLEV
Identify a variable in the input data set whose values represent the frequency of each observation	FREQ
Specify a label for a keyword	KEYLABEL
Specify a style for keyword headings	KEYWORD
Describe the table to create	TABLE

To do this	Use this statement
Identify variables in the input data set as analysis variables	VAR
Identify a variable in the input data set whose values weight each observation in the statistical calculations	WEIGHT

PROC TABULATE Statement

PROC TABULATE <*option(s)*>;

To do this	Use this option
Customize the HTML contents link to the output	CONTENTS=
Specify the input data set	DATA=
Disable floating point exception recovery	NOTRAP
Specify the output data set	OUT=
Enable floating point exception recovery	TRAP
Identify categories of data that are of interest	
Specify a secondary data set that contains the combinations of values of class variables to include in tables and output data sets	CLASSDATA=
Exclude from tables and output data sets all combinations of class variable values that are not in the CLASSDATA= data set	EXCLUSIVE
Consider missing values as valid values for class variables	MISSING
Control the statistical analysis	
Exclude observations with nonpositive weights	EXCLNPWGTS
Specify the sample size to use for the P2 quantile estimation method	QMARKERS=
Specify the quantile estimation method	QMETHOD=
Specify the mathematical definition to calculate quantiles	QNTLDEF=
Specify the variance divisor	VARDEF=
Customize the appearance of the table	
Specify a default format for each cell in the table	FORMAT=
Define the characters to use to construct the table outlines and dividers	FORMCHAR=
Eliminate horizontal separator lines from the row titles and the body of the table	NOSEPS

To do this	Use this option
Order the values of a class variable according to the specified order	ORDER=
Specify the default style element or style elements (for the Output Delivery System) to use for each cell of the table	STYLE=

Options

CLASSDATA=*SAS-data-set*
specifies a data set that contains the combinations of values of the class variables that must be present in the output. Any combinations of values of the class variables that occur in the CLASSDATA= data set but not in the input data set appear in each table or output data set and have a frequency of zero.

Restriction: The CLASSDATA= data set must contain all class variables. Their data type and format must match the corresponding class variables in the input data set.

Interaction: If you use the EXCLUSIVE option, PROC TABULATE excludes any observations in the input data set whose combinations of class variables is not in the CLASSDATA= data set.

Tip: Use the CLASSDATA= data set to filter or supplement the input data set.

Featured in: Example 2 on page 1201

CONTENTS=*link-name*
allows you to name the link in the HTML table of contents that points to the ODS output of the first table that was produced using the TABULATE procedure.

Restrictions: CONTENTS= has no effect on TABULATE procedure reports.

DATA=*SAS-data-set*
specifies the input data set.

Main Discussion: "Input Data Sets" on page 18

EXCLNPWGTS
excludes observations with nonpositive weight values (zero or negative) from the analysis. By default, PROC TABULATE treats observations with negative weights like those with zero weights and counts them in the total number of observations.

Alias: EXCLNPWGT

See also: WEIGHT= on page 1180 and "WEIGHT Statement" on page 1181

EXCLUSIVE
excludes from the tables and the output data sets all combinations of the class variable that are not found in the CLASSDATA= data set.

Requirement: If a CLASSDATA= data set is not specified, this option is ignored.

Featured in: Example 2 on page 1201

FORMAT=*format-name*
specifies a default format for the value in each table cell. You can use any SAS or user-defined format.

Default: If you omit FORMAT=, PROC TABULATE uses BEST12.2 as the default format.

Interaction: Formats that are specified in a TABLE statement override the format that is specified with FORMAT=.

Tip: This option is especially useful for controlling the number of print positions that are used to print a table.

Featured in: Example 1 on page 1199 and Example 6 on page 1212

FORMCHAR *<(position(s))>='formatting-character(s)'*
defines the characters to use for constructing the table outlines and dividers.

position(s)
identifies the position of one or more characters in the SAS formatting-character string. A space or a comma separates the positions.

Default: Omitting *position(s)* is the same as specifying all 20 possible SAS formatting characters, in order.

Range: PROC TABULATE uses 11 of the 20 formatting characters that SAS provides. Table 37.2 on page 1160 shows the formatting characters that PROC TABULATE uses. Figure 37.2 on page 1161 illustrates the use of each formatting character in the output from PROC TABULATE.

formatting-character(s)
lists the characters to use for the specified positions. PROC TABULATE assigns characters in *formatting-character(s)* to *position(s)*, in the order that they are listed. For example, the following option assigns the asterisk (*) to the third formatting character, the pound sign (#) to the seventh character, and does not alter the remaining characters:

```
formchar(3,7)='*#'
```

Interaction: The SAS system option FORMCHAR= specifies the default formatting characters. The system option defines the entire string of formatting characters. The FORMCHAR= option in a procedure can redefine selected characters.

Tip: You can use any character in *formatting-characters*, including hexadecimal characters. If you use hexadecimal characters, you must put an **x** after the closing quote. For instance, the following option assigns the hexadecimal character 2D to the third formatting character, the hexadecimal character 7C to the seventh character, and does not alter the remaining characters:

```
formchar(3,7)='2D7C'x
```

Tip: Specifying all blanks for *formatting-character(s)* produces tables with no outlines or dividers.

```
formchar(1,2,3,4,5,6,7,8,9,10,11)
        ='               ' (11 blanks)
```

See also: For more information on formatting output, see Chapter 5 "Controlling the Table's Appearance" in the *SAS Guide to TABULATE Processing*.

For information on which hexadecimal codes to use for which characters, consult the documentation for your hardware.

Table 37.2 Formatting Characters Used by PROC TABULATE

Position	Default	Used to draw
1	|	the right and left borders and the vertical separators between columns
2	-	the top and bottom borders and the horizontal separators between rows

Position	Default	Used to draw
3	-	the top character in the left border
4	-	the top character in a line of characters that separate columns
5	-	the top character in the right border
6	|	the leftmost character in a row of horizontal separators
7	+	the intersection of a column of vertical characters and a row of horizontal characters
8	|	the rightmost character in a row of horizontal separators
9	-	the bottom character in the left border
10	-	the bottom character in a line of characters that separate columns
11	-	the bottom character in the right border

Figure 37.2 Formatting Characters in PROC TABULATE Output

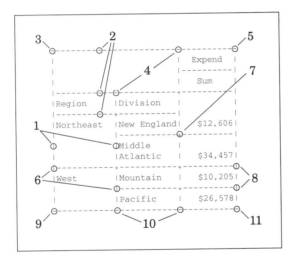

MISSING

considers missing values as valid values to create the combinations of class variables. Special missing values that are used to represent numeric values (the letters A through Z and the underscore (_) character) are each considered as a separate value. A heading for each missing value appears in the table.

Default: If you omit MISSING, PROC TABULATE does not include observations with a missing value for any class variable in the report.

Main Discussion: "Including Observations with Missing Class Variables" on page 1192

See also: *SAS Language Reference: Concepts* for a discussion of missing values that have special meaning.

NOSEPS

eliminates horizontal separator lines from the row titles and the body of the table. Horizontal separator lines remain between nested column headers.

Tip: If you want to replace the separator lines with blanks rather than remove them, use the FORMCHAR= option on page 1160.

Featured in: Example 8 on page 1216

NOTRAP

disables floating point exception (FPE) recovery during data processing. Note that normal SAS System FPE handling is still in effect so that PROC TABULATE terminates in the case of math exceptions.

Default: FPE recovery is disabled.

Tip: In operating environments where the overhead of FPE recovery is significant, NOTRAP can improve performance.

See also: TRAP on page 1165

ORDER=DATA | FORMATTED | FREQ | UNFORMATTED

specifies the sort order to create the unique combinations of the values of the class variables, which form the headings of the table, according to the specified order.

DATA

orders values according to their order in the input data set.

Interaction: If you use PRELOADFMT in the CLASS statement, the order for the values of each class variable matches the order that PROC FORMAT uses to store the values of the associated user-defined format. If you use the CLASSDATA= option, PROC TABULATE uses the order of the unique values of each class variable in the CLASSDATA= data set to order the output levels. If you use both options, PROC TABULATE first uses the user-defined formats to order the output. If you omit EXCLUSIVE, PROC TABULATE appends after the user-defined format and the CLASSDATA= values the unique values of the class variables in the input data set based on the order that they are encountered.

Tip: By default, PROC FORMAT stores a format definition in sorted order. Use the NOTSORTED option to store the values or ranges of a user defined format in the order that you define them.

FORMATTED

orders values by their ascending formatted values. This order depends on your operating environment.

Alias: FMT | EXTERNAL

FREQ

orders values by descending frequency count.

Interaction: Use the ASCENDING option in the CLASS statement to order values by ascending frequency count.

UNFORMATTED

orders values by their unformatted values, which yields the same order as PROC SORT. This order depends on your operating environment. This sort sequence is particularly useful for displaying dates chronologically.

Alias: UNFMT | INTERNAL

Default: UNFORMATTED

Interaction: If you use the PRELOADFMT option in the CLASS statement, PROC TABULATE orders the levels by the order of the values in the user-defined format.

Featured in: "Understanding the Order of Headings with ORDER=DATA" on page 1198

OUT=_SAS-data-set_
> names the output data set. If _SAS-data-set_ doesn't exist, PROC TABULATE creates it.
> The number of observations in the output data set depends on the number of categories of data that are used in the tables and the number of subtables that are generated. The output data set contains these variables (in this order):

by variables
> variables listed in the BY statement.

class variables
> variables listed in the CLASS statement.

TYPE
> a character variable that shows which combination of class variables produced the summary statistics in that observation. Each position in _TYPE_ represents one variable in the CLASS statement. If that variable is in the category that produced the statistic, the position contains a 1; if it is not, the position contains a 0. In simple PROC TABULATE steps that do not use the universal class variable ALL, all values of _TYPE_ contain only 1's because the only categories that are being considered involve all class variables. If you use the variable ALL, your tables will contain data for categories that do not include all the class variables, and values of _TYPE_ will, therefore, include both 1's and 0's.

PAGE
> The logical page that contains the observation.

TABLE
> The number of the table that contains the observation.

statistics
> statistics calculated for each observation in the data set.

> **Featured in:** Example 3 on page 1203

QMARKERS=_number_
> specifies the default number of markers to use for the P^2 quantile estimation method. The number of markers controls the size of fixed memory space.

> **Default:** The default value depends on which quantiles you request. For the median (P50), _number_ is 7. For the quartiles (P25 and P75), _number_ is 25. For the quantiles P1, P5, P10, P90, P95, or P99, _number_ is 107. If you request several quantiles, PROC TABULATE uses the largest default value of _number_.

> **Range:** an odd integer greater than 3

> **Tip:** Increase the number of markers above the default settings to improve the accuracy of the estimates; reduce the number of markers to conserve memory and computing time.

> **Main Discussion:** "Quantiles" on page 653

QMETHOD=OS | P2
> specifies the method PROC TABULATE uses to process the input data when it computes quantiles. If the number of observations is less than or equal to the QMARKERS= value and QNTLDEF=5, both methods produce the same results.

OS
> uses order statistics. This is the technique that PROC UNIVARIATE uses.

> > _Note:_ This technique can be very memory-intensive. △

P2
> uses the P^2 method to approximate the quantile.

Default: OS

Restriction: When QMETHOD=P2, PROC TABULATE does not compute weighted quantiles.

Tip: When QMETHOD=P2, reliable estimates of some quantiles (P1,P5,P95,P99) may not be possible for some types of data.

Main Discussion: "Quantiles" on page 653

QNTLDEF=1|2|3|4|5

specifies the mathematical definition that the procedure uses to calculate quantiles when QMETHOD=OS is specified. When QMETHOD=P2, you must use QNTLDEF=5.

Default: 5

Alias: PCTLDEF=

Main discussion: "Percentile and Related Statistics" on page 1463

STYLE=<*style-element-name* | <PARENT>><[*style-attribute-specification(s)*]>

specifies the style element to use for the data cells of a table when it is used in the PROC TABULATE statement. For example, the following statement specifies that the background color for data cells be red:

```
proc tabulate data=one style=[background=red];
```

Note: This option can be used in other statements, or in dimension expressions, to specify style elements for other parts of a table. △

Note: You can use braces ({ and }) instead of square brackets ([and]). △

style-element-name

is the name of a style element that is part of a style definition that is registered with the Output Delivery System. SAS Institute provides some style definitions. Users can create their own style definitions with PROC TEMPLATE.

Default: If you do not specify a style element, PROC TABULATE uses Data.

See also: For information about Institute-supplied style definitions, see "What Style Definitions Are Shipped with the Software?" on page 43. For information about PROC TEMPLATE and the Output Delivery System, see *The Complete Guide to the SAS Output Delivery System*.

PARENT

specifies that the data cell use the style element of its parent heading. The parent style element of a data cell is one of the following:

□ the style element of the leaf heading above the column that contains the data cell, if the table specifies no row dimension, or if the table specifies the style element in the column dimension expression.

□ the style element of the leaf heading above the row that contains the cell, if the table specifies the style element in the row dimension expression.

□ the Beforecaption style element, if the table specifies the style element in the page dimension expression.

□ undefined, otherwise.

Note: The parent of a heading (not applicable to STYLE= in the PROC TABULATE statement) is the heading under which the current heading is nested. △

style-attribute-specification(s)

describes the attribute to change. Each *style-attribute-specification* has this general form:

style-attribute-name=style-attribute-value

You can set or change the following attributes with the STYLE= option in the PROC TABULATE statement (or in any other statement that uses STYLE=, except for the TABLE statement):

ASIS=	FONT_WIDTH=
BACKGROUND=	HREFTARGET=
BACKGROUNDIMAGE=	HTMLCLASS=
BORDERCOLOR=	JUST=
BORDERCOLORDARK=	NOBREAKSPACE=
BORDERCOLORLIGHT=	POSTHTML=
BORDERWIDTH=	POSTIMAGE=
CELLHEIGHT=	POSTTEXT=
CELLWIDTH=	PREHTML=
FLYOVER=	PREIMAGE=
FONT=	PRETEXT=
FONT_FACE=	PROTECTSPECIALCHARS=
FONT_SIZE=	TAGATTR=
FONT_STYLE=	URL=
FONT_WEIGHT=	VJUST=

For more information about style attributes, see "What Style Attributes Can Base Procedures Specify?" on page 43.

Alias: S=

Restriction: This option affects only the HTML and Printer output.

Tip: To specify a style element for data cells with missing values, use STYLE= in the TABLE statement MISSTEXT= option.

See also: "Using Style Elements in PROC TABULATE" on page 1188

Featured in: Example 14 on page 1243

TRAP

enables floating point exception (FPE) recovery during data processing beyond that provided by normal SAS System FPE handling, which terminates PROC TABULATE in the case of math exceptions.

Default: FPE recovery is disabled.

Tip: Remove TRAP or use NOTRAP to improve performance in operating environments where the overhead of FPE recovery is significant.

See also: NOTRAP on page 1162

VARDEF=*divisor*

specifies the divisor to use in the calculation of the variance and standard deviation. Table 37.3 on page 1166 shows the possible values for *divisor* and the associated divisors.

Table 37.3 Possible Values for VARDEF=

Value	Divisor	Formula for Divisor
DF	degrees of freedom	$n-1$
N	number of observations	n
WDF	sum of weights minus one	$(\Sigma_i \, w_i) - 1$
WEIGHT |WGT	sum of weights	$\Sigma_i \, w_i$

The procedure computes the variance as $CSS/divisor$, where CSS is the corrected sums of squares and equals $\sum (x_i - \overline{x})^2$. When you weight the analysis variables, CSS equals $\sum w_i (x_i - \overline{x}_w)^2$ where $\overline{x}_w$ is the weighted mean.

Default: DF

Requirement: To compute standard error of the mean, use the default value of VARDEF=.

Tip: When you use the WEIGHT statement and VARDEF=DF, the variance is an estimate of σ^2, where the variance of the ith observation is $var(x_i) = \sigma^2/w_i$, and w_i is the weight for the ith observation. This yields an estimate of the variance of an observation with unit weight.

Tip: When you use the WEIGHT statement and VARDEF=WGT, the computed variance is asymptotically (for large n) an estimate of $\sigma^2/\overline{w}$, where $\overline{w}$ is the average weight. This yields an asymptotic estimate of the variance of an observation with average weight.

See also: the example of weighted statistics"WEIGHT" on page 73.

BY Statement

Creates a separate table on a separate page for each BY group.

Main discussion: "BY" on page 68

BY <DESCENDING> *variable-1*
   <...<DESCENDING> *variable-n*>
   <NOTSORTED>;

Required Arguments

variable
   specifies the variable that the procedure uses to form BY groups. You can specify more than one variable. If you do not use the NOTSORTED option in the BY statement, the observations in the data set must either be sorted by all the variables that you specify, or they must be indexed appropriately. Variables in a BY statement are called *BY variables*.

Options

DESCENDING
 specifies that the observations are sorted in descending order by the variable that immediately follows the word DESCENDING in the BY statement.

NOTSORTED
 specifies that observations are not necessarily sorted in alphabetic or numeric order. The observations are grouped in another way, for example, chronological order.

 The requirement for ordering or indexing observations according to the values of BY variables is suspended for BY-group processing when you use the NOTSORTED option. In fact, the procedure does not use an index if you specify NOTSORTED. The procedure defines a BY group as a set of contiguous observations that have the same values for all BY variables. If observations with the same values for the BY variables are not contiguous, the procedure treats each contiguous set as a separate BY group.

CLASS Statement

Identifies class variables for the table. Class variables determine the categories that PROC TABULATE uses to calculate statistics.

Tip: You can use multiple CLASS statements.

Tip: Some CLASS statement options are also available in the PROC TABULATE statement. They affect all CLASS variables rather than just the one(s) that you specify in a CLASS statement.

CLASS *variable(s)* <*/option(s)*>;

Required Arguments

variable(s)
 specifies one or more variables that the procedure uses to group the data. Variables in a CLASS statement are referred to as *class variables*. Class variables can be numeric or character. Class variables can have continuous values, but they typically have a few discrete values that define the classifications of the variable. You do not have to sort the data by class variables.

Options

ASCENDING
 specifies to sort the class variable values in ascending order.
 Alias: ASCEND
 Interaction: PROC TABULATE issues a warning message if you specify both ASCENDING and DESCENDING and ignores both options.

DESCENDING
 specifies to sort the class variable values in descending order.

Alias: DESCEND

Default: ASCENDING

Interaction: PROC TABULATE issues a warning message if you specify both ASCENDING and DESCENDING and ignores both options.

EXCLUSIVE

excludes from tables and output data sets all combinations of class variables that are not found in the preloaded range of user-defined formations.

Requirement: You must specify the PRELOADFMT option in the CLASS statement to preload the class variable formats.

Featured in: Example 3 on page 1203

GROUPINTERNAL

specifies not to apply formats to the class variables when PROC TABULATE groups the values to create combinations of class variables.

Interaction: If you specify the PRELOADFMT option in the CLASS statement, PROC TABULATE ignores the GROUPINTERNAL option and uses the formatted values.

Tip: This option saves computer resources when the class variables contain discrete numeric values.

MISSING

considers missing values as valid class variable levels. Special missing values that represent numeric values (the letters A through Z and the underscore (_) character) are each considered as a separate value.

Default: If you omit MISSING, PROC TABULATE excludes the observations with any missing CLASS variable values from tables and output data sets.

See also: *SAS Language Reference: Concepts* for a discussion of missing values with special meanings.

MLF

enables PROC TABULATE to use the primary and secondary format labels for a given range or overlapping ranges to create subgroup combinations when a multilabel format is assigned to a class variable.

Requirement: You must use PROC FORMAT and the MULTILABEL option in the VALUE statement to create a multilabel format.

Interaction: Using MLF with ORDER=FREQ may not produce the order that you expect for the formatted values.

Tip: If you omit MLF, PROC TABULATE uses the primary format labels, which corresponds to the first external format value, to determine the subgroup combinations.

See also: The MULTILABEL option on page 451 in the VALUE statement of the FORMAT procedure.

Featured in: Example 4 on page 1208

Note: When the formatted values overlap, one internal class variable value maps to more than one class variable subgroup combination. Therefore, the sum of the N statistics for all subgroups is greater than the number of observations in the data set (the overall N statistic). △

ORDER=DATA | FORMATTED | FREQ | UNFORMATTED

specifies the order to group the levels of the class variables in the output, where

DATA

orders values according to their order in the input data set.

Interaction: If you use PRELOADFMT, the order for the values of each class variable matches the order that PROC FORMAT uses to store the values of the associated user-defined format. If you use the CLASSDATA= option in the PROC statement, PROC MEANS uses the order of the unique values of each class variable in the CLASSDATA= data set to order the output levels. If you use both options, PROC TABULATE first uses the user-defined formats to order the output. If you omit EXCLUSIVE in the PROC statement, PROC TABULATE appends after the user-defined format and the CLASSDATA= values the unique values of the class variables in the input data set based on the order that they are encountered.

Tip: By default, PROC FORMAT stores a format definition in sorted order. Use the NOTSORTED option to store the values or ranges of a user-defined format in the order that you define them.

FORMATTED
orders values by their ascending formatted values. This order depends on your operating environment.

Alias: FMT | EXTERNAL

FREQ
orders values by descending frequency count.

Interaction: Use the ASCENDING option to order values by ascending frequency count.

UNFORMATTED
orders values by their unformatted values, which yields the same order as PROC SORT. This order depends on your operating environment. This sort sequence is particularly useful for displaying dates chronologically.

Alias: UNFMT | INTERNAL

Default: UNFORMATTED

Interaction: If you use the PRELOADFMT option in the CLASS statement, PROC TABULATE orders the levels by the order of the values in the user-defined format.

Tip: By default, all orders except FREQ are ascending. For descending orders, use the DESCENDING option.

Featured in: "Understanding the Order of Headings with ORDER=DATA" on page 1198

PRELOADFMT
specifies that all formats are preloaded for the class variables.

Requirement: PRELOADFMT has no effect unless you specify either EXCLUSIVE, ORDER=DATA, or PRINTMISS and you assign formats to the class variables.

Note: If you specify PRELOADFMT without also specifying either EXCLUSIVE or PRINTMISS, SAS writes a warning message to the SAS log. △

Interaction: To limit PROC TABULATE output to the combinations of formatted class variable values present in the input data set, use the EXCLUSIVE option in the CLASS statement.

Interaction: To include all ranges and values of the user-defined formats in the output, use the PRINTMISS option in the TABLE statement.

CAUTION:
Use care when you use PRELOADFMT with PRINTMISS. This feature creates all possible combinations of formatted class variables. Some of these combinations may not make sense. △

Featured in: Example 3 on page 1203

STYLE=<*style-element-name* | <PARENT>><[*style-attribute-specification(s)*]>
specifies the style element to use for page dimension text, continuation messages, and class variable name headings. For information about the arguments of this option, and how it is used, see STYLE= on page 1164 in the PROC TABULATE statement.

Note: When you use STYLE= in the CLASS statement, it differs slightly from its use in the PROC TABULATE statement. In the CLASS statement, the parent of the heading is the page dimension text or heading under which the current heading is nested.   △

Note: If a page dimension expression contains multiple nested elements, the Beforecaption style element is the style element of the first element in the nesting.   △

Alias: S=

Restriction: This option affects only the HTML and Printer output.

Tip: To override a style element that is specified for page dimension text in the CLASS statement, you can specify a style element in the TABLE statement page dimension expression.

Tip: To override a style element that is specified for a class variable name heading in the CLASS statement, you can specify a style element in the related TABLE statement dimension expression.

Featured in: Example 14 on page 1243

How PROC TABULATE Handles Missing Values for Class Variables

By default, if an observation contains a missing value for any class variable, PROC TABULATE excludes that observation from all tables that it creates. CLASS statements apply to all TABLE statements in the PROC TABULATE step. Therefore, if you define a variable as a class variable, PROC TABULATE omits observations that have missing values for that variable from every table even if the variable does not appear in the TABLE statement for one or more tables.

If you specify the MISSING option in the PROC TABULATE statement, the procedure considers missing values as valid levels for all class variables. If you specify the MISSING option in a CLASS statement, PROC TABULATE considers missing values as valid levels for the class variable(s) that are specified in that CLASS statement.

CLASSLEV Statement

Specifies a style element for class variable level value headings.

Restriction: This statement affects only the HTML and Printer output.

─────────

CLASSLEV *variable(s)* / *style* =<*style-element-name* | <PARENT>>
<[*style-attribute-specification(s)*] >;

Required Arguments

variable(s)
specifies one or more class variables from the CLASS statement for which you want to specify a style element.

Options

STYLE=<*style-element-name* | <**PARENT**>><[*style-attribute-specification(s)*]>
specifies a style element for class variable level value headings. For information on the arguments of this option and how it is used, see STYLE= on page 1164 in the PROC TABULATE statement.

Note: When you use STYLE= in the CLASSLEV statement, it differs slightly from its use in the PROC TABULATE statement. In the CLASSLEV statement, the parent of the heading is the heading under which the current heading is nested. △

Alias: S=

Restriction: This option affects only the HTML and Printer output.

Tip: To override a style element that is specified in the CLASSLEV statement, you can specify a style element in the related TABLE statement dimension expression.

Featured in: Example 14 on page 1243

FREQ Statement

Specifies a numeric variable that contains the frequency of each observation.

Tip: The effects of the FREQ and WEIGHT statements are similar except when calculating degrees of freedom.

See also: For an example that uses the FREQ statement, see "FREQ" on page 70.

FREQ *variable*;

Required Arguments

variable
specifies a numeric variable whose value represents the frequency of the observation. If you use the FREQ statement, the procedure assumes that each observation represents *n* observations, where *n* is the value of *variable*. If *n* is not an integer, the SAS System truncates it. If *n* is less than 1 or is missing, the procedure does not use that observation to calculate statistics.

The sum of the frequency variable represents the total number of observations.

KEYLABEL Statement

Labels a keyword for the duration of the PROC TABULATE step. PROC TABULATE uses the label anywhere that the specified keyword would otherwise appear.

KEYLABEL *keyword-1='description-1'*

> *<...keyword-n='description-n'>*;

Required Arguments

keyword
  is one of the keywords for statistics that is discussed in "Statistics Available in PROC TABULATE" on page 1181 or is the universal class variable ALL (see "Elements That You Can Use in a Dimension Expression" on page 1177).

description
  is up to 256 characters to use as a label. As the syntax shows, you must enclose *description* in quotes.

  Restriction: Each keyword can have only one label in a particular PROC TABULATE step; if you request multiple labels for the same keyword, PROC TABULATE uses the last one that is specified in the step.

KEYWORD Statement

Specifies a style element for keyword headings.

Restriction: This statement affects only the HTML and Printer output.

KEYWORD *keyword(s)* / *style* =<*style-element-name* | <PARENT>>
  <[*style-attribute-specification(s)*] >;

Required Arguments

keyword
  is one of the keywords for statistics that is discussed in "Statistics Available in PROC TABULATE" on page 1181 or is the universal class variable ALL (see "Elements That You Can Use in a Dimension Expression" on page 1177).

Options

STYLE=<*style-element-name* | <PARENT>><[*style-attribute-specification(s)*]>
  specifies a style element for the keyword headings. For information on the arguments of this option and how it is used, see STYLE= on page 1164 in the PROC TABULATE statement.

  Note: When you use STYLE= in the KEYWORD statement, it differs slightly from its use in the PROC TABULATE statement. In the KEYWORD statement, the parent of the heading is the heading under which the current heading is nested. △

  Alias: S=

  Restriction: This option affects only the HTML and Printer output.

  Tip: To override a style element that is specified in the KEYWORD statement, you can specify a style element in the related TABLE statement dimension expression.

Featured in: Example 14 on page 1243

TABLE Statement

Describes a table to print.

Requirement: All variables in the TABLE statement must appear in either the VAR statement or the CLASS statement.

Tip: Use multiple TABLE statements to create several tables.

TABLE *<<page-expression,> row-expression,>*
    column-expression </ table-option(s)>;

Required Arguments

column-expression
    defines the columns in the table. For information on constructing dimension expressions, see "Constructing Dimension Expressions" on page 1177.

   Restriction: A column dimension is the last dimension in a TABLE statement. A row dimension or a row dimension and a page dimension may precede a column dimension.

Options

To do this	Use this option
Add dimensions	
Define the pages in a table	*page-expression*
Define the rows in a table	*row-expression*
Customize the HTML contents entry link to the output	CONTENTS=
Specify a style element for various parts of the table	STYLE=
Customize text in the table	
Specify the text to place in the empty box above row titles	BOX=
Supply up to 256 characters to print in table cells that contain missing values	MISSTEXT=
Suppresses the continuation message for tables that span multiple physical pages	NOCONTINUED
Modify the layout of the table	
Print as many complete logical pages as possible on a single printed page or, if possible, print multiple pages of tables that are too wide to fit on a page one below the other on a single page, instead of on separate pages.	CONDENSE

To do this	Use this option
Create the same row and column headings for all logical pages of the table	PRINTMISS
Customize row headings	
Specify the number of spaces to indent nested row headings	INDENT=
Control allocation of space for row titles within the available space	ROW=
Specify the number of print positions available for row titles	RTSPACE=

BOX=*value*
BOX={<*label=value*>
<*style=<style-element-name><[style-attribute-specification(s)]>*> }
    specifies text and a style element for the empty box above the row titles.
    Value can be one of the following:

PAGE
    writes the page-dimension text in the box. If the page-dimension text does not fit, it is placed in its default position above the box, and the box remains empty.

'*string*'
    writes the quoted string in the box. Any string that does not fit in the box is truncated.

variable
    writes the name (or label, if the variable has one) of a variable in the box. Any name or label that does not fit in the box is truncated.

    For details about the arguments of the STYLE= option and how it is used, see STYLE= on page 1164 in the PROC TABULATE statement.
    Featured in: Example 9 on page 1218 and Example 14 on page 1243

CONDENSE
    prints as many complete logical pages as possible on a single printed page or, if possible, prints multiple pages of tables that are too wide to fit on a page one below the other on a single page, instead of on separate pages. A *logical page* is all the rows and columns that fall within one of the following:
      □ a page-dimension category (with no BY-group processing)
      □ a BY group with no page dimension
      □ a page-dimension category within a single BY group.
    Restrictions: CONDENSE has no effect on the pages that are generated by the BY statement. The first table for a BY group always begins on a new page.
      CONDENSE is ignored by the HTML destination but supported by the printer.
    Featured in: Example 9 on page 1218

CONTENTS=*link-name*
    allows you to name the link in the HTML table of contents that points to the ODS output of the table that is produced by using the TABLE statement.
    Restrictions: CONTENTS= has no effect on TABULATE procedure reports.

FUZZ=*number*
    supplies a numeric value against which analysis variable values and table cell values other than frequency counts are compared to eliminate trivial values (absolute values less than the FUZZ= value) from computation and printing. A number whose

absolute value is less than the FUZZ= value is treated as zero in computations and printing. The default value is the smallest representable floating-point number on the computer that you are using.

INDENT=*number-of-spaces*

specifies the number of spaces to indent nested row headings, and suppresses the row headings for class variables.

Tip: When there are no crossings in the row dimension, there is nothing to indent, so the value of *number-of-spaces* has no effect. However, in such cases INDENT= still suppresses the row headings for class variables.

Featured in: Example 8 on page 1216 (with crossings) and Example 9 on page 1218 (without crossings)

page-expression

defines the pages in a table. For information on constructing dimension expressions, see "Constructing Dimension Expressions" on page 1177.

Restriction: A page dimension is the first dimension in a table statement. Both a row dimension and a column dimension must follow a page dimension.

Featured in: Example 9 on page 1218

MISSTEXT=*'text'*
MISSTEXT={<*label= 'text'*
><*style=<style-element-name><[style-attribute-specification(s)]>> }*

supplies up to 256 characters of text to print and specifies a style element for table cells that contain missing values. For details on the arguments of the STYLE= option and how it is used, see STYLE= on page 1164 in the PROC TABULATE statement.

Interaction: A style element that is specified in a dimension expression overrides a style element that is specified in the MISSTEXT= option for any given cell(s).

Featured in: "Providing Text for Cells That Contain Missing Values" on page 1195 and Example 14 on page 1243

NOCONTINUED

suppresses the continuation message, **continued**, that is displayed at the bottom of tables that span multiple pages. The text is rendered with the Aftercaption style element.

Restrictions: NOCONTINUED is ignored by the HTML destination but supported by the printer.

PRINTMISS

prints all values that occur for a class variable each time headings for that variable are printed, even if there are no data for some of the cells that these headings create. Consequently, PRINTMISS creates row and column headings that are the same for all logical pages of the table, within a single BY group.

Default: If you omit PRINTMISS, PROC TABULATE suppresses a row or column for which there are no data, unless you use the CLASSDATA= option in the PROC TABULATE statement.

Restrictions: If an entire logical page contains only missing values, that page does not print regardless of the PRINTMISS option.

See also: CLASSDATA= option on page 1159

Featured in: "Providing Headings for All Categories" on page 1194

ROW=*spacing*

specifies whether all title elements in a row crossing are allotted space even when they are blank. The possible values for *spacing* are as follows:

CONSTANT

allots space to all row titles even if the title has been blanked out (for example, N=' ').

Alias: CONST

FLOAT

divides the row title space equally among the nonblank row titles in the crossing.

Default: CONSTANT

Featured in: Example 7 on page 1214

row-expression

defines the rows in the table. For information on constructing dimension expressions, see "Constructing Dimension Expressions" on page 1177.

Restriction: A row dimension is the next to last dimension in a table statement. A column dimension must follow a row dimension. A page dimension may precede a row dimension.

RTSPACE=*number*

specifies the number of print positions to allot to all of the headings in the row dimension, including spaces that are used to print outlining characters for the row headings. PROC TABULATE divides this space equally among all levels of row headings.

Alias: RTS=

Default: one-fourth of the value of the SAS system option LINESIZE=

Interaction: By default, PROC TABULATE allots space to row titles that are blank. Use ROW=FLOAT on page 1175 to divide the space among only nonblank titles.

See also: For more information about controlling the space for row titles, see Chapter 5, "Controlling the Table's Appearance" in *SAS Guide to TABULATE Processing*.

Featured in: Example 1 on page 1199

STYLE=*<style-element-name><[style-attribute-specification(s)]>*

specifies a style element to use for the entire table. For information about the arguments of this option and how it is used, see STYLE= on page 1164 in the PROC TABULATE statement.

Note: The list of attributes that you can set or change with the STYLE= option in the TABLE statement differs from that of the PROC TABULATE statement. △

You can set or change the following attributes with the STYLE= option in the TABLE statement. These attributes apply to the table as a whole. Attributes that you apply in the PROC TABULATE statement and in other locations in the PROC TABULATE step apply to cells within the table.

BACKGROUND=	FONT_WIDTH=*
BACKGROUNDIMAGE=	FOREGROUND=*
BORDERCOLOR=	FRAME=
BORDERCOLORDARK=	HTMLCLASS=
BORDERCOLORLIGHT=	JUST=
BORDERWIDTH=	OUTPUTWIDTH=
CELLPADDING=	POSTHTML=
CELLSPACING=	POSTIMAGE=

FONT=*	POSTTEXT=
FONT_FACE=*	PREHTML=
FONT_SIZE=*	PREIMAGE=
FONT_STYLE=*	PRETEXT=
FONT_WEIGHT=*	RULES=

* When you use these attributes in this location, they affect only the text that is specified with the PRETEXT=, POSTTEXT=, PREHTML=, and POSTHTML= attributes. To alter the foreground color or the font for the text that appears in the table, you must set the corresponding attribute in a location that affects the cells rather than the table.

For more information about style attributes, see "What Style Attributes Can Base Procedures Specify?" on page 43.

Note: You can use braces ({ and }) instead of square brackets ([and]). △

Alias: S=

Restriction: This option affects only the HTML and Printer output.

Tip: To override a style element specification that is made as an option in the TABLE statement, specify STYLE= in a dimension expression of the TABLE statement.

Featured in: Example 14 on page 1243

Constructing Dimension Expressions

A TABLE statement consists of from one to three dimension expressions separated by commas. Options can follow the dimension expressions. If all three dimensions are specified, the leftmost dimension defines pages, the middle dimension defines rows, and the rightmost dimension defines columns. If two dimensions are specified, the left defines rows, and the right defines columns. If a single dimension is specified, it defines columns.

A dimension expression is composed of elements and operators.

Elements That You Can Use in a Dimension Expression

analysis variables
(see "VAR Statement" on page 1179).

class variables
(see "CLASS Statement" on page 1167).

the universal class variable ALL
summarizes all of the categories for class variables in the same parenthetical group or dimension (if the variable ALL is not contained in a parenthetical group).
Featured in: Example 6 on page 1212, Example 9 on page 1218, and Example 13 on page 1233

Note: If the input data set contains a variable named ALL, enclose the name of the universal class variable in quotes. △

keywords for statistics
Requirement: To compute standard error or a *t*-test, you must use the default value of VARDEF=, which is DF.
Featured in: Example 10 on page 1220 and Example 13 on page 1233

format modifiers
> define how to format values in cells. Cross a format modifier with the elements that produce the cells that you want to format. Format modifiers have the form

>> `f=format`

> **Tip:**   Format modifiers have no effect on CLASS variables.
>
> **See also:**   For more information on specifying formats in tables, see "Formatting Values in Tables" on page 1183.
>
> **Featured in:**   Example 6 on page 1212

labels
> temporarily replace the names of variables and statistics. Labels affect only the variable or statistic that immediately precedes the label. Labels have the form

>> `stat-or-variable-name='label-text'`

> **Tip:**   PROC TABULATE eliminates the space for blank column headings from a table but by default does not eliminate the space for blank row headings. Use ROW=FLOAT in the TABLE statement to remove the space for blank row headings.
>
> **Featured in:**   Example 5 on page 1210 and Example 7 on page 1214

style—element specifications
> specify style elements for page dimension text, continuation messages, headings, or data cells. For details, see "Specifying Style Elements in Dimension Expressions" on page 1178.

You can also form dimension expressions by combining any of these elements.

Operators That You Can Use in a Dimension Expression

asterisk *
> creates categories from the combination of values of the class variables and constructs the appropriate headers for the dimension. If one of the elements is an analysis variable, the statistics for the analysis variable are calculated for the categories that are created by the class variables. This process is called *crossing*.
>
> **Featured in:**   Example 1 on page 1199

(blank)
> places the output for each element immediately after the output for the preceding element. This process is called *concatenation*.
>
> **Featured in:**   Example 6 on page 1212

parentheses ()
> group elements and associate an operator with each concatenated element in the group.
>
> **Featured in:**   Example 6 on page 1212

angle brackets <>
> specify denominator definitions, which determine the value of the denominator in the calculation of a percentage. For a discussion of how to construct denominator definitions, see "Calculating Percentages" on page 1184.
>
> **Featured in:**   Example 10 on page 1220 and Example 13 on page 1233

Specifying Style Elements in Dimension Expressions

You can specify a style element in a dimension expression to control the appearance in HTML and Printer output of the following table elements:

analysis variable name headings

class variable name headings

class variable level value headings

data cells

keyword headings

page dimension text

Specifying a style element in a dimension expression is useful when you want to override a style element that you have specified in another statement, such as the PROC TABULATE, CLASS, CLASSLEV, KEYWORD, TABLE, or VAR statements.

The syntax for specifying a style element in a dimension expression is

[STYLE<(CLASSLEV)>=<*style-element-name* | <PARENT>><[*style-attribute-specification(s)*]>]

Some examples of style elements in dimension expressions are

```
dept={label='Department'
       style=[foreground=red]}, N

dept*[style=MyDataStyle], N

dept*[format=12.2 style=MyDataStyle], N
```

Note: When used in a dimension expression, the STYLE= option must be enclosed within square brackets ([and]) or braces ({ and }). △

With the exception of (CLASSLEV), all arguments are described in STYLE= on page 1164 in the PROC TABULATE statement.

(CLASSLEV)

assigns a style element to a class variable level value heading. For example, the following TABLE statement specifies that the level value heading for the class variable, DEPT, has a foreground color of yellow:

```
table dept=[style(classlev)=
              [foreground=yellow]]*sales;
```

Note: This option is used only in dimension expressions. △

For an example that shows how to specify style elements within dimension expressions, see Example 14 on page 1243.

VAR Statement

Identifies numeric variables to use as analysis variables.

Alias: VARIABLES

Tip: You can use multiple VAR statements.

VAR *analysis-variable(s)* </ *option(s)*>;

Required Arguments

analysis-variable(s);
> identifies the analysis variables in the table. Analysis variables are numeric variables for which PROC TABULATE calculates statistics. The values of an analysis variable can be continuous or discrete.
>
> If an observation contains a missing value for an analysis variable, PROC TABULATE omits that value from calculations of all statistics except N (the number of observations with nonmissing variable values) and NMISS (the number of observations with missing variable values). For example, the missing value does not increase the SUM, and it is not counted when you are calculating statistics such as the MEAN.

Options

STYLE=<*style-element-name* | <PARENT>><[*style-attribute-specification(s)*>]
> specifies a style element for analysis variable name headings. For information on the arguments of this option and how it is used, see STYLE= on page 1164 in the PROC TABULATE statement.
>
> *Note:* When you use STYLE= in the VAR statement, it differs slightly from its use in the PROC TABULATE statement. In the VAR statement, the parent of the heading is the heading under which the current heading is nested. △
>
> **Alias:** S=
>
> **Restriction:** This option affects only the HTML and Printer output.
>
> **Tip:** To override a style element that is specified in the VAR statement, you can specify a style element in the related TABLE statement dimension expression.
>
> **Featured in:** Example 14 on page 1243

WEIGHT=*weight-variable*
> specifies a numeric variable whose values weight the values of the variables that are specified in the VAR statement. The variable does not have to be an integer. If the value of the weight variable is

Weight value...	PROC TABULATE...
0	counts the observation in the total number of observations
less than 0	converts the value to zero and counts the observation in the total number of observations
missing	excludes the observation

> To exclude observations that contain negative and zero weights from the analysis, use EXCLNPWGT. Note that most SAS/STAT procedures, such as PROC GLM, exclude negative and zero weights by default.
>
> **Restriction:** To compute weighted quantiles, use QMETHOD=OS in the PROC statement.
>
> **Tip:** When you use the WEIGHT= option, consider which value of the VARDEF= option is appropriate (see the discussion of VARDEF= on page 1165).
>
> **Tip:** Use the WEIGHT option in multiple VAR statements to specify different weights for the analysis variables.
>
> *Note:* Prior to Version 7 of the SAS System, the procedure did not exclude the observations with missing weights from the count of observations. △

WEIGHT Statement

Specifies weights for analysis variables in the statistical calculations.

See also: For information on calculating weighted statistics and for an example that uses the WEIGHT statement, see "Calculating Weighted Statistics" on page 74

WEIGHT *variable*;

Required Arguments

variable
specifies a numeric variable whose values weight the values of the analysis variables. The values of the variable do not have to be integers. If the value of the weight variable is

Weight value ...	PROC TABULATE ...
0	counts the observation in the total number of observations
less than 0	converts the value to zero and counts the observation in the total number of observations
missing	excludes the observation

To exclude observations that contain negative and zero weights from the analysis, use EXCLNPWGT. Note that most SAS/STAT procedures, such as PROC GLM, exclude negative and zero weights by default.

Restriction: To compute weighted quantiles, use QMETHOD=OS in the PROC statement.

Interaction: If you use the WEIGHT= option in a VAR statement to specify a weight variable, PROC TABULATE uses this variable instead to weight those VAR statement variables.

Tip: When you use the WEIGHT statement, consider which value of the VARDEF= option is appropriate. See the discussion of VARDEF= on page 1165 and the calculation of weighted statistics in "Keywords and Formulas" on page 1458 for more information.

Note: Prior to Version 7 of the SAS System, the procedure did not exclude the observations with missing weights from the count of observations. △

Concepts

Statistics Available in PROC TABULATE

Use the following keywords to request statistics in the TABLE statement. If a variable name (class or analysis) and a statistic name are the same, enclose the statistic name in single quotes.

Descriptive statistic keywords

COLPCTN	PCTSUM
COLPCTSUM	RANGE
CSS	REPPCTN
CV	REPPCTSUM
MAX	ROWPCTN
MEAN	ROWPCTSUM
MIN	STDDEV|STD
N	STDERR
NMISS	SUM
PAGEPCTN	SUMWGT
PAGEPCTSUM	USS
PCTN	VAR

Quantile statistic keywords

MEDIAN|P50	Q3|P75
P1	P90
P5	P95
P10	P99
Q1|P25	QRANGE

Hypothesis testing keyword

PROBT	T

To compute standard error (STD), you must use VARDEF=DF in the PROC statement. To compute weighted quantiles, you must use QMETHOD=OS in the PROC statement.

Explanations of the keywords, the formulas that are used to calculate them, and the data requirements are discussed in "Keywords and Formulas" on page 1458.

Formatting Class Variables

Use the FORMAT statement to assign a format to a class variable for the duration of a PROC TABULATE step. When you assign a format to a class variable, PROC TABULATE uses the formatted values to create categories, and it uses the formatted values in headings.

User-defined formats are particularly useful for grouping values into fewer categories. For example, if you have a class variable, Age, with values ranging from 1 to 99, you could create a user-defined format that groups the ages so that your tables contain a manageable number of categories. The following PROC FORMAT step creates a format that condenses all possible values of age into six groups of values.

```
proc format;
    value agefmt  0-29='Under 30'
                 30-39='30-39'
                 40-49='40-49'
                 50-59='50-59'
                 60-69='60-69'
                 other='70 or over';
```

```
run;
```

For information on creating user-defined formats, see Chapter 19, "The FORMAT Procedure," on page 433.

By default, PROC TABULATE includes in a table only those formats for which the frequency count is not zero and for which values are not missing. To include missing values for all class variables in the output, use the MISSING option in the PROC TABULATE statement, and to include missing values for selected class variables, use the MISSING option in a CLASS statement. To include formats for which the frequency count is zero, use the PRELOADFMT option in a CLASS statement and the PRINTMISS option in the TABLE statement, or use the CLASSDATA= option in the PROC TABULATE statement.

Formatting Values in Tables

The formats for data in table cells serve two purposes. They determine how PROC TABULATE displays the values, and they determine the width of the columns. The default format for values in table cells is 12.2. You can modify the format for printing values in table cells by

☐ changing the default format with the FORMAT= option in the PROC TABULATE statement

☐ crossing elements in the TABLE statement with the F= format modifier.

PROC TABULATE determines the format to use for a particular cell based on the following order of precedence for formats:

1 If no other formats are specified, PROC TABULATE uses the default format (12.2).

2 The FORMAT= option in the PROC TABULATE statement changes the default format. If no format modifiers affect a cell, PROC TABULATE uses this format for the value in that cell.

3 A format modifier in the page dimension applies to the values in all the table cells on the page unless you specify another format modifier for a cell in the row or column dimension.

4 A format modifier in the row dimension applies to the values in all the table cells in the row unless you specify another format modifier for a cell in the column dimension.

5 A format modifier in the column dimension applies to the values in all the table cells in the column.

For more information about formatting table cells, see "Formatting Values in Table Cells" in Chapter 5, "Controlling the Table's Appearance" in *SAS Guide to TABULATE Processing*.

How Using BY-group Processing Differs from Using the Page Dimension

Using the page-dimension expression in a TABLE statement can have an effect similar to using a BY statement.

Table 37.4 on page 1184 contrasts the two methods.

Table 37.4 Contrasting the BY Statement and the Page Dimension

Issue	PROC TABULATE with a BY statement	PROC TABULATE with a page dimension in the TABLE statement
Order of observations in the input data set	The observations in the input data set must be sorted by the BY variables. [1]	Sorting is unnecessary.
One report summarizing all BY groups	You cannot create one report for all the BY groups.	Use ALL in the page dimension to create a report for all classes. (See Example 6 on page 1212.)
Percentages	The percentages in the tables are percentages of the total for that BY group. You cannot calculate percentages for a BY group compared to the totals for all BY groups because PROC TABULATE prepares the individual reports separately. Data for the report for one BY group are not available to the report for another BY group.	You can use denominator definitions to control the meaning of PCTN (see "Calculating Percentages" on page 1184.)
Titles	You can use the #BYVAL, #BYVAR, and #BYLINE specifications in TITLE statements to customize the titles for each BY group (see "Creating Titles That Contain BY-Group Information" on page 54).	The BOX= option in the TABLE statement customizes the page headers, but you must use the same title on each page.
Ordering class variables	ORDER=DATA and ORDER=FREQ order each BY group independently.	The order of class variables is the same on every page.
Obtaining uniform headings	You may need to insert dummy observations into BY groups that do not have all classes represented.	The PRINTMISS option ensures that each page of the table has uniform headings.
Multiple ranges with the same format	PROC TABULATE produces a table for each range.	PROC TABULATE combines observations from the two ranges.

1   You can use the BY statement without sorting the data set if the data set has an index for the BY variable.

Calculating Percentages

The following statistics print the percentage of the value in a single table cell in relation to the total of the values in a group of cells. No denominator definitions are required; however, an analysis variable may be used as a denominator definition for percentage sum statistics.

REPPCTN and REPPCTSUM statistics—print the percentage of the value in a single table cell in relation to the total of the values in the report.

COLPCTN and COLPCTSUM statistics—print the percentage of the value in a single table cell in relation to the total of the values in the column.

ROWPCTN and ROWPCTSUM statistics—print the percentage of the value in a single table cell in relation to the total of the values in the row.

PAGEPCTN and PAGEPCTSUM statistics—print the percentage of the value in a single table cell in relation to the total of the values in the page.

These statistics calculate the most commonly used percentages. See Example 12 on page 1230 for an example.

PCTN and PCTSUM statistics can be used to calculate these same percentages. They allow you to manually define denominators. PCTN and PCTSUM statistics print the percentage of the value in a single table cell in relation to the value (used in the denominator of the calculation of the percentage) in another table cell or to the total of the values in a group of cells. By default, PROC TABULATE summarizes the values in all N cells (for PCTN) or all SUM cells (for PCTSUM) and uses the summarized value for the denominator. You can control the value that PROC TABULATE uses for the denominator with a denominator definition.

You place a denominator definition in angle brackets (< and >) next to the N or PCTN statistic. The denominator definition specifies which categories to sum for the denominator.

This section illustrates how to specify denominator definitions in a simple table. Example 13 on page 1233 illustrates how to specify denominator definitions in a table that is composed of multiple subtables. For more examples of denominator definitions, see "How Percentages Are Calculated" in Chapter 3, "Details of TABULATE Processing" in *SAS Guide to TABULATE Processing*.

Specifying a Denominator for the PCTN Statistic

The following PROC TABULATE step calculates the N statistic and three different versions of PCTN using the data set ENERGY on page 1199.

```
proc tabulate data=energy;
   class division type;
   table division*
            (n='Number of customers'
             pctn<type>='% of row' ❶
             pctn<division>='% of column' ❷
             pctn='% of all customers'), ❸
           type/rts=50;
   title 'Number of Users in Each Division';
run;
```

The TABLE statement creates a row for each value of Division and a column for each value of Type. Within each row, the TABLE statement nests four statistics: N and three different calculations of PCTN (see Figure 37.3 on page 1186). Each occurrence of PCTN uses a different denominator definition.

Figure 37.3 Three Different Uses of the PCTN Statistic with Frequency Counts Highlighted

```
                    Number of Users in Each Division
  1


    ----------------------------------------------------------------
    |                              |            Type               |
    |                              |-------------------------------|
    |                              |     1      |      2      |
    |------------------------------+------------+-------------|
    |Division |                    |            |             |
    |---------+--------------------+------------+-------------|
    |1        |Number of customers |      6.00  |       6.00  |
    |         |--------------------+------------+-------------|
    |         |% of row   ❶        |     50.00  |      50.00  |
    |         |--------------------+------------+-------------|
    |         |% of column ❷       |     27.27  |      27.27  |
    |         |--------------------+------------+-------------|
    |         |% of all customers ❸|     13.64  |      13.64  |
    |---------+--------------------+------------+-------------|
    |2        |Number of customers |      3.00  |       3.00  |
    |         |--------------------+------------+-------------|
    |         |% of row            |     50.00  |      50.00  |
    |         |--------------------+------------+-------------|
    |         |% of column         |     13.64  |      13.64  |
    |         |--------------------+------------+-------------|
    |         |% of all customers  |      6.82  |       6.82  |
    |---------+--------------------+------------+-------------|
    |3        |Number of customers |      8.00  |       8.00  |
    |         |--------------------+------------+-------------|
    |         |% of row            |     50.00  |      50.00  |
    |         |--------------------+------------+-------------|
    |         |% of column         |     36.36  |      36.36  |
    |         |--------------------+------------+-------------|
    |         |% of all customers  |     18.18  |      18.18  |
    |---------+--------------------+------------+-------------|
    |4        |Number of customers |      5.00  |       5.00  |
    |         |--------------------+------------+-------------|
    |         |% of row            |     50.00  |      50.00  |
    |         |--------------------+------------+-------------|
    |         |% of column         |     22.73  |      22.73  |
    |         |--------------------+------------+-------------|
    |         |% of all customers  |     11.36  |      11.36  |
```

1 `<type>` sums the frequency counts for all occurrences of Type within the same value of Division. Thus, for Division=1, the denominator is 6 + 6, or 12.

2 `<division>` sums the frequency counts for all occurrences of Division within the same value of Type. Thus, for Type=1, the denominator is 6 + 3 + 8 + 5, or 22.

3 The third use of PCTN has no denominator definition. Omitting a denominator definition is the same as including all class variables in the denominator definition. Thus, for all cells, the denominator is 6 + 3 + 8 + 5 + 6 + 3 + 8 + 5, or 44.

Specifying a Denominator for the PCTSUM Statistic

The following PROC TABULATE step sums expenditures for each combination of Type and Division and calculates three different versions of PCTSUM.

```
proc tabulate data=energy format=8.2;
   class division type;
   var expenditures;
   table division*
           (sum='Expenditures'*f=dollar10.2
            pctsum<type>='% of row' ❶
            pctsum<division>='% of column' ❷
```

```
            pctsum='% of all customers'),  ❸
         type*expenditures/rts=40;
   title 'Expenditures in Each Division';
run;
```

The TABLE statement creates a row for each value of Division and a column for each value of Type. Because Type is crossed with Expenditures, the value in each cell is the sum of the values of Expenditures for all observations that contribute to the cell. Within each row, the TABLE statement nests four statistics: SUM and three different calculations of PCTSUM (see Figure 37.4 on page 1187). Each occurrence of PCTSUM uses a different denominator definition.

Figure 37.4 Three Different Uses of the PCTSUM Statistic with Sums Highlighted

```
                 Expenditures in Each Division          1

 ----------------------------------------------------------------
 |                            |         Type             |
 |                            |--------------------------|
 |                            |    1      |    2         |
 |                            |-----------+-----------   |
 |                            |  Expend   |  Expend      |
 |----------------------------+-----------+-----------   |
 |Division         |          |           |             |
 |-----------------+----------|           |             |
 |1                |Expenditures          |$7,477.00| $5,129.00|
 |                 |--------------------- +-----------+-----------|
 |                 |% of row ❶            |    59.31|    40.69|
 |                 |--------------------- +-----------+-----------|
 |                 |% of column ❷        |    16.15|    13.66|
 |                 |--------------------- +-----------+-----------|
 |                 |% of all customers ❸ |     8.92|     6.12|
 |-----------------+--------------------- +-----------+-----------|
 |2                |Expenditures          |$19,379.00|$15,078.00|
 |                 |--------------------- +-----------+-----------|
 |                 |% of row              |    56.24|    43.76|
 |                 |--------------------- +-----------+-----------|
 |                 |% of column           |    41.86|    40.15|
 |                 |--------------------- +-----------+-----------|
 |                 |% of all customers    |    23.11|    17.98|
 |-----------------+--------------------- +-----------+-----------|
 |3                |Expenditures          | $5,476.00| $4,729.00|
 |                 |--------------------- +-----------+-----------|
 |                 |% of row              |    53.66|    46.34|
 |                 |--------------------- +-----------+-----------|
 |                 |% of column           |    11.83|    12.59|
 |                 |--------------------- +-----------+-----------|
 |                 |% of all customers    |     6.53|     5.64|
 |-----------------+--------------------- +-----------+-----------|
 |4                |Expenditures          |$13,959.00|$12,619.00|
 |                 |--------------------- +-----------+-----------|
 |                 |% of row              |    52.52|    47.48|
 |                 |--------------------- +-----------+-----------|
 |                 |% of column           |    30.15|    33.60|
 |                 |--------------------- +-----------+-----------|
 |                 |% of all customers    |    16.65|    15.05|
 ----------------------------------------------------------------
```

1 **<type>** sums the values of Expenditures for all occurrences of Type within the same value of Division. Thus, for Division=1, the denominator is $7,477 + $5,129.

2 **<division>** sums the frequency counts for all occurrences of Division within the same value of Type. Thus, for Type=1, the denominator is $7,477 + $19,379 + $5,476 + $13,959.

3 The third use of PCTN has no denominator definition. Omitting a denominator definition is the same as including all class variables in the denominator definition. Thus, for all cells, the denominator is $7,477 + $19,379 + $5,476 + $13,959 + $5,129 + $15,078 + $4,729 + $12,619.

Using Style Elements in PROC TABULATE

If you use the Output Delivery System to create both HTML and Printer output from PROC TABULATE, you can set the style element that the procedure uses for various parts of the table. Style elements determine presentation attributes, such as font face, font weight, color, and so forth. Information about the style attributes that you can set for a style element is in "Customizing the Style Definition That ODS Uses" on page 42. lists the default styles for various regions of a table.

Table 37.5 Default Styles for Table Regions

Region	Style
column headings	Header
continuation message	Aftercaption
box	Header
page dimension text	Beforecaption
row headings	Rowheader
data cells	Data
table	Table

You specify style elements for PROC TABULATE with the STYLE= option. The following shows where you can use this option. Specifications in the TABLE statement override the same specification in the PROC TABULATE statement. However, any style attributes that you specify in the PROC TABULATE statement and that you do not override in the TABLE statement are inherited. For instance, if you specify a blue background and a white foreground for all data cells in the PROC TABULATE statement, and you specify a gray background for the data cells of a particular crossing in the TABLE statement, the background for those data cells is gray, and the foreground is white (as specified in the PROC TABULATE statement).

Detailed information on STYLE= is provided in the documentation for individual statements.

Table 37.6 Using the STYLE= Option in PROC TABULATE

To set the style element for	Use STYLE in this statement
data cells	PROC TABULATE
page dimension text, continuation messages, and class variable name headings	CLASS
class level value headings	CLASSLEV
keyword headings	KEYWORD
the entire table	TABLE
analysis variable name headings	VAR

Results

Missing Values

How a missing value for a variable in the input data set affects your output depends on how you use the variable in the PROC TABULATE step. Table 37.7 on page 1189 summarizes how the procedure treats missing values.

Table 37.7 Summary of How PROC TABULATE Treats Missing Values

If . . .	PROC TABULATE, by default, . . .	To override the default . . .
an observation contains a missing value for an analysis variable	excludes that observation from the calculation of statistics (except N and NMISS) for that particular variable	no alternative
an observation contains a missing value for a class variable	excludes that observation from the table[1]	use MISSING in the PROC TABULATE statement, or MISSING in the CLASS statement
there are no data for a category	does not show the category in the table	use PRINTMISS in the TABLE statement, or use CLASSDATA= in the PROC TABULATE statement
every observation that contributes to a table cell contains a missing value for an analysis variable	displays a missing value for any statistics (except N and NMISS) in that cell	use MISSTEXT= in the TABLE statement
there are no data for a formatted value	does not display that formatted value in the table	use PRELOADFMT in the CLASS statement with PRINTMISS in the TABLE statement, or use CLASSDATA= in the PROC TABULATE statement, or add dummy observations to the input data set so that it contains data for each formatted value
a FREQ variable value is missing or is less than 1	does not use that observation to calculate statistics	no alternative
a WEIGHT variable value is missing or 0	uses a value of 0	no alternative

1 The CLASS statement applies to all TABLE statements in a PROC TABULATE step. Therefore, if you define a variable as a class variable, PROC TABULATE omits observations that have missing values for that variable even if you do not use the variable in a TABLE statement.

This section presents a series of PROC TABULATE steps that illustrate how PROC TABULATE treats missing values. The following program creates the data set and formats that are used in this section and prints the data set. The data set COMPREV contains no missing values (see Figure 37.5 on page 1190).

```
proc format;
    value cntryfmt 1='United States'
                   2='Japan';
```

```
       value compfmt  1='Supercomputer'
                      2='Mainframe'
                      3='Midrange'
                      4='Workstation'
                      5='Personal Computer'
                      6='Laptop';
   run;


   data comprev;
      input Country Computer Rev90 Rev91 Rev92;
      datalines;
   1 1 788.8 877.6 944.9
   1 2 12538.1 9855.6 8527.9
   1 3 9815.8 6340.3 8680.3
   1 4 3147.2 3474.1 3722.4
   1 5 18660.9 18428.0 23531.1
   2 1 469.9 495.6 448.4
   2 2 5697.6 6242.4 5382.3
   2 3 5392.1 5668.3 4845.9
   2 4 1511.6 1875.5 1924.5
   2 5 4746.0 4600.8 4363.7
   ;


   proc print data=comprev noobs;
      format country cntryfmt. computer compfmt.;
      title 'The Data Set COMPREV';
   run;
```

Figure 37.5   The Data Set COMPREV

```
                    The Data Set COMPREV                    1

Country        Computer              Rev90     Rev91     Rev92

United States  Supercomputer         788.8     877.6     944.9
United States  Mainframe           12538.1    9855.6    8527.9
United States  Midrange             9815.8    6340.3    8680.3
United States  Workstation          3147.2    3474.1    3722.4
United States  Personal Computer   18660.9   18428.0   23531.1
Japan          Supercomputer         469.9     495.6     448.4
Japan          Mainframe            5697.6    6242.4    5382.3
Japan          Midrange             5392.1    5668.3    4845.9
Japan          Workstation          1511.6    1875.5    1924.5
Japan          Personal Computer    4746.0    4600.8    4363.7
```

No Missing Values

The following PROC TABULATE step produces Figure 37.6 on page 1191:

```
proc tabulate data=comprev;
   class country computer;
   var rev90 rev91 rev92;
   table computer*country,rev90 rev91 rev92 /
        rts=32;
```

```
      format country cntryfmt. computer compfmt.;
      title 'Revenues from Computer Sales';
      title2 'for 1990 to 1992';
   run;
```

Figure 37.6 Computer Sales Data: No Missing Values

Because the data set contains no missing values, the table includes all observations. All headers and cells contain nonmissing values.

```
                    Revenues from Computer Sales           1
                           for 1990 to 1992


      ----------------------------------------------------------
      |                          | Rev90   | Rev91   | Rev92   |
      |                          |---------+---------+---------|
      |                          | Sum     | Sum     | Sum     |
      |--------------------------+---------+---------+---------|
      |Computer      |Country    |         |         |         |
      |--------------+-----------|         |         |         |
      |Supercomputer |United States |  788.80|  877.60|  944.90|
      |              |-----------+---------+---------+---------|
      |              |Japan      |  469.90|  495.60|  448.40|
      |--------------+-----------+---------+---------+---------|
      |Mainframe     |United States | 12538.10| 9855.60| 8527.90|
      |              |-----------+---------+---------+---------|
      |              |Japan      |  5697.60| 6242.40| 5382.30|
      |--------------+-----------+---------+---------+---------|
      |Midrange      |United States |  9815.80| 6340.30| 8680.30|
      |              |-----------+---------+---------+---------|
      |              |Japan      |  5392.10| 5668.30| 4845.90|
      |--------------+-----------+---------+---------+---------|
      |Workstation   |United States |  3147.20| 3474.10| 3722.40|
      |              |-----------+---------+---------+---------|
      |              |Japan      |  1511.60| 1875.50| 1924.50|
      |--------------+-----------+---------+---------+---------|
      |Personal      |United States | 18660.90|18428.00|23531.10|
      |Computer      |-----------+---------+---------+---------|
      |              |Japan      |  4746.00| 4600.80| 4363.70|
      ----------------------------------------------------------
```

A Missing Class Variable

The next program copies COMPREV and alters the data so that the eighth observation has a missing value for Computer. Except for specifying this new data set, the program that produces Figure 37.7 on page 1192 is the same as the program that produces Figure 37.6 on page 1191. By default, PROC TABULATE ignores observations with missing values for a class variable.

```
   data compmiss;
      set comprev;
      if _n_=8 then computer=.;
   run;


   proc tabulate data=compmiss;
      class country computer;
      var rev90 rev91 rev92;
      table computer*country,rev90 rev91 rev92 /
```

```
            rts=32;
      format country cntryfmt. computer compfmt.;
      title 'Revenues from Computer Sales';
      title2 'for 1990 to 1992';
   run;
```

Figure 37.7   Computer Sales Data: Midrange, Japan, Deleted

The observation with a missing value for Computer was the category **Midrange, Japan**. This
category no longer exists. By default, PROC TABULATE ignores observations with missing
values for a class variable, so this table contains one fewer row than Figure 37.6 on page 1191.

```
                    Revenues from Computer Sales                1
                          for 1990 to 1992


-----------------------------------------------------------------
|                          | Rev90   | Rev91   | Rev92   |
|                          |---------+---------+---------|
|                          | Sum     | Sum     | Sum     |
|--------------------------+---------+---------+---------|
|Computer      |Country    |         |         |         |
|--------------+-----------|         |         |         |
|Supercomputer |United States |  788.80|   877.60|   944.90|
|              |-----------+---------+---------+---------|
|              |Japan      |  469.90|   495.60|   448.40|
|--------------+-----------+---------+---------+---------|
|Mainframe     |United States | 12538.10|  9855.60|  8527.90|
|              |-----------+---------+---------+---------|
|              |Japan      |  5697.60|  6242.40|  5382.30|
|--------------+-----------+---------+---------+---------|
|Midrange      |United States |  9815.80|  6340.30|  8680.30|
|--------------+-----------+---------+---------+---------|
|Workstation   |United States |  3147.20|  3474.10|  3722.40|
|              |-----------+---------+---------+---------|
|              |Japan      |  1511.60|  1875.50|  1924.50|
|--------------+-----------+---------+---------+---------|
|Personal      |United States | 18660.90| 18428.00| 23531.10|
|Computer      |-----------+---------+---------+---------|
|              |Japan      |  4746.00|  4600.80|  4363.70|
-----------------------------------------------------------------
```

Including Observations with Missing Class Variables

This program adds the MISSING option to the previous program. MISSING is
available either in the PROC TABULATE statement or in the CLASS statement. If you
want MISSING to apply only to selected class variables, but not to others, specify
MISSING in a separate CLASS statement with the selected variable(s). The MISSING
option includes observations with missing values of a class variable in the report (see
Figure 37.8 on page 1193).

```
proc tabulate data=compmiss missing;
   class country computer;
   var rev90 rev91 rev92;
   table computer*country,rev90 rev91 rev92 /
         rts=32;
   format country cntryfmt. computer compfmt.;
   title 'Revenues from Computer Sales';
   title2 'for 1990 to 1992';
```

```
run;
```

Figure 37.8 Computer Sales Data: Missing Value for COMP

This table includes a category with missing values of COMP. This category makes up the first row of data in the table.

```
                  Revenues from Computer Sales            1
                        for 1990 to 1992

---------------------------------------------------------------
|                       | Rev90   | Rev91   | Rev92   |
|                       |---------+---------+---------|
|                       | Sum     | Sum     | Sum     |
|-----------------------+---------+---------+---------|
|Computer    |Country   |         |         |         |
|------------+-----------+---------+---------+---------|
|.           |Japan     |  5392.10|  5668.30|  4845.90|
|------------+-----------+---------+---------+---------|
|Supercomputer|United States|  788.80|   877.60|   944.90|
|            |-----------+---------+---------+---------|
|            |Japan     |   469.90|   495.60|   448.40|
|------------+-----------+---------+---------+---------|
|Mainframe   |United States| 12538.10|  9855.60|  8527.90|
|            |-----------+---------+---------+---------|
|            |Japan     |  5697.60|  6242.40|  5382.30|
|------------+-----------+---------+---------+---------|
|Midrange    |United States|  9815.80|  6340.30|  8680.30|
|------------+-----------+---------+---------+---------|
|Workstation |United States|  3147.20|  3474.10|  3722.40|
|            |-----------+---------+---------+---------|
|            |Japan     |  1511.60|  1875.50|  1924.50|
|------------+-----------+---------+---------+---------|
|Personal    |United States| 18660.90| 18428.00| 23531.10|
|Computer    |-----------+---------+---------+---------|
|            |Japan     |  4746.00|  4600.80|  4363.70|
---------------------------------------------------------------
```

Formatting Headings for Observations with Missing Class Variables

By default, as shown in Figure 37.8 on page 1193, PROC TABULATE displays missing values of a class variable as one of the standard SAS characters for missing values (a period, a blank, an underscore, or one of the letters A through Z). If you want to display something else instead, you must assign a format to the class variable that has missing values, as shown in the following program (see Figure 37.9 on page 1194):

```
proc format;
   value misscomp 1='Supercomputer'
                  2='Mainframe'
                  3='Midrange'
                  4='Workstation'
                  5='Personal Computer'
                  6='Laptop'
                  .='No type given';
run;


proc tabulate data=compmiss missing;
   class country computer;
   var rev90 rev91 rev92;
```

```
      table computer*country,rev90 rev91 rev92 /
           rts=32;
      format country cntryfmt. computer misscomp.;
      title 'Revenues for Computer Sales';
      title2 'for 1990 to 1992';
   run;
```

Figure 37.9   Computer Sales Data: Text Supplied for Missing COMP Value

In this table, the missing value appears as the text that the MISSCOMP. format specifies.

```
                     Revenues for Computer Sales                1
                            for 1990 to 1992

      ---------------------------------------------------------------
      |                         | Rev90  | Rev91  | Rev92  |
      |                         |--------+--------+--------|
      |                         | Sum    | Sum    | Sum    |
      |-------------+-----------+--------+--------+--------|
      |Computer     |Country    |        |        |        |
      |-------------+-----------|        |        |        |
      |No type given|Japan      | 5392.10| 5668.30| 4845.90|
      |-------------+-----------+--------+--------+--------|
      |Supercomputer|United States| 788.80| 877.60| 944.90|
      |             |-----------+--------+--------+--------|
      |             |Japan      | 469.90| 495.60| 448.40|
      |-------------+-----------+--------+--------+--------|
      |Mainframe    |United States|12538.10| 9855.60| 8527.90|
      |             |-----------+--------+--------+--------|
      |             |Japan      | 5697.60| 6242.40| 5382.30|
      |-------------+-----------+--------+--------+--------|
      |Midrange     |United States| 9815.80| 6340.30| 8680.30|
      |-------------+-----------+--------+--------+--------|
      |Workstation  |United States| 3147.20| 3474.10| 3722.40|
      |             |-----------+--------+--------+--------|
      |             |Japan      | 1511.60| 1875.50| 1924.50|
      |-------------+-----------+--------+--------+--------|
      |Personal     |United States|18660.90|18428.00|23531.10|
      |Computer     |-----------+--------+--------+--------|
      |             |Japan      | 4746.00| 4600.80| 4363.70|
      ---------------------------------------------------------------
```

Providing Headings for All Categories

By default, PROC TABULATE evaluates each page that it prints and omits columns and rows for categories that do not exist. For example, Figure 37.9 on page 1194 does not include a row for **No type given** and for **United States** or for **Midrange** and for **Japan** because there are no data in these categories. If you want the table to represent all possible categories, use the PRINTMISS option in the TABLE statement, as shown in the following program (see Figure 37.10 on page 1195):

```
proc tabulate data=compmiss missing;
   class country computer;
   var rev90 rev91 rev92;
   table computer*country,rev90 rev91 rev92 /
        rts=32 printmiss;
   format country cntryfmt. computer misscomp.;
   title 'Revenues for Computer Sales';
   title2 'for 1990 to 1992';
```

```
run;
```

Figure 37.10 Computer Sales Data: Missing Statistics Values

This table contains a row for the categories **No type given**, **United States** and **Midrange**, **Japan**. Because there are no data in these categories, the values for the statistics are all missing.

```
                        Revenues for Computer Sales              1
                             for 1990 to 1992

  -----------------------------------------------------------------
  |                       | Rev90   | Rev91   | Rev92   |
  |                       |---------+---------+---------|
  |                       | Sum     | Sum     | Sum     |
  |-----------------------+---------+---------+---------|
  |Computer    |Country   |         |         |         |
  |------------+-----------+---------+---------+---------|
  |No type given|United States|    .|      .|       .|
  |------------+-----------+---------+---------+---------|
  |            |Japan     | 5392.10| 5668.30| 4845.90|
  |------------+-----------+---------+---------+---------|
  |Supercomputer|United States| 788.80|  877.60|  944.90|
  |            |-----------+---------+---------+---------|
  |            |Japan     |  469.90|  495.60|  448.40|
  |------------+-----------+---------+---------+---------|
  |Mainframe   |United States|12538.10| 9855.60| 8527.90|
  |            |-----------+---------+---------+---------|
  |            |Japan     | 5697.60| 6242.40| 5382.30|
  |------------+-----------+---------+---------+---------|
  |Midrange    |United States| 9815.80| 6340.30| 8680.30|
  |            |-----------+---------+---------+---------|
  |            |Japan     |       .|       .|       .|
  |------------+-----------+---------+---------+---------|
  |Workstation |United States| 3147.20| 3474.10| 3722.40|
  |            |-----------+---------+---------+---------|
  |            |Japan     | 1511.60| 1875.50| 1924.50|
  |------------+-----------+---------+---------+---------|
  |Personal    |United States|18660.90|18428.00|23531.10|
  |Computer    |-----------+---------+---------+---------|
  |            |Japan     | 4746.00| 4600.80| 4363.70|
  -----------------------------------------------------------------
```

Providing Text for Cells That Contain Missing Values

If some observations in a category contain missing values for analysis variables, PROC TABULATE does not use those observations to calculate statistics (except N and NMISS). However, if each observation in a category contains a missing value, PROC TABULATE displays a missing value for the value of the statistic. To replace missing values for analysis variables with text, use the MISSTEXT= option in the TABLE statement to specify the text to use, as shown in the following program (see Figure 37.11 on page 1196).

```
proc tabulate data=compmiss missing;
    class country computer;
    var rev90 rev91 rev92;
    table computer*country,rev90 rev91 rev92 /
        rts=32 printmiss misstext='NO DATA!';
    format country cntryfmt. computer misscomp.;
    title 'Revenues for Computer Sales';
```

```
      title2 'for 1990 to 1992';
  run;
```

Figure 37.11 Computer Sales Data: Text Supplied for Missing Statistics Values

This table replaces the period normally used to display missing values with the text of the MISSTEXT= option.

```
                  Revenues for Computer Sales              1
                        for 1990 to 1992

    ---------------------------------------------------------
    |               |               | Rev90 | Rev91 | Rev92 |
    |               |               |-------+-------+-------|
    |               |               |  Sum  |  Sum  |  Sum  |
    |---------------+---------------+-------+-------+-------|
    |Computer       |Country        |       |       |       |
    |---------------+---------------+-------+-------+-------|
    |No type given  |United States  |NO DATA!|NO DATA!|NO DATA!|
    |               |---------------+-------+-------+-------|
    |               |Japan          | 5392.10| 5668.30| 4845.90|
    |---------------+---------------+-------+-------+-------|
    |Supercomputer  |United States  |  788.80|  877.60|  944.90|
    |               |---------------+-------+-------+-------|
    |               |Japan          |  469.90|  495.60|  448.40|
    |---------------+---------------+-------+-------+-------|
    |Mainframe      |United States  |12538.10| 9855.60| 8527.90|
    |               |---------------+-------+-------+-------|
    |               |Japan          | 5697.60| 6242.40| 5382.30|
    |---------------+---------------+-------+-------+-------|
    |Midrange       |United States  | 9815.80| 6340.30| 8680.30|
    |               |---------------+-------+-------+-------|
    |               |Japan          |NO DATA!|NO DATA!|NO DATA!|
    |---------------+---------------+-------+-------+-------|
    |Workstation    |United States  | 3147.20| 3474.10| 3722.40|
    |               |---------------+-------+-------+-------|
    |               |Japan          | 1511.60| 1875.50| 1924.50|
    |---------------+---------------+-------+-------+-------|
    |Personal       |United States  |18660.90|18428.00|23531.10|
    |Computer       |---------------+-------+-------+-------|
    |               |Japan          | 4746.00| 4600.80| 4363.70|
    ---------------------------------------------------------
```

Providing Headings for All Values of a Format

PROC TABULATE prints headings only for values that appear in the input data set. For example, the format COMPFMT. provides for six possible values of COMP. Only five of these values occur in the data set COMPREV. The data set contains no data for laptop computers.

If you want to include headings for all possible values of COMP (perhaps to make it easier to compare the output with tables that are created later when you do have data for laptops), you have three different ways to create such a table:

□ Use the PRELOADFMT option in the CLASS statement with the PRINTMISS option in the TABLE statement. See Example 3 on page 1203 for another example that uses PRELOADFMT.

□ Use the CLASSDATA= option in the PROC TABULATE statement. See Example 2 on page 1201 for an example that uses the CLASSDATA= option.

□ Add dummy values to the input data set so that each value that the format handles appears at least once in the data set.

The following program adds the PRELOADFMT option to a CLASS statement that contains the relevant variable.

The results are shown in Figure 37.12 on page 1197.

```
proc tabulate data=compmiss missing;
   class country;
   class computer / preloadfmt;
   var rev90 rev91 rev92;
   table computer*country,rev90 rev91 rev92 /
        rts=32 printmiss misstext='NO DATA!';
   format country cntryfmt. computer compfmt.;
   title 'Revenues for Computer Sales';
   title2 'for 1990 to 1992';
run;
```

Figure 37.12   Computer Sales Data: All Possible COMP Valued Included

This table contains a heading for each possible value of COMP.

```
                  Revenues for Computer Sales            1
                       for 1990 to 1992


---------------------------------------------------------
|                           | Rev90  | Rev91  |  Rev92  |
|                           |--------+--------+---------|
|                           | Sum    |  Sum   |   Sum   |
|---------------------------+--------+--------+---------|
|Computer     |Country      |        |        |         |
|-------------+-------------|        |        |         |
|.            |United States|NO DATA!|NO DATA!|NO DATA! |
|             |-------------+--------+--------+---------|
|             |Japan        | 5392.10| 5668.30| 4845.90 |
|-------------+-------------+--------+--------+---------|
|Supercomputer|United States| 788.80 | 877.60 | 944.90  |
|             |-------------+--------+--------+---------|
|             |Japan        | 469.90 | 495.60 | 448.40  |
|-------------+-------------+--------+--------+---------|
|Mainframe    |United States|12538.10| 9855.60| 8527.90 |
|             |-------------+--------+--------+---------|
|             |Japan        | 5697.60| 6242.40| 5382.30 |
|-------------+-------------+--------+--------+---------|
|Midrange     |United States| 9815.80| 6340.30| 8680.30 |
|             |-------------+--------+--------+------+----|
|             |Japan        |NO DATA!|NO DATA!|NO DATA! |
|-------------+-------------+--------+--------+------+----|
|Workstation  |United States| 3147.20| 3474.10| 3722.40 |
|             |-------------+--------+--------+------+----|
|             |Japan        | 1511.60| 1875.50| 1924.50 |
|-------------+-------------+--------+--------+---------|
|Personal     |United States|18660.90|18428.00|23531.10 |
|Computer     |-------------+--------+--------+---------|
|             |Japan        | 4746.00| 4600.80| 4363.70 |
|-------------+-------------+--------+--------+---------|
|Laptop       |United States|NO DATA!|NO DATA!|NO DATA! |
|             |-------------+--------+--------+---------|
|             |Japan        |NO DATA!|NO DATA!|NO DATA! |
---------------------------------------------------------
```

Understanding the Order of Headings with ORDER=DATA

The ORDER= option applies to all class variables. Occasionally, you want to order the headings for different variables differently. One method for doing this is to group the data as you want them to appear and to specify ORDER=DATA.

For this technique to work, the first value of the first class variable must occur in the data with all possible values of all the other class variables. If this criterion is not met, the order of the headings may surprise you.

The following program creates a simple data set in which the observations are ordered first by the values of Animal, then by the values of Food. The ORDER= option in the PROC TABULATE statement orders the heading for the class variables by the order of their appearance in the data set (see Figure 37.13 on page 1198). Although **bones** is the first value for Food in the group of observations where Animal= **dog**, all other values for Food appear before **bones** in the data set because **bones** never appears when Animal= **cat**. Therefore, the header for **bones** in the table in Figure 37.13 on page 1198 is not in alphabetic order.

In other words, PROC TABULATE maintains for subsequent categories the order that was established by earlier categories. If you want to reestablish the order of Food for each value of Animal, use BY-group processing. PROC TABULATE creates a separate table for each BY group, so that the ordering can differ from one BY group to the next.

```
data foodpref;
   input Animal $ Food $;
   datalines;
cat fish
cat meat
cat milk
dog bones
dog fish
dog meat
;

proc tabulate data=foodpref format=9.
              order=data;
   class animal food;
   table animal*food;
run;
```

Figure 37.13 Ordering the Headings of Class Variables

```
                                                             1

-------------------------------------------------------------
|                          Animal                            |
|------------------------------------------------------------|
|            cat             |             dog               |
|----------------------------+-------------------------------|
|            Food            |             Food              |
|----------------------------+-------------------------------|
|  fish   |  meat   |  milk  |  fish   |  meat   |  bones    |
|---------+---------+--------+---------+---------+-----------|
|    N    |    N    |    N   |    N    |    N    |    N      |
|---------+---------+--------+---------+---------+-----------|
|        1|        1|       1|        1|        1|          1|
-------------------------------------------------------------
```

Examples

Example 1: Creating a Basic Two-Dimensional Table

Procedure features:
  PROC TABULATE statement options:
    FORMAT=
  TABLE statement
    crossing (* operator)
  TABLE statement options:
    RTS=
Other features: FORMAT statement

This example

☐ creates a category for each type of user (residential or business) in each division of each region

☐ applies the same format to all cells in the table

☐ applies a format to each class variable

☐ extends the space for row headings.

Program

The data set ENERGY contains data on expenditures of energy for business and residential customers in individual states in the Northeast and West regions of the United States. A DATA step on page 1503 creates the data set.

```
data energy;
   length State $2;
   input Region Division state $ Type Expenditures;
   datalines;
1 1 ME 1 708
1 1 ME 2 379

. . . more lines of data . . .

4 4 HI 1 273
4 4 HI 2 298
;
```

PROC FORMAT creates formats for Region, Division, and Type.

```
proc format;
   value regfmt 1='Northeast'
                2='South'
                3='Midwest'
                4='West';
   value divfmt 1='New England'
                2='Middle Atlantic'
                3='Mountain'
                4='Pacific';
   value usetype 1='Residential Customers'
                 2='Business Customers';
run;
```

The FORMAT= option specifies DOLLAR12. as the default format for the value in each table cell.

```
options nodate pageno=1 linesize=80 pagesize=60;
proc tabulate data=energy format=dollar12.;
```

The CLASS statement identifies Region, Division, and Type as class variables. The VAR statement identifies Expenditures as an analysis variable.

```
   class region division type;
   var expenditures;
```

The TABLE statement creates a row for each formatted value of Region. Nested within each row are rows for each formatted value of Division. The TABLE statement also creates a column for each formatted value of Type. Each cell created by these rows and columns contains the sum of the analysis variable Expenditures for all observations that contribute to that cell.

```
   table region*division,
         type*expenditures
```

RTS= provides 25 characters per line for row headings.

```
         / rts=25;
```

The FORMAT statement assigns formats to Region, Division, and Type. The TITLE statements specify the titles.

```
   format region regfmt. division divfmt. type usetype.;
   title 'Energy Expenditures for Each Region';
   title2 '(millions of dollars)';
run;
```

Output

```
                    Energy Expenditures for Each Region                    1
                           (millions of dollars)

  ------------------------------------------------------------------
  |                            |                  Type                |
  |                            |--------------------------------------|
  |                            |Residential  |  Business             |
  |                            |Customers    |  Customers            |
  |                            |-------------+------------            |
  |                            |Expenditures |Expenditures           |
  |                            |-------------+------------            |
  |                            |    Sum      |    Sum                |
  |----------------------------+-------------+------------            |
  |Region     |Division        |             |                       |
  |-----------+----------      |             |                       |
  |Northeast  |New England|        $7,477|          $5,129|
  |           |-----------+------------+-----------|
  |           |Middle     |               |                          |
  |           |Atlantic   |       $19,379|         $15,078|
  |-----------+----------+------------+-----------|
  |West       |Mountain   |        $5,476|          $4,729|
  |           |-----------+------------+-----------|
  |           |Pacific    |       $13,959|         $12,619|
  ------------------------------------------------------------------
```

Example 2: Specifying Class Variable Combinations to Appear in a Table

Procedure features:

    PROC TABULATE Statement options:

        CLASSDATA=

        EXCLUSIVE

Data set: ENERGY on page 1199

Formats: REGFMT., DIVFMT., and USETYPE. on page 1200

This example

□ uses the CLASSDATA= option to specify combinations of class variables to appear in a table

□ uses the EXCLUSIVE option to restrict the output to only the combinations specified in the CLASSDATA= data set. Without the EXCLUSIVE option, the output would be the same as in Example 1 on page 1199.

Program

The data set CLASSES contains the combinations of class variable values that PROC TABULATE uses to create the table.

```
data classes;
   input region division type;
   datalines;
```

```
1 1 1
1 1 2
4 4 1
4 4 2
;
```

CLASSDATA= and EXCLUSIVE restrict the class level combinations to those specified in the CLASSES data set.

```
options nodate pageno=1 linesize=80 pagesize=60;
proc tabulate data=energy format=dollar12.
              classdata=classes exclusive;
```

The CLASS statement identifies Region, Division, and Type as class variables. The VAR statement identifies Expenditures as an analysis variable.

```
class region division type;
var expenditures;
```

The TABLE statement creates a row for each formatted value of Region. Nested within each row are rows for each formatted value of Division. The TABLE statement also creates a column for each formatted value of Type. Each cell created by these rows and columns contains the sum of the analysis variable Expenditures for all observations that contribute to that cell.

```
table region*division,
      type*expenditures
```

RTS= provides 25 characters per line for row headings.

```
      / rts=25;
```

The FORMAT statement assigns formats to Region, Division, and Type. The TITLE statements specify the titles.

```
format region regfmt. division divfmt. type usetype.;
title 'Energy Expenditures for Each Region';
title2 '(millions of dollars)';
run;
```

```
                    Energy Expenditures for Each Region              1
                            (millions of dollars)

        ------------------------------------------------------------
        |                         |            Type                |
        |                         |--------------------------------|
        |                         |Residential | Business          |
        |                         |Customers   | Customers         |
        |                         |------------+------------        |
        |                         |Expenditures|Expenditures        |
        |                         |------------+------------        |
        |                         |    Sum     |    Sum             |
        |-------------------------+------------+------------        |
        |Region    |Division      |            |                    |
        |----------+----------    |            |                    |
        |Northeast |New England   |    $7,477  |    $5,129          |
        |----------+----------+------------+------------            |
        |West      |Pacific       |   $13,959  |   $12,619          |
        ------------------------------------------------------------
```

Example 3: Using Preloaded Formats with Class Variables

Procedure features:
    PROC TABULATE statement option:

      OUT=

    CLASS statement options:

      EXCLUSIVE
      PRELOADFMT

    TABLE statement option:

      PRINTMISS

Other features: PRINT procedure

Data set: ENERGY on page 1199

Formats: REGFMT., DIVFMT., and USETYPE. on page 1200

This example

□ creates a table that includes all possible combinations of formatted class variable values (PRELOADFMT with PRINTMISS), even if those combinations have a zero frequency and even if they do not make sense

□ restricts the data in the table to combinations of formatted class variable values that appear in the input data set (PRELOADFMT with EXCLUSIVE).

□ writes the output to an output data set, and prints that data set.

Program

The FORMAT= option specifies DOLLAR12. as the default format for the value in each table cell.

```
options nodate pageno=1 linesize=80 pagesize=60;
proc tabulate data=energy format=dollar12.;
```

PRELOADFMT specifies that PROC TABULATE use the preloaded values of the user-defined formats for the class variables.

```
class region division type / preloadfmt;
var expenditures;
```

PRINTMISS specifies that all possible combinations of user-defined formats be used as the levels of the class variables.

```
table region*division,
      type*expenditures / rts=25 printmiss;
```

The FORMAT statement assigns formats to Region, Division, and Type. The TITLE statements specify the titles.

```
format region regfmt. division divfmt. type usetype.;
title 'Energy Expenditures for Each Region';
title2 '(millions of dollars)';
run;
```

The OUT= option specifies the name of the output data set to which PROC TABULATE writes the data.

```
proc tabulate data=energy format=dollar12. out=tabdata;
```

The EXCLUSIVE option (used with PRELOADFMT) restricts the output to only the combinations of formatted class variable values that appear in the input data set.

```
class region division type / preloadfmt exclusive;
var expenditures;
```

The PRINTMISS option is not specified in this case. If it were, it would override the EXCLUSIVE option in the CLASS statement.

```
table region*division,
      type*expenditures / rts=25;
```

The FORMAT statement assigns formats to Region, Division, and Type. The TITLE statements specify the titles.

```
    format region regfmt. division divfmt. type usetype.;
    title 'Energy Expenditures for Each Region';
    title2 '(millions of dollars)';
run;
```

The PRINT procedure lists the output data set from PROC TABULATE.

```
proc print data=tabdata;
run;
```

Output

This output, created with the PRELOADFMT and PRINTMISS options, contains all possible combinations of preloaded user-defined formats for the class variable values. It includes combinations with zero frequencies, and combinations that make no sense, such as **Northeast** and **Pacific**.

Energy Expenditures for Each Region   1
(millions of dollars)

Region	Division	Residential Customers Expenditures Sum	Business Customers Expenditures Sum
Northeast	New England	$7,477	$5,129
	Middle Atlantic	$19,379	$15,078
	Mountain	.	.
	Pacific	.	.
South	New England	.	.
	Middle Atlantic	.	.
	Mountain	.	.
	Pacific	.	.
Midwest	New England	.	.
	Middle Atlantic	.	.
	Mountain	.	.
	Pacific	.	.
West	New England	.	.
	Middle Atlantic	.	.
	Mountain	$5,476	$4,729
	Pacific	$13,959	$12,619

This output, created with the PRELOADFMT and EXCLUSIVE options, contains only those combinations of preloaded user-defined formats for the class variable values that appear in the input data set. This output is identical to the output from Example 1 on page 1199.

```
                    Energy Expenditures for Each Region                    1
                           (millions of dollars)

          ----------------------------------------------------------
          |                         |            Type               |
          |                         |-------------------------------|
          |                         |Residential  | Business        |
          |                         |Customers    | Customers       |
          |                         |-------------+-----------------|
          |                         |Expenditures |Expenditures     |
          |                         |-------------+-----------------|
          |                         |    Sum      |    Sum          |
          |-------------------------+-------------+-----------------|
          |Region     |Division     |             |                 |
          |-----------+-----------  |             |                 |
          |Northeast  |New England  |    $7,477   |      $5,129     |
          |           |-----------  +-------------+-----------------|
          |           |Middle       |             |                 |
          |           |Atlantic     |   $19,379   |     $15,078     |
          |-----------+-----------  +-------------+-----------------|
          |West       |Mountain     |    $5,476   |      $4,729     |
          |           |-----------  +-------------+-----------------|
          |           |Pacific      |   $13,959   |     $12,619     |
          ----------------------------------------------------------
```

This output is a listing of the output data set from PROC TABULATE. It contains the data created with the PRELOADFMT and EXCLUSIVE options specified.

```
                    Energy Expenditures for Each Region
                           (millions of dollars)
                                                                    E
                                                                    x
                                                                    p
                                                                    e
                                                                    n
                                                                    d
                                                                    i
                                                                    t
                          D                                         u
                          i                                         r
                          v                                         e
               R          i                                _   _  T s
               e          s                                T   P  A
               g          i                    T           Y   A  B __
       O       i          o                    y           P   G  L  S
       b       o          n                    p           E   E  E  u
       s       n          n                    e           _   _  _  m

       1   Northeast   New England      Residential Customers  111  1  1   7477
       2   Northeast   New England      Business Customers     111  1  1   5129
       3   Northeast   Middle Atlantic  Residential Customers  111  1  1  19379
       4   Northeast   Middle Atlantic  Business Customers     111  1  1  15078
       5   West        Mountain         Residential Customers  111  1  1   5476
       6   West        Mountain         Business Customers     111  1  1   4729
       7   West        Pacific          Residential Customers  111  1  1  13959
       8   West        Pacific          Business Customers     111  1  1  12619
```

Example 4: Using Multilabel Formats

Procedure features:

    CLASS statement options:

      MLF

    PROC TABULATE statement options:

      FORMAT=

    TABLE statement

      ALL class variable

      concatenation (blank operator)

      crossing (* operator)

      grouping elements (parentheses operator)

      label

      variable list

Other features:

    FORMAT procedure

    FORMAT statement

    VALUE statement options:

      MULTILABEL

This example

- shows how to specify a multilabel format in the VALUE statement of PROC FORMAT

- shows how to activate multilabel format processing using the MLF option with the CLASS statement

- demonstrates the behavior of the N statistic when multilabel format processing is activated.

Program

The CARSURVEY data set contains data from a survey distributed by a car manufacturer to a focus group of potential customers brought together to evaluate new car names. Each observation in the data set contains an id, the participant's age, and the participant's ratings of four car names. A DATA step creates the data set.

```
options nodate pageno=1 linesize=80 pagesize=64;

data carsurvey;
   input Rater Age Progressa Remark Jupiter Dynamo;
   datalines;
1    38   94   98   84   80
2    49   96   84   80   77
3    16   64   78   76   73
4    27   89   73   90   92

. . . more lines of data . . .

77   61   92   88   77   85
78   24   87   88   88   91
```

```
79   18  54  50  62  74
80   62  90  91  90  86
;
```

The FORMAT procedure creates a multilabel format for ages using the MULTILABEL option on page 451.

```
proc format;
   value agefmt (multilabel notsorted)
         15 - 29 = 'Below 30 years'
         30 - 50 = 'Between 30 and 50'
       51 - high = 'Over 50 years'
         15 - 19 = '15 to 19'
         20 - 25 = '20 to 25'
         25 - 39 = '25 to 39'
         40 - 55 = '40 to 55'
       56 - high = '56 and above';
   run;
```

The FORMAT= option specifies up to ten digits as the default format for the value in each table cell.

```
proc tabulate data=carsurvey format=10.;
```

The CLASS statement identifies Age as the class variable and uses the MLF option to activate multilabel format processing. The VAR statement identifies Progressa, Remark, Jupiter, and Dynamo as the analysis variables.

```
class age /mlf;
var progressa remark jupiter dynamo;
```

The row dimension of the TABLE statement creates a row for each formatted value of Age. Multilabel formatting allows an observation to be included in multiple rows or age categories. The row dimension uses the ALL class variable to sumarize information for all rows. The column dimension uses the N statistic to calculate the number of observations for each age group. Notice the result of the N statistic crossed with the ALL class variable in the row dimension is the total number of observations instead of the sum of the N statistics for the rows. The column dimension uses the ALL class variable at the beginning of a crossing to assign a label, **Potential Car Names** , instead of calculating statistics. The four nested columns calculate the mean ratings for the car names for each age group.

```
table age all, n all='Potential Car Names'*(progressa remark
jupiter dynamo)*mean;
```

The TITLE1 and TITLE2 statements specify the first and second titles.

```
title1 "Rating Four Potential Car Names";
title2 "Rating Scale 0-100 (100 is the highest rating)";
```

The FORMAT statement assigns the user-defined format. **agefmt.**, to Age for this analysis.

```
format age agefmt.;
run;
```

Output

Output 37.3

```
                        Rating Four Potential Car Names                        1
                    Rating Scale 0-100 (100 is the highest rating)

   --------------------------------------------------------------------------
   |               |          |           Potential Car Names              |
   |               |          ------------------------------------------------
   |               |          | Progressa | Remark  | Jupiter | Dynamo   |
   |               |          ------------+---------+---------+----------|
   |               |    N     |   Mean    |  Mean   |  Mean   |  Mean    |
   |---------------+----------+-----------+---------+---------+----------|
   | Age           |          |           |         |         |          |
   |---------------|          |           |         |         |          |
   | 15 to 19      |       14 |        75 |      78 |      81 |       73 |
   |---------------+----------+-----------+---------+---------+----------|
   | 20 to 25      |       11 |        89 |      88 |      84 |       89 |
   |---------------+----------+-----------+---------+---------+----------|
   | 25 to 39      |       26 |        84 |      90 |      82 |       72 |
   |---------------+----------+-----------+---------+---------+----------|
   | 40 to 55      |       14 |        85 |      87 |      80 |       68 |
   |---------------+----------+-----------+---------+---------+----------|
   | 56 and above  |       15 |        84 |      82 |      81 |       75 |
   |---------------+----------+-----------+---------+---------+----------|
   | Below 30 years|       36 |        82 |      84 |      82 |       75 |
   |---------------+----------+-----------+---------+---------+----------|
   | Between 30 and 50|    25 |        86 |      89 |      81 |       73 |
   |---------------+----------+-----------+---------+---------+----------|
   | Over 50 years |       19 |        82 |      84 |      80 |       76 |
   |---------------+----------+-----------+---------+---------+----------|
   | All           |       80 |        83 |      86 |      81 |       74 |
   --------------------------------------------------------------------------
```

Example 5: Customizing Row and Column Headings

Procedure features:
> TABLE statement
>> labels

Data set: ENERGY on page 1199

Formats: REGFMT., DIVFMT., and USETYPE on page 1200

This example shows how to customize row and column headings. A label specifies text for a heading. A blank label creates a blank heading. PROC TABULATE removes the space for blank column headings from the table.

Program

The FORMAT= option specifies DOLLAR12. as the default format for the value in each table cell.

```
options nodate pageno=1 linesize=80 pagesize=60;
proc tabulate data=energy format=dollar12.;
```

The CLASS statement identifies Region, Division, and Type as class variables. The VAR statement identifies Expenditures as an analysis variable.

```
class region division type;
var expenditures;
```

The TABLE statement creates a row for each formatted value of Region. Nested within each row are rows for each formatted value of Division. The TABLE statement also creates a column for each formatted value of Type. Each cell created by these rows and columns contains the sum of the analysis variable Expenditures for all observations that contribute to that cell. Text in quotation marks specifies headings for the corresponding variable or statistic. Although Sum is the default statistic, it is specified here so that you can remove the heading.

```
table region*division,
      type='Customer Base'*expenditures=' '*sum=' '
```

RTS= provides 25 characters per line for row headings.

```
      / rts=25;
```

The FORMAT statement assigns formats to Region, Division, and Type. The TITLE statements specify the titles.

```
format region regfmt. division divfmt. type usetype.;
title 'Energy Expenditures for Each Region';
title2 '(millions of dollars)';
run;
```

Output

The headings for Region, Division, and Type contain text specified in the TABLE statement. The TABLE statement eliminated the headings for Expenditures and Sum.

```
                  Energy Expenditures for Each Region                   1
                        (millions of dollars)

          --------------------------------------------------------
          |                          |       Customer Base       |
          |                          |---------------------------|
          |                          | Residential |  Business   |
          |                          |  Customers  |  Customers  |
          |--------------------------+-------------+-------------|
          |Region     |Division      |             |             |
          |-----------+--------------|             |             |
          |Northeast  |New England   |     $7,477  |     $5,129  |
          |           |--------------+-------------+-------------|
          |           |Middle        |             |             |
          |           |Atlantic      |    $19,379  |    $15,078  |
          |-----------+--------------+-------------+-------------|
          |West       |Mountain      |     $5,476  |     $4,729  |
          |           |--------------+-------------+-------------|
          |           |Pacific       |    $13,959  |    $12,619  |
          --------------------------------------------------------
```

Example 6: Summarizing Information with the Universal Class Variable ALL

Procedure features:

PROC TABULATE statement options:

FORMAT=

TABLE statement:

ALL class variable

concatenation (blank operator)

format modifiers

grouping elements (parentheses operator)

Data set: ENERGY on page 1199

Formats: REGFMT., DIVFMT., and USETYPE on page 1200

This example shows how to use the universal class variable ALL to summarize information from multiple categories.

Program

The FORMAT= option specifies COMMA12. as the default format for the value in each table cell.

```
options nodate pageno=1 linesize=64 pagesize=60;
proc tabulate data=energy format=comma12.;
```

The CLASS statement identifies Region, Division, and Type as class variables. The VAR statement identifies Expenditures as an analysis variable.

```
class region division type;
var expenditures;
```

The row dimension of the TABLE statement creates a row for each formatted value of Region. Nested within each row are rows for each formatted value of Division and a row (labeled **Subtotal**) that summarizes all divisions in the region. The last row of the report (labeled **Total for All Regions**) summarizes all regions. The format modifier f=DOLLAR12. assigns the DOLLAR12. format to the cells in this row.

```
table region*(division all='Subtotal')
          all='Total for All Regions'*f=dollar12.,
```

The column dimension of the TABLE statement creates a column for each formatted value of Type and a column labeled **All customers** that shows expenditures for all customers in a row of the table. Each cell created by these rows and columns contains the sum of the analysis variable Expenditures for all observations that contribute to that cell. Text in quotation marks specifies headings for the corresponding variable or statistic. Although Sum is the default statistic, it is specified here so that you can remove the heading.

```
type='Customer Base'*expenditures=' '*sum=' '
all='All Customers'*expenditures=' '*sum=' '
```

RTS= provides 25 characters per line for row headings.

```
/ rts=25;
```

The FORMAT statement assigns formats to Region, Division, and Type. The TITLE statements specify the titles.

```
format region regfmt. division divfmt. type usetype.;
title 'Energy Expenditures for Each Region';
title2 '(millions of dollars)';
run;
```

Output

The universal class variable ALL provides subtotals and totals in this table.

```
                Energy Expenditures for Each Region                    1
                         (millions of dollars)

     ---------------------------------------------------------------
     |                     |            Customer Base              |
     |                     |---------------------------------------|
     |                     |Residential | Business  |    All       |
     |                     | Customers  | Customers | Customers    |
     |---------------------+------------+-----------+--------------|
     |Region     |Division |            |           |              |
     |-----------+---------|            |           |              |
     |Northeast  |New England|  7,477   |    5,129  |    12,606    |
     |           |---------+------------+-----------+--------------|
     |           |Middle   |            |           |              |
     |           |Atlantic | 19,379     |   15,078  |    34,457    |
     |           |---------+------------+-----------+--------------|
     |           |Subtotal | 26,856     |   20,207  |    47,063    |
     |-----------+---------+------------+-----------+--------------|
     |West       |Division |            |           |              |
     |           |---------|            |           |              |
     |           |Mountain |  5,476     |    4,729  |    10,205    |
     |           |---------+------------+-----------+--------------|
     |           |Pacific  | 13,959     |   12,619  |    26,578    |
     |           |---------+------------+-----------+--------------|
     |           |Subtotal | 19,435     |   17,348  |    36,783    |
     |-----------+---------+------------+-----------+--------------|
     |Total for All Regions| $46,291    |  $37,555  |   $83,846    |
     ---------------------------------------------------------------
```

Example 7: Eliminating Row Headings

Procedure features:

    TABLE statement:

        labels

        ROW=FLOAT

Data set: ENERGY on page 1199

Formats: REGFMT., DIVFMT., and USETYPE on page 1200

This example shows how to eliminate blank row headings from a table. To do so, you must both provide blank labels for the row headings and specify ROW=FLOAT in the TABLE statement.

Program

The FORMAT= option specifies DOLLAR12. as the default format for the value in each table cell.

```
options nodate pageno=1 linesize=80 pagesize=60;
proc tabulate data=energy format=dollar12.;
```

The CLASS statement identifies Region, Division, and Type as class variables. The VAR statement identifies Expenditures as an analysis variable.

```
class region division type;
var expenditures;
```

The row dimension of the TABLE statement creates a row for each formatted value of Region. Nested within these rows is a row for each formatted value of Division. The analysis variable Expenditures and the Sum statistic are also included in the row dimension, so PROC TABULATE creates row headings for them as well. The text in quotation marks specifies the headings. In the case of Expenditures and Sum, the headings are blank.

```
table region*division*expenditures=' '*sum=' ',
```

The column dimension of the TABLE statement creates a column for each formatted value of Type.

```
type='Customer Base'
```

RTS= provides 25 characters per line for row headings. ROW=FLOAT eliminates blank row headings.

```
/ rts=25 row=float;
```

The FORMAT statement assigns formats to Region, Division, and Type. The TITLE statements specify the titles.

```
format region regfmt. division divfmt. type usetype.;
title 'Energy Expenditures for Each Region';
title2 '(millions of dollars)';
run;
```

Output

Compare this table with the table in Example 5 on page 1210. The two tables are identical, but the program that creates the table uses Expenditures and Sum in the column dimension. PROC TABULATE automatically eliminates blank headings from the column dimension, whereas you must specify ROW=FLOAT to eliminate blank headings from the row dimension.

```
                        Energy Expenditures for Each Region                   1
                               (millions of dollars)

                   -------------------------------------------------
                   |                     |     Customer Base        |
                   |                     |--------------------------|
                   |                     |Residential |  Business   |
                   |                     | Customers  |  Customers  |
                   |----------------------+------------+------------|
                   |Region    |Division  |            |             |
                   |----------+----------|            |             |
                   |Northeast |New England|   $7,477  |     $5,129  |
                   |          |----------+------------+------------|
                   |          |Middle    |            |             |
                   |          |Atlantic  |   $19,379  |    $15,078  |
                   |----------+----------+------------+------------|
                   |West      |Mountain  |   $5,476   |     $4,729  |
                   |          |----------+------------+------------|
                   |          |Pacific   |   $13,959  |    $12,619  |
                   -------------------------------------------------
```

Example 8: Indenting Row Headings and Eliminating Horizontal Separators

Procedure features:
    PROC TABULATE statement options:
        NOSEPS
    TABLE statement options:
        INDENT=
Data set: ENERGY on page 1199
Formats: REGFMT., DIVFMT., and USETYPE on page 1200

This example shows how to condense the structure of a table by
☐ removing row headings for class variables
☐ indenting nested rows underneath parent rows instead of placing them next to each other
☐ eliminating horizontal separator lines from the row titles and the body of the table.

Program

The FORMAT= option specifies DOLLAR12. as the default format for the value in each table cell. NOSEPS eliminates horizontal separator lines from row titles and from the body of the table.

```
options nodate pageno=1 linesize=80 pagesize=60;
proc tabulate data=energy format=dollar12. noseps;
```

The CLASS statement identifies Region, Division, and Type as class variables. The VAR statement identifies Expenditures as an analysis variable.

```
class region division type;
var expenditures;
```

The TABLE statement creates a row for each formatted value of Region. Nested within each row are rows for each formatted value of Division. The TABLE statement also creates a column for each formatted value of Type. Each cell created by these rows and columns contains the sum of the analysis variable Expenditures for all observations that contribute to that cell. Text in quotation marks in all dimensions specifies headings for the corresponding variable or statistic. Although Sum is the default statistic, it is specified here so that you can remove the heading.

```
table region*division,
      type='Customer Base'*expenditures=' '*sum=' '
```

RTS= provides 25 characters per line for row headings. INDENT= removes row headings for class variables, places values for Division beneath values for Region rather than beside them, and indents values for Division 4 spaces.

```
/ rts=25 indent=4;
```

The FORMAT statement assigns formats to Region, Division, and Type. The TITLE statements specify the titles.

```
format region regfmt. division divfmt. type usetype.;
title 'Energy Expenditures for Each Region';
title2 '(millions of dollars)';
run;
```

Output

NOSEPS removes the separator lines from the row titles and the body of the table. INDENT= eliminates the row headings for Region and Division, and indents values for Division underneath values for Region.

```
                   Energy Expenditures for Each Region                  1
                           (millions of dollars)

           ----------------------------------------------------
           |                   |     Customer Base            |
           |                   |------------------------------|
           |                   |Residential |  Business       |
           |                   | Customers  | Customers        |
           |-------------------+------------+-----------------|
           |Northeast          |            |                 |
           |    New England    |     $7,477 |     $5,129      |
           |    Middle Atlantic |   $19,379 |    $15,078      |
           |West               |            |                 |
           |    Mountain       |     $5,476 |     $4,729      |
           |    Pacific        |    $13,959 |    $12,619      |
           ----------------------------------------------------
```

Example 9: Creating Multipage Tables

Procedure features:
    TABLE statement
      ALL class variable
      BOX=
      CONDENSE
      INDENT=
      page expression
Data set: ENERGY on page 1199
Formats: REGFMT., DIVFMT., and USETYPE. on page 1200

This example creates a separate table for each region and one table for all regions. By default, PROC TABULATE creates each table on a separate page, but the CONDENSE option places them all on the same page.

Program

The FORMAT= option specifies DOLLAR12. as the default format for the value in each table cell.

```
options nodate pageno=1 linesize=80 pagesize=60;
proc tabulate data=energy format=dollar12.;
```

The CLASS statement identifies Region, Division, and Type as class variables. The VAR statement identifies Expenditures as an analysis variable.

```
class region division type;
var expenditures;
```

The page dimension of the TABLE statement creates one table for each formatted value of Region and one table for all regions. Text in quotation marks provides the heading for each page.

```
table region='Region: ' all='All Regions',
```

The row dimension creates a row for each formatted value of Division and a row for all divisions. Text in quotation marks provides the row headings.

```
division all='All Divisions',
```

The column dimension of the TABLE statement creates a column for each formatted value of Type. Each cell created by these pages, rows, and columns contains the sum of the analysis variable Expenditures for all observations that contribute to that cell. Text in quotation marks specifies headings for the corresponding variable or statistic. Although Sum is the default statistic, it is specified here so that you can remove the heading.

```
type='Customer Base'*expenditures=' '*sum=' '
```

RTS= provides 25 characters per line for row headings. BOX= places the page heading inside the box above the row headings. CONDENSE places as many tables as possible on one physical page. INDENT= eliminates the row heading for Division. (Because there is no nesting in the row dimension, there is nothing to indent.)

```
/ rts=25 box=_page_ condense indent=1;
```

The FORMAT statement assigns formats to Region, Division, and Type. The TITLE statements specify the titles.

```
format region regfmt. division divfmt. type usetype.;
title 'Energy Expenditures for Each Region and All Regions';
title2 '(millions of dollars)';
run;
```

Output

```
                 Energy Expenditures for Each Region and All Regions        1
                              (millions of dollars)

        ---------------------------------------------------------------
        |Region: Northeast        |          Customer Base            |
        |                         |-----------------------------------|
        |                         |  Residential  |   Business        |
        |                         |  Customers    |   Customers        |
        |-------------------------+---------------+-------------------|
        |New England              |      $7,477|        $5,129|
        |-------------------------+---------------+-------------------|
        |Middle Atlantic          |     $19,379|       $15,078|
        |-------------------------+---------------+-------------------|
        |All Divisions            |     $26,856|       $20,207|
        ---------------------------------------------------------------


        ---------------------------------------------------------------
        |Region: West             |          Customer Base            |
        |                         |-----------------------------------|
        |                         |  Residential  |   Business        |
        |                         |  Customers    |   Customers        |
        |-------------------------+---------------+-------------------|
        |Mountain                 |      $5,476|        $4,729|
        |-------------------------+---------------+-------------------|
        |Pacific                  |     $13,959|       $12,619|
        |-------------------------+---------------+-------------------|
        |All Divisions            |     $19,435|       $17,348|
        ---------------------------------------------------------------


        ---------------------------------------------------------------
        |All Regions              |          Customer Base            |
        |                         |-----------------------------------|
        |                         |  Residential  |   Business        |
        |                         |  Customers    |   Customers        |
        |-------------------------+---------------+-------------------|
        |New England              |      $7,477|        $5,129|
        |-------------------------+---------------+-------------------|
        |Middle Atlantic          |     $19,379|       $15,078|
        |-------------------------+---------------+-------------------|
        |Mountain                 |      $5,476|        $4,729|
        |-------------------------+---------------+-------------------|
        |Pacific                  |     $13,959|       $12,619|
        |-------------------------+---------------+-------------------|
        |All Divisions            |     $46,291|       $37,555|
        ---------------------------------------------------------------
```

Example 10: Reporting on Multiple-Response Survey Data

Procedure features:
   TABLE statement:

       denominator definition (angle bracket operators)
       N statistic
       PCTN statistic
       variable list

Other features:
   FORMAT procedure

SAS system options:
  FORMDLIM=
  NONUMBER
SYMPUT routine

The two tables in this example show

- □ which factors most influenced customers' decisions to buy products
- □ where customers heard of the company.

The reports appear on one physical page with only one page number. By default, they would appear on separate pages.

In addition to showing how to create these tables, this example shows how to

- □ use a DATA step to count the number of observations in a data set
- □ store that value in a macro variable
- □ access that value later in the SAS session.

Collecting the Data

Figure 37.14 on page 1221 shows the survey form used to collect data.

Figure 37.14 Completed Survey Form

Customer Questionnaire

ID#: ______

Please place a check beside all answers that apply.

Why do you buy our products?

___ Cost ___ Performance ___ Reliability ___ Sales staff

How did you find out about our company?

___ T.V. / Radio ___ Newspaper / Magazine ___ Word of mouth

What makes a sales person effective?

___ Product knowledge ___ Personality ___ Appearance

Program

The FORMDLIM= option replaces the character that delimits page breaks with a single blank. By default, a new physical page starts whenever a page break occurs.

```
options nodate pageno=1 linesize=80 pagesize=18
                        formdlim=' ';
```

The CUSTOMER_RESPONSE data set contains data from a customer survey. Each observation in the data set contains information about factors that influence one respondent's decisions to buy products. A DATA step on page 1496 creates the data set. Using missing values rather than 0's is crucial for calculating frequency counts in PROC TABULATE.

```
data customer_response;
   input Customer Factor1-Factor4 Source1-Source3
         Quality1-Quality3;
   datalines;
1 . . 1 1 1 1 . 1 . .
2 1 1 . 1 1 1 . 1 1 .
3 . . 1 1 1 1 . . . .

. . . more lines of data . . .

119 . . . 1 . . . 1 . .
120 1 1 . 1 . . . . 1 .
;
```

The SET statement reads the descriptor portion of CUSTOMER_RESPONSE at compile time and stores the number of observations (the number of respondents) in COUNT. The SYMPUT routine stores the value of COUNT in the macro variable NUM. This variable is available to the remainder of the SAS session. The IF 0 condition, which is always false, ensures that the SET statement, which reads the observations, never executes. (Reading observations is unnecessary.) The STOP statement ensures that the DATA step executes only once.

```
data _null_;
   if 0 then set customer_response nobs=count;
   call symput('num',left(put(count,4.)));
   stop;
run;
```

The FORMAT procedure creates a format for percentages. The PCTFMT. format writes all values with at least one digit to the left of the decimal point and with one digit to the right of the decimal point. A blank and a percent sign follow the digits.

```
proc format;
   picture pctfmt low-high='009.9 %';
run;
```

The VAR statement identifies Factor1, Factor2, Factor3, Factor4, and Customer as the analysis variables. Customer must be listed because it appears in the denominator definition.

```
proc tabulate data=customer_response;
   var factor1-factor4 customer;
```

The TABLE statement creates a row for each factor, a column for frequency counts, and a column for the percentages. Text in quotation marks supplies headers for the corresponding row or column. The format modifiers F=7. and F=PCTFMT9. provide formats for values in the associated cells and extend the column widths to accommodate the column headers.

```
table factor1='Cost'
      factor2='Performance'
      factor3='Reliability'
      factor4='Sales Staff',
      (n='Count'*f=7. pctn<customer>='Percent'*f=pctfmt9.) ;
```

The TITLE statements specify titles.

```
   title 'Customer Survey Results: Spring 1996';
   title3 'Factors Influencing the Decision to Buy';
run;
```

The SAS system option NONUMBER suppresses page numbers for subsequent pages.

```
options nonumber;
```

The VAR statement specifies the analysis variables. Customer must be in the variable list because it appears in the denominator definition.

```
proc tabulate data=customer_response;
   var source1-source3 customer;
```

The TABLE statement creates a row for each source of the company name, a column for frequency counts, and a column for the percentages. Text in quotation marks supplies a header for the corresponding row or column.

```
table source1='TV/Radio'
      source2='Newspaper'
      source3='Word of Mouth',
      (n='Count'*f=7. pctn<customer>='Percent'*f=pctfmt9.) ;
```

The TITLE and FOOTNOTE statements specify the title and footnote. The macro variable NUM resolves to the number of respondents. The FOOTNOTE statement uses double rather than single quotes so that the macro variable will resolve.

```
   title 'Source of Company Name';
   footnote "Number of Respondents: &num";
run;
```

The FORMDLIM= option resets the page delimiter to a page eject. The NUMBER option resumes the display of page numbers on subsequent pages.

```
options formdlim='' number;
```

Output

```
                      Customer Survey Results: Spring 1996              1

                     Factors Influencing the Decision to Buy

                 -----------------------------------------
                 |                 | Count | Percent |
                 |-----------------+-------+---------|
                 |Cost             |    87 |  72.5 % |
                 |-----------------+-------+---------|
                 |Performance      |    62 |  51.6 % |
                 |-----------------+-------+---------|
                 |Reliability      |    30 |  25.0 % |
                 |-----------------+-------+---------|
                 |Sales Staff      |   120 | 100.0 % |
                 -----------------------------------------
```

```
                          Source of Company Name

                 -----------------------------------------
                 |                 | Count | Percent |
                 |-----------------+-------+---------|
                 |TV/Radio         |    92 |  76.6 % |
                 |-----------------+-------+---------|
                 |Newspaper        |    69 |  57.5 % |
                 |-----------------+-------+---------|
                 |Word of Mouth    |    26 |  21.6 % |
                 -----------------------------------------




                      Number of Respondents: 120
```

Example 11: **Reporting on Multiple-Choice Survey Data**

Procedure features:
  TABLE statement:
    N statistic
Other features:
  FORMAT procedure
  TRANSPOSE procedure
  Data set options:
    RENAME=

This report of listener preferences shows how many listeners select each type of programming during each of seven time periods on a typical weekday. The data were collected by a survey, and the results were stored in a SAS data set. Although this data set contains all the information needed for this report, the information is not arranged in a way that PROC TABULATE can use.

To make this crosstabulation of time of day and choice of radio programming, you must have a data set that contains a variable for time of day and a variable for programming preference. PROC TRANSPOSE reshapes the data into a new data set that contains these variables. Once the data are in the appropriate form, PROC TABULATE creates the report.

Collecting the Data

Figure 37.15 on page 1225 shows the survey form used to collect data.

Figure 37.15   Completed Survey Form

```
                                                           phone_ _ _
                          LISTENER SURVEY

   1. _____   What is your age?

   2. _____   What is your gender?

   3. _____   On the average WEEKDAY, how many hours do you listen
                to the radio?

   4. _____   On the average WEEKEND-DAY, how many hours do you
                listen to the radio?

 Use codes 1-8 for question 5.  Use codes 0-8 for 6-19.
                 0    Do not listen at that time

                 1   Rock            5   Classical
                 2   Top 40          6   Easy Listening
                 3   Country         7   News/Information/Talk
                 4   Jazz            8   Other

   5. _____   What style of music or radio programming do you most
                often listen to?

 On a typical WEEKDAY,              On a typical WEEKEND-DAY,
 what kind of radio program-       what kind of radio programming
 ming do you listen to             do you listen to

   6. _____ from 6-9 a.m.?        13. _____ from 6-9 a.m.?

   7. _____ from 9 a.m. to noon?  14. _____ from 9 a.m. to noon?

   8. _____ from noon to 1 p.m.?  15. _____ from noon to 1 p.m.?

   9. _____ from 1-4 p.m.?        16. _____ from 1-4 p.m.?

  10. _____ from 4-6 p.m.?        17. _____ from 4-6 p.m.?

  11. _____ from 6-10 p.m.?       18. _____ from 6-10 p.m.?

  12. _____ from 10 p.m. to 2 a.m.?  19. _____ from 10 p.m. to 2 a.m.?
```

An external file on page 1522 contains the raw data for the survey. Several lines from that file appear here.

```
967 32 f 5 3 5
7 5 5 5 7 0 0 0 8 7 0 0 8 0
781 30 f 2 3 5
```

```
5 0 0 0 5 0 0 0 4 7 5 0 0 0
859 39 f 1 0 5
1 0 0 0 1 0 0 0 0 0 0 0 0 0
```

. . . more lines of data . . .

```
859 32 m .25 .25 1
1 0 0 0 0 0 0 0 1 0 0 0 0 0
```

Program

```
options nodate pageno=1 linesize=132 pagesize=40;
```

The data set RADIO contains data from a survey of 336 listeners. The data set contains information about listeners and their preferences in radio programming. The INFILE statement specifies the external file that contains the data. MISSOVER prevents the input pointer from going to the next record if it doesn't find values in the current line for all variables listed in the INPUT statement. Each raw-data record contains two lines of information about each listener. The INPUT statement reads only the information that this example needs. The / line control skips the first line of information in each record. The rest of the INPUT statement reads Time1-Time7 from the beginning of the second line. These variables represent the listener's radio programming preference for each of seven time periods on weekdays (see Figure 37.15 on page 1225). Listener=_N_ assigns a unique identifier to each listener.

```
data radio;
   infile 'input-file' missover;
   input /(Time1-Time7) ($1. +1);
   listener=_n_;
run;
```

PROC FORMAT creates formats for the time of day and the choice of programming.

```
proc format;
   value $timefmt  'Time1'='6-9 a.m.'
                   'Time2'='9 a.m. to noon'
                   'Time3'='noon to 1 p.m.'
                   'Time4'='1-4 p.m.'
                   'Time5'='4-6 p.m.'
                   'Time6'='6-10 p.m.'
                   'Time7'='10 p.m. to 2 a.m.'
                     other='*** Data Entry Error ***';
   value $pgmfmt       '0'="Don't Listen"
                   '1','2'='Rock and Top 40'
                       '3'='Country'
               '4','5','6'='Jazz, Classical, and Easy Listening'
                       '7'='News/ Information /Talk'
                       '8'='Other'
                     other='*** Data Entry Error ***';
run;
```

PROC TRANSPOSE creates RADIO_TRANSPOSED. This data set contains the variable Listener from the original data set. It also contains two transposed variables: Timespan and Choice. Timespan contains the names of the variables (Time1-Time7) from the input data set that are transposed to form observations in the output data set. Choice contains the values of these variables. (See "A Closer Look" on page 1228 for a complete explanation of the PROC TRANSPOSE step.)

```
proc transpose data=radio
               out=radio_transposed(rename=(col1=Choice))
               name=Timespan;
   by listener;
   var time1-time7;
```

The FORMAT statement permanently associates these formats with the variables in the output data set.

```
   format timespan $timefmt. choice $pgmfmt.;
run;
```

The FORMAT= option specifies the default format for the values in each table cell.

```
proc tabulate data=radio_transposed format=12.;
```

The CLASS statement identifies Timespan and Choice as class variables.

```
   class timespan choice;
```

The TABLE statement creates a row for each formatted value of Timespan and a column for each formatted value of Choice. In each column are values for the N statistic. Text in quotation marks supplies headers for the corresponding rows or columns.

```
   table timespan='Time of Day',
         choice='Choice of Radio Program'*n='Number of Listeners';
```

The TITLE statement specifies the title.

```
   title 'Listening Preferences on Weekdays';
run;
```

Output

```
                                    Listening Preferences on Weekdays                          1

-----------------------------------------------------------------------------------------------
|                             |                        Choice of Radio Program                 |
|                             |------------------------------------------------------------------|
|                             |             |             |             | Jazz,       |             |             |             |
|                             |             |             |             | Classical,  | News/       |             |
|                             |             |Rock and Top |             | and Easy    |Information  |             |
|                             |Don't Listen |     40      |  Country    | Listening   |   /Talk     |   Other     |
|                             |-------------+-------------+-------------+-------------+-------------+-------------|
|                             | Number of   | Number of   | Number of   | Number of   | Number of   | Number of   |
|                             | Listeners   | Listeners   | Listeners   | Listeners   | Listeners   | Listeners   |
|-----------------------------+-------------+-------------+-------------+-------------+-------------+-------------|
|Time of Day                  |             |             |             |             |             |             |
|-----------------------------|             |             |             |             |             |             |
|6-9 a.m.                     |          34 |         143 |           7 |          39 |          96 |          17 |
|-----------------------------+-------------+-------------+-------------+-------------+-------------+-------------|
|9 a.m. to noon               |         214 |          59 |           5 |          51 |           3 |           4 |
|-----------------------------+-------------+-------------+-------------+-------------+-------------+-------------|
|noon to 1 p.m.               |         238 |          55 |           3 |          27 |           9 |           4 |
|-----------------------------+-------------+-------------+-------------+-------------+-------------+-------------|
|1-4 p.m.                     |         216 |          60 |           5 |          50 |           2 |           3 |
|-----------------------------+-------------+-------------+-------------+-------------+-------------+-------------|
|4-6 p.m.                     |          56 |         130 |           6 |          57 |          69 |          18 |
|-----------------------------+-------------+-------------+-------------+-------------+-------------+-------------|
|6-10 p.m.                    |         202 |          54 |           9 |          44 |          20 |           7 |
|-----------------------------+-------------+-------------+-------------+-------------+-------------+-------------|
|10 p.m. to 2 a.m.            |         264 |          29 |           3 |          36 |           2 |           2 |
-----------------------------------------------------------------------------------------------
```

A Closer Look

Reshape the data

The original input data set has all the information that you need to make the crosstabular report, but PROC TABULATE cannot use the information in that form. PROC TRANSPOSE rearranges the data so that each observation in the new data set contains the variable Listener, a variable for time of day, and a variable for programming preference. PROC TABULATE uses this new data set to create the crosstabular report.

PROC TRANSPOSE restructures data so that values that were stored in one observation are written to one variable. You can specify which variables you want to transpose. This section illustrates how PROC TRANSPOSE reshapes the data. The following section explains the PROC TRANSPOSE step in this example.

When you transpose with BY processing, as this example does, you create from each BY group one observation for each variable that you transpose. In this example, Listener is the BY variable. Each observation in the input data set is a BY group because the value of Listener is unique for each observation.

This example transposes seven variables, Time1 through Time7. Therefore, the output data set has seven observations from each BY group (each observation) in the input data set.

Figure 37.16 on page 1229 uses the first two observations in the input data set to illustrate the transposition.

Figure 37.16 Transposing Two Observations

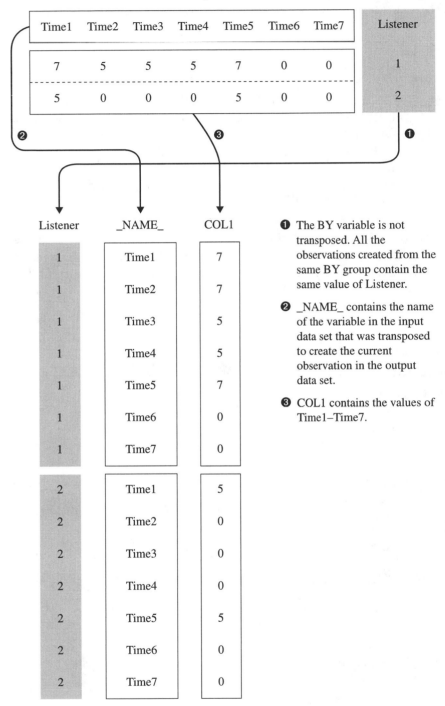

Input Data Set

① The BY variable is not transposed. All the observations created from the same BY group contain the same value of Listener.

② _NAME_ contains the name of the variable in the input data set that was transposed to create the current observation in the output data set.

③ COL1 contains the values of Time1–Time7.

Output Data Set

Understanding the PROC TRANSPOSE Step

This is the PROC TRANSPOSE step that reshapes the data:

```
proc transpose data=radio  ①
               out=radio_transposed(rename=(col1=Choice))  ②
```

```
                       name=Timespan;     ③
         by listener;     ④
         var time1-time7;     ⑤
         format timespan $timefmt. choice $pgmfmt.;     ⑥
     run;
```

1 The DATA= option in the PROC TRANSPOSE statement specifies the input data set.

2 The OUT= option in the PROC TRANSPOSE statement specifies the output data set. The RENAME= data set option renames the transposed variable from COL1 (the default name) to Choice.

3 The NAME= option in the PROC TRANSPOSE statement specifies the name for the variable in the output data set that contains the name of the variable that is being transposed to create the current observation. By default, the name of this variable is _NAME_.

4 The BY statement identifies Listener as the BY variable.

5 The VAR statement identifies Time1 through Time7 as the variables to transpose.

6 The FORMAT statement assigns formats to Timespan and Choice. The PROC TABULATE step that creates the report does not need to format Timespan and Choice because the formats are stored with these variables.

Example 12: Calculating Various Percentage Statistics

Procedure features:
PROC TABULATE statement options:
   FORMAT=
TABLE statement:
        ALL class variable
        COLPCTSUM statistic
        concatenation (blank operator)
        crossing (* operator)
        format modifiers
        grouping elements (parentheses operator)
        labels
        REPPCTSUM statistic
        ROWPCTSUM statistic
        variable list

TABLE statement options:
        ROW=FLOAT
        RTS=
Other features: FORMAT procedure

This example shows how to use three percentage sum statistics: COLPCTSUM, REPPCTSUM, and ROWPCTSUM.

The data set FUNDRAIS contains data on student sales during a school fundraiser. A DATA step creates the data set.

```
options nodate pageno=1 linesize=105 pagesize=60;
data fundrais;
   length name $ 8 classrm $ 1;
   input @1 team $ @8 classrm $ @10 name $
         @19 pencils @23 tablets;
   sales=pencils + tablets;
   cards;
BLUE    A ANN       4    8
RED     A MARY      5   10
GREEN   A JOHN      6    4
RED     A BOB       2    3
BLUE    B FRED      6    8
GREEN   B LOUISE   12    2
BLUE    B ANNETTE   .    9
RED     B HENRY     8   10
GREEN   A ANDREW    3    5
RED     A SAMUEL   12   10
BLUE    A LINDA     7   12
GREEN   A SARA      4    .
BLUE    B MARTIN    9   13
RED     B MATTHEW   7    6
GREEN   B BETH     15   10
RED     B LAURA     4    3
;
```

The FORMAT procedure creates a format for percentages. The PCTFMT. format writes all values with at least one digit, a blank, and a percent sign.

```
proc format;
   picture pctfmt low-high='009 %';
run;
```

The TITLE statement specifies the title.

```
title "Fundraiser Sales";
```

The FORMAT= option specifies up to seven digits as the default format for the value in each table cell.

```
proc tabulate format=7.;
```

The CLASS statement identifies Team and Classrm as class variables. The VAR statement identifies Sales as the analysis variable.

```
class team classrm;
var sales;
```

The row dimension of the TABLE statement creates a row for each formatted value of Team. Nested within each row is a row (labeled **sales**) that summarizes sales for the team. The last row of the report summarizes sales for all teams.

```
table (team all)*sales=' ',
```

The column dimension of the TABLE statement creates a column for each formatted value of Classrm. Nested within each column are columns that summarize sales for the class. The first nested column, labeled **sum**, is the sum of sales for the row for the classroom. The second nested column, labeled **ColPctSum**, is the percentage of the sum of sales for the row for the classroom in relation to the sum of sales for all teams in the classroom. The third nested column, labeled **RowPctSum**, is the percentage of the sum of sales for the row for the classroom in relation to the sum of sales for the row for all classrooms. The fourth nested column, labeled **RepPctSum**, is the percentage of the sum of sales for the row for the classroom in relation to the sum of sales for all teams for all classrooms. The last column of the report summarizes sales for the row for all classrooms.

```
classrm='Classroom'*(sum
colpctsum*f=pctfmt9.
rowpctsum*f=pctfmt9.
reppctsum*f=pctfmt9.)
all
```

RTS= provides 20 characters per line for row headings. ROW=FLOAT eliminates blank row headings.

```
/rts=20 row=float;
run;
```

Output

```
                                    Fundraiser Sales                                         1
----------------------------------------------------------------------------------------------
|                 |      |                          Classroom                       |     |
|                 |      |-------------------------------------------------------------|     |
|                 |      |            A            |            B            | All |
|                 |      |-------------------------+-------------------------+-------|
|                 | Sum  |ColPctSum|RowPctSum|RepPctSum| Sum  |ColPctSum|RowPctSum|RepPctSum| Sum  |
|-----------------+------+---------+---------+---------+------+---------+---------+---------+-------|
|team             |      |         |         |         |      |         |         |         |      |
|-----------------|      |         |         |         |      |         |         |         |      |
|BLUE             |   31 |   34 %  |   46 %  |   15 %  |   36 |   31 %  |   53 %  |   17 %  |   67 |
|-----------------+------+---------+---------+---------+------+---------+---------+---------+-------|
|GREEN            |   18 |   19 %  |   31 %  |    8 %  |   39 |   34 %  |   68 %  |   19 %  |   57 |
|-----------------+------+---------+---------+---------+------+---------+---------+---------+-------|
|RED              |   42 |   46 %  |   52 %  |   20 %  |   38 |   33 %  |   47 %  |   18 %  |   80 |
|-----------------+------+---------+---------+---------+------+---------+---------+---------+-------|
|All              |   91 |  100 %  |   44 %  |   44 %  |  113 |  100 %  |   55 %  |   55 %  |  204 |
----------------------------------------------------------------------------------------------
```

A Closer Look

Here are the percentage sum statistic calculations used to produce the output for the Blue Team in Classroom A:

COLPCTSUM=31/91*100=34%

ROWPCTSUM=31/67*100=46%

REPPCTSUM=31/204*100=15%

Similar calculations were used to produce the output for the remaining teams and classroom.

Example 13: Using Denominator Definitions to Display Basic Frequency Counts and Percentages

Procedure features:

TABLE statement:

ALL class variable
denominator definitions (angle bracket operators)
N statistic
PCTN statistic

Other features:

FORMAT procedure

Crosstabulation tables (also called *contingency tables* and *stub-and-banner reports*) show combined frequency distributions for two or more variables. This table shows frequency counts for females and males within each of four job classes. The table also shows the percentage that each frequency count represents of

□ the total women and men in that job class (row percentage)

□ the total for that gender in all job classes (column percentage)

□ the total for all employees.

Program

```
options nodate pageno=1 linesize=80 pagesize=60;
```

The JOBCLASS data set contains encoded information about the gender and job class of employees in a fictitious company.

```
data jobclass;
   input Gender Occupation @@;
   datalines;
1 1   1 1   1 1   1 1   1 1   1 1   1 1
1 2   1 2   1 2   1 2   1 2   1 2   1 2
1 3   1 3   1 3   1 3   1 3   1 3   1 3
1 1   1 1   1 1   1 2   1 2   1 2   1 2
1 2   1 2   1 3   1 3   1 4   1 4   1 4
1 4   1 4   1 4   1 1   1 1   1 1   1 1
1 1   1 2   1 2   1 2   1 2   1 2   1 2
1 2   1 3   1 3   1 3   1 3   1 4   1 4
1 4   1 4   1 4   1 1   1 3   2 1   2 1
2 1   2 1   2 1   2 1   2 1   2 2   2 2
2 2   2 2   2 2   2 3   2 3   2 3   2 4
2 4   2 4   2 4   2 4   2 4   2 1   2 3
2 3   2 3   2 3   2 3   2 4   2 4   2 4
2 4   2 4   2 1   2 1   2 1   2 1   2 1
2 2   2 2   2 2   2 2   2 2   2 2   2 2
2 3   2 3   2 4   2 4   2 4   2 1   2 1
```

```
2 1   2 1   2 1   2 2   2 2   2 2   2 3
2 3   2 3   2 3   2 4
;
```

PROC FORMAT creates formats for Gender and Occupation.

```
proc format;
   value gendfmt 1='Female'
                 2='Male'
              other='*** Data Entry Error ***';
   value occupfmt 1='Technical'
                  2='Manager/Supervisor'
                  3='Clerical'
                  4='Administrative'
               other='*** Data Entry Error ***';
run;
```

The FORMAT= option specifies the 8.2 format as the default format for the value in each table cell.

```
proc tabulate data=jobclass format=8.2;
```

The CLASS statement identifies Gender and Occupation as class variables.

```
   class gender occupation;
```

The TABLE statement creates a set of rows for each formatted value of Occupation and for all jobs together. Text in quotation marks supplies a header for the corresponding row.

```
   table (occupation='Job Class' all='All Jobs')
```

For detailed explanations of the structure of this table and of the use of denominator definitions, see "A Closer Look" on page 1236. The asterisk in the row dimension indicates that the statistics that follow in parentheses are nested within the values of Occupation and All to form sets of rows. Each set of rows includes four statistics:

1 N, the frequency count. The format modifier (F=9.) writes the values of N without the decimal places that the default format would use. It also extends the column width to nine characters so that the word **Employees** fits on one line.

2 the percentage of the row total (row percent).

3 the percentage of the column total (column percent).

4 the overall percent. Text in quotation marks supplies the header for the corresponding row. A comma separates the row definition from the column definition.

```
         *(n='Number of employees'*f=9.
           pctn<gender all>='Percent of row total'
           pctn<occupation all>='Percent of column total'
           pctn='Percent of total'),
```

The column dimension creates a column for each formatted value of Gender and for all employees. Text in quotation marks supplies the header for the corresponding column. The RTS= option provides 50 characters per line for row headings.

```
gender='Gender' all='All Employees'/ rts=50;
```

The FORMAT statement assigns formats to Gender and Occupation. The TITLE statements specify the titles.

```
format gender gendfmt. occupation occupfmt.;
title 'Gender Distribution';
title2 'within Job Classes';
run;
```

Output

```
                        Gender Distribution
                        within Job Classes

|-----------------------------------------------------------------------|
|                          |         Gender        |         |
|                          |-----------------------|  All    |
|                          | Female  |   Male  |Employees|
|--------------------------+---------+---------+---------|
|Job Class                 |         |         |         |
|--------------------------+---------|         |         |
|Technical  |Number of employees    |      16 |      18 |      34 |
|           |-----------------------+---------+---------+---------|
|           |Percent of row total   |   47.06 |   52.94 |  100.00 |
|           |-----------------------+---------+---------+---------|
|           |Percent of column total|   26.23 |   29.03 |   27.64 |
|           |-----------------------+---------+---------+---------|
|           |Percent of total       |   13.01 |   14.63 |   27.64 |
|-----------------------+-----------------------+---------+---------+---------|
|Manager/Supervisor     |Number of employees    |      20 |      15 |      35 |
|           |-----------------------+---------+---------+---------|
|           |Percent of row total   |   57.14 |   42.86 |  100.00 |
|           |-----------------------+---------+---------+---------|
|           |Percent of column total|   32.79 |   24.19 |   28.46 |
|           |-----------------------+---------+---------+---------|
|           |Percent of total       |   16.26 |   12.20 |   28.46 |
|-----------------------+-----------------------+---------+---------+---------|
|Clerical   |Number of employees    |      14 |      14 |      28 |
|           |-----------------------+---------+---------+---------|
|           |Percent of row total   |   50.00 |   50.00 |  100.00 |
|           |-----------------------+---------+---------+---------|
|           |Percent of column total|   22.95 |   22.58 |   22.76 |
|           |-----------------------+---------+---------+---------|
|           |Percent of total       |   11.38 |   11.38 |   22.76 |
|-----------------------+-----------------------+---------+---------+---------|
|Administrative         |Number of employees    |      11 |      15 |      26 |
|           |-----------------------+---------+---------+---------|
|           |Percent of row total   |   42.31 |   57.69 |  100.00 |
|           |-----------------------+---------+---------+---------|
|           |Percent of column total|   18.03 |   24.19 |   21.14 |
|           |-----------------------+---------+---------+---------|
|           |Percent of total       |    8.94 |   12.20 |   21.14 |
|-----------------------+-----------------------+---------+---------+---------|
|All Jobs   |Number of employees    |      61 |      62 |     123 |
|           |-----------------------+---------+---------+---------|
|           |Percent of row total   |   49.59 |   50.41 |  100.00 |
|           |-----------------------+---------+---------+---------|
|           |Percent of column total|  100.00 |  100.00 |  100.00 |
|           |-----------------------+---------+---------+---------|
|           |Percent of total       |   49.59 |   50.41 |  100.00 |
|-----------------------------------------------------------------------|
```

A Closer Look

The part of the TABLE statement that defines the rows of the table uses the PCTN statistic to calculate three different percentages.

In all calculations of PCTN, the numerator is N, the frequency count for one cell of the table. The denominator for each occurrence of PCTN is determined by the *denominator definition*. The denominator definition appears in angle brackets after the keyword PCTN. It is a list of one or more expressions. The list tells PROC TABULATE which frequency counts to sum for the denominator.

Analyzing the Structure of the Table

Taking a close look at the structure of the table helps you understand how PROC TABULATE uses the denominator definitions. The following simplified version of the TABLE statement clarifies the basic structure of the table:

```
table occupation='Job Class' all='All Jobs',
      gender='Gender' all='All Employees';
```

The table is a concatenation of four subtables. In this report, each subtable is a crossing of one class variable in the row dimension and one class variable in the column dimension. Each crossing establishes one or more categories. A *category* is a combination of unique values of class variables, such as **female, technical** or **all, clerical**. Table 37.8 on page 1237 describes each subtable.

Table 37.8 Contents of Subtables

Class variables contributing to the subtable	Description of frequency counts	Number of categories
Occupation and Gender	number of females in each job or number of males in each job	8
All and Gender	number of females or number of males	2
Occupation and All	number of people in each job	4
All and All	number of people in all jobs	1

Figure 37.17 on page 1238 highlights these subtables and the frequency counts for each category.

Figure 37.17   Illustration of the Four Subtables

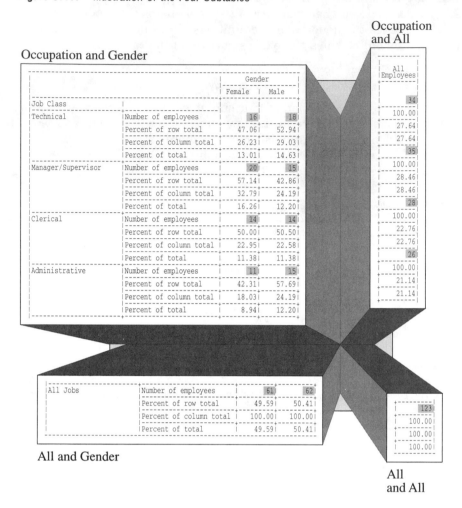

Occupation and Gender

Occupation and All

All and Gender

All and All

Interpreting Denominator Definitions

The following fragment of the TABLE statement defines the denominator definitions for this report. The PCTN keyword and the denominator definitions are underlined.

```
table (occupation='Job Class' all='All Jobs')
        *(n='Number of employees'*f=5.
          pctn<gender all>='Row percent'
          pctn<occupation all>='Column percent'
          pctn='Percent of total'),
```

Each use of PCTN nests a row of statistics within each value of Occupation and All. Each denominator definition tells PROC TABULATE which frequency counts to sum for the denominators in that row. This section explains how PROC TABULATE interprets these denominator definitions.

Row Percentages

The part of the TABLE statement that calculates the row percentages and that labels the row is

```
pctn<gender all>='Row percent'
```

Consider how PROC TABULATE interprets this denominator definition for each subtable.

Subtable 1: Occupation and Gender

PROC TABULATE looks at the first element in the denominator definition, Gender, and asks if Gender contributes to the subtable. Because Gender does contribute to the subtable, PROC TABULATE uses it as the denominator definition. This denominator definition tells PROC TABULATE to sum the frequency counts for all occurrences of Gender within the same value of Occupation.

For example, the denominator for the category **female, technical** is the sum of all frequency counts for all categories in this subtable for which the value of Occupation is **technical**. There are two such categories: **female, technical** and **male, technical**. The corresponding frequency counts are 16 and 18. Therefore, the denominator for this category is 16+18, or 34.

Subtable 2: All and Gender

PROC TABULATE looks at the first element in the denominator definition, Gender, and asks if Gender contributes to the subtable. Because Gender does contribute to the subtable, PROC TABULATE uses it as the denominator definition. This denominator definition tells PROC TABULATE to sum the frequency counts for all occurrences of Gender in the subtable.

For example, the denominator for the category **all, female** is the sum of the frequency counts for **all, female** and **all, male**. The corresponding frequency counts are 61 and 62. Therefore, the denominator for cells in this subtable is 61+62, or 123.

Subtable 3: Occupation and All

PROC TABULATE looks at the first element in the denominator definition, Gender, and asks if Gender contributes to the subtable. Because Gender does not contribute to the subtable, PROC TABULATE looks at the next element in the denominator definition, which is All. The variable All does contribute to this subtable, so PROC TABULATE uses it as the denominator definition. All is a reserved class variable with only one category. Therefore, this denominator definition tells PROC TABULATE to use the frequency count of All as the denominator.

For example, the denominator for the category `clerical, all` is the frequency count for that category, 28.

Note: In these table cells, because the numerator and the denominator are the same, the row percentages in this subtable are all 100. △

Subtable 4: All and All

PROC TABULATE looks at the first element in the denominator definition, Gender, and asks if Gender contributes to the subtable. Because Gender does not contribute to the subtable, PROC TABULATE looks at the next element in the denominator definition, which is All. The variable All does contribute to this subtable, so PROC TABULATE uses it as the denominator definition. All is a reserved class variable with only one category. Therefore, this denominator definition tells PROC TABULATE to use the frequency count of All as the denominator.

There is only one category in this subtable: `all, all`. The denominator for this category is 123.

Note: In this table cell, because the numerator and denominator are the same, the row percentage in this subtable is 100. △

Column Percentages

The part of the TABLE statement that calculates the column percentages and labels the row is

```
pctn<occupation all>='Column percent'
```

Consider how PROC TABULATE interprets this denominator definition for each subtable.

Subtable 1: Occupation and Gender

PROC TABULATE looks at the first element in the denominator definition, Occupation, and asks if Occupation contributes to the subtable. Because Occupation does contribute to the subtable, PROC TABULATE uses it as the denominator definition. This denominator definition tells PROC TABULATE to sum the frequency counts for all occurrences of Occupation within the same value of Gender.

For example, the denominator for the category **manager/supervisor, male** is the sum of all frequency counts for all categories in this subtable for which the value of Gender is **male**. There are four such categories: **technical, male**; **manager/supervisor, male**; **clerical, male**; and **administrative, male**. The corresponding frequency counts are 18, 15, 14, and 15. Therefore, the denominator for this category is 18+15+14+15, or 62.

Subtable 2: All and Gender

PROC TABULATE looks at the first element in the denominator definition, Occupation, and asks if Occupation contributes to the subtable. Because Occupation does not contribute to the subtable, PROC TABULATE looks at the next element in the denominator definition, which is All. Because the variable All does contribute to this subtable, PROC TABULATE uses it as the denominator definition. All is a reserved class variable with only one category. Therefore, this denominator definition tells PROC TABULATE to use the frequency count for All as the denominator.

For example, the denominator for the category **all, female** is the frequency count for that category, 61.

Note: In these table cells, because the numerator and denominator are the same, the column percentages in this subtable are all 100. △

Subtable 3: Occupation and All

PROC TABULATE looks at the first element in the denominator definition, Occupation, and asks if Occupation contributes to the subtable. Because Occupation does contribute to the subtable, PROC TABULATE uses it as the denominator definition. This denominator definition tells PROC TABULATE to sum the frequency counts for all occurrences of Occupation in the subtable.

For example, the denominator for the category `technical, all` is the sum of the frequency counts for `technical, all`; `manager/supervisor, all`; `clerical, all`; and `administrative, all`. The corresponding frequency counts are 34, 35, 28, and 26. Therefore, the denominator for this category is 34+35+28+26, or 123.

Subtable 4: All and All

PROC TABULATE looks at the first element in the denominator definition, Occupation, and asks if Occupation contributes to the subtable. Because Occupation does not contribute to the subtable, PROC TABULATE looks at the next element in the denominator definition, which is All. Because the variable All does contribute to this subtable, PROC TABULATE uses it as the denominator definition. All is a reserved class variable with only one category. Therefore, this denominator definition tells PROC TABULATE to use the frequency count of All as the denominator.

There is only one category in this subtable: `all, all`. The frequency count for this category is 123.

Note: In this calculation, because the numerator and denominator are the same, the column percentage in this subtable is 100. △

Total Percentages

The part of the TABLE statement that calculates the total percentages and labels the row is

```
pctn='Total percent'
```

If you do not specify a denominator definition, PROC TABULATE obtains the denominator for a cell by totaling all the frequency counts in the subtable. Table 37.9 on page 1243 summarizes the process for all subtables in this example.

Table 37.9 Denominators for Total Percentages

Class variables contributing to the subtable	Frequency counts	Total
Occupat and Gender	16, 18, 20, 15 14, 14, 11, 15	123
Occupat and All	34, 35, 28, 26	123
Gender and All	61, 62	123
All and All	123	123

Consequently, the denominator for total percentages is always 123.

Example 14: Specifying Style Elements for HTML Output

Procedure features:
    STYLE= option in
        PROC TABULATE statement
        CLASSLEV statement
        KEYWORD statement
        TABLE statement
        VAR statement

Other features: ODS HTML statement

Data set: ENERGY on page 1199

Formats: REGFMT, DIVFMT, and USETYPE on page 1200

This example creates HTML files and specifies style elements for various table regions.

Program

The ODS HTML statement produces output that is written in HTML. The output from PROC TABULATE goes to the body file.

```
ods html body='external-file';
```

The STYLE= option in the PROC TABULATE statement specifies the style element for the data cells of the table.

```
proc tabulate data=energy style=[font_weight=bold];
```

The STYLE= option in the CLASS statement specifies the style element for the class variable name headings.

```
   style=[just=center];
```

The STYLE= option in the CLASSLEV statement specifies the style element for the class variable level value headings.

```
classlev region division type / style=[just=left];
```

The STYLE= option in the VAR statement specifies a style element for the variable name headings.

```
var expenditures / style=[font_size=3];
```

The STYLE= option in the KEYWORD statement specifies a style element for keywords. The KEYLABEL statement assigns a label to the keyword.

```
keyword all sum / style=[font_width=wide];
keylabel all="Total";
```

The STYLE= option in the dimension expression overrides any other STYLE= specifications in PROC TABULATE, including the STYLE= specification after the slash in the TABLE statement.

```
table (region all)*(division all*[style=[background=yellow]]),
      (type all)*(expenditures*f=dollar10.) /
      style=[background=red]
```

The STYLE= option in the MISSTEXT option of the TABLE statement specifies a style element to use for the text in table cells that contain missing values.

```
misstext=[label="Missing" style=[font_weight=light]]
```

The STYLE= option in the BOX option of the TABLE statement specifies a style element to use for text in the empty box above the row titles.

```
box=[label="Region by Division by Type"
     style=[font_style=italic]];
```

The FORMAT statement assigns formats to Region, Division, and Type. The TITLE statements specify the titles.

```
format region regfmt. division divfmt. type usetype.;
title 'Energy Expenditures';
title2 '(millions of dollars)';
run;
```

The ODS HTML statement closes the HTML destination.

```
ods html close;
```

HTML Body File

This table uses customized style elements to control font sizes, font widths, justification, and other style attributes for the headings and data cells.

Region by Division by Type		Energy Expenditures (millions of dollars)		
		Type		Total
		Residential Customers	Business Customers	
		Expenditures	Expenditures	Expenditures
		Sum	Sum	Sum
Region	Division			
Northeast	New England	$7,477	$5,129	$12,606
	Middle Atlantic	$19,379	$15,078	$34,457
	Total	$26,856	$20,207	$47,063
West	Division			
	Mountain	$5,476	$4,729	$10,205
	Pacific	$13,959	$12,619	$26,578
	Total	$19,435	$17,348	$36,783
Total	Division			
	New England	$7,477	$5,129	$12,606
	Middle Atlantic	$19,379	$15,078	$34,457
	Mountain	$5,476	$4,729	$10,205
	Pacific	$13,959	$12,619	$26,578
	Total	$46,291	$37,555	$83,846

References

Jain, Raj and Chlamtac, Imrich (1985), "The P^2 Algorithm for Dynamic Calculation of Quantiles and Historgrams without Storing Observations," *Communications of the Association of Computing Machinery*, 28:10.

CHAPTER

38

The TIMEPLOT Procedure

Overview

The TIMEPLOT procedure plots one or more variables over time intervals. A listing of variable values accompanies the plot. Although the plot and the listing are similar to those produced by the PLOT and PRINT procedures, PROC TIMEPLOT output has these distinctive features:

☐ The vertical axis always represents the sequence of observations in the data set; thus, if the observations are in order of date or time, the vertical axis represents the passage of time.

☐ The horizontal axis represents the values of the variable that you are examining. Like PROC PLOT, PROC TIMEPLOT can overlay multiple plots on one set of axes so that each line of the plot can contain values for more than one variable.

☐ A plot produced by PROC TIMEPLOT may occupy more than one page.

☐ Each observation appears sequentially on a separate line of the plot; PROC TIMEPLOT does not hide observations as PROC PLOT sometimes does.

☐ The listing of the plotted values may include variables that do not appear in the plot.

Output 38.1 on page 1248 illustrates a simple report that you can produce with PROC TIMEPLOT. This report shows sales of refrigerators for two sales representatives during the first six weeks of the year. The statements that produce the output follow. A DATA step on page 1258 creates the data set SALES.

```
options linesize=64 pagesize=60 nodate
        pageno=1;



proc timeplot data=sales;
   plot icebox;
   id month week;
   title 'Weekly Sales of Refrigerators';
   title2 'for the';
   title3 'First Six Weeks of the Year';
run;
```

Output 38.1 Simple Report Created with PROC TIMEPLOT

```
                  Weekly Sales of Refrigerators              1
                              for the
                  First Six Weeks of the Year

 Month      Week      Icebox      min                        max
                                  2520.04                    3550.43
                                  *---------------------------------*
      1         1     3450.94     |                          I      |
      1         1     2520.04     |I                                |
      1         2     3240.67     |                     I           |
      1         2     2675.42     |       I                         |
      1         3     3160.45     |                  I              |
      1         3     2805.35     |          I                      |
      1         4     3400.24     |                       I         |
      1         4     2870.61     |            I                    |
      2         1     3550.43     |                               I |
      2         1     2730.09     |       I                         |
      2         2     3385.74     |                       I         |
      2         2     2670.93     |      I                          |
                                  *---------------------------------*
```

Output 38.2 on page 1248 is a more complicated report of the same data set that is used to create Output 38.1 on page 1248. The statements that create this report

□ create one plot for the sale of refrigerators and one for the sale of stoves

□ plot sales for both sales representatives on the same line

□ identify points on the plots by the first letter of the sales representative's last name

□ control the size of the horizontal axis

□ control formats and labels.

For an explanation of the program that produces this report, see Example 5 on page 1266.

Output 38.2 More Complex Report Created with PROC TIMEPLOT

```
                    Weekly Appliance Sales for the First Quarter              1

               Seller :Kreitz  Seller :LeGrange
   Month   Week        Stove          Stove          min                    max
                                                     $184.24             $2,910.37
                                                     *------------------------*
   January   1   $1,312.61         $728.13           |        L     K         |
   January   2     $222.35         $184.24           |!                       |
   January   3   $2,263.33         $267.35           |  L                 K   |
   January   4   $1,787.45         $274.51           |  L              K      |
   February  1   $2,910.37         $397.98           |   L                  K |
   February  2     $819.69       $2,242.24           |        K          L    |
                                                     *------------------------*
```

```
                    Weekly Appliance Sales for the First Quarter              2

                    Kreitz        LeGrange
   Month   Week     Icebox          Icebox         min                    max
                                                    $2,520.04            $3,550.43
                                                    *------------------------*
   January   1   $3,450.94       $2,520.04          |L                   K   |
   January   2   $3,240.67       $2,675.42          |    L            K      |
   January   3   $3,160.45       $2,805.35          |       L      K         |
   January   4   $3,400.24       $2,870.61          |         L       K      |
   February  1   $3,550.43       $2,730.09          |    L               K   |
   February  2   $3,385.74       $2,670.93          |    L            K       |
                                                    *------------------------*
```

Procedure Syntax

Requirements: At least one PLOT statement

Tip: Supports the Output Delivery System (see Chapter 2, "Fundamental Concepts for Using Base SAS Procedures")

Reminder: You can use the ATTRIB, FORMAT, LABEL, and WHERE statements. See Chapter 3, "Statements with the Same Function in Multiple Procedures," for details. You can also use any global statements as well. See Chapter 2, "Fundamental Concepts for Using Base SAS Procedures," for a list.

PROC TIMEPLOT <DATA=*SAS-data-set*>
  <MAXDEC=*number*> <UNIFORM>;

  BY <DESCENDING> *variable-1*
    <...<DESCENDING> *variable-n*>
    <NOTSORTED>;

  CLASS *variable(s)*;

  ID *variable(s)*;

  PLOT *plot-request(s)/option(s)*;

To do this	Use this statement
Produce a separate plot for each BY group	BY
Group data according to the values of the class variables	CLASS
Print in the listing the values of the variables that you identify	ID
Specify the plots to produce	PLOT

PROC TIMEPLOT Statement

PROC TIMEPLOT <DATA=*SAS-data-set*>
   <MAXDEC=*number*> <UNIFORM>;

Options

DATA=*SAS-data-set*
   identifies the input data set.

MAXDEC=*number*
   specifies the maximum number of decimal places to print in the listing.
   Interaction: A decimal specification in a format overrides a MAXDEC= specification.
   Default: 2
   Range: 0-12
   Featured in: Example 4 on page 1264

UNIFORM
   uniformly scales the horizontal axis across all BY groups. By default, PROC TIMEPLOT separately determines the scale of the axis for each BY group.
   Interaction: UNIFORM also affects the calculation of means for reference lines (see REF= on page 1256).

BY Statement

Produces a separate plot for each BY group.

Main discussion: "BY" on page 68

BY <DESCENDING> *variable-1*
   <...<DESCENDING> *variable-n*>
   <NOTSORTED>;

Required Arguments

variable

specifies the variable that the procedure uses to form BY groups. You can specify more than one variable. If you do not use the NOTSORTED option in the BY statement, the observations in the data set must either be sorted by all the variables that you specify, or they must be indexed appropriately. These variables are called *BY variables.*

Options

DESCENDING

specifies that the data set is sorted in descending order by the variable that immediately follows the word DESCENDING in the BY statement.

NOTSORTED

specifies that observations are not necessarily sorted in alphabetic or numeric order. The data are grouped in another way, for example, chronological order.

The requirement for ordering or indexing observations according to the values of BY variables is suspended for BY-group processing when you use the NOTSORTED option. In fact, the procedure does not use an index if you specify NOTSORTED. The procedure defines a BY group as a set of contiguous observations that have the same values for all BY variables. If observations with the same values for the BY variables are not contiguous, the procedure treats each contiguous set as a separate BY group.

CLASS Statement

Groups data according to the values of the class variables.

Tip: PROC TIMEPLOT uses the formatted values of the CLASS variables to form classes. Thus, if a format groups the values, the procedure uses those groups.

Featured in: Example 5 on page 1266

CLASS *variable(s)*;

Required Arguments

variable(s)

specifies one or more variables that the procedure uses to group the data. Variables in a CLASS statement are called *class variables*. Class variables can be numeric or character. Class variables can have continuous values, but they typically have a few discrete values that define the classifications of the variable. You do not have to sort the data by class variables.

The values of the class variables appear in the listing. PROC TIMEPLOT prints and plots one line each time the combination of values of the class variables changes. Therefore, the output typically is more meaningful if you sort or group the data according to values of the class variables.

Using Multiple CLASS Statements

You can use any number of CLASS statements. If you use more than one CLASS statement, PROC TIMEPLOT simply concatenates all variables from all of the CLASS statements. The following form of the CLASS statement includes three variables:

CLASS *variable-1 variable-2 variable-3*;

It has the same effect as this form:

CLASS *variable-1*;

CLASS *variable-2*;

CLASS *variable-3*;

Using a Symbol Variable

Normally, you use the CLASS statement with a symbol variable (see the discussion of plot requests on page 1254). In this case, the listing of the plot variable contains a column for each value of the symbol variable, and each row of the plot contains a point for each value of the symbol variable. The plotting symbol is the first character of the formatted value of the symbol variable. If more than one observation within a class has the same value of a symbol variable, PROC TIMEPLOT plots and prints only the first occurrence of that value and writes a warning message to the SAS log.

ID Statement

Prints in the listing the values of the variables that you identify.

Featured in: Example 1 on page 1258

ID *variable(s)*;

Required Arguments

variable(s)
  identifies one or more *ID variables* to print in the listing.

PLOT Statement

Specifies the plots to produce.

Tip: Each PLOT statement produces a separate plot.

PLOT *plot-request(s)/option(s)*;

Table 38.1 on page 1253 summarizes the options available in the PLOT statement.

Table 38.1 Summary of Options for the PLOT Statement

To do this	Use this option
Customize the axis	
Specify the range of values to plot on the horizontal axis, as well as the interval represented by each print position on the horizontal axis	AXIS=
Order the values on the horizontal axis with the largest value in the leftmost position	REVERSE
Control the appearance of the plot	
Connect the leftmost plotting symbol to the rightmost plotting symbol with a line of hyphens (-)	HILOC
Connect the leftmost and rightmost symbols on each line of the plot with a line of hyphens (-) regardless of whether the symbols are reference symbols or plotting symbols	JOINREF
Suppress the name of the symbol variable in column headings when you use a CLASS statement	NOSYMNAME
Suppress the listing of the values of the variables that appear in the PLOT statement	NPP
Specify the number of print positions to use for the horizontal axis	POS=
Create and customize a reference line	
Draw lines on the plot that are perpendicular to the specified values on the horizontal axis	REF=
Specify the character for drawing reference lines	REFCHAR=
Display multiple plots on the same set of axes	
Plot all requests in one PLOT statement on one set of axes	OVERLAY
Specify the character to print if multiple plotting symbols coincide	OVPCHAR=

Required Arguments

plot-request(s)
> specifies the variable or variables to plot and, optionally, the plotting symbol to use. By default, each plot request produces a separate plot.
>
> A plot request can have the following forms. You can mix different forms of requests in one PLOT statement (see Example 4 on page 1264).

variable(s)
> identifies one or more numeric variables to plot. PROC TIMEPLOT uses the first character of the variable name as the plotting symbol.
>
> Featured in: Example 1 on page 1258

(variable(s))='plotting-symbol'
> identifies one or more numeric variables to plot and specifies the plotting symbol to use for all variables in the list. You can omit the parentheses if you use only one variable.
>
> Featured in: Example 2 on page 1260

(variable(s))=symbol-variable
> identifies one or more numeric variables to plot and specifies a *symbol variable*. PROC TIMEPLOT uses the first nonblank character of the formatted value of the symbol variable as the plotting symbol for all variables in the list. The plotting symbol changes from one observation to the next if the value of the symbol variable changes. You can omit the parentheses if you use only one variable.
>
> Featured in: Example 3 on page 1262

Options

AXIS=*axis-specification*
> specifies the range of values to plot on the horizontal axis, as well as the interval represented by each print position on the axis. PROC TIMEPLOT labels the first and last ends of the axis, if space permits.
>
> ☐ For numeric values, *axis-specification* can be one of the following or a combination of both:
>
> > *n<. . .n>*
> >
> > *n* **TO** *n* **<BY** *increment>*
>
> The values must be in either ascending or descending order. Use a negative value for *increment* to specify descending order. The specified values are spaced evenly along the horizontal axis even if the values are not uniformly distributed. Numeric values can be specified in the following ways:

Specification	Comments
`axis=1 2 10`	Values are 1, 2, and 10.
`axis=10 to 100 by 5`	Values appear in increments of 5, starting at 10 and ending at 100.
`axis=12 10 to 100 by 5`	A combination of the two previous forms of specification.

> ☐ For axis variables that contain datetime values, *axis-specification* is either an explicit list of values or a starting and an ending value with an increment specified:
>
> > *'date-time-value'i <. . . 'date-time-value'i>*
> >
> > *'date-time-value'i* **TO** *'date-time-value'i*
> >   **<BY** *increment>*

'date-time-value'i
> any SAS date, time, or datetime value described for the SAS functions INTCK and INTNX. The suffix *i* is one of the following:

D	date
T	time
DT	datetime

increment
one of the valid arguments for the INTCK or INTNX functions. For dates, *increment* can be one of the following:

DAY

WEEK

MONTH

QTR

YEAR
For datetimes, *increment* can be one of the following:

DTDAY

DTWEEK

DTMONTH

DTQTR

DTYEAR
For times, *increment* can be one of the following:

HOUR

MINUTE

SECOND
For example,

```
axis='01JAN95'd to '01JAN96'd by month
axis='01JAN95'd to '01JAN96'd by qtr
```

For descriptions of individual intervals, see the chapter on dates, times, and intervals in *SAS Language Reference: Concepts*.

Note: You must use a FORMAT statement to print the tick-mark values in an understandable form. △

Interaction: The value of POS= (see POS= on page 1256) overrides an interval set with AXIS=.

Tip: If the range that you specify does not include all your data, PROC TIMEPLOT uses angle brackets (< or >) on the left or right border of the plot to indicate a value outside the range.

Featured in: Example 2 on page 1260

HILOC
connects the leftmost plotting symbol to the rightmost plotting symbol with a line of hyphens (-).

Interactions: If you specify JOINREF, PROC TIMEPLOT ignores HILOC.

JOINREF
connects the leftmost and rightmost symbols on each line of the plot with a line of hyphens (-), regardless of whether the symbols are reference symbols or plotting

symbols. However, if a line contains only reference symbols, PROC TIMEPLOT does not connect the symbols.

Featured in: Example 3 on page 1262

NOSYMNAME

suppresses the name of the symbol variable in column headings when you use a CLASS statement. If you use NOSYMNAME, only the value of the symbol variable appears in the column heading.

Featured in: Example 5 on page 1266

NPP

suppresses the listing of the values of the variables that appear in the PLOT statement.

Featured in: Example 3 on page 1262

OVERLAY

plots all requests in one PLOT statement on one set of axes. Otherwise, PROC TIMEPLOT produces a separate plot for each plot request.

Featured in: Example 4 on page 1264

OVPCHAR=*'character'*

specifies the character to print if multiple plotting symbols coincide. If a plotting symbol and a character in a reference line coincide, PROC TIMEPLOT prints the plotting symbol.

Default: at sign (@)

Featured in: Example 5 on page 1266

POS=*print-positions-for-plot*

specifies the number of print positions to use for the horizontal axis.

Default: If you omit both POS= and AXIS=, PROC TIMEPLOT initially assumes that POS=20. However, if space permits, this value increases so that the plot fills the available space.

Interaction: If you specify POS=0 and AXIS=, the plot fills the available space. POS= overrides an interval set with AXIS= (see the discussion of AXIS= on page 1254).

See also: "Page Layout" on page 1257

Featured in: Example 1 on page 1258

REF=*reference-value(s)*

draws lines on the plot that are perpendicular to the specified values on the horizontal axis. The values for *reference-value(s)* may be constants, or you may use the form

MEAN(*variable(s)*)

If you use this form of REF=, PROC TIMEPLOT evaluates the mean for each variable that you list and draws a reference line for each mean.

Interaction: If you use the UNIFORM option in the PROC TIMEPLOT statement, the procedure calculates the mean values for the variables over all observations for all BY groups. If you do not use UNIFORM, the procedure calculates the mean for each variable for each BY group.

Interaction: If a plotting symbol and a reference character coincide, PROC TIMEPLOT prints the plotting symbol.

Featured in: Example 3 on page 1262 and Example 4 on page 1264

REFCHAR=*'character'*

specifies the character for drawing reference lines.

Default: vertical bar (|)

Interaction: If you are using the JOINREF or HILOC option, do not specify a value for REFCHAR= that is the same as a plotting symbol because PROC TIMEPLOT will interpret the plotting symbols as reference characters and will not connect the symbols as you expect.

Featured in: Example 3 on page 1262

REVERSE

orders the values on the horizontal axis with the largest value in the leftmost position.

Featured in: Example 4 on page 1264

Results

Data Considerations

The input data set usually contains a date variable to use as either a class or an ID variable. Although PROC TIMEPLOT does not require an input data set sorted by date, the output is usually more meaningful if the observations are in chronological order. In addition, if you use a CLASS statement, the output is more meaningful if the input data set groups observations according to combinations of class variable values. (For more information see "CLASS Statement" on page 1251.)

Procedure Output

Page Layout

For each plot request, PROC TIMEPLOT prints a listing and a plot. PROC TIMEPLOT determines the arrangement of the page as follows:

□ If you use POS=, the procedure

  □ determines the size of the plot from the POS= value

  □ determines the space for the listing from the width of the columns of printed values, equally spaced and with a maximum of five positions between columns

  □ centers the output on the page.

□ If you omit POS=, the procedure

  □ determines the width of the plot from the value of the AXIS= option

  □ expands the listing to fill the rest of the page.

If there is not enough room to print the listing and the plot for a particular plot request, PROC TIMEPLOT produces no output and writes the following error message to the SAS log:

```
ERROR:  Too many variables/symbol values
        to print.
```

The error does not affect other plot requests.

Contents of the Listing

The listing in the output contains different information depending on whether or not you use a CLASS statement. If you do not use a CLASS statement (see Example 1 on page 1258), PROC TIMEPLOT prints (and plots) each observation on a separate line. If you do use a CLASS statement, the form of the output varies depending on whether or not you specify a symbol variable (see "Using a Symbol Variable" on page 1252).

Missing Values

Four types of variables can appear in the listing from PROC TIMEPLOT: plot variables, ID variables, class variables, and symbol variables (as part of some column headers). Plot variables and symbol variables can also appear in the plot.

Observations with missing values of a class variable form a class of observations.

In the listing, missing values appear as a period (.), a blank, or a special missing value (the letters A through Z and the underscore (_) character).

In the plot, PROC TIMEPLOT handles different variables in different ways:

□ An observation or class of observations with a missing value of the plot variable does not appear in the plot.

□ If you use a symbol variable (see the discussion of plot requests on page 1254), PROC TIMEPLOT uses a period (.) as the symbol variable on the plot for all observations with a missing value of the symbol variable.

Examples

Example 1: Plotting a Single Variable

Procedure features:
  ID statement
  PLOT statement arguments:
    simple plot request
    POS=

This example
□ uses a single PLOT statement to plot sales of refrigerators
□ specifies the number of print positions to use for the horizontal axis of the plot
□ provides context for the points in the plot by printing in the listing the values of two variables that are not in the plot.

Program

```
options nodate pageno=1 linesize=80 pagesize=60;
```

The data set SALES contains weekly information on the sales of refrigerators and stoves by two sales representatives.

```
data sales;
   input Month Week Seller $ Icebox Stove;
```

```
   datalines;
1 1 Kreitz    3450.94 1312.61
1 1 LeGrange 2520.04  728.13
1 2 Kreitz    3240.67  222.35
1 2 LeGrange 2675.42  184.24
1 3 Kreitz    3160.45 2263.33
1 3 LeGrange 2805.35  267.35
1 4 Kreitz    3400.24 1787.45
1 4 LeGrange 2870.61  274.51
2 1 Kreitz    3550.43 2910.37
2 1 LeGrange 2730.09  397.98
2 2 Kreitz    3385.74  819.69
2 2 LeGrange 2670.93 2242.24
;
```

The plot variable, Icebox, appears in both the listing and the output. POS= provides 50 print positions for the horizontal axis.

```
proc timeplot data=sales;
   plot icebox / pos=50;
```

The values of the ID variables, Month and Week, appear in the listing.

```
   id month week;
```

The TITLE statements specify titles for the report.

```
   title 'Weekly Sales of Iceboxes';
   title2 'for the';
   title3 'First Six Weeks of the Year';
run;
```

Output

The column headers in the listing are the variables' names. The plot uses the default plotting symbol, which is the first character of the plot variable's name.

```
                        Weekly Sales of Iceboxes                              1
                                for the
                        First Six Weeks of the Year

Month     Week      Icebox    min                                      max
                              2520.04                                  3550.43
                              *------------------------------------------------*
   1        1       3450.94   |                                      I         |
   1        1       2520.04   |I                                               |
   1        2       3240.67   |                                 I              |
   1        2       2675.42   |           I                                    |
   1        3       3160.45   |                            I                   |
   1        3       2805.35   |                 I                              |
   1        4       3400.24   |                                    I           |
   1        4       2870.61   |               I                                |
   2        1       3550.43   |                                            I   |
   2        1       2730.09   |            I                                   |
   2        2       3385.74   |                                  I             |
   2        2       2670.93   |        I                                       |
                              *------------------------------------------------*
```

Example 2: Customizing an Axis and a Plotting Symbol

Procedure features:
    ID statement
    PLOT statement arguments:
        using a plotting symbol
        AXIS=
Other features:
    LABEL statement
    PROC FORMAT
    SAS system options:
        FMTSEARCH=
Data set: SALES on page 1258

This example
□ specifies the character to use as the plotting symbol
□ specifies the minimum and maximum values for the horizontal axis as well as the interval represented by each print position
□ provides context for the points in the plot by printing in the listing the values of two variables that are not in the plot
□ uses a variable's label as a column header in the listing
□ creates and uses a permanent format.

Program

```
libname proclib 'SAS-data-library';
```

The SAS system option FMTSEARCH= adds the SAS data library PROCLIB to the search path that is used to locate formats.

```
options nodate pageno=1 linesize=80 pagesize=60
        fmtsearch=(proclib);
```

PROC FORMAT creates a permanent format for Month. The LIBRARY= option specifies a permanent storage location so that the formats are available in subsequent SAS sessions. This format is used for examples throughout this chapter.

```
proc format library=proclib;
   value monthfmt 1='January'
                  2='February';
run;
```

The plot variable, Icebox, appears in both the listing and the output. The plotting symbol is 'R'. AXIS= sets the minimum value of the axis to 2500 and the maximum value to 3600. BY 25 specifies that each print position on the axis represents 25 units (in this case, dollars).

```
proc timeplot data=sales;
   plot icebox='R' / axis=2500 to 3600 by 25;
```

The values of the ID variables, Month and Week, appear in the listing.

```
id month week;
```

The LABEL statement associates a label with the variable Icebox for the duration of the PROC TIMEPLOT step. PROC TIMEPLOT uses the label as the column header in the listing.

```
label icebox='Refrigerator';
```

The FORMAT statement assigns a format to use for Month in the report. The TITLE statements specify titles.

```
format month monthfmt.;
title 'Weekly Sales of Refrigerators';
title2 'for the';
title3 'First Six Weeks of the Year';
run;
```

Output

The column headers in the listing are the variables' names (for Month and Week, which have no labels) and the variable's label (for Icebox, which has a label). The plotting symbol is **R** (for Refrigerator).

```
                         Weekly Sales of Refrigerators                            1
                                    for the
                         First Six Weeks of the Year

        Month     Week    Refrigerator    min                                max
                                          2500                               3600
                                          *------------------------------------*
        January     1        3450.94      |                              R     |
        January     1        2520.04      |  R                                 |
        January     2        3240.67      |                         R          |
        January     2        2675.42      |        R                           |
        January     3        3160.45      |                    R               |
        January     3        2805.35      |             R                      |
        January     4        3400.24      |                          R         |
        January     4        2870.61      |                R                   |
        February    1        3550.43      |                                R   |
        February    1        2730.09      |          R                         |
        February    2        3385.74      |                           R        |
        February    2        2670.93      |         R                          |
                                          *------------------------------------*
```

Example 3: Using a Variable for a Plotting Symbol

Procedure features:

ID statement

PLOT statement arguments:

using a variable as the plotting symbol
JOINREF
NPP
REF=
REFCHAR=

Data set: SALES on page 1258

Formats: MONTHFMT. on page 1261

This example

□ specifies a variable to use as the plotting symbol to distinguish between points for each of two sales representatives

□ suppresses the printing of the values of the plot variable in the listing

□ draws a reference line to a specified value on the axis and specifies the character to use to draw the line

□ connects the leftmost and rightmost symbols on each line of the plot.

Program

```
libname proclib 'SAS-data-library';
```

The SAS system option FMTSEARCH= adds the SAS data library PROCLIB to the search path that is used to locate formats.

```
options nodate pageno=1 linesize=80 pagesize=60
       fmtsearch=(proclib);
```

The PLOT statement specifies both the plotting variable, Stove, and a symbol variable, Seller. The plotting symbol is the first letter of the formatted value of the Seller (in this case, **L** or **K**).

```
proc timeplot data=sales;
   plot stove=seller /
```

NPP suppresses the appearance of the plotting variable, Stove, in the listing.

```
              npp
```

REF= and REFCHAR= draw a line of colons at the sales target of $1500.

```
              ref=1500 refchar=':'
```

JOINREF connects the leftmost and rightmost symbols on each line of the plot.

```
              joinref
```

AXIS= sets the minimum value of the horizontal axis to 100 and the maximum value to 3000. BY 50 specifies that each print position on the axis represents 50 units (in this case, dollars).

```
              axis=100 to 3000 by 50;
```

The ID statement writes the values of the ID variables, Month and Week, in the listing.

```
   id month week;
```

The FORMAT statement assigns a format to use for Month in the report. The TITLE statements specify titles.

```
   format month monthfmt.;
   title 'Weekly Sales of Stoves';
   title2 'Compared to Target Sales of $1500';
   title3 'K for Kreitz; L for LaGrange';
run;
```

Output

The plot uses the first letter of the value of Seller as the plotting symbol.

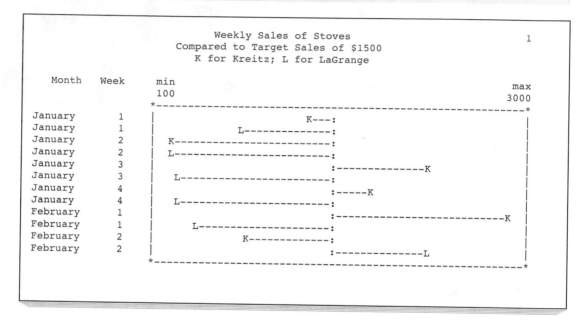

```
                          Weekly Sales of Stoves                            1
                       Compared to Target Sales of $1500
                          K for Kreitz; L for LaGrange

     Month    Week    min                                               max
                      100                                               3000
                      *-----------------------------------------------------*
     January    1     |                            K---:                    |
     January    1     |                  L--------------:                   |
     January    2     |   K---------------------:                           |
     January    2     |   L---------------------:                           |
     January    3     |                           :-------------K           |
     January    3     |       L-----------------:                           |
     January    4     |                           :-----K                   |
     January    4     |       L----------------:                            |
     February   1     |                           :------------------------K|
     February   1     |          L-----------------:                        |
     February   2     |              K-----------:                          |
     February   2     |                           :-------------L           |
                      *-----------------------------------------------------*
```

Example 4: Superimposing Two Plots

Procedure features:
　PROC TIMEPLOT statement options:
　　MAXDEC=
　PLOT statement arguments:
　　using two types of plot requests
　　OVERLAY
　　REF=MEAN(*variable(s)*)
　　REVERSE

Data set:　SALES on page 1258

This example

☐ superimposes two plots on one set of axes

☐ specifies a variable to use as the plotting symbol for one plot and a character to use as the plotting symbol for the other plot

☐ draws a reference line to the mean value of each of the two variables plotted

☐ reverses the labeling of the axis so that the largest value is at the far left of the plot.

Program

```
options nodate pageno=1 linesize=80 pagesize=60;
```

MAXDEC= specifies the number of decimal places to display in the listing.

```
proc timeplot data=sales maxdec=0;
```

The PLOT statement requests two plots. One plot uses the first letter of the formatted value of Seller to plot the values of Stove. The other uses the letter **R** (to match the label Refrigerators) to plot the value of Icebox.

```
plot stove=seller icebox='R' /
```

OVERLAY places the two plots on the same set of axes.

```
overlay
```

REF= draws two reference lines: one perpendicular to the mean of Stove, the other perpendicular to the mean of Icebox.

```
ref=mean(stove icebox)
```

REVERSE orders the values on the horizontal axis from largest to smallest.

```
reverse;
```

The LABEL statement associates a label with the variable Icebox for the duration of the PROC TIMEPLOT step. PROC TIMEPLOT uses the label as the column header in the listing. The TITLE statements specify titles.

```
label icebox='Refrigerators';
title 'Weekly Sales of Stoves and Refrigerators';
title2 'for the';
title3 'First Six Weeks of the Year';
run;
```

Output

The column header for the variable Icebox in the listing is the variable's label (Refrigerators). One plot uses the first letter of the value of Seller as the plotting symbol. The other plot uses the letter **R**.

```
                    Weekly Sales of Stoves and Refrigerators                    1
                                    for the
                          First Six Weeks of the Year

     Stove       Refrigerators      max                                      min
                                    3550.43                                184.24
                                *-----------------------------------------------*
      1313          3451         |R       |               K    |                 |
       728          2520         |        |      R             |    L            |
       222          3241         |     R  |           R        |             K   |
       184          2675         |        |       R            |              L  |
      2263          3160         |      R |        K           |                 |
       267          2805         |        |    R               |         L       |
      1787          3400         |   R    |             K      |                 |
       275          2871         |        |R                   |          L      |
      2910          3550         |R       |K                   |                 |
       398          2730         |        |    R               |      L          |
       820          3386         |  R     |                    |   K             |
      2242          2671         |        |      R     L       |                 |
                                *-----------------------------------------------*
```

Example 5: Showing Multiple Observations on One Line of a Plot

Procedure features:
>   CLASS statement
>   PLOT statement arguments:
>   creating multiple plots
>   NOSYMNAME
>   OVPCHAR=

Data set: SALES on page 1258
Formats: MONTHFMT. on page 1261

This example

□ groups observations for the same month and week so that sales for the two sales representatives for the same week appear on the same line of the plot

□ specifies a variable to use as the plotting symbol

□ suppresses the name of the plotting variable from one plot

□ specifies a size for the plots so that they both occupy the same amount of space.

Program

The SAS system option FMTSEARCH= adds the SAS data library PROCLIB to the search path that is used to locate formats.

```
libname proclib 'SAS-data-library';


options nodate pageno=1 linesize=80 pagesize=60
       fmtsearch=(proclib);
```

The CLASS statement groups all observations with the same values of Month and Week into one line in the output. Using the CLASS statement with a symbol variable produces in the listing one column of the plot variable for each value of the symbol variable.

```
proc timeplot data=sales;
   class month week;
```

Each PLOT statement produces a separate plot. The plotting symbol is the first character of the formatted value of the symbol variable: K for Kreitz; L for LaGrange. POS= specifies that each plot uses 25 print positions for the horizontal axis. OVPCHAR= designates the exclamation point as the plotting symbol when the plotting symbols coincide. NOSYMNAME suppresses the name of the symbol variable Seller from the second listing.

```
   plot stove=seller  / pos=25 ovpchar='!';
   plot icebox=seller / pos=25 ovpchar='!' nosymname;
```

The FORMAT statement assigns formats to use for Stove, Icebox, and Month in the report. The TITLE statement specifies a title.

```
   format stove icebox dollar10.2 month monthfmt.;
   title 'Weekly Appliance Sales for the First Quarter';
run;
```

Output

```
            Weekly Appliance Sales for the First Quarter          1

              Seller :Kreitz  Seller :LeGrange
 Month    Week         Stove             Stove    min              max
                                                  $184.24      $2,910.37
                                                  *---------------------*
January     1    $1,312.61        $728.13         |    L     K          |
January     2      $222.35        $184.24         |!              K     |
January     3    $2,263.33        $267.35         | L                   |
January     4    $1,787.45        $274.51         | L         K         |
February    1    $2,910.37        $397.98         |  L                 K|
February    2      $819.69      $2,242.24         |     K         L     |
                                                  *---------------------*
```

```
            Weekly Appliance Sales for the First Quarter                    2

                         Kreitz          LeGrange
      Month    Week      Icebox           Icebox       min                    max
                                                       $2,520.04      $3,550.43
                                                     *------------------------*
      January    1     $3,450.94        $2,520.04    |L                    K  |
      January    2     $3,240.67        $2,675.42    |      L          K       |
      January    3     $3,160.45        $2,805.35    |         L       K       |
      January    4     $3,400.24        $2,870.61    |            L        K   |
      February   1     $3,550.43        $2,730.09    |       L              K  |
      February   2     $3,385.74        $2,670.93    |       L         K       |
                                                     *------------------------*
```

CHAPTER

39

The TRANSPOSE Procedure

Overview

The TRANSPOSE procedure creates an output data set by restructuring the values in a SAS data set, transposing selected variables into observations. The TRANSPOSE procedure can often eliminate the need to write a lengthy DATA step to achieve the same result. Further, the output data set can be used in subsequent DATA or PROC steps for analysis, reporting, or further data manipulation.

PROC TRANSPOSE does not produce printed output. To print the output data set from the PROC TRANSPOSE step, use PROC PRINT, PROC REPORT, or another SAS reporting tool.

A *transposed variable* is a variable the procedure creates by transposing the values of an observation in the input data set into values of a variable in the output data set.

Output 39.1 on page 1270 illustrates a simple transposition. In the input data set, each *variable* represents the scores from one tester. In the output data set, each *observation* now represents the scores from one tester. Each value of _NAME_ is the name of a variable in the input data set that the procedure transposed. Thus, the value of _NAME_ identifies the source of each observation in the output data set. For example, the values in the first observation in the output data set come from the values of the variable Tester1 in the input data set. The statements that produce the output follow.

```
proc print data=proclib.product noobs;
   title 'The Input Data Set';
run;

proc transpose data=proclib.product
            out=proclib.product_transposed;
run;

proc print data=proclib.product_transposed noobs;
   title 'The Output Data Set';
run;
```

Output 39.1 A Simple Transposition

```
                        The Input Data Set                          1

            Tester1     Tester2     Tester3     Tester4

              22          25          21          21
              15          19          18          17
              17          19          19          19
              20          19          16          19
              14          15          13          13
              15          17          18          19
              10          11           9          10
              22          24          23          21
```

```
                        The Output Data Set                         2

     _NAME_    COL1   COL2   COL3   COL4   COL5   COL6   COL7   COL8

     Tester1    22     15     17     20     14     15     10     22
     Tester2    25     19     19     19     15     17     11     24
     Tester3    21     18     19     16     13     18      9     23
     Tester4    21     17     19     19     13     19     10     21
```

Output 39.2 on page 1270 is a more complex example that uses BY groups. The input data set represents measurements of fish weight and length at two lakes. The statements that create the output data set

- □ transpose only the variables that contain the length measurements
- □ create six BY groups, one for each lake and date
- □ use a data set option to name the transposed variable.

Output 39.2 A Transposition with BY Groups

```
                              Input Data Set                           1

   L
   o                    L      W      L      W      L      W      L      W
   c                    e      e      e      e      e      e      e      e
   a                    n      i      n      i      n      i      n      i
   t            D       g      g      g      g      g      g      g      g
   i            a       t      h      t      h      t      h      t      h
   o            t       h      t      h      t      h      t      h      t
   n            e       1      1      2      2      3      3      4      4

Cole Pond    02JUN95    31    0.25    32    0.30    32    0.25    33    0.30
Cole Pond    03JUL95    33    0.32    34    0.41    37    0.48    32    0.28
Cole Pond    04AUG95    29    0.23    30    0.25    34    0.47    32    0.30
Eagle Lake   02JUN95    32    0.35    32    0.25    33    0.30     .      .
Eagle Lake   03JUL95    30    0.20    36    0.45     .      .      .      .
Eagle Lake   04AUG95    33    0.30    33    0.28    34    0.42     .      .
```

```
              Fish Length Data for Each Location and Date               2

         Location        Date     _NAME_     Measurement

         Cole Pond     02JUN95    Length1          31
         Cole Pond     02JUN95    Length2          32
         Cole Pond     02JUN95    Length3          32
         Cole Pond     02JUN95    Length4          33
         Cole Pond     03JUL95    Length1          33
         Cole Pond     03JUL95    Length2          34
         Cole Pond     03JUL95    Length3          37
         Cole Pond     03JUL95    Length4          32
         Cole Pond     04AUG95    Length1          29
         Cole Pond     04AUG95    Length2          30
         Cole Pond     04AUG95    Length3          34
         Cole Pond     04AUG95    Length4          32
         Eagle Lake    02JUN95    Length1          32
         Eagle Lake    02JUN95    Length2          32
         Eagle Lake    02JUN95    Length3          33
         Eagle Lake    02JUN95    Length4           .
         Eagle Lake    03JUL95    Length1          30
         Eagle Lake    03JUL95    Length2          36
         Eagle Lake    03JUL95    Length3           .
         Eagle Lake    03JUL95    Length4           .
         Eagle Lake    04AUG95    Length1          33
         Eagle Lake    04AUG95    Length2          33
         Eagle Lake    04AUG95    Length3          34
         Eagle Lake    04AUG95    Length4           .
```

For a complete explanation of the SAS program that produces Output 39.2 on page 1270, see Example 4 on page 1282.

Procedure Syntax

Tip: Does not support the Output Delivery System

Reminder: You can use the ATTRIB, FORMAT, LABEL, and WHERE statements. See Chapter 3, "Statements with the Same Function in Multiple Procedures," for details. You can also use any global statements as well. See Chapter 2, "Fundamental Concepts for Using Base SAS Procedures," for a list.

> **PROC TRANSPOSE** <DATA=*input-data-set*> <LABEL=*label*> <LET>
>   <NAME=*name*> <OUT=*output-data-set*> <PREFIX=*prefix*>;
> **BY** <DESCENDING> *variable-1*
>   <...<DESCENDING> *variable-n*>
>   <NOTSORTED>;
> **COPY** *variable(s)*;
> **ID** *variable*;
>   **IDLABEL** *variable*;
> **VAR** *variable(s)*;

To do this	Use this statement
Transpose each BY group	BY
Copy variables directly without transposing them	COPY
Specify a variable whose values name the transposed variables	ID
Create labels for the transposed variables	IDLABEL
List the variables to transpose	VAR

PROC TRANSPOSE Statement

Reminder: You can use data set options with the DATA= and OUT= options. See Chapter 2, "Fundamental Concepts for Using Base SAS Procedures," for a list.

> **PROC TRANSPOSE** <DATA=*input-data-set*> <LABEL=*label*> <LET>
>   <NAME=*name*> <OUT=*output-data-set*> <PREFIX=*prefix*>;

Options

DATA= *input-data-set*
  names the SAS data set to transpose.
  Default: most recently created SAS data set

LABEL= *label*
  specifies a name for the variable in the output data set that contains the label of the variable that is being transposed to create the current observation.
  Default: _LABEL_

LET
  allows duplicate values of an ID variable. PROC TRANSPOSE transposes the observation containing the last occurrence of a particular ID value within the data set or BY group.
  Featured in: Example 5 on page 1284

NAME= *name*
  specifies the name for the variable in the output data set that contains the name of the variable being transposed to create the current observation.

Default: _NAME_

Featured in: Example 2 on page 1280

OUT= *output-data-set*

names the output data set. If *output-data-set* does not exist, PROC TRANSPOSE creates it using the DATA*n* naming convention.

Default: DATA*n*

Featured in: Example 1 on page 1278

PREFIX= *prefix*

specifies a prefix to use in constructing names for transposed variables in the output data set. For example, if PREFIX=VAR, the names of the variables are VAR1, VAR2, . . . ,VAR*n*.

Interaction: when you use PREFIX= with an ID statement, the value prefixes to the ID value.

Featured in: Example 2 on page 1280

BY Statement

Defines BY groups.

Main discussion: "BY" on page 68

Featured in: Example 4 on page 1282

Restriction: You cannot use PROC TRANSPOSE with a BY statement or an ID statement with an engine that supports concurrent access if another user is updating the data set at the same time.

Required Arguments

variable

specifies the variable that PROC TRANSPOSE uses to form BY groups. You can specify more than one variable. If you do not use the NOTSORTED option in the BY statement, the observations must be either sorted by all the variables that you specify, or they must be indexed appropriately. Variables in a BY statement are called *BY variables*.

Options

DESCENDING

specifies that the data set is sorted in descending order by the variable that immediately follows the word DESCENDING in the BY statement.

NOTSORTED

specifies that observations are not necessarily sorted in alphabetic or numeric order. The data are grouped in another way, for example, chronological order.

The requirement for ordering or indexing observations according to the values of BY variables is suspended for BY-group processing when you use the NOTSORTED option. In fact, the procedure does not use an index if you specify NOTSORTED. The procedure defines a BY group as a set of contiguous observations that have the same values for all BY variables. If observations with the same values for the BY variables are not contiguous, the procedure treats each contiguous set as a separate BY group.

Transpositions with BY Groups

PROC TRANSPOSE does not transpose BY groups. Instead, for each BY group, PROC TRANSPOSE creates one observation for each variable that it transposes.

Figure 39.1 on page 1274 shows what happens when you transpose a data set with BY groups. TYPE is the BY variable, and SOLD, NOTSOLD, REPAIRED, and JUNKED are the variables to transpose.

Figure 39.1   Transposition with BY Groups

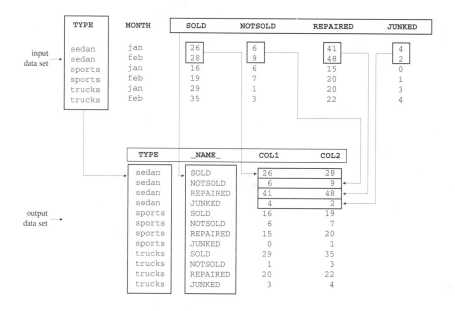

- ☐ The number of observations in the output data set (12) is the number of BY groups (3) multiplied by the number of variables that are transposed (4).

- ☐ The BY variable is not transposed.

- ☐ _NAME_ contains the name of the variable in the input data set that was transposed to create the current observation in the output data set. You can use the NAME= option to specify another name for the _NAME_ variable.

- ☐ The maximum number of observations in any BY group in the input data set is two; therefore, the output data set contains two variables, COL1 and COL2. COL1 and COL2 contain the values of SOLD, NOTSOLD, REPAIRED, and JUNKED.

Note: If a BY group in the input data set has more observations than other BY groups, PROC TRANSPOSE assigns missing values in the output data set to the variables that have no corresponding input observations. △

COPY Statement

Copies variables directly from the input data set to the output data set without transposing them.

Featured in: Example 6 on page 1286

COPY *variable(s)*;

Required Argument

variable(s)
> names one or more variables that the COPY statement copies directly from the input data set to the output data set without transposing them.

Details

Because the COPY statement copies variables directly to the output data set, the number of observations in the output data set is equal to the number of observations in the input data set.

The procedure pads the output data set with missing values if the number of observations in the input data set and the number of variables it transposes are not equal.

ID Statement

Specifies a variable in the input data set whose formatted values name the transposed variables in the output data set.

Featured in: Example 2 on page 1280

Restriction: You cannot use PROC TRANSPOSE with an ID statement or a BY statement with an engine that supports concurrent access if another user is updating the data set at the same time.

ID *variable*;

Required Argument

variable
> names the variable whose formatted values name the transposed variables.

Duplicate ID Values

Typically, each formatted ID value occurs only once in the input data set or, if you use a BY statement, only once within a BY group. Duplicate values cause PROC TRANSPOSE to issue a warning message and stop. However, if you use the LET option in the PROC TRANSPOSE statement, the procedure issues a warning message about duplicate ID values and transposes the observation containing the last occurrence of the duplicate ID value.

Making Variable Names Out of Numeric Values

When you use a numeric variable as an ID variable, PROC TRANSPOSE changes the formatted ID value into a valid SAS name.

However, SAS variable names cannot begin with a number. Thus, when the first character of the formatted value is numeric, the procedure prefixes an underscore to the value, truncating the last character of an 32-character value. Any remaining invalid characters are replaced by underscores. The procedure truncates to 32 characters any ID value that is longer than 32 characters when it uses that value to name a transposed variable.

If the formatted value looks like a numeric constant, PROC TRANSPOSE changes the characters '+', '−', and '.' to 'P','N', and 'D', respectively. If the formatted value has characters that are not numerics, PROC TRANSPOSE changes the characters '+', '−', and '.' to underscores.

Note: If the value of the VALIDVARNAME system option is V6, PROC TRANSPOSE truncates transposed variable names to eight characters. △

Missing Values

If you use an ID variable that contains a missing value, PROC TRANSPOSE writes an error message to the log. The procedure does not transpose observations that have a missing value for the ID variable.

IDLABEL Statement

Creates labels for the transposed variables.

Restriction: Must appear after an ID statement.

Featured in: Example 3 on page 1281

IDLABEL *variable*;

Required Argument

variable
   names the variable whose values the procedure uses to label the variables that the ID statement names. *variable* can be character or numeric.

Note: To see the effect of the IDLABEL statement, print the output data set with the PRINT procedure using the LABEL option, or print the contents of the output data set using the CONTENTS statement in the DATASETS procedure. △

VAR Statement

Lists the variables to transpose.

Featured in: Example 4 on page 1282 and Example 6 on page 1286

VAR *variable(s)*;

Required Argument

variable(s)
names one or more variables to transpose.

Details

☐ If you omit the VAR statement, the TRANSPOSE procedure transposes all numeric variables in the input data set that are not listed in another statement.

☐ You must list character variables in a VAR statement if you want to transpose them.

Results

Output Data Set

The TRANSPOSE procedure always produces an output data set, regardless of whether you specify the OUT= option in the PROC TRANSPOSE statement. PROC TRANSPOSE does not print the output data set. Use PROC PRINT, PROC REPORT or some other SAS reporting tool to print the output data set.

The output data set contains the following variables:

☐ variables that result from transposing the values of each variable into an observation.

☐ a variable that PROC TRANSPOSE creates to identify the source of the values in each observation in the output data set. This variable is a character variable whose values are the names of the variables transposed from the input data set. By default, PROC TRANSPOSE names this variable _NAME_. To override the default name, use the NAME= option. The label for the _NAME_ variable is NAME OF FORMER VARIABLE.

☐ variables that PROC TRANSPOSE copies from the input data set when you use either the BY or COPY statement. These variables have the same names and values as they do in the input data set.

☐ a character variable whose values are the variable labels of the variables being transposed (if any of the variables the procedure is transposing have labels). Specify the name of the variable with the LABEL= option. The default is **_LABEL_**.

Note: If the value of the LABEL= option or the NAME= option is the same as a variable that appears in a BY or COPY statement, the output data set does not contain a variable whose values are the names or labels of the transposed variables. △

Attributes of Transposed Variables

□ All transposed variables are the same type and length.
□ If all variables that the procedure is transposing are numeric, the transposed variables are numeric. Thus, if the numeric variable has a character string as a formatted value, its unformatted numeric value is transposed.
□ If any variable that the procedure is transposing is character, all transposed variables are character. Thus, if you are transposing a numeric variable that has a character string as a formatted value, the formatted value is transposed.
□ The length of the transposed variables is equal to the length of the longest variable being transposed.

Names of Transposed Variables

PROC TRANSPOSE names transposed variables using the following rules:

1 An ID statement specifies a variable in the input data set whose formatted values become names for the transposed variables.
2 The PREFIX= option specifies a prefix to use in constructing the names of transposed variables.
3 If you do not use an ID statement or the PREFIX= option, PROC TRANSPOSE looks for an input variable called _NAME_ from which to get the names of the transposed variables.
4 If you do not use an ID statement or the PREFIX= option, and the input data set does not contain a variable named _NAME_, PROC TRANSPOSE assigns the names COL1, COL2, . . . , COLn to the transposed variables.

Examples

Example 1: Performing a Simple Transposition

Procedure features:
PROC TRANSPOSE statement option:
   OUT=

This example performs a default transposition and uses no subordinate statements.

Program

```
options nodate pageno=1 linesize=80 pagesize=40;
```

The data set SCORE contains students' names, their identification numbers, and their grades on two tests and a final exam.

```
data score;
   input Student $9. +1 StudentID $ Section $ Test1 Test2 Final;
   datalines;
Capalleti 0545 1  94 91 87
Dubose    1252 2  51 65 91
Engles    1167 1  95 97 97
Grant     1230 2  63 75 80
Krupski   2527 2  80 76 71
Lundsford 4860 1  92 40 86
Mcbane    0674 1  75 78 72
;
```

PROC TRANSPOSE transposes only the numeric variables, Test1, Test2, and Final because no VAR statement appears and none of the numeric variables appear in another statement. OUT= puts the result of the transposition in the SCORE_TRANSPOSED data set.

```
proc transpose data=score out=score_transposed;
run;
```

PROC PRINT prints the output data set.

```
proc print data=score_transposed noobs;
   title 'Student Test Scores in Variables';
run;
```

Output

In the output data set SCORE_TRANSPOSED, variables COL1 through COL7 contain the individual scores for the students. Each observation contains all the scores for one test. The _NAME_ variable contains the names of the variables from the input data set that were transposed.

```
                     Student Test Scores in Variables                          1

       _NAME_    COL1    COL2    COL3    COL4    COL5    COL6    COL7

       Test1      94      51      95      63      80      92      75
       Test2      91      65      97      75      76      40      78
       Final      87      91      97      80      71      86      72
```

Example 2: Naming Transposed Variables

Procedure features:
    PROC TRANSPOSE statement options:
        NAME=
        PREFIX=
    ID statement
Data set: SCORE on page 1279

This example uses the values of a variable and a user-supplied value to name transposed variables.

Program

```
options nodate pageno=1 linesize=80 pagesize=40;
```

PROC TRANSPOSE transposes only the numeric variables, Test1, Test2, and Final because no VAR statement appears. OUT= puts the result of the transposition in the IDNUMBER data set. NAME= specifies Test as the name for the variable that contains the names of the variables in the input data set that the procedure transposes. The procedure names the transposed variables by using the value from PREFIX=, sn, and the value of the ID variable StudentID

```
proc transpose data=score out=idnumber name=Test
     prefix=sn;
   id studentid;
run;
```

PROC PRINT prints the data set.

```
proc print data=idnumber noobs;
   title 'Student Test Scores';
run;
```

Output

The output data set, IDNUMBER

```
                              Student Test Scores                              1

    Test     sn0545    sn1252    sn1167    sn1230    sn2527    sn4860    sn0674

    Test1      94        51        95        63        80        92        75
    Test2      91        65        97        75        76        40        78
    Final      87        91        97        80        71        86        72
```

Example 3: Labeling Transposed Variables

Procedure features:
PROC TRANSPOSE statement option:
PREFIX=
IDLABEL statement
Data set: SCORE on page 1279

This example uses the values of the variable in the IDLABEL statement to label transposed variables.

Program

```
options nodate pageno=1 linesize=80 pagesize=40;
```

PROC TRANSPOSE transposes only the numeric variables, Test1, Test2, and Final because no VAR statement appears. OUT= puts the result of the transposition in the IDLABEL data set. NAME= specifies Test as the name for the variable that contains the names of the variables in the input data set that the procedure transposes. The procedure names the transposed variables by using the value from PREFIX=, sn, and the value of the ID variable StudentID.

```
proc transpose data=score out=idlabel name=Test
    prefix=sn;
  id studentid;
```

PROC TRANSPOSE uses the values of the variable Student to label the transposed variables. The procedure provides

NAME OF FORMER VARIABLE

as the label for the _NAME_ variable.

```
    idlabel student;
run;
```

PROC PRINT prints the output data set and uses the variable labels as column headers. The LABEL option causes PROC PRINT to print variable labels for column headers.

```
proc print data=idlabel label noobs;
    title 'Student Test Scores';
run;
```

Output

The output data set, IDLABEL

```
                           Student Test Scores                              1

NAME OF
 FORMER
VARIABLE    Capalleti   Dubose   Engles   Grant   Krupski   Lundsford   Mcbane

  Test1        94         51       95      63       80         92         75
  Test2        91         65       97      75       76         40         78
  Final        87         91       97      80       71         86         72
```

Example 4: Transposing BY Groups

Procedure features:
>   BY statement
>   VAR statement
>
> **Other features:**   Data set option:
>   RENAME=

This example illustrates transposing BY groups and selecting variables to transpose.

Program

```
options nodate pageno=1 linesize=80 pagesize=40;
```

The input data represent length and weight measurements of fish caught at two ponds on three separate days. The data are sorted by Location and Date.

```
data fishdata;
   infile datalines missover;
   input Location & $10. Date date7.
         Length1 Weight1 Length2 Weight2 Length3 Weight3
         Length4 Weight4;
   format date date7.;
   datalines;
Cole Pond   2JUN95 31 .25 32 .3  32 .25 33 .3
Cole Pond   3JUL95 33 .32 34 .41 37 .48 32 .28
Cole Pond   4AUG95 29 .23 30 .25 34 .47 32 .3
Eagle Lake  2JUN95 32 .35 32 .25 33 .30
Eagle Lake  3JUL95 30 .20 36 .45
Eagle Lake  4AUG95 33 .30 33 .28 34 .42
;
```

OUT= puts the result of the transposition in the FISHLENGTH data set. RENAME= renames COL1 in the output data set to Measurement.

```
proc transpose data=fishdata
     out=fishlength(rename=(col1=Measurement));
```

PROC TRANSPOSE transposes only the Length1-Length4 variables because they appear in the VAR statement.

```
var length1-length4;
```

The BY statement creates BY groups for each unique combination of values of Location and Date. The procedure does not transpose the BY variables.

```
by location date;
run;
```

PROC PRINT prints the output data set.

```
proc print data=fishlength noobs;
   title 'Fish Length Data for Each Location and Date';
run;
```

Output

The output data set, FISHLENGTH. For each BY group in the original data set, PROC TRANSPOSE creates four observations, one for each variable it is transposing. Missing values appear for the variable Measurement (renamed from COL1) when the variables being transposed have no value in the input data set for that BY group. Several observations have a missing value for Measurement. For example, in the last observation, a missing value appears because there was no value for Length4 on 04AUG95 at Eagle Lake in the input data.

```
             Fish Length Data for Each Location and Date            1

             Location        Date     _NAME_      Measurement

             Cole Pond      02JUN95    Length1         31
             Cole Pond      02JUN95    Length2         32
             Cole Pond      02JUN95    Length3         32
             Cole Pond      02JUN95    Length4         33
             Cole Pond      03JUL95    Length1         33
             Cole Pond      03JUL95    Length2         34
             Cole Pond      03JUL95    Length3         37
             Cole Pond      03JUL95    Length4         32
             Cole Pond      04AUG95    Length1         29
             Cole Pond      04AUG95    Length2         30
             Cole Pond      04AUG95    Length3         34
             Cole Pond      04AUG95    Length4         32
             Eagle Lake     02JUN95    Length1         32
             Eagle Lake     02JUN95    Length2         32
             Eagle Lake     02JUN95    Length3         33
             Eagle Lake     02JUN95    Length4          .
             Eagle Lake     03JUL95    Length1         30
             Eagle Lake     03JUL95    Length2         36
             Eagle Lake     03JUL95    Length3          .
             Eagle Lake     03JUL95    Length4          .
             Eagle Lake     04AUG95    Length1         33
             Eagle Lake     04AUG95    Length2         33
             Eagle Lake     04AUG95    Length3         34
             Eagle Lake     04AUG95    Length4          .
```

Example 5: Naming Transposed Variables When the ID Variable Has Duplicate Values

Procedure features:

PROC TRANSPOSE statement option:

LET

This example shows how to use values of a variable (ID) to name transposed variables even when the ID variable has duplicate values.

Program

```
options nodate pageno=1 linesize=64 pagesize=40;
```

STOCKS contains stock prices for two competing kite manufacturers. The prices are recorded three times a day: at opening, at noon, and at closing, on two days. Notice that the input data set contains duplicate values for the Date variable.

```
data stocks;
    input Company $14. Date $ Time $ Price;
    datalines;
Horizon Kites jun11 opening 29
Horizon Kites jun11 noon    27
Horizon Kites jun11 closing 27
Horizon Kites jun12 opening 27
Horizon Kites jun12 noon    28
Horizon Kites jun12 closing 30
SkyHi Kites   jun11 opening 43
SkyHi Kites   jun11 noon    43
SkyHi Kites   jun11 closing 44
SkyHi Kites   jun12 opening 44
SkyHi Kites   jun12 noon    45
SkyHi Kites   jun12 closing 45
;
```

LET transposes only the last observation for each BY group. PROC TRANSPOSE transposes only the Price variable. OUT= puts the result of the transposition in the CLOSE data set.

```
proc transpose data=stocks out=close let;
```

The BY statement creates two BY groups, one for each company.

```
    by company;
```

The values of Date are used as names for the transposed variables.

```
    id date;
run;
```

PROC PRINT prints the output data set.

```
proc print data=close noobs;
    title 'Closing Prices for Horizon Kites and SkyHi Kites';
run;
```

Output

The output data set, CLOSE

```
             Closing Prices for Horizon Kites and SkyHi Kites          1

                Company      _NAME_     jun11    jun12

              Horizon Kites   Price      27       30
              SkyHi Kites     Price      44       45
```

Example 6: Transposing Data for Statistical Analysis

Procedure features:
 COPY statement
 VAR statement

This example arranges data to make them suitable for either a multivariate or univariate repeated-measures analysis.

The data are from Chapter 8, "Repeated-Measures Analysis of Variance" in *SAS System for Linear Models, Third Edition*.

Program 1

```
options nodate pageno=1 linesize=80 pagesize=40;
```

The data represent the results of an exercise therapy study of three weight-lifting programs: CONT is control, RI is a program in which the number of repetitions are increased, and WI is a program in which the weight is increased.

```
data weights;
   input Program $ s1-s7;
   datalines;
CONT  85 85 86 85 87 86 87
CONT  80 79 79 78 78 79 78
CONT  78 77 77 77 76 76 77
CONT  84 84 85 84 83 84 85
CONT  80 81 80 80 79 79 80
RI    79 79 79 80 80 78 80
RI    83 83 85 85 86 87 87
RI    81 83 82 82 83 83 82
RI    81 81 81 82 82 83 81
RI    80 81 82 82 82 84 86
WI    84 85 84 83 83 83 84
WI    74 75 75 76 75 76 76
WI    83 84 82 81 83 83 82
```

```
WI     86 87 87 87 87 87 86
WI     82 83 84 85 84 85 86
;
```

The DATA step rearranges WEIGHTS to create the data set SPLIT. The DATA step transposes the strength values and creates two new variables: Time and Subject. SPLIT contains one observation for each repeated measure. SPLIT can be used in a PROC GLM step for a univariate repeated-measures analysis.

```
data split;
   set weights;
   array s{7} s1-s7;
   Subject + 1;
   do Time=1 to 7;
      Strength=s{time};
      output;
   end;
   drop s1-s7;
run;
```

PROC PRINT prints the data set. The OBS= data set option limits the printing to the first 15 observations. SPLIT has 105 observations.

```
proc print data=split(obs=15) noobs;
   title 'SPLIT Data Set';
   title2 'First 15 Observations Only';
run;
```

Output 1

```
                           SPLIT Data Set                          1
                       First 15 Observations Only

             Program    Subject    Time    Strength

               CONT        1         1        85
               CONT        1         2        85
               CONT        1         3        86
               CONT        1         4        85
               CONT        1         5        87
               CONT        1         6        86
               CONT        1         7        87
               CONT        2         1        80
               CONT        2         2        79
               CONT        2         3        79
               CONT        2         4        78
               CONT        2         5        78
               CONT        2         6        79
               CONT        2         7        78
               CONT        3         1        78
```

Program 2

```
options nodate pageno=1 linesize=80 pagesize=40;
```

PROC TRANSPOSE transposes SPLIT to create TOTSPLIT. The TOTSPLIT data set contains the same variables as SPLIT and a variable for each strength measurement (Str1-Str7). TOTSPLIT can be used for either a multivariate repeated-measures analysis or for a univariate repeated-measures analysis.

```
proc transpose data=split out=totsplit prefix=Str;
```

The variables in the BY and COPY statements are not transposed. TOTSPLIT contains the variables Program, Subject, Time, and Strength with the same values that are in SPLIT. The BY statement creates the first observation in each BY group, which contains the transposed values of Strength. The COPY statement creates the other observations in each BY group by copying the values of Time and Strength without transposing them.

```
   by program subject;
   copy time strength;
```

The VAR statement specifies the Strength variable as the only variable to be transposed.

```
   var strength;
run;
```

PROC PRINT prints the output data set.

```
proc print data=totsplit(obs=15) noobs;
   title  'TOTSPLIT Data Set';
   title2 'First 15 Observations Only';
run;
```

Output 2

The variables in TOTSPLIT with missing values are used only in a multivariate repeated–measures analysis. The missing values do not preclude this data set from being used in a repeated-measures analysis because the MODEL statement in PROC GLM ignores observations with missing values.

```
                          TOTSPLIT Data Set                              1
                       First 15 Observations Only

Program Subject Time Strength  _NAME_  Str1 Str2 Str3 Str4 Str5 Str6 Str7

   CONT      1    1     85    Strength  85   85   86   85   87   86   87
   CONT      1    2     85               .    .    .    .    .    .    .
   CONT      1    3     86               .    .    .    .    .    .    .
   CONT      1    4     85               .    .    .    .    .    .    .
   CONT      1    5     87               .    .    .    .    .    .    .
   CONT      1    6     86               .    .    .    .    .    .    .
   CONT      1    7     87               .    .    .    .    .    .    .
   CONT      2    1     80    Strength  80   79   79   78   78   79   78
   CONT      2    2     79               .    .    .    .    .    .    .
   CONT      2    3     79               .    .    .    .    .    .    .
   CONT      2    4     78               .    .    .    .    .    .    .
   CONT      2    5     78               .    .    .    .    .    .    .
   CONT      2    6     79               .    .    .    .    .    .    .
   CONT      2    7     78               .    .    .    .    .    .    .
   CONT      3    1     78    Strength  78   77   77   77   76   76   77
```

CHAPTER

40

The TRANTAB Procedure

Overview

The TRANTAB procedure creates, edits, and displays customized translation tables. In addition, you can use PROC TRANTAB to view and modify translation tables that are supplied by SAS Institute. These Institute-supplied tables are stored in the SASHELP.HOST catalog. Any translation table that you create or customize is stored in your SASUSER.PROFILE catalog. Translation tables have an entry type of TRANTAB.

Translation tables are operating environment-specific SAS catalog entries that are used to translate the values of one (coded) character set to another. A translation table has two halves: table one provides a translation, such as ASCII to EBCDIC; table two provides the inverse (or reverse) translation, such as EBCDIC to ASCII. Each half of a translation table is an array of 256 two-digit *positions*, each of which contains a one-byte unsigned number that corresponds to a coded character.

The SAS System uses translation tables for the following purposes:

☐ determining the collating sequence in the SORT procedure

☐ performing transport-format translations when you transfer files with the CPORT and CIMPORT procedures

☐ performing translations between operating environments when you access remote data in SAS/CONNECT or SAS/SHARE software

☐ facilitating data communications between the operating environment and a graphics device when you run SAS/GRAPH software in an IBM environment

☐ accommodating national language character sets other than U.S. English.

PROC TRANTAB produces no output. It can display translation tables and notes in the SAS log.

Concepts

Understanding Translation Tables and Character Sets

The kth element in a translation table corresponds to the kth element of an ordered character set. For example, position 00 (which is byte 1) in a translation table contains a coded value that corresponds to the first element of the ordered character set. To determine the position of a character in your operating environment's character set, use the SAS function RANK. The following example shows how to use RANK:

```
data _null_;
   x=rank('a');
   put "The position of a is " x ".";
```

The SAS log prints the following message: **The position of a is 97 .**

Each position in a translation table contains a hexadecimal number that is within the range of 0 ('00'x) to 255 ('FF'x). Hexadecimal values always end with an x. You can represent one or more consecutive hexadecimal values within quotation marks followed by a single x. For example, a string of three consecutive hexadecimal values can be written as '08090A'x. The SAS log displays each row of a translation table as 16 hexadecimal values enclosed in quotes followed by an x. The SAS log also lists reference numbers in the vertical and horizontal margins that correspond to the positions in the table. Example 1 on page 1301 shows how the SAS log displays a translation table.

Storing Translation Tables

When you use PROC TRANTAB to create a customized translation table, the procedure automatically stores the table in your SASUSER.PROFILE catalog. This enables you to use customized translation tables without affecting other users. When you specify the translation table in the SORT procedure or in a GOPTIONS statement, the software first looks in your SASUSER.PROFILE catalog to find the table. If the specified translation table is not in your SASUSER.PROFILE catalog, the software looks in the SASHELP.HOST catalog.

If you want the translation table you create to be globally accessed, have your SAS Installation Coordinator copy the table from your SASUSER.PROFILE catalog (using the CATALOG procedure) to the SASHELP.HOST catalog.

Modifying Institute-supplied Translation Tables

If an Institute-supplied translation table does not meet your needs, you can use PROC TRANTAB to edit it and create a new table. That is, you can issue the PROC TRANTAB statement that specifies the Institute-supplied table, edit the table, and then save the table using the SAVE statement. The modified translation table is saved in your SASUSER.PROFILE catalog. If you are a SAS Installation Coordinator, you can modify a translation table with PROC TRANTAB and then use the CATALOG procedure to copy the modified table from your SASUSER.PROFILE catalog to the SASHELP.HOST catalog, as shown in the following example:

```
proc catalog c=sasuser.profile;
   copy out=sashelp.host entrytype=trantab;
run;
```

You can use PROC TRANTAB to modify translation tables stored in the SASHELP.HOST catalog only if you have update (or write) access to that data library and catalog.

Using Translation Tables Outside PROC TRANTAB

Using Translation Tables in the SORT Procedure

PROC SORT uses translation tables to determine the collating sequence to be used by the sort. You can specify an alternative translation table with the SORTSEQ= option of PROC SORT. For example, if your operating environment sorts with the EBCDIC sequence by default, and you want to sort with the ASCII sequence, you can issue the following statement to specify the ASCII translation table:

```
proc sort sortseq=ascii;
```

You can also create a customized translation table with PROC TRANTAB and specify the new table with PROC SORT. This is useful when you want to specify sorting sequences for languages other than U.S. English. The sample program TRABASE from the SAS Sample Library builds transport-format and character-operations translation tables for a number of languages and environments. The NLSSetup Application, shipped with Release 6.11 as part of the SAS Sample Library, provides an easy way to create all the necessary translation tables, device maps, and key maps simply by selecting a country name from a listbox.

See Example 6 on page 1311 for an example that uses translation tables to sort data in different ways. For information on the tables available for sorting and the SORTSEQ= option, see Chapter 33, "The SORT Procedure," on page 1005.

Using Translation Tables with the CPORT and CIMPORT Procedures

The CPORT and CIMPORT procedures use translation tables to translate characters in catalog entries that you export from one operating environment and import on another operating environment. You may specify the name of an Institute-supplied or a customized translation table in the TRANTAB statement of PROC CPORT. See

"TRANTAB Statement" on page 320 in Chapter 13, "The CPORT Procedure," on page 313 for more information.

Using Translation Tables with Remote Library Services

Remote Library Services (RLS) use translation tables to translate characters when you access remote data.
SAS/CONNECT and SAS/SHARE software use translation tables to translate characters when you transfer or share files between two operating environments that use different encoding standards.

Using Translation Tables in SAS/GRAPH Software

In SAS/GRAPH software, translation tables are most commonly used on an IBM operating environment where tables are necessary because graphics commands must leave IBM operating environments in EBCDIC representation but must reach asynchronous graphics devices in ASCII representation. Specifically, SAS/GRAPH software builds the command stream for these devices internally in ASCII representation but must convert the commands to EBCDIC representation before they can be given to the communications software for transmission to the device. SAS/GRAPH software uses a translation table internally to make the initial conversion from ASCII to EBCDIC. The communications software then translates the command stream back to ASCII representation before it reaches the graphics device.

Translation tables are operating environment-specific. In most cases, you can simply use the default translation table, SASGTAB0, or one of the Institute-supplied graphics translation tables. However, if these tables are not able to do all of the translation correctly, you can create your own translation table with PROC TRANTAB. The SASGTAB0 table may fail to do the translation correctly when it encounters characters from languages other than U.S. English.

To specify an alternative translation table for SAS/GRAPH software, you can either use the TRANTAB= option in a GOPTIONS statement or modify the TRANTAB device parameter in the device entry. For example, the following GOPTIONS statement specifies the GTABTCAM graphics translation table:

```
goptions trantab=gtabtcam;
```

Translation tables used in SAS/GRAPH software perform both *device-to-operating environment* translation and *operating environment-to-device* translation. Therefore, a translation table is made up of 512 bytes, with the first 256 bytes used to perform device-to-operating environment translation (ASCII to EBCDIC on IBM mainframes) and the second 256 bytes used to perform operating environment-to-device translation (EBCDIC to ASCII on IBM mainframes). For PROC TRANTAB, the area of a translation table for device–to–operating environment translation is considered to be *table one*, and the area for operating environment–to–device translation is considered to be *table two*. See Example 1 on page 1301 for a listing of the ASCII translation table (an Institute-provided translation table), which shows both areas of the table.

On operating environments other than IBM mainframes, translation tables can be used to translate specific characters in the data stream that are created by the driver. For example, if the driver normally generates a vertical bar in the data stream, but you want another character to be generated in place of the vertical bar, you can create a translation table that translates the vertical bar to an alternate character.

For details on how to specify translation tables with the TRANTAB= option in SAS/GRAPH software, see
SAS/GRAPH Software: Reference, Version 6, First Edition, Volume 1 and *Volume 2*.

SAS/GRAPH software also uses key maps and device maps to map codes generated by the keyboard to specified characters and to map character codes to codes required by the graphics output device. These maps are specific to SAS/GRAPH software and are discussed in "The GKEYMAP Procedure" in *SAS/GRAPH Software: Reference*.

Procedure Syntax

Tip: Supports RUN-group processing

PROC TRANTAB TABLE=*table-name* <NLS>;
   CLEAR <ONE|TWO|BOTH>;
   INVERSE;
   LIST <ONE|TWO|BOTH>;
   LOAD TABLE=*table-name* <NLS>;
   REPLACE *position value-1*<*...value-n*>;
   SAVE <TABLE=*table-name*> <ONE|TWO|BOTH>;
   SWAP;

To do this	Use this statement
Set all positions in the translation table to zero	CLEAR
Create an inverse of table one	INVERSE
Display a translation table in hexadecimal representation	LIST
Load a translation table into memory for editing	LOAD
Replace the characters in a translation table with specified values	REPLACE
Save the translation table in your SASUSER.PROFILE catalog	SAVE
Exchange table one with table two	SWAP

Note: PROC TRANTAB is an interactive procedure. Once you submit a PROC TRANTAB statement, you can continue to enter and execute statements without repeating the PROC TRANTAB statement. To terminate the procedure, submit a QUIT statement or submit another DATA or PROC statement. △

PROC TRANTAB Statement

Tip: If you specify an incorrect table name in the PROC TRANTAB statement, use the LOAD statement to load the correct table. You do not need to reinvoke PROC TRANTAB. New tables are not stored in the catalog until you issue the SAVE statement, so you will not have unwanted tables in your catalog.

PROC TRANTAB TABLE=*table-name* <NLS>;

Required Arguments

TABLE=*table-name*
specifies the translation table to create, edit, or display. The specified table name must be a valid one-level SAS name.

Options

NLS
specifies that the table you listed in the TABLE= argument is one of five special internal translation tables provided with every copy of the SAS System. You must use the NLS option when you specify one of the five special tables in the TABLE= argument:

SASXPT
the local-to-transport format translation table (used by the CPORT procedure)

SASLCL
the transport-to-local format translation table (used by the CIMPORT procedure)

SASUCS
the lowercase-to-uppercase translation table (used by the UPCASE function)

SASLCS
the uppercase-to-lowercase translation table (used by the LOWCASE macro)

SASCCL
the character classification table (used internally), which contains flag bytes that correspond to each character position that indicate the class or classes to which each character belongs.

NLS stands for National Language Support. This option and the associated translation tables provide a method to translate characters that exist in languages other than English. To make SAS use the modified NLS table, specify its name in the SAS system option TRANTAB= .

Note: When you load one of these special translation tables, the SAS log displays a note that states that table 2 is uninitialized. That is, table 2 is an empty table that contains all zeros. PROC TRANTAB does not use table 2 at all for translation in these special cases, so you do not need to be concerned about this note. △

CLEAR Statement

Sets all positions in the translation table to zero. This statement is useful when you create a new table.

CLEAR <ONE | TWO | BOTH>;

Options

ONE | TWO | BOTH
  ONE
    clears table one.
  TWO
    clears table two.
  BOTH
    clears both table one and table two.
  Default: ONE

INVERSE Statement

Creates an inverse of table one in a translation table. That is, it creates table two.

Featured in: Example 5 on page 1308

INVERSE;

Details

INVERSE does not preserve multiple translations. Suppose table one has two (or more) different characters translated to the same value; for example, "A" and "B" are both translated to "1". For table two, INVERSE uses the last translated character for the value; that is, "1" is always translated to "B" and not "A", assuming that "A" appears before "B" in the first table.

Operating environment sort programs in the SAS System require an inverse table for proper operation.

LIST Statement

Displays a translation table in hexadecimal representation. The translation table listing appears in the SAS log.

Featured in: All examples

LIST <ONE | TWO | BOTH>;

Options

ONE | TWO | BOTH

ONE
  displays table one.

TWO
  displays table two.

BOTH
  displays both table one and table two.
  Default: ONE

LOAD Statement

Loads a translation table into memory for editing.

Tip: Use LOAD when you specify an incorrect table name in the PROC TRANTAB statement. You can specify the correct name without the need to reinvoke the procedure.

Tip: Use LOAD to edit multiple translation tables in a single PROC TRANTAB step. (Be sure to save the first table before you load another one.)

Featured in: Example 4 on page 1306

LOAD TABLE=*table-name* <NLS>;

Required Arguments

TABLE=*table-name*
  specifies the name of an existing translation table to be edited. The specified table name must be a valid one-level SAS name.

Option

NLS
  specifies that the table you listed in the TABLE= argument is one of five special internal translation tables provided with every copy of the SAS System. You must use the NLS option when you specify one of the five special tables in the TABLE= argument:

SASXPT
  the local-to-transport format translation table

SASLCL
  the transport-to-local format translation table

SASUCS

the lowercase-to-uppercase translation table

SASLCS

the uppercase-to-lowercase translation table

SASCCL

the character classification table, which contains flag bytes that correspond to each character position that indicate the class or classes to which each character belongs.

NLS stands for National Language Support. This option and the associated translation tables provide a method to map characters that exist in languages other than English to programs, displays, files, or products of the SAS System.

Note: When you load one of these special translation tables, the SAS log displays a note that states that table 2 is uninitialized. That is, table 2 is an empty table that contains all zeros. PROC TRANTAB does not use table 2 at all for translation in these special cases, so you do not need to be concerned about this note. △

REPLACE Statement

Replaces characters in a translation table with the values given, starting at the specified position.

Alias: REP

Tip: To save edits, you must issue the SAVE statement.

Featured in: Example 2 on page 1302, Example 3 on page 1304, and Example 4 on page 1306

REPLACE *position value-1<...value-n>;*

Required Arguments

position

specifies the position in a translation table where the replacement is to begin. The editable positions in a translation table begin at position decimal 0 and end at decimal 255. To specify the position, you can

□ use a decimal or hexadecimal value to specify an actual location. If you specify a decimal value, for example, 20, PROC TRANTAB locates position 20 in the table, which is byte 21. If you specify a hexadecimal value, for example, '14'x, PROC TRANTAB locates the decimal position that is equivalent to the specified hexadecimal value, which in this case is position 20 (or byte 21) in the table.

□ use a quoted character. PROC TRANTAB locates the quoted character in the table (that is, the quoted character's hexadecimal value) and uses that character's position as the starting position. For example, if you specify the following REPLACE statement, the statement replaces the first occurrence of the hexadecimal value for "a" and the next two hexadecimal values with the hexadecimal equivalent of "ABC":

```
replace 'a' 'ABC';
```

This is useful when you want to locate alphabetic and numerical characters when you do not know their actual location. If the quoted character is not found, PROC TRANTAB displays an error message and ignores the statement.

To edit positions 256 through 511 (table two), follow this procedure:

1 Issue the SWAP statement.

2 Issue the appropriate REPLACE statement.

3 Issue the SWAP statement again to reposition the table.

value-1 <...value-n>

is one or more decimal, hexadecimal, or character constants that give the actual value to be put into the table, starting at *position*. You can also use a mixture of the types of values. That is, you can specify a decimal, a hexadecimal, and a character value in one REPLACE statement. Example 3 on page 1304 shows a mixture of all three types of values in the REPLACE statement.

SAVE Statement

Saves the translation table in your SASUSER.PROFILE catalog.

Featured in: Example 2 on page 1302 and Example 4 on page 1306

SAVE <TABLE=*table-name*> <ONE | TWO | BOTH>;

Options

TABLE=*table-name*

specifies the table name under which the current table is to be saved. The name must be a valid one-level SAS name.

Default: If you omit the TABLE= option, the current table is saved under the name you specify in the PROC TRANTAB statement or the LOAD statement.

ONE | TWO | BOTH

ONE

saves table one.

TWO

saves table two.

BOTH

saves both table one and table two.

Default: BOTH

SWAP Statement

Exchanges table one with table two to enable you to edit positions 256 through 511.

Tip: After you edit the table, you must issue SWAP again to reposition the table.

Featured in: Example 7 on page 1313

SWAP;

Examples

Note: All examples were produced in the UNIX environment. △

Example 1: Viewing a Translation Table

Procedure features:
    LIST statement

This example uses PROC TRANTAB to display the Institute-supplied ASCII translation table.

Program

```
options nodate pageno=1 linesize=80 pagesize=60;
proc trantab table=ascii;
```

The LIST BOTH statement displays both table one and table two.

```
list both;
```

SAS Log

```
NOTE: Table specified is ASCII.
ASCII table 1:
         0 1 2 3 4 5 6 7 8 9 A B C D E F
  00 '000102030405060708090A0B0C0D0E0F'x
  10 '101112131415161718191A1B1C1D1E1F'x
  20 '202122232425262728292A2B2C2D2E2F'x
  30 '303132333435363738393A3B3C3D3E3F'x
  40 '404142434445464748494A4B4C4D4E4F'x
  50 '505152535455565758595A5B5C5D5E5F'x
  60 '606162636465666768696A6B6C6D6E6F'x
  70 '707172737475767778797A7B7C7D7E7F'x
  80 '808182838485868788898A8B8C8D8E8F'x
  90 '909192939495969798999A9B9C9D9E9F'x
  A0 'A0A1A2A3A4A5A6A7A8A9AAABACADAEAF'x
  B0 'B0B1B2B3B4B5B6B7B8B9BABBBCBDBEBF'x
  C0 'C0C1C2C3C4C5C6C7C8C9CACBCCCDCECF'x
  D0 'D0D1D2D3D4D5D6D7D8D9DADBDCDDDEDF'x
  E0 'E0E1E2E3E4E5E6E7E8E9EAEBECEDEEEF'x
  F0 'F0F1F2F3F4F5F6F7F8F9FAFBFCFDFEFF'x


ASCII table 2:
         0 1 2 3 4 5 6 7 8 9 A B C D E F
  00 '000102030405060708090A0B0C0D0E0F'x
  10 '101112131415161718191A1B1C1D1E1F'x
  20 '202122232425262728292A2B2C2D2E2F'x
  30 '303132333435363738393A3B3C3D3E3F'x
  40 '404142434445464748494A4B4C4D4E4F'x
  50 '505152535455565758595A5B5C5D5E5F'x
  60 '606162636465666768696A6B6C6D6E6F'x
  70 '707172737475767778797A7B7C7D7E7F'x
  80 '808182838485868788898A8B8C8D8E8F'x
  90 '909192939495969798999A9B9C9D9E9F'x
  A0 'A0A1A2A3A4A5A6A7A8A9AAABACADAEAF'x
  B0 'B0B1B2B3B4B5B6B7B8B9BABBBCBDBEBF'x
  C0 'C0C1C2C3C4C5C6C7C8C9CACBCCCDCECF'x
  D0 'D0D1D2D3D4D5D6D7D8D9DADBDCDDDEDF'x
  E0 'E0E1E2E3E4E5E6E7E8E9EAEBECEDEEEF'x
  F0 'F0F1F2F3F4F5F6F7F8F9FAFBFCFDFEFF'x
```

Example 2: Creating a Translation Table

Procedures features:
   LIST statement
   REPLACE statement
   SAVE statement

This example uses PROC TRANTAB to create a customized translation table.

Program

```
options nodate pageno=1 linesize=80 pagesize=60;
proc trantab table=newtable;
```

The REPLACE statement places the values into the table starting at position 0. You can use hexadecimal strings of any length in the REPLACE statement. This example uses strings of length 16 to match the way translation tables appear in the SAS log.

```
replace 0
'00010203a309e57ff9ecc40b0c0d0e0f'x
'10111213a5e008e71819c6c51c1d1e1f'x
'c7fce9e2e40a171beaebe8efee050607'x
'c9e616f4f6f2fb04ffd6dca2b6a7501a'x
'20e1edf3faf1d1aababfa22e3c282b7c'x
'265facbdbca1abbb5f5f21242a293bac'x
'2d2f5fa6a6a6a62b2ba6a62c255f3e3f'x
'a62b2b2b2b2b2d2d603a2340273d22'x
'2b6162636465666768692d2ba6a62b2b'x
'2d6a6b6c6d6e6f7071722da62d2b2d2d'x
'2d7e737475767778787a2d2b2b2b2b2b'x
'2b2b2b5f5fa65f5f5fdf5fb65f5fb55f'x
'7b41424344454647484 95f5f5f5f5f5f'x
'7d4a4b4c4d4e4f5051525f5f5fb15f5f'x
'5c83535455565758595a5f5ff75f5fb0'x
'30313233343536373839b75f6eb25f5f'x
;
```

The SAVE statement saves the table under the name specified in the PROC TRANTAB statement. By default, the table is saved in your SASUSER.PROFILE catalog.

```
save;
```

The LIST statement specifies that both table one and table two be displayed.

```
list both;
```

SAS Log

Table 2 is empty; that is, it consists entirely of 0s. To create table 2, you can use the INVERSE statement. (See Example 5 on page 1308.) To edit table 2, you can use the SWAP statement with the REPLACE statement. (See Example 7 on page 1313.)

```
    NOTE: Table specified is NEWTABLE.
 WARNING: Table NEWTABLE not found! New table is assumed.
 NOTE: NEWTABLE table 1 is uninitialized.
 NOTE: NEWTABLE table 2 is uninitialized.

 NOTE: Saving table NEWTABLE.
 NOTE: NEWTABLE table 2 will not be saved because it is uninitialized.
 NEWTABLE table 1:
          0 1 2 3 4 5 6 7 8 9 A B C D E F
     00 '00010203A309E57FF9ECC40B0C0D0E0F'x
     10 '10111213A5E008E71819C6C51C1D1E1F'x
     20 'C7FCE9E2E40A171BEAEBE8EFEE050607'x
     30 'C9E616F4F6F2FB04FFD6DCA2B6A7501A'x
     40 '20E1EDF3FAF1D1AABABFA22E3C282B7C'x
     50 '265FACBDBCA1ABBB5F5F21242A293BAC'x
     60 '2D2F5FA6A6A6A62B2BA6A62C255F3E3F'x
     70 'A62B2B2B2B2B2D2D603A2340273D22'x
     80 '2B6162636465666768692D2BA6A62B2B'x
     90 '2D6A6B6C6D6E6F7071722DA62D2B2D2D'x
     A0 '2D7E737475767778787A2D2B2B2B2B2B'x
     B0 '2B2B2B5F5FA65F5F5FDF5FB65F5FB55F'x
     C0 '7B41424344454647484E5F5F5F5F5F5F'x
     D0 '7D4A4B4C4D4E4F5051525F5F5FB15F5F'x
     E0 '5C83535455565758595A5F5FFF75F5FB0'x
     F0 '30313233343536373839B75F6EB25F5F'x



 NOTE: NEWTABLE table 2 is uninitialized.
 NEWTABLE table 2:
          0 1 2 3 4 5 6 7 8 9 A B C D E F
     00 '00000000000000000000000000000000'x
     10 '00000000000000000000000000000000'x
     20 '00000000000000000000000000000000'x
     30 '00000000000000000000000000000000'x
     40 '00000000000000000000000000000000'x
     50 '00000000000000000000000000000000'x
     60 '00000000000000000000000000000000'x
     70 '00000000000000000000000000000000'x
     80 '00000000000000000000000000000000'x
     90 '00000000000000000000000000000000'x
     A0 '00000000000000000000000000000000'x
     B0 '00000000000000000000000000000000'x
     C0 '00000000000000000000000000000000'x
     D0 '00000000000000000000000000000000'x
     E0 '00000000000000000000000000000000'x
     F0 '00000000000000000000000000000000'x
```

Example 3: Editing by Specifying a Decimal Value for Starting Position

Procedure features:
    LIST statement

    REPLACE statement

    SAVE statement

This example edits the translation table created in Example 2 on page 1302. The decimal value specified in the REPLACE statement marks the starting position for the changes to the table.

The vertical arrow in both SAS logs marks the point at which the changes begin.

Program

```
options nodate pageno-1 linesize=80 pagesize=60;
proc trantab table=newtable;
```

The first LIST statement displays the original NEWTABLE translation table.

```
    list one;
```

SAS Log

The Original NEWTABLE Translation Table

```
NOTE: Table specified is NEWTABLE.
NOTE: NEWTABLE table 2 is uninitialized.
NEWTABLE table 1:
                              ↓
        0 1 2 3 4 5 6 7 8 9 A B C D E F
   00  '00010203A309E57FF9ECC40B0C0D0E0F'x
   10  '10111213A5E008E71819C6C51C1D1E1F'x
   20  'C7FCE9E2E40A171BEAEBE8EFEE050607'x
   30  'C9E616F4F6F2FB04FFD6DCA2B6A7501A'x
   40  '20E1EDF3FAF1D1AABABFA22E3C282B7C'x
   50  '265FACBDBCA1ABBB5F5F21242A293BAC'x
   60  '2D2F5FA6A6A62B2BA6A62C255F3E3F'x
   70  'A62B2B2B2B2B2B2D2D603A2340273D22'x
   80  '2B61626364656667686692D2BA6A62B2B'x
   90  '2D6A6B6C6D6E6F7071722DA62D2B2D2D'x
   A0  '2D7E737475767778787A2D2B2B2B2B2B'x
   B0  '2B2B2B5F5FA65F5F5FDF5FB65F5FB55F'x
   C0  '7B414243444546474849 5F5F5F5F5F5F'x
   D0  '7D4A4B4C4D4E4F5051525F5F5FB15F5F'x
   E0  '5C835354555657585 95A5F5FF75F5FB0'x
   F0  '303132333435363738 39B75F6EB25F5F'x
```

The REPLACE statement starts at position decimal 10, which is byte 11 in the original table, and performs a byte-to-byte replacement with the given values.

```
    replace 10
    20 10 200 'x' 'ux' '092040'x;
```

The SAVE statement saves the changes made to the NEWTABLE translation table.

```
save;
```

The second LIST statement displays the edited NEWTABLE translation table.

```
list one;
```

SAS Log

The Edited NEWTABLE Translation Table

```
NOTE: Saving table NEWTABLE.
NOTE: NEWTABLE table 2 will not be saved because it is uninitialized.
NEWTABLE table 1:
                              ↓
        0 1 2 3 4 5 6 7 8 9 A B C D E F
  00  '00010203A309E57FF9EC140AC8787578'x
  10  '09204013A5E008E71819C6C51C1D1E1F'x
  20  'C7FCE9E2E40A171BEAEBE8EFEE050607'x
  30  'C9E616F4F6F2FB04FFD6DCA2B6A7501A'x
  40  '20E1EDF3FAF1D1AABABFA22E3C282B7C'x
  50  '265FACBDBCA1ABBB5F5F21242A293BAC'x
  60  '2D2F5FA6A6A6A62B2BA6A62C255F3E3F'x
  70  'A62B2B2B2B2B2D2D603A2340273D22'x
  80  '2B616263646566676866692D2BA6A62B2B'x
  90  '2D6A6B6C6D6E6F7071722DA62D2B2D2D'x
  A0  '2D7E737475767778787A2D2B2B2B2B2B'x
  B0  '2B2B2B5F5FA65F5F5FDF5FB65F5FB55F'x
  C0  '7B4142434445464748495F5F5F5F5F5F'x
  D0  '7D4A4B4C4D4E4F5051525F5F5FB15F5F'x
  E0  '5C8353545556575859A5A5F5FF75F5FB0'x
  F0  '30313233343536373839B75F6EB25F5F'x
```

At position 10 (which is byte 11), a vertical arrow denotes the starting point for the changes to the translation table.

- ☐ At byte 11, decimal 20 (which is hexadecimal 14) replaces hexadecimal C4.
- ☐ At byte 12, decimal 10 (which is hexadecimal 0A) replaces hexadecimal 0B.
- ☐ At byte 13, decimal 200 (which is hexadecimal C8) replaces hexadecimal 0C.
- ☐ At byte 14, character 'x' (which is hexadecimal 78) replaces hexadecimal 0D.
- ☐ At bytes 15 and 16, characters 'ux' (which are hexadecimal 75 and 78, respectively) replace hexadecimal 0E and 0F.
- ☐ At bytes 17, 18, and 19, hexadecimal 092040 replaces hexadecimal 101112.

Example 4: Editing by Using a Quoted Character for Starting Position
Procedure features:

LIST statement
LOAD statement
REPLACE statement
SAVE statement

This example creates a new translation table by editing the Institute-supplied ASCII translation table. The first occurrence of the hexadecimal equivalent of the quoted character specified in the REPLACE statement is the starting position for the changes to the table. This differs from Example 3 on page 1304 in that you do not need to know the exact position at which to start the changes to the table. PROC TRANTAB finds the correct position for you.

The edited table is saved under a new name. Horizontal arrows in both SAS logs denote the edited rows in the translation table.

Program

```
options nodate pageno=1 linesize=80 pagesize=60;
proc trantab table=ascii;
```

The LIST statement displays the translation table in the SAS log.

```
    list one;
```

SAS Log

```
NOTE: Table specified is ASCII.
ASCII table 1:
          0 1 2 3 4 5 6 7 8 9 A B C D E F
    00 '000102030405060708090A0B0C0D0E0F'x
    10 '101112131415161718191A1B1C1D1E1F'x
    20 '202122232425262728292A2B2C2D2E2F'x
    30 '303132333435363738393A3B3C3D3E3F'x
    40 '404142434445464748494A4B4C4D4E4F'x
    50 '505152535455565758595A5B5C5D5E5F'x
    60 '606162636465666768696A6B6C6D6E6F'x    ←
    70 '707172737475767778797A7B7C7D7E7F'x    ←
    80 '808182838485868788898A8B8C8D8E8F'x
    90 '909192939495969798999A9B9C9D9E9F'x
    A0 'A0A1A2A3A4A5A6A7A8A9AAABACADAEAF'x
    B0 'B0B1B2B3B4B5B6B7B8B9BABBBCBDBEBF'x
    C0 'C0C1C2C3C4C5C6C7C8C9CACBCCCDCECF'x
    D0 'D0D1D2D3D4D5D6D7D8D9DADBDCDDDEDF'x
    E0 'E0E1E2E3E4E5E6E7E8E9EAEBECEDEEEF'x
    F0 'F0F1F2F3F4F5F6F7F8F9FAFBFCFDFEFF'x
```

The REPLACE statement finds the first occurrence of the hexadecimal "a" (which is 61) and replaces it and the next 25 hexadecimal values with the hexadecimal values for uppercase "A" through "Z."

```
replace 'a' 'ABCDEFGHIJKLMNOPQRSTUVWXYZ';
```

The SAVE statement saves the changes made to the ASCII translation table under the new table name UPPER.

```
save table=upper;
```

The LOAD statement loads the edited translation table UPPER. The LIST statement displays the translation table UPPER in the SAS log.

```
load table=upper;
list one;
```

SAS Log

The UPPER Translation Table

The horizontal arrows in the SAS log denote the rows in which the changes are made.

```
NOTE: Table UPPER being loaded.
UPPER table 1:
          0 1 2 3 4 5 6 7 8 9 A B C D E F
    00 '000102030405060708090A0B0C0D0E0F'x
    10 '101112131415161718191A1B1C1D1E1F'x
    20 '202122232425262728292A2B2C2D2E2F'x
    30 '303132333435363738393A3B3C3D3E3F'x
    40 '404142434445464748494A4B4C4D4E4F'x
    50 '505152535455565758595A5B5C5D5E5F'x
    60 '604142434445464748494A4B4C4D4E4F'x   ←
    70 '505152535455565758595A7B7C7D7E7F'x   ←
    80 '808182838485868788898A8B8C8D8E8F'x
    90 '909192939495969798999A9B9C9D9E9F'x
    A0 'A0A1A2A3A4A5A6A7A8A9AAABACADAEAF'x
    B0 'B0B1B2B3B4B5B6B7B8B9BABBBCBDBEBF'x
    C0 'C0C1C2C3C4C5C6C7C8C9CACBCCCDCECF'x
    D0 'D0D1D2D3D4D5D6D7D8D9DADBDCDDDEDF'x
    E0 'E0E1E2E3E4E5E6E7E8E9EAEBECEDEEEF'x
    F0 'F0F1F2F3F4F5F6F7F8F9FAFBFCFDFEFF'x
```

Example 5: Creating the Inverse of a Table

Procedure features:
   INVERSE statement

LIST statement
SAVE statement

This example creates the inverse of the translation table that was created in Example 4 on page 1306. The new translation table created in this example is the operating environment-to-device translation for use in data communications.

Program

```
options nodate pageno=1 linesize=80 pagesize=60;
proc trantab table=upper;
```

The INVERSE statement creates table two by inverting the original table one (called UPPER). The SAVE statement saves the translation tables. The LIST BOTH statement displays both the original translation table and its inverse.

```
inverse;
save;
list both;
```

SAS Log

The UPPER Translation Table and Its Inverse

The SAS log lists all of the duplicate values that it encounters as it creates the inverse of table one. To conserve space, most of these messages are deleted in this example.

```
NOTE: Table specified is UPPER.
NOTE: This table cannot be mapped one to one.
 duplicate of '41'x found at '61'x in table one.
 duplicate of '42'x found at '62'x in table one.
 duplicate of '43'x found at '63'x in table one.
         .
         .
         .
 duplicate of '58'x found at '78'x in table one.
 duplicate of '59'x found at '79'x in table one.
 duplicate of '5A'x found at '7A'x in table one.
NOTE: Saving table UPPER.
UPPER table 1:
        0 1 2 3 4 5 6 7 8 9 A B C D E F
   00 '000102030405060708090A0B0C0D0E0F'x
   10 '101112131415161718191A1B1C1D1E1F'x
   20 '202122232425262728292A2B2C2D2E2F'x
   30 '303132333435363738393A3B3C3D3E3F'x
   40 '404142434445464748494A4B4C4D4E4F'x
   50 '505152535455565758595A5B5C5D5E5F'x
   60 '604142434445464748494A4B4C4D4E4F'x
   70 '505152535455565758595A7B7C7D7E7F'x
   80 '808182838485868788898A8B8C8D8E8F'x
   90 '909192939495969798999A9B9C9D9E9F'x
   A0 'A0A1A2A3A4A5A6A7A8A9AAABACADAEAF'x
   B0 'B0B1B2B3B4B5B6B7B8B9BABBBCBDBEBF'x
   C0 'C0C1C2C3C4C5C6C7C8C9CACBCCCDCECF'x
   D0 'D0D1D2D3D4D5D6D7D8D9DADBDCDDDEDF'x
   E0 'E0E1E2E3E4E5E6E7E8E9EAEBECEDEEEF'x
   F0 'F0F1F2F3F4F5F6F7F8F9FAFBFCFDFEFF'x


UPPER table 2:
        0 1 2 3 4 5 6 7 8 9 A B C D E F
   00 '000102030405060708090A0B0C0D0E0F'x
   10 '101112131415161718191A1B1C1D1E1F'x
   20 '202122232425262728292A2B2C2D2E2F'x
   30 '303132333435363738393A3B3C3D3E3F'x
   40 '404142434445464748494A4B4C4D4E4F'x
   50 '505152535455565758595A5B5C5D5E5F'x
   60 '600000000000000000000000000000000'x
   70 '000000000000000000000007B7C7D7E7F'x
   80 '808182838485868788898A8B8C8D8E8F'x
   90 '909192939495969798999A9B9C9D9E9F'x
   A0 'A0A1A2A3A4A5A6A7A8A9AAABACADAEAF'x
   B0 'B0B1B2B3B4B5B6B7B8B9BABBBCBDBEBF'x
   C0 'C0C1C2C3C4C5C6C7C8C9CACBCCCDCECF'x
   D0 'D0D1D2D3D4D5D6D7D8D9DADBDCDDDEDF'x
   E0 'E0E1E2E3E4E5E6E7E8E9EAEBECEDEEEF'x
   F0 'F0F1F2F3F4F5F6F7F8F9FAFBFCFDFEFF'x
```

The INVERSE statement lists in the SAS log all of the multiple translations that it encounters as it inverts the translation table. In Example 4 on page 1306, all the lowercase letters were converted to uppercase in the translation table UPPER, which means that there are two sets of uppercase letters in UPPER. When INVERSE cannot make a translation, PROC TRANTAB fills the value with 00. Note that the inverse of the translation table UPPER has numerous 00 values.

Example 6: Using Different Translation Tables for Sorting

Procedure features:
 PROC SORT statement option:
  SORTSEQ=

Other features:
 PRINT procedure

This example shows how to specify a different translation table to sort data in an order that is different from the default sort order. Characters that are written in a language other than U.S. English may require a sort order that is different from the default order.

Note: You can use the TRABASE program in the SAS Sample Library to create translation tables for several different languages. △

Program

```
options nodate pageno=1 linesize=80 pagesize=60;
```

The DATA step creates a SAS data set with four pairs of words, each pair differing only in the case of the first letter.

```
data testsort;
   input Values $10.;
   datalines;
Always
always
Forever
forever
Later
later
Yesterday
yesterday
;
```

PROC SORT sorts the data using the default translation table, which sorts all lowercase words first, then all uppercase words. PROC PRINT prints the sorted data set.

```
proc sort;
   by values;
run;
proc print noobs;
   title 'Default Sort Sequence';
run;
```

SAS Output

Output from Sorting Values with Default Translation Table

The default sort sequence sorts all the capitalized words in alphabetical order before it sorts any lowercase words.

```
                        Default Sort Sequence                      1

                            Values

                            Always
                            Forever
                            Later
                            Yesterday
                            always
                            forever
                            later
                            yesterday
```

The SORTSEQ= option specifies that PROC SORT sort the data according to the customized translation table UPPER, which treats lowercase and uppercase letters alike. This is useful for sorting without regard for case. PROC PRINT prints the sorted data set.

```
proc sort sortseq=upper;
   by values;
run;
proc print noobs;
   title 'Customized Sort Sequence';
run;
```

SAS Output

Output from Sorting Values with Customized Translation Table

The customized sort sequence sorts all the words in alphabetical order, without regard for the case of the letters.

```
                      Customized Sort Sequence                     2

                            Values

                            Always
                            always
                            Forever
                            forever
                            Later
                            later
                            Yesterday
                            yesterday
```

Example 7: Editing Table One and Table Two

Procedure features:
   LIST statement
   REPLACE statement
   SAVE statement
   SWAP statement

This example shows how to edit both areas of a translation table. To edit positions 256 through 511 (table two), you must

1 Issue the SWAP statement to have table two change places with table one.

2 Issue an appropriate REPLACE statement to make changes to table two.

3 Issue the SWAP statement again to reposition the table.

Arrows in the SAS logs mark the rows and columns that are changed.

Program

```
options nodate pageno=1 linesize=80 pagesize=60;
proc trantab table=upper;
```

The LIST statement displays the original UPPER translation table.

```
    list both;
```

SAS Log

The Original UPPER Translation Table

```
NOTE: Table specified is UPPER.
UPPER table 1:
        ↓
        0 1 2 3 4 5 6 7 8 9 A B C D E F
00  '000102030405060708090A0B0C0D0E0F'x   ←
10  '101112131415161718191A1B1C1D1E1F'x
20  '202122232425262728292A2B2C2D2E2F'x
30  '303132333435363738393A3B3C3D3E3F'x
40  '404142434445464748494A4B4C4D4E4F'x
50  '505152535455565758595A5B5C5D5E5F'x
60  '604142434445464748494A4B4C4D4E4F'x
70  '505152535455565758595A7B7C7D7E7F'x
80  '808182838485868788898A8B8C8D8E8F'x
90  '909192939495969798999A9B9C9D9E9F'x
A0  'A0A1A2A3A4A5A6A7A8A9AAABACADAEAF'x
B0  'B0B1B2B3B4B5B6B7B8B9BABBBCBDBEBF'x
C0  'C0C1C2C3C4C5C6C7C8C9CACBCCCDCECF'x
D0  'D0D1D2D3D4D5D6D7D8D9DADBDCDDDEDF'x
E0  'E0E1E2E3E4E5E6E7E8E9EAEBECEDEEEF'x
F0  'F0F1F2F3F4F5F6F7F8F9FAFBFCFDFEFF'x

UPPER table 2:
        ↓
        0 1 2 3 4 5 6 7 8 9 A B C D E F
00  '000102030405060708090A0B0C0D0E0F'x   ←
10  '101112131415161718191A1B1C1D1E1F'x
20  '202122232425262728292A2B2C2D2E2F'x
30  '303132333435363738393A3B3C3D3E3F'x
40  '404142434445464748494A4B4C4D4E4F'x
50  '505152535455565758595A5B5C5D5E5F'x
60  '600000000000000000000000000000000'x
70  '00000000000000000000000007B7C7D7E7F'x
80  '808182838485868788898A8B8C8D8E8F'x
90  '909192939495969798999A9B9C9D9E9F'x
A0  'A0A1A2A3A4A5A6A7A8A9AAABACADAEAF'x
B0  'B0B1B2B3B4B5B6B7B8B9BABBBCBDBEBF'x
C0  'C0C1C2C3C4C5C6C7C8C9CACBCCCDCECF'x
D0  'D0D1D2D3D4D5D6D7D8D9DADBDCDDDEDF'x
E0  'E0E1E2E3E4E5E6E7E8E9EAEBECEDEEEF'x
F0  'F0F1F2F3F4F5F6F7F8F9FAFBFCFDFEFF'x
```

The REPLACE statement starts at position 1 and replaces the current value of 01 with '0A'.

```
replace 1 '0A'x;
```

The first SWAP statement positions table two so that it can be edited. The second REPLACE statement makes the same change on table two that was made on table one.

```
swap;
replace 1 '0A'x;
```

The second SWAP statement restores table one and table two to their original positions. The SAVE statement saves both areas of the translation table by default. The LIST statement displays both areas of the table.

```
swap;
save;
list both;
```

SAS Log

The Edited UPPER Translation Table

In byte 2, in both areas of the translation table, hexadecimal value '0A' replaces hexadecimal 01. Arrows denote the rows and columns of the table in which this change is made.

```
NOTE: Table specified is UPPER.
UPPER table 1:
            ↓
          0 1 2 3 4 5 6 7 8 9 A B C D E F
     00  '000A02030405060708090A0B0C0D0E0F'x   ←
     10  '101112131415161718191A1B1C1D1E1F'x
     20  '202122232425262728292A2B2C2D2E2F'x
     30  '303132333435363738393A3B3C3D3E3F'x
     40  '404142434445464748494A4B4C4D4E4F'x
     50  '505152535455565758595A5B5C5D5E5F'x
     60  '604142434445464748494A4B4C4D4E4F'x
     70  '505152535455565758595A7B7C7D7E7F'x
     80  '808182838485868788898A8B8C8D8E8F'x
     90  '909192939495969798999A9B9C9D9E9F'x
     A0  'A0A1A2A3A4A5A6A7A8A9AAABACADAEAF'x
     B0  'B0B1B2B3B4B5B6B7B8B9BABBBCBDBEBF'x
     C0  'C0C1C2C3C4C5C6C7C8C9CACBCCCDCECF'x
     D0  'D0D1D2D3D4D5D6D7D8D9DADBDCDDDEDF'x
     E0  'E0E1E2E3E4E5E6E7E8E9EAEBECEDEEEF'x
     F0  'F0F1F2F3F4F5F6F7F8F9FAFBFCFDFEFF'x

UPPER table 2:
            ↓
          0 1 2 3 4 5 6 7 8 9 A B C D E F
     00  '000A02030405060708090A0B0C0D0E0F'x   ←
     10  '101112131415161718191A1B1C1D1E1F'x
     20  '202122232425262728292A2B2C2D2E2F'x
     30  '303132333435363738393A3B3C3D3E3F'x
     40  '404142434445464748494A4B4C4D4E4F'x
     50  '505152535455565758595A5B5C5D5E5F'x
     60  '600000000000000000000000000000000'x
     70  '000000000000000000000007B7C7D7E7F'x
     80  '808182838485868788898A8B8C8D8E8F'x
     90  '909192939495969798999A9B9C9D9E9F'x
     A0  'A0A1A2A3A4A5A6A7A8A9AAABACADAEAF'x
     B0  'B0B1B2B3B4B5B6B7B8B9BABBBCBDBEBF'x
     C0  'C0C1C2C3C4C5C6C7C8C9CACBCCCDCECF'x
     D0  'D0D1D2D3D4D5D6D7D8D9DADBDCDDDEDF'x
     E0  'E0E1E2E3E4E5E6E7E8E9EAEBECEDEEEF'x
     F0  'F0F1F2F3F4F5F6F7F8F9FAFBFCFDFEFF'x
```

CHAPTER
41

The **UNIVARIATE Procedure**

Overview

The UNIVARIATE procedure provides data summarization tools, high-resolution graphics displays, and information on the distribution of numeric variables. For example, PROC UNIVARIATE

 □ calculates descriptive statistics based on moments

 □ calculates the median, mode, range, and quantiles

 □ calculates the robust estimates of location and scale

 □ calculates confidence limits

- □ tabulates extreme observations and extreme values
- □ generates frequency tables
- □ plots the data distribution
- □ performs tests for location and normality
- □ performs goodness-of-fit tests for fitted parametric and nonparametric distributions.
- □ creates histograms and optionally superimposes density curves for fitted continuous distributions (beta, exponential, gamma, lognormal, and Weibull) and for kernel density estimates
- □ creates quantile-quantile plots and probability plots for various theoretical distributions and optionally superimposes a reference line that corresponds to the specified or estimated location and scale parameters for the theoretical distribution
- □ creates one-way and two-way comparative histograms, comparative quantile-quantile plots, and comparative probability plots
- □ insets tables of statistics in the graphical displays (high-resolution graphs)
- □ creates output data sets with requested statistics, histogram intervals, and parameters of the fitted distributions.

Output 41.1 on page 1319 shows a default univariate analysis for student exam scores. The statements that produce the output follow:

```
options pagesize=36;
proc univariate data=score;
run;
```

By default, the tests for location examine the hypothesis that the mean is equal to zero. Optionally, you can request a test for the hypothesis that the mean is equal to a specified value μ_0.

Output 41.2 on page 1321 and Output 41.3 on page 1324 are the result of a more extensive univariate analysis. The analysis examines the data distribution of student exam scores and creates an output data set that saves percentiles that were not computed by default. The statements that produce the analysis also

- □ specify the null hypothesis for the tests for locations
- □ perform tests for normality
- □ plot the data distribution
- □ specify the analysis variables
- □ request confidence limits for parameters and quantiles
- □ list the five highest and lowest extreme values
- □ print an output data set that contains percentiles.

For an explanation of the program that produces both these reports, see Example 5 on page 1432.

Output 41.1 The Default Univariate Analysis

```
                        The SAS System                         1

                      The UNIVARIATE Procedure
                         Variable:  Test1

                              Moments

N                        12   Sum Weights                 12
Mean                  79.25   Sum Observations           951
Std Deviation    13.3152339   Variance            177.295455
Skewness         -0.7841891   Kurtosis            0.27709746
Uncorrected SS        77317   Corrected SS           1950.25
Coeff Variation   16.801557   Std Error Mean      3.84377695


                    Basic Statistical Measures

          Location                      Variability

     Mean      79.25000    Std Deviation          13.31523
     Median    79.50000    Variance              177.29545
     Mode      75.00000    Range                  44.00000
                           Interquartile Range    17.50000


                  Tests for Location: Mu0=0

        Test           -Statistic-      -----p Value------

        Student's t    t  20.61774      Pr > |t|    <.0001
        Sign           M         6      Pr >= |M|   0.0005
        Signed Rank    S        39      Pr >= |S|   0.0005
```

```
                        The SAS System                        2

                    The UNIVARIATE Procedure
                       Variable:  Test1

                  Quantiles (Definition 5)

                     Quantile      Estimate

                     100% Max        95.0
                     99%             95.0
                     95%             95.0
                     90%             94.0
                     75% Q3          90.5
                     50% Median      79.5
                     25% Q1          73.0
                     10%             63.0
                     5%              51.0
                     1%              51.0
                     0% Min          51.0


                    Extreme Observations

              ----Lowest----        ----Highest---

           Value      Obs        Value      Obs

              51        2           87       12
              63        4           89        8
              71       10           92        6
              75       11           94        1
              75        7           95        3
```

Output 41.2 A Univariate Analysis with Tests for Normality and Plots of the Data Distribution

```
            Examining the Distribution of Final Exam Scores          1

                       The UNIVARIATE Procedure
                          Variable:  Final

                               Moments

N                            12    Sum Weights                     12
Mean                  82.4166667    Sum Observations               989
Std Deviation         8.59659905    Variance                73.9015152
Skewness              0.22597472    Kurtosis                -1.0846549
Uncorrected SS             82323    Corrected SS            812.916667
Coeff Variation       10.4306561    Std Error Mean          2.48162439


                     Basic Statistical Measures

         Location                          Variability

     Mean      82.41667    Std Deviation               8.59660
     Median    81.50000    Variance                   73.90152
     Mode      80.00000    Range                      26.00000
                           Interquartile Range        14.50000


                 Basic Confidence Limits Assuming Normality

         Parameter           Estimate      Lower 90% CL

         Mean                82.41667         79.03314
         Std Deviation        8.59660          6.85984
         Variance            73.90152         47.05738


                  Tests for Location: Mu0=80

         Test            -Statistic-      -----p Value------

         Student's t     t  0.973825      Pr > |t|    0.3511
         Sign            M         1      Pr >= |M|   0.7539
         Signed Rank     S         8      Pr >= |S|   0.4434


                       Tests for Normality

  Test                    --Statistic---      ------p Value------

  Shapiro-Wilk            W    0.952903      Pr < W        0.6797
  Kolmogorov-Smirnov      D    0.113328      Pr > D       >0.1500
  Cramer-von Mises        W-Sq 0.028104      Pr > W-Sq    >0.2500
  Anderson-Darling        A-Sq 0.212693      Pr > A-Sq    >0.2500
```

```
Examining the Distribution of Final Exam Scores          2

              The UNIVARIATE Procedure
                Variable:  Final

           Quantiles (Definition 5)

                            90% Confidence Limits
 Quantile     Estimate      Assuming Normality

100% Max        97.0
 99%            97.0       96.30698    114.6289
 95%            97.0       91.55028    105.9399
 90%            93.0       88.89956    101.4163
 75% Q3         89.0       84.12815     94.1623
 50% Median     81.5       77.95996     86.8734
 25% Q1         74.5       70.67102     80.7052
 10%            72.0       63.41705     75.9338
  5%            71.0       58.89343     73.2831
  1%            71.0       50.20448     68.5264
  0% Min        71.0


              Extreme Observations

      ----Lowest----        ----Highest---

      Value     Obs         Value     Obs

        71       5            86       6
        72       7            87       1
        73      11            91       2
        76      12            93       8
        80       9            97       3


Stem Leaf                       #      Boxplot
  96 0                          1         |
  94                                      |
  92 0                          1         |
  90 0                          1         |
  88                                   +-----+
  86 00                         2      |     |
  84                                   |     |
  82 0                          1      |  +  |
  80 00                         2      *-----*
  78                                   |     |
  76 0                          1      |     |
  74                                   +-----+
  72 00                         2         |
  70 0                          1         |
     ----+----+----+----+
```

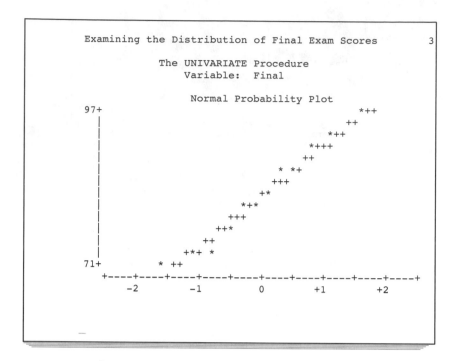

Output 41.3   An Output Data Set That Contains Univariate Statistics

```
              Quantile Statistics for Final Exam Scores              4
                  Output Data Set from PROC UNIVARIATE

       Median      Pctl_Top     Pctl_Mid      Pctl_Low     Pctl_70

        81.5          97          81.5           73           87
```

Procedure Syntax

Tip: Supports the Output Delivery System. See "Output Delivery System" on page 19

Reminder: You can use the ATTRIB, FORMAT, LABEL, and WHERE statements. See Chapter 3, "Statements with the Same Function in Multiple Procedures," for details. You can also use any global statements as well. See Chapter 2, "Fundamental Concepts for Using Base SAS Procedures," for a list.

PROC UNIVARIATE *<option(s)>*;

> **BY** <DESCENDING> *variable-1* <...<DESCENDING> *variable-n>*
> <NOTSORTED>;
>
> **CLASS** *variable-1<(variable-option(s))> <variable-2<(variable-option(s))>>*
> </ **KEYLEVEL**='*value1*' | ('*value1*' '*value2*')>;
>
> **FREQ** *variable*;
>
> **HISTOGRAM** *<variable(s)> </ option(s)>*;
>
> **ID** *variable(s)*;
>
> **INSET** *<keyword(s)* DATA=*SAS-data-set> </ option(s)>*;
>
> **OUTPUT** <OUT=*SAS-data-set> statistic-keyword-1=name(s)*
> *<... statistic-keyword-n=name(s)> <percentiles-specification>*;

PROBPLOT *<variable(s)> </ option(s)>*;
QQPLOT *<variable(s)> </ option(s)>*;
VAR *variable(s)*;
WEIGHT *variable*;

To do this	Use this statement
Calculate separate statistics for each BY group	BY
Specify up to two class variables to categorize the analysis	CLASS
Specify a variable that contains the frequency of each observation	FREQ
Create a high-resolution graph of a histogram	HISTOGRAM
Specify one or more variables whose values identify the extreme observations	ID
Inset a table of summary statistics in a high-resolution graph	INSET
Create an output data set that contains specified statistics	OUTPUT
Create a high-resolution graph of a probability plot	PROBPLOT
Create a high-resolution graph of a quantile-quantile plot	QQPLOT
Select the analysis variables and determine their order in the report	VAR
Identify a variable whose values weight each observation in the statistical calculations	WEIGHT

PROC UNIVARIATE Statement

PROC UNIVARIATE *<option(s)>*;

To do this	Use this option
Specify the input data set	DATA=
Specify the input data set that contains annotate variables	ANNOTATE=
Specify the SAS catalog to save high-resolution graphics output	GOUT=
Control the statistical analysis	
Request all statistics and tables that the FREQ, MODES, NEXTRVAL=, PLOT, and CIBASIC options generate	ALL
Specify the confidence level for the confidence limits	ALPHA=
Request confidence limits for the mean, standard deviation, and variance based on normally distributed data	CIBASIC
Request confidence limits for quantiles using a distribution-free method	CIPCTLDF
Request confidence limits for quantiles based on normally distributed data	CIPCTLNORMAL

To do this	Use this option
Exclude observations with nonpositive weights from the analysis	EXCLNPWGT
Specify the value of the mean or location parameter	MU0=
Specify the number of extreme observations displayed	NEXTROBS=
Specify the number of extreme values displayed	NEXTRVAL=
Request tests for normality	NORMAL
Specify the mathematical definition used to compute quantiles	PCTLDEF=
Compute robust estimates of scale	ROBUSTSCALE
Specify the units to round the analysis variable prior to computing statistics	ROUND=
Compute trimmed means	TRIMMED=
Specify the variance divisor	VARDEF=
Compute Winsorized means	WINSORIZED=
Control the displayed output	
Request a frequency table	FREQ
Request a table that shows number of observations greater than, equal to, and less than MU0=	LOCCOUNT
Request a table of all possible modes	MODES
Suppress side-by-side plots	NOBYPLOT
Suppress tables of descriptive statistics	NOPRINT
Create low-resolution stem-and-leaf, box, and normal probability plots	PLOTS
Specify the approximate number of rows the plots use	PLOTSIZE=

Options

ALL
> requests all statistics and tables that the FREQ, MODES, NEXTRVAL=5, PLOT, and CIBASIC options generate. If the analysis variables are not weighted, this option also requests the statistics and tables that the CIPCTLDF, CIPCTLNORMAL, LOCCOUNT, NORMAL, ROBUSTSCALE, TRIMMED=.25, and WINSORIZED=.25 options generate. PROC UNIVARIATE also uses any values that you specify for ALPHA=, MU0=, NEXTRVAL=, CIBASIC, CIPCTLDF, CIPCTLNORMAL, TRIMMED=, or WINSORIZED= to produce the output.

ALPHA=*value*
> specifies the default confidence level to compute confidence limits. The percentage for the confidence limits is $(1-value) \times 100$. For example, ALPHA=.05 results in a 95 percent confidence limit.
> **Default:** .05
> **Range:** between 0 and 1
> **Main discussion:** "Confidence Limits for Parameters of the Normal Distribution" on page 1393
> **Featured in:** Example 4 on page 1428 and Example 5 on page 1432

ANNOTATE=*SAS-data-set*

specifies an input data set that contains annotate variables as described in *SAS/ GRAPH Software: Reference*. You can use this data set to add features to your high-resolution graphics. PROC UNIVARIATE adds the features in this data set to every high-resolution graph that is produced in the PROC step.

Alias: ANNO=

Interaction: PROC UNIVARIATE does not use the ANNOTATE= data set unless you create a high-resolution graph with the HISTOGRAM, PROBPLOT, or QQPLOT statement.

Tip: Use the ANNOTATE= option in the HISTOGRAM, PROBPLOT, or QQPLOT statement if you want to add a feature to a specific graphics display.

CIBASIC<(<TYPE=*keyword***> <ALPHA=***value***>)>**

requests confidence limits for the mean, standard deviation, and variance based on the assumption that the data are normally distributed. For large sample sizes, this assumption is not required for the mean because of the Central Limit Theorem.

TYPE=*keyword*

specifies the type of confidence limit, where *keyword* is LOWER, UPPER, or TWOSIDED.

Default: TWOSIDED

ALPHA=*value*

specifies the confidence level to compute the confidence limit. The percentage for the confidence limits is $(1-value) \times 100$. For example, ALPHA=.05 results in a 95 percent confidence limit.

Default: The value of ALPHA= in the PROC statement

Range: between 0 and 1

Requirement: You must use the default value of VARDEF=, which is DF.

Main discussion: "Confidence Limits for Parameters of the Normal Distribution" on page 1393

Featured in: Example 4 on page 1428 and Example 5 on page 1432

CIPCTLDF<(<TYPE=*keyword***> <ALPHA=***value***>)>**

requests confidence limits for quantiles by using a method that is distribution-free. In other words, no specific parametric distribution such as the normal is assumed for the data. PROC UNIVARIATE uses order statistics (ranks) to compute the confidence limits as described by Hahn and Meeker (1991).

TYPE=*keyword*

specifies the type of confidence limit, where *keyword* is LOWER, UPPER, SYMMETRIC, or ASYMMETRIC.

Default: SYMMETRIC

ALPHA=*value*

specifies the confidence level to compute the confidence limit. The percentage for the confidence limits is $(1-value) \times 100$. For example, ALPHA=.05 results in a 95 percent confidence limit.

Default: The value of ALPHA= in the PROC statement

Range: between 0 and 1

Alias: CIQUANTDF

Restriction: This option is not available if you specify a WEIGHT statement.

Main discussion: "Confidence Limits for Quantiles" on page 1404

Featured in: Example 4 on page 1428

CIPCTLNORMAL <(<TYPE=*keyword*> <ALPHA=*value*>)>
requests confidence limits for quantiles based on the assumption that the data are normally distributed.

TYPE=*keyword*
specifies the type of confidence limit, where *keyword* is LOWER, UPPER, or TWOSIDED.

Default: TWOSIDED

ALPHA=*value*
specifies the confidence level to compute the confidence limit. The percentage for the confidence limits is (1–*value*) × 100. For example, ALPHA=.05 results in a 95 percent confidence limit.

Default: The value of ALPHA= in the PROC statement

Range: between 0 and 1

Alias: CIQUANTNORMAL

Requirement: You must use the default value of VARDEF=, which is DF.

Restriction: This option is not available if you specify a WEIGHT statement.

Main discussion: "Confidence Limits for Quantiles" on page 1404

Featured in: Example 5 on page 1432

DATA=*SAS-data-set*
specifies the input SAS data set.

Main discussion: "Input Data Sets" on page 18

EXCLNPWGT
excludes observations with nonpositive weight values (zero or negative) from the analysis. By default, PROC UNIVARIATE treats observations with negative weights like those with zero weights and counts them in the total number of observations.

Requirement: You must use a WEIGHT statement.

See also: "WEIGHT Statement" on page 1387

FREQ
requests a frequency table that consists of the variable values, frequencies, cell percentages, and cumulative percentages.

Interaction: If you specify the WEIGHT statement, PROC UNIVARIATE includes the weighted count in the table and uses this value to compute the percentages.

Featured in: Example 2 on page 1421

GOUT=*graphics-catalog*
specifies the SAS catalog that PROC UNIVARIATE uses to save the high-resolution graphics output.

Tip: If you omit the libref, PROC UNIVARIATE looks for the catalog in the temporary library called WORK and creates the catalog if it does not exist.

See also: For information on storing graphics output in SAS catalogs, see *SAS/ GRAPH Software: Reference*

LOCCOUNT
requests a table that shows the number of observations greater than, equal to, and less than the value of MU0=. PROC UNIVARIATE uses these values to construct the sign test and the signed rank test.

Restriction: This option is not available if you specify a WEIGHT statement.

See also: MU0= on page 1329

Featured in: Example 4 on page 1428

MODES

requests a table of all possible modes. By default, when the data contain multiple modes, PROC UNIVARIATE displays the lowest mode in the table of basic statistical measures. When all the values are unique, PROC UNIVARIATE does not produce a table of modes.

Alias: MODE

Main discussion: "Calculating the Mode" on page 1406

Featured in: Example 4 on page 1428

MU0=*value(s)*

specifies the value of the mean or location parameter (μ_o) in the null hypothesis for tests of location. If you specify one value, PROC UNIVARIATE tests the same null hypothesis for all analysis variables. If you specify multiple values, a VAR statement is required, and PROC UNIVARIATE tests a different null hypothesis for each analysis variable in the corresponding order.

Alias: LOCATION=

Default: 0

Main discussion: "Tests for Location" on page 1394

Example: The following statement tests if the mean of the first variable equals 0 and the mean of the second variable equals 0.5.

```
proc univariate mu0=0 0.5;
```

Featured in: Example 5 on page 1432

NEXTROBS=*n*

specifies the number of extreme observations that PROC UNIVARIATE lists in the table of extreme observations. The table lists the *n* lowest observations and the *n* highest observations.

Default: 5

Range: an integer between 0 and the half the maximum number of observations

Tip: Use NEXTROBS=0 to suppress the table of extreme observations.

Featured in: Example 2 on page 1421 and Example 7 on page 1439

NEXTRVAL=*n*

specifies the number of extreme values that PROC UNIVARIATE lists in the table of extreme values. The table lists the *n* lowest unique values and the *n* highest unique values.

Default: 0

Range: an integer between 0 and half the maximum number of observations

Featured in: Example 2 on page 1421

NOBYPLOT

suppresses side-by-side box plots when you use the BY statement and the ALL option or the PLOT option in the PROC statement.

NOPRINT

suppresses all the tables of descriptive statistics that the PROC UNIVARIATE statement creates. NOPRINT does not suppress the tables that the HISTOGRAM statement creates.

Tip: Use NOPRINT when you want to create an OUT= output data set only.

Featured in: Example 6 on page 1437 and Example 8 on page 1444

NORMAL

requests tests for normality that include the Shapiro-Wilk test and a series of goodness-of-fit tests based on the empirical distribution function.

Alias: NORMALTEST

Restriction: This option is not available if you specify a WEIGHT statement.

Main discussion: "Goodness-of-Fit Tests" on page 1396

Featured in: Example 5 on page 1432

PCTLDEF=*value*

specifies the definition that PROC UNIVARIATE uses to calculate quantiles.

Alias: DEF=

Default: 5

Range: 1, 2, 3, 4, 5

Restriction: You cannot use PCTLDEF= when you compute weighted quantiles.

Main discussion:

PLOTS

produces a stem-and-leaf plot (or a horizontal bar chart), a box plot, and a normal probability plot. If you use a BY statement, side-by-side box plots that are labeled **Schematic Plots** appear after the univariate analysis for the last BY group.

Alias: PLOT

Main discussion: "Generating Line Printer Plots" on page 1389

Featured in: Example 5 on page 1432 and Example 7 on page 1439

PLOTSIZE=*n*

specifies the approximate number of rows that the plots use. If n is larger than the value of the SAS system option PAGESIZE=, PROC UNIVARIATE uses the value of PAGESIZE=. If n is less than eight, PROC UNIVARIATE uses eight rows to draw the plots.

Default: the value of PAGESIZE=

Range: 8 to the value of PAGESIZE=

Featured in: Example 5 on page 1432 and Example 7 on page 1439

ROBUSTSCALE

produces a table with robust estimates of scale. The statistics include the interquartile range, Gini's mean difference, the median absolute deviation about the median (*MAD*), and two statistics proposed by Rousseeuw and Croux (1993), Q_n, and S_n.

Restriction: This option is not available if you specify a WEIGHT statement.

Main discussion: "Robust Measures of Scale" on page 1403

Featured in: Example 3 on page 1424

ROUND=*unit(s)*

specifies the units to use to round the analysis variables prior to computing statistics. If you specify one unit, PROC UNIVARIATE uses this unit to round all analysis variables. If you specify multiple units, a VAR statement is required, and each unit rounds the values of the corresponding analysis variable. If ROUND=0, no rounding occurs.

Default: 0

Tip: ROUND= reduces the number of unique variable values, thereby reducing the memory requirements.

Range: ≥ 0

Main discussion: "Rounding" on page 1388

Example: To make 1 the rounding unit for the first analysis variable and 0.5 the rounding unit for second analysis variable, submit the statement

```
proc univariate round=1 0.5;
```

Featured in: Example 2 on page 1421

TRIMMED=*value(s)* <(<TYPE=*keyword*> <ALPHA=*value*>)>
requests a table of trimmed means, where *value* specifies the number or the proportion of observations that PROC UNIVARIATE trims. If *value* is a proportion *p* between 0 and .5, the number of observations that PROC UNIVARIATE trims is the smallest integer that is greater than or equal to *np*, where *n* is the number of observations.

TYPE=*keyword*
specifies the type of confidence limit for the mean, where *keyword* is LOWER, UPPER, or TWOSIDED.

Default: TWOSIDED

ALPHA=*value*
specifies the confidence level to compute the confidence limit. The percentage for the confidence limits is (1–*value*) × 100. For example, ALPHA=.05 results in a 95 percent confidence limit.

Default: The value of ALPHA= in the PROC statement

Range: between 0 and 1

Alias: TRIM=

Range: between 0 and half the number of nonmissing observations. When a proportion is specified, *value* must be less than .5.

Requirement: To compute confidence limits for the mean and the Student's *t* test, you must use the default value of VARDEF=, which is DF.

Restriction: This option is not available if you specify a WEIGHT statement.

Main discussion "Trimmed Means" on page 1402

Featured in: Example 3 on page 1424

VARDEF=*divisor*
specifies the divisor to use in the calculation of variances and standard deviation. Table 41.1 on page 1331 shows the possible values for *divisor* and associated divisors.

Table 41.1 Possible Values for VARDEF=

Value	Divisor	Formula for Divisor
DF	degrees of freedom	$n - 1$
N	number of observations	n
WDF	sum of weights minus one	$(\Sigma_i \, w_i) - 1$
WEIGHT |WGT	sum of weights	$\Sigma_i \, w_i$

The procedure computes the variance as $CSS/divisor$, where CSS is the corrected sums of squares and equals $\sum (x_i - \overline{x})^2$. When you weight the analysis variables, CSS equals $\sum w_i (x_i - \overline{x}_w)^2$, where $\overline{x}_w$ is the weighted mean.

Default: DF

Requirement: To compute the standard error of the mean, confidence limits, and Student's *t* test, use the default value of VARDEF=.

> **Tip:** When you use the WEIGHT statement and VARDEF=DF, the variance is an estimate of σ^2, where the variance of the ith observation is $var\,(x_i) = \sigma^2/w_i$ and w_i is the weight for the ith observation. This yields an estimate of the variance of an observation with unit weight.

> **Tip:** When you use the WEIGHT statement and VARDEF=WGT, the computed variance is asymptotically (for large n) an estimate of $\sigma^2/\overline{w}$, where $\overline{w}$ is the average weight. This yields an asymptotic estimate of the variance of an observation with average weight.

> **See also:** "Keywords and Formulas" on page 1458 and "WEIGHT Statement" on page 1387

WINSORIZED=*value(s)* <(<TYPE=*keyword*> <ALPHA=*value*>)>
requests of a table of Winsorized means, where *value* is the number or the proportion of observations that PROC UNIVARIATE uses to compute the Winsorized mean. If *value* is a proportion p between 0 and .5, the number of observations that PROC UNIVARIATE uses is equal to the smallest integer that is greater than or equal to np, where n is the number of observations.

TYPE=*keyword*
  specifies the type of confidence limit for the mean, where *keyword* is LOWER, UPPER, or TWOSIDED.

  Default: TWOSIDED

ALPHA=*value*
  specifies the confidence level to compute the confidence limit. The percentage for the confidence limits is $(1-value) \times 100$. For example, ALPHA=.05 results in a 95 percent confidence limit.

  Default: The value of ALPHA= in the PROC statement

  Range: between 0 and 1

> **Alias:** WINSOR=

> **Range:** between 0 and half the number of nonmissing observations. When a proportion is specified, *value* must be less than .5.

> **Requirement:** To compute confidence limits and the Student's t test, you must use the default value of VARDEF=, which is DF.

> **Restriction:** This option is not available if you specify a WEIGHT statement.

> **Main discussion** "Winsorized Means" on page 1401

> **Featured in:** Example 3 on page 1424

BY Statement

Calculates univariate statistics separately for each BY group.

Main discussion: "BY" on page 68

Featured in: Example 7 on page 1439

BY <DESCENDING> *variable-1* <...<DESCENDING> *variable-n*><NOTSORTED>;

Required Arguments

variable

specifies the variable that the procedure uses to form BY groups. You can specify more than one variable. If you do not use the NOTSORTED option in the BY statement, the observations in the data set must either be sorted by all the variables that you specify, or they must be indexed appropriately. These variables are called *BY variables*.

Options

DESCENDING

specifies that the data set is sorted in descending order by the variable that immediately follows the word DESCENDING in the BY statement.

NOTSORTED

specifies that observations are not necessarily sorted in alphabetic or numeric order. The data are grouped in another way, for example, chronological order.

The requirement for ordering or indexing observations according to the values of BY variables is suspended for BY-group processing when you use the NOTSORTED option. In fact, the procedure does not use an index if you specify NOTSORTED. The procedure defines a BY group as a set of contiguous observations that have the same values for all BY variables. If observations with the same values for the BY variables are not contiguous, the procedure treats each contiguous set as a separate BY group.

CLASS Statement

Specifies up to two variables whose values define the classification levels for the analysis.

Interaction: When you use the HISTOGRAM, PROBPLOT, or QQPLOT statement, PROC UNIVARIATE creates comparative histograms, comparative probability plots, or comparative quantile-quantile plots.

Featured in: Example 10 on page 1450

CLASS *variable-1<(variable-option(s))>* *<variable-2<(variable-option(s))>>*
    </ **KEYLEVEL**=*'value1'* | *('value1' 'value2')>*;

Required Arguments

variable-n

specifies one or two variables that the procedure uses to group the data into classification levels. Variables in a CLASS statement are referred to as *class variables*.

Class variables can be numeric or character. Class variables can have continuous values, but they typically have a few discrete values that define levels of the variable.

You do not have to sort the data by class variables. PROC UNIVARIATE uses the formatted values of the class variables to determine the classification levels.

You can use the HISTOGRAM, PROBPLOT, or QQPLOT statement with the CLASS statement to create one-way and two-way comparative plots. When you use one class variable, PROC UNIVARIATE displays an array of component plots (stacked or side-by-side), one for each level of the classification variable. When you use two class variables, PROC UNIVARIATE displays a matrix of component plots, one for each combination of levels of the classification variables. The observations in a given level are referred to collectively as a *cell*.

Restriction: The length of a character class variable cannot exceed 16.

Interaction: When you create a one-way comparative plot, the observations in the input data set are sorted by the formatted values (levels) of the variable. PROC UNIVARIATE creates a separate plot for the analysis variable values in each level, and arranges these component plots in an array to form the comparative plot with uniform horizontal and vertical axes.

When you create a two-way comparative plot, the observations in the input data set are cross-classified according to the values (levels) of these variables. PROC UNIVARIATE creates a separate plot for the analysis variable values in each cell of the cross-classification and arranges these component plots in a matrix to form the comparative plot with uniform horizontal and vertical axes. The levels of *variable–1* are the labels for the rows of the matrix, and the levels of *variable–2* are the labels for the columns of the matrix.

Interaction: If you associate a label with a variable, PROC UNIVARIATE displays the variable label in the comparative plot and this label is parallel to the column (or row) labels.

Tip: Use the MISSING option to treat missing values as valid levels.

Tip: To reduce the number of classification levels, use a FORMAT statement to combine variable values.

Options

KEYLEVEL='value1' | ('value1' 'value2')
specifies the *key cell* in a comparative plot. PROC UNIVARIATE first determines the bin size and midpoints for the key cell, and then extends the midpoint list to accommodate the data ranges for the remaining cells. Thus, the choice of the key cell determines the uniform horizontal axis that PROC UNIVARIATE uses for all cells.

If you specify only one class variable and use a HISTOGRAM statement, KEYLEVEL='value' identifies the key cell as the level for which *variable* is equal to *value*. By default, PROC UNIVARIATE sorts the levels in the order that is determined by the ORDER= option. Then, the key cell is the first occurrence of a level in this order. The cells display in order from top to bottom or left to right. Consequently, the key cell appears at the top (or left). When you specify a different key cell with the KEYLEVEL= option, this cell appears at the top (or left).

Likewise, with the PROBPLOT statement and the QQPLOT statement the key cell determines uniform axis scaling.

If you specify two class variables, use KEYLEVEL=('value1' 'value2') to identify the key cell as the level for which *variable-n* is equal to *value-n*. By default, PROC UNIVARIATE sorts the levels of the first variable in the order that is determined by its ORDER= option and, within each of these levels, it sorts the levels of the second variable in the order that is determined by its ORDER= option. Then, the default key cell is the first occurrence of a combination of levels for the two variables in this order. The cells display in the order of *variable–1* from top to bottom and in the order of *variable–2* from left to right. Consequently, the default key cell appears at the upper left corner. When you specify a different key cell with the KEYLEVEL= option, this cell appears at the upper left corner.

Restriction: The length of the KEYLEVEL= value cannot exceed 16 characters and you must specify a formatted value.

Requirement: This option is ignored unless you specify a HISTOGRAM, PROBPLOT, or QQPLOT statement.

See also: the ORDER= option on page 1335

MISSING
specifies to treat the missing values for the class variable as valid classification levels. Special missing values that represent numeric values (the letters A through Z and the underscore (_) character) are each considered as a separate value.

Default: If you omit MISSING, PROC UNIVARIATE excludes the observations with a missing class variable value from the analysis.

Requirement: Enclose this option in parentheses after the class variable.

See also: *SAS Language Reference: Concepts* for a discussion of missing values that have special meaning.

ORDER=DATA | FORMATTED | FREQ | INTERNAL
specifies the display order for the class variable values, where

DATA
orders values according to their order in the input data set.

Interaction: When you use a HISTOGRAM, PROBPLOT, or QQPLOT statement, PROC UNIVARIATE displays the rows (columns) of the comparative plot from top to bottom (left to right) in the order that the class variable values first appear in the input data set.

FORMATTED
orders values by their ascending formatted values. This order depends on your operating environment.

Interaction: When you use a HISTOGRAM, PROBPLOT, or QQPLOT statement, PROC UNIVARIATE displays the rows (columns) of the comparative plot from top to bottom (left to right) in increasing order of the formatted class variable values. For example, a numeric class variable DAY (with values 1, 2, and 3) has a user-defined format that assigns **Wednesday** to the value 1, **Thursday** to the value 2, and **Friday** to the value 3. The rows of the comparative plot will appear in alphabetical order (Friday, Thursday, Wednesday) from top to bottom.

FREQ
orders values by descending frequency count so that levels with the most observations are listed first. If two or more values have the same frequency count, PROC UNIVARIATE uses the formatted values to determine the order.

Interaction: When you use a HISTOGRAM, PROBPLOT, or QQPLOT statement, PROC UNIVARIATE displays the rows (columns) of the comparative plot from top to bottom (left to right) in order of decreasing frequency count for the class variable values.

INTERNAL
orders values by their unformatted values, which yields the same order as PROC SORT. This order depends on your operating environment.

If there are two or more distinct internal values with the same formatted value then PROC UNIVARIATE determines the order by the internal value that occurs first in the input data set.

Interaction: When you use a HISTOGRAM, PROBPLOT, or QQPLOT statement, PROC UNIVARIATE displays the rows (columns) of the comparative plot from top to bottom (left to right) in increasing order of the internal (unformatted) values of the class variable. The first class variable is used to label the rows of the comparative plots (top to bottom). The second class variable are used to label the columns of the comparative plots (left to right). For example, a numeric class variable DAY (with values 1, 2, and 3) has a user-defined format that assigns **Wednesday** to the value 1, **Thursday** to the value 2, and **Friday** to the value 3. The rows of the comparative plot will appear in day-of-the-week order (Wednesday, Thursday, Friday) from top to bottom.

Default: INTERNAL

Requirement: Enclose this option in parentheses after the class variable.

Interaction: When you use a HISTOGRAM, PROBPLOT, or QQPLOT statement and ORDER=INTERNAL, PROC UNIVARIATE constructs the levels of the class variables by using the formatted values of the variables. The formatted values of the first class variable are used to label the rows of the comparative plots (top to bottom). The formatted values of a second class variable are used to label the columns of the comparative plots (left to right).

PROC UNIVARIATE determines the layout of a two-way comparative plot by using the order for the first class variable to obtain the order of the rows from top to bottom. Then it applies the order for the second class variable to the observations that correspond to the first row to obtain the order of the columns from left to right. If any columns remain unordered (that is, the categories are unbalanced), PROC UNIVARIATE applies the order for the second class variable to the observations in the second row, and so on, until all the columns have been ordered.

Featured in: Example 10 on page 1450

FREQ Statement

Specifies a numeric variable whose values represent the frequency of the observation.

Tip: The FREQ statement affects the degrees of freedom, but the WEIGHT statement does not.

See also: For an example that uses the FREQ statement, see "FREQ" on page 70

FREQ *variable*;

Required Arguments

variable
specifies a numeric variable whose value represents the frequency of the observation. If you use the FREQ statement, the procedure assumes that each observation represents *n* observations, where *n* is the value of *variable*. If *variable* is not an integer, the SAS System truncates it. If *variable* is less than 1 or is missing, the procedure excludes that observation from the analysis.

HISTOGRAM Statement

Creates histograms using high-resolution graphics and optionally superimposes parametric and nonparametric density curve estimates.

Alias: HIST

Tip: You can use multiple HISTOGRAM statements.

Featured in: Example 8 on page 1444 and Example 10 on page 1450

HISTOGRAM *<variable(s)> </ option(s)>*;

To do this	Use this option
Create output data set with information on histogram intervals	OUTHISTOGRAM=
Request estimated density curve	
Fit beta density with threshold parameter θ, scale parameter σ, and shape parameters α and β	BETA(*beta-suboptions*)
Fit exponential density with threshold parameter θ and scale parameter σ	EXPONENTIAL(*exponential-suboptions*)
Fit gamma density with threshold parameter θ, scale parameter σ, and shape parameter α	GAMMA(*gamma-suboptions*)
Fit nonparametric kernel density estimates	KERNEL(*kernel-suboptions*)
Fit lognormal density with threshold parameter θ, scale parameter ζ, and shape parameter σ	LOGNORMAL(*lognormal-suboptions*)
Fit normal density with mean μ and standard deviation σ	NORMAL(*normal-suboptions*)
Fit Weibull density with threshold parameter θ, scale parameter σ, and shape parameter c	WEIBULL(*Weibull-suboptions*)
Parametric density curve suboptions	
Specify shape parameter α for fitted beta or gamma curve	ALPHA=
Specify second shape parameter β for beta fitted curve	BETA=
Specify shape parameter c for fitted Weibull curve	C=
Specify the mean μ for fitted normal curve	MU=
Specify scale parameter σ for the fitted beta curve, exponential curve, gamma curve and Weibull curve; standard deviation σ for fitted normal curve; or the scale parameter σ for the fitted lognormal curve	SIGMA=
Specify threshold parameter θ for fitted beta curve, exponential curve, gamma curve, lognormal curve, and Weibull curve	THETA=

To do this	Use this option
Specify scale parameter ζ for fitted lognormal curve	ZETA=
Nonparametric density curve suboptions	
Specify standardized bandwidth parameter c for fitted kernel density estimates	C=
Specify type of kernel density curve	K=
Control appearance of fitted density curves	
Specify color of fitted curve	COLOR=
Fill area under fitted curve	FILL
Specify line type of fitted curve	L=
Display table of histogram interval midpoints	MIDPERCENTS
Suppress the table summarizing the fitted curve	NOPRINT
List percentages for calculated and estimated quantiles	PERCENTS=
Specify width of fitted density curve	W=
Control general histogram layout	
Specify width for the bars	BARWIDTH=
Force creation of a histogram	FORCEHIST
Create a grid	GRID
Specify offset for horizontal axis	HOFFSET=
Specify reference lines perpendicular to the horizontal axis	HREF=
Specify labels for HREF= lines	HREFLABELS=
Specify vertical position of labels for HREF= lines	HREFLABPOS=
Specify a line style for grid lines	LGRID=
List percentages for histogram intervals	MIDPOINTS=
Suppress histogram bars	NOBARS
Suppress frame around plotting area	NOFRAME
Suppress label for horizontal axis	NOHLABEL
Suppress plot	NOPLOT
Suppress label for vertical axis	NOVLABEL
Suppress tick marks and tick mark labels for vertical axis	NOVTICK
Include right endpoint in interval	RTINCLUDE
Turn and vertically string out characters in labels for vertical axis	TURNVLABELS
Specify tick mark values for vertical axis	VAXIS=
Specify label for vertical axis	VAXISLABEL=
Specify length of offset at upper end of vertical axis	VOFFSET=

To do this	Use this option
Specify reference lines perpendicular to the vertical axis	VREF=
Specify labels for VREF= lines	VREFLABELS=
Specify horizontal position of labels for VREF= lines	VREFLABPOS=
Specify scale for vertical axis	VSCALE=
Specify line thickness for axes and frame	WAXIS=
Specify line thickness for grid	WGRID=
Enhance the graph	
Specify annotate data set	ANNOTATE=
Specify color for axis	CAXIS=
Specify color of outlines of histogram bars	CBARLINE=
Specify color for filling under curve	CFILL=
Specify color for frame	CFRAME=
Specify color for grid lines	CGRID=
Specify color for HREF= lines	CHREF=
Specify color for text	CTEXT=
Specify color for VREF= lines	CVREF=
Specify description for plot in graphics catalog	DESCRIPTION=
Specify software font for text	FONT=
Specify height of text used outside framed areas	HEIGHT=
Specify number of horizontal minor tick marks	HMINOR=
Specify software font for text inside framed areas	INFONT=
Specify height of text inside framed areas	INHEIGHT=
Specify line style for HREF= lines	LHREF=
Specify line style for VREF= lines	LVREF=
Specify name for plot in graphics catalog	NAME=
Specify pattern for filling under curve	PFILL=
Specify number of vertical minor tick marks	VMINOR=
Specify line thickness for bar outlines	WBARLINE=
Enhance comparative histograms	
Apply annotation requested in ANNOTATE= data set to key cell only	ANNOKEY
Specify color for filling frame for row labels	CFRAMESIDE=
Specify color for filling frame for column labels	CFRAMETOP=
Specify color for proportion of frequency bar	CPROP=
Specify distance between tiles	INTERTILE=
Specify maximum number of bins to display	MAXNBIN=

To do this	Use this option
Limit the number of bins that display to within a specified number of standard deviations above and below mean of data in key cell	MAXSIGMAS=
Specify number of columns in comparative histogram	NCOLS=
Specify number of rows in comparative histogram	NROWS=

Arguments

variable(s)

identifies one or more analysis variables that the procedure uses to create histograms.

Default: If you omit *variable(s)* in the HISTOGRAM statement, then the procedure creates a histogram for each variable that you list in the VAR statement, or for each numeric variable in the DATA= data set if you omit a VAR statement.

Requirement: If you specify a VAR statement, use a subset of the *variable(s)* that you list in the VAR statement. Otherwise, *variable(s)* are any numeric variables in the DATA= data set.

Options

ALPHA=*value*

specifies the shape parameter α for fitted density curves when you request the BETA and GAMMA options.

Alias: A= if you use it as a *beta-suboption*. SHAPE= if you use it as a *gamma-suboption*

Default: a maximum likelihood estimate

Requirement: Enclose this suboption in parentheses after the BETA option or GAMMA option.

ANNOKEY

specifies to apply the annotation requested with the ANNOTATE= option to the *key cell* only. By default, PROC UNIVARIATE applies annotation to all of the cells.

Requirement: This option is ignored unless you specify the CLASS statement.

Tip: Use the KEYLEVEL= option in the CLASS statement to specify the key cell.

See also: the KEYLEVEL= option on page 1334

ANNOTATE=*SAS-data-set*

specifies an input data set that contains annotate variables as described in *SAS/ GRAPH Software: Reference*.

Alias: ANNO=

Tip: You can also specify an ANNOTATE= data set in the PROC UNIVARIATE statement to enhance all the graphic displays that the procedure creates.

See also: ANNOTATE= on page 1327 in the PROC UNIVARIATE statement

BARWIDTH=*value*

specifies the width of the histogram bars in screen percent units.

BETA<(*beta-suboptions***)>**

displays a fitted beta density curve on the histogram.

Restriction: The BETA option can occur only once in a HISTOGRAM statement.

Interaction: The beta distribution is bounded below by the parameter θ and above by the value $\theta + \sigma$. Use the THETA= and SIGMA= suboptions to specify these parameters. The default values for THETA= and SIGMA= are 0 and 1, respectively. You can specify THETA=EST and SIGMA=EST to request maximum likelihood estimates for θ and σ.

Note: Three- and four-parameter maximum likelihood estimation may not always converge. △

Interaction: The beta distribution has two shape parameters, α and β. If these parameters are known, you can specify their values with the ALPHA= and BETA= options. By default, PROC UNIVARIATE computes maximum likelihood estimates for α and β.

Main Discussion: See "Beta Distribution" on page 1406

See also: the ALPHA= suboption on page 1340, BETA= suboption on page 1341, SIGMA= suboption on page 1350, and THETA= suboption on page 1350

BETA=*value*

specifies the second shape parameter β for the fitted beta density curves when you request the BETA option.

Alias: B=

Default: a maximum likelihood estimate

Requirement: Enclose this suboption in parentheses after the BETA option.

C=*value*

specifies the shape parameter c for the fitted Weibull density curve when you request the WEIBULL option.

Default: a maximum likelihood estimate

Requirement: Enclose this suboption in parentheses after the WEIBULL option.

C=*value(s)*|MISE

specifies the standardized bandwidth parameter c for kernel density estimates when you request the KERNEL option.

Default: the bandwidth that minimizes the approximate MISE.

Restriction: You can specify up to five values to request multiple estimates.

Requirement: Enclose this suboption in parentheses after the KERNEL option.

Interaction: You can also use the C= suboption with the K= suboption, which specifies the kernel function, to compute multiple estimates. If you specify more kernel functions than bandwidths, PROC UNIVARIATE repeats the last bandwidth in the list for the remaining estimates. Likewise, if you specify more bandwidths than kernel functions, then PROC UNIVARIATE repeats the last kernel function for the remaining estimates. For example, the following statements compute three density estimates:

```
proc univariate;
   var length;
   histogram length / kernel(c=1 2 3 k=normal quadratic);
   run;
```

The first uses a normal kernel and a bandwidth of 1, the second uses a quadratic kernel and a bandwidth of 2, and the third uses a quadratic kernel and a bandwidth of 3.

Tip: To estimate a bandwidth that minimizes the approximate mean integrated square error (MISE) use the C=MISE suboption. For example, the following statements compute three density estimates:

```
proc univariate;
  var length;
  histogram length / kernel(c=0.5 1.0 mise);
  run;
```

The first two estimates have standardized bandwidths of 0.5 and 1.0, respectively, and the third has a bandwidth that minimizes the approximate MISE.

CAXIS=*color*

specifies the color for the axes and tick marks.

Alias: CAXES= and CA=

Default: the first color in the device color list

CBARLINE=*color*

specifies the color for the outline of the histogram bars.

Default: the first color in the device color list

Featured in: Example 8 on page 1444

CFILL=*color*

specifies the color to fill the bars of the histogram (or the area under a fitted density curve if you also specify the FILL option).

See also: FILL option on page 1343 and PFILL=option on page 1350

Featured in: Example 8 on page 1444 and Example 10 on page 1450

CFRAME=*color*

specifies the color for the area that is enclosed by the axes and frame.

Alias: CRF=

Default: The area is not filled.

CFRAMESIDE=*color*

specifies the color to fill the frame area for the row labels that display along the left side of the comparative histogram. This color also fills the frame area for the label of the corresponding class variable (if you associate a label with the variable).

Default: These areas are not filled.

Requirement: This option is ignored unless you specify the CLASS statement.

CFRAMETOP=*color*

specifies the color to fill the frame area for the column labels that display across the top of the comparative histogram. This color also fills the frame area for the label of the corresponding class variable (if you associate a label with the variable).

Default: These areas are not filled.

Requirement: This option is ignored unless you specify the CLASS statement.

CGRID=*color*

specifies the color for grid lines when a grid displays on the histogram.

Default: the first color in the device color list

Interaction: This option automatically invokes the GRID= option.

CHREF=*color*

specifies the color for horizontal axis reference lines when you specify the HREF= option.

Default: the first color in the device color list

COLOR=*color*

specifies the color of the density curve.

Requirement: You must enclose this suboption in parentheses after the density curve option or the KERNEL option.

Interaction: You can specify as a KERNEL suboption a list of up to five colors in parentheses for multiple kernel density estimates. If there are more estimates than colors, the remaining estimates use the last color that you specify.

CPROP=*color*| EMPTY
specifies the color for a horizontal bar whose length (relative to the width of the tile) indicates the proportion of the total frequency that is represented by the corresponding cell in a comparative histogram.

Default: bars do not display

Requirement: This option is ignored unless you specify the CLASS statement.

Tip: Use the keyword EMPTY to display empty bars.

CTEXT=*color*
specifies the color for tick mark values and axis labels.

Alias: CT=

Default: The color that you specify for the CTEXT= option in the GOPTIONS statement. If you omit the GOPTIONS statement, the default is the first color in the device color list.

CVREF=*color*
specifies the color for the reference lines that you request with the VREF= option.

Alias: CV=

Default: the first color in the device color list

DESCRIPTION=*'string'*
specifies a description, up to 40 characters long, that appears in the PROC GREPLAY master menu.

Alias: DES=

Default: the variable name

EXPONENTIAL<(*exponential-suboptions*)>
displays a fitted exponential density curve on the histogram.

Alias EXP

Restriction: The EXPONENTIAL option can occur only once in a HISTOGRAM statement.

Interaction: The parameter θ must be less than or equal to the minimum data value. Use the THETA= suboption to specify θ. The default value for θ is zero. Specify THETA=EST to request the maximum likelihood estimate for θ.

Interaction: Use the SIGMA= suboption to specify σ. By default, PROC UNIVARIATE computes a maximum likelihood estimate for σ. For example, the following statements fit an exponential curve with $\theta = 10$ and with a maximum likelihood estimate for σ:

```
proc univariate;
   var length;
   histogram / exponential(theta=10 l=2 color=red);
run;
```

Main discussion: See "Exponential Distribution" on page 1407

See also: the SIGMA= suboption on page 1350 and THETA= suboption on page 1350

Featured in: Example 8 on page 1444

FILL
fills areas under the fitted density curve or the kernel density estimate with colors and patterns.

Restriction: The FILL suboption can occur with only one fitted curve.

Requirement: Enclose the FILL suboption in parentheses after a density curve option or the KERNEL option.

Interaction: The CFILL= and PFILL= options specify the color and pattern for the area under the curve.

See also: For a list of available colors and patterns, see *SAS/GRAPH Software: Reference*

Featured in: Example 8 on page 1444

FONT=*font*
specifies a software font for the axis labels.

Default: hardware characters

Interaction: The FONT= *font* takes precedence over the FTEXT= *font* that you specify in the GOPTIONS statement.

FORCEHIST
forces PROC UNIVARIATE to create a histogram when there is only one unique observation. By default, if the standard deviation of the data is zero then PROC UNIVARIATE does not create a histogram.

GAMMA<(*gamma-suboptions*)>
displays a fitted gamma density curve on the histogram.

Restriction: The GAMMA option can occur only once in a HISTOGRAM statement.

Interaction: The parameter θ must be less than the minimum data value. Use the THETA= suboption to specify θ. The default value for θ is zero. Specify THETA=EST to request the maximum likelihood estimate for θ.

Interaction: Use the ALPHA= and the SIGMA= suboptions to specify the shape parameter α and the scale parameter σ. By default, PROC UNIVARIATE computes maximum likelihood estimates for α and σ. For example, the following statements fit a gamma curve with $\theta = 4$ and with a maximum likelihood estimate for α and σ:

```
proc univariate;
   var length;
   histogram length/ gamma(theta=4);
run;
```

PROC UNIVARIATE calculates the maximum likelihood estimate of α iteratively using the Newton-Raphson approximation.

Main discussion: See "Gamma Distribution" on page 1407

See also: the SIGMA= suboption on page 1350, ALPHA= suboption on page 1340, and the THETA= suboption on page 1350

GRID
specifies to display a grid on the histogram. Grid lines are horizontal lines that are positioned at major tick marks on the vertical axis.

See also: the CGRID= option on page 1342

HEIGHT=*value*
specifies the height in percentage screen units of text for axis labels, tick mark labels, and legends. This option takes precedence over the HTEXT= option in the GOPTIONS statement.

HMINOR=*n*
specifies the number of minor tick marks between each major tick mark on the horizontal axis. PROC UNIVARIATE does not label minor tick marks.

Alias: HM=

Default: 0

HOFFSET=*value*

specifies the offset in percentage screen units at both ends of the horizontal axis.

Tip: Use HOFFSET=0 to eliminate the default offset.

HREF=*value(s)*

draws reference lines that are perpendicular to the horizontal axis at the values that you specify.

See also: CHREF= option on page 1342 and LHREF= option on page 1346.

HREFLABELS=*'label1' ... 'labeln'*

specifies labels for the reference lines that you request with the HREF= option.

Alias: HREFLABEL= and HREFLAB=

Restriction: The number of labels must equal the number of reference lines. Labels can have up to 16 characters.

HREFLABPOS=*n*

specifies the vertical position of HREFLABELS= labels, where *n* is

1	positions the labels along the top of the histogram
2	staggers the labels from top to bottom
3	positions the labels along the bottom.

Default: 1

INFONT=*font*

specifies a software font to use for text inside the framed areas of the histogram. The INFONT= option takes precedence over the FTEXT= option in the GOPTIONS statement.

See also: For a list of fonts, see *SAS/GRAPH Software: Reference*.

INHEIGHT=*value*

specifies the height, in percentage screen units of text, to use inside the framed areas of the histogram.

Default: The height that you specify with the HEIGHT= option. If you do not specify the HEIGHT= option, the default height is the height that you specify with the HTEXT= option in the GOPTIONS statement.

INTERTILE=*value*

specifies the distance in horizontal percentage screen units between the framed areas, which are called *tiles*.

Default: .75 in percentage screen units.

Requirement: This option is ignored unless you specify the CLASS statement.

Featured in: Example 10 on page 1450

K=NORMAL | QUADRATIC | TRIANGULAR

specifies the kernel function (normal, quadratic, or triangular) that PROC UNIVARIATE uses to compute a kernel density estimate.

Default: normal kernel

Restriction: You can specify up to five values to request multiple estimates.

Requirement: You must enclose this suboption in parentheses after the KERNEL option.

Interaction: You can also use the K= suboption with the C= suboption, which specifies standardized bandwidths. If you specify more kernel functions than bandwidths, PROC UNIVARIATE repeats the last bandwidth in the list for the remaining estimates. Likewise, if you specify more bandwidths than kernel functions, PROC UNIVARIATE repeats the last kernel function for the remaining estimates. For example, the following statements compute three estimates with bandwidths of 0.5, 1.0, and 1.5:

```
proc univariate;
   var length;
   histogram length / kernel(c=0.5 1.0 1.5 k=normal quadratic);
run;
```

The first estimate uses a normal kernel, and the last two estimates use a quadratic kernel.

KERNEL<(*kernel-suboptions*)>

superimposes up to five kernel density estimates on the histogram. By default, PROC UNIVARIATE uses the AMISE method to compute kernel density estimates.

Tip: To request multiple kernel density estimates on the same histogram, specify a list of values for either the C= suboption or K= suboption.

Main discussion: "Kernel Density Estimates" on page 1410

See also: C= suboption on page 1341 and K= suboption on page 1345

L=*linetype*

specifies the line type for a fitted density curve or kernel density estimate curve.

Default: 1, which produces a solid line.

Requirement: You must enclose the L= suboption in parentheses after a density curve option or the KERNEL option.

Interaction: If you use the L= suboption with the KERNEL option, you can specify a single line type or a list of line types.

See also: For a list of available line types, see *SAS/GRAPH Software: Reference*

Featured in: Example 8 on page 1444

LGRID=*linetype*

specifies the line type for the grid when a grid displays on the histogram.

Default: 1, which produces a solid line

Interaction: This option automatically invokes the GRID= option.

LHREF=*linetype*

specifies the line type for the reference lines that you request with the HREF= option.

Alias: LH=

Default: 2, which produces a dashed line

LOGNORMAL<(*lognormal-suboptions*)>

displays a fitted lognormal density curve on the histogram.

Restriction: The LOGNORMAL option can occur only once in a HISTOGRAM statement.

Interaction: The parameter θ must be less than the minimum data value. Use the THETA= suboption to specify θ. The default value for θ is zero. Specify THETA=EST to request the maximum likelihood estimate for θ.

Interaction: Use the SIGMA= and ZETA= suboptions to specify σ and ζ. By default, PROC UNIVARIATE computes a maximum likelihood estimate for σ and ζ. For example, the following statements fit a lognormal distribution function with a default value of $\theta = 0$ and with maximum likelihood estimates for σ and ζ:

```
proc univariate;
   var length;
```

```
      histogram length/ lognormal;
   run;
```

Main discussion: See "Lognormal Distribution" on page 1408

See also: the ZETA= suboption on page 1352, SIGMA= suboption on page 1350, and THETA= suboption on page 1350

LVREF=*linetype*

specifies the line type for the reference lines that you request with the VREF= option.

Alias: LV=

Default: 2, which produces a dashed line

MAXNBIN=*n*

specifies the maximum number of bins in the comparative histogram that display. This option is useful when the scales or ranges of the data distributions differ greatly from cell to cell.

By default, PROC UNIVARIATE determines the bin size and midpoints for the key cell, and then extends the midpoint list to accommodate the data ranges for the remaining cells. However, if the cell scales differ considerably, the resulting number of bins may be so great that each cell histogram is scaled into a narrow region. By using MAXNBIN= to limit the number of bins, you can narrow the window about the data distribution in the key cell.

Requirement: This option is ignored unless you specify the CLASS statement.

Tip: MAXNBIN= provides an alternative to the MAXSIGMAS= option.

MAXSIGMAS=*value*

specifies to limit the number of bins in the comparative histogram that display to a range of *value* standard deviations (of the data in the key cell) above and below the mean of the data in the key cell. This option is useful when the scales or ranges of the data distributions differ greatly from cell to cell.

By default, PROC UNIVARIATE determines the bin size and midpoints for the key cell, and then extends the midpoint list to accommodate the data ranges for the remaining cells. However, if the cell scales differ considerably, the resulting number of bins may be so great that each cell histogram is scaled into a narrow region. By using MAXSIGMAS= to limit the number of bins, you can narrow the window that surrounds the data distribution in the key cell.

Requirement: This option is ignored unless you specify the CLASS statement.

MIDPERCENTS

requests a table that lists the midpoints and percentage of observations in each histogram interval.

Interaction: If you specify MIDPERCENTS in parentheses after a density estimate option, PROC UNIVARIATE displays a table that lists the midpoints, the observed percentage of observations, and the estimated percentage of the population in each interval (estimated from the fitted distribution).

MIDPOINTS=*value(s)* | KEY | UNIFORM

specifies how to determine the midpoints for the histogram intervals, where

value(s)

determines the width of the histogram bars as the difference between consecutive midpoints. PROC UNIVARIATE uses the same *value(s)* for all variables.

Range: The range of midpoints, extended at each end by half of the bar width, must cover the range of the data. For example, if you specify

```
   midpoints=2 to 10 by 0.5
```

then all of the observations should fall between 1.75 and 10.25.

Requirement: You must use evenly spaced midpoints which you list in increasing order.

KEY

determines the midpoints for the data in the key cell. The initial number of midpoints is based on the number of observations in the key cell that use the method of Terrell and Scott (1985). PROC UNIVARIATE extends the midpoint list for the key cell in either direction as necessary until it spans the data in the remaining cells.

Requirement: This option is ignored unless you specify the CLASS statement.

UNIFORM

determines the midpoints by using all the observations as if there were no cells. In other words, the number of midpoints is based on the total sample size by using the method of Terrell and Scott (1985).

Requirement: This option does not apply unless you specify the CLASS statement.

Default: If you use a CLASS statement, MIDPOINTS=KEY; however, if the key cell is empty then MIDPOINTS=UNIFORM. Otherwise, PROC UNIVARIATE computes the midpoints by using an algorithm (Terrell and Scott, 1985) that is primarily applicable to continuous data that are approximately normally distributed.

Featured in: Example 8 on page 1444 and Example 10 on page 1450

MU=*value*

specifies the parameter μ for normal density curves.

Default: the sample mean

Requirement: You must enclose this suboption in parentheses after the NORMAL option.

NAME='*string*'

specifies a name for the plot, up to eight characters long, that appears in the PROC GREPLAY master menu.

Default: UNIVAR

NCOLS=*n*

specifies the number of columns in the comparative histogram.

Alias: NCOL=

Default: NCOLS=1, if you specify only one class variable, and NCOLS=2, if you specify two class variables.

Requirement: This option is ignored unless you specify the CLASS statement.

Interaction: If you specify two class variables, you can use the NCOLS= option with the NROWS= option.

Featured in: Example 10 on page 1450

NOBARS

suppresses drawing of histogram bars.

Tip: Use this option to display only the fitted curves.

NOFRAME

suppresses the frame that surrounds the subplot area.

NOHLABEL

suppresses the label for the horizontal axis.

Tip: Use this option to reduce clutter.

NOPLOT

suppresses the creation of a plot.

Alias: NOCHART

Tip: Use NOPLOT when you want to display only descriptive statistics for a fitted density or create an OUTHISTOGRAM= data set.

NOPRINT
suppresses the table of statistics that summarizes the fitted density curve.

Requirement: Enclose this option in the parentheses that follow the density curve option.

Featured in: Example 8 on page 1444

NORMAL<(*normal-suboptions*)>
displays a fitted lognormal density curve on the histogram.

Restriction: The NORMAL option can occur only once in a HISTOGRAM statement.

Interaction: Use the MU= and SIGMA= suboptions to specify μ and σ. By default, PROC UNIVARIATE uses the sample mean and sample standard deviation for μ and σ.

Main discussion: See "Normal Distribution" on page 1409

See also: the MU= suboption on page 1348 and the SIGMA= suboption on page 1350

Featured in: Example 8 on page 1444

NOVLABEL
suppresses the label for the vertical axis.

NOVTICK
suppresses the tick marks and tick mark labels for the vertical axis.

Interaction: This option automatically invokes the NOVLABEL option.

NROWS=*n*
specifies the number of rows in the comparative histogram.

Alias: NROW=

Default: 2

Requirement: This option is ignored unless you specify the CLASS statement.

Interaction: If you specify two class variables, you can use the NCOLS= option with the NROWS= option.

Featured in: Example 10 on page 1450

OUTHISTOGRAM=*SAS-data-set*
creates a SAS data set that contains information about histogram intervals. Specifically, the data set contains the midpoints of the histogram intervals, the observed percentage of observations in each interval, and the estimated percentage of observations in each interval (estimated from each of the specified fitted curves).

Alias: OUTHIST=

See also: "OUTHISTOGRAM= Data Set" on page 1417

PERCENTS=*value(s)*
specifies a list of percentages that PROC UNIVARIATE uses to calculate quantiles from the data and to estimate quantiles from the fitted density curve.

Alias: PERCENT=

Default: 1, 5, 10, 25, 50, 75, 90, 95, and 99 percent

Range: between 0 and 100

Requirement: You must enclose this suboption in parentheses after the curve option.

PFILL=*pattern*

specifies a pattern to fill the bars of the histograms (or the areas that are under a fitted density curve if you also specify the FILL option).

Default: The bars and curve areas are not filled.

See also: CFILL= option on page 1342 and FILL option on page 1343

See also: *SAS/GRAPH Software: Reference*

RTINCLUDE

includes the right endpoint of each histogram interval in that interval. By default, PROC UNIVARIATE includes the left endpoint in the histogram interval.

SCALE=*value*

is an alias for the SIGMA= suboption when you request density curves with the BETA, EXPONENTIAL, GAMMA, and WEIBULL options and an alias for the ZETA= suboption when you request density curves with the LOGNORMAL option.

See also: SIGMA= suboption on page 1350 and ZETA= suboption on page 1352

SHAPE=*value*

is an alias for the ALPHA= suboption when you request gamma curves with the GAMMA option, the SIGMA= suboption when you request lognormal curves with the LOGNORMAL option, and the C= suboption when you request Weibull curves with the WEIBULL option.

See also: ALPHA suboption on page 1340, SIGMA suboption on page 1350, and C= suboption on page 1341

SIGMA=*value***|EST**

specifies the parameter σ for the fitted density curve when you request the BETA, EXPONENTIAL, GAMMA, LOGNORMAL, NORMAL, and WEIBULL options. See Table 41.2 on page 1350 for a summary of how to use the SIGMA= suboption.

Default: see Table 41.2 on page 1350

Requirement: You must enclose this suboption in parentheses after the density curve option.

Tip: As a BETA suboption, you can specify SIGMA=EST to request a maximum likelihood estimate for σ.

Table 41.2 Uses of the SIGMA suboption

Distribution Keyword	SIGMA= Specifies	Default Value	Alias
BETA	scale parameter σ	1	SCALE=
EXPONENTIAL	scale parameter σ	maximum likelihood estimate	SCALE=
GAMMA	scale parameter σ	maximum likelihood estimate	SCALE=
WEIBULL	scale parameter σ	maximum likelihood estimate	SCALE=
LOGNORMAL	shape parameter σ	maximum likelihood estimate	SCALE=
NORMAL	scale parameter σ	standard deviation	SHAPE=

THETA=*value***|EST**

specifies the lower threshold parameter θ for the fitted density curve when you request the BETA, EXPONENTIAL, GAMMA, LOGNORMAL, and WEIBULL options.

Default: 0

Requirement: You must enclose this suboption in parentheses after the curve option.

Tip: To compute a maximum likelihood estimate for θ, specify THETA=EST.

THRESHOLD= *value*

is an alias for the THETA= option. See the THETA= suboption on page 1350.

TURNVLABELS

specifies that PROC UNIVARIATE turn the characters in the vertical axis labels so that they display vertically. This happens by default when you use a hardware font.

Alias: TURNVLABEL

VAXIS= *value(s)*

specifies tick mark values for the vertical axis.

Requirement: Use evenly spaced values which you list in increasing order. The first value must be zero and the last value must be greater than or equal to the height of the largest bar. You must scale the values in the same units as the bars.

See also: the VSCALE= option on page 1351

Featured in: Example 10 on page 1450

VAXISLABEL= *'label'*

specifies a label for the vertical axis.

Requirement: Labels can have up to 40 characters.

Featured in: Example 10 on page 1450

VMINOR= *n*

specifies the number of minor tick marks between each major tick mark on the vertical axis. PROC UNIVARIATE does not label minor tick marks.

Alias: VM=

Default: 0

VOFFSET= *value*

specifies the offset in percentage screen units at the upper end of the vertical axis.

VREF= *value(s)*

draws reference lines that are perpendicular to the vertical axis at the *value(s)* that you specify.

See also: CVREF= option on page 1343 and LVREF= option on page 1347.

VREFLABELS= *' label1'... 'labeln'*

specifies labels for the reference lines that you request with the VREF= option.

Alias: VREFLABEL= and VREFLAB=

Restriction: The number of labels must equal the number of reference lines. Labels can have up to 16 characters.

VREFLABPOS= *n*

specifies the horizontal position of VREFLABELS= labels, where *n* is

1	positions the labels at the left of the histogram.
2	positions the labels at the right of the histogram.

Default: 1

VSCALE= *scale*

specifies the scale of the vertical axis, where *scale* is

COUNT

scales the data in units of the number of observations per data unit.

PERCENT

scales the data in units of percentage of observations per data unit.

PROPORTION

scales the data in units of proportion of observations per data unit.

Default: PERCENT

Featured in: Example 10 on page 1450

W=*n*

specifies the width in pixels of the fitted density curve or the kernel density estimate curve.

Default: 1

Requirement: You must enclose this suboption in parentheses after the density curve option or the KERNEL option.

Interaction: As a KERNEL suboption, you can specify a list of up to five W= values.

WAXIS=*n*

specifies the line thickness (in pixels) for the axes and frame.

Default: 1

WBARLINE=*n*

specifies the line thickness for the histogram bar outlines.

Default: 1

WEIBULL<(*Weibull-suboptions*)>

displays a fitted Weibull density curve on the histogram.

Restriction: The WEIBULL option can occur only once in a HISTOGRAM statement.

Interaction: The parameter θ must be less than the minimum data value. Use the THETA= suboption to specify θ. The default value for θ is zero. Specify THETA=EST to request the maximum likelihood estimate for θ.

Interaction: Use ALPHA= and the SIGMA= suboptions to specify the shape parameter c and the scale parameter σ. By default, PROC UNIVARIATE computes the maximum likelihood estimates for c and σ. For example, the following statements fit a Weibull curve with $\theta = 15$ and with a maximum likelihood estimate for c and σ:

```
proc univariate;
   var length;
   histogram length/ weibull(theta=4);
run;
```

PROC UNIVARIATE calculates the maximum likelihood estimate of α iteratively by using the Newton-Raphson approximation.

Main discussion: See "Weibull Distribution" on page 1409

See also: the C= suboption on page 1341, SIGMA= suboption on page 1350, and THETA= suboption on page 1350

WGRID=*n*

specifies the line thickness for the grid.

ZETA= *value*

specifies a value for the scale parameter ζ for the lognormal density curve when you request the LOGNORMAL option.

Default: a maximum likelihood estimate

> **Requirement:** You must enclose this suboption in parentheses after the
> LOGNORMAL option.

ID Statement

Identifies the extreme observations in the table of extreme observations.

Featured in: Example 2 on page 1421

ID *variable(s)*;

Required Arguments

variable(s)
    specifies one or more variables to include in the table of extreme observations. The
    corresponding values of the ID variables appear beside the n largest and n smallest
    observations, where n is the value of NEXTROBS= option.

    See also: NEXTROBS= on page 1329

INSET Statement

Places a box or table of summary statistics, called an *inset*, directly in the high-resolution graph.

Requirement: The INSET statement must follow the HISTOGRAM, PROBPLOT, or
QQPLOT statement that creates the plot that you want to augment. The inset appears
in all the graphs that the preceding plot statement produces.

Tip: You can use multiple INSET statements.

Featured in: Example 9 on page 1448 and Example 10 on page 1450

INSET *<keyword(s)* DATA=*SAS-data-set> </ option(s)>*;

Arguments

keyword(s)
    specifies one or more keywords that identify the information to display in the inset.
    PROC UNIVARIATE displays the information in the order that you request the
    keywords.
       You can specify statistical keywords, primary keywords, and secondary keywords.
    The available statistical keywords are

Descriptive statistic keywords

CSS	CV	KURTOSIS
MAX	MEAN	N
MIN	MODE	RANGE
NMISS	NOBS	STDMEAN
SKEWNESS	STD	USS
SUM	SUMWGT	VAR

Quantile statistic keywords

MEDIAN	P1	P5
P10	P90	P95
P99	Q1	Q3
QRANGE		

Robust statistic keywords

GINI	MAD	QN
SN	STD_GINI	STD_MAD
STD_QN	STD_QRANGE	STD_SN

Hypothesis testing keywords

MSIGN	PROBM	PROBT
NORMALTEST	PROBN	SIGNRANK
PNORMAL	PROBS	T

A *primary keyword* allows you to specify *secondary keywords* in parentheses immediately after the primary keyword. Primary keywords are BETA, EXPONENTIAL, GAMMA, LOGNORMAL, NORMAL, WEIBULL, WEIBULL2, KERNEL, and KERNELn. If you specify a primary keyword but omit a secondary keyword, the inset displays a colored line and the distribution name as a key for the density curve. For a list of the secondary keywords, see Table 41.3 on page 1354.

By default, PROC UNIVARIATE identifies inset statistics with appropriate labels and prints numeric values using appropriate formats. To customize the label, specify the keyword followed by an equal sign (=) and the desired label in quotes. To customize the format, specify a numeric format in parentheses after the keyword. Labels can have up to 24 characters. If you specify both a label and a format for a statistic, the label must appear before the format. For example,

```
inset n='Sample Size' std='Std Dev' (5.2);
```

requests customized labels for two statistics and displays the standard deviation with field width of 5 and two decimal places.

Table 41.3   Available Secondary Keywords

Keyword	Alias	Description
For BETA primary keyword		
ALPHA	SHAPE1	first shape parameter α

Keyword	Alias	Description
BETA	SHAPE2	second shape parameter β
SIGMA	SCALE	scale parameter σ
THETA	THRESHOLD	lower threshold parameter θ

For EXP primary keyword

SIGMA	SCALE	scale parameter σ
THETA	THRESHOLD	threshold parameter θ

For GAMMA primary keyword

ALPHA	SHAPE	shape parameter α
SIGMA	SCALE	scale parameter σ
THETA	THRESHOLD	threshold parameter θ

For LOGNORMAL primary keyword

SIGMA	SHAPE	shape parameter σ
THETA	THRESHOLD	threshold parameter θ
ZETA	SCALE	scale parameter ζ

For NORMAL primary keyword

MU	MEAN	mean parameter μ
SIGMA	STD	shape parameter σ

For WEIBULL primary keyword

C	SHAPE	shape parameter c
SIGMA	SCALE	scale parameter σ
THETA	THRESHOLD	threshold parameter θ

For WEIBULL2 primary keyword

C	SHAPE	shape parameter c
SIGMA	SCALE	scale parameter σ
THETA	THRESHOLD	known lower threshold parameter θ_0

For any parametric distribution primary keyword*

AD		Anderson-Darling EDF test statistic
ADPVAL		Anderson-Darling EDF test p-value
CVM		Cramer-von Mises EDF test statistic
CVMPVAL		Cramer-von Mises EDF test p-value
KSD		Kolmogorov-Smirnov EDF test statistic
KSDPVAL		Kolmogorov-Smirnov EDF test p-value

For KERNEL or KERNEL*n* primary keyword*

TYPE		kernel type: normal, quadratic, or triangular

Keyword	Alias	Description
BANDWIDTH	BWIDTH	bandwidth λ for the density estimate
C		standardized bandwidth c for the density estimate: $c = \frac{\lambda}{Q} n^{\frac{1}{5}}$ where n =sample size, λ =bandwidth, and Q =interquartile range
AMISE		approximate mean integrated square error (MISE) for the kernel density

* Available with only the HISTOGRAM statement and a BETA, EXPONENTIAL, LOGNORMAL, NORMAL, or WEIBULL distribution.

Requirement: Some inset statistics are not available unless you request a plot statement and options that calculate these statistics. For example:

```
proc univariate data=score;
    histogram final / normal;
    inset mean std normal(ad adpval);
run;
```

The MEAN and STD keywords display the sample mean and standard deviation of FINAL. The NORMAL keyword with the *secondary keywords* AD and ADPVAL display the Anderson-Darling goodness-of-fit test statistic and *p*-value. The statistics that are specified with the NORMAL keyword are available only because the NORMAL option is requested in the HISTOGRAM statement.

The KERNEL or KERNEL*n* keyword is available only if you request a kernel density estimate in a HISTOGRAM statement. The WEIBULL2 keyword is available only if you request a two-parameter Weibull distribution in the PROBPLOT or QQPLOT statement.

Tip: To specify the same format for all the statistics in the INSET statement, use the FORMAT= option.

Tip: To create a completely customized inset, use a DATA= data set. The data set contains the label and the value that you want to display in the inset.

Tip: If you specify multiple kernel density estimates, you can request inset statistics for all the estimates with the KERNEL keyword. Alternatively, you can display inset statistics for individual curves with KERNEL*n* keyword, where *n* is the curve number between 1 and 5.

Featured in: Example 9 on page 1448 and Example 10 on page 1450

DATA=*SAS-data-set*

requests that PROC UNIVARIATE display customized statistics from a SAS data set in the inset table. The data set must contain two variables:

LABEL	a character variable whose values provide labels for inset entries.
VALUE	a variable that is either character or numeric and whose values provide values for inset entries.

The label and value from each observation in the data set occupy one line in the inset. The position of the DATA= keyword in the keyword list determines the position of its lines in the inset.

Options

Figure 41.1 on page 1357 illustrates the meaning of terms that are used in this section.

Figure 41.1 The Inset

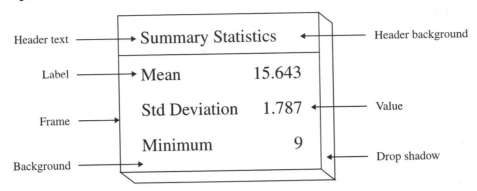

CFILL=*color* | BLANK
specifies the color of the background which, if you omit the CFILLH= option, includes the header background.

> **Default** The background is empty which causes items that overlap the inset (such as curves, histogram bars, or specification limits) to show through the inset.
>
> **Tip:** Specify a value for CFILL= so that items that overlap no longer show through the inset. Use CFILL=BLANK to leave the background uncolored.

CFILLH=*color*
specifies the color of the header background.

> **Default:** the CFILL= *color*

CFRAME=*color*
specifies the color of the frame.

> **Default:** the same color as the axis of the plot

CHEADER=*color*
specifies the color of the header text.

> **Default:** the CTEXT=*color*

CSHADOW=*color*
specifies the color of the drop shadow.

> **Default:** A drop shadow is not displayed.

CTEXT=*color*
specifies the color of the text.

> **Default:** the same color as the other text on the plot

DATA
specifies how to use data coordinates to position the inset with the POSITION= option.

> **Requirement:** The DATA option is available only when you specify POSITION=(x,y). You must place DATA immediately after the coordinates (x,y).
>
> **Main Discussion:** "Positioning the Inset Using Coordinates" on page 1360
>
> **See also:** POSITION= option on page 1358

FONT=*font*
specifies the font of the text.

> **Default:** If you locate the inset in the interior of the plot then the font is SIMPLEX. If you locate the inset in the exterior of the plot then the font is the same as the other text on the plot.

Featured in: Example 10 on page 1450

FORMAT=*format*
specifies a format for all the values in the inset.

Interaction: If you specify a format for a particular statistic, then this format overrides FORMAT=*format*.

See also: For more information about SAS formats, see *SAS Language Reference: Dictionary*

Featured in: Example 9 on page 1448

HEADER=*string*
specifies the header text where *string* cannot exceed 40 characters.

Default: No header line appears in the inset.

Interaction: If all the keywords that you list in the INSET statement are secondary keywords that correspond to a fitted curve on a histogram, PROC UNIVARIATE displays a default header that indicates the distribution and identifies the curve.

Featured in: Example 9 on page 1448

HEIGHT=*value*
specifies the height of the text.

Featured in: Example 10 on page 1450

NOFRAME
suppresses the frame drawn around the text.

Featured in: Example 10 on page 1450

POSITION=*position*
determines the position of the inset. The *position* is a compass point keyword, a margin keyword, or a pair of coordinates (x,y).

Alias: POS=

Default: NW, which positions the inset in the upper left (northwest) corner of the display.

Requirement: You must specify coordinates in axis percentage units or axis data units.

Main discussion: "Positioning the Inset Using Compass Point" on page 1359, "Positioning the Inset in the Margins" on page 1359, and "Positioning the Inset Using Coordinates" on page 1360

Featured in: Example 9 on page 1448 and Example 10 on page 1450

REFPOINT=BR | BL | TR | TL
specifies the reference point for an inset that PROC UNIVARIATE positions by a pair of coordinates with the POSITION= option. The REFPOINT= option specifies which corner of the inset frame that you want to position at coordinates (x,y). The reference points are

BL	bottom left
BR	bottom right
TL	top left
TR	top right

Default: BL

Requirement: You must use REFPOINT= with POSITION=(x,y) coordinates.

Featured in: Example 9 on page 1448

Positioning the Inset Using Compass Point

To position the inset by using a compass point position, use the keyword N, NE, E, SE, S, SW, W, or NW in the POSITION= option. The default position of the inset is NW.

The following statements produce a histogram to show the position of the inset for the eight compass points:

```
proc univariate data=score noprint;
   histogram final / cfill=gray midpoints=45 to 95 by 10 barwidth=5;
   inset n     / cfill=blank header='Position = NW' pos=nw;
   inset mean  / cfill=blank header='Position = N ' pos=n ;
   inset sum   / cfill=blank header='Position = NE' pos=ne;
   inset max   / cfill=blank header='Position = E ' pos=e ;
   inset min   / cfill=blank header='Position = SE' pos=se;
   inset nobs  / cfill=blank header='Position = S ' pos=s ;
   inset range / cfill=blank header='Position = SW' pos=sw;
   inset mode  / cfill=blank header='Position = W ' pos=w ;
   label final='Final Examination Score';
   title 'Test Scores for a College Course';
run;
```

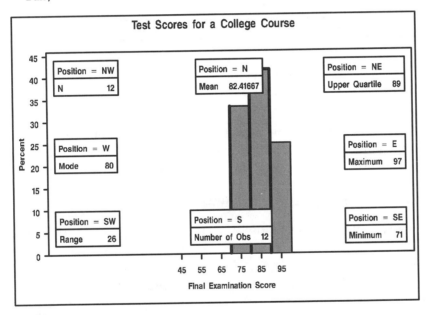

Positioning the Inset in the Margins

To position the inset in one of the four margins that surround the plot area use the margin keywords LM, RM, TM, or BM in the POSITION= option. Figure 41.2 on page 1360 shows the location of the inset in the margin.

Figure 41.2   Locating the Inset in the Margins

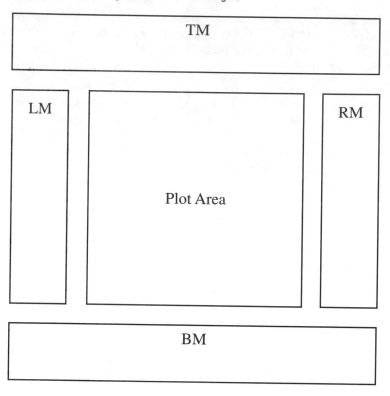

Margin positions are recommended if you list a large number of statistics in the INSET statement. If you attempt to display a lengthy inset in the interior of the plot, it is most likely that the inset will collide with the data display.

Positioning the Inset Using Coordinates

To position the inset with coordinates, use POSITION=(x,y). You specify the coordinates in axis data units or in axis percentage units (the default).

data unit

If you specify the DATA option immediately following the coordinates, PROC UNIVARIATE positions the inset by using axis data units. For example, the following statements place the bottom left corner of the inset at 12.5 on the horizontal axis and 10 on the vertical axis:

```
proc univariate data=score;
   histogram final / midpoints 45 to 95 by 10 barwidth=5
                     cfill=gray ;
   inset n / header   = 'Position=(12.5,10)'
             position = (12.5,10) data;
run;
```

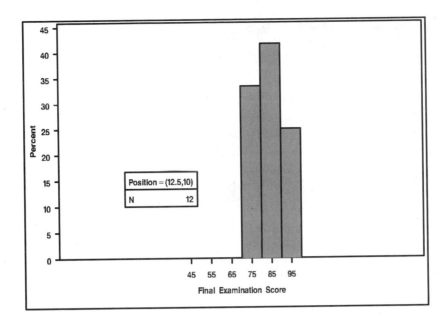

By default, the specified coordinates determine the position of the bottom left corner of the inset. To change this reference point, use the REFPOINT= option (see the next example).

axis percent unit

If you omit the DATA option, PROC UNIVARIATE positions the inset by using axis percentage units. The coordinates in axis percentage units must be *between* 0 and 100. The coordinates of the bottom left corner of the display are (0,0), while the upper right corner is (100,100). For example, the following statements create a histogram and use coordinates in axis percentage units to position the two insets:

```
proc univariate data=sccore;
    histogram final / midpoints 45 to 95 by 10 barwidth=5
                      cfill=gray;
    inset min / position = (5,25)
                header    = 'Position=(5,25)'
                refpoint = tl;
    inset max / position = (95,95)
                header    = 'Position=(95,95)'
                refpoint = tr;
    run;
```

The REFPOINT= option determines which corner of the inset to place at the coordinates that are specified with the POSITION= option. The first inset uses REFPOINT=TL, so that the top left corner of the inset is positioned 5% of the way across the horizontal axis and 25% of the way up the vertical axis. The second inset uses REFPOINT=TR, so that the top right corner of the inset is positioned 95% of the way across the horizontal axis and 95% of the way up the vertical axis.

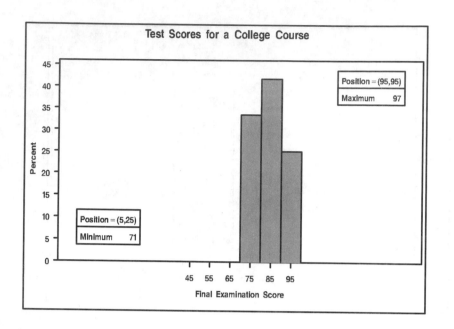

OUTPUT Statement

Saves statistics and BY variables in an output data set.

Tip: You can save percentiles that are not automatically computed.

Tip: You can use multiple OUTPUT statements to create several OUT= data sets.

Main discussion: "Output Data Set" on page 1417

Featured in: Example 5 on page 1432, Example 6 on page 1437, and Example 7 on page 1439

OUTPUT <OUT=*SAS-data-set*> *statistic-keyword-1=name(s)*
    <...*statistic-keyword-n=name(s)*> <*percentiles-specification*> ;

Options

OUT=*SAS-data-set*
    identifies the output data set. If *SAS-data-set* does not exist, PROC UNIVARIATE
    creates it. If you omit OUT=, the data set is named DATA*n*, where *n* is the smallest
    integer that makes the name unique.
    Default: DATA*n*

statistic-keyword=name(s)
    specifies a statistic to store in the OUT= data set and names the new variable that
    will contain the statistic. The available statistical keywords are

Descriptive statistic keywords

CSS	CV	KURTOSIS
MAX	MEAN	N
MIN	MODE	RANGE

NMISS	NOBS	STDMEAN
SKEWNESS	STD	USS
SUM	SUMWGT	VAR

Quantile statistic keywords

MEDIAN	P1	P5
P10	P90	P95
P99	Q1	Q3
QRANGE		

Robust statistic keywords

GINI	MAD	QN
SN	STD_GINI	STD_MAD
STD_QN	STD_QRANGE	STD_SN

Hypothesis testing keywords

NORMAL	PROBN	MSIGN
PROBM	SIGNRANK	PROBS
T	PROBT	

See Appendix 1, "SAS Elementary Statistics Procedures," on page 1457 and "Statistical Computations" on page 1393 for the keyword definitions and statistical formulas.

To store the same statistic for several analysis variables, specify a list of names. The order of the names corresponds to the order of the analysis variables in the VAR statement. PROC UNIVARIATE uses the first name to create a variable that contains the statistic for the first analysis variable, the next name to create a variable that contains the statistic for the second analysis variable, and so on. If you do not want to output statistics for all the analysis variables, specify fewer names than the number of analysis variables.

percentiles-specification

specifies one or more percentiles to store in the OUT= data set and names the new variables that contain the percentiles. The form of *percentiles-specification* is

PCTLPTS=*percentile(s)* PCTLPRE=*prefix-name(s)* <PCTLNAME=*suffix-name(s)*>

PCTLPTS=*percentile(s)*

specifies one or more percentiles to compute. You can specify percentiles with the expression *start* TO *stop* BY *increment* where *start* is a starting number, *stop* is an ending number, and *increment* is a number to increment by.

Range: any decimal numbers between 0 and 100, inclusive

Example: To compute the 50th, 95th, 97.5th, and 100th percentiles, submit the statement

```
output pctlpre=P_ pctlpts=50,95 to 100 by 2.5;
```

PCTLPRE=*prefix-name(s)*

specifies one or more prefixes to create the variable names for the variables that contain the PCTLPTS= percentiles. To save the same percentiles for more than one analysis variable, specify a list of prefixes. The order of the prefixes corresponds to the order of the analysis variables in the VAR statement.

Interaction: PROC UNIVARIATE creates a variable name by combining the PCTLPRE= value and either *suffix-name* or (if you omit PCTLNAME= or if you specify too few *suffix-name(s)*) the PCTLPTS= value.

PCTLNAME=*suffix-name(s)*

specifies one or more suffixes to create the names for the variables that contain the PCTLPTS= percentiles. PROC UNIVARIATE creates a variable name by combining the PCTLPRE= value and *suffix-name*. Because the suffix names are associated with the percentiles that are requested, list the suffix names in the same order as the PCTLPTS= percentiles.

Requirement: You must specify PCTLPRE= to supply prefix names for the variables that contain the PCTLPTS= percentiles.

Interaction: If the number of PCTLNAME= values is fewer than the number of *percentile(s)* or if you omit PCTLNAME=, PROC UNIVARIATE uses *percentile* as the suffix to create the name of the variable that contains the percentile. For an integer percentile, PROC UNIVARIATE uses *percentile*. For a noninteger percentile, PROC UNIVARIATE truncates decimal values of *percentile* to two decimal places and replaces the decimal point with an underscore.

Interaction: If either the prefix and suffix name combination or the prefix and percentile name combination is longer than 32 characters, PROC UNIVARIATE truncates the prefix name so that the variable name is 32 characters.

Saving Percentiles Not Automatically Computed

You can use PCTLPTS= to output percentiles that are not in the list of quantile statistics. PROC UNIVARIATE computes the requested percentiles based on the method that you specify with the PCTLDEF= option in the PROC UNIVARIATE statement. You must use PCTLPRE=, and optionally PCTLNAME=, to specify variable names for the percentiles. For example, the following statements create an output data set that is named PCTLS that contains the 20th and 40th percentiles of the analysis variables Test1 and Test2:

```
proc univariate data=score;
   var Test1 Test2;
   output out=pctls pctlpts=20 40 pctlpre=Test1_ Test2_
           pctlname=P20 P40;
run;
```

PROC UNIVARIATE saves the 20th and 40th percentiles for Test1 and Test2 in the variables Test1_P20, Test2_P20, Test1_P40, and Test2_P40.

Using the BY Statement with the OUTPUT Statement

When you use a BY statement, the number of observations in the OUT= data set corresponds to the number of BY groups. Otherwise, the OUT= data set contains only one observation.

PROBPLOT Statement

Creates a probability plot by using high-resolution graphs, which compare ordered variable values with the percentiles of a specified theoretical distribution.

Alias: PROB

Default: Normal probability plot

Restriction: You can specify only one theoretical distribution.

Tip: You can use multiple PROBPLOT statements.

Main discussion:

Featured in: "Quantile–Quantile and Probability Plots" on page 1391

PROBPLOT *<variable(s)> </ option(s)>;*

To do this:	Use this option:
Request a distribution	
Specify beta probability plot with required shape parameters α, β.	BETA(*beta-suboptions*)
Specify exponential probability plot	EXPONENTIAL(*exponential-suboptions*)
Specify gamma probability plot with a required shape parameter α	GAMMA(*gamma-suboptions*)
Specify lognormal probability plot with a required shape parameter σ	LOGNORMAL(*lognormal-suboptions*)
Specify normal probability plot	NORMAL(*normal-suboptions*)
Specify three-parameter Weibull probability plot with a required shape parameter c	WEIBULL(*Weibull-suboptions*)
Specify two-parameter Weibull probability plot	WEIBULL2(*Weibull2-suboptions*)
Distribution suboptions	
Specify shape parameter α for the beta or gamma distribution	ALPHA=
Specify shape parameter β for the beta distribution	BETA=
Specify shape parameter c for the Weibull distribution or c_0 for distribution reference line of the Weibull2 distribution	C=
Specify μ_0 for distribution reference line for the normal distribution	MU=
Specify σ_0 for distribution reference line for the beta, exponential, gamma, normal, Weibull, or Weibull2 distribution or the required shape parameter σ for the lognormal option	SIGMA=
Specify slope of distribution reference line for the lognormal or Weibull2 distribution	SLOPE=

To do this:	Use this option:
Specify θ_0 for distribution reference line for the beta, exponential, gamma, lognormal, or Weibull distribution, or the lower known threshold θ_0 for the Weibull2 distribution	THETA=
Specify ζ_0 for distribution reference line for the lognormal distribution	ZETA=
Control appearance of distribution reference line	
Specify color of distribution reference line	COLOR=
Specify line type of distribution reference line	L=
Specify width of distribution reference line	W=
Control general plot layout	
Create a grid	GRID
Specify reference lines perpendicular to the horizontal axis	HREF=
Specify labels for HREF lines	HREFLABELS=
Specify a line style for grid lines	LGRID=
Adjust sample size when computing percentiles	NADJ=
Suppress frame around plotting area	NOFRAME
Request minor tick marks for percentile axis	PCTLMINOR
Specify tick mark labels for percentile axis	PCTLORDER=
Adjust ranks when computing percentiles	RANKADJ=
Display plot in square format	SQUARE
Specify reference lines perpendicular to the vertical axis	VREF=
Specify labels for VREF lines	VREFLABELS=
Enhance the probability plot	
Specify annotate data set	ANNOTATE=
Specify color for axis	CAXIS=
Specify color for frame	CFRAME=
Specify color for HREF= lines	CHREF=
Specify color for text	CTEXT=
Specify color for VREF= lines	CVREF=
Specify description for plot in graphics catalog	DESCRIPTION=
Specify software font for text	FONT=
Specify number of horizontal minor tick marks	HMINOR=
Specify line style for HREF= lines	LHREF=
Specify line style for VREF= lines	LVREF=
Specify name for plot in graphics catalog	NAME=
Specify number of vertical minor tick marks	VMINOR=

To do this:	Use this option:
Enhance the comparative probability plot	
Apply annotation requested in ANNOTATE= data set to key cell only	ANNOKEY
Specify color for filling frame for row labels	CFRAMESIDE=
Specify color for filling frame for column labels	CFRAMETOP=
Specify distance between tiles	INTERTILE=
Specify number of columns in comparative probability plot	NCOLS=
Specify number of rows in comparative probability plot	NROWS=

Arguments

variable(s)
    identifies one or more variables that the procedure uses to create probability plots.

    Default: If you omit *variable(s)* in the PROBPLOT statement then the procedure creates a probability plot for each variable that you list in the VAR statement, or for each numeric variable in the DATA= data set if you omit a VAR statement.

    Requirement: If you specify a VAR statement, use a subset of the *variable(s)* that you list in the VAR statement. Otherwise, *variable(s)* are any numeric variables in the DATA= data set.

Options

ALPHA=*value(s)*|EST
    specifies the required shape parameter $\alpha(\alpha > 0)$ for probability plots when you request the BETA or GAMMA options. The PROBPLOT statement creates a plot for each value that you specify.

    Requirement: Enclose this suboption in parentheses following the BETA or GAMMA options.

    Tip: To compute a maximum likelihood estimate for α, specify ALPHA=EST.

ANNOKEY
    specifies to apply the annotation requested with the ANNOTATE= option to the *key cell* only. By default, PROC UNIVARIATE applies annotation to all of the cells.

    Requirement: This option is ignored unless you specify the CLASS statement.

    Tip: Use the KEYLEVEL= option in the CLASS statement to specify the key cell.

    See also: the KEYLEVEL= option on page 1334

ANNOTATE=*SAS-data-set*
    specifies an input data set that contains annotate variables as described in *SAS/GRAPH Software: Reference*.

    Alias: ANNO=

    Tip: The ANNOTATE = data set that you specify in the PROBPLOT statement is used by all plots that this statement creates. You can also specify an ANNOTATE= data set in the PROC UNIVARIATE statement to enhance all the graphics displays that the procedure creates.

See also: the ANNOTATE= option on page 1327 in the PROC UNIVARIATE statement

BETA(ALPHA=*value(s)*|EST BETA=*value(s)*|EST <*beta-suboptions*>)
displays a beta probability plot for each combination of the required shape parameters α and β.

Requirement: You must specify the shape parameters with the ALPHA= and BETA= suboptions.

Interaction: To create a plot that is based on maximum likelihood estimates for α and β, specify ALPHA=EST and BETA=EST.

Tip: To obtain graphical estimates of α and β, specify lists of values in the ALPHA= and BETA= suboptions. Then select the combination of α and β that most nearly linearizes the point pattern.

To assess the point pattern, add a diagonal distribution reference line that corresponds to the lower threshold parameter θ_0 and the scale parameter σ_0 with the THETA= and SIGMA= suboptions. Alternatively, you can add a line that corresponds to estimated values of θ_0 and σ_0 with THETA=EST and SIGMA=EST.

Agreement between the reference line and the point pattern indicates that the beta distribution with parameters α, β, θ_0, and σ_0 is a good fit.

Main discussion: "Beta Distribution" on page 1412

See also: the ALPHA= on page 1367 suboption and BETA= suboption on page 1368

BETA=*value(s)*|EST
specifies the shape parameter β $(\beta > 0)$ for probability plots when you request the BETA distribution option. PROC UNIVARIATE creates a plot for each value that you specify.

Alias: B=

Requirement: Enclose this suboption in parentheses after the BETA option.

Tip: To compute a maximum likelihood estimate for β, specify BETA=EST.

C=*value(s)*|EST
specifies the shape parameter c $(c > 0)$ for probability plots when you request the WEIBULL option or WEIBULL2 option. C= is a required suboption in the WEIBULL option.

Requirement: Enclose this suboption in parentheses after the WEIBULL option or WEIBULL2 option.

Interaction: To request a distribution reference line in the WEIBULL2 option, you must specify both the C= and SIGMA= suboptions.

Tip: To compute a maximum likelihood estimate for c, specify C=EST.

CAXIS=*color*
specifies the color for the axes.

Alias: CAXES=

Default: the first color in the device color list

Interaction: This option overrides any COLOR= specification.

CFRAME=*color*
specifies the color for the area that is enclosed by the axes and frame.

Default: the area is not filled

CFRAMESIDE=*color*
specifies the color to fill the frame area for the row labels that display along the left side of the comparative probability plot. This color also fills the frame area for the label of the corresponding class variable (if you associate a label with the variable).

Default: These areas are not filled.

Requirement: This option is ignored unless you specify the CLASS statement.

CFRAMETOP=*color*

specifies the color to fill the frame area for the column labels that display across the top of the comparative probability plot. This color also fills the frame area for the label of the corresponding class variable (if you associate a label with the variable).

Default: These areas are not filled.

Requirement: This option does not apply unless you specify the CLASS statement.

CHREF=*color*

specifies the color for horizontal axis reference lines when you specify the HREF= option.

Default: the first color in the device color list

COLOR=*color*

specifies the color of the diagonal distribution reference line.

Default: the first color in the device color list

Requirement: You must enclose this suboption in parentheses after a distribution option keyword.

CTEXT=*color*

specifies the color for tick mark values and axis labels.

Default: the color that you specify for the CTEXT= option in the GOPTIONS statement. If you omit the GOPTIONS statement, the default is the first color in the device color list.

CVREF=*color*

specifies the color for the reference lines that you request with the VREF= option.

Alias: CV=

Default: the first color in the device color list

DESCRIPTION=*'string'*

specifies a description, up to 40 characters long, that appears in the PROC GREPLAY master menu.

Alias: DES=

Default: the variable name

EXPONENTIAL<(*exponential-options***)>**

displays an exponential probability plot.

Alias: EXP

Tip: To assess the point pattern, add a diagonal distribution reference line that corresponds to θ_0 and σ_0 with the THETA= and SIGMA= suboptions. Alternatively, you can add a line that corresponds to estimated values of the threshold parameter θ_0 and the scale parameter σ_0 with the THETA=EST and SIGMA=EST suboptions.

Agreement between the reference line and the point pattern indicates that the exponential distribution with parameters θ_0 and σ_0 is a good fit.

Main discussion: "Exponential Distribution" on page 1412

See also: the SIGMA= suboption on page 1373 and the THETA= suboption on page 1374

FONT=*font*

specifies a software font for the reference lines and the axis labels.

Default: hardware characters

Interaction: FONT=*font* takes precedence over the FTEXT=*font* that you specify in the GOPTIONS statement.

GAMMA(ALPHA=*value(s)* | EST *<gamma-suboptions>*)

displays a gamma probability plot for each value of the required shape parameter α.

Requirement: You must specify the shape parameter with the ALPHA= suboption.

Interaction: To create a plot that is based on a maximum likelihood estimate for α, specify ALPHA=EST.

Tip: To obtain a graphical estimate of α, specify a list of values in the ALPHA= suboption. Then select the value that most nearly linearizes the point pattern.

To assess the point pattern, add a diagonal distribution reference line that corresponds to the threshold parameter θ_0 and the scale parameter σ_0 with the THETA= and SIGMA= suboptions. Alternatively, you can add a line that corresponds to estimated values of θ_0 and σ_0 with THETA=EST and SIGMA=EST.

Agreement between the reference line and the point pattern indicates that the exponential distribution with parameters α, θ_0, and σ_0 is a good fit.

Main discussion: "Gamma Distribution" on page 1412

See also: the ALPHA= on page 1367 suboption, SIGMA suboption on page 1373, and THETA suboption on page 1374

GRID

displays a grid, drawing reference lines that are perpendicular to the percentile axis at major tick marks.

Default: 1

HMINOR=*n*

specifies the number of minor tick marks between each major tick mark on the horizontal axis. PROC UNIVARIATE does not label minor tick marks.

Alias: HM=

Default: 0

HREF=*value(s)*

draws reference lines that are perpendicular to the horizontal axis at the values you specify.

See also: CHREF= option on page 1369

HREFLABELS='*label1*' ... '*labeln*'

specifies labels for the reference lines that you request with the HREF= option.

Alias: HREFLABEL= and HREFLAB=

Restriction: The number of labels must equal the number of reference lines. Labels can have up to 16 characters.

HREFLABPOS=*n*

specifies the vertical position of HREFLABELS= labels, where *n* is

1	positions the labels at the left of the plot
2	positions the labels along the top of the plot
3	positions the labels from top to bottom

Default: 1

INTERTILE=*value*

specifies the distance in horizontal percentage screen units between the framed areas, which are called *tiles*.

Default: The tiles are contiguous.

Requirement: This option is ignored unless you specify the CLASS statement.

L=*linetype*
specifies the line type for a diagonal distribution reference line.

Default: 1, which produces a solid line

Requirement: You must enclose this suboption in parentheses after a distribution option.

LGRID=*linetype*
specifies the line type for the grid that you request with the GRID= option.

Default: 1, which produces solid lines

LHREF=*linetype*
specifies the line type for the reference lines that you request with the HREF= option.

Alias: LH=

Default: 2, which produces a dashed line

LOGNORMAL(SIGMA=*value(s)***|EST <***lognormal-suboptions***>)**
displays a lognormal probability plot for each value of the required shape parameter σ.

Alias: LNORM

Requirement: You must specify the shape parameter with the SIGMA= suboption.

Interaction: To compute a maximum likelihood estimate for σ, specify SIGMA=EST.

Tip: To obtain a graphical estimate of σ, specify a list of values for the SIGMA= suboption, and select the value that most nearly linearizes the point pattern.
   To assess the point pattern, add a diagonal distribution reference line that corresponds to the threshold parameter θ_0 and the scale parameter ζ_0 with the THETA= and ZETA= suboptions. Alternatively, you can add a line that corresponds to estimated values of θ_0 and ζ_0 with THETA=EST and ZETA=EST.
   Agreement between the reference line and the point pattern indicates that the lognormal distribution with parameters σ, θ_0, and ζ_0 is a good fit.

Main discussion: "Lognormal Distribution" on page 1413

See also: the SIGMA= suboption on page 1373, SLOPE= suboption on page 1373, THETA= suboption on page 1374, and ZETA= suboption on page 1375

LVREF=*linetype*
specifies the line type for the reference lines that you request with the VREF= option.

Default: 2, which produces a dashed line

MU=*value***|EST**
specifies the mean μ_0 for a normal probability plot requested with the NORMAL option.

Default: the sample mean

Requirement: You must enclose this suboption in parentheses after the NORMAL option.

Tip: Specify the MU= and SIGMA= suboptions together to request a distribution reference line. Specify MU=EST to request a distribution reference line with μ_0 equal to the sample mean.

Featured in: Example 9 on page 1448

NADJ=*value*
specifies the adjustment value that is added to the sample size in the calculation of theoretical percentiles. For additional information, see Chambers et al. (1983)

Default: $\frac{1}{4}$ as recommended by Blom (1958)

NAME=*'string'*

specifies a name for the plot, up to eight characters long, that appears in the PROC GREPLAY master menu.

Default: UNIVAR

NCOLS=*n*

specifies the number of columns in the comparative probability plot.

Alias: NCOL=

Default: NCOLS=1, if you specify only one class variable, and NCOLS=2, if you specify two class variables.

Requirement: This option is ignored unless you specify the CLASS statement.

Interaction: If you specify two class variables, you can use the NCOLS= option with the NROWS= option.

NOFRAME

suppresses the frame around the area that is bounded by the axes.

NORMAL<(*normal-suboptions***)>**

displays a normal probability plot. This is the default if you omit a distribution option.

Tip: To assess the point pattern, add a diagonal distribution reference line that corresponds to μ_0 and σ_0 with the MU= and SIGMA= suboptions. Alternatively, you can add a line that corresponds to estimated values of μ_0 and σ_0 with the THETA=EST and SIGMA=EST; the estimates of the mean μ_0 and the standard deviation σ_0 are the sample mean and sample standard deviation.

Agreement between the reference line and the point pattern indicates that the normal distribution with parameters μ_0 and σ_0 is a good fit.

Main discussion: "Normal Distribution" on page 1413

See also: the MU= suboption on page 1371 and SIGMA= suboption on page 1373

Featured in: Example 9 on page 1448

NROWS=*n*

specifies the number of rows in the comparative probability plot.

Alias: NROW=

Default: 2

Requirement: This option is ignored unless you specify the CLASS statement.

Interaction: If you specify two class variables, you can use the NCOLS= option with the NROWS= option.

PCTLMINOR

requests minor tick marks for the percentile axis.

Featured in: Example 9 on page 1448

PCTLORDER=*value(s)*

specifies the tick marks that are labeled on the theoretical percentile axis.

Default: 1, 5, 10, 25, 50, 75, 90, 95, and 99

Range: $0 \le value \le 100$

Restriction: The values that you specify must be in increasing order and cover the plotted percentile range. Otherwise, PROC UNIVARIATE uses the default.

RANKADJ=*value*

specifies the adjustment value that PROC UNIVARIATE adds to the ranks in the calculation of theoretical percentiles. For additional information, see Chambers et al. (1983).

Default: $-\frac{3}{8}$ as recommended by Blom (1958)

SCALE=*value*

is an alias for the SIGMA= option when you request probability plots with the BETA, EXPONENTIAL, GAMMA, and WEIBULL options and for the ZETA= option when you request the LOGNORMAL option.

See also: the SIGMA= suboption on page 1373 and ZETA= suboption on page 1375

SHAPE=*value(s)* **| EST**

is an alias for the ALPHA=option when you request gamma plots with the GAMMA option, for the SIGMA= option when you request lognormal plots with the LOGNORMAL option, and for the C= option when you request Weibull plots with the WEIBULL and WEIBULL2 options.

See also: the ALPHA= suboption on page 1367, SIGMA= suboption on page 1373, and C= suboption on page 1368

SIGMA=*value(s)* **| EST**

specifies the parameter σ, where $\sigma > 0$. The interpretation and use of the SIGMA= option depend on which distribution you specify, as shown Table 41.4 on page 1373.

Table 41.4 Uses of the SIGMA Suboption

Distribution Option	Uses of the SIGMA= Option
BETA, EXPONENTIAL GAMMA, WEIBULL	THETA=θ_0 and SIGMA=σ_0 request a distribution reference line that corresponds to θ_0 and σ_0.
LOGNORMAL	SIGMA=$\sigma_1 \ldots \sigma_n$ requests n probability plots with shape parameters $\sigma_1 \ldots \sigma_n$. The SIGMA= option is required.
NORMAL	MU=μ_0 and SIGMA=σ_0 request a distribution reference line that corresponds to μ_0 and σ_0. SIGMA=EST requests a line with σ_0 equal to the sample standard deviation.
WEIBULL2	SIGMA=σ_0 and C=c_0 request a distribution reference line that corresponds to σ_0 and c_0.

Requirement: You must enclose this suboption in parentheses after the distribution option.

Tip: To compute a maximum likelihood estimate for σ_0, specify SIGMA=EST.

Featured in: Example 9 on page 1448

SLOPE=*value* **| EST**

specifies the slope for a distribution reference when you request the LOGNORMAL option or WEIBULL2 option.

Requirement: You must enclose this suboption in parentheses after the distribution option.

Tip: When you use the LOGNORMAL option and SLOPE= to request the line, you must also specify a threshold parameter value θ_0 with the THETA= suboption. SLOPE= is an alternative to the ZETA= suboption for specifying ζ_0, because the slope is equal to $\exp\left(\zeta_0\right)$.

When you use the WEIBULL2 option and SLOPE= option to request the line, you must also specify a scale parameter value σ_0 with the SIGMA= suboption. SLOPE= is an alternative to the C= suboption for specifying c_0, because the slope is equal to $\frac{1}{c_0}$.

For example, the first and second PROBPLOT statements produce the same probability plots as the third and fourth PROBPLOT statements:

```
proc univariate data=measures;
    probplot width /lognormal(sigma=2 theta=0 zeta=0);
    probplot width /lognormal(sigma=2 theta=0 slope=1);
    probplot width /weibull2(sigma=2 theta=0 c=.25);
    probplot width /weibull2(sigma=2 theta=0 slope=4);
```

Main Discussion: "Three-Parameter Weibull Distribution" on page 1413

SQUARE

displays the probability plot in a square frame.

Default: rectangular frame

THETA=*value*|EST

specifies the lower threshold parameter θ for probability plots when you request the BETA, EXPONENTIAL, GAMMA, LOGNORMAL, WEIBULL, or WEIBULL2 option.

Default: 0

Requirement: You must enclose this suboption in parentheses after the distribution option.

Interaction: When you use the WEIBULL2 option, the THETA= suboption specifies the known lower threshold θ_0, which by default is 0.

When you use the THETA= suboption with another distribution option, THETA= specifies θ_0 for a distribution reference line. To compute a maximum likelihood estimate for θ_0, specify THETA=EST. To request the line, you must also specify a scale parameter.

THRESHOLD= *value*

is an alias for the THETA= option. See the THETA= suboption on page 1374.

VMINOR=*n*

specifies the number of minor tick marks between each major tick mark on the vertical axis. PROBPLOT does not label minor tick marks.

Alias: VM=

Default: 0

VREF=*value(s)*

draws reference lines that are perpendicular to the vertical axis at the *value(s)* that you specify.

See also: CVREF= option on page 1369 and LVREF= option on page 1371.

VREFLABELS=' *label1*'... '*labeln*'

specifies labels for the reference lines that you request with the VREF= option.

Alias: VREFLABEL= and VREFLAB=

Restriction: The number of labels must equal the number of reference lines. Labels can have up to 16 characters.

W=*n*

specifies the width in pixels for a diagonal distribution line.

Default: 1

Requirement: You must enclose this suboption in parentheses after the distribution option.

WEIBULL(C=*value(s)*|EST <*Weibull-suboptions*>)

creates a three-parameter Weibull probability plot for each value of the required shape parameter *c*.

Alias: WEIB

Requirement: You must specify the shape parameter with the C= suboption.

Interaction: To create a plot that is based on a maximum likelihood estimate for c, specify C=EST.

Tip: To obtain a graphical estimate of c, specify a list of values in the C= suboption. Then select the value that most nearly linearizes the point pattern.

To assess the point pattern, add a diagonal distribution reference line that corresponds to θ_0 and σ_0 with the THETA= and SIGMA= suboptions. Alternatively, you can add a line that corresponds to estimated values of θ_0 and σ_0 with THETA=EST and SIGMA=EST.

Agreement between the reference line and the point pattern indicates that the Weibull distribution with parameters c, θ_0, and σ_0 is a good fit.

Main discussion: "Three-Parameter Weibull Distribution" on page 1413

See also the C= suboption on page 1368, SIGMA= suboption on page 1373, and THETA= suboption on page 1374

WEIBULL2<(*Weibull-suboptions*)>

creates a two-parameter Weibull probability plot. Use this distribution when your data have a *known* lower threshold θ_0, which by default is 0. To specify the threshold value θ_0, use the THETA= suboption.

Alias: W2

Tip: An advantage of the two-parameter Weibull plot over the three-parameter Weibull plot is that the parameters c and σ can be estimated from the slope and intercept of the point pattern. A disadvantage is that the two-parameter Weibull distribution applies only in situations where the threshold parameter is known.

Tip: To obtain a graphical estimate of c, specify a list of values for the C= suboption. Then select the value that most nearly linearizes the point pattern.

To assess the point pattern, add a diagonal distribution reference line that corresponds to σ_0 and c_0 with the SIGMA= and C= suboptions. Alternatively, you can add a distribution reference line that corresponds to estimated values of σ_0 and c_0 with SIGMA=EST and C=EST.

Agreement between the reference line and the point pattern indicates that the Weibull2 distribution with parameters c_0, θ_0, and σ_0 is a good fit.

Main discussion: "Two-Parameter Weibull Distribution" on page 1414

See also: the C= suboption on page 1368, SIGMA= suboption on page 1373, SLOPE= suboption on page 1373, and THETA= suboption on page 1374

ZETA= *value*|EST

specifies a value for the scale parameter ζ for the lognormal probability plots when you request the LOGNORMAL option.

Requirement: You must enclose this suboption in parentheses after the LOGNORMAL option.

Interaction: To request a distribution reference line with intercept θ_0 and slope $\exp(\zeta_0)$, specify THETA= θ_0 and ZETA= ζ_0.

QQPLOT Statement

Creates a quantile-quantile plot (Q-Q plot) (using high-resolution graphics) compares ordered variable values with quantiles of a specified theoretical distribution.

Alias: QQ

Default: Normal Q–Q plot

Restriction: You can specify only one theoretical distribution.

Tip: You can use multiple QQPLOT statements.

Main Discussion: "Quantile–Quantile and Probability Plots" on page 1391

QQPLOT *<variable(s)> </ option(s)>*;

To do this:	Use this option:
Request a distribution	
Specify beta probability plot with required shape parameters α, β.	BETA(*beta-suboptions*)
Specify exponential probability plot	EXPONENTIAL(*exponential-suboptions*)
Specify gamma probability plot with a required shape parameter α	GAMMA(*gamma-suboptions*)
Specify lognormal probability plot with a required shape parameter σ	LOGNORMAL(*lognormal-suboptions*)
Specify normal probability plot	NORMAL(*normal-suboptions*)
Specify three-parameter Weibull probability plot with a required shape parameter c	WEIBULL(*Weibull-suboptions*)
Specify two-parameter Weibull probability plot	WEIBULL2(*Weibull2-suboptions*)
Distribution suboptions	
Specify shape parameter α for the beta or gamma distribution	ALPHA=
Specify shape parameter β for the beta distribution	BETA=
Specify shape parameter c for the Weibull distribution or c_0 for distribution reference line of the Weibull2 distribution	C=
Specify μ_0 for distribution reference line of the normal distribution	MU=
Specify σ_0 for distribution reference line for the beta, exponential, gamma, normal, Weibull, or Weibull2 distribution or the required shape parameter σ for the lognormal option	SIGMA=
Specify slope of distribution reference line for the lognormal or Weibull2 distribution	SLOPE=

To do this:	Use this option:
Specify θ_0 for distribution reference line for the beta, exponential, gamma. lognormal, or Weibull distribution, or the lower known threshold θ_0 for the Weibull2 distribution	THETA=
Specify ζ_0 for distribution reference line for the lognormal distribution	ZETA=
Control appearance of distribution reference line	
Specify color of distribution reference line	COLOR=
Specify line type of distribution reference line	L=
Specify width of distribution reference line	W=
Control general plot layout	
Specify reference lines perpendicular to the horizontal axis	HREF=
Specify labels for HREF lines	HREFLABELS=
Adjust sample size when computing quantiles	NADJ=
Suppress frame around plotting area	NOFRAME
Request minor tick marks for percentile axis	PCTLMINOR
Replace theoretical quantiles with percentiles	PCTLSCALE
Adjust ranks when computing quantiles	RANKADJ=
Display Q-Q plot in square format	SQUARE
Specify reference lines perpendicular to the vertical axis	VREF=
Specify labels for VREF lines	VREFLABELS=
Enhance the Q-Q plot	
Specify annotate data set	ANNOTATE=
Specify color for axis	CAXIS=
Specify color for frame	CFRAME=
Specify color for HREF= lines	CHREF=
Specify color for text	CTEXT=
Specify color for VREF= lines	CVREF=
Specify description for plot in graphics catalog	DESCRIPTION=
Specify software font for text	FONT=
Specify number of minor tick marks on horizontal axis	HMINOR=
Specify line style for HREF= lines	LHREF=
Specify line style for VREF= lines	LVREF=
Specify name for plot in graphics catalog	NAME=
Specify number of minor tick marks on vertical axis	VMINOR=
Enhance the comparative Q-Q plot	

To do this:	Use this option:
Apply annotation requested in ANNOTATE= data set to key cell only	ANNOKEY
Specify color for filling frame for row labels	CFRAMESIDE=
Specify color for filling frame for column labels	CFRAMETOP=
Specify distance between tiles	INTERTILE=
Specify number of columns in comparative Q-Q plot	NCOLS=
Specify number of rows in comparative Q-Q plot	NROWS=

Arguments

variable(s)
> identifies one or more variables that the procedure uses to create Q-Q plots.
>
> **Default:** If you omit *variable(s)* in the QQPLOT statement, then the procedure creates a Q-Q plot for each variable that you list in the VAR statement, or for each numeric variable in the DATA= data set if you omit a VAR statement.
>
> **Requirement:** If you specify a VAR statement, use the *variable(s)* that you list in the VAR statement. Otherwise, *variable(s)* are any numeric variables in the DATA= data set.

Options

ALPHA=*value(s)*|EST
> specifies the required shape parameter $\alpha(\alpha > 0)$ for quantile plots when you request the BETA or GAMMA options. The QQPLOT statement creates a plot for each value that you specify.
>
> **Requirement:** Enclose this suboption in parentheses when it follows the BETA or GAMMA options.
>
> **Tip:** To compute a maximum likelihood estimate for α, specify ALPHA=EST.

ANNOKEY
> specifies to apply the annotation that you requested with the ANNOTATE= option to the *key cell* only. By default, PROC UNIVARIATE applies annotation to all of the cells.
>
> **Requirement:** This option is ignored unless you specify the CLASS statement.
>
> **Tip:** Use the KEYLEVEL= option in the CLASS statement to specify the key cell.
>
> **See also:** the KEYLEVEL= option on page 1334

ANNOTATE=*SAS-data-set*
> specifies an input data set that contains annotate variables as described in *SAS/GRAPH Software: Reference*.
>
> **Alias:** ANNO=
>
> **Tip:** The ANNOTATE = data set that you specify in the QQPLOT statement is used by all plots that this statement creates. You can also specify an ANNOTATE= data set in the PROC UNIVARIATE statement to enhance all the graphic displays that the procedure creates.
>
> **See also:** ANNOTATE= on page 1327 in the PROC UNIVARIATE statement

BETA(ALPHA=*value(s)*|EST BETA=*value(s)*|EST <*beta-suboptions*>)
    displays a beta Q-Q plot for each combination of the required shape parameters α and β.

    Requirement: You must specify the shape parameters with the ALPHA= and BETA= suboptions

    Interaction: To create a plot that is based on maximum likelihood estimates for α and β, specify ALPHA=EST and BETA=EST.

    Tip: To obtain graphical estimates of α and β, specify lists of values in the ALPHA= and BETA= suboptions. Then select the combination of α and β that most nearly linearizes the point pattern.

        To assess the point pattern, add a diagonal distribution reference line that corresponds to the lower threshold parameter θ_0 and the scale parameter σ_0 with the THETA= and SIGMA= suboptions. Alternatively, you can add a line that corresponds to estimated values of lower threshold parameter θ_0 and σ_0 with THETA=EST and SIGMA=EST.

        Agreement between the reference line and the point pattern indicates that the beta distribution with parameters α, β, θ_0, and σ_0 is a good fit.

    Main discussion: "Beta Distribution" on page 1412

    See also: the ALPHA= suboption on page 1378, BETA= suboption on page 1379, SIGMA= suboption on page 1383, and THETA= suboption on page 1384.

BETA=*value(s)*|EST
    specifies the shape parameter $\beta\,(\beta > 0)$ for Q-Q plots when you request the BETA distribution option. PROC UNIVARIATE creates a plot for each value that you specify.

    Alias: B=

    Requirement: You must enclose this suboption in parentheses after the BETA option.

    Tip: To compute a maximum likelihood estimate for β, specify BETA=EST.

C=*value(s)*|EST
    specifies the shape parameter $c\,(c > 0)$ for Q-Q plots when you request the WEIBULL option or WEIBULL2 option. C= is a required suboption in the WEIBULL option.

    Requirement: Enclose this suboption in parentheses after the WEIBULL option or WEIBULL2 option.

    Interaction: To request a distribution reference line in the WEIBULL2 option, you must specify both the C= and SIGMA= suboptions.

    Tip: To compute a maximum likelihood estimate for c, specify C=EST.

CAXIS=*color*
    specifies the color for the axes.

    Alias: CAXES=

    Default: the first color in the device color list

    Interaction: This option overrides any COLOR= specification.

CFRAME=*color*
    specifies the color for the area that is enclosed by the axes and frame.

    Default: the area is not filled

CFRAMESIDE=*color*
    specifies the color to fill the frame area for the row labels that display along the left side of the comparative probability plot. This color also fills the frame area for the label of the corresponding class variable (if you associate a label with the variable).

Default: These areas are not filled.

Requirement: This option is ignored unless you specify the CLASS statement.

CFRAMETOP=*color*

specifies the color to fill the frame area for the column labels that display across the top of the comparative probability plot. This color also fills the frame area for the label of the corresponding class variable (if you associate a label with the variable).

Default: These areas are not filled.

Requirement: This option is ignored unless you specify the CLASS statement.

CHREF=*color*

specifies the color for horizontal axis reference lines when you specify the HREF= option.

Default: the first color in the device color list

COLOR=*color*

specifies the color for a distribution reference line.

Default: the fourth color in the device color list

Requirement: You must enclose this suboption in parentheses after a distribution option keyword.

CTEXT=*color*

specifies the color for tick mark values and axis labels.

Default: the color that you specify for the CTEXT= option in the GOPTIONS statement. If you omit the GOPTIONS statement, the default is the first color in the device color list.

CVREF=*color*

specifies the color for the reference lines that you request with the VREF= option.

Alias: CV=

Default: the first color in the device color list.

DESCRIPTION=*'string'*

specifies a description, up to 40 characters long, that appears in the PROC GREPLAY master menu.

Alias: DES=

Default: the variable name

EXPONENTIAL<(*exponential-suboptions***)>**

displays an exponential Q–Q plot.

Alias: EXP

Tip: To assess the point pattern, add a diagonal distribution reference line that corresponds to θ_0 and σ_0 with the THETA= and SIGMA= suboptions. Alternatively, you can add a line that corresponds to estimated values of the threshold parameter θ_0 and the scale parameter σ_0 with the THETA=EST and SIGMA=EST suboptions.

Agreement between the reference line and the point pattern indicates that the exponential distribution with parameters θ_0 and σ_0 is a good fit.

Main discussion: "Exponential Distribution" on page 1412

See also: the SIGMA suboption on page 1383 and THETA suboption on page 1384

FONT=*font*

specifies a software font for the reference lines and the axis labels.

Default: hardware characters

Interaction: FONT=*font* takes precedence over FTEXT=*font* that you specify in the GOPTIONS statement.

GAMMA(ALPHA=*value(s)* | EST <*gamma-suboptions*>)
displays a gamma Q–Q plot for each value of the required shape parameter α.

Requirement: You must specify the shape parameter with the ALPHA= suboption.

Interaction: To create a plot that is based on a maximum likelihood estimate for α, specify ALPHA=EST.

Tip: To obtain a graphical estimate of α, specify a list of values in the ALPHA= suboption. Then select the value that most nearly linearizes the point pattern.

To assess the point pattern, add a diagonal distribution reference line that corresponds to θ_0 and σ_0 with the THETA= and SIGMA= suboptions. Alternatively, you can add a line that corresponds to estimated values of the threshold parameter θ_0 and the scale parameter σ_0 with THETA=EST and SIGMA=EST.

Agreement between the reference line and the point pattern indicates that the exponential distribution with parameters α, θ_0, and σ_0 is a good fit.

Main discussion: "Gamma Distribution" on page 1412

See also: the ALPHA= suboption on page 1378, SIGMA= suboption on page 1383, and THETA= suboption on page 1384

HMINOR=*n*
specifies the number of minor tick marks between each major tick mark on the horizontal axis. PROC UNIVARIATE does not label minor tick marks.

Alias: HM=

Default: 0

HREF=*value(s)*
draws reference lines that are perpendicular to the horizontal axis at the values you specify.

See also: CHREF= option on page 1380

HREFLABELS='*label1*' ... '*labeln*'
specifies labels for the reference lines that you request with the HREF= option.

Alias: HREFLABEL= and HREFLAB=

Restriction: The number of labels must equal the number of reference lines. Labels can have up to 16 characters.

INTERTILE=*value*
specifies the distance in horizontal percentage screen units between the framed areas, which are called *tiles*.

Default: The tiles are contiguous.

Requirement: This option is ignored unless you specify the CLASS statement.

L=*linetype*
specifies the line type for a diagonal distribution reference line.

Default: 1, which produces a solid line

Requirement: You must enclose this suboption in parentheses after a distribution option keyword.

LHREF=*linetype*
specifies the line type for the reference lines that you request with the HREF= option.

Alias: LH=

Default: 2, which produces a dashed line

LOGNORMAL(SIGMA=*value(s)* | EST <*lognormal-suboptions*>)
displays a lognormal Q-Q plot for each value of the required shape parameter σ.

Alias: LNORM

Requirement: You must specify the shape parameter with the SIGMA= suboption.

Tip: To obtain a graphical estimate of σ, specify a list of values for the SIGMA= suboption, and select the value that most nearly linearizes the point pattern.

To assess the point pattern, add a diagonal distribution reference line that corresponds to the threshold parameter θ_0 and the scale parameter ζ_0 with the THETA= and ZETA= suboptions. Alternatively, you can add a line that corresponds to estimated values of θ_0 and ζ_0 with THETA=EST and ZETA=EST. This line has intercept θ_0, and slope $\exp(\zeta_0)$.

Agreement between the reference line and the point pattern indicates that the lognormal distribution with parameters σ, θ_0 and ζ_0 is a good fit.

Main discussion: "Lognormal Distribution" on page 1413

See also: the SIGMA= suboption on page 1383, SLOPE= suboption on page 1384, THETA= suboption on page 1384, and ZETA= suboption on page 1386

LVREF=*linetype*

specifies the line type for the reference lines that you request with the VREF= option.

Alias: LV=

Default: 2, which produces a dashed line

MU=*value* | EST

specifies the mean μ for a normal Q-Q plot requested with the NORMAL option.

Default: the sample mean

Requirement: You must enclose this suboption in parentheses after the NORMAL option.

Tip: Specify the MU= and SIGMA= suboptions together to request a distribution reference line. Specify MU=EST to request a distribution reference line with μ_0 equal to the sample mean.

NADJ=*value*

specifies the adjustment value that is added to the sample size in the calculation of theoretical quantiles. For additional information, see Chambers et al. (1983).

Default: $\frac{1}{4}$ as recommended by Blom (1958)

NAME='*string*'

specifies a name for the plot, up to eight characters long, that appears in the PROC GREPLAY master menu.

Default: UNIVAR

NCOLS=*n*

specifies the number of columns in the comparative probability plot.

Alias: NCOL=

Default: NCOLS=1, if you specify only one class variable, and NCOLS=2, if you specify two class variables.

Requirement: This option is ignored unless you specify the CLASS statement.

Interaction: If you specify two class variables, you can use the NCOLS= option with the NROWS= option.

NOFRAME

suppresses the frame around the area that is bounded by the axes.

NORMAL<(*normal-suboptions*)>

displays a normal Q-Q plot. This is the default if you omit a distribution option.

Tip: To assess the point pattern, add a diagonal distribution reference line that corresponds to μ_0 and σ_0 with the MU= and SIGMA= suboptions. Alternatively, you can add a line that corresponds to estimated values of μ_0 and σ_0 with the THETA=EST and SIGMA=EST; the estimates of the mean μ_0 and the standard deviation σ_0 are the sample mean and sample standard deviation.

Agreement between the reference line and the point pattern indicates that the normal distribution with parameters μ_0 and σ_0 is a good fit.

Main discussion: "Normal Distribution" on page 1413

See also: the MU= suboption on page 1382 and SIGMA= suboption on page 1383

NROWS=*n*
specifies the number of rows in the comparative probability plot.

Alias: NROW=

Default: 2

Requirement: This option is ignored unless you specify the CLASS statement.

Interaction: If you specify two class variables, you can use the NCOLS= option with the NROWS= option.

PCTLMINOR
requests minor tick marks for the percentile axis.

PCTLSCALE
requests scale labels for the theoretical quantile axis in percentile units, resulting in a nonlinear axis scale.

Tip: Tick marks are drawn uniformly across the axis based on the quantile scale. In all other respects, the plot remains the same, and you must specify HREF= values in quantile units. For a true nonlinear axis, use the PROBPLOT statement.

RANKADJ=*value*
specifies the adjustment value that PROC UNIVARIATE adds to the ranks in the calculation of theoretical quantiles. For additional information, see Chambers et al. (1983).

Default: $-\frac{3}{8}$ as recommended by Blom (1958)

SCALE=*value*
is an alias for the SIGMA= option when you request Q-Q plots with the BETA, EXPONENTIAL, GAMMA, WEIBULL, and WEIBULL2 options and for the ZETA= option when you request the LOGNORMAL option.

See also: SIGMA= on page 1383 and ZETA= on page 1386

SHAPE=*value(s)*|EST
is an alias for the ALPHA=option when you request gamma plots with the GAMMA option, for the SIGMA= option when you request lognormal plots with the LOGNORMAL option, and for the C= option when you request Weibull plots with the WEIBULL, and WEIBULL2 options.

See also: ALPHA= on page 1378, SIGMA= on page 1383, and C= on page 1379

SIGMA=*value(s)*|EST
specifies the distribution parameter σ, where $\sigma > 0$ for the quantile plot. The interpretation and use of the SIGMA= option depend on which distribution you specify, as shown in Table 41.5 on page 1384.

Table 41.5 Uses of the SIGMA Suboption

Distribution Option	Uses of the SIGMA= Option
BETA, EXPONENTIAL GAMMA, WEIBULL	THETA=θ_0 and SIGMA=σ_0 request a distribution reference line with intercept θ_0 and slope σ_0.
LOGNORMAL	SIGMA=$\sigma_1 \ldots \sigma_n$ requests n Q-Q plots with shape parameters $\sigma_1 \ldots \sigma_n$. The SIGMA= option is required.
NORMAL	MU=μ_0 and SIGMA=σ_0 request a distribution reference line with intercept μ_0 and slope σ_0. SIGMA=EST requests a slope σ_0 equal to the sample standard deviation.
WEIBULL2	SIGMA=σ_0 and C=c_0 request a distribution reference line with intercept $\log\left(\sigma_0\right)$ and slope $\frac{1}{c_0}$.

Requirement: Enclose this suboption in parentheses after the distribution option.

Tip: To compute a maximum likelihood estimate for σ_0, specify SIGMA=EST .

SLOPE=*value*|EST
specifies the slope for a distribution reference when you request the LOGNORMAL option or WEIBULL2 option.

Requirement: Enclose this suboption in parentheses after the distribution option.

Tip: When you use the LOGNORMAL option and SLOPE= to request the line, you must also specify a threshold parameter value θ_0 with the THETA= suboption. SLOPE= is an alternative to the ZETA= suboption for specifying ζ_0, because the slope is equal to $\exp\left(\zeta_0\right)$.

When you use the WEIBULL2 option and SLOPE= option to request the line, you must also specify a scale parameter value σ_0 with the SIGMA= suboption. SLOPE= is an alternative to the C= suboption for specifying c_0, because the slope is equal to $\frac{1}{c_0}$.

For example, the first and second QQPLOT statements produce the same quantile-quantile plots as the third and fourth QQPLOT statements:

```
proc univariate data=measures;
   qqplot width /lognormal(sigma=2 theta=0 zeta=0);
   qqplot width /lognormal(sigma=2 theta=0 slope=1);
   qqplot width /weibull2(sigma=2 theta=0 c=.25);
   qqplot width /weibull2(sigma=2 theta=0 slope=4);
```

Main Discussion: "Shape Parameters" on page 1414

SQUARE
displays the Q-Q plot in a square frame.

Default: rectangular frame

THETA=*value*|EST
specifies the lower threshold parameter θ for Q-Q plots when you request BETA, EXPONENTIAL, GAMMA, LOGNORMAL, WEIBULL, or WEIBULL2 option.

Default: 0

Requirement: You must enclose this suboption in parentheses after the distribution option.

Interaction: When you use the WEIBULL2 option, the THETA= suboption specifies the known lower threshold θ_0, which by default is 0.

When you use the THETA= suboption with another distribution option, THETA= specifies θ_0 for a distribution reference line. To compute a maximum likelihood estimate for θ_0, specify THETA=EST. To request the line, you must also specify a scale parameter.

THRESHOLD= *value* | EST
is an alias for the THETA= option. See the THETA= suboption on page 1384.

VMINOR=*n*
specifies the number of minor tick marks between each major tick mark on the vertical axis. QQPLOT does not label minor tick marks.

Alias: VM=

Default: 0

VREF=*value(s)*
draws reference lines that are perpendicular to the vertical axis at the *value(s)* you specify.

See also: CVREF= option on page 1380 and LVREF= option on page 1382

VREFLABELS=' *label1*'... '*labeln*'
specifies labels for the reference lines that you request with the VREF= option.

Alias: VREFLABEL= and VREFLAB=

Restriction: The number of labels must equal the number of reference lines. Labels can have up to 16 characters.

W=*n*
specifies the width in pixels for a distribution reference line.

Default: 1

Requirement: You must enclose this suboption in parentheses after the distribution option.

WEIBULL(C=*value(s)* | EST <*Weibull-suboptions*>)
creates a three-parameter Weibull Q–Q plot for each value of the required shape parameter c.

Alias: WEIB

Requirement: You must specify the shape parameter with the C= suboption.

Interaction: To create a plot that is based on a maximum likelihood estimate for c, specify C=EST.
   To specify the threshold value θ_0, use the THETA= suboption.

Tip: To obtain a graphical estimate of c, specify a list of values in the C= suboption. Then select the value that most nearly linearizes the point pattern.
   To assess the point pattern, add a diagonal distribution reference line with intercept θ_0 and slope σ_0 with the THETA= and SIGMA= suboptions. Alternatively, you can add a line that corresponds to estimated values of θ_0 and σ_0 with THETA=EST and SIGMA=EST.
   Agreement between the reference line and the point pattern indicates that the Weibull distribution with parameters c, θ_0, and σ_0 is a good fit.

Main discussion: "Three-Parameter Weibull Distribution" on page 1413

See also the C= suboption on page 1379, SIGMA= suboption on page 1383, and THETA= suboption on page 1384

WEIBULL2<(*Weibull-suboptions*)>
creates a two-parameter Weibull Q-Q plot. Use this distribution when your data have a *known* lower threshold θ_0, which by default is 0. To specify the threshold value θ_0, use the THETA= suboption.

Note: The C= shape parameter option is not required with the Weibull2 option. △

Alias: W2

Default: 0

Interaction: To specify the threshold value θ_0, use the THETA= suboption.

Tip: An advantage of the two-parameter Weibull plot over the three-parameter Weibull plot is that the parameters c and σ can be estimated from the slope and intercept of the point pattern. A disadvantage is that the two-parameter Weibull distribution applies only in situations where the threshold parameter is known.

Tip: To obtain a graphical estimate of θ_0, specify a list of values for the THETA= suboption. Then select the value that most nearly linearizes the point pattern.

To assess the point pattern, add a diagonal distribution reference line that corresponds to σ_0 and c_0 with the SIGMA= and C= suboptions. Alternatively, you can add a distribution reference line that corresponds to estimated values of σ_0 and c_0 with SIGMA=EST and C=EST.

Agreement between the reference line and the point pattern indicates that the Weibull2 distribution with parameters c_0, θ_0, and σ_0 is a good fit.

Main discussion: "Two-Parameter Weibull Distribution" on page 1414

See also: the C= suboption on page 1379, SIGMA= suboption on page 1383, SLOPE= suboption on page 1384, and THETA= suboption on page 1384

ZETA= *value* | **EST**
specifies a value for the scale parameter ζ for the lognormal Q-Q plots when you request the LOGNORMAL option.

Requirement: You must enclose this suboption in parentheses after the LOGNORMAL option.

Interaction: To request a distribution reference line with intercept θ_0 and slope $\exp(\zeta_0)$, specify THETA= θ_0 and ZETA= ζ_0.

Theoretical Percentiles of Quantile-Quantile Plots

To estimate percentiles from a Q-Q plot

□ Specify the PCTLAXIS option, which adds a percentile axis opposite the theoretical quantile axis. The scale for the percentile axis ranges between 0 and 100 with tick marks at percentile values such as 1, 5, 10, 25, 50, 75, 90, 95, and 99.

□ Specify the PCTLSCALE option, which relabels the horizontal axis tick marks with their percentile equivalents but does not alter their spacing. For example, on a normal Q-Q plot, the tick mark labeled 0 is relabeled as 50 because the 50th percentile corresponds to the zero quantile.

You can also use the PROBPLOT statement to estimate percentiles.

VAR Statement

Specifies the analysis variables and their order in the results.

Default: If you omit the VAR statement, PROC UNIVARIATE analyzes all numeric variables that are not listed in the other statements.

Featured in: Example 1 on page 1418 and Example 6 on page 1437

VAR *variable(s)*;

Required Arguments

variable(s)
identifies one or more analysis variables.

Using the Output Statement with the VAR Statement

Use a VAR statement when you use an OUTPUT statement. To store the same statistic for several analysis variables in the OUT= data set, you specify a list of names in the OUTPUT statement. PROC UNIVARIATE makes a one-to-one correspondence between the order of the analysis variables in the VAR statement and the list of names that follow a statistic keyword.

WEIGHT Statement

Specifies weights for analysis variables in the statistical calculations.

See also: For information about how to calculate weighted statistics and for an example that uses the WEIGHT statement, see "Calculating Weighted Statistics" on page 74

WEIGHT *variable*;

Required Arguments

variable
specifies a numeric variable whose values weight the values of the analysis variables. The values of the variable do not have to be integers. If the value of the weight variable is

Weight value...	PROC UNIVARIATE...
0	counts the observation in the total number of observations
less than 0	converts the weight value to zero and counts the observation in the total number of observations
missing	excludes the observation

To exclude observations that contain negative and zero weights from the analysis, use EXCLNPWGT. Note that most SAS/STAT procedures, such as PROC GLM, exclude negative and zero weights by default.

The weight variable does not change how the procedure determines the range, mode, extreme values, extreme observations, or number of missing values. The Student's *t* test is the only test of location that PROC UNIVARIATE computes when you weight the analysis variables.

Restriction: The CIPCTLDF, CIPCTLNORMAL, LOCCOUNT, NORMAL, ROBUSTSCALE, TRIMMED=, and WINSORIZED= options are not available with the WEIGHT statement.

> **Restriction:** To compute weighted skewness or kurtosis, use VARDEF=DF or VARDEF=N in the PROC statement.

> **Tip:** When you use the WEIGHT statement, consider which value of the VARDEF= option is appropriate. See VARDEF= on page 1331 and the calculation of weighted statistics in "Keywords and Formulas" on page 1458 for more information.

> *Note:* Prior to Version 7 of the SAS System, the procedure did not exclude the observations with missing weights from the count of observations. △

Concepts

Rounding

When you specify ROUND=u, PROC UNIVARIATE rounds a variable by using the rounding unit to divide the number line into intervals with midpoints $u*i$, where u is the nonnegative rounding unit and i equals the integers (..., -4, -3, -2, -1, 0, 1, 2, 3, 4,...). The interval width is u. Any variable value that falls in an interval rounds to the midpoint of that interval. A variable value that is midway between two midpoints, and is therefore on the boundary of two intervals, rounds to the even midpoint. Even midpoints occur when i is an even integer (0,±2,±4,...).

When ROUND=1 and the analysis variable values are between -2.5 and 2.5, the intervals are as follows:

i	Interval	Midpoint	Left endpt rounds to	Right endpt rounds to
-2	[-2.5,-1.5]	-2	-2	-2
-1	[-1.5,-0.5]	-1	-2	0
0	[-0.5,0.5]	0	0	0
1	[0.5,1.5]	1	0	2
2	[1.5,2.5]	2	2	2

When ROUND=.5 and the analysis variable values are between -1.25 and 1.25, the intervals are as follows:

i	Interval	Midpoint	Left endpt rounds to	Right endpt rounds to
-2	[-1.25,-0.75]	-1.0	-1	-1
-1	[-0.75,-0.25]	-0.5	-1	0
0	[-0.25,0.25]	0.0	0	0
1	[0.25,0.75]	0.5	0	1
2	[0.75,1.25]	1.0	1	1

As the rounding unit increases, the interval width also increases. This reduces the number of unique values and decreases the amount of memory that PROC UNIVARIATE needs.

Generating Line Printer Plots

The PLOTS option in the PROC UNIVARIATE statement provides up to four diagnostic line printer plots to examine the data distribution. These plots are the stem-and-leaf plot or horizontal bar chart, the box plot, the normal probability plot, and the side-by-side box plots. If you specify the WEIGHT statement, PROC UNIVARIATE provides a weighted histogram, a weighted box plot based on the weighted quantiles, and a weighted normal probability plot.

Stem-and-Leaf Plot

The first plot in the output is either a stem-and-leaf plot (Tukey 1977) or a horizontal bar chart. If any single interval contains more than 49 observations, the horizontal bar chart appears. Otherwise, the stem-and-leaf plot appears. The stem-and-leaf plot is like a horizontal bar chart in that both plots provide a method to visualize the overall distribution of the data. The stem-and-leaf plot provides more detail because each point in the plot represents an individual data value.

To change the number of stems that the plot displays, use PLOTSIZE= to increase or decrease the number of rows. Instructions that appear below the plot explain how to determine the values of the variable. If no instructions appear, you multiply *Stem.Leaf* by 1 to determine the values of the variable. For example, if the stem value is 10 and the leaf value is 1, then the variable value is approximately 10.1.

For the stem-and-leaf plot, the procedure rounds a variable value to the nearest leaf. If the variable value is exactly halfway between two leaves, the value rounds to the nearest leaf with an even integer value. For example, a variable value of 3.15 has a stem value of 3 and a leaf value of 2.

Box Plot

The box plot, also known as a schematic plot, appears beside the stem-and-leaf plot. Both plots use the same vertical scale. The box plot provides a visual summary of the data and identifies outliers. The bottom and top edges of the box correspond to the sample 25th (Q1) and 75th (Q3) percentiles. The box length is one *interquartile range* (Q3 - Q1). The center horizontal line with asterisk endpoints corresponds to the sample median. The central plus sign (+) corresponds to the sample mean. If the mean and median are equal, the plus sign falls on the line inside the box. The vertical lines that project out from the box, called *whiskers*, extend as far as the data extend, up to a distance of 1.5 interquartile ranges. Values farther away are potential outliers. The procedure identifies the extreme values with a zero or an asterisk (*). If zero appears, the value is between 1.5 and 3 interquartile ranges from the top or bottom edge of the box. If an asterisk appears, the value is more extreme.

To generate box plot using high-resolution graphics, use the BOXPLOT procedure in SAS/STAT software.

Normal Probability Plot

The normal probability plot is a quantile-quantile plot of the data. The procedure plots the empirical quantiles against the quantiles of a standard normal distribution. Asterisks (*) indicate the data values. The plus signs (+) provide a straight reference line that is drawn by using the sample mean and standard deviation. If the data are from a normal distribution, the asterisks tend to fall along the reference line. The vertical coordinate is the data value, and the horizontal coordinate is $\Phi^{-1}(v_i)$ where

$$\Phi^{-1}\left(\left(r_i - 3/8\right)/\left(n + 1/4\right)\right)$$

and where

v_i is $\left(r_i - \frac{3}{8} \right) / \left(n + \frac{1}{4} \right)$.

Φ^{-1} is the inverse of the standard normal distribution function.

r_i is the rank of the ith data value when ordered from smallest to largest.

n is the number of nonmissing data values.

For weighted normal probability plot, the ith ordered observation is plotted against the normal quantile $\Phi^{-1}(v_i)$, where Φ^{-1} is the inverse standard cumulative normal distribution and

$$
v_i = \frac{\sum_{j=1}^{i} w_{(j)} \left(1 - \frac{3}{8i} \right)}{W \left(1 + \frac{1}{4n} \right)}
$$

where $w_{(j)}$ is weight that is associated with $y_{(j)}$ for the jth ordered observation and $W = \sum_{i=1}^{n} w_i$ is the sum of the individual weights.

When each observation has an identical weight, $w_{(j)} = w$, the formula for v_i reduces to the expression for v_i in the unweighted normal probability plot

$$
v_i = \frac{i - \frac{3}{8}}{n + \frac{1}{4}}
$$

When the value of VARDEF= is WDF or WEIGHT, PROC UNIVARIATE draws a reference line with intercept $\widehat{\mu}$ and slope $\widehat{\sigma}$ and when the value of VARDEF= is DF or N, the slope is $\widehat{\sigma}/\sqrt{\overline{w}}$ where $\overline{w} = W/n$ is the average weight.

When each observation has an identical weight and the value of VARDEF= is DF, N, or WEIGHT, the reference line reduces to the usual reference line with intercept $\widehat{\mu}$ and slope $\widehat{\sigma}$ in the unweighted normal probability plot.

If the data are normally distributed with mean μ, standard deviation σ, and each observation has an identical weight w, then, as in the unweighted normal probability plot, the points on the plot should lie approximately on a straight line. The intercept is μ and slope is σ when VARDEF= is WDF or WEIGHT, and the slope is $\sigma/\sqrt{w}$ when VARDEF= is DF or N.

Side-by-Side Box Plots

When you use a BY statement with the PLOT option, PROC UNIVARIATE produces full-page side-by-side box plots, one for each BY group. The box plots (also known as schematic plots) use a common scale that allows you to compare the data distribution across BY groups. This plot appears after the univariate analyses of all BY groups. Use the NOBYPLOT option to suppress this plot.

For more information on how to interpret these plots see *SAS System for Elementary Statistical Analysis* and *SAS System for Statistical Graphics*.

Generating High-Resolution Graphics

If your site licenses SAS/GRAPH software, you can use the HISTOGRAM statement, PROBPLOT statement, and QQPLOT statement to create high-resolution graphs.

The HISTOGRAM statement generates histograms and comparative histograms that allow you to examine the data distribution. You can optionally fit families of density curves and superimpose kernel density estimates on the histograms. For additional information about the fitted distributions and kernel density estimates, see "Formulas for Fitted Continuous Distributions" on page 1406.

The PROBPLOT statement generates a probability plot, which compares ordered values of a variable with percentiles of a specified theoretical distribution. The QQPLOT statement generates a quantile-quantile plot, which compares ordered values of a variable with quantiles of a specified theoretical distribution. Thus, you can use these plots to determine how well a theoretical distribution models a set of measures.

Quantile–Quantile and Probability Plots

The following figure illustrates how to construct a Q-Q plot for a specified theoretical distribution $F(x)$ with the QQPLOT statement.

Figure 41.3 Construction of a Q-Q Plot

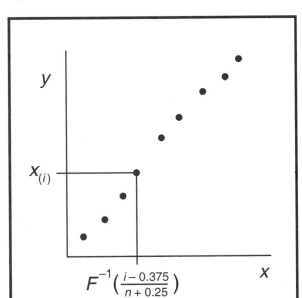

First, the n nonmissing values of the variable are ordered from smallest to largest: $x_{(1)} \leq x_{(2)} \leq \cdots \leq x_{(n)}$. Then, the ith ordered value $x_{(i)}$ is represented on the plot by a point whose y-coordinate is $x_{(i)}$ and whose x-coordinate is $F^{-1}\left(\frac{i-0.375}{n+0.25}\right)$, where $F(.)$ is the theoretical distribution with a zero location parameter and a unit scale parameter. For additional information about the theoretical distributions that you can request, see "Theoretical Distributions for Quantile-Quantile and Probability Plots" on page 1411.

You can modify the adjustment constants -0.375 and 0.25 with the RANKADJ= and NADJ= options. The default combination is recommended by Blom (1958). For additional information, see Chambers et al. (1983). Since $x_{(i)}$ is a quantile of the empirical cumulative distribution function (ecdf), a Q-Q plot compares quantiles of the ecdf with quantiles of a theoretical distribution. Probability plots are constructed the same way, except that the x-axis is scaled nonlinearly in percentiles.

Interpreting Quantile–Quantile and Probability Plots

If the data distribution matches the theoretical distribution, the points on the plot form a linear pattern. Thus, you can use a Q–Q plot or a probability plot to determine how well a theoretical distribution models a set of measurements. The following properties of these plots make them useful diagnostics to test how well a specified theoretical distribution fits a set of measurements:

- □ If the quantiles of the theoretical and data distributions agree, the plotted points fall on or near the line $y = x$.

- □ If the theoretical and data distributions differ only in their location or scale, the points on the plot fall on or near the line $y = ax + b$. The slope a and intercept b are visual estimates of the scale and location parameters of the theoretical distribution.

Q-Q plots are more convenient than probability plots for graphical estimation of the location and scale parameters because the x-axis of a Q-Q plot is scaled linearly. On the other hand, probability plots are more convenient for estimating percentiles or probabilities. There are many reasons why the point pattern in a Q-Q plot may not be linear. Chambers et al. (1983) and Fowlkes (1987) discuss the interpretations of commonly encountered departures from linearity, and these are summarized in the following table.

Table 41.6   Quantile-Quantile Plot Diagnostics

Description of Point Pattern	Possible Interpretation
All but a few points fall on a line	Outliers in the data
Left end of pattern is below the line; right end of pattern is above the line	Long tails at both ends of the data distribution
Left end of pattern is above the line; right end of pattern is below the line	Short tails at both ends of the distribution
Curved pattern with slope increasing from left to right	Data distribution is skewed to the right
Curved pattern with slope decreasing from left to right	Data distribution is skewed to the left
Staircase pattern (plateaus and gaps)	Data have been rounded or are discrete

In some applications, a nonlinear pattern may be more revealing than a linear pattern. However as noted by Chambers et al. (1983), departures from linearity can also be due to chance variation.

Determining Computer Resources

Because PROC UNIVARIATE computes quantile statistics, it requires additional memory to store a copy of the data in memory. By default, the report procedures PROC MEANS, PROC SUMMARY, and PROC TABULATE require less memory because they do not automatically compute quantiles. These procedures also provide an option to use a new fixed-memory quantiles estimation method that is usually less memory intense. For more information, see "Quantiles" on page 653.

The only factor that limits the number of variables that you can analyze is the computer resources that are available. The amount of temporary storage and CPU time that PROC UNIVARIATE requires depends on the statements and the options that you specify. To calculate the computer resources the procedure needs, let

N be the number of observations in the data set

V be the number of variables in the VAR statement

U_i be the number of unique values for the ith variable.

Then the minimum memory requirement in bytes to process all variables is

$$M = 24 \sum U_i$$

If M bytes are not available, PROC UNIVARIATE must process the data multiple times to compute all the statistics. This reduces the minimum memory requirement to

$$M = 24 \max (U_i)$$

ROUND= reduces the number of unique values (U_i), thereby reducing memory requirements. ROBUSTSCALE requires $40U_i$ bytes of temporary storage.

Several factors affect the CPU time requirement:

- □ The time to create V tree structures to internally store the observations is proportional to $NV \log (N)$.
- □ The time to compute moments and quantiles for the ith variable is proportional to U_i.
- □ The time to compute the NORMAL option test statistics is proportional to N.
- □ The time to compute the ROBUSTSCALE option test statistics is proportional to $U_i \log (U_i)$.
- □ The time to compute the exact significance level of the sign rank statistic may increase when the number of nonzero values is less than or equal to 20.

Each of these factors has a different constant of proportionality. For additional information on how to optimize CPU performance and memory usage, see the SAS documentation for your operating environment.

Statistical Computations

PROC UNIVARIATE uses standard algorithms to compute the moment statistics (such as the mean, variance, skewness, and kurtosis). See Appendix 1, "SAS Elementary Statistics Procedures," on page 1457 for the statistical formulas. The computational details for confidence limits, hypothesis test statistics, and quantile statistics follow.

Confidence Limits for Parameters of the Normal Distribution

The two-sided $100 (1 - \alpha)$ percent confidence interval for the mean has upper and lower limits

$$\overline{x} \pm t_{(1-\alpha/2;n-1)}\frac{s}{\sqrt{n}}$$

where s is $\sqrt{\frac{1}{n-1}\sum\left(x_i - \overline{x}\right)^2}$ and $t_{(1-\alpha/2;n-1)}$ is the $(1-\alpha/2)$ percentile of the t distribution with $n-1$ degrees of freedom.

The one-sided $100\,(1-\alpha)$ percent confidence limit is computed as

$$\overline{x} + t_{(1-\alpha;n-1)}\frac{s}{\sqrt{n}} \qquad \textbf{(upper)}$$

$$\overline{x} - t_{(1-\alpha;n-1)}\frac{s}{\sqrt{n}} \qquad \textbf{(lower)}$$

The two-sided $100\,(1-\alpha)$ percent confidence interval for the standard deviation has lower and upper limits

$$s\sqrt{\frac{n-1}{\chi^2_{(1-\alpha/2;n-1)}}} \,,\; s\sqrt{\frac{n-1}{\chi^2_{(\alpha/2;n-1)}}}$$

where $\chi^2_{(1-\alpha/2;n-1)}$ and $\chi^2_{(\alpha/2;n-1)}$ are the $(1-\alpha/2)$ and $\alpha/2$ percentiles of the chi-square distribution with $n-1$ degrees of freedom. A one-sided $100\,(1-\alpha)$ percent confidence limit is computed by replacing $\alpha/2$ with α.

A $100\,(1-\alpha)$ percent confidence interval for the variance has upper and lower limits equal to the squares of the corresponding upper and lower limits for the standard deviation.

When you use the WEIGHT statement and specify VARDEF=DF in the PROC statement, the $100\,(1-\alpha)$ percent confidence interval for the weighted mean is

$$\overline{x}_w \pm t_{(1-\alpha/2)}\frac{s_w}{\sqrt{\sum\limits_{i=1}^{n} w_i}}$$

where $\overline{x}_w$ is the weighted mean, s_w is the weighted standard deviation, w_i is the weight for ith observation, and $t_{(1-\alpha/2)}$ is the $(1-\alpha/2)$ critical percentage for the t distribution with $n-1$ degrees of freedom.

Tests for Location

PROC UNIVARIATE computes tests for location that include Student's t test, the sign test, and the Wilcoxon signed rank test. All three tests produce a test statistic for the null hypothesis that the mean or median is equal to a given value μ_0 against the two-sided alternative that the mean or median is not equal to μ_0. By default, PROC UNIVARIATE sets the value of μ_0 to zero. Use the MU0= option in the PROC UNIVARIATE statement to test that the mean or median is equal to another value.

The Student's t test is appropriate when the data are from an approximately normal population; otherwise, use nonparametric tests such as the sign test or the signed rank test. For large sample situations, the t test is asymptotically equivalent to a z test.

If you use the WEIGHT statement, PROC UNIVARIATE computes only one weighted test for location, the t test. You must use the default value for the VARDEF= option in the PROC statement.

You can also compare means or medians of *paired data*. Data are said to be paired when subjects or units are matched in pairs according to one or more variables, such as pairs of subjects with the same age and gender. Paired data also occur when each subject or unit is measured at two times or under two conditions. To compare the means or medians of the two times, create an analysis variable that is the difference between the two measures. The test that the mean or the median difference of the variables equals zero is equivalent to the test that the means or medians of the two original variables are equal. See Example 4 on page 1428.

Student's *t* Test

PROC UNIVARIATE calculates the t statistic as

$$t = \frac{\overline{x} - \mu_0}{s/\sqrt{n}}$$

where $\overline{x}$ is the sample mean, n is the number of nonmissing values for a variable, and s is the sample standard deviation. Under the null hypothesis, the population mean equals μ_0. When the data values are approximately normally distributed, the probability under the null hypothesis of a t statistic that is as extreme, or more extreme, than the observed value (the p-value) is obtained from the t distribution with $n-1$ degrees of freedom. For large n, the t statistic is asymptotically equivalent to a z test.

When you use the WEIGHT statement and the default value of VARDEF=, which is DF, the t statistic is calculated as

$$t_w = \frac{\overline{x}_w - \mu_0}{s_w/\sqrt{\sum_{i=1}^{n} w_i}}$$

where $\overline{x}_w$ is the weighted mean, s_w is the weighted standard deviation, and w_i is the weight for ith observation. The t_w statistic is treated as having a Student's t distribution with $n-1$ degrees of freedom. If you specify the EXCLNPWGT option in the PROC statement, n is the number of nonmissing observations when the value of the WEIGHT variable is positive. By default, n is the number of nonmissing observations for the WEIGHT variable.

Sign Test

PROC UNIVARIATE calculates the sign test statistic as

$$\mathbf{M} = \left(n^+ - n^- \right)/2$$

where n^+ is the number of values that is greater than u_0 and n^- is the number of values that is less than u_0. Values equal to u_0 are discarded.

Under the null hypothesis that the population median is equal to u_0, the p-value for the observed statistic M is

$$\mathrm{Prob}\left\{|\mathbf{M}| \geq |M|\right\} = 0.5^{(n_t - 1)} \sum_{j=0}^{\min(n^+, n^-)} \binom{n_t}{j}$$

where $n_t = n^+ + n^-$ is the number of x_i values not equal to u_0.

Wilcoxon Signed Rank Test

PROC UNIVARIATE calculates the Wilcoxon signed rank test statistic as

$$S = \sum r_i^+ - n_t \left(n_t + 1\right)/4$$

where r_i^+ is the rank of $|x_i - \mu_0|$ after discarding values of x_i equal to u_0, n_t is the number of x_i values not equal to u_0, and the sum is calculated for values of $x_i - \mu_0$ greater than 0. Average ranks are used for tied values.

The *p*-value is the probability of obtaining a signed rank statistic greater in absolute value than the absolute value of the observed statistic S. If $n_t \leq 20$, the significance level of S is computed from the exact distribution of S, which can be enumerated under the null hypothesis that the distribution is symmetric about u_0. When $n_t > 20$, the significance of level S is computed by treating

$$\frac{S\sqrt{n_t - 1}}{\sqrt{n_t V - S^2}}$$

as a Student's *t* variate with $n_t - 1$ degrees of freedom. V is computed as

$$V = \frac{1}{24}n_t \left(n_t + 1\right)\left(2n_t + 1\right) - 0.5\sum t_i \left(t_i + 1\right)\left(t_i - 1\right)$$

where the sum is calculated over groups that are tied in absolute value, and t_i is the number of tied values in the ith group (Iman 1974; Conover 1980).

The Wilcoxon signed rank test assumes that the distribution is symmetric. If the assumption is not valid, you can use the sign test to test that the median is u_0. See Lehmann (1975) for more details.

Goodness-of-Fit Tests

When you specify the NORMAL option in the PROC UNIVARIATE statement or you request a fitted parametric distribution in the HISTOGRAM statement, the procedure computes test statistics for the null hypothesis that the values of the analysis variable are a random sample from the specified theoretical distribution. When you specify the normal distribution, the test statistics depend on the sample size. If the sample size is less than or equal to 2000, PROC UNIVARIATE calculates the Shapiro-Wilk *W* statistic. For a specified distribution, the procedure attempts to calculate three goodness-of-fit tests that are based on the empirical distribution function (EDF): the Kolmogorov-Smirnov *D* statistic, the Anderson-Darling statistic, and the Cramer-von Mises statistic. However, some of the EDF tests are currently not supported when the parameters of a specified distribution are estimated. See Table 41.7 on page 1400 for more information.

You determine whether to reject the null hypothesis by examining the probability that is associated with a test statistic. When the *p*-value is less than the predetermined critical value (alpha value), you reject the null hypothesis and conclude that the data came from the theoretical distribution.

If you want to test the normality assumptions that underlie analysis of variance methods, beware of using a statistical test for normality alone. A test's ability to reject the null hypothesis (known as the *power* of the test) increases with the sample size. As the sample size becomes larger, increasingly smaller departures from normality can be detected. Since small deviations from normality do not severely affect the validity of analysis of variance tests, it is important to examine other statistics and plots to make a final assessment of normality. The skewness and kurtosis measures and the plots that are provided by the PLOTS option, the HISTOGRAM statement, PROBPLOT statement, and QQPLOT statement can be very helpful. For small sample sizes, power is low for detecting larger departures from normality that may be important. To increase the test's ability to detect such deviations, you may want to declare significance at higher levels, such as 0.15 or 0.20, rather than the often-used 0.05 level. Again, consulting plots and additional statistics will help you assess the severity of the deviations from normality.

Shapiro-Wilk Statistic

If the sample size is less than or equal to 2000 and you specify the NORMAL option, PROC UNIVARIATE computes the Shapiro-Wilk statistic, W. The W statistic is the ratio of the best estimator of the variance (based on the square of a linear combination of the order statistics) to the usual corrected sum of squares estimator of the variance (Shapiro, 1965). W must be greater than zero and less than or equal to one. Small values of W lead to the rejection of the null hypothesis of normality. The distribution of W is highly skewed. Seemingly large values of W (such as 0.90) may be considered small and lead you to reject the null hypothesis. When the sample size is greater than three, the coefficients to compute the linear combination of the order statistics are approximated by the method of Royston (1992).

$$Z_n = \left(-\log \left(\gamma - \log \left(1 - W_n \right) \right) - \mu \right) / \sigma$$

when $4 \leq n \leq 11$ and

$$Z_n = \left(\log \left(1 - W_n \right) - \mu \right) / \sigma$$

when $12 \leq n \leq 2000$, where γ, μ, and σ are functions of n, obtained from simulation results, and Z_n is a standard normal variate. Large values of Z_n indicate departure from normality.

EDF Goodness-of-Fit Tests

When you fit a parametric distribution, PROC UNIVARIATE provides a series of goodness-of-fit tests that are based on the empirical distribution function (EDF). The empirical distribution function is defined for a set of n independent observations $X_1, \ldots, X_n$ with a common distribution function $F(x)$. The observations that are ordered from smallest to largest as $X_{(1)}, \ldots, X_{(n)}$. The empirical distribution function, $F_n(x)$, is defined as

$$F_n(x) = 0, \quad x < X_{(1)}$$
$$F_n(x) = \frac{i}{n}, \quad X_{(i)} \leq x < X_{(i+1)} \quad i = 1, \ldots, n-1$$
$$F_n(x) = 1, \quad X_{(n)} \leq x$$

Note that $F_n(x)$ is a step function that takes a step of height $\frac{1}{n}$ at each observation. This function estimates the distribution function $F(x)$. At any value x, $F_n(x)$ is the proportion of observations that is less than or equal to x while $F(x)$ is the theoretical probability of an observation that is less than or equal to x. EDF statistics measure the discrepancy between $F_n(x)$ and $F(x)$.

The computational formulas for the EDF statistics use the probability integral transformation $U = F(X)$. If $F(X)$ is the distribution function of X, the random variable U is uniformly distributed between 0 and 1.

Given n observations $X_{(1)}, \ldots, X_{(n)}$, PROC UNIVARIATE computes the values $U_{(i)} = F\left(X_{(i)}\right)$ by applying the transformation, as follows.

When you specify the NORMAL option in the PROC UNIVARIATE statement or use the HISTOGRAM statement to fit a parametric distribution, PROC UNIVARIATE provides a series of goodness-of-fit tests that are based on the empirical distribution function (EDF):

□ Kolmogorov-Smirnov

□ Anderson-Darling

□ Cramer-von Mises

These tests are based on various measures of the discrepancy between the empirical distribution function $F_n(x)$ and the proposed cumulative distribution function $F(x)$.

Once the EDF test statistics are computed, the associated p-values are calculated. PROC UNIVARIATE uses internal tables of probability levels that are similar to those given by D'Agostino and Stephens (1986). If the value lies between two probability levels, then linear interpolation is used to estimate the probability value.

Note: PROC UNIVARIATE does not support some of the EDF tests when you use the HISTOGRAM statement and you estimate the parameters of the specified distribution. See Table 41.7 on page 1400 for more information. △

Kolmogorov *D* Statistic

The Kolmogorov-Smirnov statistic (D) is defined as

$$D = \sup_x \left| F_n(x) - F_{(x)} \right|$$

The Kolmogorov-Smirnov statistic belongs to the supremum class of EDF statistics. This class of statistics is based on the largest vertical difference between $F(x)$ and $F_n(x)$.

The Kolmogorov-Smirnov statistic is computed as the maximum of D^+ and D^-. D^+ is the largest vertical distance between the EDF and the distribution function when the EDF is greater than the distribution function. D^- is the largest vertical distance when the EDF is less than the distribution function.

$$D^+ = \max_i \left(\frac{i}{n} - U_{(i)} \right)$$

$$D^- = \max_i \left(U_{(i)} - \frac{i-1}{n} \right)$$

$$D = \max \left(D^+, D^- \right)$$

PROC UNIVARIATE uses a modified Kolmogorov D statistic to test the data against a normal distribution with mean and variance equal to the sample mean and variance.

Anderson-Darling Statistic

The Anderson-Darling statistic and the Cramer-von Mises statistic belong to the quadratic class of EDF statistics. This class of statistics is based on the squared difference $(F_n(x) - F(x))^2$. Quadratic statistics have the following general form:

$$Q = n \int_{-\infty}^{+\infty} (F_n(x) - F(x))^2 \, \psi(x) \, dF(x)$$

The function $\psi(x)$ weights the squared difference $(F_n(x) - F(x))^2$.
The Anderson-Darling statistic (A^2) is defined as

$$A^2 = n \int_{-\infty}^{+\infty} (F_n(x) - F(x))^2 \left[F(x)(1 - F(x)) \right]^{-1} dF(x)$$

where the weight function is $\psi(x) = \left[F(x)(1 - F(x)) \right]^{-1}$.
The Anderson-Darling statistic is computed as

$$A^2 = -n - \frac{1}{n} \sum_{i=1}^{n} \left[(2i-1) \left(\log U_{(i)} + \log\left(1 - U_{(n+1-i)} \right) \right) \right]$$

Cramer-von Mises Statistic

The Cramer-von Mises statistic (W^2) is defined as

$$W^2 = n \int_{-\infty}^{+\infty} (F_n(x) - F(x))^2 \, dF(x)$$

where the weight function is $\psi(x) = 1$.
The Cramer-von Mises statistic is computed as

$$W^2 = \sum_{i=1}^{n} \left(U_{(i)} - \frac{2i-1}{2n} \right)^2 + \frac{1}{12n}$$

Probability Values of EDF Tests

Once the EDF test statistics are computed, PROC UNIVARIATE computes the associated probability values.

The probability value depends upon the parameters that are known and the parameters that PROC UNIVARIATE estimates for the fitted distribution. Table 41.7 on page 1400 summarizes different combinations of estimated parameters for which EDF tests are available.

Note: PROC UNIVARIATE assumes that the threshold (THETA=) parameter for the beta, exponential, gamma, lognormal, and Weibull distributions is known. If you omit its value, PROC UNIVARIATE assumes that it is zero and that it is known. Likewise, PROC UNIVARIATE assumes that the SIGMA= parameter, which determines the upper threshold (SIGMA) for the beta distribution, is known. If you omit its value, PROC UNIVARIATE assumes that the value is one. These parameters are not listed in Table 41.7 on page 1400 because they are assumed to be known in all cases, and they do not affect which EDF statistics PROC UNIVARIATE computes. △

Table 41.7   Availability of EDF Tests

Distribution	Parameters	EDF
Beta	α and β unknown	none
	α known, β unknown	none
	α unknown, β known	none
	α and β known	all
Exponential	σ unknown	all
	σ known	all
Gamma	α and σ unknown	none
	α known, σ unknown	none
	α unknown, σ known	none
	α and σ known	all
Lognormal	ζ and σ unknown	all
	ζ known, σ unknown	A^2 and W^2
	ζ unknown, σ known	A^2 and W^2
	ζ and σ known	all

Distribution	Parameters	EDF
Normal	μ and σ unknown	all
	μ known, σ unknown	A^2 and W^2
	μ unknown, σ known	A^2 and W^2
	μ and σ known	all
Weibull	c and σ unknown	A^2 and W^2
	c known, σ unknown	A^2 and W^2
	c unknown, σ known	A^2 and W^2
	c and σ known	all

Robust Estimators

A statistical method is robust if the method is insensitive to slight departures from the assumptions that justify the method. PROC UNIVARIATE provides several methods for robust estimation of location and scale.

Winsorized Means

When outliers are present in the data, the Winsorized mean is a robust estimator of the location that is relatively insensitive to the outlying values. The k-times Winsorized mean is calculated as

$$\overline{x}_{wk} = \frac{1}{n} \left((k+1)\, x_{(k+1)} + \sum_{i=k+2}^{n-k-1} x_{(i)} + (k+1)\, x_{(n-k)} \right)$$

The Winsorized mean is computed after the k smallest observations are replaced by the $(k+1)$ smallest observation, and the k largest observations are replaced by the $(k+1)$ largest observation.

For a symmetric distribution, the symmetrically Winsorized mean is an unbiased estimate of the population mean. But the Winsorized mean does not have a normal distribution even if the data are from a normal population.

The Winsorized sum of squared deviations is defined as

$$s_{wk}^2 = (k+1)\left(x_{(k+1)} - \overline{x}_{wk} \right)^2 + \sum_{i=k+2}^{n-k-1} \left(x_{(i)} - \overline{x}_{wk} \right)^2$$
$$+ (k+1)\left(x_{(n-k)} - \overline{x}_{wk} \right)^2$$

A Winsorized t test is given by

$$t_{wk} = \frac{\left(\overline{x}_{wk} - \mu_0 \right)}{STDERR\left(\overline{x}_{wk} \right)}$$

where the standard error of the Winsorized mean is

$$STDERR\left(\overline{x}_{wk}\right) = \frac{n-1}{n-2k-1}\frac{s_{wk}}{\sqrt{n\left(n-1\right)}}$$

When the data are from a symmetric distribution, the distribution of the Winsorized t statistic t_{wk} is approximated by a Student's t distribution with $n-2k-1$ degrees of freedom (Tukey and McLaughlin 1963, Dixon and Tukey 1968).

A $100\left(1-\alpha\right)$ percent confidence interval for the Winsorized mean has upper and lower limits

$$\overline{x}_{wk} \pm t_{(1-\alpha/2)}STDERR\left(\overline{x}_{wk}\right)$$

and the $(1-\alpha/2)$ critical value of the Student's t statistics has $n-2k-1$ degrees of freedom.

Trimmed Means

When outliers are present in the data, the trimmed mean is a robust estimator of the location that is relatively insensitive to the outlying values. The k-times trimmed mean is calculated as

$$\overline{x}_{tk} = \frac{1}{n-2k}\sum_{i=k+1}^{n-k} x_{(i)}$$

The trimmed mean is computed after the k smallest and k largest observations are deleted from the sample. In other words, the observations are trimmed at each end.

For a symmetric distribution, the symmetrically trimmed mean is an unbiased estimate of the population mean. But the trimmed mean does not have a normal distribution even if the data are from a normal population.

A robust estimate of the variance of the trimmed mean t_{tk} can be based on the Winsorized sum of squared deviations (Tukey and McLaughlin 1963). The resulting trimmed t test is given by

$$t_{tk} = \frac{\left(\overline{x}_{tk} - \mu_0\right)}{STDERR\left(\overline{x}_{tk}\right)}$$

where the standard error of the trimmed mean is

$$STDERR\left(\overline{x}_{tk}\right) = \frac{s_{wk}}{\sqrt{\left(n-2k\right)\left(n-2k-1\right)}}$$

and s_{wk} is the square root of the Winsorized sum of squared deviations

When the data are from a symmetric distribution, the distribution of the trimmed t statistic t_{tk} is approximated by a Student's t distribution with $n-2k-1$ degrees of freedom (Tukey and McLaughlin 1963, Dixon and Tukey 1968).

A $100\left(1-\alpha\right)$ percent confidence interval for the trimmed mean has upper and lower limits

$$\overline{x}_{tk} \pm t_{(1-\alpha/2)} STDERR\left(\overline{x}_{tk}\right)$$

and the $(1 - \alpha/2)$ critical value of the Student's t statistics has $n - 2k - 1$ degrees of freedom.

Robust Measures of Scale

The sample standard deviation is a commonly used estimator of the population scale. However, it is sensitive to outliers and may not remain bounded when a single data point is replaced by an arbitrary number. With robust scale estimators, the estimates remain bounded even when a portion of the data points are replaced by arbitrary numbers.

PROC UNIVARIATE computes robust measures of scale that include statistics of interquartile range, Gini's mean difference G, *MAD*, Q_n, and S_n, with their corresponding estimates of σ.

The interquartile range is a simple robust scale estimator, which is the difference between the upper and lower quartiles. For a normal population, the standard deviation σ can be estimated by dividing the interquartile range by 1.34898.

Gini's mean difference is also a robust estimator of the standard deviation σ. For a normal population, Gini's mean difference has expected value $2\sigma/\sqrt{\pi}$. Thus, multiplying Gini's mean difference by $\sqrt{\pi}/2$ yields a robust estimator of the standard deviation when the data are from a normal sample. The constructed estimator has high efficiency for the normal distribution relative to the usual sample standard deviation. It is also less sensitive to the presence of outliers than the sample standard deviation.

Gini's mean difference is computed as

$$G = \frac{1}{\binom{n}{2}} \sum_{i<j} |x_i - x_j|$$

If the observations are from a normal distribution, then $\sqrt{\pi}\, G/2$ is an unbiased estimator of the standard deviation σ.

A very robust scale estimator is the *MAD*, the median absolute deviation about the median (Hampel, 1974.)

$$MAD = \text{med}_i \left(|x_i - \text{med}_j \left(x_j \right)| \right)$$

where the inner median, $\text{med}_j(x_j)$, is the median of the n observations and the outer median, med_i, is the median of the n absolute values of the deviations about the median.

For a normal distribution, 1.4826·*MAD* can be used to estimate the standard deviation σ.

The *MAD* statistic has low efficiency for normal distributions, and it may not be appropriate for symmetric distributions. Rousseeuw and Croux (1993) proposed two new statistics as alternatives to the *MAD* statistic.

The first statistic is

$$S_n = 1.1926 \,\text{med}_i(\text{med}_j(|x_i - x_j|))$$

where the outer median, med_i, is the median of the n medians of $(|x_i - x_j|)$; $j = 1, 2, \ldots, n$.

To reduce the small-sample bias, $c_{sn} S_n$ is used to estimate the standard deviation σ, where c_{sn} is a the correction factor (Croux and Rousseeuw, 1992.)

The second statistic is

$$Q_n = 2.219 \left\{ |x_i - x_j|; \ i < j \right\}_{(k)}$$

where $k = \binom{h}{2}$, $h = [n/2] + 1$, and $[n/2]$ is the integer part of $n/2$. That is, Q_n is

2.2219 times the kth order statistic of the $\binom{n}{2}$ distances between data points.

The bias-corrected statistic, $c_{qn} Q_n$, is used to estimate the standard deviation σ, where c_{qn} is a correction factor.

Calculating Percentiles

The UNIVARIATE procedure automatically computes the minimum, 1st, 5th, 10th, 25th, 50th, 75th, 90th, 95th, 99th, and maximum percentiles. You use the PCTLDEF= option in the PROC UNIVARIATE statement to specify one of five methods to compute quantile statistics. See for more information.

To compute the quantile that each observation falls in, use PROC RANK with the GROUP= option. To calculate percentiles other than the default percentiles, use PCTLPTS= and PCTLPRE= in the OUTPUT statement.

Confidence Limits for Quantiles

The CIPCTLDF option and CIPCTLNORMAL option compute confidence limits for quantiles using methods described in Hahn and Meeker (1991).

When $0.0 < p < 0.5$, the two-sided $100 (1 - \alpha)$ percent confidence interval for quantiles that are based on normal data has lower and upper limits

$$\overline{x} - g'_{(\alpha/2;1-p,n)} s, \overline{x} - g'_{(1-\alpha/2;1-p,n)} s$$

where p is the percentile $100 \times p$.

When $0.5 \le p < 1.0$, the lower and upper limits are

$$\overline{x} + g'_{(\alpha/2;p,n)} s, \ \overline{x} + g'_{(1-\alpha/2;p,n)} s$$

A one-sided $100 (1 - \alpha)$ percent confidence limit is computed by replacing $\alpha/2$ with α. The factor $g'_{(\gamma,p,n)}$ is described in Owen and Hua (1977) and Odeh and Owen (1980).

The two-sided distribution-free $100 (1 - \alpha)\%$ confidence interval for quantiles from a sample of size n is

$$x_{(l)}, x_{(u)}$$

where $x_{(j)}$ is jth order statistic. The lower rank l and upper rank u are integers that are symmetric or nearly symmetric around $i = [np] + 1$, where $[np]$ is the integral part of np.

The l and u are chosen so that the order statistics $x_{(l)}$ and $x_{(u)}$

□ are approximately symmetric about $x_{((n+1)p)}$

□ are as close to $x_{((n+1)p)}$ as possible

□ satisfy the coverage probability requirement.

$$Q_b (u - 1; n, p) - Q_b (l - 1; n, p) \geq 1 - \alpha$$

where Q_b is the cumulative binomial probability, $0 < l < u \leq n$, and $0 < p < 1$.

The coverage probability is sometimes less that $1 - \alpha$. This can occur in the tails of the distribution when the sample size is small. To avoid this problem, you can specify the option TYPE=ASYMMETRIC, which causes PROC UNIVARIATE to use asymmetric values of l and u. However, PROC UNIVARIATE first attempts to compute confidence limits that satisfy all three conditions. If the last condition is not satisfied, then the first condition is relaxed. Thus, some of the confidence limits may be symmetric while others, especially in the extremes, are not.

A one-sided distribution-free lower $100 (1 - \alpha)$ percent confidence limit is computed as $x_{(l)}$ when l is the largest integer that satisfies the inequality

$$1 - Q_b (l - 1; n, p) \geq 1 - \alpha$$

where $0 < l \leq n$, and $0 < p < 1$. Likewise, a one-sided distribution-free upper $100 (1 - \alpha)\%$ confidence limit is computed as $x_{(u)}$ when u is the smallest integer that satisfies the inequality

$$Q_b (u - 1; n, p) \geq 1 - \alpha$$

where $0 < u \leq n$, and $0 < p < 1$.

Weighted Quantiles

When you use the WEIGHT statement the percentiles are computed as follows. Let x_i be the ith ordered nonmissing value, $x_1 \leq x_2 \leq \ldots \leq x_n$. Then, for a given value of p between 0 and 1, the pth weighted quantile (or 100 pth weighted percentile), y, is computed from the empirical distribution function with averaging

$$y = \begin{cases} \frac{1}{2} (x_i + x_{i+1}) & \text{if } \sum_{j=1}^{i} w_j = pW \\ x_{i+1} & \text{if } \sum_{j=1}^{i} w_j < pW < \sum_{j=1}^{i+1} w_j \end{cases}$$

where w_j is the weight associated with x_i, $W = \sum_{i=1}^{n} w_i$ is the sum of the weights and w_i is the weight for ith observation.

When the observations have identical weights, the weighted percentiles are the same as the unweighted percentiles with PCTLDEF=5.

Calculating the Mode

The mode is the value that occurs most often in the data. PROC UNIVARIATE counts repetitions of the actual values or, if you specify the ROUND= option, the rounded values. If a tie occurs for the most frequent value, the procedure reports the lowest value. To list all possible modes, use the MODES option in the PROC UNIVARIATE statement. When no repetitions occur in the data (as with truly continuous data), the procedure does not report the mode.

The WEIGHT statement has no effect on the mode.

Formulas for Fitted Continuous Distributions

The following sections provide information about the families of parametric distributions that you can fit with the HISTOGRAM statement. Properties of the parametric curves are discussed by Johnson, et al. (1994).

Beta Distribution

The fitted density function is

$$p(x) = \begin{cases} \frac{(x-\theta)^{\alpha-1}(\sigma+\theta-x)^{\beta-1}}{B(\alpha,\beta)\sigma^{(\alpha+\beta-1)}} h \times 100\% & \text{for } \theta < x < \theta + \sigma \\ 0 & \text{for } x \leq \theta \text{ or } x \geq \theta + \sigma \end{cases}$$

where $B(\alpha, \beta) = \frac{\Gamma(\alpha)\Gamma(\beta)}{\Gamma(\alpha+\beta)}$ and

θ = lower threshold parameter (lower endpoint parameter)
σ = scale parameter ($\sigma > 0$)
α = shape parameter ($\alpha > 0$)
β = shape parameter ($\beta > 0$)
h = width of histogram interval

This notation is consistent with that of other distributions that you can fit with the HISTOGRAM statement. However, many texts, including Johnson, et al. (1994), write the beta density function as:

$$p(x) = \begin{cases} \frac{(x-a)^{p-1}(b-x)^{q-1}}{B(p,q)(b-a)^{p+q-1}} & \text{for } a < x < b \\ 0 & \text{for } x \leq a \text{ or } x \geq b \end{cases}$$

The two notations are related as follows:

$$\sigma = b - a$$
$$\theta = a$$
$$\alpha = p$$
$$\beta = q$$

The range of the beta distribution is bounded below by a threshold parameter $\theta = a$ and above by $\theta + \sigma = b$. If you specify a fitted beta curve using the BETA option, θ must be less than the minimum data value, and $\theta + \sigma$ must be greater than the maximum data value. You can specify θ and σ with the THETA= and SIGMA= *value* in parentheses after the keyword BETA. By default, $\sigma = 1$ and $\theta = 0$. If you specify THETA=EST and SIGMA=EST, maximum likelihood estimates are computed for θ and σ.

Note: However, three- and four-parameter maximum likelihood estimation may not always converge. △

In addition, you can specify α and β with the ALPHA= and BETA= *beta-options*, respectively. By default, the procedure calculates maximum likelihood estimates for α and β. For example, to fit a beta density curve to a set of data bounded below by 32 and above by 212 with maximum likelihood estimates for α and β, use the following statement:

```
histogram length / beta(theta=32 sigma=180);
```

The beta distributions are also referred to as Pearson Type I or II distributions. These include the *power-function* distribution ($\beta = 1$), the *arc-sine* distribution ($\alpha = \beta = \frac{1}{2}$), and the generalized *arc-sine* distributions ($\alpha + \beta = 1, \beta \neq \frac{1}{2}$). You can use the DATA step function BETAINV to compute beta quantiles and the DATA step function PROBBETA to compute beta probabilities.

Exponential Distribution

The fitted density function is

$$
p(x) = \begin{cases} \frac{h \times 100\%}{\sigma} \exp\left(-\left(\frac{x-\theta}{\sigma}\right)\right) & \text{for} x \geq \theta \\ 0 & \text{for } x < \theta \end{cases}
$$

where

$$
\begin{aligned}
\theta &= \text{threshold parameter} \\
\sigma &= \text{scale parameter } (\sigma > 0) \\
h &= \text{width of histogram interval}
\end{aligned}
$$

The threshold parameter θ must be less than or equal to the minimum data value. You can specify θ with the THRESHOLD= *exponential-option*. By default, $\theta = 0$. If you specify THETA=EST, a maximum likelihood estimate is computed for θ. In addition, you can specify σ with the SCALE= *exponential-option*. By default, the procedure calculates a maximum likelihood estimate for σ. Note that some authors define the scale parameter as $\frac{1}{\sigma}$.

The exponential distribution is a special case of both the gamma distribution (with $\alpha = 1$ and the Weibull distribution (with $c = 1$). A related distribution is the *extreme value* distribution. If $Y = \exp(-X)$ has an exponential distribution, then X has an extreme value distribution.

Gamma Distribution

The fitted density function is

$$p\left(x\right) = \begin{cases} \frac{h \times 100\%}{\Gamma(\alpha)\sigma} \left(\frac{x-\theta}{\sigma}\right)^{\alpha-1} \exp\left(-\left(\frac{x-\theta}{\sigma}\right)\right) & \text{for } x > \theta \\ 0 & \text{for } x \leq \theta \end{cases}$$

where

$$\theta = \text{threshold parameter}$$
$$\sigma = \text{scale parameter} \ (\sigma > 0)$$
$$\alpha = \text{shape parameter} \ (\alpha > 0)$$
$$h = \text{width of histogram interval}$$

The threshold parameter θ must be less than the minimum data value. You can specify θ with the THRESHOLD= *gamma-option*. By default, $\theta = 0$. If you specify THETA=EST, a maximum likelihood estimate is computed for θ. In addition, you can specify σ and α with the SCALE= and ALPHA= *gamma-options*. By default, the procedure calculates maximum likelihood estimates for σ and α.

The gamma distributions are also referred to as Pearson Type III distributions, and they include the chi-square, exponential, and Erlang distributions. The probability density function for the chi-square distribution is

$$p\left(x\right) = \begin{cases} \frac{1}{2\Gamma\left(\frac{\nu}{2}\right)} \left(\frac{x}{2}\right)^{\frac{\nu}{2}-1} \exp\left(-\frac{x}{2}\right) & \text{for } x > 0 \\ 0 & \text{for } x \leq 0 \end{cases}$$

Notice that this is a gamma distribution with $\alpha = \frac{\nu}{2}$, and $\theta = 0$. The exponential distribution is a gamma distribution with $\alpha = 1$, and the Erlang distribution is a gamma distribution with α being a positive integer. A related distribution is the Rayleigh distribution. If $R = \frac{\max(X_1,...,X_n)}{\min(X_1,...,X_n)}$ where the X_i's are independent χ^2_ν variables, then $\log R$ is distributed with a χ_ν distribution having a probability density function of

$$p\left(x\right) = \begin{cases} \left[2^{\frac{\nu}{2}-1}\Gamma\left(\frac{\nu}{2}\right)\right]^{-1} x^{\nu-1} \exp\left(-\frac{x^2}{2}\right) & \text{for } x > 0 \\ 0 & \text{for } x \leq 0 \end{cases}$$

If $\nu = 2$, the preceding distribution is referred to as the Rayleigh distribution. You can use the DATA step function GAMINV to compute gamma quantiles and the DATA step function PROBGAM to compute gamma probabilities.

Lognormal Distribution

The fitted density function is

$$p\left(x\right) = \begin{cases} \frac{h \times 100\%}{\sigma\sqrt{2\pi}(x-\theta)} \exp\left(-\frac{(\log(x-\theta)-\zeta)^2}{2\sigma^2}\right) & \text{for } x > \theta \\ 0 & \text{for } x \leq \theta \end{cases}$$

where

$$\theta = \text{threshold parameter}$$
$$\zeta = \text{scale parameter } (-\infty < \zeta < \infty)$$
$$\sigma = \text{shape parameter } (\sigma > 0)$$
$$h = \text{width of histogram interval}$$

The threshold parameter θ must be less than the minimum data value. You can specify θ with the THRESHOLD= *lognormal-option*. By default, $\theta = 0$. If you specify THETA=EST, a maximum likelihood estimate is computed for θ. You can specify ζ and σ with the SCALE= and SHAPE= *lognormal-options*, respectively. By default, the procedure calculates maximum likelihood estimates for these parameters.

Note: σ denotes the shape parameter of the lognormal distribution, whereas σ denotes the scale parameter of the beta, exponential, gamma, normal, and Weibull distributions. The use of σ to denote the lognormal shape parameter is based on the fact that $\frac{1}{\sigma} (\log (X - \theta) - \zeta)$ has a standard normal distribution if X is lognormally distributed. △

Normal Distribution

The fitted density function is

$$p(x) = \frac{h \times 100\%}{\sigma \sqrt{2\pi}} \exp\left(-\frac{1}{2}\left(\frac{x - \mu}{\sigma}\right)^2\right) \text{ for } -\infty < x < \infty$$

where

$$\mu = \text{mean}$$
$$\sigma = \text{standard deviation } (\sigma > 0)$$
$$h = \text{width of histogram interval}$$

You can specify μ and σ with the MU= and SIGMA= *normal-options*, respectively. By default, the procedure estimates μ with the sample mean and σ with the sample standard deviation. You can use the DATA step function PROBIT to compute normal quantiles and the DATA step function PROBNORM to compute probabilities.

Weibull Distribution

The fitted density function is

$$p(x) = \begin{cases} \frac{ch \times 100\%}{\sigma} \left(\frac{x-\theta}{\sigma}\right)^{c-1} \exp\left(-\left(\frac{x-\theta}{\sigma}\right)^c\right) & \text{for } x > \theta \\ 0 & \text{for } x \leq \theta \end{cases}$$

where

$$\theta = \text{threshold parameter}$$
$$\sigma = \text{scale parameter } (\sigma > 0)$$
$$c = \text{shape parameter } (\alpha > 0)$$
$$h = \text{width of histogram interval}$$

The threshold parameter θ must be less than the minimum data value. You can specify θ with the THRESHOLD= *Weibull-option*. By default, $\theta = 0$. If you specify THETA=EST, a maximum likelihood estimate is computed for θ. You can specify σ and c with the SCALE= and SHAPE= *Weibull-options*, respectively. By default, the procedure calculates maximum likelihood estimates for σ and c.

The exponential distribution is a special case of the Weibull distribution where $c = 1$.

Kernel Density Estimates

You can use the KERNEL option to superimpose kernel density estimates on histograms. Smoothing the data distribution with a kernel density estimate can be more effective than using a histogram to visualize features that might be obscured by the choice of histogram bins or sampling variation. For example, a kernel density estimate can also be more effective when the data distribution is multimodal. The general form of the kernel density estimator is

$$\hat{f}_\lambda(x) = \frac{1}{n\lambda} \sum_{i=1}^{n} K_0\left(\frac{x - x_i}{\lambda}\right)$$

where $K_0(.)$ is a kernel function, λ is the bandwidth, n is the sample size, and x_i is the ith observation.

The KERNEL option provides three kernel functions (K_0): normal, quadratic, and triangular. You can specify the function with the K=*kernel-function* in parentheses after the KERNEL option. Values for the K= option are NORMAL, QUADRATIC, and TRIANGULAR (with aliases of N, Q, and T, respectively). By default, a normal kernel is used. The formulas for the kernel functions are

Normal $K_0(t) = \frac{1}{\sqrt{2\pi}} \exp\left(-\frac{1}{2}t^2\right)$ for $-\infty < t < \infty$

Quadratic $K_0(t) = \frac{3}{4}\left(1 - t^2\right)$ for $|t| \leq 1$

Triangular $K_0(t) = 1 - |t|$ for $|t| \leq 1$

The value of λ, referred to as the bandwidth parameter, determines the degree of smoothness in the estimated density function. You specify λ indirectly by specifying a standardized bandwidth c with the C=*kernel-option*. If Q is the interquartile range, and n is the sample size, then c is related to λ by the formula

$$\lambda = cQn^{-\frac{1}{5}}$$

For a specific kernel function, the discrepancy between the density estimator $\hat{f}_\lambda(x)$ and the true density $f(x)$ is measured by the mean integrated square error (MISE):

$$\text{MISE}(\lambda) = \int_x \left\{ E\left(\hat{f}_\lambda(x)\right) - f(x) \right\}^2 dx + \int_x var\left(\hat{f}_\lambda(x)\right) dx$$

The MISE is the sum of the integrated squared bias and the variance. An approximate mean integrated square error (AMISE) is

$$\text{AMISE}(\lambda) = \frac{1}{4}\lambda^4 \left(\int_t t^2 K(t)\, dt \right)^2 \int_x \left(f''(x) \right)^2 dx + \frac{1}{n\lambda} \int_t K(t)^2\, dt$$

A bandwidth that minimizes AMISE can be derived by treating $f(x)$ as the normal density having parameters μ and σ estimated by the sample mean and standard deviation. If you do not specify a bandwidth parameter or if you specify C=MISE, the bandwidth that minimizes AMISE is used. The value of AMISE can be used to compare different density estimates. For each estimate, the bandwidth parameter c, the kernel function type, and the value of AMISE are reported in the SAS log.

Theoretical Distributions for Quantile-Quantile and Probability Plots

You can use the PROBPLOT and QQPLOT statements to request probability and Q-Q plots that are based on the theoretical distributions that are summarized in the following table:

Table 41.8 Distributions and Parameters

Distribution	Density Function $p(x)$	Range	Location	Scale	Shape
Beta	$\dfrac{(x-\theta)^{\alpha-1}(\theta+\sigma-x)^{\beta-1}}{\beta(\alpha,\beta)\sigma^{(\alpha+\beta-1)}}$	$\theta < x < \theta + \sigma$	θ	σ	α, β
Exponential	$\frac{1}{\sigma}\exp\left(-\frac{x-\theta}{\sigma}\right)$	$x \geq \theta$	θ	σ	
Gamma	$\frac{1}{\sigma\Gamma(\alpha)}\left(\frac{x-\theta}{\sigma}\right)^{\alpha-1}\exp\left(-\frac{x-\theta}{\sigma}\right)$	$x > \theta$	θ	σ	α
Lognormal (3-parameter)	$\frac{1}{\sigma\sqrt{2\pi}(x-\theta)}\exp\left(-\frac{(\log(x-\theta)-\zeta)^2}{2\sigma^2}\right)$	$x > \theta$	θ	ζ	σ
Normal	$\frac{1}{\sigma\sqrt{2\pi}}\exp\left(-\frac{(x-\mu)^2}{2\sigma^2}\right)$	*all x*	μ	σ	
Weibull (3-parameter)	$\frac{c}{\sigma}\left(\frac{x-\theta}{\sigma}\right)^{c-1}\exp\left(-\left(\frac{x-\theta}{\sigma}\right)^c\right)$	$x > \theta$	θ	σ	c
Weibull2 (2-parameter)	$\frac{c}{\sigma}\left(\frac{x-\theta_0}{\sigma}\right)^{c-1}\exp\left(-\left(\frac{x-\theta_0}{\sigma}\right)^c\right)$	$x > \theta_0$	θ_0 (known)	σ	c

You can request these distributions with the BETA, EXPONENTIAL, GAMMA, LOGNORMAL, NORMAL, WEIBULL, and WEIBULL2 options, respectively. If you omit a distribution option, the PROBPLOT statement creates a normal probability plot and the QQPLOT statement creates a normal Q-Q plot.

The following sections provide the details for constructing Q-Q plots that are based on these distributions. Probability plots are constructed similarly except that the horizontal axis is scaled in percentile units.

Beta Distribution

To create a plot that is based on the beta distribution, PROC UNIVARIATE orders the observations from smallest to largest, and plots the ith ordered observation against the quantile $B_{\alpha\beta}^{-1}\left(\frac{i-0.375}{n+0.25}\right)$ where $B_{\alpha\beta}^{-1}(.)$ is the inverse normalized incomplete beta function, n is the number of nonmissing observations, and α and β are the shape parameters of the beta distribution.

The point pattern on the plot for ALPHA=α and BETA=β tends to be linear with intercept θ and slope σ if the data are beta distributed with the specific density function

$$p(x) = \begin{cases} \frac{(x-\theta)^{\alpha-1}(\theta+\sigma-x)^{\beta-1}}{B(\alpha,\beta)\sigma^{(\alpha+\beta-1)}} & \text{for } \theta < x < \theta+\sigma \\ 0 & \text{for } x \leq \theta \text{ or } x \geq \theta+\sigma \end{cases}$$

where $B(\alpha,\beta) = \frac{\Gamma(\alpha)\Gamma(\beta)}{\Gamma(\alpha+\beta)}$ and θ is the lower threshold parameter, σ is the scale parameter $(\sigma > 0)$, α the first shape parameter $(\alpha > 0)$ and β is the second shape parameter $(\beta > 0)$.

Exponential Distribution

To create a plot that is based on the exponential distribution, PROC UNIVARIATE orders the observations from smallest to largest, and plots the ith ordered observation against the quantile $-\log\left(1 - \frac{i-0.375}{n+0.25}\right)$ where n is the number of nonmissing observations.

The point pattern on the plot tends to be linear with intercept θ and slope σ if the data are exponentially distributed with the specific density function

$$p(x) = \begin{cases} \frac{1}{\sigma}\exp\left(-\frac{x-\theta}{\sigma}\right) & \text{for } x \geq \theta \\ 0 & \text{for } x < \theta \end{cases}$$

where θ is a threshold parameter and σ is a positive scale parameter.

Gamma Distribution

To create a plot that is based on the gamma distribution, PROC UNIVARIATE orders the observations from smallest to largest, and plots the ith ordered observation against the quantile $G_{\alpha}^{-1}\left(\frac{i-0.375}{n+0.25}\right)$ where G_{α}^{-1} is the inverse normalized incomplete gamma function, n is the number of nonmissing observations, and α is the shape parameter of the gamma distribution.

The point pattern on the plot tends to be linear with intercept θ and slope σ if the data are gamma distributed with the specific density function

$$p(x) = \begin{cases} \frac{1}{\sigma\Gamma(\alpha)}\left(\frac{x-\theta}{\sigma}\right)^{\alpha-1}\exp\left(-\frac{x-\theta}{\sigma}\right) & \text{for } x > \theta \\ 0 & \text{for } x \leq \theta \end{cases}$$

where θ is the threshold parameter, σ is the scale parameter $(\sigma > 0)$, and α is the shape parameter $(\alpha > 0)$.

Lognormal Distribution

To create a plot that is based on the lognormal distribution, PROC UNIVARIATE orders the observations from smallest to largest, and plots the ith ordered observation against the quantile $\exp\left(\sigma\Phi^{-1}\left(\frac{i-0.375}{n+0.25}\right)\right)$ where $\Phi^{-1}(.)$ is the inverse standard cumulative normal distribution, n is the number of nonmissing observations, and σ is the shape parameter of the lognormal distribution.

The point pattern on the plot for SIGMA=σ tends to be linear with intercept θ and slope $\exp(\zeta)$ if the data are lognormally distributed with the specific density function

$$p(x) = \begin{cases} \frac{1}{\sigma\sqrt{2\pi}(x-\theta)} \exp\left(-\frac{(\log(x-\theta)-\zeta)^2}{2\sigma^2}\right) & \text{for } x > \theta \\ 0 & \text{for } x \leq \theta \end{cases}$$

where θ is the threshold parameter, ζ is the scale parameter, and σ is the shape parameter $(\sigma > 0)$.

Normal Distribution

To create a plot that is based on the normal distribution, PROC UNIVARIATE orders the observations from smallest to largest, and plots the ith ordered observation against the quantile $\Phi^{-1}\left(\frac{i-0.375}{n+0.25}\right)$ where $\Phi^{-1}(.)$ is the inverse cumulative standard normal distribution and n is the number of nonmissing observations.

The point pattern on the plot tends to be linear with intercept μ and slope σ if the data are normally distributed with the specific density function

$$p(x) = \frac{1}{\sigma\sqrt{2\pi}} \exp\left(-\frac{(x-\mu)^2}{2\sigma^2}\right) \quad \text{for all } x$$

where μ is the mean and σ is the standard deviation $(\sigma > 0)$.

Three-Parameter Weibull Distribution

To create a plot that is based on a three-parameter Weibull distribution, PROC UNIVARIATE orders the observations from smallest to largest, and plots the ith ordered observation against the quantile $\left(-\log\left(1-\frac{i-0.375}{n+0.25}\right)\right)^{\frac{1}{c}}$ where n is the number of nonmissing observations, and α and c are the Weibull distribution shape parameters.

The point pattern on the plot for C=c tends to be linear with intercept θ and slope σ if the data are Weibull distributed with the specific density function

$$p(x) = \begin{cases} \frac{c}{\sigma}\left(\frac{x-\theta}{\sigma}\right)^{c-1} \exp\left(-\left(\frac{x-\theta}{\sigma}\right)^c\right) & \text{for } x > \theta \\ 0 & \text{for } x \leq \theta \end{cases}$$

where θ is the threshold parameter, σ is the scale parameter $(\sigma > 0)$, and c is the shape parameter $(c > 0)$.

Two-Parameter Weibull Distribution

To create a plot that is based on a two-parameter Weibull distribution, PROC UNIVARIATE orders the observations from smallest to largest, and plots the log of the shifted i^{th} ordered observation $x_{(i)}$, denoted by $\log\left(x_{(i)} - \theta_0\right)$, against the quantile $\left(-\log\left(1 - \frac{i-0.375}{n+0.25}\right)\right)$ where n is the number of nonmissing observations.

Unlike the three-parameter Weibull quantile, the preceding expression is free of distribution parameters. This is why the C= shape parameter is not required in the WEIBULL2 option.

The point pattern on the plot for THETA=θ_0 tends to be linear with intercept $\log(\sigma)$ and slope $\frac{1}{c}$ if the data are Weibull distributed with the specific density function

$$
p(x) = \begin{cases} \frac{c}{\sigma}\left(\frac{x-\theta_0}{\sigma}\right)^{c-1} \exp\left(-\left(\frac{x-\theta_0}{\sigma}\right)^c\right) & \text{for} x > \theta_0 \\ 0 & \text{for } x \leq \theta_0 \end{cases}
$$

where θ_0 is the known lower threshold, σ is the scale parameter $(\sigma > 0)$, and c is the shape parameter $(c > 0)$.

Shape Parameters

Some distribution options in the PROBPLOT and QQPLOT statements require that you specify one or two shape parameters in parentheses after the distribution keyword. These are summarized in the following table:

Table 41.9 Shape Parameter Options

Distribution Keyword	Required Shape Parameter Option	Range
BETA	ALPHA=α, BETA=β	$\alpha > 0,\ \beta > 0$
EXPONENTIAL	None	
GAMMA	ALPHA=α	$\alpha > 0$
LOGNORMAL	SIGMA=σ	$\sigma > 0$
NORMAL	None	
WEIBULL	C=c	$c > 0$
WEIBULL2	None	

You can visually estimate the value of a shape parameter by specifying a list of values for the shape parameter option. PROC UNIVARIATE produces a separate plot for each value. Then you can use the value of the shape parameter that produces the most nearly linear point pattern. Alternatively, you can request that PROC UNIVARIATE use an estimated shape parameter to create the plot.

Note: For Q-Q plots that are requested with the WEIBULL2 option, you can estimate the shape parameter c from a linear pattern by using the fact that the slope of the pattern is $\frac{1}{c}$. △

Location and Scale Parameters

When you use the PROBPLOT statement to specify or estimate the location and scale parameters for a distribution, a diagonal distribution reference line appears on the probability plot. (An exception is the two-parameter Weibull distribution, where the line appears when you specify or estimate the scale and shape parameters.) Agreement between this line and the point pattern indicates that the distribution with these parameters is a good fit.

Note: Close visual agreement may not necessarily mean that the distribution is a good fit based on the criteria that are used by formal goodness-of-fit tests. △

When the point pattern on a Q-Q plot is linear, its intercept and slope provide estimates of the location and scale parameters. (An exception to this rule is the two-parameter Weibull distribution, for which the intercept and slope are related to the scale and shape parameters.) When you use the QQPLOT statement to specify or estimate the slope and intercept of the line, a diagonal distribution reference line appears on the Q-Q plot. This line allows you to check the linearity of the point pattern.

The following table shows which parameters to specify to determine the intercept and slope of the line:

Table 41.10 Intercept and Slope of Distribution Reference Line

Distribution	Parameters			Linear Pattern	
	Location	Scale	Shape	Intercept	Slope
BETA	θ	σ	α, β	θ	σ
EXPONENTIAL	θ	σ		θ	σ
GAMMA	θ	σ	α	θ	σ
LOGNORMAL	θ	ζ	σ	θ	$\exp(\zeta)$
NORMAL	μ	σ		μ	σ
WEIBULL (3-parameter)	θ	σ	c	θ	σ
WEIBULL2 (2-parameter)	θ_0 (known)	σ	c	$\log(\sigma)$	$\frac{1}{c}$

For the LOGNORMAL and WEIBULL2 options, you can specify the slope directly with the SLOPE= option. That is, for the LOGNORMAL option, when you specify THETA=θ_0 and SLOPE=$\exp(\zeta_0)$, PROC UNIVARIATE displays the same line as that which is specified by THETA=θ_0 and ZETA=ζ_0. For the WEIBULL2 option, when you specify SIGMA=σ_0 and SLOPE=$\frac{1}{c_0}$, PROC UNIVARIATE displays the same line when you specify SIGMA=σ_0 and C=c_0. Alternatively, you can request to use the estimated values of the parameters to determine the reference line.

Results

By default, PROC UNIVARIATE produces tables of moments, basic statistical measures, tests for location, quantiles, and extreme observations. You must specify options in the PROC UNIVARIATE statement to produce other statistics and tables.

The CIBASIC option produces the table of the basic confidence measures that includes the confidence limits for the mean, standard deviation, and variance. The CIPCTLDF option and CIPCTLNORMAL option produce tables of confidence limits for the quantiles. The LOCCOUNT option produces the table that shows the number of values greater than, equal to, and less than the value of MU0=. The FREQ option produces the table of frequencies counts. The NEXTRVAL= option produces the table with the frequencies of the extreme values. The NORMAL option produces the table with the tests for normality. The TRIMMED=, WINSORIZED=, and ROBUSTCALE options produce tables with robust estimators.

The table of trimmed or Winsorized means includes the percentage and the number of observations that are trimmed or Winsorized at each end, the mean and standard error, confidence limits, and the Student's t test. The table with robust measures of scale includes interquartile range, Gini's mean difference G, *MAD*, Q_n, and S_n, with their corresponding estimates of σ.

Missing Values

PROC UNIVARIATE excludes missing values for the analysis variable before calculating statistics. Each analysis variable is treated individually; a missing value for an observation in one variable does not affect the calculations for other variables. The statements handle missing values as follows:

- □ If a BY or an ID variable value is missing, PROC UNIVARIATE treats it like any other BY or ID variable value. The missing values form a separate BY group.
- □ If the FREQ variable value is missing or nonpositive, PROC UNIVARIATE excludes the observation from the analysis.
- □ If the WEIGHT variable value is missing, PROC UNIVARIATE excludes the observation from the analysis.

PROC UNIVARIATE tabulates the number of the missing values and reports this information in the procedure output. Before the number of missing values is tabulated, PROC UNIVARIATE excludes observations when

- □ you use the FREQ statement and the frequencies are nonpositive
- □ you use the WEIGHT statement and the weights are missing or nonpositive (you must specify the EXCLNPWGT option).

Histograms

If you request a fitted parametric distribution with a HISTOGRAM statement, PROC UNIVARIATE creates a report that summarizes the fit in addition to the graphical display. The report includes information about

- □ parameters for the fitted curve, estimated mean, and estimated standard deviation
- □ EDF goodness-of-fit tests
- □ histogram intervals
- □ quantiles.

Histogram Intervals

If you specify the MIDPERCENTS suboption in parentheses after a density estimate option, PROC UNIVARIATE includes a table that lists the interval midpoints along with the observed and estimated percentages of the observations that lie in the interval.

The estimated percentages are based on the fitted distribution. You can also specify the MIDPERCENTS suboption to request a table of interval midpoints with the observed percentage of observations that lie in the interval.

Quantiles

By default, PROC UNIVARIATE displays a table that lists observed and estimated quantiles for the 1, 5, 10, 25, 50, 75, 90, 95, and 99 percent of a fitted parametric distribution. You can use the PERCENTS= suboption to request that the quantiles for specfic percentiles appear in the table.

Output Data Set

PROC UNIVARIATE can create one or more output SAS data sets. When you specify an OUTPUT statement and no BY statement, PROC UNIVARIATE creates an output data set that contains one observation. If you use a BY statement, the corresponding output data set contains an observation with statistics for each BY group. The procedure does not print the output data set. Use PROC PRINT, PROC REPORT, or another SAS reporting tool to print the output data set.

The output data set includes

☐ BY statement variables

☐ variables that contain statistics

☐ variables that contain percentiles.

The BY variables indicate which BY group each observation summarizes. When you omit a BY statement, the procedure computes statistics and percentiles by using all the observations in the input data set. When you use a BY statement, the procedure computes statistics and percentiles by using the observations within each BY group.

OUTHISTOGRAM= Data Set

You can create a OUTHISTOGRAM= data in the HISTOGRAM statement that contains information about histogram intervals. Because you can specify multiple HISTOGRAM statements with the UNIVARIATE procedure, you can create multiple OUTHISTOGRAM= data sets.

The data set contains a group of observations for each variable that the HISTOGRAM statement plots. The group contains an observation for each interval of the histogram, beginning with the leftmost interval that contains a value of the variable and ending with the rightmost interval that contains a value of the variable. These intervals will not necessarily coincide with the intervals displayed in the histogram since the histogram may be padded with empty intervals at either end. If you superimpose one or more fitted curves on the histogram, the OUTHISTOGRAM= data set contains multiple groups of observations for each variable (one group for each curve). If you use a BY statement, the OUTHISTOGRAM= data set contains groups of observations for each BY group. ID variables are not saved in the OUTHISTOGRAM= data set.

The variables in OUTHISTOGRAM= data set are

CURVE   name of fitted distribution (if requested in HISTOGRAM statement)

EXPPCT   estimated percent of population in histogram interval determined from optional fitted distribution

MIDPT   midpoint of fitted distribution

OBSPCT	percent of variable values in histogram interval
VAR	variable name

Examples

Example 1: Univariate Analysis for Multiple Variables

Procedure features:
   VAR statement

This example computes the univariate statistics for two variables.

Program

```
options nodate pageno=1 linesize=80 pagesize=72;
```

The data set STATEPOP contains information from the 1980 and 1990 U.S. Census on the population in metropolitan and nonmetropolitan areas. The 50 states and District of Columbia are divided into four geographic regions. The data are organized by state within each region. The metropolitan and nonmetropolitan population counts are stored in one observation for both census years. A DATA step "STATEPOP" on page 1534 creates the data set.

```
data statepop;
   input State $ citypop_80 citypop_90
         Noncitypop_80 Noncitypop_90 Region @@;
   label citypop_80='1980 metropolitan pop in millions'
         noncitypop_80='1980 nonmetropolitan pop in millions'
         citypop_90='1990 metropolitan pop in millions'
         noncitypop_90='1990 nonmetropolitan pop in million'
         region='Geographic region';
   datalines;
ME    .405    .443   .721   .785 1    NH  .535    .659   .386   .450  1
NY  16.144 16.515 1.414 1.475 1    NJ 7.365   7.730   .A     .A    1
PA  10.067 10.083 1.798 1.799 1    DE  .496    .553   .098   .113  2
        ...more lines of data...
IA   1.198  1.200 1.716 1.577 3    MO 3.314   3.491 1.603 1.626 3
MT    .189   .191   .598   .608 4    ID  .257    .296   .687   .711  4
HI    .763   .836  2.02    .272 4
;
```

The VAR statement specifies the analysis variables and their order in the output.

```
proc univariate data=statepop;
   var citypop_90 citypop_80;
```

The TITLE statement specifies a title.

```
   title 'United States Census of Population and Housing';
run;
```

Output

Univariate statistics for both analysis variables appear on separate pages. Because each population value is unique, the mode is missing.

By comparing the two sums in the Moments table, you find that the metropolitan population increased by 20 million (197.7 - 176.9) in ten years. By comparing the two medians in Basic Statistical Measures table or the Quantiles table, you find that the 1990 median metropolitan population increased to 2.423 million.

```
            United States Census of Population and Housing                1

                          The UNIVARIATE Procedure
               Variable:  CityPop_90  (1990 metropolitan pop in millions)

                                    Moments

    N                         51      Sum Weights                     51
    Mean                3.87701961    Sum Observations           197.728
    Std Deviation       5.16465302    Variance                26.6736408
    Skewness            2.87109259    Kurtosis                 10.537867
    Uncorrected SS      2100.27737    Corrected SS            1333.68204
    Coeff Variation      133.21194    Std Error Mean          0.72319608


                          Basic Statistical Measures

          Location                            Variability

      Mean      3.877020      Std Deviation            5.16465
      Median    2.423000      Variance                26.67364
      Mode         .          Range                   28.66500
                              Interquartile Range      3.60000


                        Tests for Location: Mu0=0

          Test            -Statistic-      -----p Value------

          Student's t    t  5.360952      Pr > |t|    <.0001
          Sign           M      25.5      Pr >= |M|   <.0001
          Signed Rank    S       663      Pr >= |S|   <.0001


                        Quantiles (Definition 5)

                          Quantile      Estimate

                          100% Max        28.799
                          99%             28.799
                          95%             14.166
                          90%              9.574
                          75% Q3           4.376
                          50% Median       2.423
                          25% Q1           0.776
                          10%              0.257
                          5%               0.191
                          1%               0.134
                          0% Min           0.134


                          Extreme Observations

          -----Lowest----          -----Highest----

          Value      Obs            Value      Obs

          0.134       41           10.083        9
          0.152        3           12.023       18
          0.191       39           14.166       26
          0.221       36           16.515        7
          0.226       50           28.799       49
```

```
                  United States Census of Population and Housing          2

                         The UNIVARIATE Procedure
                Variable:  CityPop_80  (1980 metropolitan pop in millions)

                                  Moments

N                          51    Sum Weights                       51
Mean                 3.46847059  Sum Observations             176.892
Std Deviation          4.427991  Variance                19.6071043
Skewness             2.47255319  Kurtosis                 7.3709192
Uncorrected SS       1593.89992  Corrected SS             980.355217
Coeff Variation      127.664078  Std Error Mean           0.62004276


                          Basic Statistical Measures

           Location                       Variability

        Mean      3.468471    Std Deviation          4.42799
        Median    2.114000    Variance              19.60710
        Mode         .        Range                 22.77400
                              Interquartile Range    3.21000


                      Tests for Location: Mu0=0

          Test            -Statistic-      -----p Value------

          Student's t   t  5.593922    Pr > |t|    <.0001
          Sign          M     25.5     Pr >= |M|   <.0001
          Signed Rank   S      663     Pr >= |S|   <.0001


                        Quantiles (Definition 5)

                        Quantile      Estimate

                        100% Max       22.907
                        99%            22.907
                        95%            11.539
                        90%             9.039
                        75% Q3          3.885
                        50% Median      2.114
                        25% Q1          0.675
                        10%             0.234
                        5%              0.174
                        1%              0.133
                        0% Min          0.133


                          Extreme Observations

               -----Lowest----        -----Highest----

               Value      Obs          Value     Obs

               0.133       3           9.461      29
               0.141      41          10.067       9
               0.174      50          11.539      26
               0.189      39          16.144       7
               0.194      36          22.907      49
```

Example 2: Rounding an Analysis Variable and Identifying Extreme Values

Procedure features:

> PROC UNIVARIATE statement options:
>   FREQ
>   NEXTROBS=
>   NEXTRVAL=
>   ROUND=
> ID statement

Data set: STATEPOP on page 1418

This example

□ rounds the values of an analysis variable

□ generates a frequency table

□ identifies extreme observations.

Rounding affects all statistical computations. For this example, when the round unit is 1, all the nonnegative values below .5 round to zero.

Program

```
options nodate pageno=1 linesize=80 pagesize=68;
```

FREQ produces a frequency table. ROUND=1 rounds each value to the nearest integer.

```
proc univariate data=statepop freq round=1 nextrobs=2
                nextrval=4;
```

The VAR statement specifies an analysis variable.

```
    var citypop_90;
```

The ID statement specifies the variables to identify extreme observations. The TITLE statement specifies a title.

```
    id region state;
    title 'United States Census of Population and Housing';
run;
```

Output

The output includes a message to indicate that the values are rounded to the nearest integer. The Extreme Observations table lists values of the ID variables, Region and State. Region 4 reports the lowest metropolitan populations, while region 1 and region 4 report the highest populations. The states with the four most extreme observations are AK, WY, NY, and CA.

```
             United States Census of Population and Housing              1

                        The UNIVARIATE Procedure
            Variable:  CityPop_90  (1990 metropolitan pop in millions)
                  Values Rounded to the Nearest Multiple of 1

                                  Moments

        N                         51   Sum Weights                  51
        Mean                3.8627451   Sum Observations            197
        Std Deviation      5.23457585   Variance              27.4007843
        Skewness           2.85345529   Kurtosis              10.3550751
        Uncorrected SS           2131   Corrected SS          1370.03922
        Coeff Variation      135.5144   Std Error Mean        0.73298723


                         Basic Statistical Measures

             Location                        Variability

        Mean      3.862745     Std Deviation             5.23458
        Median    2.000000     Variance                 27.40078
        Mode      1.000000     Range                    29.00000
                               Interquartile Range       3.00000


                       Tests for Location: Mu0=0

           Test             -Statistic-      -----p Value------

           Student's t    t  5.269867    Pr > |t|     <.0001
           Sign           M      21.5    Pr >= |M|    <.0001
           Signed Rank    S       473    Pr >= |S|    <.0001


                          Quantiles (Definition 5)

                           Quantile      Estimate

                           100% Max          29
                           99%               29
                           95%               14
                           90%               10
                           75% Q3             4
                           50% Median         2
                           25% Q1             1
                           10%                0
                           5%                 0
                           1%                 0
                           0% Min             0


                          Extreme Observations

      --------------Lowest--------------      --------------Highest-------------

      Value   Region   State      Obs      Value   Region   State      Obs

          0        4   AK          50         17        1   NY           7
          0        4   WY          41         29        4   CA          49
```

The Extreme Values table lists the four lowest unique values and the four highest unique values. Because ties occur in the values, the frequency counts of the values are shown.

The Frequency Counts table lists the variable values, the frequencies, the percentages, and the cumulative percentages.

```
                     United States Census of Population and Housing              2

                            The UNIVARIATE Procedure
                  Variable:  CityPop_90  (1990 metropolitan pop in millions)
                         Values Rounded to the Nearest Multiple of 1

                                    Extreme Values

                  ---------Lowest--------      --------Highest--------

                   Order   Value    Freq      Order   Value    Freq

                      1       0       8         11      12       1
                      2       1      14         12      14       1
                      3       2       4         13      17       1
                      4       3       9         14      29       1


                                  Frequency Counts

              Percents                      Percents                       Percents
 Value Count  Cell   Cum    Value Count  Cell   Cum     Value Count  Cell    Cum

     0     8  15.7  15.7        5     1   2.0  80.4        12     1   2.0   94.1
     1    14  27.5  43.1        6     1   2.0  82.4        14     1   2.0   96.1
     2     4   7.8  51.0        8     2   3.9  86.3        17     1   2.0   98.0
     3     9  17.6  68.6        9     1   2.0  88.2        29     1   2.0  100.0
     4     5   9.8  78.4       10     2   3.9  92.2
```

Example 3: Computing Robust Estimators

Procedure features:

PROC UNIVARIATE statement options:

ROBUSTSCALE

TRIMMED=

WINSORIZED=

Data set: STATEPOP on page 1418

This example

☐ computes robust estimates of location

☐ computes two trimmed means

☐ computes a Winsorized mean.

Program

TRIMMED= computes two trimmed means after removing 6 observations and 25 percent of the observations. WINSORIZED= computes a Winsorized mean that replaces 10 percent of the observations.

```
options nodate pageno=1 linesize=80 pagesize=72;

proc univariate data=statepop robustscale trimmed=6 .25
              winsorized=.1;
```

The VAR statement specifies an analysis variable.

```
   var citypop_90;
```

The TITLE statement specifies a title.

```
   title 'United States 1990 Census of Population and Housing';
run;
```

Output

Because each value of population is unique, the mode is missing.

Both the trimmed and Winsorized means are smaller than the arithmetic mean. This may be due to the positive skewness of the data. PROC UNIVARIATE trims 6 observations or 11.76 percent of the data from the tails. When you request to trim 25 percent of the data, PROC UNIVARIATE trims 13 observations or 25.49 percent of the data from the tails. This is because the number of observations trimmed is the smallest integer greater than or equal to 12.75 ($.25 \times 51$). Likewise, when you compute a Winsorized mean for 10 percent of the data ($.1 \times 51 = 5.1$), PROC UNIVARIATE uses 6 observations or 11.76 percent of the data from the tails.

```
        United States 1990 Census of Population and Housing          1

                      The UNIVARIATE Procedure
           Variable:  CityPop_90  (1990 metropolitan pop in millions)

                                Moments

   N                           51    Sum Weights                  51
   Mean                 3.87701961    Sum Observations        197.728
   Std Deviation        5.16465302    Variance             26.6736408
   Skewness             2.87109259    Kurtosis              10.537867
   Uncorrected SS       2100.27737    Corrected SS         1333.68204
   Coeff Variation       133.21194    Std Error Mean       0.72319608


                      Basic Statistical Measures

           Location                        Variability

        Mean     3.877020    Std Deviation           5.16465
        Median   2.423000    Variance               26.67364
        Mode        .        Range                  28.66500
                             Interquartile Range     3.60000


                     Tests for Location: Mu0=0

         Test            -Statistic-      -----p Value------

         Student's t    t  5.360952    Pr > |t|     <.0001
         Sign           M      25.5    Pr >= |M|    <.0001
         Signed Rank    S       663    Pr >= |S|    <.0001
```

Trimmed Means

Percent Trimmed in Tail	Number Trimmed in Tail	Trimmed Mean	Std Error Trimmed Mean	95% Confidence Limits		DF
11.76	6	2.702231	0.535235	1.618705	3.785756	38
25.49	13	2.307000	0.438141	1.402721	3.211279	24

Trimmed Means

Percent Trimmed in Tail	t for H0: Mu0=0.00	Pr > |t|
11.76	5.048686	<.0001
25.49	5.265424	<.0001

Winsorized Means

Percent Winsorized in Tail	Number Winsorized in Tail	Winsorized Mean	Std Error Winsorized Mean	95% Confidence Limits		DF
11.76	6	3.139588	0.536889	2.052713	4.226463	38

Winsorized Means

Percent Winsorized in Tail	t for H0: Mu0=0.00	Pr > |t|
11.76	5.847741	<.0001

United States 1990 Census of Population and Housing   2

The UNIVARIATE Procedure
Variable: CityPop_90 (1990 metropolitan pop in millions)

Robust Measures of Scale

Measure	Value	Estimate of Sigma
Interquartile Range	3.600000	2.668683
Gini's Mean Difference	4.614921	4.089867
MAD	1.675000	2.483355
Sn	2.626105	2.673281
Qn	2.230788	2.171186

Quantiles (Definition 5)

Quantile	Estimate
100% Max	28.799
99%	28.799
95%	14.166
90%	9.574
75% Q3	4.376
50% Median	2.423
25% Q1	0.776
10%	0.257
5%	0.191
1%	0.134
0% Min	0.134

Extreme Observations

-----Lowest----		-----Highest----	
Value	Obs	Value	Obs
0.134	41	10.083	9
0.152	3	12.023	18
0.191	39	14.166	26
0.221	36	16.515	7
0.226	50	28.799	49

Example 4: Performing a Sign Test Using Paired Data

Procedure features:

PROC UNIVARIATE statement option:

ALPHA=
CIBASIC
CIPCTLDF
LOCCOUNT
MODES

Other features:

LABEL statement

This example

□ computes difference scores for paired data

□ lists all values of the mode

□ examines the tests for location to determine if the median difference between scores is zero

□ lists the number of observations less than, greater than, and equal to zero

□ specifies the confidence levels for the confidence limits

□ generates distribution-free confidence limits for the quantiles.

Program

```
options nodate pageno=1 linesize=80 pagesize=60;
```

The data set SCORE contains test scores for college students who took two tests and a final exam. ScoreChange contains the difference in the score between the first test and the second test.

```
data score;
   input Student $ Test1 Test2 Final @@;
   ScoreChange=test2-test1;
   datalines;
Capalleti  94 91 87  Dubose     51 65 91
Engles     95 97 97  Grant      63 75 80
Krupski    80 75 71  Lundsford  92 55 86
Mcbane     75 78 72  Mullen     89 82 93
Nguyen     79 76 80  Patel      71 77 83
Si         75 70 73  Tanaka     87 73 76
;
```

LOCCOUNT produces a Location Counts table. MODES produces a Modes table. ALPHA= specifies a 99 percent confidence limit as the default for all statistics. CIBASIC(ALPHA=.05) specifies a 95 percent confidence limit for the basic measures. CIPCTLDF produces distribution–free confidence limits for the quantiles.

```
proc univariate data=score loccount modes alpha=.01
               cibasic(alpha=.05) cipctldf;
```

The VAR statement specifies the analysis variable as the test scores differences.

```
var scorechange;
```

The LABEL statement associates a label with the analysis variable for the duration of the PROC step. The TITLE statement specifies a title.

```
label scorechange='Change in Test Scores';
title 'Test Scores for a College Course';
run;
```

Output

PROC UNIVARIATE includes the variable label in the report. The report also provides a message to indicate that the lowest mode is shown in the Basic Statistical Measures table. The Modes table reports all the mode values.

The mean of -3.08 indicates an average decrease in test scores from Test1 to Test2. The 95 percent confidence limits (-11.56, 5.39), which includes 0, and the tests for location indicate that the decrease is not statistically significant.

The Tests for Location table includes three hypothesis tests. The Student's **t** statistic assumes that the data are approximately normally distributed. The sign test and signed rank test are nonparametric tests. The signed rank test requires a symmetric distribution. If the distribution is symmetric you expect a skewness value that is close to zero. Because the value -1.42 indicates some distribution skewness, examine the sign test to determine if the difference in test scores is zero. The large **p**-value (.7744) provides insufficient evidence of a difference in test score medians.

```
                        Test Scores for a College Course                      1

                            The UNIVARIATE Procedure
                  Variable:   ScoreChange   (Change in Test Scores)

                                    Moments

        N                          12     Sum Weights                 12
        Mean                -3.0833333     Sum Observations           -37
        Std Deviation       13.3379727     Variance            177.901515
        Skewness            -1.4191368     Kurtosis            3.35291936
        Uncorrected SS            2071     Corrected SS        1956.91667
        Coeff Variation      -432.5829     Std Error Mean      3.85034106


                          Basic Statistical Measures

              Location                          Variability

          Mean      -3.08333     Std Deviation           13.33797
          Median    -3.00000     Variance               177.90152
          Mode      -5.00000     Range                   51.00000
                                 Interquartile Range     10.50000

      NOTE: The mode displayed is the smallest of 2 modes with a count of 2.
```

```
                          Modes

                    Mode    Count

                     -5       2
                     -3       2


           Basic Confidence Limits Assuming Normality

     Parameter          Estimate      95% Confidence Limits

     Mean               -3.08333     -11.55788       5.39121
     Std Deviation      13.33797       9.44856      22.64625
     Variance          177.90152      89.27519     512.85267


                 Tests for Location: Mu0=0

          Test          -Statistic-      -----p Value------

          Student's t   t  -0.80079    Pr >  |t|    0.4402
          Sign          M       -1     Pr >= |M|    0.7744
          Signed Rank   S     -8.5     Pr >= |S|    0.5278


                 Location Counts: Mu0=0.00

              Count                 Value

              Num Obs > Mu0           5
              Num Obs ^= Mu0         12
              Num Obs < Mu0          7
```

Because PROC UNIVARIATE computes a symmetric confidence interval, some coverages for the confidence limits are less than 99 percent. In some cases, there are also insufficient data to compute a symmetric confidence interval and a missing value is shown. Use the TYPE=ASYMMETRIC option to increase the coverage and reduce the number of missing confidence limits.

```
                    Test Scores for a College Course                    2

                         The UNIVARIATE Procedure
               Variable:  ScoreChange  (Change in Test Scores)

                          Quantiles (Definition 5)

                    Quantile        Estimate

                    100% Max          14.0
                    99%               14.0
                    95%               14.0
                    90%               12.0
                    75% Q3             4.5
                    50% Median        -3.0
                    25% Q1            -6.0
                    10%             -14.0
                    5%              -37.0
                    1%              -37.0
                    0% Min          -37.0


                          Quantiles (Definition 5)

                       99% Confidence Limits    -------Order Statistics-------
      Quantile          Distribution Free       LCL Rank  UCL Rank   Coverage

   100% Max
   99%                 6               14          10        12       11.34
   95%                 6               14          10        12       44.01
   90%                 2               14           8        12       71.32
   75% Q3             -3               14           6        12       95.41
   50% Median        -14               12           2        11       99.37
   25% Q1            -37               -3           1         7       95.41
   10%              -37               -5           1         5       71.32
   5%               -37               -7           1         3       44.01
   1%               -37               -7           1         3       11.34
   0% Min



                             Extreme Observations

                  ----Lowest----          ----Highest---

                  Value       Obs         Value       Obs

                   -37         6            2          3
                   -14        12            3          7
                    -7         8            6         10
                    -5        11           12          4
                    -5         5           14          2
```

Example 5: Examining the Data Distribution and Saving Percentiles

Procedure features:

    PROC UNIVARIATE statement options:

       ALPHA=

      CIBASIC
      CIPCTLNORMAL
      MU0=
      NORMAL
      PLOTS
      PLOTSIZE=
   OUTPUT statement

Other features:
   PRINT procedure

Data set: SCORE on page 1428

This example

- specifies the confidence level for the confidence limits
- computes a lower confidence limit for the parameters
- computes two-sided confidence limits for the quantiles based on the assumption of normal data
- specifies the null hypothesis mean for the tests for locations
- tests the hypothesis that the data are normally distributed
- produces a stem-and-leaf plot, box plot, and normal probability plot and increase the plot size
- computes additional percentiles
- creates an output data set with percentiles
- prints the output data set.

Program

```
options nodate pageno=1 linesize=64 pagesize=58;
```

MU0= requests a test that the population mean equals 80. ALPHA= specifies a 90 percent confidence limit for all statistics. CIBASIC computes lower confidence limits for the basic measures. CIPCTLNORMAL computes two-sided confidence limits for the quantiles. NORMAL computes tests for normality. PLOTS requests plots of the data distribution. PLOTSIZE= specifies the number of rows to display the plot.

```
proc univariate data=score mu0=80 alpha=.1 cibasic(type=lower)
                cipctlnormal normal plots plotsize=26;
```

The VAR statement specifies the analysis variable.

```
    var final;
```

The OUTPUT statement creates the PCTSCORE data set with five variables. MEDIAN= saves the median. PCTLPTS= saves four percentiles. PCTLPRE= specifies a prefix name. PCTLNAME= specifies suffix names for the variables that contain the first three percentiles. The name of the variable that contains the 70th percentile uses the default suffix.

```
      output out=pctscore median=Median pctlpts=98 50 20 70
              pctlpre=Pctl_ pctlname=Top Mid Low;
      title 'Examining the Distribution of Final Exam Scores';
   run;
```

PROC PRINT prints the PCTSCORE data set. The TITLE statement specifies a title.

```
proc print data=pctscore noobs;
   title1 'Quantile Statistics for Final Exam Scores';
   title2 'Output Data Set from PROC UNIVARIATE';
run;
```

Output

The estimate of the mean test score is 82.4, with a standard deviation of 8.6. The 90 percent lower confidence limit for the mean is 79.

The Tests for Location table includes three hypothesis tests. To determine whether the Student's **t** statistic is appropriate, you must determine if the data are approximately normally distributed. PROC UNIVARIATE calculates the Shapiro-Wilk W statistic because the sample size is below 2000. All **p**-values from the tests for normality are >0.15, which provides insufficient evidence to reject the assumption of normality. The probability plot also supports the assumption that the data are normal. Therefore, the **t** statistic appears appropriate. The **p**-value of .35 for this test provides insufficient evidence to reject the null hypothesis that the mean test score is 80.

Examination of the box plot, which is nonsymmetric, and the small sample size, which causes low power, make the sign test a more appropriate test of location. The **p**-value of .75 for this test provides insufficient evidence to reject the null hypothesis that the mean test score is 80.

```
              Examining the Distribution of Final Exam Scores        1

                        The UNIVARIATE Procedure
                          Variable:  Final

                               Moments

N                       12      Sum Weights                12
Mean             82.4166667     Sum Observations          989
Std Deviation    8.59659905     Variance           73.9015152
Skewness         0.22597472     Kurtosis           -1.0846549
Uncorrected SS        82323     Corrected SS       812.916667
Coeff Variation  10.4306561     Std Error Mean     2.48162439


                   Basic Statistical Measures

         Location                     Variability

     Mean     82.41667      Std Deviation           8.59660
     Median   81.50000      Variance               73.90152
     Mode     80.00000      Range                  26.00000
                            Interquartile Range    14.50000


         Basic Confidence Limits Assuming Normality

         Parameter          Estimate     Lower 90% CL

         Mean               82.41667        79.03314
         Std Deviation       8.59660         6.85984
         Variance           73.90152        47.05738


              Tests for Location: Mu0=80

     Test            -Statistic-      -----p Value------

     Student's t    t  0.973825      Pr > |t|    0.3511
     Sign           M         1      Pr >= |M|   0.7539
     Signed Rank    S         8      Pr >= |S|   0.4434


              Tests for Normality

Test                --Statistic---      ------p Value------

Shapiro-Wilk        W   0.952903      Pr < W        0.6797
Kolmogorov-Smirnov  D   0.113328      Pr > D       >0.1500
Cramer-von Mises    W-Sq 0.028104     Pr > W-Sq    >0.2500
Anderson-Darling    A-Sq 0.212693     Pr > A-Sq    >0.2500
```

The three plots display the data distribution. The PLOTSIZE= option enlarges the plots so that you can easily see if the data are approximately normal.

```
          Examining the Distribution of Final Exam Scores          2

                       The UNIVARIATE Procedure
                         Variable:  Final

                       Quantiles (Definition 5)

                                        90% Confidence Limits
          Quantile       Estimate         Assuming Normality

          100% Max         97.0
          99%              97.0         96.30698      114.6289
          95%              97.0         91.55028      105.9399
          90%              93.0         88.89956      101.4163
          75% Q3           89.0         84.12815       94.1623
          50% Median       81.5         77.95996       86.8734
          25% Q1           74.5         70.67102       80.7052
          10%              72.0         63.41705       75.9338
          5%               71.0         58.89343       73.2831
          1%               71.0         50.20448       68.5264
          0% Min           71.0


                         Extreme Observations

              ----Lowest----            ----Highest---

              Value      Obs            Value      Obs

                 71        5               86        6
                 72        7               87        1
                 73       11               91        2
                 76       12               93        8
                 80        9               97        3


     Stem Leaf                           #          Boxplot
       96 0                              1             |
       94                                              |
       92 0                              1             |
       90 0                              1             |
       88                                          +-----+
       86 00                             2          |     |
       84                                           |     |
       82 0                              1           |  +  |
       80 00                             2          *-----*
       78                                           |     |
       76 0                              1           |     |
       74                                          +-----+
       72 00                             2             |
       70 0                              1             |
          ----+----+----+----+
```

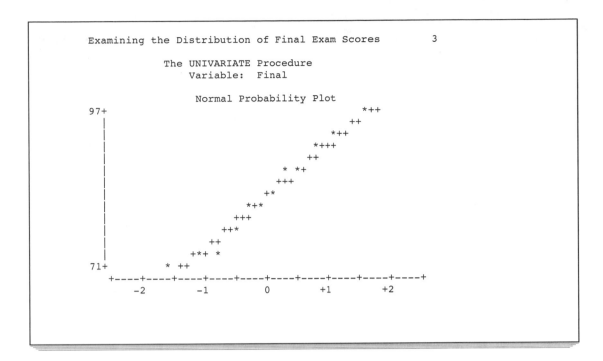

The PCTSCORE data set contains one observation. The median value in Median is equivalent to the 50th percentile in PCTL_MID.

```
        Quantile Statistics for Final Exam Scores        4
           Output Data Set from PROC UNIVARIATE

   Median    Pctl_Top    Pctl_Mid    Pctl_Low    Pctl_70

    81.5        97         81.5         73          87
```

Example 6: Creating an Output Data Set with Multiple Analysis Variables

Procedure features:
    PROC UNIVARIATE statement option:
        NOPRINT
    OUTPUT statement
    VAR statement
Other features:
    PRINT procedure
Data set: SCORE on page 1428

This example
□ suppresses the reporting of univariate statistics
□ computes additional percentiles for two variables

□ creates an output data set with descriptive statistics and percentiles

□ prints the output data set.

Program

```
options nodate pageno=1 linesize=80 pagesize=60;
```

NOPRINT suppresses all the tables of statistics.

```
proc univariate data=score noprint;
```

The VAR statement specifies the analysis variables and their order in the output.

```
var test1 test2;
```

The OUTPUT statement creates the TESTSTAT data set with nine variables. MEAN= saves the mean for Test1 and Test2. STD= saves the standard deviation for Test1. PCTLPTS= calculates three percentiles and PCTLPRE= specifies prefix names for the analysis variables. PCTLNAME= specifies a suffix name for the 33.3 percentile.

```
output out=teststat mean=MeanTest1 MeanTest2
       std=StdDeviationTest1
       pctlpts=33.3 66 99.9
       pctlpre=Test1_
       Test2_ pctlname=Low ;
run;
```

PROC PRINT prints the TESTSTAT data set. The TITLE statement specifies a title.

```
proc print data=teststat noobs;
   title1 'Univariate Statistics for Two College Tests';
   title2 'Output Data Set from PROC UNIVARIATE';
run;
```

Output

The TESTSTAT data set contains one observation with the mean for the two analysis variables and the standard deviation for the first analysis variable. The remaining six variables contain computed percentiles.

```
                      Univariate Statistics for Two College Tests                  1
                          Output Data Set from PROC UNIVARIATE

                    Std
  Mean    Mean   Deviation   Test1_              Test1_   Test2_             Test2_
  Test1   Test2    Test1      Low    Test1_66    99_9      Low    Test2_66   99_9

  79.25  76.1667  13.3152      75       87        95        73      77        97
```

Example 7: Creating Schematic Plots and an Output Data Set with BY Groups

Procedure features:
    PROC UNIVARIATE statement options:

        NEXTROBS=
        PLOT
        PLOTSIZE=
    BY statement
    OUTPUT statement

Other features:
    FORMAT statement
    FORMAT procedure
    PRINT procedure
    SORT procedure

Data set: STATEPOP on page 1418

This example
- creates a data set with observations that are separated by census year
- sorts the data set by geographic region and census year
- calculates univariate statistics and produces a stem-and-leaf plot, box plot, and normal probability plot for each BY group
- creates schematic plots to compare the BY groups
- creates an output data set with descriptive statistics and percentiles
- prints the output data set.

Program

```
options nodate pageno=1 linesize=120 pagesize=80;
```

PROC FORMAT creates a format to identify regions with a character value.

```
proc format;
   value Regnfmt 1='Northeast'
D                2='South'
                 3='Midwest'
                 4='West';
run;
```

The METROPOP data set contains one variable, Populationcount, with the metropolitan and nonmetropolitan population counts. DECADE indicates the census year for the observation. The OUTPUT statements create two observations for each state and decade combination.

```
data metropop;
   set statepop;
   keep Region Decade Populationcount;
   label PopulationCount='US Census Population (millions)'
         Decade='Census year';
   decade=1980;
   populationcount=sum(citypop_80,noncitypop_80);
   output;
   decade=1990;
   populationcount=sum(citypop_90,noncitypop_90);
   output;
```

PROC SORT sorts the observations by Region and Decade.

```
proc sort data=metropop;
   by region decade;
run;
```

NEXTROBS= suppresses the Extreme Observations table. PLOTS produces plots that show the data distribution. PLOTSIZE= specifies the number of rows used to display the plots.

```
proc univariate data=metropop nextrobs=0
               plots plotsize=20 ;
```

The VAR statement specifies the analysis variable.

```
   var populationcount;
```

The BY statement produces a separate section of the report for each BY group and prints a heading above each one.

```
   by region decade;
```

The OUTPUT statement creates the CENSTAT data set with six variables and eight observations. SUM= saves the sum. MEAN= saves the mean. STD= saves the standard deviation. PCTLPTS= calculates three percentiles. PCTLPRE= specifies the prefix name.

```
output out=censtat sum=PopulationTotal mean=PopulationMean
       std=PopulationStdDeviation pctlpts=50 to 100 by 25
       pctlpre=Pop_ ;
```

The FORMAT statement assigns a format to Region. The output data set contains the formatted values of Region. The TITLE statement specifies a title.

```
    format region regnfmt.;
    title 'United States Census of Population and Housing';
run;
```

PROC PRINT prints the CENSTAT data set.

```
proc print data=censtat;
    title1 'Statistics for Census Data by Decade and Region';
    title2 'Output Dataset From PROC UNIVARIATE';
run;
```

Output

The UNIVARIATE procedure output that is shown does not include univariate statistics for each BY group. Only univariate statistics for the first BY group and schematic plots for all BY groups are shown.

The BY statement requests separate reports for each BY group. The first report contains univariate statistics for the 1980 Census, Northeast region.

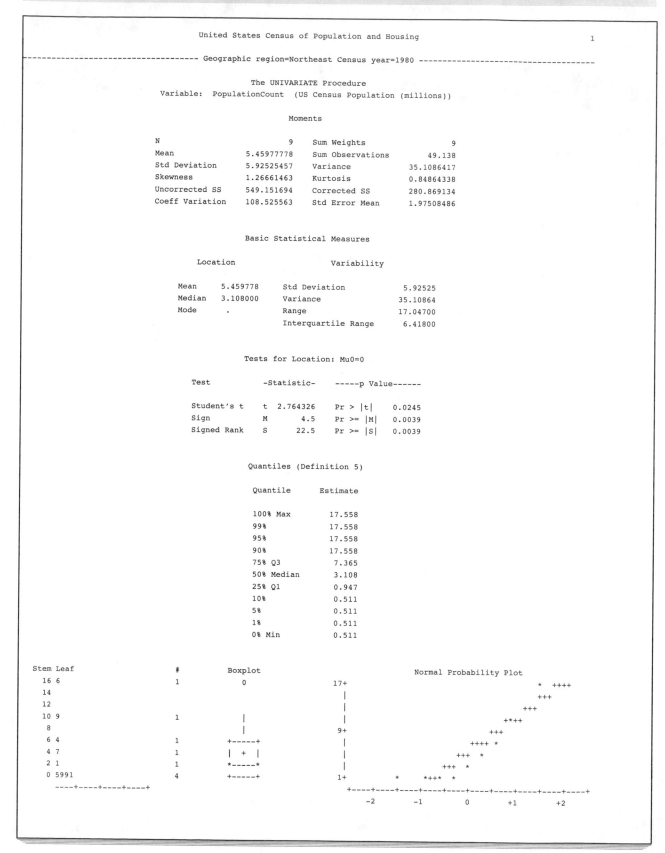

```
                    United States Census of Population and Housing                      1

----------------------- Geographic region=Northeast Census year=1980 -----------------------

                             The UNIVARIATE Procedure
              Variable:  PopulationCount  (US Census Population (millions))

                                     Moments

     N                         9    Sum Weights                  9
     Mean                5.45977778  Sum Observations        49.138
     Std Deviation       5.92525457  Variance            35.1086417
     Skewness            1.26661463  Kurtosis            0.84864338
     Uncorrected SS      549.151694  Corrected SS        280.869134
     Coeff Variation     108.525563  Std Error Mean      1.97508486


                            Basic Statistical Measures

               Location                        Variability

          Mean     5.459778     Std Deviation          5.92525
          Median   3.108000     Variance              35.10864
          Mode        .         Range                 17.04700
                                 Interquartile Range    6.41800


                          Tests for Location: Mu0=0

            Test             -Statistic-      -----p Value------

            Student's t    t  2.764326     Pr > |t|     0.0245
            Sign           M       4.5     Pr >= |M|    0.0039
            Signed Rank    S      22.5     Pr >= |S|    0.0039


                           Quantiles (Definition 5)

                           Quantile     Estimate

                           100% Max       17.558
                           99%            17.558
                           95%            17.558
                           90%            17.558
                           75% Q3          7.365
                           50% Median      3.108
                           25% Q1          0.947
                           10%             0.511
                           5%              0.511
                           1%              0.511
                           0% Min          0.511


Stem Leaf                #     Boxplot                  Normal Probability Plot
 16 6                    1        0          17+                             *  ++++
 14                                           |                                ++++
 12                                           |                              +++
 10 9                    1        |           |                           +*++
  8                               |          9+                         +++
  6 4                    1     +-----+        |                     ++++ *
  4 7                    1     | + |          |                 +++  *
  2 1                    1     *-----*        |              +++  *
  0 5991                 4     +-----+       1+        *    *+++  *
   ----+----+----+----+                       +----+----+----+----+----+----+----+----+----+----+
                                                  -2        -1         0        +1        +2
```

The BY statement and a PLOT option in PROC statement produce schematic plots on the last page of the report. Use the graph to compare the data distribution for each region-year combination.

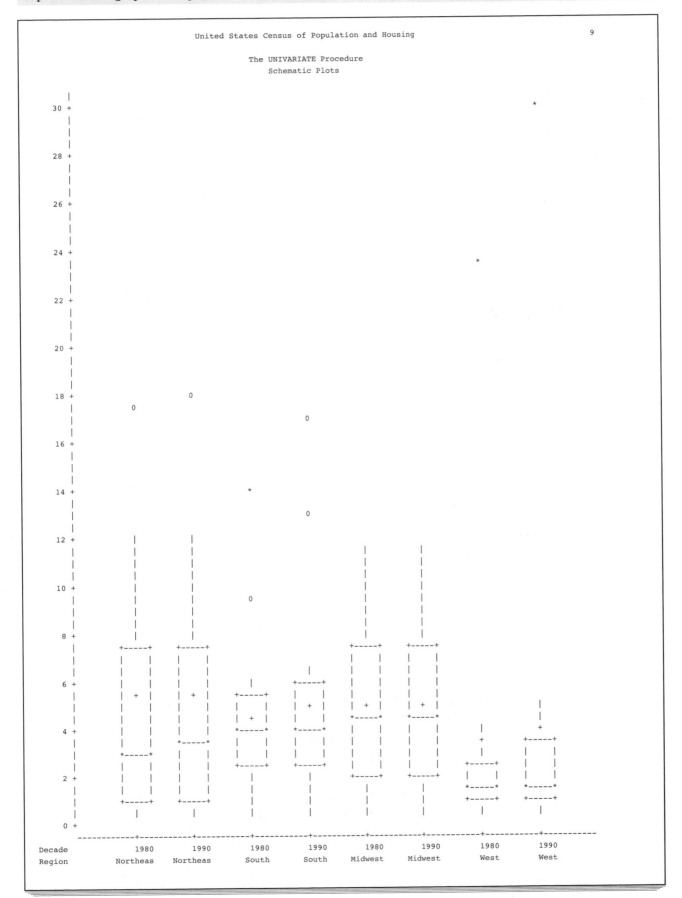

The CENSTAT data set includes the BY variables Region and Decade and contains eight observation, one for each BY group.

```
                   Statistics for Census Data by Decade and Region          10
                         Output Dataset From PROC UNIVARIATE

                                        Population
                           Population      Std       Population
     Obs   Region   Decade     Mean     Deviation      Total     Pop_50  Pop_75  Pop_100

      1   Northeast  1980     5.45978    5.92525       49.138    3.1080   7.365   17.558
      2   Northeast  1990     5.64556    6.00833       50.810    3.2880   7.730   17.990
      3   South      1980     4.43329    3.32034       75.366    3.8940   5.347   14.225
      4   South      1990     5.02647    4.20752       85.450    4.0410   6.187   16.987
      5   Midwest    1980     4.90567    3.75037       58.868    4.3910   7.376   11.428
      6   Midwest    1990     4.97242    3.75702       59.669    4.6335   7.420   11.431
      7   West       1980     3.32154    6.21703       43.180    1.3030   2.717   23.667
      8   West       1990     4.06000    7.83953       52.780    1.5150   3.294   29.760
```

Example 8: Fitting Density Curves

Procedure features:

PROC UNIVARIATE statement options:

NOPRINT

HISTOGRAM statement options:

CBARLINE=

CFILL=

EXP

FILL

L=

MIDPOINTS=

NOPRINT

NORMAL

VAR statement

Other features:

GOPTIONS statement

RANNOR function

RANEXP function

This example

□ creates a sample of 100 observations from a normal distribution and an exponential distribution

□ suppresses the tables of descriptive statistics

□ creates histograms with superimposed density curves for the normal and exponential distributions

□ requests goodness-of-fit tests for a fitted exponential distribution

□ specifies the midpoints for histogram intervals

□ requests graphical enhancements that change plot colors and line types.

Program

```
options nodate pageno=1 linesize=80 pagesize=60;
```

The GOPTIONS statement sets the graphics environment to control the appearance of graphics elements. HTITLE= and HTEXT= specify text height. FTEXT= and FTITLE= specify the font.*

```
goptions htitle=4 htext=3 ftext=swissb ftitle=swissb;
```

The data set DISTRDATA contains two variables and 100 observations. The RANNOR function creates a random variate from a normal distribution with a mean of 50 and standard deviation of 10 that is stored in the Normal_x variable. The RANEXP function creates a random variate from a exponential distribution that is stored in the Exponential_x variable.

```
data distrdata;
   drop n;
   label Normal_x='Normal Random Variable'
         Exponential_x='Exponential Random Variable';
   do n=1 to 100;
      Normal_x=10*rannor(53124)+50;
      Exponential_x=ranexp(18746363);
      output;
   end;
run;
```

NOPRINT suppresses the tables of statistics that the PROC UNIVARIATE statement creates. The VAR statement specifies the analysis variable.

```
proc univariate data=distrdata noprint;
   var Normal_x;
```

The HISTOGRAM statement creates a histogram for the analysis variable Normal_x. The NORMAL option superimposes the fitted density curve for a normal distribution. NOPRINT suppresses the tables of statistics that summarize the fitted density curve. The CBARLINE= option specifies the color to outline the histogram bars.

```
histogram Normal_x /normal(noprint) cbarline=grey ;
```

The TITLE statement specifies a title.

```
title '100 Obs Sampled from a Normal Distribution';
run;
```

Another PROC step will execute so that output displays a new customized title. The VAR statement specifies the analysis variable.

```
proc univariate data=distrdata noprint;
   var Exponential_x;
```

The HISTOGRAM statement creates a histogram for the analysis variable Exponential_x. The EXP option superimposes a fitted density curve for an exponential distribution . The FILL option specifies to fill the area under the exponential density curve with the CFILL= color. The L= option specifies a distinct line type for the density curve. The MIDPOINTS= option specifies a list of values to use as bin midpoints.

---

* For additional information about the GOPTIONS statement, see *SAS/GRAPH Software: Reference*.

```
histogram /exp(fill l=3) cfill=yellow midpoints=.05 to 5.55 by .25;
```

The TITLE statement specifies a title.

```
title '100 Obs Sampled from an Exponential Distribution';
run;
```

Output

Figure 41.4 A Histogram Superimposed with Normal Curve

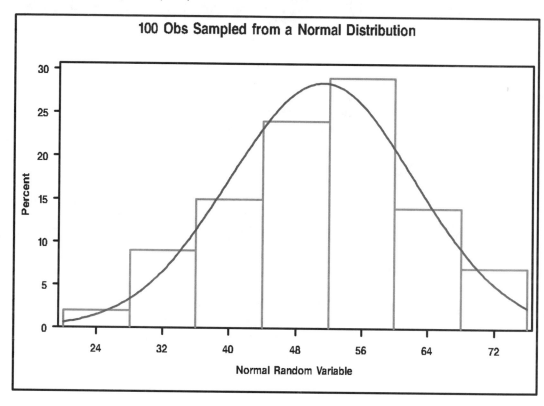

The output includes parameters estimates for the exponential curve. The exponential parameter threshold parameter θ is 0 because the THETA= option was omitted. A maximum likelihood estimate is computed for the scale parameter σ.

PROC UNIVARIATE provides three goodness-of-fit tests for the exponential distribution that are based on the empirical distribution function. The **p**–values for the exponential distribution are larger than the usual cutoff values of 0.05 and 0.10, which indicates not to reject the null hypothesis that the data are exponentially distributed.

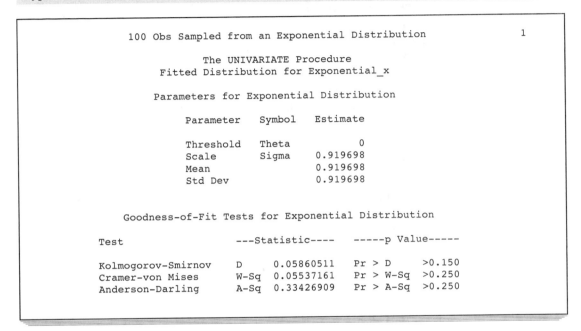

```
           100 Obs Sampled from an Exponential Distribution                1

                         The UNIVARIATE Procedure
                     Fitted Distribution for Exponential_x

                   Parameters for Exponential Distribution

                   Parameter    Symbol    Estimate

                   Threshold    Theta            0
                   Scale        Sigma     0.919698
                   Mean                   0.919698
                   Std Dev                0.919698


              Goodness-of-Fit Tests for Exponential Distribution

         Test                  ---Statistic----    -----p Value-----

         Kolmogorov-Smirnov    D    0.05860511     Pr > D       >0.150
         Cramer-von Mises      W-Sq 0.05537161     Pr > W-Sq    >0.250
         Anderson-Darling      A-Sq 0.33426909     Pr > A-Sq    >0.250
```

Figure 41.5 A Histogram Superimposed with an Exponential Curve

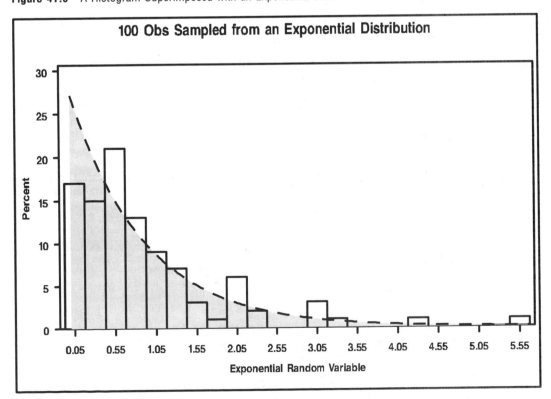

Example 9: Displaying a Reference Line on a Normal Probability Plot

Procedure features:
    PROC UNIVARIATE statement options:
        NOPRINT
    INSET statement options:
        FORMAT=
        HEADER=
        POSITION=
        REFPOINT=
        statistical-keyword
    PROBPLOT statement options:
        MU=
        NORMAL
        PCTLMINOR
        SIGMA=
    VAR statement

Other features:
    GOPTIONS statement
    SYMBOL statement

Data Set: DISTRDATA on page 1445

This example
- suppresses the tables of descriptive statistics
- creates a normal probability plot
- requests a diagonal reference line that corresponds to the normal distribution with estimated parameters μ and σ
- displays minor tick marks between major tick marks on the percentile axis
- enhances the plot by insetting a table of summary statistics
- requests graphical enhancements that change symbol type and text font.

Program

The GOPTIONS statement sets the graphics environment to control the appearance of graphics elements. HTITLE= and HTEXT= specify text height. FTEXT= and FTITLE= specify the font.*

```
goptions htitle=4 htext=3 ftext=swissb ftitle=swissb;
```

The SYMBOL statement defines the characteristics of the symbol that appears in the plot. VALUE= specifies a star for the plot symbol. By default, the plot symbol is the plus sign (+).

```
symbol value=star;
```

NOPRINT suppresses the tables of statistics that the PROC UNIVARIATE statement creates. The VAR statement specifies the analysis variable.

---

* For additional information about the GOPTIONS statement, see *SAS/GRAPH Software: Reference*.

```
proc univariate data=distrdata noprint;
   var Normal_x;
```

The PROBPLOT statement creates a normal probability plot for the analysis variable Normal_x. The NORMAL option superimposes a reference line that corresponds to the normal distribution by using estimated parameters for MU= and SIGMA=. PCTMINOR specifies that minor tick marks that appear between the major tick marks on the horizontal axis.

```
probplot normal_x /normal(mu=est sigma=est) pctlminor;
```

The INSET statement insets a table on the plot. The keywords MEAN and STD request that the mean and standard deviation display. FORMAT= specifies to use a format of field width 3. HEADER= displays a header at the top of the inset. POSITION= specifies to use axis percentage coordinates to position the inset. REFPOINT= specifies to place the bottom right corner of the inset 95% of the way across the horizontal axis and 5% of the way up the vertical axis.

```
inset mean std / format=3.0 header='Normal Parameters'
                 position=(95,5) refpoint=br;
```

The TITLE statements specify a title.

```
title1 '100 Obs Sampled from a Normal Distribution';
title2 'Normal Probability Plot';
run;
```

Output

Figure 41.6 Normal Probability Plot with a Normal Reference Line and a Customized Inset

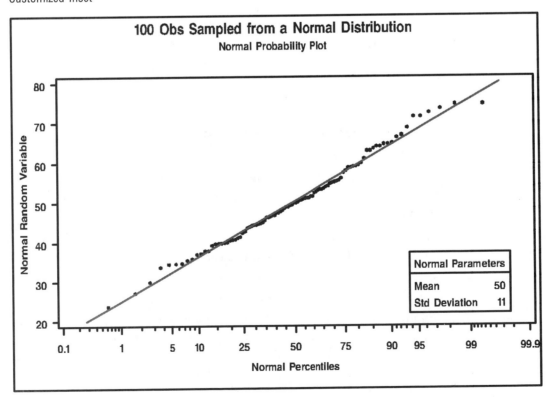

Example 10: Creating a Two-Way Comparative Histogram

Procedure features:
    PROC UNIVARIATE statement options:
        NOPRINT
    CLASS statement options:
        ORDER=
    HISTOGRAM statement options:
        CFILL=
        INTERTILE=
        MIDPOINTS=
        NCOLS=
        NROWS=
        VAXIS=
        VAXISLABEL=
        VSCALE=
    INSET statement options:
        FONT=
        HEIGHT=
        NOFRAME
        POSITION=
        statistical-keyword
    VAR statement

Other features:
    FORMAT statement
    FORMAT procedure
    GOPTIONS statement

Data set: METROPOP on page 1440

- □ suppresses the tables of descriptive statistics
- □ specifies two classification variables
- □ specifies the order of the component histograms
- □ creates a two-way comparative histogram with a specified number of rows and columns
- □
- □ specifies the distance between the component histogram tiles
- □ specifies the scale, values, and labels of the vertical axis
- □ specifies the midpoints for histogram intervals
- □ enhances the component histograms by insetting a table of summary statistics
- □ requests graphical enhancements that change fill color and font types.

Program

The GOPTIONS statement sets the graphics environment to control the appearance of graphic elements. HTITLE= and HTEXT= specify text height. FTEXT= and FTITLE= specify the font.*

```
goptions htitle=4 htext=3 ftext=swiss ftitle=swiss;
```

PROC FORMAT creates a format to identify regions with a character value.

```
proc format;
   value Regnfmt 1='Northeast'
                 2='South'
                 3='Midwest'
                 4='West';
run;
```

NOPRINT suppresses the tables of statistics that the PROC UNIVARIATE statement creates. The VAR statement specifies the analysis variable.

```
proc univariate data=metropop noprint;
    var populationcount;
```

The CLASS statement specifies Region and Decade as the classification variables. PROC UNIVARIATE produces a component histogram for each level (distinct combination of values) of these variables. ORDER= orders the classification levels by the frequency of Decade so that the year with greatest population count displays first.

```
    class region decade(order=freq);
```

The HISTOGRAM statement creates a two–way comparative histogram for the analysis variable PopulationCount. NROWS= and NCOLS= specify a 4 × 2 arrangement for the tiles. INTERTILE= inserts a space of one percentage screen unit between the tiles. CFILL= specifies a fill color for the histogram bars. VSCALE= requests the vertical axis scale in units of the number of observations per data unit. VAXIS= specifies the tick mark labels and VAXISLABEL= specifies a label for the vertical axis. MIDPOINTS= specifies a list of values to use as bin midpoints. FONT= requests a software font for the text.

```
    histogram /nrows=4 ncols=2 intertile=1 cfill=cyan vscale=count
              vaxis=0 4 8 12 vaxislabel='No. of States'
              midpoints=0 to 30 by 5;
```

---

* For additional information about the GOPTIONS statement, see *SAS/GRAPH Software: Reference*.

The INSET statement insets a table directly on each component histogram with the sum of PopulationCount. SUM= requests a customized label and a field width of five and two decimal places for the sum statistic. NOFRAME suppresses the frame around the inset table. POSITION= specifies a compass point to position the inset. HEIGHT= specifies the height of the text. FONT= requests a software font for the text.

```
inset sum='Total Population:' (4.1) / noframe position=ne
                                       height=2 font=swissxb;
```

The FORMAT statement assigns a format to Region. The TITLE statement specifies a title.

```
    format region regnfmt.;
    title 'United States Census of Population and Housing';
run;
```

Output

Figure 41.7 Two-way Comparative Histogram

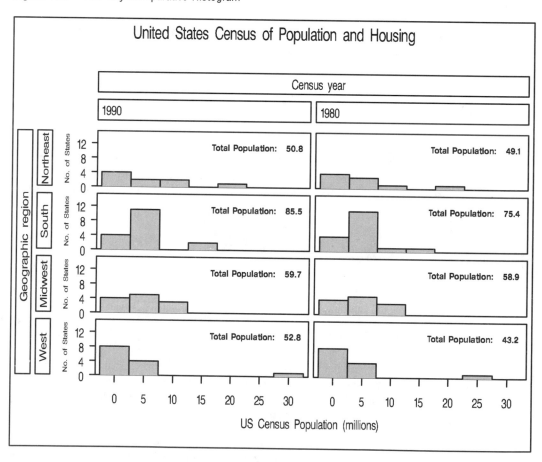

References

Blom, G. (1958), *Statistical Estimates and Transformed Beta Variables*, New York: John Wiley & Sons, Inc.

Chambers, J. M., Cleveland, W. S., Kleiner, B., and Tukey, P. A. (1983), *Graphical Methods for Data Analysis*, Belmont, CA: Wadsworth International Group.

Conover, W.J. (1980), *Practical Nonparametric Statistics*, 2nd Edition, New York: John Wiley & Sons, Inc.

Croux, C. and Rousseeuw, P.J. (1992), "Time-Efficient Algorithms for Two Highly Robust Estimators of Scale," *Computational Statistics*, Volume 1, 411-428.

D'Agostino, R.B. and Stephens, M.A. (1986), *Goodness-of-Fit Techniques*, New York: Marcel Dekker, Inc.

Dixon, W.J. and Tukey, J.W. (1968), "Approximate Behavior of the Distribution of Winsorized *t* (Trimming/Winsorization 2)," *Technometrics*, 10, 83-98.

Frigge, M., Hoaglin, D.C., and Iglewicz, B. (1989), "Some Implementations of the Boxplot," *The American Statistician*, 43:1, 50–54.

Friendly, M. (1991) *SAS System for Statistical Graphics, First Edition*, Cary, NC: SAS Institute Inc.

Hahn, G.J. and Meeker, W. Q. (1991) *Statistical Intervals: A Guide for Practitioners*, New York: John Wiley & Sons, Inc.

Hampel, F.R. (1974), "The Influence Curve and Its Role in Robust Estimation," *Journal of the American Statistical Association*, 69, 383-393.

Iman, R.L. (1974), "Use of a t-statistic as an Approximation to the Exact Distribution of the Wilcoxon Signed Ranks Test Statistic," *Communications in Statistics*, 3, 795–806.

Johnson, N.L., Kotz, S., and Balakrishnan, N. (1994), *Continuous Univariate Distributions, Volume 1*, New York: John Wiley & Sons, Inc.

Johnson, N.L., Kotz, S., and Balakrishnan, N. (1995), *Continuous Univariate Distributions, Volume 2*, New York: John Wiley & Sons, Inc.

Lehmann, E.L. (1975), *Nonparametrics: Statistical Methods Based on Ranks*, San Francisco: Holden-Day, Inc.

Odeh, R.E. and Owen, D.B. (1980), *Tables for Normal Tolerance Limits, Sampling Plans, and Screening*, New York: Marcel Dekker, Inc.

Owen, D.B. and Hua, T.A. (1977), "Tables of Confidence Limits on the Tail Area of the Normal Distribution," *Communication and Statistics, Part B – – Simulation and Computation*, 6, 285–311.

Rousseeuw, P.J. and Croux, C. (1993), "Alternatives to the Median Absolute Deviation," *Journal of the American Statistical Association*. 88, 1273-1283.

Royston, J.P. (1992), "Approximating the Shapiro-Wilk's W-Test for Non-normality," *Statistics and Computing*, 2, 117–119.

Royston, J.P. (1982), "An Extension of Shapiro and Wilk's W Test for Normality to Large Samples," *Applied Statistics*, 31, 115–124.

Shapiro, S.S. and Wilk, M.B. (1965), "An Analysis of Variance Test for Normality (complete samples)," *Biometrika*, 52, 591–611.

Schlotzhauer, S.D. and Littell, R.C. (1997) *SAS System for Elementary Statistical Analysis, Second Edition*, Cary, NC: SAS Institute Inc.

Stephens, M.A. (1974), "EDF Statistics for Goodness of Fit and Some Comparisons," *Journal of the American Statistical Association*, 69, 730–737.

Terrell, G.R. and Scott, D.W. (1985), "Oversmoothed Nonparametric Density Estimates," *Journal of the American Statistical Association*, 80, 209–214.

Tukey, J.W. (1977), *Exploratory Data Analysis*, Reading, Massachusetts: Addison-Wesley.

Tukey, J.W. and McLaughlin, D.H. (1963), "Less Vulnerable Confidence and Significance Procedures for Location Based on a Single Sample: Trimming/ Winsorization 1," *Sankhya A*, 25, 331-352.

U.S. Bureau of the Census (1994), *Statistical Abstract of the United States: 1994 (114th Edition)*, Washington, D.C.: U.S. Government Printing Office.

Appendices

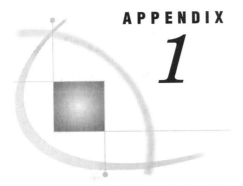

APPENDIX

1

SAS Elementary Statistics Procedures

Overview

This appendix provides a brief description of some of the statistical concepts necessary for you to interpret the output of base SAS procedures for elementary statistics. In addition, this appendix lists statistical notation, formulas, and standard keywords used for common statistics in base SAS procedures. Brief examples illustrate the statistical concepts.

Table A1.1 on page 1459 lists the most common statistics and the procedures that compute them.

Keywords and Formulas

The base SAS procedures use a standardized set of keywords to refer to statistics. You specify these keywords in SAS statements to request the statistics to be displayed or stored in an output data set.

In the following notation, summation is over observations that contain nonmissing values of the analyzed variable and, except where shown, over nonmissing weights and frequencies of one or more:

x_i
   is the nonmissing value of the analyzed variable for observation i.

f_i
   is the frequency that is associated with x_i if you use a FREQ statement. If you omit the FREQ statement, then $f_i = 1$ for all i.

w_i
   is the weight that is associated with x_i if you use a WEIGHT statement. The base procedures automatically exclude the values of x_i with missing weights from the analysis.

   By default, the base procedures treat a negative weight as if it is equal to zero. However, if you use the EXCLNPWGT option in the PROC statement, the procedure also excludes those values of x_i with nonpositive weights. Note that most SAS/STAT procedures, such as PROC TTEST and PROC GLM, exclude values with nonpositive weights by default.

   If you omit the WEIGHT statement, then $w_i = 1$ for all i.

n
   is the number of nonmissing value of x_i, $\sum f_i$. If you use the EXCLNPWGT option and the WEIGHT statement, then n is the number of nonmissing values with positive weights.

$\bar{x}$
   is the mean

$$\sum w_i x_i / \sum w_i$$

s^2
   is the variance

$$\frac{1}{d} \sum w_i \left(x_i - \bar{x} \right)^2$$

where d is the variance divisor (the VARDEF= option) that you specify in the PROC statement. Valid values are as follows:

When VARDEF=	d equals . . .
N	n
DF	$n - 1$
WEIGHT	$\sum w_i$
WDF	$\sum w_i - 1$

The default is DF.

z_i

is the standardized variable

$$(x_i - \bar{x}) / s$$

The standard keywords and formulas for each statistic follow. Some formulas use keywords to designate the corresponding statistic.

Table A1.1 The Most Common Simple Statistics

Statistic	PROC MEANS and SUMMARY	PROC UNIVARIATE	PROC TABULATE	PROC REPORT	PROC CORR	PROC SQL
Number of missing values	X	X	X	X		X
Number of nonmissing values	X	X	X	X	X	X
Number of observations	X	X				X
Sum of weights	X	X	X	X	X	X
Mean	X	X	X	X	X	X
Sum	X	X	X	X	X	X
Extreme values	X	X				
Minimum	X	X	X	X	X	X
Maximum	X	X	X	X	X	X
Range	X	X	X	X		X
Uncorrected sum of squares	X	X	X	X	X	X
Corrected sum of squares	X	X	X	X	X	X
Variance	X	X	X	X	X	X
Covariance					X	
Standard deviation	X	X	X	X	X	X
Standard error of the mean	X	X	X	X		X

Statistic	PROC MEANS and SUMMARY	PROC UNIVARIATE	PROC TABULATE	PROC REPORT	PROC CORR	PROC SQL
Coefficient of variation	X	X	X	X		X
Skewness	X	X	X			
Kurtosis	X	X	X			
Confidence Limits						
of the mean	X	X				
of the variance		X				
of quantiles		X				
Median	X	X	X		X	
Mode		X				
Percentiles/Deciles/ Quartiles	X	X	X			
t test						
for mean=0	X	X	X	X		X
for mean=μ_0		X				
Nonparametric tests for location		X				
Tests for normality		X				
Correlation coefficients					X	
Cronbach's alpha					X	

Descriptive Statistics

The keywords for descriptive statistics are

CSS
> is the sum of squares corrected for the mean, computed as

$$\sum w_i \left(x_i - \bar{x} \right)^2$$

CV
> is the percent coefficient of variation, computed as

$$\left(100s\right)/\bar{x}$$

KURTOSIS | KURT
> is the kurtosis, which measures heaviness of tails. When VARDEF=DF, the kurtosis is computed as

$$c_{4_n} \sum z_i^4 - \frac{3\left(n-1\right)}{\left(n-2\right)\left(n-3\right)}$$

where c_{4_n} is $\frac{n(n+1)}{(n-1)(n-2)(n-3)}$. The weighted kurtosis is computed as

$$= c_{4_n} \sum \left((x_i - \overline{x})/\hat{\sigma}_i \right)^4 - \frac{3(n-1)}{(n-2)(n-3)}$$

$$= c_{4_n} \sum w_i^2 \left((x_i - \overline{x})/\hat{\sigma} \right)^4 - \frac{3(n-1)}{(n-2)(n-3)}$$

When VARDEF=N, the kurtosis is computed as

$$= \frac{1}{n} \sum z_i^4 - 3$$

and the weighted kurtosis is computed as

$$= \frac{1}{n} \sum \left((x_i - \overline{x})/\hat{\sigma}_i \right)^4 - 3$$

$$= \frac{1}{n} \sum w_i^2 \left((x_i - \overline{x})/\hat{\sigma} \right)^4 - 3$$

where σ_i^2 is σ^2/w_i. The formula is invariant under the transformation $w_i^* = z w_i$, $z > 0$. When you use VARDEF=WDF or VARDEF=WEIGHT, the kurtosisis set to missing.

Note: PROC MEANS and PROC TABULATE do not compute weighted kurtosis. △

MAX
is the maximum value of x_i.

MEAN
is the arithmetic mean $\overline{x}$.

MIN
is the minimum value of x_i.

MODE
is the most frequent value of x_i.

N
is the number of x_i values that are not missing. Observations with f_i less than one and w_i equal to missing or $w_i \leq 0$ (when you use the EXCLNPWGT option) are excluded from the analysis and are not included in the calculation of N.

NMISS
is the number of x_i values that are missing. Observations with f_i less than one and w_i equal to missing or $w_i \leq 0$ (when you use the EXCLNPWGT option) are excluded from the analysis and are not included in the calculation of NMISS.

NOBS
is the total number of observations and is calculated as the sum of N and NMISS. However, if you use the WEIGHT statement, then NOBS is calculated as the sum of N, NMISS, and the number of observations excluded because of missing or nonpositive weights.

RANGE
   is the range and is calculated as the difference between maximum value and minimum value.

SKEWNESS | SKEW
   is skewness, which measures the tendency of the deviations to be larger in one direction than in the other. When VARDEF=DF, the skewness is computed as

$$c_{3_n} \sum z_i^3$$

where c_{3_n} is $\frac{n}{(n-1)(n-2)}$. The weighted skewness is computed as

$$= c_{3_n} \sum \left((x_i - \overline{x}) / \hat{\sigma}_j \right)^3$$
$$= c_{3_n} \sum w_i^{3/2} \left((x_i - \overline{x}) / \hat{\sigma} \right)^3$$

When VARDEF=N, the skewness is computed as

$$= \frac{1}{n} \sum z_i^3$$

and the weighted skewness is computed as

$$= \frac{1}{n} \sum \left((x_i - \overline{x}) / \hat{\sigma}_j \right)^3$$
$$= \frac{1}{n} \sum w_i^{3/2} \left((x_i - \overline{x}) / \hat{\sigma} \right)^3$$

The formula is invariant under the transformation $w_i^* = z w_i$, $z > 0$. When you use VARDEF=WDF or VARDEF=WEIGHT, the skewnessis set to missing.

   Note: PROC MEANS and PROC TABULATE do not compute weighted skewness. △

STDDEV|STD
   is the standard deviation s and is computed as the square root of the variance, s^2.

STDERR | STDMEAN
   is the standard error of the mean, computed as

$$s / \sqrt{\sum w_i}$$

when VARDEF=DF, which is the default. Otherwise, STDERR is set to missing.

SUM
   is the sum, computed as

$$\sum w_i x_i$$

SUMWGT
: is the sum of the weights, W, computed as

$$\sum w_i$$

USS
: is the uncorrected sum of squares, computed as

$$\sum w_i x_i^2$$

VAR
: is the variance s^2.

Percentile and Related Statistics

The keywords for percentiles and related statistics are

MEDIAN
: is the middle value.

P1
: is the 1st percentile.

P5
: is the 5th percentile.

P10
: is the 10th percentile.

P90
: is the 90th percentile.

P95
: is the 95th percentile.

P99
: is the 99th percentile.

Q1
: is the lower quartile (25th percentile).

Q3
: is the upper quartile (75th percentile).

QRANGE
: is interquartile range and is calculated as

$$Q_3 - Q_1$$

You use the PCTLDEF= option to specify the method that the procedure uses to compute percentiles. Let n be the number of nonmissing values for a variable, and let $x_1, x_2, \ldots, x_n$ represent the ordered values of the variable such that x_1 is the smallest value, x_2 is next smallest value, and x_n is the largest value. For the tth percentile between 0 and 1, let $p = t/100$. Then define j as the integer part of np and g as the fractional part of np or $(n+1)\,p$, so that

$$np = j + g \qquad \text{when PCTLDEF} = 1, 2, 3, \text{or } 5$$
$$(n+1)\, p = j + g \qquad \text{when PCTLDEF} = 4$$

Here, PCTLDEF= specifies the method that the procedure uses to compute the tth percentile, as shown in the table that follows.

When you use the WEIGHT statement, the tth percentile is computed as

$$
y = \begin{cases}
\frac{1}{2}\left(x_i + x_{i+1}\right) & \text{if } \sum_{j=1}^{i} w_j = pW \\[2ex]
x_{i+1} & \text{if } \sum_{j=1}^{i} w_j < pW < \sum_{j=1}^{i+1} w_j
\end{cases}
$$

where w_j is the weight associated with x_i and $W = \sum_{i=1}^{n} w_i$ is the sum of the weights.

When the observations have identical weights, the weighted percentiles where the same as the unweighted percentiles with PCTLDEF=5.

Table A1.2 Methods for Computing Percentile Statistics

PCTLDEF=	Description	Formula	
1	weighted average at x_{np}	$y = (1 - g)\, x_j + g x_{j+1}$ where x_o is taken to be x_1	
2	observation numbered closest to np	$y = x_i$	if $g \neq \frac{1}{2}$
		$y = x_j$	if $g = \frac{1}{2}$ and j is even
		$y = x_{j+1}$	if $g = \frac{1}{2}$ and j is odd
		where i is the integer part of $np + \frac{1}{2}$	
3	empirical distribution function	$y = x_j$	if $g = 0$
		$y = x_{j+1}$	if $g > 0$
4	weighted average aimed at $x_{(n+1)p}$	$y = (1 - g)\, x_j + g x_{j+1}$ where x_{n+1} is taken to be x_n	
5	empirical distribution function with averaging	$y = \frac{1}{2}\left(x_j + x_{j+1}\right)$	if $g = 0$
		$y = x_{j+1}$	if $g > 0$

Hypothesis Testing Statistics

The keywords for hypothesis testing statistics are

T

is the Student's t statistic to test the null hypothesis that the population mean is equal to μ_0 and is calculated as

$$\frac{\overline{x} - \mu_0}{s / \sqrt{\sum w_i}}$$

By default, μ_0 is equal to zero. You can use the MU0= option in the PROC UNIVARIATE statement to specify μ_0. You must use VARDEF=DF, which is the default variance divisor, otherwise T is set to missing.

By default, when you use a WEIGHT statement, the procedure counts the x_i values with nonpositive weights in the degrees of freedom. Use the EXCLNPWGT option in the PROC statement to exclude values with nonpositive weights. Most SAS/STAT procedures, such as PROC TTEST and PROC GLM automatically exclude values with nonpositive weights.

PROBT

is the two-tailed p-value for Student's t statistic, T, with $n - 1$ degrees of freedom. This is the probability under the null hypothesis of obtaining a more extreme value of T than is observed in this sample.

Confidence Limits for the Mean

fThe keywords for confidence limits are

CLM

is the two-sided confidence limit for the mean. A two-sided $100\,(1 - \alpha)$percent confidence interval for the mean has upper and lower limits

$$\overline{x} \pm t_{(1-\alpha/2;n-1)} \frac{s}{\sqrt{\sum w_i}}$$

where s is $\sqrt{\frac{1}{n-1} \sum (x_i - \overline{x})^2}$, $t_{(1-\alpha/2;n-1)}$ is the $(1 - \alpha/2)$ critical value of the Student's t statistics with $n - 1$ degrees of freedom, and α is the value of the ALPHA= option which by default is 0.05. Unless you use VARDEF=DF, which is the default variance divisor, CLM is set to missing.

LCLM

is the one-sided confidence limit below the mean. The one-sided $100\,(1 - \alpha)$percent confidence interval for the mean has the lower limit

$$\overline{x} - t_{(1-\alpha;n-1)} \frac{s}{\sqrt{\sum w_i}}$$

Unless you use VARDEF=DF, which is the default variance divisor, LCLM is set to missing.

UCLM

is the one-sided confidence limit above the mean. The one-sided $100\,(1 - \alpha)$percent confidence interval for the mean has the upper limit

$$\overline{x} + t_{(1-\alpha;n-1)} \frac{s}{\sqrt{\sum w_i}}$$

Unless you use VARDEF=DF, which is the default variance divisor, UCLM is set to missing.

Using Weights

For more information on using weights and an example, see on page 73.

Data Requirements for Summarization Procedures

The following are the minimal data requirements to compute unweighted statistics and do not describe recommended sample sizes. Statistics are reported as missing if VARDEF=DF (the default) and these requirements are not met:

- □ N and NMISS are computed regardless of the number of missing or nonmissing observations.
- □ SUM, MEAN, MAX, MIN, RANGE, USS, and CSS require at least one nonmissing observation.
- □ VAR, STD, STDERR, CV, T, and PRT require at least two nonmissing observations.
- □ SKEWNESS requires at least three nonmissing observations.
- □ KURTOSIS requires at least four nonmissing observations.
- □ SKEWNESS, KURTOSIS, T, and PROBT require that STD is greater than zero.
- □ CV requires that MEAN is not equal to zero.
- □ CLM, LCLM, UCLM, STDERR, T, and PROBT require that VARDEF=DF.

Statistical Background

The rest of this appendix provides text descriptions and SAS code examples that explain some of the statistical concepts and terminology that you may encounter when you interpret the output of SAS procedures for elementary statistics. For a more thorough discussion, consult an introductory statistics textbook such as Mendenhall and Beaver (1994); Ott and Mendenhall; or Snedecor and Cochran (1989).

Populations and Parameters

Usually, there is a clearly defined set of elements in which you are interested. This set of elements is called the *universe*, and a set of values associated with these elements is called a *population* of values. The statistical term *population* has nothing to do with people per se. A statistical population is a collection of values, not a collection of people. For example, a universe is all the students at a particular school, and there could be two populations of interest: one of height values and one of weight values. Or, a universe is the set of all widgets manufactured by a particular company, while the population of values could be the length of time each widget is used before it fails.

A population of values can be described in terms of its *cumulative distribution function*, which gives the proportion of the population less than or equal to each possible value. A discrete population can also be described by a *probability function*, which gives the proportion of the population equal to each possible value. A continuous population can often be described by a *density function*, which is the derivative of the cumulative distribution function. A density function can be approximated by a histogram that gives the proportion of the population lying within each of a series of intervals of values. A probability density function is like a histogram with an infinite number of infinitely small intervals.

In technical literature, when the term *distribution* is used without qualification, it generally refers to the cumulative distribution function. In informal writing, *distribution* sometimes means the density function instead. Often the word *distribution* is used simply to refer to an abstract population of values rather than some concrete population. Thus, the statistical literature refers to many types of abstract distributions, such as normal distributions, exponential distributions, Cauchy distributions, and so on. When a phrase such as *normal distribution* is used, it frequently does not matter whether the cumulative distribution function or the density function is intended.

It may be expedient to describe a population in terms of a few measures that summarize interesting features of the distribution. One such measure, computed from the population values, is called a *parameter*. Many different parameters can be defined to measure different aspects of a distribution.

The most commonly used parameter is the (arithmetic) *mean*. If the population contains a finite number of values, the population mean is computed as the sum of all the values in the population divided by the number of elements in the population. For an infinite population, the concept of the mean is similar but requires more complicated mathematics.

$E(x)$ denotes the mean of a population of values symbolized by x, such as height, where E stands for *expected value*. You can also consider expected values of derived functions of the original values. For example, if x represents height, then $E\left(x^2\right)$ is the expected value of height squared, that is, the mean value of the population obtained by squaring every value in the population of heights.

Samples and Statistics

It is often impossible to measure all of the values in a population. A collection of measured values is called a *sample*. A mathematical function of a sample of values is called a *statistic*. A statistic is to a sample as a parameter is to a population. It is customary to denote statistics by Roman letters and parameters by Greek letters. For example, the population mean is often written as μ, whereas the sample mean is written as $\bar{x}$. The field of *statistics* is largely concerned with the study of the behavior of sample statistics.

Samples can be selected in a variety of ways. Most SAS procedures assume that the data constitute a *simple random sample*, which means that the sample was selected in such a way that all possible samples were equally likely to be selected.

Statistics from a sample can be used to make inferences, or reasonable guesses, about the parameters of a population. For example, if you take a random sample of 30 students from the high school, the mean height for those 30 students is a reasonable guess, or *estimate*, of the mean height of all the students in the high school. Other statistics, such as the standard error, can provide information about how good an estimate is likely to be.

For any population parameter, several statistics can estimate it. Often, however, there is one particular statistic that is customarily used to estimate a given parameter. For example, the sample mean is the usual estimator of the population mean. In the case of the mean, the formulas for the parameter and the statistic are the same. In other cases, the formula for a parameter may be different from that of the most commonly used estimator. The most commonly used estimator is not necessarily the best estimator in all applications.

Measures of Location

Measures of location include the mean, the median, and the mode. These measures describe the center of a distribution. In the definitions that follows, notice that if the entire sample changes by adding a fixed amount to each observation, then these measures of location are shifted by the same fixed amount.

The Mean

The population mean $\mu = \mathrm{E}(x)$ is usually estimated by the sample mean $\bar{x}$.

The Median

The population median is the central value, lying above and below half of the population values. The sample median is the middle value when the data are arranged in ascending or descending order. For an even number of observations, the midpoint between the two middle values is usually reported as the median.

The Mode

The mode is the value at which the density of the population is at a maximum. Some densities have more than one local maximum (peak) and are said to be *multimodal*. The sample mode is the value that occurs most often in the sample. By default, PROC UNIVARIATE reports the lowest such value if there is a tie for the most-often-occurring sample value. PROC UNIVARIATE lists all possible modes when you specify the MODES option in the PROC statement. If the population is continuous, then all sample values occur once, and the sample mode has little use.

Percentiles

Percentiles, including quantiles, quartiles, and the median, are useful for a detailed study of a distribution. For a set of measurements arranged in order of magnitude, the pth percentile is the value that has p percent of the measurements below it and $(100-p)$ percent above it. The median is the 50th percentile. Because it may not be possible to divide your data so that you get exactly the desired percentile, the UNIVARIATE procedure uses a more precise definition.

The upper quartile of a distribution is the value below which 75 percent of the measurements fall (the 75th percentile). Twenty-five percent of the measurements fall below the lower quartile value.

In the following example, SAS artificially generates the data with a pseudorandom number function. The UNIVARIATE procedure computes a variety of quantiles and measures of location, and outputs the values to a SAS data set. A DATA step then uses the SYMPUT routine to assign the values of the statistics to macro variables. The macro %FORMGEN uses these macro variables to produce value labels for the FORMAT procedure. PROC CHART uses the resulting format to display the values of the statistics on a histogram.

```
options nodate pageno=1 linesize=64 pagesize=52;

title 'Example of Quantiles and Measures of Location';

data random;
   drop n;
   do n=1 to 1000;
```

```
         X=floor(exp(rannor(314159)*.8+1.8));
         output;
      end;
   run;

   proc univariate data=random nextrobs=0;
      var x;
      output out=location
              mean=Mean mode=Mode median=Median
              q1=Q1 q3=Q3 p5=P5 p10=P10 p90=P90 p95=P95
              max=Max;
   run;


   proc print data=location noobs;
   run;


   data _null_;
      set location;
      call symput('MEAN',round(mean,1));
      call symput('MODE',mode);
      call symput('MEDIAN',round(median,1));
      call symput('Q1',round(q1,1));
      call symput('Q3',round(q3,1));
      call symput('P5',round(p5,1));
      call symput('P10',round(p10,1));
      call symput('P90',round(p90,1));
      call symput('P95',round(p95,1));
      call symput('MAX',min(50,max));
   run;

   %macro formgen;
   %do i=1 %to &max;
      %let value=&i;
      %if &i=&p5      %then %let value=&value  P5;
      %if &i=&p10     %then %let value=&value  P10;
      %if &i=&q1      %then %let value=&value  Q1;
      %if &i=&mode    %then %let value=&value  Mode;
      %if &i=&median %then %let value=&value  Median;
      %if &i=&mean    %then %let value=&value  Mean;
      %if &i=&q3      %then %let value=&value  Q3;
      %if &i=&p90     %then %let value=&value  P90;
      %if &i=&p95     %then %let value=&value  P95;
      %if &i=&max     %then %let value=>=&value;
      &i="&value"
   %end;
   %mend;

   proc format print;
      value stat %formgen;
   run;
   options pagesize=42 linesize=64;
```

```
proc chart data=random;
   vbar x / midpoints=1 to &max by 1;
   format x stat.;
   footnote  'P5  =   5TH PERCENTILE';
   footnote2 'P10 = 10TH PERCENTILE';
   footnote3 'P90 = 90TH PERCENTILE';
   footnote4 'P95 = 95TH PERCENTILE';
   footnote5 'Q1  =   1ST QUARTILE  ';
   footnote6 'Q3  =   3RD QUARTILE  ';
run;
```

```
        Example of Quantiles and Measures of Location              1

                    The UNIVARIATE Procedure
                         Variable:  X

                             Moments

N                        1000   Sum Weights               1000
Mean                    7.605   Sum Observations          7605
Std Deviation      7.38169794   Variance            54.4894645
Skewness           2.73038523   Kurtosis            11.1870588
Uncorrected SS         112271   Corrected SS          54434.975
Coeff Variation    97.0637467   Std Error Mean      0.23342978


                   Basic Statistical Measures

        Location                        Variability

   Mean      7.605000      Std Deviation          7.38170
   Median    5.000000      Variance              54.48946
   Mode      3.000000      Range                 62.00000
                           Interquartile Range    6.00000


                 Tests for Location: Mu0=0

      Test              -Statistic-        -----p Value------

   Student's t      t  32.57939       Pr > |t|    <.0001
   Sign             M     494.5       Pr >= |M|   <.0001
   Signed Rank      S  244777.5       Pr >= |S|   <.0001


                  Quantiles (Definition 5)

                 Quantile        Estimate

                 100% Max          62.0
                 99%               37.5
                 95%               21.5
                 90%               16.0
                 75% Q3             9.0
                 50% Median         5.0
                 25% Q1             3.0
                 10%                2.0
                 5%                 1.0
                 1%                 0.0
                 0% Min             0.0
```

```
         Example of Quantiles and Measures of Location          2

 Mean   Max    P95   P90   Q3   Median   Q1   P10   P5   Mode

7.605    62    21.5   16    9      5      3     2    1     3
```

```
         Example of Quantiles and Measures of Location          3

Frequency

120 +   *
    |   *
    |   **
    |   ***
 90 +*****
    |*****
    |******
    |******
 60 +*******
    |********
    |********
    |********
 30 +************
    |***********    *
    |***************  *
    |**********************  *  *
    -------------------------------------------------------
    12345678911111111112222222222333333333344444444444>
             0123456789012345678901234567890123456789=
                                                      5
    PPQ M  MQ                                         0
    511 e  e3        P      P
    0   d  a         9      9
        i  n         0      5
     M  a
     o  n
     d
     e

                    X Midpoint


           P5  =  5TH PERCENTILE
           P10 = 10TH PERCENTILE
           P90 = 90TH PERCENTILE
           P95 = 95TH PERCENTILE
           Q1  =  1ST QUARTILE
           Q3  =  3RD QUARTILE
```

Measures of Variability

Another group of statistics is important in studying the distribution of a population. These statistics measure the *variability*, also called the spread, of values. In the definitions given in the sections that follow, notice that if the entire sample is changed by the addition of a fixed amount to each observation, then the values of these statistics are unchanged. If each observation in the sample is multiplied by a constant, however, the values of these statistics are appropriately rescaled.

The Range

The sample range is the difference between the largest and smallest values in the sample. For many populations, at least in statistical theory, the range is infinite, so the sample range may not tell you much about the population. The sample range tends to increase as the sample size increases. If all sample values are multiplied by a constant, the sample range is multiplied by the same constant.

The Interquartile Range

The interquartile range is the difference between the upper and lower quartiles. If all sample values are multiplied by a constant, the sample interquartile range is multiplied by the same constant.

The Variance

The population variance, usually denoted by σ^2, is the expected value of the squared difference of the values from the population mean:

$$\sigma^2 = \mathrm{E}\,(x - \mu)^2$$

The sample variance is denoted by s^2. The difference between a value and the mean is called a *deviation from the mean*. Thus, the variance approximates the mean of the squared deviations.

When all the values lie close to the mean, the variance is small but never less than zero. When values are more scattered, the variance is larger. If all sample values are multiplied by a constant, the sample variance is multiplied by the square of the constant.

Sometimes values other than $n - 1$ are used in the denominator. The VARDEF= option controls what divisor the procedure uses.

The Standard Deviation

The standard deviation is the square root of the variance, or root-mean-square deviation from the mean, in either a population or a sample. The usual symbols are σ for the population and s for a sample. The standard deviation is expressed in the same units as the observations, rather than in squared units. If all sample values are multiplied by a constant, the sample standard deviation is multiplied by the same constant.

Coefficient of Variation

The coefficient of variation is a unitless measure of relative variability. It is defined as the ratio of the standard deviation to the mean expressed as a percentage. The coefficient of variation is meaningful only if the variable is measured on a ratio scale. If all sample values are multiplied by a constant, the sample coefficient of variation remains unchanged.

Measures of Shape

Skewness

The variance is a measure of the overall size of the deviations from the mean. Since the formula for the variance squares the deviations, both positive and negative deviations contribute to the variance in the same way. In many distributions, positive deviations may tend to be larger in magnitude than negative deviations, or vice versa. *Skewness* is a measure of the tendency of the deviations to be larger in one direction than in the other. For example, the data in the last example are skewed to the right.

Population skewness is defined as

$$\mathrm{E}\left(x-\mu\right)^3/\sigma^3$$

Because the deviations are cubed rather than squared, the signs of the deviations are maintained. Cubing the deviations also emphasizes the effects of large deviations. The formula includes a divisor of σ^3 to remove the effect of scale, so multiplying all values by a constant does not change the skewness. Skewness can thus be interpreted as a tendency for one tail of the population to be heavier than the other. Skewness can be positive or negative and is unbounded.

Kurtosis

The heaviness of the tails of a distribution affects the behavior of many statistics. Hence it is useful to have a measure of tail heaviness. One such measure is *kurtosis*. The population kurtosis is usually defined as

$$\frac{\mathrm{E}\left(x-\mu\right)^4}{\sigma^4}-3$$

Note: Some statisticians omit the subtraction of 3. △

Because the deviations are raised to the fourth power, positive and negative deviations make the same contribution, while large deviations are strongly emphasized. Because of the divisor σ^4, multiplying each value by a constant has no effect on kurtosis.

Population kurtosis must lie between -2 and $+\infty$, inclusive. If M_3 represents population skewness and M_4 represents population kurtosis, then

$$M_4 > \left(M_3\right)^2 - 2$$

Statistical literature sometimes reports that kurtosis measures the *peakedness* of a density. However, heavy tails have much more influence on kurtosis than does the shape of the distribution near the mean (Kaplansky 1945; Ali 1974; Johnson, et al. 1980).

Sample skewness and kurtosis are rather unreliable estimators of the corresponding parameters in small samples. They are better estimators when your sample is very large. However, large values of skewness or kurtosis may merit attention even in small samples because such values indicate that statistical methods that are based on normality assumptions may be inappropriate.

The Normal Distribution

One especially important family of theoretical distributions is the *normal* or *Gaussian* distribution. A normal distribution is a smooth symmetric function often referred to as "bell-shaped." Its skewness and kurtosis are both zero. A normal distribution can be completely specified by only two parameters: the mean and the standard deviation. Approximately 68 percent of the values in a normal population are within one standard deviation of the population mean; approximately 95 percent of the values are within two standard deviations of the mean; and about 99.7 percent are within three standard deviations. Use of the term *normal* to describe this particular kind of distribution does not imply that other kinds of distributions are necessarily abnormal or pathological.

Many statistical methods are designed under the assumption that the population being sampled is normally distributed. Nevertheless, most real-life populations do not have normal distributions. Before using any statistical method based on normality assumptions, you should consult the statistical literature to find out how sensitive the method is to nonnormality and, if necessary, check your sample for evidence of nonnormality.

In the following example, SAS generates a sample from a normal distribution with a mean of 50 and a standard deviation of 10. The UNIVARIATE procedure performs tests for location and normality. Because the data are from a normal distribution, all *p*-values from the tests for normality are greater than 0.15. The CHART procedure displays a histogram of the observations. The shape of the histogram is a belllike, normal density.

```
options nodate pageno=1 linesize=64 pagesize=52;

title '10000 Obs Sample from a Normal Distribution';
title2 'with Mean=50 and Standard Deviation=10';

data normaldat;
   drop n;
   do n=1 to 10000;
      X=10*rannor(53124)+50;
      output;
   end;
run;

proc univariate data=normaldat nextrobs=0 normal
                        mu0=50 loccount;
   var x;
run;


proc format;
   picture msd
      20='20 3*Std' (noedit)
      30='30 2*Std' (noedit)
      40='40 1*Std' (noedit)
      50='50 Mean ' (noedit)
      60='60 1*Std' (noedit)
      70='70 2*Std' (noedit)
      80='80 3*Std' (noedit)
   other=' ';
run;
options linesize=64 pagesize=42;
```

```
proc chart;
   vbar x / midpoints=20 to 80 by 2;
   format x msd.;
run;
```

```
                10000 Obs Sample from a Normal Distribution            1
                    with Mean=50 and Standard Deviation=10

                         The UNIVARIATE Procedure
                             Variable:  X

                                 Moments

N                         10000   Sum Weights                  10000
Mean                 50.0323744   Sum Observations         500323.744
Std Deviation        9.92013874   Variance                 98.4091525
Skewness              -0.019929   Kurtosis                 -0.0163755
Uncorrected SS         26016378   Corrected SS             983993.116
Coeff Variation      19.8274395   Std Error Mean           0.09920139


                       Basic Statistical Measures

            Location                     Variability

        Mean      50.03237   Std Deviation            9.92014
        Median    50.06492   Variance                98.40915
        Mode          .      Range                   76.51343
                             Interquartile Range     13.28179


                     Tests for Location: Mu0=50

          Test             -Statistic-     -----p Value------

          Student's t   t   0.32635     Pr > |t|    0.7442
          Sign          M        26     Pr >= |M|   0.6101
          Signed Rank   S    174063     Pr >= |S|   0.5466


                    Location Counts: Mu0=50.00

                    Count                Value

                    Num Obs > Mu0         5026
                    Num Obs ^= Mu0       10000
                    Num Obs < Mu0         4974


                        Tests for Normality

          Test               --Statistic---     -----p Value------

          Kolmogorov-Smirnov   D  0.006595     Pr > D      >0.1500
          Cramer-von Mises     W-Sq 0.049963   Pr > W-Sq   >0.2500
          Anderson-Darling     A-Sq 0.371151   Pr > A-Sq   >0.2500
```

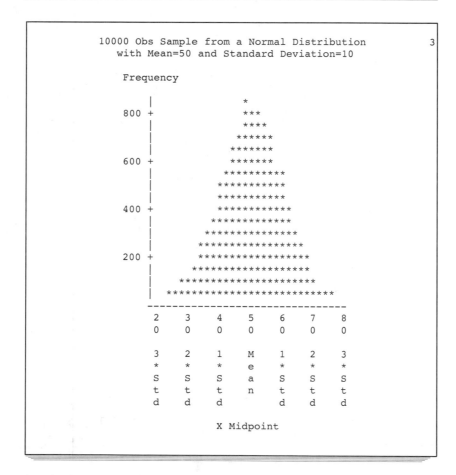

```
              10000 Obs Sample from a Normal Distribution          2
                 with Mean=50 and Standard Deviation=10

                        The UNIVARIATE Procedure
                               Variable:  X

                        Quantiles (Definition 5)

                        Quantile        Estimate

                        100% Max         90.2105
                        99%              72.6780
                        95%              66.2221
                        90%              62.6678
                        75% Q3           56.7280
                        50% Median       50.0649
                        25% Q1           43.4462
                        10%              37.1139
                        5%               33.5454
                        1%               26.9189
                        0% Min           13.6971
```

```
              10000 Obs Sample from a Normal Distribution          3
                 with Mean=50 and Standard Deviation=10

         Frequency

             |                    *
         800 +                   ***
             |                  ****
             |                 ******
             |                *******
         600 +                *******
             |               *********
             |              ***********
             |             ***********
         400 +             ************
             |            *************
             |           ***************
             |          ****************
         200 +          ******************
             |         *******************
             |        *********************
             |       ***************************
             -----------------------------------
                2    3    4    5    6    7    8
                0    0    0    0    0    0    0

                3    2    1    M    1    2    3
                *    *    *    e    *    *    *
                S    S    S    a    S    S    S
                t    t    t    n    t    t    t
                d    d    d         d    d    d

                         X Midpoint
```

Sampling Distribution of the Mean

If you repeatedly draw samples of size *n* from a population and compute the mean of each sample, then the sample means themselves have a distribution. Consider a new population consisting of the means of all the samples that could possibly be drawn from the original population. The distribution of this new population is called a *sampling distribution*.

It can be proven mathematically that if the original population has mean μ and standard deviation σ, then the sampling distribution of the mean also has mean μ, but its standard deviation is $\sigma/\sqrt{n}$. The standard deviation of the sampling distribution of the mean is called the *standard error of the mean*. The standard error of the mean provides an indication of the accuracy of a sample mean as an estimator of the population mean.

If the original population has a normal distribution, then the sampling distribution of the mean is also normal. If the original distribution is not normal but does not have excessively long tails, then the sampling distribution of the mean can be approximated by a normal distribution for large sample sizes.

The following example consists of three separate programs that show how the sampling distribution of the mean can be approximated by a normal distribution as the sample size increases. The first DATA step uses the RANEXP function to create a sample of 1000 observations from an exponential distribution. The theoretical population mean is 1.00, while the sample mean is 1.01, to two decimal places. The population standard deviation is 1.00; the sample standard deviation is 1.04.

This is an example of a nonnormal distribution. The population skewness is 2.00, which is close to the sample skewness of 1.97. The population kurtosis is 6.00, but the sample kurtosis is only 4.80.

```
options nodate pageno=1 linesize=64 pagesize=42;

title '1000 Observation Sample';
title2 'from an Exponential Distribution';

data expodat;
   drop n;
   do n=1 to 1000;
      X=ranexp(18746363);
      output;
   end;
run;
proc format;
    value axisfmt
      .05='0.05'
      .55='0.55'
     1.05='1.05'
     1.55='1.55'
     2.05='2.05'
     2.55='2.55'
     3.05='3.05'
     3.55='3.55'
     4.05='4.05'
     4.55='4.55'
     5.05='5.05'
     5.55='5.55'
     other=' ';
run;

proc chart data=expodat ;
   vbar x / axis=300
            midpoints=0.05 to 5.55 by .1;
   format x axisfmt.;
```

```
        run;


        options pagesize=64;

        proc univariate data=expodat noextrobs=0 normal
                        mu0=1;
           var x;
        run;
```

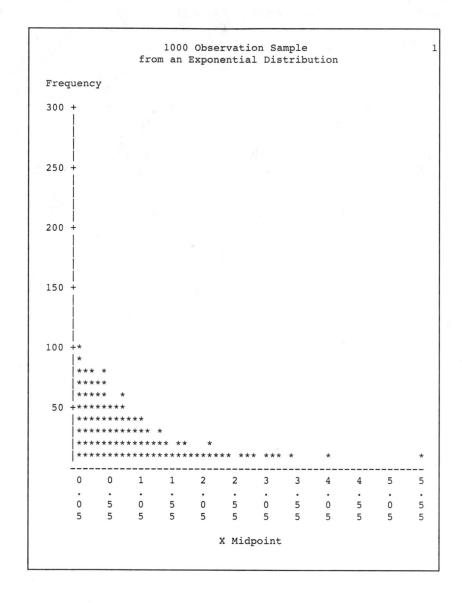

```
                         1000 Observation Sample                    2
                     from an Exponential Distribution

                        The UNIVARIATE Procedure
                             Variable:  X

                                Moments

N                      1000    Sum Weights                  1000
Mean             1.01176214    Sum Observations       1011.76214
Std Deviation    1.04371187    Variance                1.08933447
Skewness         1.96963112    Kurtosis                4.80150594
Uncorrected SS   2111.90777    Corrected SS           1088.24514
Coeff Variation   103.15783    Std Error Mean          0.03300507


                    Basic Statistical Measures

           Location                     Variability

      Mean      1.011762     Std Deviation          1.04371
      Median    0.689502     Variance               1.08933
      Mode        .          Range                  6.63851
                             Interquartile Range    1.06252


              Tests for Location: Mu0=1

      Test            -Statistic-     -----p Value------

      Student's t    t  0.356374    Pr > |t|     0.7216
      Sign           M      -140    Pr >= |M|    <.0001
      Signed Rank    S    -50781    Pr >= |S|    <.0001


                  Tests for Normality

   Test                 --Statistic---     -----p Value------

   Shapiro-Wilk         W    0.801498    Pr < W     <0.0001
   Kolmogorov-Smirnov   D    0.166308    Pr > D     <0.0100
   Cramer-von Mises     W-Sq 9.507975    Pr > W-Sq  <0.0050
   Anderson-Darling     A-Sq 54.5478     Pr > A-Sq  <0.0050


                  Quantiles (Definition 5)

              Quantile         Estimate

              100% Max        6.63906758
              99%             5.04491651
              95%             3.13482318
              90%             2.37803632
              75% Q3          1.35733401
              50% Median      0.68950221
              25% Q1          0.29481436
              10%             0.10219011
              5%              0.05192799
              1%              0.01195590
              0% Min          0.00055441
```

The next DATA step generates 1000 different samples from the same exponential distribution. Each sample contains ten observations. The MEANS procedure computes the mean of each sample. In the data set that is created by PROC MEANS, each observation represents the mean of a sample of ten observations from an exponential distribution. Thus, the data set is a sample from the sampling distribution of the mean for an exponential population.

PROC UNIVARIATE displays statistics for this sample of means. Notice that the mean of the sample of means is .99, almost the same as the mean of the original population. Theoretically, the standard deviation of the sampling distribution is $\sigma/\sqrt{n} = 1.00/\sqrt{10} = .32$, whereas the standard deviation of this sample from thesampling distribution is .30. The skewness (.55) and kurtosis (-.006) are closer to zero in the sample from the sampling distribution than in the original sample from the exponential distribution. This is so because the sampling distribution is closer to a normal distribution than is the original exponential distribution. The CHART procedure displays a histogram of the 1000-sample means. The shape of the histogram is much closer to a belllike, normal density, but it is still distinctly lopsided.

```
options nodate pageno=1 linesize=64 pagesize=48;

title '1000 Sample Means with 10 Obs per Sample';
title2 'Drawn from an Exponential Distribution';

data samp10;
   drop n;
   do Sample=1 to 1000;
      do n=1 to 10;
         X=ranexp(433879);
         output;
      end;
   end;

proc means data=samp10 noprint;
   output out=mean10 mean=Mean;
   var x;
   by sample;
run;


 proc format;
    value axisfmt
      .05='0.05'
       .55='0.55'
      1.05='1.05'
      1.55='1.55'
      2.05='2.05'
      other=' ';
 run;

proc chart data=mean10;
   vbar mean/axis=300
              midpoints=0.05 to 2.05 by .1;
   format mean axisfmt.;
run;


options pagesize=64;
proc univariate data=mean10 noextrobs=0 normal
                mu0=1;
   var mean;
run;
```

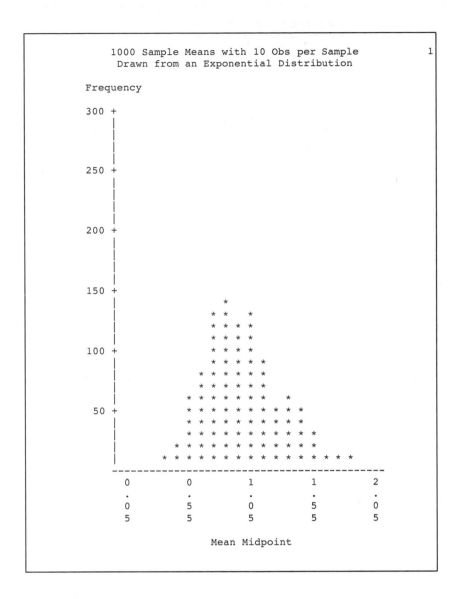

```
                1000 Sample Means with 10 Obs per Sample          2
                  Drawn from an Exponential Distribution

                          The UNIVARIATE Procedure
                              Variable:  Mean

                                   Moments

  N                         1000   Sum Weights                  1000
  Mean                 0.9906857   Sum Observations       990.685697
  Std Deviation       0.30732649   Variance               0.09444957
  Skewness            0.54575615   Kurtosis               -0.0060892
  Uncorrected SS      1075.81327   Corrected SS           94.3551193
  Coeff Variation     31.0215931   Std Error Mean         0.00971852


                      Basic Statistical Measures

            Location                       Variability

     Mean      0.990686    Std Deviation            0.30733
     Median    0.956152    Variance                 0.09445
     Mode         .        Range                    1.79783
                           Interquartile Range      0.41703


                  Tests for Location: Mu0=1

        Test            -Statistic-      -----p Value------

        Student's t    t   -0.95841   Pr > |t|     0.3381
        Sign           M      -53     Pr >= |M|    0.0009
        Signed Rank    S    -22687    Pr >= |S|    0.0129


                        Tests for Normality

    Test                   --Statistic---      -----p Value------

    Shapiro-Wilk        W      0.9779      Pr < W      <0.0001
    Kolmogorov-Smirnov  D      0.055498    Pr > D      <0.0100
    Cramer-von Mises    W-Sq   0.953926    Pr > W-Sq   <0.0050
    Anderson-Darling    A-Sq   5.945023    Pr > A-Sq   <0.0050


                     Quantiles (Definition 5)

                     Quantile        Estimate

                     100% Max        2.053899
                     99%             1.827503
                     95%             1.557175
                     90%             1.416611
                     75% Q3          1.181006
                     50% Median      0.956152
                     25% Q1          0.763973
                     10%             0.621787
                     5%              0.553568
                     1%              0.433820
                     0% Min          0.256069
```

In the following DATA step, the size of each sample from the exponential distribution is increased to 50. The standard deviation of the sampling distribution is smaller than in the previous example because the size of each sample is larger. Also, the sampling distribution is even closer to a normal distribution, as can be seen from the histogram and the skewness.

```
options nodate pageno=1 linesize=64 pagesize=48;

title '1000 Sample Means with 50 Obs per Sample';
title2 'Drawn from an Exponential Distribution';

data samp50;
   drop n;
   do sample=1 to 1000;
      do n=1 to 50;
         X=ranexp(72437213);
         output;
      end;
   end;

proc means data=samp50 noprint;
   output out=mean50 mean=Mean;
   var x;
   by sample;
run;


proc format;
   value axisfmt
       .05='0.05'
       .55='0.55'
      1.05='1.05'
      1.55='1.55'
      2.05='2.05'
      2.55='2.55'
      other=' ';
run;

proc chart data=mean50;
   vbar mean / axis=300
               midpoints=0.05 to 2.55 by .1;
   format mean axisfmt.;
run;


options pagesize=64;

proc univariate data=mean50 nextrobs=0 normal
               mu0=1;
   var mean;
run;
```

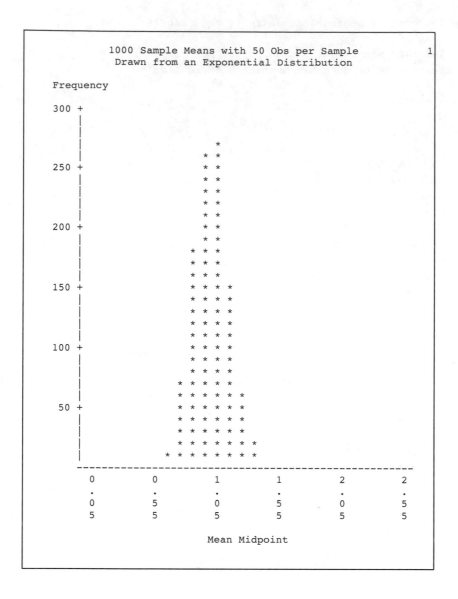

```
              1000 Sample Means with 50 Obs per Sample          2
                 Drawn from an Exponential Distribution

                      The UNIVARIATE Procedure
                         Variable:  Mean

                              Moments

N                      1000    Sum Weights              1000
Mean             0.99679697    Sum Observations   996.796973
Std Deviation    0.13815404    Variance           0.01908654
Skewness         0.19062633    Kurtosis           -0.1438604
Uncorrected SS   1012.67166    Corrected SS         19.067451
Coeff Variation  13.8597969    Std Error Mean      0.00436881


                   Basic Statistical Measures

         Location                      Variability

    Mean      0.996797    Std Deviation         0.13815
    Median    0.996023    Variance              0.01909
    Mode         .        Range                 0.87040
                          Interquartile Range   0.18956


                 Tests for Location: Mu0=1

        Test             -Statistic-     -----p Value------

        Student's t    t  -0.73316    Pr > |t|    0.4636
        Sign           M      -13     Pr >= |M|   0.4292
        Signed Rank    S    -10767    Pr >= |S|   0.2388


                      Tests for Normality

    Test               --Statistic---     -----p Value------

    Shapiro-Wilk       W     0.996493    Pr < W       0.0247
    Kolmogorov-Smirnov D     0.023687    Pr > D      >0.1500
    Cramer-von Mises   W-Sq  0.084468    Pr > W-Sq    0.1882
    Anderson-Darling   A-Sq  0.66039     Pr > A-Sq    0.0877


                   Quantiles (Definition 5)

                   Quantile        Estimate

                   100% Max        1.454957
                   99%             1.337016
                   95%             1.231508
                   90%             1.179223
                   75% Q3          1.086515
                   50% Median      0.996023
                   25% Q1          0.896953
                   10%             0.814906
                   5%              0.780783
                   1%              0.706588
                   0% Min          0.584558
```

Testing Hypotheses

The purpose of the statistical methods that have been discussed so far is to estimate a population parameter by means of a sample statistic. Another class of statistical methods is used for testing hypotheses about population parameters or for measuring the amount of evidence against a hypothesis.

Consider the universe of students in a college. Let the variable X be the number of pounds by which a student's weight deviates from the ideal weight for a person of the same sex, height, and build. You want to find out whether the population of students is, on the average, underweight or overweight. To this end, you have taken a random sample of X values from nine students, with results as given in the following DATA step:

```
title 'Deviations from Normal Weight';

data x;
   input X @@;
   datalines;
-7 -2 1 3 6 10 15 21 30
;
```

You can define several hypotheses of interest. One hypothesis is that, on the average, the students are of exactly ideal weight. If μ represents the population mean of the X values, you can write this hypothesis, called the *null* hypothesis, as $H_0 : \mu = 0$. The other two hypotheses, called *alternative* hypotheses, are that the students are underweight on the average, $H_1 : \mu < 0$, and that the students are overweight on the average, $H_2 : \mu > 0$.

The null hypothesis is so called because in many situations it corresponds to the assumption of "no effect" or "no difference." However, this interpretation is not appropriate for all testing problems. The null hypothesis is like a straw man that can be toppled by statistical evidence. You decide between the alternative hypotheses according to which way the straw man falls.

A naive way to approach this problem would be to look at the sample mean $\bar{x}$ and decide among the three hypotheses according to the following rule:

- If $\bar{x} < 0$, decide on $H_1 : \mu < 0$.
- If $\bar{x} = 0$, decide on $H_0 : \mu = 0$.
- If $\bar{x} > 0$, decide on $H_2 : \mu > 0$.

The trouble with this approach is that there may be a high probability of making an incorrect decision. If H_0 is true, you are nearly certain to make a wrong decision because the chances of $\bar{x}$ being exactly zero are almost nil. If μ is slightly less than zero, so that H_1 is true, there may be nearly a 50 percent chance that $\bar{x}$ will be greater than zero in repeated sampling, so the chances of incorrectly choosing H_2 would also be nearly 50 percent. Thus, you have a high probability of making an error if $\bar{x}$ is near zero. In such cases, there is not enough evidence to make a confident decision, so the best response may be to reserve judgment until you can obtain more evidence.

The question is, how far from zero must $\bar{x}$ be for you to be able to make a confident decision? The answer can be obtained by considering the sampling distribution of $\bar{x}$. If X has a roughly normal distribution, then $\bar{x}$ has an approximately normal sampling distribution. The mean of the sampling distribution of $\bar{x}$ is μ. Assume temporarily that σ, the standard deviation of X, is known to be 12. Then the standard error of $\bar{x}$ for samples of nine observations is $\sigma/\sqrt{n} = 12/\sqrt{9} = 4$.

You know that about 95 percent of the values from a normal distribution are within two standard deviations of the mean, so about 95 percent of the possible samples of nine X values have a sample mean $\bar{x}$ between $0 - 2\,(4)$ and $0 + 2\,(4)$, or between –8 and 8. Consider the chances of making an error with the following decision rule:

- If $\bar{x} < -8$, decide on $H_1 : \mu < 0$.
- If $-8 \le \bar{x} \le 8$, reserve judgment.
- If $\bar{x} > 8$, decide on $H_2 : \mu > 0$.

If H_0 is true, then in about 95 percent of the possible samples $\bar{x}$ will be between the *critical values* -8 and 8, so you will reserve judgment. In these cases the statistical evidence is not strong enough to fell the straw man. In the other 5 percent of the samples you will make an error; in 2.5 percent of the samples you will incorrectly choose H_1, and in 2.5 percent you will incorrectly choose H_2.

The price you pay for controlling the chances of making an error is the necessity of reserving judgment when there is not sufficient statistical evidence to reject the null hypothesis.

Significance and Power

The probability of rejecting the null hypothesis if it is true is called the *Type I error rate* of the statistical test and is typically denoted as α. In this example, an $\bar{x}$ value less than -8 or greater than 8 is said to be *statistically significant* at the 5 percent level. You can adjust the type I error rate according to your needs by choosing different critical values. For example, critical values of -4 and 4 would produce a significance level of about 32 percent, while -12 and 12 would give a type I error rate of about 0.3 percent.

The decision rule is a *two-tailed test* because the alternative hypotheses allow for population means either smaller or larger than the value specified in the null hypothesis. If you were interested only in the possibility of the students being overweight on the average, you could use a *one-tailed test*:

- □ If $\bar{x} \le 8$, reserve judgment.
- □ If $\bar{x} > 8$, decide on $H_2 : \mu > 0$.

For this one-tailed test, the type I error rate is 2.5 percent, half that of the two-tailed test.

The probability of rejecting the null hypothesis if it is false is called the *power* of the statistical test and is typically denoted as $1 - \beta$. β is called the *Type II error rate*, which is the probability of not rejecting a false null hypothesis. The power depends on the true value of the parameter. In the example, assume the population mean is 4. The power for detecting H_2 is the probability of getting a sample mean greater than 8. The critical value 8 is one standard error higher than the population mean 4. The chance of getting a value at least one standard deviation greater than the mean from a normal distribution is about 16 percent, so the power for detecting the alternative hypothesis H_2 is about 16 percent. If the population mean were 8, the power for H_2 would be 50 percent, whereas a population mean of 12 would yield a power of about 84 percent.

The smaller the type I error rate is, the less the chance of making an incorrect decision, but the higher the chance of having to reserve judgment. In choosing a type I error rate, you should consider the resulting power for various alternatives of interest.

Student's *t* Distribution

In practice, you usually cannot use any decision rule that uses a critical value based on σ because you do not usually know the value of σ. You can, however, use s as an estimate of σ. Consider the following statistic:

$$t = \frac{\bar{x} - \mu_0}{s/\sqrt{n}}$$

This t statistic is the difference between the sample mean and the hypothesized mean μ_0 divided by the estimated standard error of the mean.

If the null hypothesis is true and the population is normally distributed, then the t statistic has what is called a *Student's t distribution* with $n - 1$ degrees of freedom. This distribution looks very similar to a normal distribution, but the tails of the

Student's t distribution are heavier. As the sample size gets larger, the sample standard deviation becomes a better estimator of the population standard deviation, and the t distribution gets closer to a normal distribution.

You can base a decision rule on the t statistic:

- ☐ If $t < -2.3$, decide on $H_1 : \mu < 0$.
- ☐ If $-2.3 \leq t \leq 2.3$, reserve judgment.
- ☐ If $t > 2.3$, decide on $H_0 : \mu > 0$.

The value 2.3 was obtained from a table of Student's t distribution to give a type I error rate of 5 percent for 8 (that is, $9 - 1 = 8$) degrees of freedom. Most common statistics texts contain a table of Student's t distribution. If you do not have a statistics text handy, you can use the DATA step and the TINV function to print any values from the t distribution.

By default, PROC UNIVARIATE computes a t statistic for the null hypothesis that $\mu_0 = 0$, along with related statistics. Use the MU0= option in the PROC statement to specify another value for the null hypothesis.

This example uses the data on deviations from normal weight, which consist of nine observations. First, PROC MEANS computes the t statistic for the null hypothesis that $\mu = 0$. Then, the TINV function in a DATA step computes the value of Student's t distribution for a two-tailed test at the 5 percent level of significance and 8 degrees of freedom.

```
data devnorm;
   title 'Deviations from Normal Weight';
   input X @@;
   datalines;
-7 -2 1 3 6 10 15 21 30
;


proc means data=devnorm maxdec=3 n mean
           std stderr t probt;
run;


title 'Student''s t Critical Value';


data _null_;
   file print;
   t=tinv(.975,8);
   put t 5.3;
run;
```

		Deviations from Normal Weight				1
		The MEANS Procedure				
		Analysis Variable : X				
N	Mean	Std Dev	Std Error	t Value	Pr > |t|	
9	8.556	11.759	3.920	2.18	0.0606	

Student's t Critical Value	2
2.306	

In the current example, the value of the *t* statistic is 2.18, which is less than the critical *t* value of 2.3 (for a 5 percent significance level and 8 degrees of freedom). Thus, at a 5 percent significance level you must reserve judgment. If you had elected to use a 10 percent significance level, the critical value of the *t* distribution would have been 1.86 and you could have rejected the null hypothesis. The sample size is so small, however, that the validity of your conclusion depends strongly on how close the distribution of the population is to a normal distribution.

Probability Values

Another way to report the results of a statistical test is to compute a *probability value* or *p-value*. A *p*-value gives the probability in repeated sampling of obtaining a statistic as far in the direction(s) specified by the alternative hypothesis as is the value actually observed. A two-tailed *p*-value for a *t* statistic is the probability of obtaining an absolute *t* value that is greater than the observed absolute *t* value. A one-tailed *p*-value for a *t* statistic for the alternative hypothesis $\mu > \mu_0$ is the probability of obtaining a *t* value greater than the observed *t* value. Once the *p*-value is computed, you can perform a hypothesis test by comparing the *p*-value with the desired significance level. If the *p*-value is less than or equal to the type I error rate of the test, the null hypothesis can be rejected. The two-tailed *p*-value, labeled `Pr > |t|` in the PROC MEANS output, is .0606, so the null hypothesis could be rejected at the 10 percent significance level but not at the 5 percent level.

A *p*-value is a measure of the strength of the evidence against the null hypothesis. The smaller the *p*-value, the stronger the evidence for rejecting the null hypothesis.

References

Ali, M.M. (1974), "Stochastic Ordering and Kurtosis Measure," *Journal of the American Statistical Association*, 69, 543–545.

Johnson, M.E., Tietjen, G.L., and Beckman, R.J. (1980), "A New Family of Probability Distributions With Applications to Monte Carlo Studies," *Journal of the American Statistical Association*, 75, 276-279.

Kaplansky, I. (1945), "A Common Error Concerning Kurtosis," *Journal of the American Statistical Association*, 40, 259-263.

Mendenhall, W. and Beaver, R.. (1994), *Introduction to Probability and Statistics*, 9th Edition, Belmont, CA: Wadsworth Publishing Company.

Ott, R. and Mendenhall, W. (1994) *Understanding Statistics*, 6th Edition, North Scituate, MA: Duxbury Press.

Schlotzhauer, S.D. and Littell, R.C. (1997), *SAS System for Elementary Statistical Analysis*, Second Edition, Cary, NC: SAS Institute Inc.

Snedecor, G.W. and Cochran, W.C. (1989), *Statistical Methods*, 8th Edition, Ames, IA: Iowa State University Press.

APPENDIX

2

Operating Environment-Specific Procedures

The following table gives a brief description and the relevant releases for some common operating environment-specific procedures. All of these procedures are described in more detail in operating environment-companion documentation.

Table A2.1 Host-Specific Procedures

Procedure	Description	Releases
BMDP	Calls any BMDP program to analyze data in a SAS data set.	All
CONVERT	Converts BMDP, OSIRIS, and SPSS system files to SAS data sets.	All
C16PORT	Converts a 16-bit SAS data library or catalog created in Release 6.08 to a transport file, which you can then convert to a 32-bit format for use in the current release of SAS by using the CIMPORT procedure.	6.10 - 6.12
FSDEVICE	Creates, copies, modifies, deletes, or renames device descriptions in a catalog.	All
PDS	Lists, deletes, or renames the members of a partitioned data set.	6.09E
PDSCOPY	Copies partitioned data sets from disk to disk, disk to tape, tape to tape, or tape to disk.	6.09E
RELEASE	Releases unused space at the end of a disk data set.	6.09E
SOURCE	Provides an easy way to back up and process source library data sets.	6.09E
TAPECOPY	Copies an entire tape volume, or files from one or more tape volumes, to one output tape volume.	6.09E
TAPELABEL	Writes the label information of an IBM standard-labeled tape volume to the SAS procedure output file.	6.09E

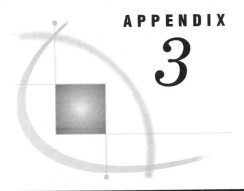

APPENDIX

3

Raw Data and DATA Steps

Overview

The programs for examples in this document generally show you how to create the data sets that are used. Some examples show only partial data. For these examples, the complete data are shown in this appendix.

CENSUS

```
data census;
    input Density CrimeRate State $ 14-27 PostalCode $ 29-30;
    datalines;
```

```
263.3 4575.3 Ohio           OH
62.1 7017.1  Washington     WA
103.4 5161.9 South Carolina SC
53.4 3438.6  Mississippi    MS
180.0 8503.2 Florida        FL
80.8 2190.7  West Virginia  WV
428.7 5477.6 Maryland       MD
71.2 4707.5  Missouri       MO
43.9 4245.2  Arkansas       AR
7.3 6371.4   Nevada         NV
264.3 3163.2 Pennsylvania   PA
11.5 4156.3  Idaho          ID
44.1 6025.6  Oklahoma       OK
51.2 4615.8  Minnesota      MN
55.2 4271.2  Vermont        VT
27.4 6969.9  Oregon         OR
205.3 5416.5 Illinois       IL
94.1 5792.0  Georgia        GA
9.1 2678.0   South Dakota   SD
9.4 2833.0   North Dakota   ND
102.4 3371.7 New Hampshire  NH
54.3 7722.4  Texas          TX
76.6 4451.4  Alabama        AL
307.6 4938.8 Delaware       DE
151.4 6506.4 California      CA
111.6 4665.6 Tennessee      TN
120.4 4649.9 North Carolina NC
;
```

CHARITY

```
data Charity;
    input School $ 1-7 Year 9-12 Name $ 14-20 MoneyRaised 22-26
          HoursVolunteered 28-29;
    datalines;
Monroe  1992 Allison 31.65 19
Monroe  1992 Barry   23.76 16
Monroe  1992 Candace 21.11  5
Monroe  1992 Danny    6.89 23
Monroe  1992 Edward  53.76 31
Monroe  1992 Fiona   48.55 13
Monroe  1992 Gert    24.00 16
Monroe  1992 Harold  27.55 17
Monroe  1992 Ima     15.98  9
Monroe  1992 Jack    20.00 23
Monroe  1992 Katie   22.11  2
Monroe  1992 Lisa    18.34 17
Monroe  1992 Tonya   55.16 40
Monroe  1992 Max     26.77 34
Monroe  1992 Ned     28.43 22
Monroe  1992 Opal    32.66 14
```

```
Monroe    1993 Patsy    18.33 18
Monroe    1993 Quentin  16.89 15
Monroe    1993 Randall  12.98 17
Monroe    1993 Sam      15.88  5
Monroe    1993 Tyra     21.88 23
Monroe    1993 Myrtle   47.33 26
Monroe    1993 Frank    41.11 22
Monroe    1993 Cameron  65.44 14
Monroe    1993 Vern     17.89 11
Monroe    1993 Wendell  23.00 10
Monroe    1993 Bob      26.88  6
Monroe    1993 Leah     28.99 23
Monroe    1994 Becky    30.33 26
Monroe    1994 Sally    35.75 27
Monroe    1994 Edgar    27.11 12
Monroe    1994 Dawson   17.24 16
Monroe    1994 Lou       5.12 16
Monroe    1994 Damien   18.74 17
Monroe    1994 Mona     27.43  7
Monroe    1994 Della    56.78 15
Monroe    1994 Monique  29.88 19
Monroe    1994 Carl     31.12 25
Monroe    1994 Reba     35.16 22
Monroe    1994 Dax      27.65 23
Monroe    1994 Gary     23.11 15
Monroe    1994 Suzie    26.65 11
Monroe    1994 Benito   47.44 18
Monroe    1994 Thomas   21.99 23
Monroe    1994 Annie    24.99 27
Monroe    1994 Paul     27.98 22
Monroe    1994 Alex     24.00 16
Monroe    1994 Lauren   15.00 17
Monroe    1994 Julia    12.98 15
Monroe    1994 Keith    11.89 19
Monroe    1994 Jackie   26.88 22
Monroe    1994 Pablo    13.98 28
Monroe    1994 L.T.     56.87 33
Monroe    1994 Willard  78.65 24
Monroe    1994 Kathy    32.88 11
Monroe    1994 Abby     35.88 10
Kennedy   1992 Arturo   34.98 14
Kennedy   1992 Grace    27.55 25
Kennedy   1992 Winston  23.88 22
Kennedy   1992 Vince    12.88 21
Kennedy   1992 Claude   15.62  5
Kennedy   1992 Mary     28.99 34
Kennedy   1992 Abner    25.89 22
Kennedy   1992 Jay      35.89 35
Kennedy   1992 Alicia   28.77 26
Kennedy   1992 Freddy   29.00 27
Kennedy   1992 Eloise   31.67 25
Kennedy   1992 Jenny    43.89 22
Kennedy   1992 Thelma   52.63 21
Kennedy   1992 Tina     19.67 21
```

```
Kennedy 1992 Eric    24.89 12
Kennedy 1993 Bubba   37.88 12
Kennedy 1993 G.L.    25.89 21
Kennedy 1993 Bert    28.89 21
Kennedy 1993 Clay    26.44 21
Kennedy 1993 Leeann  27.17 17
Kennedy 1993 Georgia 38.90 11
Kennedy 1993 Bill    42.23 25
Kennedy 1993 Holly   18.67 27
Kennedy 1993 Benny   19.09 25
Kennedy 1993 Cammie  28.77 28
Kennedy 1993 Amy     27.08 31
Kennedy 1993 Doris   22.22 24
Kennedy 1993 Robbie  19.80 24
Kennedy 1993 Ted     27.07 25
Kennedy 1993 Sarah   24.44 12
Kennedy 1993 Megan   28.89 11
Kennedy 1993 Jeff    31.11 12
Kennedy 1993 Taz     30.55 11
Kennedy 1993 George  27.56 11
Kennedy 1993 Heather 38.67 15
Kennedy 1994 Nancy   29.90 26
Kennedy 1994 Rusty   30.55 28
Kennedy 1994 Mimi    37.67 22
Kennedy 1994 J.C.    23.33 27
Kennedy 1994 Clark   27.90 25
Kennedy 1994 Rudy    27.78 23
Kennedy 1994 Samuel  34.44 18
Kennedy 1994 Forrest 28.89 26
Kennedy 1994 Luther  72.22 24
Kennedy 1994 Trey     6.78 18
Kennedy 1994 Albert  23.33 19
Kennedy 1994 Che-Min 26.66 33
Kennedy 1994 Preston 32.22 23
Kennedy 1994 Larry   40.00 26
Kennedy 1994 Anton   35.99 28
Kennedy 1994 Sid     27.45 25
Kennedy 1994 Will    28.88 21
Kennedy 1994 Morty   34.44 25
;
```

CUSTRESP

```
data customer_response;
   input Customer Factor1-Factor4 Source1-Source3
         Quality1-Quality3;
   datalines;
1 . . 1 1 1 1 . 1 . .
2 1 1 . 1 1 1 . 1 1 .
3 . . 1 1 1 1 . . . .
4 1 1 . 1 . 1 . . . 1
```

```
 5 . 1 . 1 1 . . . . 1
 6 . 1 . 1 1 . . . . .
 7 . 1 . 1 1 . . 1 . .
 8 1 . . 1 1 1 . 1 1 .
 9 1 1 . 1 1 . . . . 1
10 1 . . 1 1 1 . 1 1 .
11 1 1 1 1 . 1 . 1 1 1
12 1 1 . 1 1 1 . . . .
13 1 1 . 1 . 1 . 1 1 .
14 1 1 . 1 1 1 . . . .
15 1 1 . 1 . 1 . 1 1 1
16 1 . . 1 1 . . 1 . .
17 1 1 . 1 1 1 . . 1 .
18 1 1 . 1 1 1 1 . . 1
19 . 1 . 1 1 1 1 . 1 .
20 1 . . 1 1 1 . 1 1 1
21 . . . 1 1 1 . 1 . .
22 . . . 1 1 1 . 1 1 .
23 1 . . 1 . . . . . 1
24 . 1 . 1 1 . . 1 . 1
25 1 1 . 1 1 . . . 1 1
26 1 1 . 1 1 . . 1 . .
27 1 . . 1 1 . . . 1 .
28 1 1 . 1 . . . 1 1 1
29 1 . . 1 1 1 . 1 . 1
30 1 . 1 1 1 . . 1 1 .
31 . . . 1 1 . . 1 1 .
32 1 1 1 1 1 . . 1 1 1
33 1 . . 1 1 . . 1 . 1
34 . . 1 1 . . . 1 1 .
35 1 1 1 1 1 . 1 1 . .
36 1 1 1 1 . 1 . 1 . .
37 1 1 . 1 . . . 1 . .
38 . . . 1 1 1 . 1 . .
39 1 1 . 1 1 . . 1 . 1
40 1 . . 1 . . 1 1 . 1
41 1 . . 1 1 1 1 1 . 1
42 1 1 1 1 . . 1 1 . .
43 1 . . 1 1 1 . 1 . .
44 1 . 1 1 . 1 . 1 . 1
45 . . . 1 . . 1 . . 1
46 . . . 1 1 . . . 1 .
47 1 1 . 1 . . 1 1 . .
48 1 . 1 1 1 . 1 1 . .
49 . . 1 1 1 1 . 1 . 1
50 . 1 . 1 1 . . 1 1 .
51 1 . 1 1 1 1 . . . .
52 1 1 1 1 1 1 . 1 . .
53 . 1 1 1 . 1 . 1 1 1
54 1 . . 1 1 . . 1 1 .
55 1 1 . 1 1 1 . 1 . .
56 1 . . 1 1 . . 1 1 .
57 1 1 . 1 1 . 1 . . 1
58 . 1 . 1 . 1 . . 1 1
```

```
 59  1 1 1 1 . . 1 1 1 .
 60  . 1 1 1 1 1 . . 1 1
 61  1 1 1 1 1 1 . 1 . .
 62  1 1 . 1 1 . . 1 1 .
 63  . . . 1 . . . 1 1 1
 64  1 . . 1 1 1 . 1 . .
 65  1 . . 1 1 1 . 1 . .
 66  1 . . 1 1 1 1 1 . 
 67  1 1 . 1 1 1 . 1 1 .
 68  1 1 . 1 1 1 . 1 1 .
 69  1 1 . 1 1 . 1 . . .
 70  . . . 1 1 1 . 1 . .
 71  1 . . 1 1 . 1 . . 1
 72  1 . 1 1 1 1 . . 1 .
 73  1 1 . 1 . 1 . 1 1 .
 74  1 1 1 1 1 1 . 1 . .
 75  . 1 . 1 1 1 . . 1 .
 76  1 1 . 1 1 1 . 1 1 1
 77  . . . 1 1 1 . . . .
 78  1 1 1 1 1 1 . 1 1 .
 79  1 . . 1 1 1 . 1 1 .
 80  1 1 1 1 1 . 1 1 . 1
 81  1 1 . 1 1 1 1 1 1 .
 82  . . . 1 1 1 1 . . .
 83  1 1 . 1 1 1 . 1 1 .
 84  1 . . 1 1 . . 1 1 .
 85  . . . 1 . 1 . 1 . .
 86  1 . . 1 1 1 . 1 1 1
 87  1 1 . 1 1 1 . 1 . .
 88  . . . 1 . 1 . . . .
 89  1 . . 1 . 1 . . 1 1
 90  1 1 . 1 1 1 . 1 . 1
 91  . . . 1 1 . . . 1 .
 92  1 . . 1 1 1 . 1 1 .
 93  1 . . 1 1 . . 1 1 .
 94  1 . . 1 1 1 1 1 . .
 95  1 . . 1 . 1 1 1 1 .
 96  1 . 1 1 1 1 . . 1 .
 97  1 1 . 1 1 . . . 1 .
 98  1 . 1 1 1 1 1 1 . .
 99  1 1 . 1 1 1 1 1 1 .
100  1 . 1 1 1 . . . 1 1
101  1 . 1 1 1 1 . . . .
102  1 . . 1 1 . 1 1 . .
103  1 1 . 1 1 1 . 1 . .
104  . . . 1 1 1 . 1 1 1
105  1 . 1 1 1 . . 1 . 1
106  1 1 1 1 1 1 1 1 1 1
107  1 1 1 1 . . . 1 . 1
108  1 . . 1 . 1 1 1 . .
109  . 1 . 1 1 . . 1 1 .
110  1 . . 1 . . . . . .
111  1 . . 1 1 1 . 1 1 .
112  1 1 . 1 1 1 . . . 1
```

```
113 1 1 . 1 1 . 1 1 1 .
114 1 1 . 1 1 . . . . .
115 1 1 . 1 1 . . 1 . .
116 . 1 . 1 1 1 1 1 . .
117 . 1 . 1 1 1 . . . .
118 . 1 1 1 1 . . 1 1 .
119 . . . 1 . . . 1 . .
120 1 1 . 1 . . . . 1 .
;
```

DJIA

```
data djia;
        input Year @7 HighDate date7. High @24 LowDate date7. Low;
        format highdate lowdate date7.;
        datalines;
1954    31DEC54   404.39    11JAN54   279.87
1955    30DEC55   488.40    17JAN55   388.20
1956    06APR56   521.05    23JAN56   462.35
1957    12JUL57   520.77    22OCT57   419.79
1958    31DEC58   583.65    25FEB58   436.89
1959    31DEC59   679.36    09FEB59   574.46
1960    05JAN60   685.47    25OCT60   568.05
1961    13DEC61   734.91    03JAN61   610.25
1962    03JAN62   726.01    26JUN62   535.76
1963    18DEC63   767.21    02JAN63   646.79
1964    18NOV64   891.71    02JAN64   768.08
1965    31DEC65   969.26    28JUN65   840.59
1966    09FEB66   995.15    07OCT66   744.32
1967    25SEP67   943.08    03JAN67   786.41
1968    03DEC68   985.21    21MAR68   825.13
1969    14MAY69   968.85    17DEC69   769.93
1970    29DEC70   842.00    06MAY70   631.16
1971    28APR71   950.82    23NOV71   797.97
1972    11DEC72  1036.27    26JAN72   889.15
1973    11JAN73  1051.70    05DEC73   788.31
1974    13MAR74   891.66    06DEC74   577.60
1975    15JUL75   881.81    02JAN75   632.04
1976    21SEP76  1014.79    02JAN76   858.71
1977    03JAN77   999.75    02NOV77   800.85
1978    08SEP78   907.74    28FEB78   742.12
1979    05OCT79   897.61    07NOV79   796.67
1980    20NOV80  1000.17    21APR80   759.13
1981    27APR81  1024.05    25SEP81   824.01
1982    27DEC82  1070.55    12AUG82   776.92
1983    29NOV83  1287.20    03JAN83  1027.04
1984    06JAN84  1286.64    24JUL84  1086.57
1985    16DEC85  1553.10    04JAN85  1184.96
1986    02DEC86  1955.57    22JAN86  1502.29
1987    25AUG87  2722.42    19OCT87  1738.74
1988    21OCT88  2183.50    20JAN88  1879.14
```

```
1989   09OCT89 2791.41   03JAN89 2144.64
1990   16JUL90 2999.75   11OCT90 2365.10
1991   31DEC91 3168.83   09JAN91 2470.30
1992   01JUN92 3413.21   09OCT92 3136.58
1993   29DEC93 3794.33   20JAN93 3241.95
1994   31JAN94 3978.36   04APR94 3593.35
;
```

EDUC

```
data education;
   input State $14. +1 Code $ DropoutRate Expenditures MathScore Region $;
   label dropoutrate='Dropout Percentage - 1989'
         expenditures='Expenditure Per Pupil - 1989'
         mathscore='8th Grade Math Exam - 1990';
   datalines;
Alabama          AL 22.3 3197 252 SE
Alaska           AK 35.8 7716 .   W
Arizona          AZ 31.2 3902 259 W
Arkansas         AR 11.5 3273 256 SE
California       CA 32.7 4121 256 W
Colorado         CO 24.7 4408 267 W
Connecticut      CT 16.8 6857 270 NE
Delaware         DE 28.5 5422 261 NE
Florida          FL 38.5 4563 255 SE
Georgia          GA 27.9 3852 258 SE
Hawaii           HI 18.3 4121 251 W
Idaho            ID 21.8 2838 272 W
Illinois         IL 21.5 4906 260 MW
Indiana          IN 13.8 4284 267 MW
Iowa             IA 13.6 4285 278 MW
Kansas           KS 17.9 4443 .   MW
Kentucky         KY 32.7 3347 256 SE
Louisiana        LA 43.1 3317 246 SE
Maine            ME 22.5 4744 .   NE
Maryland         MD 26.0 5758 260 NE
Massachusetts    MA 28.0 5979 .   NE
Michigan         MI 29.3 5116 264 MW
Minnesota        MN 11.4 4755 276 MW
Mississippi      MS 39.9 2874 .   SE
Missouri         MO 26.5 4263 .   MW
Montana          MT 15.0 4293 280 W
Nebraska         NE 13.9 4360 276 MW
Nevada           NV 28.1 3791 .   W
New Hampshire    NH 25.9 4807 273 NE
New Jersey       NE 20.4 7549 269 NE
New Mexico       NM 28.5 3473 256 W
New York         NY 35.0 .    261 NE
North Carolina   NC 31.2 3874 250 SE
North Dakota     ND 12.1 3952 281 MW
Ohio             OH 24.4 4649 264 MW
```

;

EMPDATA

```
data empdata;
input IdNumber $ 1-4 LastName $ 9-19 FirstName $ 20-29
      City $ 30-42 State $ 43-44 /
      Gender $ 1 JobCode $ 9-11 Salary 20-29 @30 Birth date7.
      @43 Hired date7. HomePhone $ 54-65;
format birth hired date7.;
datalines;
1919    Adams      Gerald    Stamford      CT
M       TA2        34376     15SEP48       07JUN75    203/781-1255
1653    Alexander  Susan     Bridgeport    CT
F       ME2        35108     18OCT52       12AUG78    203/675-7715
1400    Apple      Troy      New York      NY
M       ME1        29769     08NOV55       19OCT78    212/586-0808
1350    Arthur     Barbara   New York      NY
F       FA3        32886     03SEP53       01AUG78    718/383-1549
1401    Avery      Jerry     Paterson      NJ
M       TA3        38822     16DEC38       20NOV73    201/732-8787
1499    Barefoot   Joseph    Princeton     NJ
M       ME3        43025     29APR42       10JUN68    201/812-5665
1101    Baucom     Walter    New York      NY
M       SCP        18723     09JUN50       04OCT78    212/586-8060
1333    Blair      Justin    Stamford      CT
M       PT2        88606     02APR49       13FEB69    203/781-1777
1402    Blalock    Ralph     New York      NY
M       TA2        32615     20JAN51       05DEC78    718/384-2849
1479    Bostic     Marie     New York      NY
F       TA3        38785     25DEC56       08OCT77    718/384-8816
1403    Bowden     Earl      Bridgeport    CT
M       ME1        28072     31JAN57       24DEC79    203/675-3434
1739    Boyce      Jonathan  New York      NY
M       PT1        66517     28DEC52       30JAN79    212/587-1247
1658    Bradley    Jeremy    New York      NY
M       SCP        17943     11APR55       03MAR80    212/587-3622
1428    Brady      Christine Stamford      CT
F       PT1        68767     07APR58       19NOV79    203/781-1212
1782    Brown      Jason     Stamford      CT
M       ME2        35345     07DEC58       25FEB80    203/781-0019
1244    Bryant     Leonard   New York      NY
M       ME2        36925     03SEP51       20JAN76    718/383-3334
1383    Burnette   Thomas    New York      NY
M       BCK        25823     28JAN56       23OCT80    718/384-3569
1574    Cahill     Marshall  New York      NY
M       FA2        28572     30APR48       23DEC80    718/383-2338
1789    Caraway    Davis     New York      NY
M       SCP        18326     28JAN45       14APR66    212/587-9000
1404    Carter     Donald    New York      NY
M       PT2        91376     27FEB41       04JAN68    718/384-2946
```

1437	Carter	Dorothy	Bridgeport	CT	
F	A3	33104	23SEP48	03SEP72	203/675-4117
1639	Carter	Karen	Stamford	CT	
F	A3	40260	29JUN45	31JAN72	203/781-8839
1269	Caston	Franklin	Stamford	CT	
M	NA1	41690	06MAY60	01DEC80	203/781-3335
1065	Chapman	Neil	New York	NY	
M	ME2	35090	29JAN32	10JAN75	718/384-5618
1876	Chin	Jack	New York	NY	
M	TA3	39675	23MAY46	30APR73	212/588-5634
1037	Chow	Jane	Stamford	CT	
F	TA1	28558	13APR52	16SEP80	203/781-8868
1129	Cook	Brenda	New York	NY	
F	ME2	34929	11DEC49	20AUG79	718/383-2313
1988	Cooper	Anthony	New York	NY	
M	FA3	32217	03DEC47	21SEP72	212/587-1228
1405	Davidson	Jason	Paterson	NJ	
M	SCP	18056	08MAR54	29JAN80	201/732-2323
1430	Dean	Sandra	Bridgeport	CT	
F	TA2	32925	03MAR50	30APR75	203/675-1647
1983	Dean	Sharon	New York	NY	
F	FA3	33419	03MAR50	30APR75	718/384-1647
1134	Delgado	Maria	Stamford	CT	
F	TA2	33462	08MAR57	24DEC76	203/781-1528
1118	Dennis	Roger	New York	NY	
M	PT3	111379	19JAN32	21DEC68	718/383-1122
1438	Donaldson	Karen	Stamford	CT	
F	TA3	39223	18MAR53	21NOV75	203/781-2229
1125	Dunlap	Donna	New York	NY	
F	FA2	28888	11NOV56	14DEC75	718/383-2094
1475	Eaton	Alicia	New York	NY	
F	FA2	27787	18DEC49	16JUL78	718/383-2828
1117	Edgerton	Joshua	New York	NY	
M	TA3	39771	08JUN51	16AUG80	212/588-1239
1935	Fernandez	Katrina	Bridgeport	CT	
F	NA2	51081	31MAR42	19OCT69	203/675-2962
1124	Fields	Diana	White Plains	NY	
F	FA1	23177	13JUL46	04OCT78	914/455-2998
1422	Fletcher	Marie	Princeton	NJ	
F	FA1	22454	07JUN52	09APR79	201/812-0902
1616	Flowers	Annette	New York	NY	
F	TA2	34137	04MAR58	07JUN81	718/384-3329
1406	Foster	Gerald	Bridgeport	CT	
M	ME2	35185	11MAR49	20FEB75	203/675-6363
1120	Garcia	Jack	New York	NY	
M	ME1	28619	14SEP60	10OCT81	718/384-4930
1094	Gomez	Alan	Bridgeport	CT	
M	FA1	22268	05APR58	20APR79	203/675-7181
1389	Gordon	Levi	New York	NY	
M	BCK	25028	18JUL47	21AUG78	718/384-9326
1905	Graham	Alvin	New York	NY	
M	PT1	65111	19APR60	01JUN80	212/586-8815
1407	Grant	Daniel	Mt. Vernon	NY	
M	PT1	68096	26MAR57	21MAR78	914/468-1616

```
1114    Green     Janice    New York    NY
F       TA2       32928     21SEP57     30JUN75     212/588-1092
;
```

ENERGY

```
data energy;
   length State $2;
   input Region Division state $ Type Expenditures;
   datalines;
1 1 ME 1 708
1 1 ME 2 379
1 1 NH 1 597
1 1 NH 2 301
1 1 VT 1 353
1 1 VT 2 188
1 1 MA 1 3264
1 1 MA 2 2498
1 1 RI 1 531
1 1 RI 2 358
1 1 CT 1 2024
1 1 CT 2 1405
1 2 NY 1 8786
1 2 NY 2 7825
1 2 NJ 1 4115
1 2 NJ 2 3558
1 2 PA 1 6478
1 2 PA 2 3695
4 3 MT 1 322
4 3 MT 2 232
4 3 ID 1 392
4 3 ID 2 298
4 3 WY 1 194
4 3 WY 2 184
4 3 CO 1 1215
4 3 CO 2 1173
4 3 NM 1 545
4 3 NM 2 578
4 3 AZ 1 1694
4 3 AZ 2 1448
4 3 UT 1 621
4 3 UT 2 438
4 3 NV 1 493
4 3 NV 2 378
4 4 WA 1 1680
4 4 WA 2 1122
4 4 OR 1 1014
4 4 OR 2 756
4 4 CA 1 10643
4 4 CA 2 10114
4 4 AK 1 349
```

```
4 4 AK 2 329
4 4 HI 1 273
4 4 HI 2 298
;
```

GROC

```
data groc;
   input Region $9. Manager $ Department $ Sales;
   datalines;
Southeast    Hayes       Paper        250
Southeast    Hayes       Produce      100
Southeast    Hayes       Canned       120
Southeast    Hayes       Meat          80
Southeast    Michaels    Paper         40
Southeast    Michaels    Produce      300
Southeast    Michaels    Canned       220
Southeast    Michaels    Meat          70
Northwest    Jeffreys    Paper         60
Northwest    Jeffreys    Produce      600
Northwest    Jeffreys    Canned       420
Northwest    Jeffreys    Meat          30
Northwest    Duncan      Paper         45
Northwest    Duncan      Produce      250
Northwest    Duncan      Canned       230
Northwest    Duncan      Meat          73
Northwest    Aikmann     Paper         45
Northwest    Aikmann     Produce      205
Northwest    Aikmann     Canned       420
Northwest    Aikmann     Meat          76
Southwest    Royster     Paper         53
Southwest    Royster     Produce      130
Southwest    Royster     Canned       120
Southwest    Royster     Meat          50
Southwest    Patel       Paper         40
Southwest    Patel       Produce      350
Southwest    Patel       Canned       225
Southwest    Patel       Meat          80
Northeast    Rice        Paper         90
Northeast    Rice        Produce       90
Northeast    Rice        Canned       420
Northeast    Rice        Meat          86
Northeast    Fuller      Paper        200
Northeast    Fuller      Produce      300
Northeast    Fuller      Canned       420
Northeast    Fuller      Meat         125
;
```

MATCH_11

```
data match_11;
   input Pair Low Age Lwt Race Smoke Ptd Ht UI @@;
   select(race);
      when (1) do;
         race1=0;
         race2=0;
      end;
      when (2) do;
         race1=1;
         race2=0;
      end;
      when (3) do;
         race1=0;
         race2=1;
      end;
   end;
   datalines;
1  0 14 135 1 0 0 0 0        1  1 14 101 3 1 1 0 0
2  0 15  98 2 0 0 0 0        2  1 15 115 3 0 0 0 1
3  0 16  95 3 0 0 0 0        3  1 16 130 3 0 0 0 0
4  0 17 103 3 0 0 0 0        4  1 17 130 3 1 1 0 1
5  0 17 122 1 1 0 0 0        5  1 17 110 1 1 0 0 0
6  0 17 113 2 0 0 0 0        6  1 17 120 1 1 0 0 0
7  0 17 113 2 0 0 0 0        7  1 17 120 2 0 0 0 0
8  0 17 119 3 0 0 0 0        8  1 17 142 2 0 0 1 0
9  0 18 100 1 1 0 0 0        9  1 18 148 3 0 0 0 0
10 0 18  90 1 1 0 0 1        10 1 18 110 2 1 1 0 0
11 0 19 150 3 0 0 0 0        11 1 19  91 1 1 1 0 1
12 0 19 115 3 0 0 0 0        12 1 19 102 1 0 0 0 0
13 0 19 235 1 1 0 1 0        13 1 19 112 1 1 0 0 1
14 0 20 120 3 0 0 0 1        14 1 20 150 1 1 0 0 0
15 0 20 103 3 0 0 0 0        15 1 20 125 3 0 0 0 1
16 0 20 169 3 0 1 0 1        16 1 20 120 2 1 0 0 0
17 0 20 141 1 0 1 0 1        17 1 20  80 3 1 0 0 1
18 0 20 121 2 1 0 0 0        18 1 20 109 3 0 0 0 0
19 0 20 127 3 0 0 0 0        19 1 20 121 1 1 1 0 1
20 0 20 120 3 0 0 0 0        20 1 20 122 2 1 0 0 0
21 0 20 158 1 0 0 0 0        21 1 20 105 3 0 0 0 0
22 0 21 108 1 1 0 0 1        22 1 21 165 1 1 0 1 0
23 0 21 124 3 0 0 0 0        23 1 21 200 2 0 0 0 0
24 0 21 185 2 1 0 0 0        24 1 21 103 3 0 0 0 0
25 0 21 160 1 0 0 0 0        25 1 21 100 3 0 1 0 0
26 0 21 115 1 0 0 0 0        26 1 21 130 1 1 0 1 0
27 0 22  95 3 0 0 1 0        27 1 22 130 1 1 0 0 0
28 0 22 158 2 0 1 0 0        28 1 22 130 1 1 1 0 1
29 0 23 130 2 0 0 0 0        29 1 23  97 3 0 0 0 1
30 0 23 128 3 0 0 0 0        30 1 23 187 2 1 0 0 0
31 0 23 119 3 0 0 0 0        31 1 23 120 3 0 0 0 0
32 0 23 115 3 1 0 0 0        32 1 23 110 1 1 1 0 0
33 0 23 190 1 0 0 0 0        33 1 23  94 3 1 0 0 0
34 0 24  90 1 1 1 0 0        34 1 24 128 2 0 1 0 0
35 0 24 115 1 0 0 0 0        35 1 24 132 3 0 0 1 0
36 0 24 110 3 0 0 0 0        36 1 24 155 1 1 1 0 0
37 0 24 115 3 0 0 0 0        37 1 24 138 1 0 0 0 0
```

```
      38  0  24  110  3  0  1  0  0        38  1  24  105  2  1  0  0  0
      39  0  25  118  1  1  0  0  0        39  1  25  105  3  0  1  1  0
      40  0  25  120  3  0  0  0  1        40  1  25   85  3  0  0  0  1
      41  0  25  155  1  0  0  0  0        41  1  25  115  3  0  0  0  0
      42  0  25  125  2  0  0  0  0        42  1  25   92  1  1  0  0  0
      43  0  25  140  1  0  0  0  0        43  1  25   89  3  0  1  0  0
      44  0  25  241  2  0  0  1  0        44  1  25  105  3  0  1  0  0
      45  0  26  113  1  1  0  0  0        45  1  26  117  1  1  1  0  0
      46  0  26  168  2  1  0  0  0        46  1  26   96  3  0  0  0  0
      47  0  26  133  3  1  1  0  0        47  1  26  154  3  0  1  1  0
      48  0  26  160  3  0  0  0  0        48  1  26  190  1  1  0  0  0
      49  0  27  124  1  1  0  0  0        49  1  27  130  2  0  0  0  1
      50  0  28  120  3  0  0  0  0        50  1  28  120  3  1  1  0  1
      51  0  28  130  3  0  0  0  0        51  1  28   95  1  1  0  0  0
      52  0  29  135  1  0  0  0  0        52  1  29  130  1  0  0  0  1
      53  0  30   95  1  1  0  0  0        53  1  30  142  1  1  1  0  0
      54  0  31  215  1  1  0  0  0        54  1  31  102  1  1  1  0  0
      55  0  32  121  3  0  0  0  0        55  1  32  105  1  1  0  0  0
      56  0  34  170  1  0  1  0  0        56  1  34  187  2  1  0  1  0
      ;
```

PROCLIB.DELAY

```
      data proclib.delay;
         input flight $3. +5 date date7. +2 orig $3. +3 dest $3. +3
               delaycat $15. +2 destype $15. +8 delay;
         informat date date7.;
         format date date7.;
         datalines;
      114      01MAR94   LGA    LAX    1-10 Minutes     Domestic          8
      202      01MAR94   LGA    ORD    No Delay         Domestic         -5
      219      01MAR94   LGA    LON    11+ Minutes      International     18
      622      01MAR94   LGA    FRA    No Delay         International     -5
      132      01MAR94   LGA    YYZ    11+ Minutes      International     14
      271      01MAR94   LGA    PAR    1-10 Minutes     International      5
      302      01MAR94   LGA    WAS    No Delay         Domestic         -2
      114      02MAR94   LGA    LAX    No Delay         Domestic          0
      202      02MAR94   LGA    ORD    1-10 Minutes     Domestic          5
      219      02MAR94   LGA    LON    11+ Minutes      International     18
      622      02MAR94   LGA    FRA    No Delay         International      0
      132      02MAR94   LGA    YYZ    1-10 Minutes     International      5
      271      02MAR94   LGA    PAR    1-10 Minutes     International      4
      302      02MAR94   LGA    WAS    No Delay         Domestic          0
      114      03MAR94   LGA    LAX    No Delay         Domestic         -1
      202      03MAR94   LGA    ORD    No Delay         Domestic         -1
      219      03MAR94   LGA    LON    1-10 Minutes     International      4
      622      03MAR94   LGA    FRA    No Delay         International     -2
      132      03MAR94   LGA    YYZ    1-10 Minutes     International      6
      271      03MAR94   LGA    PAR    1-10 Minutes     International      2
      302      03MAR94   LGA    WAS    1-10 Minutes     Domestic          5
      114      04MAR94   LGA    LAX    11+ Minutes      Domestic         15
```

```
202      04MAR94   LGA   ORD   No Delay        Domestic           -5
219      04MAR94   LGA   LON   1-10 Minutes    International        3
622      04MAR94   LGA   FRA   11+ Minutes     International       30
132      04MAR94   LGA   YYZ   No Delay        International       -5
271      04MAR94   LGA   PAR   1-10 Minutes    International        5
302      04MAR94   LGA   WAS   1-10 Minutes    Domestic            7
114      05MAR94   LGA   LAX   No Delay        Domestic           -2
202      05MAR94   LGA   ORD   1-10 Minutes    Domestic            2
219      05MAR94   LGA   LON   1-10 Minutes    International        3
622      05MAR94   LGA   FRA   No Delay        International       -6
132      05MAR94   LGA   YYZ   1-10 Minutes    International        3
271      05MAR94   LGA   PAR   1-10 Minutes    International        5
114      06MAR94   LGA   LAX   No Delay        Domestic           -1
202      06MAR94   LGA   ORD   No Delay        Domestic           -3
219      06MAR94   LGA   LON   11+ Minutes     International       27
132      06MAR94   LGA   YYZ   1-10 Minutes    International        7
302      06MAR94   LGA   WAS   1-10 Minutes    Domestic            1
114      07MAR94   LGA   LAX   No Delay        Domestic           -1
202      07MAR94   LGA   ORD   No Delay        Domestic           -2
219      07MAR94   LGA   LON   11+ Minutes     International       15
622      07MAR94   LGA   FRA   11+ Minutes     International       21
132      07MAR94   LGA   YYZ   No Delay        International       -2
271      07MAR94   LGA   PAR   1-10 Minutes    International        4
302      07MAR94   LGA   WAS   No Delay        Domestic            0
;
```

PROCLIB.EMP95

```
data proclib.emp95;
   input #1 idnum $4. @6 name $15.
         #2 address $42.
         #3 salary 6.;
   datalines;
2388 James Schmidt
100 Apt. C Blount St. SW Raleigh NC 27693
92100
2457 Fred Williams
99 West Lane  Garner NC 27509
33190
2776 Robert Jones
12988 Wellington Farms Ave. Cary NC 27512
29025
8699 Jerry Capalleti
222 West L St. Oxford NC 27587
39985
2100 Lanny Engles
293 Manning Pl. Raleigh NC 27606
30998
9857 Kathy Krupski
1000 Taft Ave. Morrisville NC 27508
38756
```

```
0987 Dolly Lunford
2344 Persimmons Branch   Apex NC 27505
44010
3286 Hoa Nguyen
2818 Long St. Cary NC 27513
87734
6579 Bryan Samosky
3887 Charles Ave. Garner NC 27508
50234
3888 Kim Siu
5662 Magnolia Blvd Southeast Cary NC 27513
77558
;
```

PROCLIB.EMP96

```
data proclib.emp96;
   input #1 idnum $4. @6 name $15.
         #2 address $42.
         #3 salary 6.;
   datalines;
2388 James Schmidt
100 Apt. C Blount St. SW Raleigh NC 27693
92100
2457 Fred Williams
99 West Lane   Garner NC 27509
33190
2776 Robert Jones
12988 Wellington Farms Ave. Cary NC 27511
29025
8699 Jerry Capalleti
222 West L St. Oxford NC 27587
39985
3278 Mary Cravens
211 N. Cypress St. Cary NC 27512
35362
2100 Lanny Engles
293 Manning Pl. Raleigh NC 27606
30998
9857 Kathy Krupski
100 Taft Ave. Morrisville NC 27508
40456
0987 Dolly Lunford
2344 Persimmons Branch Trail Apex NC 27505
45110
3286 Hoa Nguyen
2818 Long St. Cary NC 27513
89834
6579 Bryan Samosky
3887 Charles Ave. Garner NC 27508
```

```
50234
3888 Kim Siu
5662 Magnolia Blvd Southwest Cary NC 27513
79958
6544 Roger Monday
3004 Crepe Myrtle Court Raleigh NC 27604
47007
;
```

PROCLIB.INTERNAT

```
data proclib.internat;
   input flight $3.  +5 date date7. +2 dest $3. +8 boarded;
   informat date date7.;
   format date date7.;
   datalines;
219      01MAR94  LON      198
622      01MAR94  FRA      207
132      01MAR94  YYZ      115
271      01MAR94  PAR      138
219      02MAR94  LON      147
622      02MAR94  FRA      176
132      02MAR94  YYZ      106
271      02MAR94  PAR      172
219      03MAR94  LON      197
622      03MAR94  FRA      180
132      03MAR94  YYZ       75
271      03MAR94  PAR      147
219      04MAR94  LON      232
622      04MAR94  FRA      137
132      04MAR94  YYZ      117
271      04MAR94  PAR      146
219      05MAR94  LON      160
622      05MAR94  FRA      185
132      05MAR94  YYZ      157
271      05MAR94  PAR      177
219      06MAR94  LON      163
132      06MAR94  YYZ      150
219      07MAR94  LON      241
622      07MAR94  FRA      210
132      07MAR94  YYZ      164
271      07MAR94  PAR      155
;
```

PROCLIB.LAKES

```
data proclib.lakes;
   input region $ 1-2 lake $ 5-13 pol_a1 pol_a2 pol_b1-pol_b4;
```

```
    datalines;
NE  Carr        0.24    0.99    0.95    0.36    0.44    0.67
NE  Duraleigh   0.34    0.01    0.48    0.58    0.12    0.56
NE  Charlie     0.40    0.48    0.29    0.56    0.52    0.95
NE  Farmer      0.60    0.65    0.25    0.20    0.30    0.64
NW  Canyon      0.63    0.44    0.20    0.98    0.19    0.01
NW  Morris      0.85    0.95    0.80    0.67    0.32    0.81
NW  Golf        0.69    0.37    0.08    0.72    0.71    0.32
NW  Falls       0.01    0.02    0.59    0.58    0.67    0.02
SE  Pleasant    0.16    0.96    0.71    0.35    0.35    0.48
SE  Juliette    0.82    0.35    0.09    0.03    0.59    0.90
SE  Massey      1.01    0.77    0.45    0.32    0.55    0.66
SE  Delta       0.84    1.05    0.90    0.09    0.64    0.03
SW  Alumni      0.45    0.32    0.45    0.44    0.55    0.12
SW  New Dam     0.80    0.70    0.31    0.98    1.00    0.22
SW  Border      0.51    0.04    0.55    0.35    0.45    0.78
SW  Red         0.22    0.09    0.02    0.10    0.32    0.01
;
```

PROCLIB.MARCH

```
data proclib.march;
    input flight $3. +5 date date7. +3 depart time5. +2 orig $3.
          +3 dest $3.   +7 miles +6 boarded +6 capacity;
    format date date7. depart time5.;
    informat date date7. depart time5.;
    datalines;
114     01MAR94     7:10    LGA     LAX     2475    172     210
202     01MAR94    10:43    LGA     ORD      740    151     210
219     01MAR94     9:31    LGA     LON     3442    198     250
622     01MAR94    12:19    LGA     FRA     3857    207     250
132     01MAR94    15:35    LGA     YYZ      366    115     178
271     01MAR94    13:17    LGA     PAR     3635    138     250
302     01MAR94    20:22    LGA     WAS      229    105     180
114     02MAR94     7:10    LGA     LAX     2475    119     210
202     02MAR94    10:43    LGA     ORD      740    120     210
219     02MAR94     9:31    LGA     LON     3442    147     250
622     02MAR94    12:19    LGA     FRA     3857    176     250
132     02MAR94    15:35    LGA     YYZ      366    106     178
302     02MAR94    20:22    LGA     WAS      229     78     180
271     02MAR94    13:17    LGA     PAR     3635    104     250
114     03MAR94     7:10    LGA     LAX     2475    197     210
202     03MAR94    10:43    LGA     ORD      740    118     210
219     03MAR94     9:31    LGA     LON     3442    197     250
622     03MAR94    12:19    LGA     FRA     3857    180     250
132     03MAR94    15:35    LGA     YYZ      366     75     178
271     03MAR94    13:17    LGA     PAR     3635    147     250
302     03MAR94    20:22    LGA     WAS      229    123     180
114     04MAR94     7:10    LGA     LAX     2475    178     210
202     04MAR94    10:43    LGA     ORD      740    148     210
219     04MAR94     9:31    LGA     LON     3442    232     250
```

```
622      04MAR94    12:19   LGA   FRA      3857       137       250
132      04MAR94    15:35   LGA   YYZ       366       117       178
271      04MAR94    13:17   LGA   PAR      3635       146       250
302      04MAR94    20:22   LGA   WAS       229       115       180
114      05MAR94     7:10   LGA   LAX      2475       117       210
202      05MAR94    10:43   LGA   ORD       740       104       210
219      05MAR94     9:31   LGA   LON      3442       160       250
622      05MAR94    12:19   LGA   FRA      3857       185       250
132      05MAR94    15:35   LGA   YYZ       366       157       178
271      05MAR94    13:17   LGA   PAR      3635       177       250
114      06MAR94     7:10   LGA   LAX      2475       128       210
202      06MAR94    10:43   LGA   ORD       740       115       210
219      06MAR94     9:31   LGA   LON      3442       163       250
132      06MAR94    15:35   LGA   YYZ       366       150       178
302      06MAR94    20:22   LGA   WAS       229        66       180
114      07MAR94     7:10   LGA   LAX      2475       160       210
202      07MAR94    10:43   LGA   ORD       740       175       210
219      07MAR94     9:31   LGA   LON      3442       241       250
622      07MAR94    12:19   LGA   FRA      3857       210       250
132      07MAR94    15:35   LGA   YYZ       366       164       178
271      07MAR94    13:17   LGA   PAR      3635       155       250
302      07MAR94    20:22   LGA   WAS       229       135       180
;
```

PROCLIB.PAYLIST2

```
proc sql;
   create table proclib.paylist2
        (IdNum char(4),
         Gender char(1),
         Jobcode char(3),
         Salary num,
         Birth num informat=date7.
                  format=date7.,
         Hired num informat=date7.
                  format=date7.);

insert into proclib.paylist2
values('1919','M','TA2',34376,'12SEP66'd,'04JUN87'd)
values('1653','F','ME2',31896,'15OCT64'd,'09AUG92'd)
values('1350','F','FA3',36886,'31AUG55'd,'29JUL91'd)
values('1401','M','TA3',38822,'13DEC55'd,'17NOV93'd)
values('1499','M','ME1',23025,'26APR74'd,'07JUN92'd);

title 'PROCLIB.PAYLIST2 Table';
select * from proclib.paylist2;
```

PROCLIB.PAYROLL

This data set (table) is updated in Example 3 on page 1104 and its updated data are used in subsequent examples.

```
data proclib.payroll;
    input IdNumber $4. +3 Sex $1. +4 Jobcode $3. +9 Salary 5.
        +2 Birth date7. +2 Hired date7.;
    informat birth date7. hired date7.;
    format birth date7. hired date7.;
    datalines;
1919    M    TA2        34376    12SEP60    04JUN87
1653    F    ME2        35108    15OCT64    09AUG90
1400    M    ME1        29769    05NOV67    16OCT90
1350    F    FA3        32886    31AUG65    29JUL90
1401    M    TA3        38822    13DEC50    17NOV85
1499    M    ME3        43025    26APR54    07JUN80
1101    M    SCP        18723    06JUN62    01OCT90
1333    M    PT2        88606    30MAR61    10FEB81
1402    M    TA2        32615    17JAN63    02DEC90
1479    F    TA3        38785    22DEC68    05OCT89
1403    M    ME1        28072    28JAN69    21DEC91
1739    M    PT1        66517    25DEC64    27JAN91
1658    M    SCP        17943    08APR67    29FEB92
1428    F    PT1        68767    04APR60    16NOV91
1782    M    ME2        35345    04DEC70    22FEB92
1244    M    ME2        36925    31AUG63    17JAN88
1383    M    BCK        25823    25JAN68    20OCT92
1574    M    FA2        28572    27APR60    20DEC92
1789    M    SCP        18326    25JAN57    11APR78
1404    M    PT2        91376    24FEB53    01JAN80
1437    F    FA3        33104    20SEP60    31AUG84
1639    F    TA3        40260    26JUN57    28JAN84
1269    M    NA1        41690    03MAY72    28NOV92
1065    M    ME2        35090    26JAN44    07JAN87
1876    M    TA3        39675    20MAY58    27APR85
1037    F    TA1        28558    10APR64    13SEP92
1129    F    ME2        34929    08DEC61    17AUG91
1988    M    FA3        32217    30NOV59    18SEP84
1405    M    SCP        18056    05MAR66    26JAN92
1430    F    TA2        32925    28FEB62    27APR87
1983    F    FA3        33419    28FEB62    27APR87
1134    F    TA2        33462    05MAR69    21DEC88
1118    M    PT3       111379    16JAN44    18DEC80
1438    F    TA3        39223    15MAR65    18NOV87
1125    F    FA2        28888    08NOV68    11DEC87
1475    F    FA2        27787    15DEC61    13JUL90
1117    M    TA3        39771    05JUN63    13AUG92
1935    F    NA2        51081    28MAR54    16OCT81
1124    F    FA1        23177    10JUL58    01OCT90
1422    F    FA1        22454    04JUN64    06APR91
1616    F    TA2        34137    01MAR70    04JUN93
1406    M    ME2        35185    08MAR61    17FEB87
```

1120	M	ME1	28619	11SEP72	07OCT93
1094	M	FA1	22268	02APR70	17APR91
1389	M	BCK	25028	15JUL59	18AUG90
1905	M	PT1	65111	16APR72	29MAY92
1407	M	PT1	68096	23MAR69	18MAR90
1114	F	TA2	32928	18SEP69	27JUN87
1410	M	PT2	84685	03MAY67	07NOV86
1439	F	PT1	70736	06MAR64	10SEP90
1409	M	ME3	41551	19APR50	22OCT81
1408	M	TA2	34138	29MAR60	14OCT87
1121	M	ME1	29112	26SEP71	07DEC91
1991	F	TA1	27645	07MAY72	12DEC92
1102	M	TA2	34542	01OCT59	15APR91
1356	M	ME2	36869	26SEP57	22FEB83
1545	M	PT1	66130	12AUG59	29MAY90
1292	F	ME2	36691	28OCT64	02JUL89
1440	F	ME2	35757	27SEP62	09APR91
1368	M	FA2	27808	11JUN61	03NOV84
1369	M	TA2	33705	28DEC61	13MAR87
1411	M	FA2	27265	27MAY61	01DEC89
1113	F	FA1	22367	15JAN68	17OCT91
1704	M	BCK	25465	30AUG66	28JUN87
1900	M	ME2	35105	25MAY62	27OCT87
1126	F	TA3	40899	28MAY63	21NOV80
1677	M	BCK	26007	05NOV63	27MAR89
1441	F	FA2	27158	19NOV69	23MAR91
1421	M	TA2	33155	08JAN59	28FEB90
1119	M	TA1	26924	20JUN62	06SEP88
1834	M	BCK	26896	08FEB72	02JUL92
1777	M	PT3	109630	23SEP51	21JUN81
1663	M	BCK	26452	11JAN67	11AUG91
1106	M	PT2	89632	06NOV57	16AUG84
1103	F	FA1	23738	16FEB68	23JUL92
1477	M	FA2	28566	21MAR64	07MAR88
1476	F	TA2	34803	30MAY66	17MAR87
1379	M	ME3	42264	08AUG61	10JUN84
1104	M	SCP	17946	25APR63	10JUN91
1009	M	TA1	28880	02MAR59	26MAR92
1412	M	ME1	27799	18JUN56	05DEC91
1115	F	FA3	32699	22AUG60	29FEB80
1128	F	TA2	32777	23MAY65	20OCT90
1442	F	PT2	84536	05SEP66	12APR88
1417	M	NA2	52270	27JUN64	07MAR89
1478	M	PT2	84203	09AUG59	24OCT90
1673	M	BCK	25477	27FEB70	15JUL91
1839	F	NA1	43433	29NOV70	03JUL93
1347	M	TA3	40079	21SEP67	06SEP84
1423	F	ME2	35773	14MAY68	19AUG90
1200	F	ME1	27816	10JAN71	14AUG92
1970	F	FA1	22615	25SEP64	12MAR91
1521	M	ME3	41526	12APR63	13JUL88
1354	F	SCP	18335	29MAY71	16JUN92
1424	F	FA2	28978	04AUG69	11DEC89
1132	F	FA1	22413	30MAY72	22OCT93

```
1845   M   BCK        25996   20NOV59   22MAR80
1556   M   PT1        71349   22JUN64   11DEC91
1413   M   FA2        27435   16SEP65   02JAN90
1123   F   TA1        28407   31OCT72   05DEC92
1907   M   TA2        33329   15NOV60   06JUL87
1436   F   TA2        34475   11JUN64   12MAR87
1385   M   ME3        43900   16JAN62   01APR86
1432   F   ME2        35327   03NOV61   10FEB85
1111   M   NA1        40586   14JUL73   31OCT92
1116   F   FA1        22862   28SEP69   21MAR91
1352   M   NA2        53798   02DEC60   16OCT86
1555   F   FA2        27499   16MAR68   04JUL92
1038   F   TA1        26533   09NOV69   23NOV91
1420   M   ME3        43071   19FEB65   22JUL87
1561   M   TA2        34514   30NOV63   07OCT87
1434   F   FA2        28622   11JUL62   28OCT90
1414   M   FA1        23644   24MAR72   12APR92
1112   M   TA1        26905   29NOV64   07DEC92
1390   M   FA2        27761   19FEB65   23JUN91
1332   M   NA1        42178   17SEP70   04JUN91
1890   M   PT2        91908   20JUL51   25NOV79
1429   F   TA1        27939   28FEB60   07AUG92
1107   M   PT2        89977   09JUN54   10FEB79
1908   F   TA2        32995   10DEC69   23APR90
1830   F   PT2        84471   27MAY57   29JAN83
1882   M   ME3        41538   10JUL57   21NOV78
1050   M   ME2        35167   14JUL63   24AUG86
1425   F   FA1        23979   28DEC71   28FEB93
1928   M   PT2        89858   16SEP54   13JUL90
1480   F   TA3        39583   03SEP57   25MAR81
1100   M   BCK        25004   01DEC60   07MAY88
1995   F   ME1        28810   24AUG73   19SEP93
1135   F   FA2        27321   20SEP60   31MAR90
1415   M   FA2        28278   09MAR58   12FEB88
1076   M   PT1        66558   14OCT55   03OCT91
1426   F   TA2        32991   05DEC66   25JUN90
1564   F   SCP        18833   12APR62   01JUL92
1221   F   FA2        27896   22SEP67   04OCT91
1133   M   TA1        27701   13JUL66   12FEB92
1435   F   TA3        38808   12MAY59   08FEB80
1418   M   ME1        28005   29MAR57   06JAN92
1017   M   TA3        40858   28DEC57   16OCT81
1443   F   NA1        42274   17NOV68   29AUG91
1131   F   TA2        32575   26DEC71   19APR91
1427   F   TA2        34046   31OCT70   30JAN90
1036   F   TA3        39392   19MAY65   23OCT84
1130   F   FA1        23916   16MAY71   05JUN92
1127   F   TA2        33011   09NOV64   07DEC86
1433   F   FA3        32982   08JUL66   17JAN87
1431   F   FA3        33230   09JUN64   05APR88
1122   F   FA2        27956   01MAY63   27NOV88
1105   M   ME2        34805   01MAR62   13AUG90
;
```

PROCLIB.PAYROLL2

```
data proclib.payroll2;
    input idnum $4. +3 sex $1. +4 jobcode $3. +9 salary 5.
          +2 birth date7. +2 hired date7.;
    informat birth date7. hired date7.;
    format birth date7. hired date7.;
    datalines;
1639    F    TA3         42260   26JUN57  28JAN84
1065    M    ME3         38090   26JAN44  07JAN87
1561    M    TA3         36514   30NOV63  07OCT87
1221    F    FA3         29896   22SEP67  04OCT91
1447    F    FA1         22123   07AUG72  29OCT92
1998    M    SCP         23100   10SEP70  02NOV92
1036    F    TA3         42465   19MAY65  23OCT84
1106    M    PT3         94039   06NOV57  16AUG84
1129    F    ME3         36758   08DEC61  17AUG91
1350    F    FA3         36098   31AUG65  29JUL90
1369    M    TA3         36598   28DEC61  13MAR87
1076    M    PT1         69742   14OCT55  03OCT91
;
```

PROCLIB.SCHEDULE

```
data proclib.schedule;
    input flight $3. +5 date date7. +2 dest $3. +3 idnum $4.;
    format date date7.;
    informat date date7.;
    datalines;
132     01MAR94   YYZ    1739
132     01MAR94   YYZ    1478
132     01MAR94   YYZ    1130
132     01MAR94   YYZ    1390
132     01MAR94   YYZ    1983
132     01MAR94   YYZ    1111
219     01MAR94   LON    1407
219     01MAR94   LON    1777
219     01MAR94   LON    1103
219     01MAR94   LON    1125
219     01MAR94   LON    1350
219     01MAR94   LON    1332
271     01MAR94   PAR    1439
271     01MAR94   PAR    1442
271     01MAR94   PAR    1132
271     01MAR94   PAR    1411
271     01MAR94   PAR    1988
271     01MAR94   PAR    1443
622     01MAR94   FRA    1545
622     01MAR94   FRA    1890
```

622	01MAR94	FRA	1116
622	01MAR94	FRA	1221
622	01MAR94	FRA	1433
622	01MAR94	FRA	1352
132	02MAR94	YYZ	1556
132	02MAR94	YYZ	1478
132	02MAR94	YYZ	1113
132	02MAR94	YYZ	1411
132	02MAR94	YYZ	1574
132	02MAR94	YYZ	1111
219	02MAR94	LON	1407
219	02MAR94	LON	1118
219	02MAR94	LON	1132
219	02MAR94	LON	1135
219	02MAR94	LON	1441
219	02MAR94	LON	1332
271	02MAR94	PAR	1739
271	02MAR94	PAR	1442
271	02MAR94	PAR	1103
271	02MAR94	PAR	1413
271	02MAR94	PAR	1115
271	02MAR94	PAR	1443
622	02MAR94	FRA	1439
622	02MAR94	FRA	1890
622	02MAR94	FRA	1124
622	02MAR94	FRA	1368
622	02MAR94	FRA	1477
622	02MAR94	FRA	1352
132	03MAR94	YYZ	1739
132	03MAR94	YYZ	1928
132	03MAR94	YYZ	1425
132	03MAR94	YYZ	1135
132	03MAR94	YYZ	1437
132	03MAR94	YYZ	1111
219	03MAR94	LON	1428
219	03MAR94	LON	1442
219	03MAR94	LON	1130
219	03MAR94	LON	1411
219	03MAR94	LON	1115
219	03MAR94	LON	1332
271	03MAR94	PAR	1905
271	03MAR94	PAR	1118
271	03MAR94	PAR	1970
271	03MAR94	PAR	1125
271	03MAR94	PAR	1983
271	03MAR94	PAR	1443
622	03MAR94	FRA	1545
622	03MAR94	FRA	1830
622	03MAR94	FRA	1414
622	03MAR94	FRA	1368
622	03MAR94	FRA	1431
622	03MAR94	FRA	1352
132	04MAR94	YYZ	1428
132	04MAR94	YYZ	1118

```
132    04MAR94   YYZ    1103
132    04MAR94   YYZ    1390
132    04MAR94   YYZ    1350
132    04MAR94   YYZ    1111
219    04MAR94   LON    1739
219    04MAR94   LON    1478
219    04MAR94   LON    1130
219    04MAR94   LON    1125
219    04MAR94   LON    1983
219    04MAR94   LON    1332
271    04MAR94   PAR    1407
271    04MAR94   PAR    1410
271    04MAR94   PAR    1094
271    04MAR94   PAR    1411
271    04MAR94   PAR    1115
271    04MAR94   PAR    1443
622    04MAR94   FRA    1545
622    04MAR94   FRA    1890
622    04MAR94   FRA    1116
622    04MAR94   FRA    1221
622    04MAR94   FRA    1433
622    04MAR94   FRA    1352
132    05MAR94   YYZ    1556
132    05MAR94   YYZ    1890
132    05MAR94   YYZ    1113
132    05MAR94   YYZ    1475
132    05MAR94   YYZ    1431
132    05MAR94   YYZ    1111
219    05MAR94   LON    1428
219    05MAR94   LON    1442
219    05MAR94   LON    1422
219    05MAR94   LON    1413
219    05MAR94   LON    1574
219    05MAR94   LON    1332
271    05MAR94   PAR    1739
271    05MAR94   PAR    1928
271    05MAR94   PAR    1103
271    05MAR94   PAR    1477
271    05MAR94   PAR    1433
271    05MAR94   PAR    1443
622    05MAR94   FRA    1545
622    05MAR94   FRA    1830
622    05MAR94   FRA    1970
622    05MAR94   FRA    1441
622    05MAR94   FRA    1350
622    05MAR94   FRA    1352
132    06MAR94   YYZ    1333
132    06MAR94   YYZ    1890
132    06MAR94   YYZ    1414
132    06MAR94   YYZ    1475
132    06MAR94   YYZ    1437
132    06MAR94   YYZ    1111
219    06MAR94   LON    1106
219    06MAR94   LON    1118
```

```
219      06MAR94    LON    1425
219      06MAR94    LON    1434
219      06MAR94    LON    1555
219      06MAR94    LON    1332
132      07MAR94    YYZ    1407
132      07MAR94    YYZ    1118
132      07MAR94    YYZ    1094
132      07MAR94    YYZ    1555
132      07MAR94    YYZ    1350
132      07MAR94    YYZ    1111
219      07MAR94    LON    1905
219      07MAR94    LON    1478
219      07MAR94    LON    1124
219      07MAR94    LON    1434
219      07MAR94    LON    1983
219      07MAR94    LON    1332
271      07MAR94    PAR    1410
271      07MAR94    PAR    1777
271      07MAR94    PAR    1103
271      07MAR94    PAR    1574
271      07MAR94    PAR    1115
271      07MAR94    PAR    1443
622      07MAR94    FRA    1107
622      07MAR94    FRA    1890
622      07MAR94    FRA    1425
622      07MAR94    FRA    1475
622      07MAR94    FRA    1433
622      07MAR94    FRA    1352
;
```

PROCLIB.STAFF

```
data proclib.staff;
   input idnum $4. +3 lname $15. +2 fname $15. +2 city $15. +2
         state $2. +5 hphone $12.;
   datalines;
1919   ADAMS          GERALD        STAMFORD       CT    203/781-1255
1653   ALIBRANDI      MARIA         BRIDGEPORT     CT    203/675-7715
1400   ALHERTANI      ABDULLAH      NEW YORK       NY    212/586-0808
1350   ALVAREZ        MERCEDES      NEW YORK       NY    718/383-1549
1401   ALVAREZ        CARLOS        PATERSON       NJ    201/732-8787
1499   BAREFOOT       JOSEPH        PRINCETON      NJ    201/812-5665
1101   BAUCOM         WALTER        NEW YORK       NY    212/586-8060
1333   BANADYGA       JUSTIN        STAMFORD       CT    203/781-1777
1402   BLALOCK        RALPH         NEW YORK       NY    718/384-2849
1479   BALLETTI       MARIE         NEW YORK       NY    718/384-8816
1403   BOWDEN         EARL          BRIDGEPORT     CT    203/675-3434
1739   BRANCACCIO     JOSEPH        NEW YORK       NY    212/587-1247
1658   BREUHAUS       JEREMY        NEW YORK       NY    212/587-3622
1428   BRADY          CHRISTINE     STAMFORD       CT    203/781-1212
1782   BREWCZAK       JAKOB         STAMFORD       CT    203/781-0019
```

1244	BUCCI	ANTHONY	NEW YORK	NY	718/383-3334
1383	BURNETTE	THOMAS	NEW YORK	NY	718/384-3569
1574	CAHILL	MARSHALL	NEW YORK	NY	718/383-2338
1789	CARAWAY	DAVIS	NEW YORK	NY	212/587-9000
1404	COHEN	LEE	NEW YORK	NY	718/384-2946
1437	CARTER	DOROTHY	BRIDGEPORT	CT	203/675-4117
1639	CARTER-COHEN	KAREN	STAMFORD	CT	203/781-8839
1269	CASTON	FRANKLIN	STAMFORD	CT	203/781-3335
1065	COPAS	FREDERICO	NEW YORK	NY	718/384-5618
1876	CHIN	JACK	NEW YORK	NY	212/588-5634
1037	CHOW	JANE	STAMFORD	CT	203/781-8868
1129	COUNIHAN	BRENDA	NEW YORK	NY	718/383-2313
1988	COOPER	ANTHONY	NEW YORK	NY	212/587-1228
1405	DACKO	JASON	PATERSON	NJ	201/732-2323
1430	DABROWSKI	SANDRA	BRIDGEPORT	CT	203/675-1647
1983	DEAN	SHARON	NEW YORK	NY	718/384-1647
1134	DELGADO	MARIA	STAMFORD	CT	203/781-1528
1118	DENNIS	ROGER	NEW YORK	NY	718/383-1122
1438	DABBOUSSI	KAMILLA	STAMFORD	CT	203/781-2229
1125	DUNLAP	DONNA	NEW YORK	NY	718/383-2094
1475	ELGES	MARGARETE	NEW YORK	NY	718/383-2828
1117	EDGERTON	JOSHUA	NEW YORK	NY	212/588-1239
1935	FERNANDEZ	KATRINA	BRIDGEPORT	CT	203/675-2962
1124	FIELDS	DIANA	WHITE PLAINS	NY	914/455-2998
1422	FUJIHARA	KYOKO	PRINCETON	NJ	201/812-0902
1616	FUENTAS	CARLA	NEW YORK	NY	718/384-3329
1406	FOSTER	GERALD	BRIDGEPORT	CT	203/675-6363
1120	GARCIA	JACK	NEW YORK	NY	718/384-4930
1094	GOMEZ	ALAN	BRIDGEPORT	CT	203/675-7181
1389	GOLDSTEIN	LEVI	NEW YORK	NY	718/384-9326
1905	GRAHAM	ALVIN	NEW YORK	NY	212/586-8815
1407	GREGORSKI	DANIEL	MT. VERNON	NY	914/468-1616
1114	GREENWALD	JANICE	NEW YORK	NY	212/588-1092
1410	HARRIS	CHARLES	STAMFORD	CT	203/781-0937
1439	HASENHAUER	CHRISTINA	BRIDGEPORT	CT	203/675-4987
1409	HAVELKA	RAYMOND	STAMFORD	CT	203/781-9697
1408	HENDERSON	WILLIAM	PRINCETON	NJ	201/812-4789
1121	HERNANDEZ	ROBERTO	NEW YORK	NY	718/384-3313
1991	HOWARD	GRETCHEN	BRIDGEPORT	CT	203/675-0007
1102	HERMANN	JOACHIM	WHITE PLAINS	NY	914/455-0976
1356	HOWARD	MICHAEL	NEW YORK	NY	212/586-8411
1545	HERRERO	CLYDE	STAMFORD	CT	203/781-1119
1292	HUNTER	HELEN	BRIDGEPORT	CT	203/675-4830
1440	JACKSON	LAURA	STAMFORD	CT	203/781-0088
1368	JEPSEN	RONALD	STAMFORD	CT	203/781-8413
1369	JONSON	ANTHONY	NEW YORK	NY	212/587-5385
1411	JOHNSEN	JACK	PATERSON	NJ	201/732-3678
1113	JOHNSON	LESLIE	NEW YORK	NY	718/383-3003
1704	JONES	NATHAN	NEW YORK	NY	718/384-0049
1900	KING	WILLIAM	NEW YORK	NY	718/383-3698
1126	KIMANI	ANNE	NEW YORK	NY	212/586-1229
1677	KRAMER	JACKSON	BRIDGEPORT	CT	203/675-7432
1441	LAWRENCE	KATHY	PRINCETON	NJ	201/812-3337
1421	LEE	RUSSELL	MT. VERNON	NY	914/468-9143

1119	LI	JEFF	NEW YORK	NY	212/586-2344
1834	LEBLANC	RUSSELL	NEW YORK	NY	718/384-0040
1777	LUFKIN	ROY	NEW YORK	NY	718/383-4413
1663	MARKS	JOHN	NEW YORK	NY	212/587-7742
1106	MARSHBURN	JASPER	STAMFORD	CT	203/781-1457
1103	MCDANIEL	RONDA	NEW YORK	NY	212/586-0013
1477	MEYERS	PRESTON	BRIDGEPORT	CT	203/675-8125
1476	MONROE	JOYCE	STAMFORD	CT	203/781-2837
1379	MORGAN	ALFRED	STAMFORD	CT	203/781-2216
1104	MORGAN	CHRISTOPHER	NEW YORK	NY	718/383-9740
1009	MORGAN	GEORGE	NEW YORK	NY	212/586-7753
1412	MURPHEY	JOHN	PRINCETON	NJ	201/812-4414
1115	MURPHY	ALICE	NEW YORK	NY	718/384-1982
1128	NELSON	FELICIA	BRIDGEPORT	CT	203/675-1166
1442	NEWKIRK	SANDRA	PRINCETON	NJ	201/812-3331
1417	NEWKIRK	WILLIAM	PATERSON	NJ	201/732-6611
1478	NEWTON	JAMES	NEW YORK	NY	212/587-5549
1673	NICHOLLS	HENRY	STAMFORD	CT	203/781-7770
1839	NORRIS	DIANE	NEW YORK	NY	718/384-1767
1347	O'NEAL	BRYAN	NEW YORK	NY	718/384-0230
1423	OSWALD	LESLIE	MT. VERNON	NY	914/468-9171
1200	OVERMAN	MICHELLE	STAMFORD	CT	203/781-1835
1970	PARKER	ANNE	NEW YORK	NY	718/383-3895
1521	PARKER	JAY	NEW YORK	NY	212/587-7603
1354	PARKER	MARY	WHITE PLAINS	NY	914/455-2337
1424	PATTERSON	RENEE	NEW YORK	NY	212/587-8991
1132	PEARCE	CAROL	NEW YORK	NY	718/384-1986
1845	PEARSON	JAMES	NEW YORK	NY	718/384-2311
1556	PENNINGTON	MICHAEL	NEW YORK	NY	718/383-5681
1413	PETERS	RANDALL	PRINCETON	NJ	201/812-2478
1123	PETERSON	SUZANNE	NEW YORK	NY	718/383-0077
1907	PHELPS	WILLIAM	STAMFORD	CT	203/781-1118
1436	PORTER	SUSAN	NEW YORK	NY	718/383-5777
1385	RAYNOR	MILTON	BRIDGEPORT	CT	203/675-2846
1432	REED	MARILYN	MT. VERNON	NY	914/468-5454
1111	RHODES	JEREMY	PRINCETON	NJ	201/812-1837
1116	RICHARDS	CASEY	NEW YORK	NY	212/587-1224
1352	RIVERS	SIMON	NEW YORK	NY	718/383-3345
1555	RODRIGUEZ	JULIA	BRIDGEPORT	CT	203/675-2401
1038	RODRIGUEZ	MARIA	BRIDGEPORT	CT	203/675-2048
1420	ROUSE	JEREMY	PATERSON	NJ	201/732-9834
1561	SANDERS	RAYMOND	NEW YORK	NY	212/588-6615
1434	SANDERSON	EDITH	STAMFORD	CT	203/781-1333
1414	SANDERSON	NATHAN	BRIDGEPORT	CT	203/675-1715
1112	SANYERS	RANDY	NEW YORK	NY	718/384-4895
1390	SMART	JONATHAN	NEW YORK	NY	718/383-1141
1332	STEPHENSON	ADAM	BRIDGEPORT	CT	203/675-1497
1890	STEPHENSON	ROBERT	NEW YORK	NY	718/384-9874
1429	THOMPSON	ALICE	STAMFORD	CT	203/781-3857
1107	THOMPSON	WAYNE	NEW YORK	NY	718/384-3785
1908	TRENTON	MELISSA	NEW YORK	NY	212/586-6262
1830	TRIPP	KATHY	BRIDGEPORT	CT	203/675-2479
1882	TUCKER	ALAN	NEW YORK	NY	718/384-0216
1050	TUTTLE	THOMAS	WHITE PLAINS	NY	914/455-2119

```
1425    UNDERWOOD       JENNY           STAMFORD        CT      203/781-0978
1928    UPCHURCH        LARRY           WHITE PLAINS    NY      914/455-5009
1480    UPDIKE          THERESA         NEW YORK        NY      212/587-8729
1100    VANDEUSEN       RICHARD         NEW YORK        NY      212/586-2531
1995    VARNER          ELIZABETH       NEW YORK        NY      718/384-7113
1135    VEGA            ANNA            NEW YORK        NY      718/384-5913
1415    VEGA            FRANKLIN        NEW YORK        NY      718/384-2823
1076    VENTER          RANDALL         NEW YORK        NY      718/383-2321
1426    VICK            THERESA         PRINCETON       NJ      201/812-2424
1564    WALTERS         ANNE            NEW YORK        NY      212/587-3257
1221    WALTERS         DIANE           NEW YORK        NY      718/384-1918
1133    WANG            CHIN            NEW YORK        NY      212/587-1956
1435    WARD            ELAINE          NEW YORK        NY      718/383-4987
1418    WATSON          BERNARD         NEW YORK        NY      718/383-1298
1017    WELCH           DARIUS          NEW YORK        NY      212/586-5535
1443    WELLS           AGNES           STAMFORD        CT      203/781-5546
1131    WELLS           NADINE          NEW YORK        NY      718/383-1045
1427    WHALEY          CAROLYN         MT. VERNON      NY      914/468-4528
1036    WONG            LESLIE          NEW YORK        NY      212/587-2570
1130    WOOD            DEBORAH         NEW YORK        NY      212/587-0013
1127    WOOD            SANDRA          NEW YORK        NY      212/587-2881
1433    YANCEY          ROBIN           PRINCETON       NJ      201/812-1874
1431    YOUNG           DEBORAH         STAMFORD        CT      203/781-2987
1122    YOUNG           JOANN           NEW YORK        NY      718/384-2021
1105    YOUNG           LAWRENCE        NEW YORK        NY      718/384-0008
;
```

PROCLIB.SUPERV

```
data proclib.superv;
   input supid $4. +8 state $2. +5  jobcat  $2.;
   label supid='Supervisor Id' jobcat='Job Category';
   datalines;
1677         CT     BC
1834         NY     BC
1431         CT     FA
1433         NJ     FA
1983         NY     FA
1385         CT     ME
1420         NJ     ME
1882         NY     ME
1935         CT     NA
1417         NJ     NA
1352         NY     NA
1106         CT     PT
1442         NJ     PT
1118         NY     PT
1405         NJ     SC
1564         NY     SC
1639         CT     TA
1401         NJ     TA
```

```
1126        NY    TA
;
```

RADIO

This DATA step uses an INFILE statement to read data that are stored in an external file.

```
data radio;
   infile 'input-file' missover;
   input /(time1-time7) ($1. +1);
   listener=_n_;
run;
```

Here are the data that are in the external file:

```
967 32 f 5 3 5
7 5 5 5 7 0 0 0 8 7 0 0 8 0
781 30 f 2 3 5
5 0 0 0 5 0 0 0 4 7 5 0 0 0
859 39 f 1 0 5
1 0 0 0 1 0 0 0 0 0 0 0 0 0
859 40 f 6 1 5
7 5 0 5 7 0 0 0 0 0 0 5 0 0
467 37 m 2 3 1
1 5 5 5 5 4 4 8 8 0 0 0 0 0
220 35 f 3 1 7
7 0 0 0 7 0 0 0 7 0 0 0 0 0
833 42 m 2 2 4
7 0 0 0 7 5 4 7 4 0 1 4 4 0
967 39 f .5 1 7
7 0 0 0 7 7 0 0 0 0 0 0 8 0
677 28 m .5 .5 7
7 0 0 0 0 0 0 0 0 0 0 0 0 0
833 28 f 3 4 1
1 0 0 0 0 1 1 1 1 0 0 0 1 1
677 24 f 3 1 2
2 0 0 0 0 0 0 2 0 8 8 0 0 0
688 32 m 5 2 4
5 5 0 4 8 0 0 5 0 8 0 0 0 0
542 38 f 6 8 5
5 0 0 5 5 5 0 5 5 5 5 5 5 0
677 27 m 6 1 1
1 1 0 4 4 0 0 1 4 0 0 0 0 0
779 37 f 2.5 4 7
7 0 0 0 7 7 0 7 7 4 4 7 8 0
362 31 f 1 2 2
8 0 0 0 8 0 0 0 0 0 8 8 0 0
859 29 m 10 3 4
4 4 0 2 2 0 0 4 0 0 0 4 4 0
467 24 m 5 8 1
7 1 1 1 7 1 1 0 1 7 1 1 1 1
851 34 m 1 2 8
```

```
0 0 0 0 8 0 0 0 4 0 0 0 8 0
859 23 f 1 1 8
8 0 0 0 8 0 0 0 0 0 0 0 0 8
781 34 f 9 3 1
2 1 0 1 4 4 4 0 1 1 1 1 4 4
851 40 f 2 4 5
5 0 0 0 5 0 0 5 0 0 5 5 0 0
783 34 m 3 2 4
7 0 0 0 7 4 4 0 0 4 4 0 0 0
848 29 f 4 1.5 7
7 4 4 1 7 0 0 0 7 0 0 7 0 0
851 28 f 1 2 2
2 0 2 0 2 0 0 0 0 2 2 2 0 0
856 42 f 1.5 1 2
2 0 0 0 0 0 0 2 0 0 0 0 0 0
859 29 m .5 .5 5
5 0 0 0 1 0 0 0 0 0 0 8 8 5 0
833 29 m 1 3 2
2 0 0 0 2 2 0 0 4 2 0 2 0 0
859 23 f 10 3 1
1 5 0 8 8 1 4 0 1 1 1 1 1 4
781 37 f .5 2 7
7 0 0 0 1 0 0 0 1 7 0 1 0 0
833 31 f 5 4 1
1 0 0 0 1 0 0 0 4 0 4 0 0 0
942 23 f 4 2 1
1 0 0 0 1 0 1 0 1 1 0 0 0 0
848 33 f 5 4 1
1 1 0 1 1 0 0 0 1 1 1 0 0 0
222 33 f 2 0 1
1 0 0 0 1 0 0 0 0 0 0 0 0 0
851 45 f .5 1 8
8 0 0 0 8 0 0 0 0 0 8 0 0 0
848 27 f 2 4 1
1 0 0 0 1 1 0 0 4 1 1 1 1 1
781 38 m 2 2 1
5 0 0 0 1 0 0 0 0 0 1 1 0 0
222 27 f 3 1 2
2 0 2 0 2 2 0 0 2 0 0 0 0 0
467 34 f 2 2 1
1 0 0 0 0 1 0 1 0 0 0 0 1 0
833 27 f 8 8 1
7 0 1 0 7 4 0 0 1 1 1 4 1 0
677 49 f 1.5 0 8
8 0 8 0 8 0 0 0 0 0 0 0 0 0
849 43 m 1 4 1
1 0 0 0 4 0 0 0 4 0 1 0 0 0
467 28 m 2 1 7
7 0 0 0 7 0 0 7 0 0 1 0 0 0
732 29 f 1 0 2
2 0 0 0 2 0 0 0 0 0 0 0 0 0
851 31 m 2 2 2
2 5 0 6 0 0 8 0 2 2 8 2 0 0
779 42 f 8 2 2
```

```
7 2 0 2 7 0 0 0 0 0 0 0 0 2 0
493 40 m 1 3 3
3 0 0 0 5 3 0 5 5 0 0 0 1 1
859 30 m 1 0 7
7 0 0 0 7 0 0 0 0 0 0 0 0 0 0
833 36 m 4 2 5
7 5 0 5 0 5 0 0 7 0 0 0 5 0
467 30 f 1 4 1
0 0 0 0 1 0 6 0 0 1 1 1 0 6
859 32 f 3 5 2
2 2 2 2 2 2 6 6 2 2 2 2 2 6
851 43 f 8 1 5
7 5 5 5 0 0 0 4 0 0 0 0 0 0
848 29 f 3 5 1
7 0 0 0 7 1 0 0 1 1 1 1 1 0
833 25 f 2 4 5
7 0 0 0 5 7 0 0 7 5 0 0 5 0
783 33 f 8 3 8
8 0 8 0 7 0 0 0 8 0 5 4 0 5
222 26 f 10 2 1
1 1 0 1 1 0 0 0 3 1 1 0 0 0
222 23 f 3 2 2
2 2 2 2 7 0 0 2 2 0 0 0 0 0
859 50 f 1 5 4
7 0 0 0 7 0 0 5 4 4 4 7 0 0
833 26 f 3 2 1
1 0 0 1 1 0 0 5 5 0 1 0 0 0
467 29 m 7 2 1
1 1 1 1 1 0 0 1 1 1 0 0 0 0
859 35 m .5 2 2
7 0 0 0 2 0 0 7 5 0 0 4 0 0
833 33 f 3 3 6
7 0 0 0 6 8 0 8 0 0 0 8 6 0
221 36 f .5 1 5
0 7 0 0 0 7 0 0 7 0 0 7 7 0
220 32 f 2 4 5
5 0 5 0 5 5 5 0 5 5 5 5 5 5
684 19 f 2 4 2
0 2 0 2 0 0 0 0 0 2 2 0 0 0
493 55 f 1 0 5
5 0 0 5 0 0 0 0 7 0 0 0 0 0
221 27 m 1 1 7
7 0 0 0 0 0 0 0 5 0 0 0 5 0
684 19 f 0 .5 1
7 0 0 0 0 1 1 0 0 0 0 0 1 1
493 38 f .5 .5 5
0 8 0 0 5 0 0 0 5 0 0 0 0 0
221 26 f .5 2 1
0 1 0 0 0 1 0 0 5 5 5 1 0 0
684 18 m 1 .5 1
0 2 0 0 0 0 1 0 0 0 0 1 1 0
684 19 m 1 1 1
0 0 0 1 1 0 0 0 0 0 0 1 0 0 0
221 29 m .5 .5 5
```

```
0 0 0 0 0 5 5 0 0 0 0 0 5 5
683 18 f 2 4 8
0 0 0 0 8 0 0 0 8 8 8 0 0 0
966 23 f 1 2 1
1 5 5 5 1 0 0 0 0 1 0 0 1 0
493 25 f 3 5 7
7 0 0 0 7 2 0 0 7 0 2 7 7 0
683 18 f .5 .5 2
1 0 0 0 0 0 5 0 0 1 0 0 0 1
382 21 f 3 1 8
0 8 0 0 5 8 8 0 0 8 8 0 0 0
683 18 f 4 6 2
2 0 0 0 2 2 2 0 2 0 2 2 2 0
684 19 m .5 2 1
0 0 0 0 1 1 0 0 0 1 1 1 1 5
684 19 m 1.5 3.5 2
2 0 0 0 2 0 0 0 0 0 2 5 0 0
221 23 f 1 5 1
7 5 1 5 1 3 1 7 5 1 5 1 3 1
684 18 f 2 3 1
2 0 0 1 1 1 1 7 2 0 1 1 1 1
683 19 f 3 5 2
2 0 0 2 0 6 1 0 1 1 2 2 6 1
683 19 f 3 5 1
2 0 0 2 0 6 1 0 1 1 2 0 2 1
221 35 m 3 5 5
7 5 0 1 7 0 0 5 5 5 0 0 0 0
221 43 f 1 4 5
1 0 0 0 5 0 0 5 5 0 0 0 0 0
493 32 f 2 1 6
0 0 0 6 0 0 0 0 0 0 0 0 4 0
221 24 f 4 5 2
2 0 5 0 0 2 4 4 4 5 0 0 2 2
684 19 f 2 3 2
0 5 5 2 5 0 1 0 5 5 2 2 2 2
221 19 f 3 3 8
0 1 1 8 8 8 4 0 5 4 1 8 8 4
221 29 m 1 1 5
5 5 5 5 5 5 5 5 5 5 5 5 5 5
221 21 m 1 1 1
1 0 0 0 0 0 5 1 0 0 0 0 0 5
683 20 f 1 2 2
0 0 0 0 2 0 0 0 2 0 0 0 0 0
493 54 f 1 1 5
7 0 0 5 0 0 0 0 0 0 5 0 0 0
493 45 m 4 6 5
7 0 0 0 7 5 0 0 5 5 5 5 5 5
850 44 m 2.5 1.5 7
7 0 7 0 4 7 5 0 5 4 3 0 0 4
220 33 m 5 3 5
1 5 0 5 1 0 0 0 0 0 0 0 5 5
684 20 f 1.5 3 1
1 0 0 0 1 0 1 0 1 0 0 1 1 0
966 63 m 3 5 3
```

```
5 4 7 5 4 5 0 5 0 0 5 5 4 0
683 21 f 4 6 1
0 1 0 1 1 1 1 0 1 1 1 1 1 1
493 23 f 5 2 5
7 5 0 4 0 0 0 0 1 1 1 1 1 0
493 32 f 8 8 5
7 5 0 0 7 0 5 5 5 0 0 7 5 5
942 33 f 7 2 5
0 5 5 4 7 0 0 0 0 0 0 7 8 0
493 34 f .5 1 5
5 0 0 0 5 0 0 0 0 0 6 0 0 0
382 40 f 2 2 5
5 0 0 0 5 0 0 5 0 0 5 0 0 0
362 27 f 0 3 8
0 0 0 0 0 0 0 0 0 0 0 0 8 0
542 36 f 3 3 7
7 0 0 0 7 1 0 0 0 7 1 1 0 0
966 39 f 3 6 5
7 0 0 0 7 5 0 0 7 0 5 0 5 0
849 32 m 1 .5 7
7 0 0 0 5 0 0 0 7 4 4 5 7 0
677 52 f 3 2 3
7 0 0 0 0 7 0 0 0 7 0 0 3 0
222 25 m 2 4 1
1 0 0 0 1 0 0 0 1 0 1 0 0 0
732 42 f 3 2 7
7 0 0 0 1 7 5 5 7 0 0 3 4 0
467 26 f 4 4 1
7 0 1 0 7 1 0 0 7 7 4 7 0 0
467 38 m 2.5 0 1
1 0 0 0 1 0 0 0 0 0 0 0 0 0
382 37 f 1.5 .5 7
7 0 0 0 7 0 0 0 3 0 0 0 3 0
856 45 f 3 3 7
7 0 0 0 7 5 0 0 7 7 4 0 0 0
677 33 m 3 2 7
7 0 0 4 7 0 0 0 7 0 0 0 0 0
490 27 f .5 1 2
2 0 0 0 2 0 0 0 2 0 2 0 0 0
362 27 f 1.5 2 2
2 0 0 0 1 0 4 0 1 0 0 0 4 4
783 25 f 2 1 1
1 0 0 0 1 7 0 0 0 0 1 1 1 0
546 30 f 8 3 1
1 1 1 1 1 0 0 1 0 5 5 0 0 0
677 30 f 2 0 1
1 0 0 0 0 1 0 0 0 0 0 0 0 1
221 35 f 2 2 1
1 0 0 0 1 0 1 0 1 1 1 0 0 0
966 32 f 6 1 7
7 1 1 1 7 4 0 1 7 1 8 8 4 0
222 28 f 1 5 4
7 0 0 0 4 0 0 4 4 4 4 0 0 0
467 29 f 5 3 4
```

```
4 5 5 5 1 4 4 5 1 1 1 1 4 4
467 32 m 3 4 1
1 0 1 0 4 0 0 0 4 0 0 0 1 0
966 30 m 1.5 1 7
7 0 0 0 7 5 0 7 0 0 0 0 5 0
967 38 m 14 4 7
7 7 7 7 7 0 4 8 0 0 0 0 4 0
490 28 m 8 1 1
7 1 1 1 1 0 0 7 0 0 8 0 0 0
833 30 f .5 1 6
6 0 0 0 6 0 0 0 0 6 0 0 6 0
851 40 m 1 0 7
7 5 5 5 7 0 0 0 0 0 0 0 0 0
859 27 f 2 5 2
6 0 0 0 2 0 0 0 0 0 0 2 2 2
851 22 f 3 5 2
7 0 2 0 2 2 0 0 2 0 8 0 2 0
967 38 f 1 1.5 7
7 0 0 0 7 5 0 7 4 0 0 7 5 0
856 34 f 1.5 1 1
0 1 0 0 0 1 0 0 4 0 0 0 0 0
222 33 m .1 .1 7
7 0 0 0 7 0 0 0 0 0 7 0 0 0
856 22 m .50 .25 1
0 1 0 0 1 0 0 0 0 0 0 0 0 0
677 30 f 2 2 4
1 0 4 0 4 0 0 0 4 0 0 0 0 0
859 25 m 2 3 7
0 0 0 0 0 7 0 0 7 0 2 0 0 1
833 35 m 2 6 7
7 0 0 0 7 1 1 0 4 7 4 7 1 1
677 35 m 10 4 1
1 1 1 1 1 8 6 8 1 0 0 8 8 8
848 29 f 5 3 8
8 0 0 0 8 8 0 0 0 8 8 8 0 0
688 26 m 3 1 1
1 1 7 1 1 7 0 0 0 8 8 0 0 0
490 41 m 2 2 5
5 0 0 0 0 0 5 5 0 0 0 0 0 5
493 35 m 4 4 7
7 5 0 5 7 0 0 7 7 7 7 0 0 0
677 27 m 15 11 1
1 1 1 1 1 1 1 1 1 1 1 1 1 1
848 27 f 3 5 1
1 1 0 0 1 1 0 0 1 1 1 1 0 0
362 30 f 1 0 1
1 0 0 0 7 5 0 0 0 0 0 0 0 0
783 29 f 1 1 4
4 0 0 0 4 0 0 0 4 0 0 0 4 0
467 39 f .5 2 4
7 0 4 0 4 4 0 0 4 4 4 4 4 4
677 27 m 2 2 7
7 0 0 0 7 0 0 7 7 0 0 7 0 0
221 23 f 2.5 1 1
```

```
1 0 0 0 1 0 0 0 0 0 0 0 0 0
677 29 f 1 1 7
0 0 0 0 7 0 0 0 7 0 0 0 0 0
783 32 m 1 2 5
4 5 5 5 4 2 0 0 0 0 3 2 2 0
833 25 f 1 0 1
1 1 0 0 0 0 0 0 0 0 0 0 0 0
859 24 f 7 3 7
1 0 0 0 1 0 0 0 0 1 0 0 1 0
677 29 m 2 2 8
0 8 8 0 8 0 0 0 8 8 8 0 0 0
688 31 m 8 2 5
7 5 5 5 5 7 0 0 7 7 0 0 0 0
856 31 m 9 4 1
1 1 1 1 1 0 0 0 0 0 0 0 1 0
856 44 f 1 0 6
6 0 0 0 6 0 0 0 0 0 0 0 0 0
677 37 f 3 3 1
0 0 1 0 0 0 0 0 4 4 0 0 0 0
859 27 m 2 .5 2
2 2 2 2 2 2 2 0 0 0 0 0 0 2
781 30 f 10 4 2
2 0 0 0 2 0 2 0 0 0 0 0 0 2
362 27 m 12 4 3
3 1 1 1 1 3 3 3 0 0 0 0 3 0
362 33 f 2 4 1
1 0 0 0 7 0 0 7 1 1 1 1 1 0
222 26 f 8 1 1
1 1 1 1 0 0 0 1 0 0 0 0 0 0
779 37 f 6 3 1
1 1 1 1 1 0 0 1 1 0 0 0 1 0
467 32 f 1 1 2
2 0 0 0 0 0 0 0 2 0 0 2 0 0
859 23 m 1 1 1
1 0 0 0 1 1 0 1 0 0 0 0 1 1
781 33 f 1 .5 6
6 0 0 0 6 0 0 0 0 0 0 0 0 0
779 28 m 5 2 1
1 1 1 1 1 0 0 0 0 7 7 1 1 0
677 28 m 3 1 5
7 5 5 5 5 6 0 0 6 6 6 6 6 0
677 25 f 9 2 5
1 5 5 5 5 1 1 0 1 1 1 1 1 1
848 30 f 6 2 8
8 0 0 0 2 7 0 0 0 0 2 0 2 0
546 36 f 4 6 4
7 0 0 0 4 4 0 5 5 5 5 2 4 4
222 30 f 2 3 2
2 2 0 0 2 0 0 0 2 0 2 2 0 0
383 32 m 4 1 2
2 0 0 0 2 0 0 2 0 0 0 0 0 0
851 43 f 8 1 6
4 6 0 6 4 0 0 0 0 0 0 0 0 0
222 27 f 1 3 1
```

```
1 1 0 1 1 1 0 0 1 0 0 0 4 0
833 22 f 1.5 2 1
1 0 0 0 1 1 0 0 1 1 1 0 0 0
467 29 f 2 1 8
8 0 8 0 8 0 0 0 0 0 8 0 0 0
856 28 f 2 3 1
1 0 0 0 1 0 0 0 1 0 0 1 0 0
580 31 f 2.5 2.5 6
6 6 6 6 6 6 6 6 1 1 1 1 6 6
688 39 f 8 8 3
3 3 3 3 3 3 3 3 3 3 3 3 3 3
677 37 f 1.5 .5 1
6 1 1 1 6 6 0 0 1 1 6 6 6 0
859 38 m 3 6 3
7 0 0 0 7 3 0 0 3 0 3 0 0 0
677 25 f 7 1 1
0 1 1 1 2 0 0 0 1 2 1 1 1 0
848 36 f 7 1 1
0 1 0 1 1 0 0 0 0 0 0 1 1 0
781 31 f 2 4 1
1 0 0 0 1 1 0 1 1 1 1 1 0 0
781 40 f 2 2 8
8 0 0 8 8 0 0 0 0 0 8 8 0 0
677 25 f 3 5 1
1 6 1 6 6 3 0 0 2 2 1 1 1 1
779 33 f 3 2 1
1 0 1 0 0 0 1 0 1 0 0 0 1 0
677 25 m 7 1.5 1
1 1 0 1 1 0 0 0 0 0 1 0 0 0
362 35 f .5 0 1
1 0 0 0 1 0 0 0 0 0 0 0 0 0
677 41 f 6 2 7
7 7 0 7 7 0 0 0 0 0 8 0 0 0
677 24 m 5 1 5
1 5 0 5 0 0 0 0 1 0 0 0 0 0
833 29 f .5 0 6
6 0 0 0 6 0 0 0 0 0 0 0 0 0
362 30 f 1 1 1
1 0 0 0 1 0 0 0 1 0 0 0 0 0
850 26 f 6 12 6
6 0 0 0 2 2 6 6 6 0 0 6 6
467 25 f 2 3 1
1 0 0 6 1 1 0 0 0 0 1 1 1 1
967 29 f 1 2 7
7 0 0 0 7 0 0 7 7 0 0 0 0 0
833 31 f 1 1 7
7 0 7 0 7 3 0 0 3 3 0 0 0 0
859 40 f 7 1 5
1 5 0 5 5 1 0 0 1 0 0 0 0 0
848 31 m 1 2 1
1 0 0 0 1 1 0 0 4 4 1 4 0 0
222 32 f 2 3 3
3 0 0 0 0 7 0 0 3 0 8 0 0 0
783 33 f 2 0 4
```

```
7 0 0 0 7 0 0 0 4 0 4 0 0 0
856 28 f 8 4 2
0 2 0 2 2 0 0 0 2 0 2 0 4 0
781 30 f 3 5 1
1 1 1 1 1 1 0 0 1 1 1 1 1 0
850 25 f 6 3 1
7 5 0 5 7 1 0 0 7 0 1 0 1 0
580 33 f 2.5 4 2
2 0 0 0 2 0 0 0 0 0 8 8 0 0
677 38 f 3 3 1
1 0 0 0 1 0 1 1 1 0 1 0 0 4
677 26 f 2 2 1
1 0 1 0 1 0 0 0 1 1 1 0 0 0
467 52 f 3 2 2
2 6 6 6 6 2 0 0 2 2 2 2 0 0
542 31 f 1 3 1
1 0 1 0 1 0 0 0 1 1 1 1 1 0
859 50 f 9 3 6
6 6 6 6 6 6 6 6 6 3 3 3 6 6
779 26 f 1 2 1
7 0 1 0 1 1 4 1 4 1 1 1 4 4
779 36 m 1.5 2 4
1 4 0 4 4 0 0 4 4 4 4 0 0 0
222 31 f 0 3 7
1 0 0 0 7 0 0 0 0 0 0 0 0 0
362 27 f 1 1 1
1 0 1 0 1 4 0 4 4 1 0 4 4 0
967 32 f 3 2 7
7 0 0 0 7 0 0 0 1 0 0 1 0 0
362 29 f 10 2 2
2 2 2 2 2 2 2 2 2 2 7 0 0
677 27 f 3 4 1
0 5 1 1 0 5 0 0 0 1 1 1 0 0
546 32 m 5 .5 8
8 0 0 0 8 0 0 0 8 0 0 0 0 0
688 38 m 2 3 2
2 0 0 0 2 0 0 0 2 0 0 0 1 0
362 28 f 1 1 1
1 0 0 0 1 1 0 4 0 0 0 0 4 0
851 32 f .5 2 4
5 0 0 0 4 0 0 0 0 0 0 0 2 0
967 43 f 2 2 1
1 0 0 0 1 0 0 1 7 0 0 0 1 0
467 44 f 10 4 6
7 6 0 6 6 0 6 0 0 0 0 0 0 6
467 23 f 5 3 1
0 2 1 2 1 0 0 0 1 1 1 1 1 1
783 30 f 1 .5 1
1 0 0 0 1 0 0 0 0 0 0 7 0 0
677 29 f 3 1 2
2 2 2 2 2 0 0 0 0 0 0 0 0 0
859 26 f 9.5 1.5 2
2 2 2 2 2 0 0 2 2 0 0 0 0 0
222 28 f 3 0 2
```

```
2 0 0 0 2 0 0 0 0 0 2 0 0 0
966 37 m 2 1 1
7 1 1 1 7 0 0 0 7 0 0 0 0 0
859 31 f 10 10 1
0 1 1 1 1 0 0 0 1 1 0 0 1 0
781 27 f 2 1 2
2 0 0 0 1 0 0 0 4 0 0 0 0 0
677 31 f .5 .5 6
7 0 0 0 0 0 0 0 6 0 0 0 0 0
848 28 f 5 1 2
2 2 0 2 0 0 0 0 2 0 0 0 0 0
781 24 f 3 3 6
1 6 6 6 1 6 0 0 0 0 1 0 1 1
856 27 f 1.5 1 6
2 6 6 6 2 5 0 2 0 0 5 2 0 0
382 30 m 1 2 7
7 0 0 0 7 0 4 7 0 0 0 7 4 4
848 25 f 9 3 1
7 1 1 5 1 0 0 0 1 1 1 1 1 0
382 30 m 1 2 4
7 0 0 0 7 0 4 7 0 0 0 7 4 4
688 40 m 2 3 1
1 0 0 0 1 3 1 0 5 0 4 4 7 1
856 40 f .5 5 5
3 0 0 0 3 0 0 0 0 0 5 5 0 0
966 25 f 2 .5 2
1 0 0 0 2 6 0 0 4 0 0 0 0 0
859 30 f 2 4 2
2 0 0 0 0 2 0 0 0 0 2 0 0 0
849 29 m 10 1 5
7 5 5 5 7 5 5 0 0 0 0 0 7 0
781 28 m 1.5 3 4
1 0 0 0 1 4 4 0 4 4 1 1 4 0
467 35 f 4 2 6
7 6 7 6 6 7 6 7 7 7 7 7 7 6
222 32 f 10 5 1
1 1 0 1 1 0 0 1 1 1 0 0 1 0
677 32 f 1 0 1
1 0 1 0 0 0 0 0 0 0 0 0 0 0
222 54 f 21 4 3
5 0 0 0 7 0 0 7 0 0 0 0 0 0
677 30 m 4 6 1
7 0 0 0 0 1 1 1 7 1 1 0 8 1
683 29 f 1 2 8
8 0 0 0 8 0 0 0 0 8 8 0 0 0
467 38 m 3 5 1
1 0 0 0 1 0 0 1 1 0 0 0 0 0
781 29 f 2 3 8
8 0 0 0 8 8 0 0 8 8 0 8 8 0
781 30 f 1 0 5
5 0 0 0 0 5 0 0 0 0 0 0 0 0
783 40 f 1.5 3 1
1 0 0 0 1 4 0 0 1 1 1 0 0 0
851 30 f 1 1 6
```

```
6 0 0 0 6 0 0 0 6 0 0 6 0 0
851 40 f 1 1 5
5 0 0 0 5 0 0 0 0 1 0 0 0 0
779 40 f 1 0 2
2 0 0 0 2 0 0 0 0 0 0 0 0 0
467 37 f 4 8 1
1 0 0 0 1 0 3 0 3 1 1 1 0 0
859 37 f 4 3 3
0 3 7 0 0 7 0 0 0 7 8 3 7 0
781 26 f 4 1 2
2 2 0 2 1 0 0 0 2 0 0 0 0 0
859 23 f 8 3 3
3 2 0 2 3 0 0 0 1 0 0 3 0 0
967 31 f .5 0 1
1 0 0 0 0 0 0 0 0 0 0 0 0 0
851 38 m 4 2 5
7 5 0 5 4 0 4 7 7 0 4 0 8 0
467 30 m 2 1 2
2 2 0 2 0 0 0 0 2 0 2 0 0 0
848 33 f 2 2 7
7 0 0 0 0 7 0 7 7 0 0 0 7 0
688 35 f 5 8 3
2 2 2 2 2 0 0 3 3 3 3 3 0 0
467 27 f 2 3 1
1 0 1 0 0 1 0 0 1 1 1 0 0 0
783 42 f 3 1 1
1 0 0 0 1 0 0 0 1 0 1 1 0 0
687 40 m 1.5 2 1
7 0 0 0 1 1 0 0 1 0 7 0 1 0
779 30 f 4 8 7
7 0 0 0 7 0 6 7 4 2 2 0 0 6
222 34 f 9 0 8
8 2 0 2 8 0 0 0 0 0 0 0 0 0
467 28 m 3 1 2
2 0 0 0 2 2 0 0 0 2 2 0 0 0
222 28 f 8 4 2
1 2 1 2 2 0 0 1 2 2 0 0 2 0
542 35 m 2 3 2
6 0 7 0 7 0 7 0 0 0 2 2 0 0
677 31 m 12 4 3
7 3 0 3 3 4 0 0 4 4 4 0 0 0
783 45 f 1.5 2 6
6 0 0 0 6 0 0 6 6 0 0 0 0 0
942 34 f 1 .5 4
4 0 0 0 1 0 0 0 0 0 2 0 0 0
222 30 f 8 4 1
1 1 1 1 1 0 0 0 1 1 0 0 0 0
967 38 f 1.5 2 7
7 0 0 0 7 0 0 7 1 1 1 1 0 0
783 37 f 2 1 1
6 6 1 1 6 6 0 0 6 1 1 1 6 0
467 31 f 1.5 2 2
2 0 7 0 7 0 0 7 7 0 0 0 7 0
859 48 f 3 0 7
```

```
7 0 0 0 0 0 0 0 0 7 0 0 0 0
490 35 f 1 1 7
7 0 0 0 7 0 0 0 0 0 0 0 8 0
222 27 f 3 2 3
8 0 0 0 3 8 0 3 3 0 0 0 0 0
382 36 m 3 2 4
7 0 5 4 7 4 4 0 7 7 4 7 0 4
859 37 f 1 1 2
7 0 0 0 0 2 0 2 2 0 0 0 0 2
856 29 f 3 1 1
1 0 0 0 1 1 1 1 0 0 1 1 0 1
542 32 m 3 3 7
7 0 0 0 0 7 7 7 0 0 0 0 7 7
783 31 m 1 1 1
1 0 0 0 1 0 0 0 0 1 1 1 0 0 0
833 35 m 1 1 1
5 4 1 5 1 0 0 1 1 0 0 0 0 0
782 38 m 30 8 5
7 5 5 5 5 0 0 4 4 4 4 4 0 0
222 33 m 3 3 1
1 1 1 1 1 1 1 1 4 1 1 1 1 1
467 24 f 2 4 1
0 0 1 0 1 0 0 0 1 1 1 0 0 0
467 34 f 1 1 1
1 0 0 0 1 0 0 1 1 0 0 0 0 0
781 53 f 2 1 5
5 0 0 0 5 5 0 0 0 0 5 5 5 0
222 30 m 2 5 3
6 3 3 3 6 0 0 0 3 3 3 3 0 0
688 26 f 2 2 1
1 0 0 0 1 0 0 0 1 0 1 1 0 0
222 29 m 8 5 1
1 6 0 6 1 0 0 1 1 1 1 0 0 0
783 33 m 1 2 7
7 0 0 0 7 0 0 0 7 0 0 0 7 0
781 39 m 1.5 2.5 2
2 0 2 0 2 0 0 0 2 2 2 0 0 0
850 22 f 2 1 1
1 0 0 0 1 1 1 0 5 0 0 1 0 0
493 36 f 1 0 5
0 0 0 0 7 0 0 0 0 0 0 0 0 0
967 46 f 2 4 7
7 5 0 5 7 0 0 0 4 7 4 0 0 0
856 41 m 2 2 4
7 4 0 0 7 4 0 4 0 0 0 7 0 0
546 25 m 5 5 8
8 8 0 0 0 0 0 0 0 0 0 0 0 0
222 27 f 4 4 3
2 2 2 3 7 7 0 2 2 2 3 3 3 0
688 23 m 9 3 3
3 3 3 3 3 7 0 0 3 0 0 0 0 0
849 26 m .5 .5 8
8 0 0 0 8 0 0 0 0 8 0 0 0 0
783 29 f 3 3 1
```

```
1 0 0 0 4 0 0 4 1 0 1 0 0 0
856 34 f 1.5 2 1
7 0 0 0 7 0 0 7 4 0 0 7 0 0
966 33 m 3 5 4
7 0 0 0 7 4 5 0 7 0 0 7 4 4
493 34 f 2 5 1
1 0 0 0 1 0 0 0 7 0 1 1 8 0
467 29 m 2 4 2
2 0 0 0 2 0 0 2 2 2 2 2 2 2
677 28 f 1 4 1
1 1 1 1 0 0 0 1 0 1 0 0 0
781 27 m 2 2 1
1 0 1 0 4 2 4 0 2 2 1 0 1 4
467 24 m 4 4 1
7 1 0 1 1 1 0 7 1 0 0 0 0 0
859 26 m 5 5 1
1 1 1 1 1 1 1 1 1 1 1 1 1 1
848 27 m 7 2 5
7 5 0 5 4 5 0 0 0 7 4 4 0 4
677 25 f 1 2 8
8 0 0 0 0 5 0 0 8 0 0 0 2 0
222 26 f 3.5 0 2
2 0 0 0 2 0 0 0 0 0 0 0 0 0
833 32 m 1 2 1
1 0 0 0 1 0 0 0 5 0 1 0 0 0
781 28 m 2 .5 7
7 0 0 0 7 0 0 0 4 0 0 0 0 0
783 28 f 1 1 1
1 0 0 0 1 0 0 0 0 0 1 1 0 0
222 28 f 5 5 2
2 6 6 2 2 0 0 0 2 2 0 0 2 2
851 33 m 4 5 3
1 0 0 0 7 3 0 3 3 3 3 3 7 5
859 39 m 2 1 1
1 0 0 0 1 0 0 0 0 0 0 1 0 0
848 45 m 2 2 7
7 0 0 0 7 0 0 0 7 0 0 0 0 0
467 37 m 2 2 7
7 0 0 0 0 7 0 0 0 7 0 0 7 0
859 32 m .25 .25 1
1 0 0 0 0 0 0 0 1 0 0 0 0 0
```

STATEPOP

```
data statepop;
   input State $ CityPop_80 CityPop_90 NonCityPop_80 NonCityPop_90
Region @@;
   label citypop_80=   '1980 metropolitan pop in millions'
         noncitypop_80='1980 nonmetropolitan pop in millions'
         citypop_90=   '1990 metropolitan pop in millions'
         noncitypop_90='1990 nonmetropolitan pop in million'
```

```
            region='Geographic region';
        datalines;
ME    .405    .443    .721    .785  1   NH    .535    .659    .386    .450  1
VT    .133    .152    .378    .411  1   MA   5.530   5.788    .207    .229  1
RI    .886    .938    .061    .065  1   CT   2.982   3.148    .126    .140  1
NY  16.144  16.515   1.414   1.475  1   NJ   7.365   7.730     .A      .A   1
PA  10.067  10.083   1.798   1.799  1   DE    .496    .553    .098    .113  2
MD   3.920   4.439    .297    .343  2   DC    .638    .607      .       .   2
VA   3.966   4.773   1.381   1.414  2   WV    .796    .748   1.155   1.045  2
NC   3.749   4.376   2.131   2.253  2   SC   2.114   2.423   1.006   1.064  2
GA   3.507   4.352   1.956   2.127  2   FL   9.039  12.023    .708    .915  2
KY   1.735   1.780   1.925   1.906  2   TN   3.045   3.298   1.546   1.579  2
AL   2.560   2.710   1.334   1.331  2   MS    .716    .776   1.805   1.798  2
AR    .963   1.040   1.323   1.311  2   LA   3.125   3.160   1.082   1.060  2
OK   1.724   1.870   1.301   1.276  2   TX  11.539  14.166   2.686   2.821  2
OH   8.791   8.826   2.007   2.021  3   IN   3.885   3.962   1.605   1.582  3
IL   9.461   9.574   1.967   1.857  3   MI   7.719   7.698   1.543   1.598  3
WI   3.176   3.331   1.530   1.561  3   MN   2.674   3.011   1.402   1.364  3
IA   1.198   1.200   1.716   1.577  3   MO   3.314   3.491   1.603   1.626  3
ND    .234    .257    .418    .381  3   SD    .194    .221    .497    .475  3
NE    .728    .787    .842    .791  3   KS   1.184   1.333   1.180   1.145  3
MT    .189    .191    .598    .608  4   ID    .257    .296    .687    .711  4
WY    .141    .134    .329    .319  4   CO   2.326   2.686    .563    .608  4
NM    .675    .842    .628    .673  4   AZ   2.264   3.106    .453    .559  4
UT   1.128   1.336    .333    .387  4   NV    .666   1.014    .135    .183  4
WA   3.366   4.036    .776    .830  4   OR   1.799   1.985    .834    .858  4
CA  22.907  28.799    .760    .961  4   AK    .174    .226    .227    .324  4
HI    .763    .836    .202    .272  4
;
run;
```

APPENDIX

4

Alternate ODS HTML Statements for Running Examples in Different Operating Environments

Using an OS/390 UNIX System Services HFS Directory for HTML Output

```
/* Specify the files to create for the HTML output. */
/* The PATH= option specifies the location for all  */
/* the HTML files. The URL= suboption prevents       */
/* information from PATH= from appearing in the      */
/* links and references that ODS creates. The URLs   */
/* will be the same as the file specifications.      */
ods html body='odsexample-body.htm'
        contents='odsexample-contents.htm'
        page='odsexample-page.htm'
        frame='odsexample-frame.htm'
        path='~'(url=none);
```

Using an OS/390 PDSE for EBCDIC HTML Output

```
/* Allocate a PDSE for the HTML Output. */
filename pdsehtml '.example.htm'
                dsntype=library dsorg=po
                disp=(new, catlg, delete);

/* Specify the files to create for the HTML output. */
/* These files are PDSE members.                     */
/* The PATH= option specifies the location for all   */
/* the HTML files. The URL= suboption prevents       */
/* information from PATH= from appearing in the      */
/* links and references that ODS creates. The URLs   */
/* will be the same as the file specifications.      */
/* The RS= option creates HTML that you can work     */
/* with in an editor and use on an MVS Web server.   */
```

```
ods html body='odsexb'
         contents='odsexc'
         page='odsexp'
         frame='odsexf'
         path='.example.htm'(url=none)
         rs=none;
```

Using an OS/390 PDSE for ASCII HTML Output

```
/* Allocate a PDSE for the HTML Output. */
filename pdsehtml '.example.htm'
                    dsntype=library dsorg=po
                    disp=(new, catlg, delete);

/* Specify the files to create for the HTML output. */
/* These files are PDSE members.                    */
/* The URL= suboption in the HTML-file              */
/* specifications provides a URL that will be valid */
/* after the PDSE members have been moved to an     */
/* ASCII file system. When the files are            */
/* transferred, they must retain their member names */
/* and have the ".htm" extension added in order for */
/* these URLs to be correct.                        */
/* The PATH= option specifies the location for all  */
/* the HTML files. The URL= suboption in the PATH=  */
/* option prevents information from PATH= from      */
/* appearing in the links and references that ODS   */
/* creates because it will not be a valid URL for   */
/* the ASCII file system.                           */
/* The TRANTAB= option creates ASCII HTML that      */
/* you can send to an ASCII-based web server.       */

ods html body='odsexb' (url='odsexb.htm')
         contents='odsexc' (url='odsexc.htm')
         page='odsexp' (url='odsexp.htm')
         frame='odsexf'
         path='.example.htm'(url=none)
         trantab=ascii;
```

Note: Use a binary transfer to move the files to the Web server. △

Using CMS to Create EBCDIC HTML Output

```
/* You must use the URL= suboption to specify a  */
/* valid string for the URL.                     */
/* The RS= option creates HTML that you can work */
/* with in an editor and use on a CMS Web server.*/
ods html body='odsexb htm' (url='odsexb.htm')
         contents='odsexc htm' (url='odsexc.htm')
         page='odsexp htm' (url='odsexp.htm')
```

```
frame='odsexf htm'
rs=none;
```

Operating Environment Information: In the CMS operating environment, you must use the URL= suboption in the HTML file specifications for the body, contents, and page files because CMS filenames do not form valid URLs. For the same reason, you must use the suboption if you use the GPATH= or the PATH= option in the ODS HTML statement. (See the discussion of these options in the documentation for the ODS HTML statement in Chapter 3, "The ODS Statements," in *The Complete Guide to the SAS Output Delivery System.*) △

Using CMS to Create ASCII HTML Output

```
/* You must use the URL= suboption to specify a */
/* valid string for the URL.                    */
/* The TRANTAB= option creates ASCII HTML that  */
/* you can send to an ASCII-based Web server.    */
ods html body='odsexb htm' (url='odsexb.htm')
        contents='odsexc htm' (url='odsexc.htm')
        page='odsexp htm' (url='odsexp.htm')
        frame='odsexf htm'
        trantab=ascii;
```

Note: Use a binary transfer to move the files to the web server. △

Operating Environment Information: In the CMS operating environment, you must use the URL= suboption in the HTML-file specifications for the body, contents, and page files because CMS filenames do not form valid URLs. For the same reason, you must use the suboption if you use the GPATH= or the PATH= option in the ODS HTML statement. (See the discussion of these options in the documentation for the ODS HTML statement in Chapter 3, "The ODS Statements," in *The Complete Guide to the SAS Output Delivery System.*) △

ndex

Your Turn

If you have comments or suggestions about *SAS® Procedures Guide, Version 8*, please send them to us on a photocopy of this page or send us electronic mail.

Send comments about this book to

SAS Institute
Publications Division
SAS Campus Drive
Cary, NC 27513
email: yourturn@sas.com

Send suggestions about the software to

SAS Institute
Technical Support Division
SAS Campus Drive
Cary, NC 27513
email: suggest@sas.com

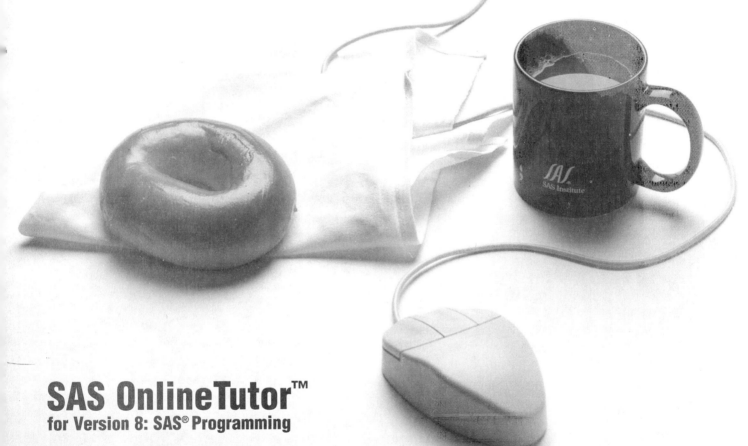

*Welcome * Bienvenue * Willkommen * Yohkoso * Bienvenido*

SAS® Publications Is Easy to Reach

Visit our SAS Publications Web page located at www.sas.com/pubs

You will find product and service details, including

- **sample chapters**
- **tables of contents**
- **author biographies**
- **book reviews**

Learn about

- **regional user groups conferences**
- **trade show sites and dates**
- **authoring opportunities**
- **custom textbooks**

Order books with ease at our secured Web page!

Explore all the services that Publications has to offer!

Your Listserv Subscription Brings the News to You Automatically

Do you want to be among the first to learn about the latest books and services available from SAS Publications? Subscribe to our listserv **newdocnews-l** and automatically receive the following once each month: a description of the new titles, the applicable environments or operating systems, and the applicable SAS release(s). To subscribe:

1. Send an e-mail message to **listserv@vm.sas.com**

2. Leave the "Subject" line blank

3. Use the following text for your message:

    subscribe newdocnews-l *your-first-name your-last-name*

For example: subscribe newdocnews-l John Doe

Please note: newdocnews-l ◄——— that's the letter "l" not the number "1".

For customers outside the U.S., contact your local SAS office for listserv information.

Create Customized Textbooks Quickly, Easily, and Affordably

SelecText® offers instructors at U.S. colleges and universities a way to create custom textbooks for courses that teach students how to use SAS software.

For more information, see our Web page at **www.sas.com/selectext**, or contact our SelecText coordinators by sending e-mail to **selectext@sas.com**.

You're Invited to Publish with SAS Institute's User Publishing Program

If you enjoy writing about SAS software and how to use it, the User Publishing Program at SAS Institute Inc. offers a variety of publishing options. We are actively recruiting authors to publish books, articles, and sample code. Do you find the idea of writing a book or an article by yourself a little intimidating? Consider writing with a co-author. Keep in mind that you will receive complete editorial and publishing support, access to our users, technical advice and assistance, and competitive royalties. Please contact us for an author packet. E-mail us at **sasbbu@sas.com** or call 919-677-8000, then press 1-6479. See the SAS Publications Web page at **www.sas.com/pubs** for complete information.

Read All about It in *Authorline*®!

Our User Publishing newsletter, *Authorline*, features author interviews, conference news, and informational updates and highlights from our User Publishing Program. Published quarterly, *Authorline* is available free of charge. To subscribe, send e-mail to **sasbbu@sas.com** or call 919-677-8000, then press 1-6479.

See *Observations*®, Our Online Technical Journal

Feature articles from *Observations*®: *The Technical Journal for SAS*® *Software Users* are now available online at **www.sas.com/obs**. Take a look at what your fellow SAS software users and SAS Institute experts have to tell you. You may decide that you, too, have information to share. If you are interested in writing for *Observations*, send e-mail to **sasbbu@sas.com** or call 919-677-8000, then press 1-6479.

Book Discount Offered at SAS Public Training Courses!

When you attend one of our SAS Public Training Courses at any of our regional Training Centers in the U.S., you will receive a 15% discount on any book orders placed during the course. Each course has a list of recommended books to choose from, and the books are displayed for you to see. Take advantage of this offer at the next course you attend!

SAS Institute
SAS Campus Drive
Cary, NC 27513-2414
Fax 919-677-4444

E-mail: sasbook@sas.com
Web page: www.sas.com/pubs
To order books, call Fulfillment Services at 800-727-3228*
For other SAS Institute business, call 919-677-8000*

* Note: Customers outside the U.S. should contact their local SAS office.